D1577891

Legal and Regulatory Issues in Human Resources Management

A volume in
Contemporary Human Resources Management:
Issues, Challenges, and Opportunities
Ronald R. Sims, *Series Editor*

Legal and Regulatory Issues in Human Resources Management

edited by

Ronald R. Sims
College of William and Mary

William I. Sauser, Jr.
Auburn University

INFORMATION AGE PUBLISHING, INC.
Charlotte, NC • www.infoagepub.com

Library of Congress Cataloging-in-Publication Data

A CIP record for this book is available from the Library of Congress
http://www.loc.gov

ISBN: 978-1-62396-841-0 (Paperback)
         978-1-62396-842-7 (Hardcover)
         978-1-62396-843-4 (ebook)

CONTENTS

LIST OF FIGURES

LIST OF TABLES

ACKNOWLEDGMENTS

We are indebted to George F. Johnson at Information Age Publishing, Inc., who once again has provided the collective outlet for our ideas. A most deserved thank you and Acknowledgment goes to our top-notch group of contributors. Without their collective professional and personal efforts, based upon their own human resources management (HRM) experiences as practitioners, academics, and researchers of the legal and regulatory issues, this book ceases to exist. We believe that when reading through the impressive content of their chapters you will wholeheartedly agree that they have made a significant contribution to the overall HRM field and the corresponding legal and regulatory issues. We are indebted to them all as colleagues and friends.

A very, very special thanks goes to my colleague, friend, and co-editor, William I. Sauser, Jr. and Herrington Bryce who continues to serve as my colleague, mentor, and valued friend. The administrative support of the Mason School of Business at the College of William and Mary is also acknowledged.

Thanks and appreciation goes to Nandi, Dangaia, and Sieya, who have supported me throughout my work on this book.

—**Ronald R. Sims**

I am grateful for the fine work of my colleagues in the preparation of the chapters comprising this book, the encouragement of George Johnson as Ron and I worked on this project, and the skill of the professionals at

Legal and Regulatory Issues in Human Resources Management, pages xi–xii
Copyright © 2015 by Information Age Publishing

Information Age Publishing in assembling the final product. I hope the readers find this volume to be interesting and informative. I wish especially to thank my friend and co-editor, Ronald Sims. "Ron, thanks for helping to keep me focused as we worked together this year. It was a difficult year for me personally, and your friendship means so much." I dedicate this book to my "one and only," my dear wife Lane. To God be the glory.

—**William I. Sauser, Jr.**

CHAPTER 1

AN INTRODUCTION TO LEGAL ISSUES IN HUMAN RESOURCES MANAGEMENT

Ronald R. Sims and William I. Sauser, Jr.

INTRODUCTION

Human resources management (HRM) professionals and their organizations face a myriad of challenges with today's workforce. For example, there are issues concerning the diverse workforce, technology, and legislation and regulations affecting the workplace and technology matters that rise to the top of the list of challenges. HRM professionals who encounter these challenges use their leadership skills, expertise, knowledge, and experience to avert issues that might arise from these challenges. In reality, legal issues pervade all that occurs in the HRM function. More specifically, each day HRM professionals interpret a variety of state, federal, and local laws associated with various employment-related situations. In addition, HRM professionals have firsthand experience with legal realities as employers face increased numbers of employment-based complaints, charges, and lawsuits filed by current or former employees. These all have escalated rapidly in the past decade. HRM experts have identified many factors that may explain this increase, including an expansion of the employment laws, a greater

Legal and Regulatory Issues in Human Resources Management, pages 1–25
Copyright © 2015 by Information Age Publishing
All rights of reproduction in any form reserved.

awareness by employees of their rights under the law, and an increase in the number of attorneys who are willing to represent disgruntled employees.

There continues to be an increased need to provide an ongoing update or look at the legal and regulatory issues and laws that impact organizations and those HRM professionals whose job it is to help employees and organizations understand and leverage the laws to their competitive advantage. This chapter first takes a brief look at the key responsibilities of HRM before focusing on the history of HRM. Next the chapter provides an overview of major HRM laws. A discussion of the importance of changing HRM laws and legislation to HRM professionals and their role in ensuring compliance with such laws and legislation is the focus of the next portion of the chapter. The chapter concludes with a brief overview of the remaining chapters in this book.

HUMAN RESOURCE MANAGEMENT: KEY RESPONSIBILITIES AND ITS HISTORY

HRM is the term used to describe formal systems devised for the management of people within an organization. HRM is concerned with the development of both individuals and the organization in which they operate. HRM, then, is engaged not only in securing and developing the talents of individual workers, but also in implementing programs that enhance communication and cooperation among those individual workers in order to nurture organizational development. A more specific look at the primary responsibilities associated with HRM include: job analysis; recruitment and staffing; organization and utilization of work force; measurement and appraisal of work force performance; implementation of reward systems for employees; professional development of workers; and maintenance of work force to include safety, wellness, benefits, employee motivation, communication, administration, training and staff reduction. HRM is also a strategic and comprehensive approach to people and organizations and involves culture management that helps to heighten effectiveness, accomplish organizational objectives, and add value to the organization's performance. As classical definitions of HRM state, HRM is a strategic approach to the acquisition, motivation, development and management of the organization's human resources. It is devoted to shaping an appropriate corporate culture and introducing programs that reflect and support the core values of the enterprise and ensure its success (Armstrong, 2006).

Essentially, the purpose of HRM is to maximize the productivity of an organization by optimizing the effectiveness of its employees. This mandate is unlikely to change in any fundamental way, despite the ever-increasing pace of change in the business world or any future laws or regulations.

Until fairly recently, an organization's HRM professionals and department were often consigned to lower rungs of the corporate hierarchy, despite the fact that its mandate is to replenish and nourish what is often cited—legitimately—as an organization's greatest resource, its work force. But in recent years, recognition of the importance of HRM to an organization's overall health has grown dramatically. Perhaps one of the main reasons for this increased recognition is HRM's role in helping the organization achieve its goals of obtaining and maintaining excellent employees while also navigating the never-ending plethora of employment laws and regulations or legal issues in HRM.

Key principles and practices associated with HRM date back to the beginning of mankind. During prehistoric times for example, mechanisms were developed for the selection of tribal leaders, and knowledge was recorded and passed on from generation to generation about the practice of safety, health, hunting, and gathering. More advanced HRM functions were developed as early as 1000 and 2000 B.C. Employee screening tests have been traced back to 1115 B.C. in China, for instance. And the earliest form of industrial education, the apprentice system, was started in ancient Greek and Babylonian civilizations (Khilawala, 2010) before gaining prominence during medieval times.

Since the inception of modern management theory, the terminology used to describe the role and function of workers has evolved from "personnel" to "industrial relations" to "employee relations" to "human resources." While all of these terms remain in use, "human resources management" (typically abbreviated "HRM") most accurately represents the view of workers by contemporary management theory: as valuable resources managed in the same manner as all other valuable resources.

The need for an organized form of HRM emerged during the industrial revolution as the manufacturing process evolved from a cottage system to factory production. More specifically, during the late 1700s and early 1800s, because of the rapid industrialization of Great Britain, the United States shifted from an agricultural economy to an industrial economy. British factories were being built with innovative manufacturing processes, and British immigrants brought their new knowledge to the United States. U.S. organizations were forced to develop and implement effective ways of recruiting and keeping skilled workers. In addition, industrialization helped spur immigration, as the country opened its borders to fill industrial positions. Filling these jobs with immigrants, however, created an even greater need for adequate management of employees as there developed a separate class of managers and employees in the factories (Thompson, 2010). Labor unions flourished from 1790 to 1820, and with their rise, labor organization membership represented different types of skilled employees, such as carpenters or printers, to ensure that these employees were treated fairly by management. Byars and Rue (2011) note that job security, fair wages, and shorter working hours for employees were the main focus of labor unions. As a result of this dramatic change in the U.S. economy, there arose a need for a system in the workplace to manage both employees and management—the *human resources* of these new types of organizations. Labor unions became powerful advocates for employee rights despite the numerous court battles attempting to mitigate the power of unions.

Between the 1880s and the 1940s, immigration rose significantly and remained robust until World War II. Advertisements circulated throughout the world promoting the United States as the land of opportunity where good-paying industrial jobs were plentiful. And as noted previously, as a result, the United States experienced a steady stream of low-skill, low-cost immigrant workers who occupied manufacturing, construction, and machinery operation positions. Even though these employees performed largely routine tasks, companies and their managers faced serious obstacles when trying to manage them since they spoke different languages.

Early HRM techniques included social welfare approaches aimed at helping immigrants adjust to their jobs and to life in the United States. These programs assisted immigrants in learning English and obtaining housing and healthcare. In addition, these techniques promoted training and developing supervisors in order to increase organizational productivity.

While some organizations paid attention to the "human" side of employment, others did not. Therefore, other factors such as hazardous working conditions and pressure from labor unions also increased the importance of effective management of human resources. Along with the manufacturing efficiencies brought about by industrialization came several shortcomings related to working conditions. These problems included hazardous tasks, long hours, and unhealthy work environments. The direct cause of employers seeking better HRM programs was not poor working conditions, but rather the protests and pressures generated by workers and organized labor unions. Indeed, labor unions, which had existed as early as 1790 in the United States, became much more powerful during the late 1800s and early 1900s.

Union membership represented more than 25% of the U.S. workforce from 1950 to 1970. From 1980 to 1990, as the U.S. economy focused less on manufacturing and evolved into a more service economy, union membership declined (Mathis & Jackson, 2010). Union membership fell to 11.3%, down from 11.8% in 2011, according to the Bureau of Labor Statistics 2012 report (Bureau of Labor Statistics, 2013). That brought union membership to its lowest level since 1916, when it was 11.2% (Bureau of Labor Statistics, 2013; Greenhouse, 2013). Although union membership has continued to decline since 1990, labor unions can truly be seen as the predecessors of HRM departments as both share the goal of equitable treatment of employees by management.

Two other particularly important contributing factors to the origination of modem HRM occurred during the same period. The first was the industrial welfare movement, which represented a shift in the way that managers viewed employees—from nonhuman resources to human beings. That movement resulted in the creation of medical care and educational facilities. The second factor was Frederick W. Taylor's (b. 1856–d. 1915) *The Principles of Scientific Management* (1911/1998), a landmark book that outlined management methods for attaining greater productivity from low-level production workers. Taylor's book was timely as it coincided with a labor shortage that existed in the early 20th century and management's increased focus on the productivity of its employees. Taylor promoted scientific management through four principles:

1. Evaluate a task by discussing its components.
2. Select employees that had the appropriate skills for a task.
3. Provide workers with incentives and training to do a task.
4. Use science to plan how workers perform their jobs (Kinicki & Williams, 2008).

Taylor developed a different pay system that rewarded employees who performed at a higher level. This idea within HRM is still used today.

The B. F. Goodrich Company pioneered the establishment of an employee department to address labor concerns in 1900. In 1902, National Cash Register formed a separate department to handle worker grievances, wage administration, record keeping, and many other functions (Khilawala, 2010). As expected, more organizations followed the lead of B. F. Goodrich Company and National Cash Register in HRM.

A federal agency, the U.S. Department of Labor (DOL), was established in 1913 by President Taft in response to the economic revolution in the United States. The DOL's mission was and is to promote the welfare of working people and their work conditions. By the end of World I, the DOL had established policies to ensure that fair wages and work conditions existed so that human resources, the workers, were treated fairly (Department of Labor, 2010).

A Harvard research group implemented the "Hawthorne studies" in the 1920s that focused on changing the physical work environments of employees to assess any changes in their work habits. The results of the studies indicated an increase in productivity as their work environment was improved. While these experiments were eventually criticized for having a poor research design, they illustrated the importance of management treating employees well as an impetus to improved worker performance (Kinicki & Williams, 2008).

During the 1930s and 1940s, the general focus of HRM changed from a focus on worker efficiency and skills to employee satisfaction. That shift became especially pronounced after World War II, when a shortage of skilled labor forced companies to pay more attention to workers' needs. Employers, influenced by the famous Hawthorne productivity studies (mentioned above) and similar behavioral research, began to emphasize personal development and improved working conditions as a means of motivating employees.

HRM as a professional discipline was especially bolstered by the passage of the Wagner Act in 1935 (also known as the National Labor Relations Act), which remained the basic U.S. labor law through the 1990s (Sauser, 1998). It augmented the power of labor unions and increased the role and importance of personnel managers. The Social Security Act, which insured a modicum of income to old age people after retirement, also came to fruition in 1935. The Fair Labor Standards Act of 1938, enforced by the DOL, established federal minimum wage standards, child labor laws, and increased wages for overtime. Both laws helped contribute to the establishment of HRM today. In addition to providing security, these enacted laws also helped in increasing employees' standard of living.

In the 1960s and 1970s, the federal government furthered the HRM movement with a battery of regulations created to enforce fair treatment of workers, such as the Equal Pay Act of 1963, the Civil Rights Act of 1964, the Employee Retirement Income Security Act of 1974 (ERISA), the Occupational Safety and Health Act of 1970, and the Pregnancy Discrimination Act of 1978. Because of these acts, companies began placing greater emphasis on HRM in order to avoid lawsuits for violating this legislation, which was intended to ensure the safety and protect the rights of employees. This Civil Rights legislation stressed that no discrimination in any form would be committed against an organization's employees. These regulations created an entirely new legal role for HRM professionals. Furthermore, during the 1970s, HRM gained status as a recognized profession with the advent of human resource management programs in colleges.

By the end of the 1970s, virtually all medium-sized and large companies and institutions had some type of HRM program in place to handle recruitment, training, regulatory compliance, dismissal, and other related issues. The importance of HRM continued to grow during the 1980s and 1990s. Changing workforce values, for example, required the skills of HRM professionals to adapt organizational structures to a new generation of workers with different attitudes about authority and conformity (Sauser & Sims, 2012). Shifting demographics forced changes in the way workers were hired, fired, and managed. Other factors contributing to the importance of HRM during the 1980s and 1990s were legislation such as the Americans with Disabilities Act of 1990 and the Older Workers Benefit Protection Act of 1990 (both of which supported employee rights), increasing education levels, growth of service and white-collar jobs, corporate restructuring (including reductions in middle management), more women in the workforce, slower domestic market growth, greater international competition, and new federal and state regulations. The advent of all these laws regulating organizations placed an increase emphasis on HRM. More recently, legislation such as the Genetic Information Nondiscrimination Act of 2008, the Lilly Ledbetter Fair Pay Act of 2009 (which continued to focus on employment discrimination), and the Patient Protection and Affordability Act of 2010 (the goal of which is to increase the number of individuals who have health-care insurance) have continued to add complexity and importance to the role of HRM departments in organizations.

In looking at the history of HRM, it is clear that proactive organizations include a department responsible for managing their recruitment, performance management, employee relations, wage and benefits, and other important employee-related functions. In the early 20th century and prior to World War II, the personnel function (the precursor to the term human resource management) was primarily involved in record keeping of employee information; in other words, it fulfilled the role of a "caretaker." At this point, there were very few government influences in employment relations, and thus employment terms, practices, and conditions were left to those who owned the organization. As a result, worker abuses such as child labor and unsafe working conditions were prevalent. Some employers set up labor welfare and administration departments to look after the interests of employees by maintaining records on health and safety as well as recording hours worked and payroll. Since that time, HRM has increased dramatically in importance as most evident in the strategic role that HRM departments now play in organizations. HRM professionals and the organizations that employ them must continually respond to an economic landscape made up of radical changes to include increasing globalization, technological breakthroughs, hyper-competition, and of course legal issues.

HUMAN RESOURCES MANAGEMENT
LAWS AND LEGAL ISSUES

HRM professionals are charged with a great deal of responsibility in assisting their organizations in the legal framework of the employer–employee relationship. HRM professionals must be aware of and ensure that their organizations effectively respond to the public policy considerations that have shaped and are continuing to shape the broad range of federal and state regulatory initiatives in the world of work. This also means that there needs to be an understanding of the changing nature of the employer–employee relationship as viewed by the courts. It is also important that HRM professionals and other managers/leaders in organizations are aware of the differences in the status of employees in the private sector versus the public sector. For example, specific areas of interest include employment discrimination and equal employment opportunity, affirmative action, workplace safety and health, employee benefits, legally required insurance protection, personal rights of employees, labor relations and collective bargaining, and the employment-at-will doctrine. This also means that HRM professionals and others in the organization must continue to learn to recognize issues, analyze situations in the workplace, and develop strategies to avoid legal liability.

The network of state and federal laws that exists to regulate employment and labor relations is extensive. In many cases, rules only apply to organizations with a specified minimum number of employees and thus do not regulate small companies. But other regulations apply to all employee–employer relationships, regardless of organization size. So organizations of all sizes and their HRM professionals must make an effort to stay abreast of legislative and regulatory developments like those briefly described in the remainder of this section.

The Civil Rights Act of 1868, enacted during the Reconstruction era, was largely ignored for 100 years until 1968 when the United States Supreme Court declared it valid. Section 1981 of the Act offers the same "Equal Rights under the Law" to all persons "as is enjoyed by white citizens" and states that all persons "shall have the same right to make and enforce contracts" as "white citizens." In 1975, the Supreme Court ruled that Section 1981 prohibits racial discrimination in employment. A year later, the Court ruled that the section applies to all discrimination, including discrimination against people of Arabic and Hispanic descent. Section 1981 applies to all employers regardless of size, has no specified deadline for filing a complaint, and allows money damages.

Title VII of the Civil Rights Act of 1964 prohibits employers with 15 or more employees from discriminating against individuals because of their race, color, religion, sex, or national origin. Employers who discharge or otherwise discriminate against an employee based on one of these protected characteristics have engaged in illegal discrimination. Employees can establish a violation of Title VII through one of two distinct legal theories:

- *Disparate Treatment:* Employees can claim they are the victims of intentional discrimination because of a protected characteristic. They must offer direct or circumstantial proof of discriminatory intent. Employees may accuse their employers who treat them differently because of their race, color, religion, sex, or national origin of disparate treatment.

- *Adverse Impact*: Employees can also establish a violation by showing that, although an employer's practice does not seem discriminatory, it nonetheless adversely affects employees in a protected class. For example, employees have established a violation by showing that a specific employment requirement—such as a minimum weight of 165 pounds—denies employment opportunities to a disproportionately high number of women or other minority employees.

Title VII influences every aspect of employment from the initial job posting to promotions and training. Under Title VII, if an employee claims discrimination, the employer must prove it has not violated the law. The court may remedy violations by ordering reinstatement, with or without back pay, and may grant any other equitable relief it feels is appropriate. With the passage of the *Civil Rights Act of 1991*, monetary damages are available for intentional discrimination.

A 1978 amendment to Title VII provides in part that the term "because of sex" includes "because of or on the basis of pregnancy, childbirth or related medical conditions." The *Pregnancy Discrimination Act* specifically prohibits employers from discriminating against women based upon the fact that they are pregnant. This includes recruitment, hiring, promotion, discipline, discharge, and training.

Affirmative action programs permit employers to engage in limited preferences based upon race or sex. These plans must meet certain criteria to be lawful. This issue is currently under increased scrutiny. We, therefore, suggest that employers who have an affirmative action plan or wish to establish one, confer with their employment attorney and the Equal Employment Opportunity Commission (EEOC).

The Equal Pay Act of 1963 requires equal pay for equal work within the same establishment regardless of the employee's gender. The law states, in part, that

> No employer . . . shall discriminate, within any establishment in which such employees are employed, between employees on the basis of sex by paying wages to employees in such establishment at a rate less than the rate at which he pays wages to employees of the opposite sex in such establishment for equal work on jobs the performance of which requires equal skill, effort, and responsibility, and which are performed under similar working conditions.

The Act permits exceptions where unequal pay for equal work is legitimately based on a seniority system or a merit system, when earnings are based on quantity or quality of production, or where a differential based on any other factor than sex exists.

The Age Discrimination in Employment Act of 1967 (ADEA) forbids employment discrimination against employees who are forty years of age or older.

Covered employers may not discharge protected employees solely because of their age. The ADEA does not protect certain types of employees, such as high-level managers, public safety personnel, and tenured college professors. In 1996, the Court ruled that replacing an older worker with a younger one who is forty years of age or older does not protect the employer from charges of age discrimination.

The best defense against charges of age discrimination is proving that age is a bona fide occupational qualification (BFOQ) for a particular job. For example, airlines have successfully argued that mandatory retirement at age sixty for pilots is a BFOQ because of concerns about safety. An employer can also defend against ADEA suits by showing that he or she dismissed the employee for reasons unrelated to his/her age. If, however, age was a factor that made a difference in the employer's decision to discharge, an ADEA violation still exists.

The Occupational Safety and Health Act (OSHA) of 1970 prohibits employers from discharging employees solely because they file complaints or institute proceedings under OSHA. Section 18 of OSHA permits states to create and enforce their own health and safety plans.

Section 504 of the Vocational Rehabilitation Act of 1973 prohibits employers who receive federal funds from discriminating against employees with disabilities who possess the necessary qualifications for particular positions. Employers must provide these employees with "reasonable accommodations" to allow them to hold a job that they might otherwise be unable to perform. Under Section 504, employers may not dismiss employees solely because they have disabilities. Employers may dismiss employees if their disabilities affect job performance and there are no reasonable measures the employer can take to accommodate the disabilities.

The Employment Retirement Security Act of 1970 (ERISA) prohibits discrimination against employees for invoking their rights concerning certain benefit plans.

The National Labor Relations Act (NLRA) encourages workers to organize and engage in collective bargaining. It also prohibits discrimination in employment as a means of encouraging or discouraging membership or participation in any labor organization. It protects employees who either choose or refuse to engage in labor activity.

The Immigration Reform and Control Act of 1986 forbids discrimination based on citizenship and national origin. It also prohibits the hiring, recruitment, or referral for a fee for employment the following individuals:

a. Aliens, knowing they are not legally entitled to work or are not lawfully admitted for permanent residence.
b. Any individual, without complying with the verification procedures the Act requires.

Employers must examine each prospective employee's eligibility and complete Form I–9. To satisfy the requirements of the Act, prospective employees must produce specified documents.

The Drug-Free Workplace Act of 1988 provides that recipients of federal grants must institute a drug-free workplace program to help curb workplace drug abuse. Specific requirements include:

- Creation of a drug-free workplace statement
- Establishment of a drug-free awareness program
- Notification to all employees that adherence to workplace drug restrictions is a condition of employment
- A good faith effort to maintain a drug-free workplace by implementing all the requirements of the Act

Although the Act does not apply to private sector employers, it has created widespread acceptance of drug testing. As a result, employers must be sensitive to issues of privacy and fairness if they institute a drug testing requirement. Federal laws may require employees who drive company vehicles to comply with CDL requirements that include random drug testing.

Title I of the Americans with Disabilities Act of 1990 (ADA) provides that employers may not discriminate against individuals with disabilities who have the qualifications to perform the essential functions of the job. The ADA touches all stages of the employment process from recruitment to termination.

The Family and Medical Leave Act (1993) requires employers to provide an employee with up to 12 weeks of unpaid leave under specific conditions. These include the birth, adoption, or serious illness of a child; to care for a spouse or dependent parent; or for an employee's illness. The law requires employers to balance their interests with the legitimate needs of employees.

As a means of making noncustodial parents pay child support payments, the *Personal Responsibility and Work Opportunity Reconciliation Act of 1996* (Welfare Reform) requires organizations to report certain information regarding newly hired employees. The *PRWORA* is considered to be a fundamental shift in both the method and goal of federal cash assistance to the poor. The bill added a workforce development component to welfare legislation, encouraging employment among the poor. The law requires employers, for example, in the state of Michigan to report the name, address, and social security number of every new employee within 20 days of hire to the Michigan Department of Treasury. The information is then reported to the National Directory of New Hires, which is maintained by the federal government. In addition to child support, the information is also used to detect and prevent payments of unemployment, workers compensation, and public benefit payments to those employed.

The *Health Insurance Portability and Accountability Act* (HIPAA, 1996) has also had a major impact on HRM. In passing this law, Congress addressed concerns about employees who change jobs and might not qualify for healthcare coverage as a result of preexisting conditions. HIPAA creates new standards for medical privacy, portability, disclosure, medical savings accounts, and COBRA *(the Consolidated Omnibus Budget Reconciliation Act of 1985)* benefits. HIPAA allows criminal prosecution for violations of the privacy provision. It is important for employers to review the *Freedom of Information Act* at the federal and state level before answering any requests for medical information from any employee's files. The portability provision limits the length of any preexisting condition exclusions that an employer may impose. Parts of this provision require the tracking of information beginning in 1996.

The intent of the *Fair Labor Standards Act* (FLSA) is to maintain a minimum standard of living for the well-being of workers. Since its enactment, there have been more than 25 amendments to the Act to expand coverage. Provisions of the FLSA cover minimum wages, employment relationships, child labor laws, overtime calculations, wage recordkeeping requirements, required postings, as well as determining compensation for hours worked. Employers should review the various "tests" in the law to determine if they are "covered employers" and which employees are "exempt" or "nonexempt" from the Act. The FLSA is vigorously enforced by the Department of Labor and can lead to substantial penalties if violated.

The courts may sometimes require employers to garnish employee wages and to direct funds to a prescribed destination. Laws protect the affected employee's right to privacy. The federal *Consumer Credit Protection Act* and state guidelines regulate and limit wages that are subject to garnishment.

The *Fair Credit Reporting Act* (FCRA) regulates the use of credit checks for employment purposes. The Act allows credit checks for positions that involve financial responsibility or the handling of large sums of money. When conducting credit checks, HRM professionals should:

- Consider carefully before checking credit history unless the position requires financial responsibility or the handling of large sums of money. HRM professionals must inform potential employees that their credit may be checked and must also obtain their written permission before doing so.
- Candidates should be informed by HRM professionals if they are denied employment based on factors in a credit report. The law requires that the individual be provided with the name of the credit agency that issued the report. The candidate must be allowed to discuss any problems in the report with the HRM professionals.

- Under the provisions of the Bankruptcy Act it may be unlawful to terminate an employee or to refuse employment to a candidate solely because the individual has sought protection under the act.

The *Recovery Act of 2009* and the health care reform bill, which passed in March 2010, promised immediate impact on the workplace. The requirements of the Recovery Act had an enormous effect on businesses that provide health care insurance to workers who lost their jobs. The Act mandated an employer-paid 65% subsidy for former employees receiving COBRA, short for Consolidated Omnibus Budget Reconciliation Act, benefits. On the other hand, the Recovery Act created thousands of jobs and contracting opportunities for small businesses. In addition, the guarantee for U.S. Small Business Administration loans was increased to 90%.

Now that the U.S. Supreme Court has ruled that the *Patient Protection and Affordable Care Act* (ACA) is constitutional, it is moving ahead full speed. Together with the *Health Care and Education Reconciliation Act*, the ACA represents the most significant regulatory overhaul of the U.S. healthcare system since the passage of Medicare and Medicaid in 1965. The ACA puts in place comprehensive health insurance reforms that will roll out over four years and beyond. The ACA was enacted with the goals of increasing the quality and affordability of health insurance, lowering the number of uninsured by expanding public and private insurance coverage, and reducing the costs of healthcare for individuals and the government. The ACA introduced a number of mechanisms—including mandates, subsidies, and insurance exchanges—meant to increase coverage and affordability. The law also requires insurance companies to cover all applicants within new minimum standards and offer the same rates regardless of preexisting conditions or sex. In short, the ACA is intended to lessen the threshold for procuring insurance coverage. Additional reforms aimed to reduce costs and improve healthcare outcomes by shifting the system towards quality over quantity through increased competition, regulation, and incentives to streamline the delivery of healthcare.

In addition to dealing with this plethora of federal laws and regulations, HRM professionals must also negotiate requirements of the various state and local laws in the jurisdictions in which their organization operates. For example, the states promulgate and enforce *worker compensation laws* protecting employees who are injured on the job, and *unemployment compensation laws* protecting employees who are laid off from work due to economic conditions (as opposed to dismissal for cause). One can see that it is essential for HRM professionals to have a clear working knowledge of federal, state, and local laws that affect employment issues, decisions, and conditions. It is also important that organizations have available—through in-house legal departments

or attorneys on retainer—immediate and effective counsel in the interpretation of ever-changing laws and regulations.

CHANGING LAWS AND LEGAL ISSUES: IMPORTANCE TO HRM PROFESSIONALS

As noted earlier in this chapter, historically HRM professionals and their
departments simply provided operational support and performed what often is seen as back-office personnel tasks in most organizations. However, as
will be evident in the chapters that follow, today's and tomorrow's competitive and highly regulated marketplace and changing legal landscape will
continue to create significant challenges for HRM professionals and the
organizations that employ them, regardless of whether those organizations
are in the not-for-profit, for-profit, or government sectors.

HRM professionals and their departments continue to take on an increasingly significant strategic and advisory role within organizations. Today's senior executives and administrators rely heavily on HRM professionals and their departments to ensure that the organization's overall strategy
is consistent with the many complex laws and regulations that govern the
workplace environment.

As the contributors in this book make clear, new legislation is passed or
substantively changed (and interpreted by the courts) each year, bringing
about more concerns and issues for human resources professionals and
highlighting the importance of ensuring that their organizations remain
compliant no matter the law or legal issue. This means HRM professionals must aggressively ensure that their organizations successfully operate by
effectively dealing with the many legal issues affecting the modern workplace—healthcare; employment discrimination; harassment; immigration;
employee privacy; unemployment; workers' compensation; age, race, and
sex discrimination; and employee benefits, to name only a few.

As each of these areas continues to change, HRM professionals and
HRM departments must evolve and change as well. It is critical that HRM
professionals make sure they do not allow their organizations to become
complacent or to develop a culture that is resistant to change; they simply
must stay informed of the constant changes affecting labor and employment law. This means that HRM professional must proactively revise and
implement policies on a timely basis in order to ensure efficient compliance with the changing regulations and legislation that governs today's and
tomorrow's workplace.

As is evident in our earlier discussion offering a definition and brief
history of HRM, there should be no doubt that HRM capabilities extend
beyond complying with laws and legal issues. HRM professionals' daily

activities require that they spend time working on the complete HRM cycle including interviewing and hiring, employee documentation, job descriptions, training and development initiatives for all levels of employees, performance evaluations (as part of the overall performance management system), and implementing various organizational development efforts.

Given such an extensive list of responsibilities, it is clearly difficult—yet essential—for HRM professionals to stay informed of changes in HRM-related laws, regulations, court decisions, and legal issues. Well-informed and proactive HRM professionals are likely to operate more efficiently and cost-effectively than those who are reactive, complacent, and resistant to change. HRM professionals who proactively implement organizational policies that align with changes in HRM laws best help their organizations avoid liability for being noncompliant or simply "caught off guard" when legal issues or challenges do arise.

When working proactively as it relates to HRM laws and legal issues HRM professionals decrease the likelihood of engaging in unfortunate cost/benefit analyses that assess the benefits of *not* complying with HRM laws with the costs associated with compliance. HRM professionals have a responsibility to make sure the organization's employees fully understand the potentially disastrous ramifications of noncompliance, which can include various penalties, the risk of civil action, and lost profits. In most cases the costs of noncompliance often are greater than the costs associated with fully obeying HRM laws. Ensuring that the organization's employees understand the impact that noncompliance may have on the overall success of the organization is essential for understanding and appreciating HRM's role given the requirements of the various HRM legislation and laws.

CONCLUSIONS

As will be evidenced by the chapters in this book, the HRM legal issues and regulatory and legal environment are critical to every organization today. This is also quite likely the area that changes more than any other in HRM. Consider the fact that every court case that deals with the HRM environment inside any organization across the nation has the potential to set a legal precedent, thus affecting every organization in the United States with its results. Even if the court ruling does not change the way an organization has to do business, if Congress sees that a ruling was unfair, they may change the law at either the federal or the state level, and that affects each organization under their jurisdiction. This, briefly, is how the *Lilly Ledbetter Fair Pay Act* (among other laws) was created. The Supreme Court ruled in a case of unequal pay based on existing laws, and because the U.S. Congress felt that the ruling was unfair, a new law was enacted to change certain rules on how and when an equal pay complaint can be filed.

So, if every court case that deals with compensation and benefits, equal opportunity, harassment, or discrimination in any form has the opportunity to change the way every organization does business, then one can quickly see that this is an area of critical importance to HRM professionals and their organizations. Clearly, individuals with strong understanding and expertise in HRM law are critical to the organization. So for those individuals who want a job where they *really* never do the same thing twice, then they should seriously look at HRM and its legal and regulatory environment as a challenging and satisfying career choice.

The objective of this book is to focus on legal or regulatory issues and HRM in the United States. More specifically, the intent of this book is to bring together a very diverse group of contributors who have real-world practical, research, and legal experience in the HRM field and who are in a position to offer a unique and updated perspective related to HRM laws and regulations. While the contributors offer their unique perspectives on the oldest and most current legal or regulatory issues, challenges, and opportunities related to the employment cycle, it is our belief as editors that the combined chapters result in a comprehensive view of the topic and its import to HRM professionals, employees, and their organizations. While comprehensive in nature, the book emphasizes the importance of managing HRM programs, policies, and procedures with attention to the various state and federal laws and regulations and their import to organizational success (i.e., navigating the legal and regulatory environment toward sustainable competitive advantage in today's and tomorrow's ever changing environment).

PREVIEW OF CHAPTER CONTENTS

In this final section, we preview and summarize the contents of the chapters our group of experts has produced. The first four chapters provide an introduction of sorts to the rest of the book by considering legal and regulatory issues from the perspective of the HRM professional. The fifth chapter provides a transition by examining the origins of the laws and regulations that impact the work of the HRM professional. The next five chapters explore challenges HRM professionals face with respect to laws affecting employee selection, accommodations for persons with disabilities, immigration, age discrimination, and sexual harassment; all of these are "hot topics" within the current regulatory environment.

The information age in which we live has also generated some important issues; these are addressed in chapters dealing with current topics like new (electronic) forms of employee selection, information technology and employee privacy, "big data," and electronic surveillance in the workplace. The next four chapters focus on special topics of interest to HRM professionals: person–organization fit, international HRM laws, the emerging role of the organizational ombudsperson, and practical advice for HRM professionals facing a federal lawsuit. In the final chapter, we argue that effective HRM managers must be leaders of change if the organizations in which they work are to be effective in meeting current and future legal and regulatory challenges.

Chapter 1: An Introduction to Legal Issues in Human Resources Management

Ronald R. Sims and William I. Sauser, Jr.

In the present chapter, Ronald R. Sims and William I. Sauser, Jr. note that there continues to be an increased need to provide an ongoing update or look at the legal and regulatory issues and laws that impact organizations and those HRM professionals whose job it is to help employees and organizations understand and leverage the laws to their competitive advantage. Sims and Sauser first take a brief look at the key responsibilities of HRM before focusing on the history of HRM. The chapter next provides an overview of major HRM laws. A discussion of the importance of changing HRM laws and legislation to HRM professionals and their role in ensuring compliance with such laws and legislation is the focus of the next portion of the chapter. The chapter concludes with a brief overview of the remaining chapters in this book.

Chapter 2: Human Resources Management Audit: Ensuring Compliance with HRM Laws and Regulations

Ronald R. Sims and William I. Sauser, Jr.)

Ronald Sims and William Sauser offer a detailed look at auditing HRM compliance to include an example of an HRM checklist and practical actions for effectively completing audits. The authors also discuss the role of HRM professionals, HRM audits, and international compliance efforts before taking a look at the HRM professional's role in creating a culture of compliance in organizations with HRM laws and regulations.

Chapter 3: HR and the Law: The HR Practitioner's Point of View

Sheri Bias and Barry Hoy

Sheri Bias and Barry Hoy first discuss the environment within which three groups (i.e., policymakers, HR practitioners or managers, and the legal staff) must interact in pursuance of the process of performing HR functions for the good of the organization. The discussion starts from the premise that the policymakers, that is to say the general management of the organization, will be called upon to make decisions that consider all of the available information balancing risk tolerance with risk averseness. Bias and Hoy then move to a more focused examination of the laws (beginning with the Emancipation Proclamation of 1863 and jumping to 1964) that guide the manner in which organizations interact with their stakeholders. In offering their examination, the authors note that while the first segment of the chapter may be seen as somewhat philosophical in its approach, the second half is more informational in nature as it presents the second consideration under which HR professionals operate, and that neither of these considerations in the practice of HRM enjoys preeminence and must be considered in tandem. In the end, members of each of the three groups must be in tune to the law and the statutes that implement the law; however, they must also consider the good of the organization from a holistic standpoint when the law cannot be relied upon to provide all of the answers.

Chapter 4: Aligning Respect and Dignity With Organizational Infrastructure and External Regulation

George Denninghoff and Sheri Bias

George Denninghoff and Sheri Bias suggest that in a knowledge-based workplace, no company can retain a competitive advantage by engaging in arbitrary or illegal discrimination. Additionally, however, they note that the dignity of employment can be lost when an organization begins to view employees as potential lawsuits. Given this, Denninghoff and Bias seek to answer the question of "how [can] an organization minimize the risk of these potential lawsuits based on its HR policies, practices, and procedures?" The chapter examines compliance and the regulatory environment in three interrelated areas: first, how values and operating principles may set the stage for values conflict and resulting compliance issues; second, recognizing the job, the basic unit of human production, as a system which incorporates key competencies provides both compliance and performance benefits; and third, to better manage risk the organization must assess, not audit, its processes and systems.

Chapter 5: From Idea to Implementation: Statutes, Regulations, and Cases

Robert A. Tufts and William I. Sauser, Jr.

Robert A. Tufts and William I. Sauser, Jr. provide answers to three key questions: (a) What is the source of these statutes, regulations, and court decisions? Where do they come from and who makes them? (b) How are the statutes, regulations, and court decisions interrelated? How do they come together to provide guidance to organizations seeking to comply fully with the law? (c) How can HR professionals—acting individually or through their companies or professional associations—influence the law and help to shape it? More specifically, after discussing the concept of "the law," Tufts and Sauser illustrate the interplay of *organic law, statutory law, administrative law,* and *case law* as the legislative, executive, and judicial branches of government all play their parts in shaping "the law" by tracing the history of one particular HR-related law, the Equal Pay Act, as it has been shaped over the past five decades. The authors highlight the important roles for HR professionals to play at every step of the process and how HR professionals can impact how "the law" is to be interpreted and applied.

Chapter 6: Legal Issues in Employee Selection: Negotiating the Obstacles and Avoiding the Landmines

Brian L. Bellenger and Kenneth A. Yusko

Brian Bellenger and Kenneth Yusko suggest that decisions regarding employee selection are arguably some of the most critical and, as such, most legally vulnerable an organization can make. Bellenger and Yusko first examine the legal requirements and standards for employee selection. Next, they discuss strategies for ensuring effective and legally defensible selection decisions. Finally, the chapter looks at the role of human resource consultants and practitioners in encouraging and guiding organizations in appropriately using and defending selection procedures.

Chapter 7: Navigating the HRM Responsibilities of the ADA

Christine Ledvinka Rush

Christine Rush focuses on the employment setting, highlighting employer responsibilities under the Americans with Disability Act (ADA). Rush first offers a brief overview of the growth of the disability rights movement and considers the similarities and differences between civil rights and benefits. Her analysis then turns to the technical elements of the ADA, clarifying the definitions, applications, and judicial interpretations that are essential to understanding both the original law and the 2008 amendments. The chapter concludes with an exploration of the potential penalties associated with ADA violations and practical strategies to avoid liability.

Chapter 8: Immigration in a Nutshell

Sue Ann Balch

Sue Ann Balch provides the reader with basic terminology, a brief history behind the current immigration law, and, in conclusion, a short guide on how to find more in-depth information on immigration law and regulations. An important theme of the chapter is the importance of HRM professionals working with an experienced immigration attorney to better navigate the ever-changing and sweeping area of immigration law and regulations, since these continue to evolve and be debated by the U.S. Congress. Additionally, the chapter emphasizes practical advice for HRM professionals, to include keeping their I-9s up to date, attending training on the new I-9 when available, and doing a self-audit or hiring someone who is trained to do one in preparation for what will eventually happen: a government audit.

Chapter 9: Combating Age Discrimination: Legal and Regulatory Issues, Challenges and Opportunities

Jonathan P. West

Jonathan West begins the chapter by highlighting demographic trends and economic restructuring initiatives that compel interest in the issue of mature workers. West next focuses on the extent and nature of discrimination complaints, ageism, and negative age-related stereotypes. He also provides an in-depth discussion of the relevant laws, court decisions, and regulatory actions surrounding aging workers and assessments of legal scholars regarding their effectiveness. Before offering a summary and conclusion, West provides the reader with some HRM strategies for creatively coping with aging workers' special needs along with several practical examples and profiles of best organizational practices in meeting the needs of older workers.

Chapter 10: The Continuing Development of the Law on Sexual Harassment

William J. Woska

William Woska traces the history of the concept of sexual harassment from its earliest days as a topic of discussion, through its inclusion in the EEOC guidelines as an illegal form of sex discrimination in 1980, to the continuing development of the concept in the present time. Woska shows how important court decisions over the past 34 years have shaped the interpretation of the concept and discusses several current issues with respect to sexual harassment, including nontraditional forms of sexual harassment such as cyber-stalking and cyber-harassment. He concludes his chapter with some clear guidance on (a) how to educate the public about the seriousness of the problem of sexual harassment and (b) how to train employees to prevent the occurrence of sexual harassment in the workplace. Woska argues forcefully that "employers will have to handle such situations with tact and understanding, and with a full recognition of (a) the rights of all involved, (b) the need for fair and equal treatment for persons thought by some to be 'different,' and (c) the morale problem that can arise from improper handling of explosive sexual situations."

Chapter 11: The Use of Technology in Employee Selection and Development: Advantages and Pitfalls

Martinique Alber

Martinique Alber explores some of the latest technological advances and how they have been used throughout HRM processes, citing their advantages as well as their potential legal pitfalls. Throughout the chapter, Alber discusses the organizational benefits—including saving time, money, and resources—that derive from the use of technology in HRM processes such as recruiting, testing, development, and applicant tracking. Alber also notes that the very same things that make the use of technology so great are also what can cripple an organization if not implemented properly. To this end, the chapter argues that organizations need to focus their searches for prospective employees in order to recruit high quality candidates rather than anyone and everyone looking at the job posting. In addition, there needs to be an emphasis on the security and responsibility of applicant and current employee personal information.

Chapter 12: Technology and Employee Privacy Challenges

Sheri K. Bias and Karin L. Bogue

Sheri Bias and Karin Bogue first review the history of employee privacy to lay the foundation for their discussion. Next, they discuss current issues and case law surrounding technology such as cell phones and laptops before taking a look at other legal areas that have impacts such as credit reports. In doing the latter, Bias and Bogue emphasize the importance of employer and employee rights associated with these areas and what employers are doing with policy creation. In concluding the chapter, the authors share their insights and perspectives on the future and where they believe technology and employee privacy challenges may be headed.

Chapter 13: Negotiating Contract Management and Personnel in High-Technology, High-Complexity Domains: Issues of Inherently Governmental and Critical Functions in Big Data Analytics Teams

Sara R. Jordan

Sara Jordan argues that there are two major and unique problems associated with Big Data Management: nondiscriminate staffing and contracting that abides by relevant regulations. In particular, Jordan suggests that the problems with staffing relate to issues of compliance with relevant antidiscrimination policies in the federal government, whereas the problems related to contracting relate to issues of compliance with Office of Management and Budget requirements for contract management under conditions where contractors may perform "inherently governmental" tasks.

Jordan offers an introduction to Big Data in government and the demographic challenges of hiring for Big Data, then offers an exploration of the meaning of "inherently governmental," "critical," and "closely associated" functions in government. She next argues that Big Data analytics are inherently governmental activities. In concluding the chapter she elaborates on some key workforce planning strategies that government agencies ought to pursue to manage a recentralization of Big Data into the hands of federal employees.

Chapter 14: Electronic Surveillance in the Workplace: Legal, Ethical, and Management Issues

Jonathan P. West, James S. Bowman, and Sally Gertz

Jonathan West, James Bowman, and Sally Gertz begin with the premise that electronic surveillance at work is pervasive, but little understood. Following the introduction, the background section reviews the extent, form, and purpose of workplace monitoring, as well as differing perceptions of it. The core of West, Bowman, and Gertz's chapter examines relevant legal, ethical, and management issues. The discussion of the legal section analyzes pertinent statutes, while the ethics section assesses a case study, followed by the management section, which discusses notification, performance, leadership, and ethical practices. West, Bowman, and Gertz conclude the chapter with a discussion of the implications of the analysis and speculate on alternative futures for electronic surveillance in organizations and beyond.

Chapter 15: Person-Organization Fit and Its Implications for Human Resource Management Practices

Daniel J. Svyantek, Kristin L. Cullen, and Alexa Doerr

Daniel Svyantek, Kristin Cullen and Alexa Doerr first review the literature on person–organization fit. Next, the chapter discusses the role of organizational culture as the variable defining the organization component of the fit construct. Then the authors describe Schneider's Attraction-Selection-Attrition (ASA) model and how the model describes person–organization fit. The chapter concludes with a review of the potential legal issues facing organizations that use person–organization fit in human resource management practices.

Chapter 16: Toward a Better Understanding of International Human Resources Management Laws and Legal Issues

Ronald R. Sims

Ronald Sims notes that ensuring legal and regulatory compliance can be very challenging in a foreign environment where laws and business practices may be different. As a result, Sims stresses the point that HRM professionals must make sure that their companies take note of local laws impacting not only how their business is run, but also how their employees are managed. More specifically, this means ensuring that their organizations comply with a wide range of labor and employment laws by developing and maintaining related policies for their organizations. The chapter first takes a look at managing organizations and human resources across borders. Next, the discussion turns to the internationalization of business and factors affecting HRM in global markets before focusing on domestic versus international human resources management (IHRM). The chapter then considers some specific HRM activities and laws within an international business before concluding with a comparison of HRM laws in China and the United States and antidiscrimination laws around the world.

Chapter 17: The Role and Function of the Organizational Ombudsperson

C. Kevin Coonrod

Kevin Coonrod discusses the important role the ombudsperson plays in today's organizations. In doing so, Coonrod notes that the organizational ombudsperson assists people in conflict within their particular institution. This assistance is supplemental to such offices as human resources, management, and legal departments and is distinguished by its confidentiality, neutrality, informality, and the ombuds' independence from direction or control by others. According to Coonrod, the organizational ombudsperson helps community members navigate institutional policies and problems, coaches them in ways to deal with conflict, intervenes as a facilitator when appropriate, and provides unbiased data to the administration for consideration when discussing systemic change. Coonrod first provides an overview of the role and functions of the organizational ombudsperson, then highlights the benefits to the organization for maintaining an ombuds office. Before concluding the chapter with a look at the legal issues facing the ombuds practitioner, Coonrod discusses the relationship between the organizational ombudsperson and human resources departments.

Chapter 18: Practical Advice for HRM Professionals When Facing a Federal Lawsuit

William I. Sauser, Jr., Ronald R. Sims, and John G. Veres, III

William Sauser, Ronald Sims, and John Veres, first offer a brief discussion of the roles of (and differences among) three types of court-appointed agents (i.e., special masters, receivers, and monitors). Next, some background on the class-action federal lawsuit the authors were involved in is offered before we recommend some specific actions HRM professionals can take to help their organizations better respond to the challenges accompanying a federal lawsuit and the need for change that may result from such a lawsuit. Sauser, Sims, and Veres conclude the chapter with a list of recommendations HRM professionals should consider when confronted with legal issues or a federal lawsuit that may well require changes for them, their HRM department, and the organization as a whole.

Chapter 19: Human Resources Management, the Law, and Organizational Change

Ronald R. Sims and William I. Sauser, Jr.

Ronald R. Sims and William I. Sauser, Jr., stress how important it is for HRM professionals to prepare themselves to be effective leaders of change. Sims and Sauser first discuss how HRM departments and professionals can and do help shape the organization's culture. Next, the chapter highlights several cultural responses organizations might take in response to HRM laws and regulations. The discussion then focuses on how HRM professionals can use traditional HRM practices to help their organizations best introduce and institutionalize HRM laws in the organization. The chapter concludes by offering a number of things HRM professionals can do to help their organizations adapt or change in response to the introduction of new HRM laws and regulations.

REFERENCES

Armstrong, M. (2006). *A handbook of human resource management practice.* London, UK: Kogan Page Publishers.

Bureau of Labor Statistics. (2013). Union membership summary. Retrieved from http://www.bls.gov/news.release/union2.nr0.htm

Byars, L., & Rue, L. (2011). *Human resource management* (10th ed.). New York, NY: McGraw-Hill/Irwin.

Department of Labor. (2010). Chapter 1: Start-up of the department. Retrieved from http://www.dol.gov/osarn/programs/history/dolchp01.htm

Greenhouse, S. (2013). Share of the work force in a union falls to a 97-year low, 11.3%. Retrieved from http://www.nytimes.com/2013/01/24/business/union-membership-drops-despite-job-growth.html?_r=0

Khilawala, R. (2010). History of human resource management. Retrieved from http://www.buzzle.com/articles/history-of-human-resource-management.html

Kinicki, A., & Wlliams, B. (2008). *Management: A paradoxical introduction.* (3rd ed.). New York, NY: McGraw-Hill/Irwin.

Mathis, R. L., & Jackson, J. (2010). *Human resource management* (13th ed.). Mason, OH: Thomson/Southwestern.

Sauser, W. I., Jr. (1998). Understanding unionism in the USA: A guide for internationals. *SAM Management in Practice, 2*(1), 1–4.

Sauser, W. I., Jr., & Sims, R. R. (Eds.). (2012). *Managing human resources for the millennial generation.* Charlotte, NC: Information Age.

Taylor, F. W. (1998). *The principles of scientific management.* Mineola, NY: Dover. (Unabridged republication of original 1911 volume.)

Thompson, W. I. (2010). *The emergence of modern industrialization.* Retrieved from http://www/industrial-revolution.us

CHAPTER 2

HUMAN RESOURCES MANAGEMENT AUDIT

Ensuring Compliance With HRM Laws and Regulations

Ronald R. Sims and William I. Sauser, Jr.

INTRODUCTION

Compliance with HRM laws is essential for any organization to be successful in today's and tomorrow's legal environment and for creating and maintaining an organizational culture of character and integrity (Sauser & Sims, 2007; Sauser, 2008). But achieving and maintaining compliance can be elusive goals for organizations that do not recognize the challenges and develop an effective strategy to meet them.

Compliance should be treated as a process of defining both individual and group behaviors to ensure the organization's applicable laws and policies are followed. The HRM department has an obligation to hire and retain individuals that are knowledgeable about HRM-specific laws and are able to create policies and procedures in relation to these laws. This is especially important given that just writing policies and procedures and placing them

Legal and Regulatory Issues in Human Resources Management, pages 27–49
Copyright © 2015 by Information Age Publishing

in a repository is not enough. Once these various policies and procedures are established, HRM professionals and other organizational leaders must effectively communicate them throughout the organization.

Effective communication is most likely to happen in cases where compliance with relevant HRM laws has been integrated with the organization's overall business strategy and culture, and HRM professionals and other organizational leaders have taken steps to ensure all employees understand the importance of HRM compliance. The following basic principles increase the likelihood of achieving these goals:

1. Hire the right talent: Hiring the right talent within the organization's HRM department's area of responsibilities (compensation, employee benefits, legal requirements, talent management) continues to be one of the most important issues in today's organizations. HRM professionals must have the important knowledge, skills, and experience, or at minimum be able to access it through third-party relationships.
2. Educate, train, and develop: Individuals in the HRM department must be well versed in employment law and the legal/regulatory requirements that affect an organization. These laws and requirements are changing all the time and its imperative for the HRM professionals to stay apprised of the latest information available.
3. Create an employee handbook and update it regularly: An organization's employee handbook is one of its most important documents. The employee handbook is a communications tool that should clearly articulate the organization's policies and procedures and how business should be conducted. All HRM professionals and legal counsel should regularly review the handbook and any new policies and procedures before distribution to (and education of) all employees.
4. Conduct scheduled HRM compliance audits: Noncompliance can be the basis for financial and reputational risks for organizations. Conducting scheduled HRM compliance audits should be a part of an organization's overall strategy to avoid any legal liabilities.
5. Communicate, communicate, and communicate some more: HRM professionals and their department are a critical component of any organization. Whether there are compliance issues or not, it is critical for HRM professionals to keep organizational leaders aware of potential HRM compliance risks and recommended remediation.

All these actions will help HRM professionals take a large step toward achieving the important goal of maintaining HRM compliance for the overall organization. In our view, the most important actions in this regard are (a) proactively auditing the organization's compliance with HRM laws, and (b) working with other organizational leaders to create a culture of compliance with these laws.

The chapter first offers a detailed look at auditing HRM compliance. Next, the chapter offers an example of an HRM checklist and practical actions for effectively completing audits. Then, the role of HRM professionals, HRM audits, and international compliance efforts is offered before the chapter concludes with a look at the HRM professional's role in creating a culture of compliance in organizations with HRM laws and regulations.

AUDITING HRM COMPLIANCE: A CLOSER LOOK

Perhaps one of the most basic things HRM professionals should do as it relates to various HRM laws and legislation is to proactively audit *all* of their organization's compliance efforts. This includes adopting appropriate checks and balances systems to ensure that an audit in the end can help keep track of the overall level of compliance. In reality, audits examine the effectiveness of not only HRM professionals but more specifically the HRM department's current policies, procedures, and systems as they relate to the latest changes and developments given the various laws or legislation and regulations governing the contemporary workplace. Beyond the HRM department, the audit also determines the extent to which these policies and procedures are being followed throughout the organization; thus, it is a measure of the effectiveness of leadership at all levels of the organization.

HRM auditing is an extensive process that HRM professionals should periodically conduct to determine whether the organization's HRM practices are current and whether they meet legal guidelines. HRM audits shed light on legal issues that an organization must address to comply with federal and state laws and to align with HRM best practices. An HRM audit's purpose is to assess whether an organization's policies and procedures are consistent with federal, state, and local labor and employment laws. As an unbiased examination and evaluation of systems and processes of an organization to demonstrate whether an organization is in compliance with a standard, for example, HRM audits determine whether an organization's practices, workplace policies, and recordkeeping measures follow all applicable laws governing the employment relationship, employers' obligations, and HRM best practices.

Whether conducted internally (by HRM professionals of the organization) or externally (by consultants), an audit of an organization's HRM systems simply put should focus on the following:

- Demonstrate that organizational leaders and managers are in compliance with organization policies on treatment of employees.
- Ensure that the organization's HRM practices are in compliance with international, federal, state, and local laws.

- Find improvements the organization can make in organizational efficiency.
- Prepare for expansion and growth by taking HRM systems to the next level.

The reality is that smart or proactive organizations should regularly monitor employee treatment and have objective data that communicate whether or not employees are treated fairly and well. An audit report can answer such questions, for example, as:

- Are the HRM policies clear enough that employees can abide by them and organizational leaders and managers can carry them out?
- Are there people being paid outside the pay range for their job on the pay scale? Are there outliers within pay ranges that cannot be explained clearly by reference to hire date or past evaluations?
- Is the grievance procedure robust enough to handle all types of employee complaints so that they will not end up resulting in grievances or lawsuits?
- Are documentation, security, and retention of HRM/personnel records adequate to comply with employment laws, prevent identity theft, and provide information for HRM decisions?

In monitoring employee treatment, for example, HRM audits complement employee surveys. Surveys can tell the HRM professional and other organizational leaders how satisfied employees are with (a) their pay and benefits, (b) how HRM policies are applied, and (c) how corrective action is handled. In contrast, HRM audits tell the HRM professional and other organizational leaders whether the organization's pay and benefits, HRM policies, and corrective actions are being administered fairly and consistently (without favoritism or arbitrariness).

Employees are not necessarily in a position to know whether certain HRM practices are being followed consistently for everyone. Surveys reflect their point of view, which is vitally important for the HRM professional and other organizational leaders to know and to address because perceptions drive behavior. But those perceptions aren't the same as an unbiased evaluation of actual HRM practices.

The simplest approach to an audit is for HRM professionals to develop a checklist of the best available practices within the most heavily regulated compliance areas in labor and employment law and then compare and contrast these best practices with the actual practices in use within their host organization. These practices include such things as the organization's relationship with its employees: HRM policies, hiring, orientation and training, performance evaluation, wages and hours, benefits, workers' compensation, corrective actions including termination, employee rights, safety, recordkeeping, employee relations overall, and organizational and employee relations, to name a few.

When developing the checklist, HRM professionals should determine whether each key legal or compliance area conforms to the laws that govern them, be they local, state, or federal. Of course, HRM professionals must update the checklist periodically but also they should be sure to do it any time substantive changes to existing laws or newly enacted laws become available. Further, because so many of the key laws or compliance areas are regulated by employee threshold (i.e., 15 or more employees, 20 or more employees, and so on), it makes sense for HRM professionals to also make updates in accordance with their organization's ongoing growth and development. Additionally, the extent to which HRM professionals can examine their organization's practices and policies depends on their company's size and the resources that are available to conduct an HRM audit.

Whether HRM professionals make use of a simple audit checklist or more comprehensive audit, some important elements in HRM audits include determining who is responsible for conducting the audit and the types of HRM processes the audit should examine, as briefly discussed below.

- *Policies and procedures*: As a starting point, HRM professionals must make sure the organization has clearly defined policies and procedures in writing and they have been made available or presented to all employees. In order to prevent lawsuits regarding such actions as wrongful termination or discrimination, HRM professionals should regularly conduct a new employee orientation. Explaining organizational policies and the discipline process to all employees and having them sign a waiver of acknowledgment can be documented as part of the HRM audit. The HRM audit checklists should contain information about when the orientation is conducted and what is included.
- *Employment applications*: An HRM audit might reveal to HRM professionals that there are legal issues concerning the organization's recruitment and selection process—for example, problems with the type of employment application the organization is using. HRM professionals must make sure employment applications do not contain questions that ask the applicant's age, sex, national origin, or other non-job-related characteristics. Additionally, many applications also contain an employment at-will disclaimer that protects the organization's interests in case of terminated employees' filing legal action for wrongful discharge. If such a disclaimer is missing, it may be wise to include one in a new revision of the employee application.
- *Employment eligibility*: U.S. Immigration and Customs Enforcement (USICE) routinely conducts audits of employers' records, looking for violations related to employment eligibility. HRM professionals

must make sure organizational employees understand that federal law requires employers to obtain documentation from workers, such as proof of citizenship or a work visa that proves the employee is eligible to work for a U.S. employer. HRM professionals need to recognize that this part of an HRM audit is a proactive measure. By incorporating this step into an HRM audit HRM professionals can significantly reduce liability if issues related to employment eligibility come to light. Employment eligibility is like the foundation of a house—if an organization's employees are not eligible to work for an organization, ineligibility can snowball into other serious concerns about employment practices, such as paying and reporting legal wages and deductions.

- *Affirmative action compliance*: Organizations that provide goods or services to the federal government may have affirmative action obligations under *Executive Order 11246*. This law mandates the compilation of data pertaining to the organization's affirmative action plan. An HRM audit looks at compliance with affirmative action requirements such as gathering information for the company's applicant flow log. The audit may also examine whether the organization has fair compensation practices, such as paying equal wages to employees, regardless of race, sex, religion, and other non-job-related factors.

- *Required postings*: Auditing whether the organization posts required notices is a relatively simple aspect of an HRM audit. Despite this fact, legal issues can arise when the organization does not post notices such as the minimum wage poster required by the Fair Labor Standards Act. An HRM audit will also increase the likelihood that an organization posts legal notices concerning employees' civil rights, equal employment practices, and workplace safety notices, as mandated by agencies such as the U.S. Equal Employment Opportunity Commission (EEOC) and the U.S. Department of Labor (DOL).

- *Workplace issues/environment*: Organizations have an obligation to provide their employees with a safe working environment, free from discrimination and harassment. An HRM audit of employee relations practices does not always reveal outstanding legal matters. Instead, the audit determines whether the organization is taking the necessary precautions and proactive measures to protect its interests should legal matters arise from HRM departmental practices. For example, an audit can examine how the organization receives employees' complaints, the process for investigating complaints, and at what point employee complaints are referred to in-house counsel or the organization's outside attorney. In addition, an audit can ensure that organizations are following occupational safety guidelines (as referenced briefly related posting of legal notices) to reduce the incidence of workplace injuries and fatalities. This component of an HRM audit requires that organizations look at their recruitment and selection processes, workplace safety and risk management practices, and the manner in which they sustain the employer–employee relationship. EEOC enforces employment laws concerning fair employment practices, of which all HRM professionals should be aware. The U.S. Occupational Safety and Health Administration (OSHA) oversees organizational compliance with regulations pertaining to handling of complex machinery, dangerous equipment, and hazardous substances. HRM professionals should include components in the audit that address compliance with federal guidelines.

- *Privacy*: Employee confidentiality continues to be a principal element of HRM practices. Organizations maintain confidential information concerning employees' personal data, compensation, and performance. More importantly, organizations must retain information about employees' medical information separately from standard employment actions. For example, HRM professionals must make sure information about an employee's health benefits, medical leaves of absence, and workers compensation matters are segregated from information in the employment file. HRM departments or functions typically designate a privacy officer who has sole access to employees' medical-related information. Confidentiality measures are required under the *Health Insurance Portability and Accountability Act* and the *Americans with Disabilities Act.*

- *Employee records/File inspection*: Audit checklists should include questions about the use and storage of employee records. As noted previously, there are legal requirements associated with the hiring of employees and maintenance of records. One checklist question may be where and with whom these files are being held. HRM professionals who work for larger organizations usually pull a sample of files to determine if they have sound recordkeeping practices concerning employment. However, smaller organizations, on the other hand, tend to examine all of their employment files and conduct a full inspection of proper documentation methods. Employment-related materials, such as employment applications, resumes, attendance and performance records, disciplinary actions, and salary and wage information should be filed by HRM professionals in employee personnel files. However, all medical information as noted previously must be stored and maintained separately, pursuant to employee privacy regulations in the *Health Insurance Portability and Accountability Act.*

- *Company benefits/Compensation*: Employee benefits are a major part of HRM responsibilities, and it is important to keep records of the medical and dental plans their organization offers. Audit checklists with questions about programs offered with the requirements and limits for coverage can provide the HRM professional and other

organizational leaders with a comprehensive view of what is working for the organization and its employees. This information is
helpful when making decisions about what programs offer the best
return on benefit investment. Additionally, how an organization
pays employees is critical to its performance and success. HRM is
responsible for recruiting and hiring the most skilled employees
the organization can afford. Thus, they must maintain information
about salaries, bonuses, and other types of payment. For an HRM
audit, HRM professionals should use checklists containing questions
about determining factors for salaries, when employees are eligible
for increases, and who is responsible for managing the process to
help evaluate areas for improvement.

Striving for improvement in organizations and their HRM processes is one
of the goals of an audit. Producing a summary of HRM audit findings is helpful to organizational leaders concerned about legal compliance, as well as the
strength of the organization–employee relationship. An audit summary identifies workplace deficiencies and ultimately should also include an action plan
for improving HRM processes in support of the organization's broader strategy.

In those instances where HRM professionals and their departments lack
the staff to implement and execute such audits, there are various consultants they can hire that specialize in compliance and ethics (C&E) programs. In some instances, it would make most sense for HRM professionals
to hire C&E professionals to develop an audit checklist and other initiatives
designed to prevent and detect illegal conduct, for example, or simply noncompliance with relevant HRM laws or legislation. Such proactive planning
on the part of HRM professionals can prove to be more than worth the
investment in the long run. The use of C&E professionals, for example,
increases the likelihood that organizational members understand, follow,
or comply with the various HRM laws.

AN HRM CHECKLIST AND PRACTICAL ACTIONS
FOR EFFECTIVELY COMPLETING AUDITS

While an HRM compliance audit is preferable HRM professionals and their
organizations should at a minimum review their employment practices to
ensure that they are complying with all state and federal laws during any
part of the employment process. Violation of these laws can range from
monetary fines to extensive punitive damages determined by juries. Aside
from avoiding liability exposures, HRM professionals must ensure that their
organizations comply with laws because they make good business sense.

And one way of doing this is for HRM professionals to review the following checklist and identify and correct any deficiencies as soon as possible:

Does Your Organization:

Yes   No

1. Establish the validity and job relatedness of all employment requirements such as minimum hiring prerequisites and screening measures? Are requirements necessary to perform the job?

2. Treat all candidates for employment equally and without regard to race, color, religion, sex, or national origin?

3. Comply with the ADA (Americans With Disabilities Act) by considering all requests for accommodations, providing reasonable accommodations, establishing essential job functions, and eliminating pre-employment medical inquiries?

4. Provide family and medical leave time as well as healthcare benefits for employees who qualify under the FMLA? Follow a written policy consistently?

5. Review issues relating to the Fair Labor Standards Act such as overtime, number of hours worked, and exempt versus nonexempt status? Employers not covered by the FLSA should comply with the corresponding state minimum wage law.

6. Place only that information in personnel files that federal or corresponding state laws permit?

7. Adequately document all disciplinary actions taken, including the work rules or policies violated, compliance with the organization's "progressive discipline" policy (e.g., oral warning, written warning, suspension, dismissal), and compliance with the organization's appeals process?

8. When hiring minors, meet the federal or corresponding state child law requirements and require working papers when applicable?

9. Review all affirmative action programs with the organization's legal counsel, the EEOC, and the corresponding state department of civil rights?

10. Assure that female employees who perform jobs that are equal in required skills, effort, responsibility, and under similar working conditions to those of male employees receive the same pay?

11. Comply with the Immigration Reform and Control Act by requiring all new employees to complete the I-9 form and produce a required document for verification of eligibility status?

12. Communicate retirement benefits to employees in compliance with the Employment Retirement Security Act?
13. Establish and communicate a written safety and health policy in compliance with the Occupational Safety and Health Act (and any corresponding state safety and health compliance policy)?
14. Retain all employee and candidate information that federal and state and laws require for the minimum retention period and make it available upon request of a federal or state official?
15. Keep information about employees confidential and accessible only to internal individuals who have a legitimate business reason to review it?
16. Retain competent legal counsel when dealing with labor organizations?
17. Have policies and procedures in place to handle requests for information about employees?

- Does a specific written policy govern the release of information to external individuals?
- Does the policy should comply with the Freedom of Information Act and the Health Insurance Portability & Accountability Act?
- Is the release documented with a signed employee release?
- Is all information accurate and factual?
- Do supervisory employees follow the release of information policy?

18. Post all required state and federal notices?

Note: Because the laws frequently change and organizations may have different posting requirements depending on their size, HRM professionals should always verify accuracy with the federal or state agency responsible for compliance.

Yes   No

Federal Posting Requirements

- Fair Labor Standard Act—Minimum Wage
- Employee Polygraph Protection Act

- Family and Medical Leave Act
- Combined Equal Opportunity
- OSHA

If you were able to answer "yes" to all eighteen questions and your organization follows most or all of the suggested practices, then your organization has reduced its exposure to future employment claims. You should congratulate yourself.

If you were unable to answer "yes" to one or more of the eighteen questions, your organization may have an exposure to claims resulting from your employment practices. Missing components of one or more of the recommended practices may also indicate a deficiency in your current program. You should take one or more of the following actions:

- Correct any deficiency that may exist
- Contact your organization's legal counsel for advice

An audit can clearly show whether or not the organization is complying with HRM laws and legislation to include, for example, whether an organization's documentation of HRM actions is robust enough to stand up to outside inquiry, such as an administrative hearing for unemployment benefits claims, an EEOC complaint, or a wrongful termination lawsuit. By reviewing randomly selected HRM/personnel files of current and recent employees, an auditor looks for answers to questions like these:

- Are the HRM policies themselves legally compliant?
- Does documentation for corrective action dovetail with the organization's own policies?
- Are performance problems documented with a similar degree of detailed evidence from one employee to another?
- Do evaluations reference corrective actions that occurred during the period covered by the evaluation?
- If the basis for termination was violation of an organization policy, is there evidence that the employee knew about the policy?
- Are employees eligible for benefits receiving them? If not, are there signed waivers showing that they declined the offered benefit?
- Are accidents and injuries properly recorded?

Small organizations without experienced full-time HRM professionals benefit from HRM audits because they need help putting in place basic structures—filing systems that ensure appropriate content, HRM policies that cover all the bases, hiring procedures that attract and select the best workers, and performance evaluation procedures that provide clear goals and help employees achieve them. An audit can help ensure that the organization is not inadvertently breaking laws. In one instance, an audit of a small business with $1 million in sales revealed that the pay rate of department managers was too low (less than $560 a week as of this writing) to permit them to be paid on a salary basis. Such a violation of the Fair Labor Standards Act could have resulted in stiff fines if the Department of Labor Wages & Hours Division had audited the business.

But larger organizations are often out of compliance, too. A multistore retailer subjected to a Wages & Hours division audit did get fined for not paying overtime on bonuses based on hours worked. Sometimes legally required posters are missing from the break room. It is not unusual either when audits are done to find some incomplete I-9 forms.

Over time, especially after a period of rapid growth, HRM systems that once worked well no longer serve the organization. Layers of policies and forms can build up that contain internal contradictions or inconsistencies. If HRM professionals labor under a mountain of paperwork, trying to keep track of dozens of different forms for each employee, that is a sign that there may be too many policies or contradictory policies.

A proliferation of HRM policies and procedures can also make it difficult for HRM professionals and others in the organization to be on the same page when it comes to hiring, pay raises, and corrective action. Policies can fall behind the times and fail to reflect changes in HRM laws and regulations and technology. Pay scales too can become obsolete if new employees get hired at pay rates well above the base of their pay range and longtime employees get raises that take them beyond the top. In response to out-of-date or unworkable HRM policies and systems, different leaders or managers may go different ways, creating workarounds or "underground or guerilla HRM systems" in the process. As a result, the HRM department's workload is increased in the effort to administer multiple systems.

Inefficiencies in HRM systems can also occur when organizational leaders and managers attempt to manage by policy instead of addressing individual abuses. For example, in some instances in one organization, employees took advantage of benefits by failing to maintain the required number of worked hours. In response, restrictions were written into the policies limiting how paid time off could be used, details that at the time of this writing require HRM oversight.

An HRM audit can ask these questions to find areas for efficiency improvements:

- Are the personnel policies all in one easily accessible place, with individual policies found through a table of contents or index or search engine?

- Is there written guidance for supervisors and other organizational leaders on how to implement the policies? Is that guidance succinct and easy to follow?
- Do forms for HRM/personnel recordkeeping cover several bases instead of requiring a multitude of separate forms?
- Is a uniform template used for all types of job descriptions? Is the template overloaded with "boilerplate" or does it allow the unique job duties to be easily grasped?
- Are performance evaluations timely? If not, is the process unduly cumbersome?
- Is benefits enrollment high? If not, is enough information on benefits provided to all employees? Is it easy for employees to access straightforward information about their benefits, written in easily comprehensible language (as opposed to "insurance-speak")?

Furthermore, if an organization is planning to expand the workforce by moving to a larger location or opening a plant or office or going global, HRM systems must be considered in planning along with all the other operational systems. Planning for expansion requires building capacity in HRM. With more employees comes more risk of interpersonal conflicts; policy abuses and legal violations, even if inadvertent; and accidents and injuries. If there is a lack of accountability in organizational leadership now, the problems will be compounded with a larger number of employees. An audit can show organizational leaders where the HRM departments' or functions' efforts need to be focused in order to ensure sound systems are in place prior to expansion.

Completing an HRM audit should be done on a regular or planned schedule. However, this is not enough: There must be specific actions undertaken to address the findings and pave the way for the necessary organizational responses, changes, transition, or transformation. That is, an HRM audit should help HRM professionals and their organizations identify opportunities for transformation. (Examples of such organizational transformation efforts may be found in the volume edited by Sims, 2010). Many transformation initiatives start with determining the data needed, collecting and analyzing the data, and looking for patterns. Here are some ways HRM professionals can practice transformational HRM:

Staff Turnover

Analyze where in the organization and when in the employee life cycle turnover tends to occur. Conduct face-to-face exit interviews with open-ended questions if the employee size and turnover rate permit. HRM professionals should consider interviewing perhaps one in every three departing employees and ask the others to fill out a questionnaire online. HRM professionals should also ask about on-the-job training, pay and benefits, evaluations, employee–employer relations, and at every opportunity, mine employee survey data.

HRM professionals should also identify opportunities for increasing retention, such as more supervisor, manager, or senior leadership development, and when possible create more paths to promotion. If high turnover in certain departments and labor markets is unavoidable, HRM professionals should create super-efficient training and development programs and other practices.

Safety

HRM professionals should analyze the circumstances in which accidents occur: departments, types of injuries, time of day, and so on, and at every opportunity interview injured employees and witnesses with the goal of identifying underlying causes—lack of thorough training, faulty equipment, understaffing—and work with organizational leaders and managers to develop solutions that address these causes.

Benefits

Instead of just accepting what an insurance broker hands them, HRM professionals should research creative benefits solutions, such as Healthcare Reimbursement Accounts and Healthcare Savings Accounts, self-funded dental, short-term disability insurance, and of course what is available under the Patient Protection and Affordable Care Act as it continues to evolve.

Hiring

HRM professionals should identify recruiting sources that bring to their organizations the best candidates and focus their attention there. Instead of just posting job announcements on the organization's website, HRM professionals and others in the organization should constantly sell the organization as a great workplace or an "employer of choice" and do everything possible to communicate the organization's expectations with a dynamic jobs page.

Orientations

HRM professionals should think strategically about the organization's goals and objectives and how employees contribute to them—and then design programs that involve others in the organization to teach new employees about the organization's strategy/direction, organizational culture, and behavioral requirements related to HRM laws and regulations.

Communication Opportunities

HRM professionals should be very familiar with the flow of information—top-down, bottom-up, and interdepartmentally throughout the organization—to locate bottlenecks and breakdowns that might impact the dissemination and understanding of HRM laws and regulations. Employee survey data can be useful here to the HRM professional too. And, of course, HRM professionals should partner with others in the organization—for example, with IT staff and other managers to develop more effective systems.

Employee Discipline

HRM professionals should study records, notes, and transcripts of all disciplinary hearings held to make certain these hearings were carried out according to policy and that the rights of all were protected. While conducting these reviews, the HRM professionals should identify themes: What rules or policies are most frequently violated? Where might more training be necessary? How can supervisors ensure that policies and rules are not broken such that formal discipline becomes unnecessary? Are the organization's "progressive discipline" and appeals policies effective, or do they need to be revised?

These are only some examples of ideas that can come out of an HRM audit. Obviously, in order to devote time to transformational work, HRM professionals must find ways to streamline their transactional workload. An audit can suggest ways to move some transactional tasks off the HRM professional's plate as well as point to opportunities to invest saved time in projects that will transform the organization.

In sum, the careful, objective evaluation provided by an HRM audit can yield information critical to the successful development of the organization's human resources and compliance with HRM laws and regulations. With more effective people management, organizations can create the momentum necessary for success and sustainability in today's and tomorrow's world of work. An HRM audit can help HRM professionals and their organizations become the employer of choice.

HRM PROFESSIONALS, AUDITS
AND INTERNATIONAL COMPLIANCE

While everything discussed thus far in this chapter on HRM audits is applicable to any organization, such audits conducted by HRM professionals or others in global or multinational (or for purposes of this chapter, international) organizations are much more complicated, because each country's laws and regulations are unique, as highlighted in Chapter 16. Given this reality, this section takes a closer look at how international organizations and HRM professionals can effectively audit their compliance with HRM laws and regulations.

As the world has become smaller and smaller, the global economy has pushed international organizations to effectively align more and more aspects of their human resources across borders. Increasingly, international organizations now routinely internationalize their HRM programs, policies, benefits, and other "offerings" that used to be essentially local.

As an organization's headquarters oversees its cross-border HRM initiatives, compliance initiatives are international as well. An organization's headquarters also has a strong incentive to oversee compliance with the growing list of "extraterritorial" laws that will have an impact upon workforces internationally. International organizations must also regularly, effectively, and efficiently audit compliance with HRM laws and regulations across borders, and this means identifying those responsible for the audit, involving headquarters, local HRM professionals, and the in-house legal and compliance functions. In addition, it is wise for HRM professionals and other organizational leaders to consider including external counsel with attorney–client privilege or an outside international HRM consultant.

For HRM professionals and others in the organization, the question in need of answer is how to cost-effectively and efficiently best manage a cross-border HRM audit. The temptation may be to use the "quick-and-dirty approach"—grab an "international HRM audit checklist" off the shelf, dive in, and just do the audit. But the "quick-and-dirty approaches" are never really successful, because no one-size-fits-all "international HRM audit checklist" exists that can do what needs to be done. Each international HRM audit initiative goes in its own direction, with its own particular goals, its own pool of affected countries, and its own clear focus in its own particular industry. An international HRM compliance audit requires that HRM professionals take an organic, holistic approach that includes steps like the following:

1. *Communicate the context and scope.* HRM professionals and others should first identify the context and delineate the scope of the international HRM audit initiative. HRM audits/assessments arise in very different contexts: for example, implementing a new orga-

nizational structure, preparing for a restructuring, doing a merger or acquisition (spin-off or post-merger integration), responding to litigation/government investigation, or simply toughening compliance through a vigorous HRM practices check-up. Some international HRM audits focus externally on outside supplier compliance, while others focus internally, but on specific legal challenges such as health/safety, wage/hour, data privacy, bribery, whistleblower hotlines, or—increasingly—corporate social responsibility and ethics.

Isolating the context of the audit is vital for HRM professionals and others because it lets them put aside all irrelevant issues not germane to the situation at hand. After setting context, it is important that those responsible for the audit delineate the scope of the audit. Should the audit focus on compliance with employment laws, with collective agreements, with organizational policies—or with all three? As to legal compliance, should the audit look at local employment laws, at laws of the country in which headquarters is located that reach "extraterritorially"—or at both? Should the audit be confined to local employees, or should it reach expatriates, consultants, independent contractors, and suppliers? Should the audit go beyond employment laws and policies to assess compliance with HRM-context data privacy, corporate, and tax laws? What industry-specific issues require special focus—like health/safety in manufacturing, conflicts of interest/insider trading in professional services, wage/hour in retail?

2. *Create an HRM audit master template.* "Compliance" with HRM laws and regulations means following mandates. Because HRM law and regulation law mandates differ significantly by jurisdiction, for example, localized HRM compliance audit checklists (or questionnaires) are essential, and HRM professionals should ensure that they align to allow for "apples-to-apples" comparisons across jurisdictions. This means aligning local HRM audit checklists by ensuring each one derives from a single master template (or outline). HRM professionals should create the audit master template organically—tailoring it to fit the unique audit at hand. And, it should include all topics consistent with the audit scope (step 1), but exclude all other topics.

Depending on the context, international HRM compliance audit topics might include:

- *Local labor/employment laws*, including rules regulating candidate interviewing, recruiting and "onboarding," union/collective labor/ works councils, wage/hour (including overtime and flat caps on hours), holiday/vacation, health/safety, employee communications/

language, discrimination/harassment, complaints and internal investigation procedures, termination/release/pay-out at separation

- *Internal policies and collective (union or works council)* agreements, including local HRM policies, international code of conduct, industry codes, bribery/corruption policy, internationally applicable HRM policies issued by headquarters, "framework"/union neutrality agreement, collective agreements to which the organization is a party, and "sectoral" agreements that apply by force of law
- *Benefits and compensation issues,* including employee benefits, equity plans, statutory mandatory benefits, profit sharing, payroll compliance (deductions, withholding, reporting)
- *Individual employment contract issues,* including contract/offer letter template, restrictive covenants, employee Acknowledgments/consents/waivers, computer-click intranet assents (electronic signatures)
- *Contingent and irregular employment* issues, including contractor/consultant misclassification, fixed-term/part-time employees, secondees/ leased/agency employees, non-employee directors, expatriates (including visas/work permits)
- *Headquarters-country employment* laws that reach overseas, such as laws on accounting, bribery/foreign corruption, discrimination, Sarbanes-Oxley whistleblower procedures, securities, terrorism watch list, trade sanctions
- *Corporate and tax issues reaching employment,* including employer entity, employer registrations/corporate forms, dual-employer exposure, "permanent establishment" exposure from "floating employees," employee powers of attorney
- *Data privacy laws* that reach employee data, personnel files and global human resources information systems (HRIS), including employee notification/consents, registrations with data protection authorities, "sensitive" employee data, data security, HRM data retention/purging practices, cross-border data transmissions

3. *Ensure local-country checklists are aligned with the master.* HRM professionals have to localize the master HRM audit template into a set of aligned audit checklists (or questionnaires), one per jurisdiction. Additionally, they should create a local checklist for each jurisdiction and localize each point with the applicable local standard. For example, if bullet #11 on the master HRM audit template says "check compliance with local vacation laws," then the local Belgium checklist (for example), at its bullet #11, might say something like "confirm employees get 30+ vacation days per year and draw down vacation in periods of 10+ days per vacation break." HRM professionals need to make sure each local checklist captures any relevant

one-off local rules that are not addressed in the master HRM audit template. (For example, a local HRM audit checklist for Scotland might address overtime opt-outs; one for Bahrain might address gender segregation; one for Japan might address maternity leave).

4. *Conduct the HRM audit.* HRM professionals should take the local checklists into the field and conduct the international audit. Additionally, HRM professionals should gather data in each jurisdiction or territory, applying appropriate metrics in addition to deciding how the audit process will work. For example, will headquarters-based HRM auditors or professionals travel onsite, or can the field piece be conducted remotely? Will inspections be preannounced or not? How will local HRM professionals who fail to respond adequately be dealt with, and by whom? What translations will be needed? Will HRM professionals or other auditors look only at HRM policies/protocols/agreements, or will they inspect specific employment agreements, Acknowledgments, payroll information, timesheets, safety logs, and so on? Will HRM professionals or other auditors interview employees? What will be the role of local outside providers like payroll agencies and benefits administrators? How will the HRM audit process itself comply with local data laws?

5. *Analyze, report and implement remedial and then longer-term measures.* After analyzing the results of the HRM audit, HRM professionals should then summarize the findings and implement remedial and longer-term measures/solutions. Any summary report should avoid identifying specific employees (to minimize data protection and defamation exposure) and should account for privilege and evidentiary "admissions" issues. Could the report later get used against the organization as evidence of deliberate noncompliance? Finally, HRM professionals and others should propose specific remedial and longer-term measures—and then ensure the solutions actually get implemented locally.

Like non-international HRM audits, HRM professionals and others in the organization must take the time to think through, in advance, the challenges to a cross-border HRM compliance audit. Like the transformation role mentioned earlier, HRM professionals responsible for HRM audits internationally should proceed strategically and develop and align locally tailored checklists from a master HRM audit template.

In the end, be it an international organization or not, HRM professionals should view HRM audits as a way to take things to the next level. More specifically, it is accepted that HRM work can be transactional or transformational. Transactional HRM works within existing systems and concentrates on recordkeeping, documentation, and legal compliance. A transformational approach to HRM focuses on identifying and analyzing problems and creating solutions, or partnering with others in the organization to create solutions. Major changes or challenges confronting today's and tomorrow's organizations include but are not limited to globalization, increased competition, workforce diversity, technological advances, and changes in the political and legal environment. All these challenges increase the pressure on HRM professionals and their organizations to attract, retain, and nurture talented employees. HRM professionals cannot ignore these challenges, which really call for transformational HRM and for HRM professionals to create a culture of compliance in their host organizations.

CREATING A CULTURE OF COMPLIANCE

Making use of HRM compliance audits and self-assessments, HRM professionals can take the lead in the years to come in helping their organizations create a culture of compliance with HRM laws or legislation. Perhaps a model or framework for such an effort is what has been done in the past few years at the DOL. The DOL (2010) implemented a program, "Plan/Prevent/Protect," that is committed to ensuring that organizations comply with labor and employment laws. While the program is a federal regulatory enforcement strategy that targets all employers and falls under the purview of the OSHA, Mine Safety and Health Administration (MSHA), the Office of Federal Contract Compliance Programs, and the DOL's wage and hour division, such an effort is critical to establishing a culture of compliance as it relates to HRM laws. The plan requires the development of a compliance action plan and other programs that address certain employment law compliance issues within each organization's portfolio. More specifically, the DOL's three-part plan/prevent/protect strategy involves the creation of a compliance plan to identify and mitigate the risk of legal violation; implementation of the plan throughout all levels of an organization in a way that prevents legal violations; and careful monitoring, or protection, to ensure that the plan's objectives are being met. The strategy involves taking the following steps to ensure compliance with applicable laws:

- *Plan*: Create a plan for identifying and remediating risks of legal violations and other risks to workers. HRM should provide employees with opportunities to participate in the creation of the plans. Additionally, HRM departments should make the plans available to organizational members so they can fully understand them and help to monitor their implementation. This level of communication helps to ensure that the plan becomes a part of the organization's strategy, goals, culture, and possibly even its mission statement and not simply another HRM procedure.

- *Prevent:* The plan should be implemented in a manner that thoroughly and completely prevents legal violations. The plan should not be a mere paper process. HRM professionals should not expect merely to draft a plan and then "put in on a shelf." An effective plan should be fully implemented and communicated throughout all levels of the organization.

- *Protect:* HRM professionals should ensure that the plan's objectives are met on a regular basis, and one way of doing this is via an audit. In the end, the plan must actually protect employees from violations of their workplace rights.

While the DOL's regulatory enforcement strategy is not a requirement for all organizations, it is, in our view, one example of a compliance action plan that any HRM department could easily implement. An action plan that could help in the creation and institutionalization of a culture of compliance is based on establishing organization-wide norms on "the way we do things around here." In actuality, an action plan, such as the DOL's *Plan/Prevent/Protect* regulatory enforcement strategy, adds another layer of regulatory compliance to any already existing measures taken by HRM departments and serves as an additional reminder of the importance of remaining compliant with labor and employment laws. Such reminders should always be welcome by HRM professionals.

By creating an effective, long-term compliance action plan, HRM professionals and other organizational leaders are more likely to create a culture of compliance. And such a culture ensures that future leaders and employees will continue to follow the plan and remain committed to the vision of proactively interacting with HRM laws in an increasingly evolving and dynamic world of work.

CONCLUSION

An HRM compliance audit is a systematic, objective tool for how well the organization is complying with legal, regulatory, and policy requirements. A well-run HRM audit has various long-reaching benefits. It can help an organization avoid exposure to legal liability by ensuring its HRM practices and policies comply with the dizzying array of local, state, federal, and international HRM laws and regulations. An effective or well-run HRM audit can also serve as an educational tool by increasing the awareness of an organization's leaders and employees of the HRM's department's or function's commitment to compliance. It can also identify ways to improve the efficiency and cost-effectiveness of the HRM department.

HRM audits can be performed in-house or through the use of an external third-party auditor. External audits may provide a fresh perspective that a self-audit may not necessarily be able to capture. However, regardless of who performs it (internal HRM or outside third-party), the HRM professionals or other auditors must be aware that HRM laws and regulations are governed by international, federal, state, and often city law and that the laws can vary greatly from state to state and city to city and country to country—what is legal in one might expose the employer to liability in another. In addition, an HRM audit must examine the organization's own policies to determine if the organization's practices are in accordance with those policies.

Because each organization's needs may be different, there really is no one exact "how-to" formula for performing an HRM audit that meets every organization's needs. What is better is to identify the various areas that typically fall under the purview of an HRM audit, regardless of whether it is international or not, and to highlight some of the key issues that HRM professionals and others should look at, and for, when performing a comprehensive HRM audit.

As noted at different points in this chapter, the main goals of an HRM audit are to (a) determine whether an organization's employment-related materials and practices are complying with the law and the organization's own policies and (b) identify and *bring into compliance* any area that may not be in compliance. An HRM audit should identify what the organization is doing right or wrong, as well as gray areas that could use improvement. Practically, this means that HRM professionals when doing an audit should typically review the organization's

- Printed materials, such as employment applications and any organization handbooks or manuals
- Practices, such as those involved in recruitment, hiring, compensation, promotion, and termination
- Policies, such as sick and vacation leave policies
- Procedures, such as those governing performance reviews and discipline
- The organization's unwritten practices to determine whether or not they should be finalized and/or changed

In addition, they should carefully read the materials, conduct interviews with other HRM professionals and other relevant personnel, and observe first-hand the workings of the HRM department.

Before beginning an HRM audit, it is important for HRM professionals and others to define its scope as the organization may only want to examine a few particular areas and not others. Once the scope of the audit is defined, the next step is to identify all the international, federal, state, and local laws that apply to the areas being audited. Identifying all the laws that apply can be a very long and complicated process. Therefore, the assistance of legal counsel can be very helpful to HRM professionals at this step.

We would be remiss if we did not conclude this chapter by noting that generally there are very few if any drawbacks when an HRM audit is properly conducted. There are, however, some considerations HRM professionals should keep in mind when deciding to conduct an audit. First, any material produced during the audit could potentially be used in litigation against the organization. This risk can possibly be reduced by using a lawyer to conduct the review. But *caveat emptor*—simply using a lawyer does not guarantee the confidentiality of the audit documents.

Invoking the protection of doctrines, such as attorney–client privilege or attorney work-product, requires fulfilling many conditions. An organization and HRM professionals interested in maintaining the confidentiality of the HRM audit should consult with legal counsel. Additionally, if non-compliance is discovered during an audit, it is very important that HRM professionals and the organization's senior leaders implement appropriate corrective action in a timely fashion. Failure to correct problems identified during an audit can lead to many more problems because if problems are identified through the audit and nothing is done to correct them, the organization's non-action can lead to lawsuits and also be used against the organization in future enforcement proceedings.

REFERENCES

Department of Labor. (2010). *Department-wide regulatory and enforcement strategies—"Plan/prevent/protect" and openness and transparency.* Retrieved from http://www.dol.gov/regulations/2010RegNarrative.htm"

Sauser, W. I., Jr. (2008). Crafting a culture of character: The role of the executive suite. In S. Quatro & R. R. Sims (Eds.), *Executive ethics: Ethical dilemmas and challenges for the C suite* (pp. 1–17). Charlotte, NC: Information Age Publishing.

Sauser, W. I., Jr., & Sims, R. R. (2007). Fostering an ethical culture for business: The role of HR managers. In R. R. Sims (Ed.), *Human resource management: Contemporary issues, challenges and opportunities* (pp. 253–285). Charlotte, NC: Information Age Publishing.

Sims, R. R. (Ed.). (2010). *Change (transformation) in government organizations.* Charlotte, NC: Information Age Publishing.

CHAPTER 3

HR AND THE LAW

The HR Practitioner's Point of View

Sheri Bias and Barry Hoy

INTRODUCTION

Human resources professionals may be involved in many legal situations that occur within the conduct of the business day. The majority of these professionals are not lawyers by education, yet they are expected to provide guidance and subject-matter expertise with regard to the applicability of the laws to their organizations—in other words "put on your lawyer hat." What the organization is seeking is the legal opinion of the HR professional.

Managers manage risk. Throughout the daily business operation, managers are confronted by decisions in which they must select from a range of options. Each of the options, to some extent, presents the manager with a risk versus gain scenario. In order to make the right decision—or more correctly, in order to avoid making the wrong decision—the manager needs information. When the HR practitioner is the source of that information, more times than not, the manager wants to know the legal risks associated with the various options that are available. Under these auspices,

Legal and Regulatory Issues in Human Resources Management, pages 51–72
Copyright © 2015 by Information Age Publishing

management is engaging in a basic and proven technique of decision making in seeking the opinion of the subject-matter expert. According to Paul and Elder (2009), information is one of the elements of thought. It is one of the underpinnings of critical thinking and hence is an essential component in the making of sound decisions.

HR practitioners, when cast in the roll of the legal expert, are asked for "advice." For several reasons the characterization does not quite fit. When a person asks for advice, there is an associated implication that the advice will likely be taken. No such compulsion is placed upon the manager who receives only an opinion. In addition, when acting in the role of an advisor, the HR practitioner might assume some accountability for the effects of the advice. But if the manager seeks and the practitioner provides an opinion, then the bulk of the responsibility for the effect of acting upon the opinion rests on the shoulders of the manager.

This chapter opens with a discussion of the environment within which three groups must interact in pursuance of the process of performing HR functions for the good of the organization. The groups—the policymakers, the HR practitioner or manager, and the legal staff—have the responsibility to guard for the interests of all of the stakeholders. The discussion proceeds from the premise that the policymakers, that is to say the general management of the organization, will be called upon to make decisions that consider all of the available information balancing risk tolerance with risk averseness. In this chapter, the three groups will be referred to interchangeably as "groups" or as "interests" as the nuances of the situation dictate.

The chapter then moves to a more focused examination of the laws that guide the manner in which organizations interact with their stakeholders. The examination will be as comprehensive as is possible given the limitations of space and the fact that this text is intended to serve the HR practitioner or manager rather than the attorney. The journey begins with the Emancipation Proclamation of 1863 and then leaps to 1964.

The first segment of the chapter may be seen as somewhat philosophical in its approach. Conversely, the second half is a bit more informational as it presents the second consideration under which HR professionals operate. Neither of these considerations in the practice of human resource management enjoys preeminence. They must be considered in tandem. Members of each of the three groups mentioned above must be in tune to the law and the statutes that implement the law. But they must also consider the good of the organization from a holistic standpoint even when the law cannot be relied upon to provide all of the answers. For this reason, the two aspects are explored in one single chapter.

THE LAY OF THE LAND

Let's lay the foundation for the discussion through an example. In a small organization, the operations manager (let's call her Jill) comes into the HR practitioner's (Jack's) office and says, "I want you to put on your lawyer hat." What Jill means is that she needs a legal opinion. Jill is a member of the policymaker group for the organization. She has been confronted by a decision, and she is smart enough to realize that her decision has a component that might involve litigation. So she turns to the closest thing to a legal department she has—the organization's internal HR practitioner, Jack. So Jill is asking Jack, a member of the HR practitioner group, to speak to her as though he were a member of the legal group.

Human Resources Response

Jack's opinion will fall into one or the other of two fairly well defined categories. In the first category, Jack will be asked if an option that Jill proposes to take is clearly actionable or clearly not actionable. He will render an opinion as to the likelihood that the option contemplated would expose the organization to a complaint—for example, with the EEOC or an action filed under some other statute. Parenthetically, some might erroneously declare that an option is either legal or not legal. While it is not always technically correct, it is informative to use the expression "legal" or "not legal" because it qualifies the situation as essentially go or no-go. To the manager, this means that the action presents significant risk or no risk. Use of the terms "legal" or "not legal" adds a weighty character to the decision and hence encourages sobriety as the options are considered. As well, it makes the situation more comprehensible to persons who might not be intimately familiar with the finer points of "illegality" as compared with "actionability."

In the second category, Jack might be asked to assess the various litigious risks associated with several different options. Among these options might be one in which there is no clear violation of the law and no absolute danger of legal action, but which possesses the potential for litigious involvement. Jack might describe four options followed by a request for his opinion as to the relative risk of each option. In this second category, black and white fade into shades of grey.

In either category, the HR practitioner will be encouraged to render an opinion regarding the level of exposure, that is to say the extent to which the organization might suffer because they have had to defend the manager's action in the legal system. The practitioner must understand that the manager who is receiving and who will make use of the opinion will view the situation from a standpoint of risk. This is because managers are accustomed to viewing their management decisions as risk versus gain relationships. Risk has two components: (a) the likelihood that the "worst case scenario" occurs, and (b) the seriousness of the damage to the organization should the "worst case scenario" occur.

INFORMATION AS AN ELEMENT OF DECISION MAKING

Managers manage risk. That is to say that as they move through their day, they are confronted by decisions in which they must select from a range of options. Each of the options, to some extent, presents the manager with a risk versus gain scenario. In order to make the right decision—or, more correctly, in order to avoid making the wrong decision—the manager needs information. When the HR practitioner is the source of that information, more times than not, the manager wants to know the legal risks associated with the various options that are available. Jill wants Jack to render his opinion as to the legal ramifications of the decision that Jill has to make.

Nearly all decision making models have a commonality. In each model, the first step is *problem identification*. No decision can be properly made unless all of the alternatives are accurately understood (Betsch & Glockner, 2010). We start the decision-making process by understanding all of the alternatives. Once the alternatives have been fully comprehended, along with all of the ramifications, the information search should stop. Intuition is useful in decision making. Intuition becomes more useful as an antecedent to the decision process as experience in a given field of inquiry informs the intuition. Essentially a hunch becomes an informed opinion.

The Jack and Jill scenario provides us with a classic, and often repeated, example in which the HR practitioner is providing information input to a policymaker so that the policymaker can make a decision. Lee and Dry (2006) hypothesize that as managers make decisions, they consider two things about the information that is presented to them. Primarily, they consider how accurate they think the information is. This is the basis of the first hypothesis presented in the research. In the second hypothesis, the authors state that the decision maker will also consider how frequently or how often the information is presented.

The first hypothesis is self-evident, but the second requires a bit of exploration to solidify understanding. In their study, Lee and Dry (2006) demonstrated that the likelihood that a decision maker will permit a bit of information to influence her decision is directly proportional to the number of times she is presented with the information. As an example, let's assume that a manager is considering a change in human resource management policy that will impact the morale of the employees of the organization. Let's also assume that in a separate initiative, the organization is in the middle of an energetic campaign to communicate the concept that employee morale is a top organizational priority. According to the conclusions emerging from Lee and Dry's (2006) study, the frequent messages that are part of the campaign will prompt the manager to be more likely to come down on the side of the employee.

In addition to accuracy of information and frequency of the message, decision makers will likely consider the degree to which the information comports with their view of the issue as they use the information to inform their decision (Ferrary, 2009). Stakeholder theory (Freeman, 1984) presents a model of organizations in which the organization is understood as a politico-economic system. In this system, each interest group or entity will view a given decision and the associated range of options against their own frame of reference. The legal interests will likely emphasize adherence to specific statutes or policies. The human resource interest must match the impact of the various options on the members of the organization. The policymakers care about either profit or mission depending upon what type of organization they are managing.

The Nature of Information Processing

The three groups that were identified previously—(a) the legal interest, (b) the policymakers, and (c) the HR interest—behave in accordance with the tenets of this theory. Each interest group is a member of a stratified triadic relationship, as depicted in Figure 3.1.

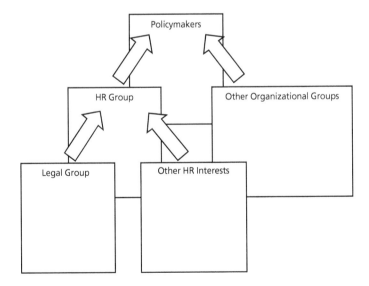

Figure 3.1 Stratified triadic relationship of three groups in the organization.

It is incumbent upon the policymakers to carefully consider the information received from the HR interest, along with the information about the interest of all organizational stakeholders. Concomitantly, the HR practitioner must present the information from the legal interest, as well as information from all other HR interests.

The organization has been described as a politico-economic system. Freeman (1984) portrays the organization as "an entity enmeshed within a set of interactions between parties inside the organization" (p. 46). The different interests emerge as stakeholders who are attempting in their own interest to influence the functioning of the organization in a way that the stakeholder perceives as "legitimate." In this case, the term *legitimate* is defined as meeting the stakeholder's needs and matching the stakeholder's viewpoints. Freeman defines *stakeholders* as "the ensemble of parties who can have an effect on the organization or who can be affected by it" (Freeman, 1984, p. 46).

The present discussion focuses upon the legal issues confronting the HR manager. Consequently, it might be tempting to equate the "legitimacy" to the "legality" of a point in question. However, this equality may not be universally perceived by members of the various groups. Certainly, to the legal group, legality is the primary consideration. Organizational lawyers may look at themselves as benevolent dictators (Ayers, 2011) attempting to mold their society in accordance with their own view of ethics.

The policymakers will demand that the legal group view the situation from the standpoint of legality because it is their job. Indeed, this is why Jill asked Jack to put on his "lawyer hat." She wanted him to give her an opinion that was based solely upon the law, knowing full well that other information would eventually find its way into the decision. But to other stakeholders, legality may be less important. The policymakers will observe the norms not only of the law but of the implementation of that law in the environment in which they are operating.

As regards the comparison of legitimacy versus legality, it should be repeated that the relative importance of these two aspects of a situation are not universally accepted as being equal. Two things impact this perception. They are:

1. The question of who is doing the perceiving
2. The question of when the issue is being raised

The first instance proposes that different groups will perceive different things to be important to the decision at hand. To those in the legal group, it will be absolutely unacceptable to select an option that is potentially actionable. However, if that viewpoint restricts the options available to the policymakers, such that they are left with only those that are tremendously expensive to implement, the policymakers may be forced to bend the rules simply to permit the organization to survive.

Comprehension of the second instance is facilitated when one considers the statement, "What is acceptable today may not be acceptable tomorrow." As an example, we may consider a decision in which rules are bent until it becomes too dangerous to bend them. An example is provided via a construction company manager who must decide to strictly observe, or cautiously dispense with, safety rules and protocol that are tremendously expensive to implement and that provide little in the way of improved employee safety. In the absence of any additional danger to workers, the single consideration faced by the manager is the potential that his project might be cited for the safety violation and fined. This fine would be levied after an inspection by a representative of the Occupational Safety and Health Administration (OSHA) visits the manager's project for the purpose of inspecting to verify that safety precautions are being observed in accordance with the rules. When the OSHA inspector detects a violation, he or she writes a report that cites the statute and suggests a fine. In most construction environments, there are far more projects being built than there are OSHA inspectors available to write citations. Consequently, the likelihood that a violation would be detected is quite low, and the manager will likely avoid the citation. But now the manager learns that an OSHA inspector will be traveling through his area, increasing the possibility that the inspector will stop to visit the manager's project. At this point, the issue of legality becomes significantly more important.

As a very real part of stakeholder theory (Freeman, 1984), each stakeholder will try to protect his or her interest by attempting to influence management decisions (Ferrary, 2009). In effect, stakeholders gain credibility when decisions go their way. So the legal stakeholder will present an opinion. If the policymaker decides the issue based solely upon the information provided by the legal stakeholder, the credibility of the legal stakeholder is reinforced.

In some cases, the legal aspect of the decision is sufficiently compelling that the information originating with the legal stakeholder must be the sole consideration. But it is the policymaker who must make the decision, and hence, it is up to the policymaker to decide which information guides the decision. In decisions that have a legal component, the policymakers determine the risk presented in the legal framework while the legal experts merely provide information to the stakeholders who will establish the framework.

Reexamination of the construction project example above is helpful. The legal group would tell the project manager (the policymaker) that he must always follow all safety rules. This opinion would be based upon the desire of the persons in the legal group to promote the safety of employees and to avoid fines by OSHA. The policymaker might know that a given safety requirement provides no additional safety and is very unlikely to result in a fine. He may also know that enforcing the rule scrupulously will make his project unprofitable during the times when the rule is enforced. It is then up to the policymaker to decide which option is the more prudent. This fits the risk versus gain model presented previously.

The role played by the HR practitioner in this instance is that of the gate-keeper. In organizations in which the legal function resides within HR or in which the HR function includes acquiring legal advice externally, it may be appropriate for the HR manager or practitioner to perform a reality check on the information or opinion that is being conveyed. At the very least, the person who receives the advice or opinion and then forwards it to the policymakers should review the advice or opinion before presenting it to the policymakers. In so doing, they must realize that the advice or opinion will likely be couched in terms that represent absolute minimum risk from a legal standpoint. Policymakers have a right to receive that unvarnished opinion. However, policymakers will also exercise their judgment arriving at a conclusion that embodies what the policymakers consider to be acceptable risk. It is the function of management and an activity of policymakers to balance all potential harms as opposed to all potential benefits in scenarios in which risk is part of the decision.

The Universal Intellectual Standards Applied to the Information

Whether she knows it or not, Jill is engaging a basic and proven technique in decision making as she approaches Jack. The decision-making process has driven her to invoke the tenets of critical thinking. She is seeking as much information as she can get in order to make a prudent decision. She visits Jack because she needs to completely understand the legal aspects of the various options. As we consider the connection between critical thinking and decision making, we must refer to the work of Richard Paul and Linda Elder, two major contributors to the field. According to Paul and Elder (2009), information is one of the elements of thought. It is one of the underpinnings of critical thinking and hence is an essential component in the making of sound decisions.

These authors gave us some universal intellectual standards that should be applied primarily to the information component of every decision (Paul & Elder, 2009). In the Jack and Jill scenario, the information includes the opinion rendered by the HR practitioner along with the opinion's supporting rationale. The universal intellectual standards may be helpful in informing the HR practitioner's response to the manager's questions. They are partially summarized below, with an associated description of the way they should be understood by the HR practitioner:

- Clarity—the extent to which the information is understandable
- Accuracy—the extent to which the information is properly descriptive
- Precision—the extent to which the information is expressed in terms of resolution
- Relevance—the extent to which the information should be part of the decision-making process
- Depth—the extent to which the information presents all possible effects in detail
- Breadth—the extent to which the information comprehensively covers all of the possible effects

As we examine these universal intellectual standards, it is important to remember that the two parties involved in the interchange, the HR practitioner and the policymaker, will view the information from differing viewpoints. The HR practitioner's contribution will be necessarily focused on the aspects of information attaching to the field of inquiry covered by the role he or she is asked to assume. In our scenario, Jack has been asked to "put on his lawyer hat." As he does this, as he assumes the legal role, he will be presenting information of a legal nature. On the other hand, Jill does not have the luxury of such a narrow focus. If she did, she would simply turn this decision and all similar decisions over to Jack. In doing so, she would be abdicating her responsibility to manage the organization.

To arrive at the right decision, the policymaker must consider the legal input along with all other information that informs the decision. Failure to do so is falling into a trap that scholars encourage the HR practitioner, and for that matter the policymaker as well, to guard against. Adjibolosoo (2011) refers to the pitfall as "the indiscriminate application of solutions dealing with HR problems" (p. 95) and employment of human resources regulations and policies. He goes on to state that this over-reliance on legal considerations is largely "impotent" and may "not deal effectively and efficiently with the root causes of the problems" of human resources use (p. 95). Adjibolosoo is not advocating lawlessness. Clearly, if a decision is informed by the law to the extent that there is a potential for a law to be broken, the organization is compelled to proceed with a full understanding of the ramifications of that eventuality.

Other scholars encourage the HR practitioner to operate in his or her "legal advisor" role in a way that is subservient to the primary role as an advocate for the organization (Nielsen, 2005). As he or she provides an input to the decision-making process, he or she must acknowledge both roles in their proper perspective. The flurry of statutes governing the relationship between employer and employee and the judicial system's interpretation of those statues has left the HR practitioner in the unenviable position of reacting to two forces that frequently pull the policymakers in different directions (Roehling & Wright, 2006). HR practitioners may view HR law as an overly restrictive influence on their profession, blaming growing government regulation for their plight. The researchers acknowledge the situation in which the legal advice that policymakers must consider cannot be practically justified.

It is important to understand the dynamic in this situation. In his or her role as a legal advisor, the HR practitioner must remember that he or she is only providing information. That information will be used by another person who is in the role of the policymaker to make a decision.

THE ORGANIZATIONAL LEGAL SUPPORT STRUCTURE

As previously discussed, Jill is asking Jack to step outside of his HR practitioner role and step into the role of the legal group and advisor. As the HR person, Jack is the most natural resource for questions of a legal nature. This example demonstrates the most basic organizational legal support structure. Organizations have four options with regard to the structure of the legal support system to which the managers must turn. The four levels of the legal structure within an organization are almost always directly proportional to the size of the organization. Briefly, the four levels of legal support, which will be discussed in detail, include first-level support, which equates to no legal support at all. Second-level support is that support which is executed by the HR practitioner as best he or she sees fit. In this case, the practitioner may see the advice of an attorney, but these requests would be episodic in nature. Third-level support embodies the use of an attorney on retainer, and finally, the fourth level of support incorporates a full-time legal staff. The form or level of legal support is driven by three factors: (a) the available resources, (b) the legal need, and (c) attitude of the policymakers.

The Available Resources Translation: What Can We Afford?

Of course, it costs money to staff a legal department within an organization. The legal department makes no profit and consequently the cost becomes an expenditure that attacks profitability. The cost breakdown includes:

- Salary plus burden of the attorney or attorneys
- Salary plus burden of the non-attorney legal staff

- Cost to physically house the legal structure
- Administrative cost such as dues, fees, travel, etc.
- Costs for supplies and incidentals

A small permanent legal structure can cost a quarter million dollars per year. Every dollar of that amount comes from the bottom line. In order for the Policy Makers to arrive at the conclusion that a permanent legal staff is worth the expenditure, they must see that the anticipated value of the legal department's contribution exceeds the cost. McDowell and Leavitt (2011) speak of five activities that occupy the lion's share of the organizational legal function's time (p. 240):

1. Presenting the employer's case in hearings when an employee files an unofficial or official charge
2. Drafting the employer's position in response to a charge brought by an employee against the organization
3. Reviewing standards, rules, and policies under which the organization's HR functions operate
4. Auditing employer practices to ensure compliance with appropriate standards and statutes
5. Preparing and conducting training sessions for managers and supervisors to raise awareness

These five activities combine to form the value of the legal department and, hence, are the basis for the decision to form a permanent legal group within the organization.

The activities can be broken down into those activities that must happen in reaction to some event (1 and 2) and to those activities that are prudent to reduce or avoid risk (3, 4, and 5). Each of these activities has a value. The value of the two mandatory activities, (a) presenting a case in a judicial proceeding and (b) writing the organization's position when a dispute arises, can be easily quantified. They are essentially a fixed cost that is determined based upon the character of the activity. That is to say, for example, that it may cost $2,000.00 to pay an average attorney to report to a courthouse for one day.

The value associated with the remaining three activities of mitigating risk is a bit more difficult to determine since that value is based upon some nondescript harm that will be avoided at a date some distance into the future. Standards, rules, and policies are reviewed in part to reduce the likelihood that employees will file a grievance. The cost to process a grievance and the chances of one being filed are not easily ascertainable. Practices are audited for compliance to place the organization on firm footing when those practices are reviewed by an external entity that has the power to inflict harm on the organization. Some regulatory organizations have the power to levy fines and even to direct that an activity be suspended until the practice is brought into compliance. Training is done to improve employee treatment and hence employee morale. A happy employee is less likely to lodge a complaint than an unhappy one. While it may be hard to ascribe a dollar figure or to predict when that value will be realized, the value is still there and is very real.

The Legal Need, Translation: How Much Legal Work Are We Doing?

Depending upon the nature of the business being conducted, some organizations might undergo a large volume of legal activity, while others have little need for legal support. According to Massey and Campbell (2013) the three most frequently litigated complaints are discrimination, harassment, and wrongful termination. The lessons to the policymakers as they approach the decision to establish or expand the legal structure within the organization are clear. Those organizations in which the employee population is characterized by wide diversity and especially when different demographic groups within the organization are represented disproportionately in groups of work assignment might anticipate problems resulting in exercise of the legal structure. As an example, the nursing field has been a traditional employer of females. If the vast majority of the nurses in a particular medical facility happen to be females, the organization may be in danger of a suit citing disparate impact to attack the practices in the facility. An organization in which the level of awareness among employees as to appropriate and acceptable interpersonal communication behaviors is low might anticipate a high number of harassment complaints. Finally, a business that relies on high turnover rates to accommodate a fluctuating operational tempo may be at higher risk of a wrongful termination suit than one in which the employee workforce is relatively static.

The Attitude of the Policymakers, Translation: How Do We Feel About the Function?

Notwithstanding the two previous factors motivating the policymakers' decision to engage a legal function, some managers simply resist adding to the existing organizational structure. Their rationale has less to do with empirical data and more to do with business philosophy or their own personal prejudices.

Certainly there may be additional factors to consider as the organization and structure of the legal function is developed. However, the three factors enumerated above will consistently enjoy prominence among considerations as the effort proceeds. The reader will quickly note the similarities between these considerations applied to legal structure decisions and management decisions attaching to any other functional expansion within the organization. For example, let us examine a decision of a heavy construction company to make use of contract haulers (the rough equivalent of seeking advice from an attorney in terms of the parameters of the relationship) as opposed to assembling an organizationally owned fleet of dump trucks (akin to hiring a full time attorney.) The three "translation" questions are equally applicable in both decisions.

It might seem somewhat out of sequence to have explored the structure in which the HR Group covers the legal needs of the organization followed directly by a discussion of the rationale for building a structure within the organization. In effect we moved from Level 2 structure directly to Level 4 structure (see Table 3.1). However, when one considers that the Level 3 structure is simply that structure in which all legal support is acquired as by a contractor, the logic of the progression is more evident.

All that needs to be said about Level 3 structure is that it represents a point at which more services are needed than can be provided by the Level 2 structure but the legal activities have not risen to a volume that would prompt a move to Level 4. The various levels of legal support are examined in Table 3.1.

It is appropriate at this point to expand on the discussion of the five primary legal activities in the list assembled by McDowell and Leavitt (2011). Recall that the activities are (p. 240):

1. Presenting the employer's case in hearings when an employee files an unofficial or official charge
2. Drafting the employer's position in response to a charge brought by an employee against the organization

TABLE 3.1 Levels of Legal Support

Legal Support Structure	Appropriate For	Considerations
No legal support (Level 1)	Very small organizations	This situation exposes the organization to a high degree of risk.
HR Practitioner only with external legal support as needed (Level 2)	Very small organizations	The HR practitioner must be familiar with the law, must take an active part in reviewing policy, and must have good knowledge of the legal support available.
Attorney on retainer (Level 3)	Medium size organizations	This structure is appropriate when the risk environment is relatively relaxed.
Full time attorney(s) and or staff (Level 4)	Large organizations	Large organizations have high levels of risk and also have a lot to lose.

3. Reviewing standards, rules and policies under which the organization's HR functions operate
4. Auditing employer practices to ensure compliance with appropriate standards and statutes
5. Preparing and conducting training sessions for managers and supervisors to raise awareness

An expansion is described in Table 3.2.

Activities 1 and 2 must be engaged regardless of the existence of a legal support structure within the organization. That is to say, once an employee has filed a charge either officially or unofficially, the organization will be compelled, either by the judicial system or as an exigency to the demands of prudence, to react and respond. On the other hand, activities 3, 4, and 5 are executed as a matter of good business. They amount to things that the organization should do rather than things the organization must do. Ironically, the proper application of activities 3, 4, and 5 will go a long way to obviate the likelihood that activities 1 or 2 will be needed. An ounce of prevention is worth a pound of cure.

Organizations that operate at the lowest level, with no existing legal structure, are at pains to react when needed. Resources must be allocated at the expense of other organizational functions (Calvasina, Calvasina, & Calvasina, 1999) or they must be contracted at significant financial investment. Since there is no structure, there is very likely a commensurate failure to perform the steps (activities 3, 4, and 5) that are predicated on the motivational imperative provided by due diligence. It is only logical

TABLE 3.2   An Expansion of the Legal Activities

Activity	Executed by	Remarks
Presenting a case	An attorney	While HR practitioners are finding themselves more welcome in the courtroom, the official presentation should be done by an attorney.
Drafting a position	An attorney	The HR practitioner will coordinate the gathering of information to be provided by the drafter.
Review	An attorney or an HR practitioner	This is fairly easy work to do except in rare cases. If the HR practitioner does the actual review, the results should be reviewed by an attorney.
Audit	An attorney or an HR practitioner	Again, this work is fairly simple, but an audit by an HR practitioner should be validated by the attorney.
Training	HR practitioner	Two distinctly different skills are engaged in this function. Initially the attorney should provide the input for the authoring of the training materials. But the actual training should be conducted by a person who is an adept trainer. This skill is generally to be found in the HR Department.

to suggest that organizations that are not prepared to do the things they may be compelled to do are similarly unlikely to do the things that rest upon due diligence.

The level two legal structures occur in small organizations that are operated responsibly. These organizations admit to the needs of the organization regardless of its size to protect itself and to do the legal activities that due diligence demands (Massey & Campbell, 2013). In the absence of resources required to fund a permanent legal staff or to keep an attorney on retainer, the organization deliberately relies upon the HR practitioner for legal support.

The HR practitioner is the first line of defense. This is what brought Jill into Jack's office. In our scenario, we mentioned two options available to Jack, but there is actually a third. Instead of giving advice or rendering an opinion, Jack might declare that he is unprepared to assist without the services of an attorney who is intimately familiar with the applicable statutes. With limited training in the law, the HR practitioner may be competent to interpret existing policies and to declare that some activity was clearly in keeping with those policies. But sooner or later, an event will present itself that the HR practitioner can't handle on his or her own.

When the HR practitioner in the small organization finds that he or she is unprepared, he or she must resort to seeking the help of an attorney from outside of the company. This may occur as an emergent response to an employee complaint. It might also flow from an event within the organization that it might be anticipated will impact employees in a way that will likely be unpopular. As an example, the closing of a location at which numerous employees work might be followed by grievances that only an attorney could address. In such cases, it would be helpful to work with an attorney before the closing so as to proceed in a way that softens the blow or accommodates the displaced employees.

Since one of the five fundamental areas for which the HR practitioner is responsible is EEO/employment law/labor law, it is natural to assume that the HR practitioner would be called upon to arrange these services. Good familiarity with the areas of expertise of the various law firms in the vicinity is essential in choosing the right attorney or the right firm.

In organizations that have an attorney on retainer or a permanent legal staff, the opinions forthcoming will not likely involve the HR practitioner except to the extent that the HR practitioner must be cognizant of them and may be called upon to implement them. In such structures, the job of the HR practitioner can be somewhat less complex. The position of the policymaker is substantially identical regardless of which level of legal structure exists. The single difference is the source of the information upon which to base his or her decisions.

THE SYNERGY AMONG THE GROUPS

Frequently, HR practitioners, when cast in the role of the legal expert are asked for "advice." For several reasons, the characterization does not quite fit. In the first place, when a person asks for advice, there is an associated implication that the advice will likely be taken. No such compulsion is placed upon the manager, who receives only an opinion. In addition, when acting in the role of an advisor, the HR practitioner might assume some accountability for the effects of the advice. But if the manager seeks and the practitioner provides an opinion, then the bulk of the responsibility for the effect of acting upon the opinion rests exactly where it should. It is on the shoulders of the manager.

McDowell and Leavitt (2011) report a declining reluctance on the part of courts to admit the testimony of HR practitioners. This means that as the manager defends the decision or action that has resulted in the legal proceeding, the HR practitioner may be called upon to endorse or denounce that action. Careful deliberation as the decision is being made will help to forestall the situation in which the opinions of the policymaker and the HR practitioner are in conflict. Once the decision is made, it is most desirable that the two interests speak with one voice.

The manager has a right to hold the HR practitioner accountable for carefully adhering to the standards as he or she provides the opinion. Concomitantly, the practitioner must approach the task with sober resoluteness. The legal environment attached to employment and labor decisions changes constantly. It is applied in ways that may seem illogical and complex. To stay on top, the practitioner must be carefully trained in the law, including the interpretation of the law by the courts. In level two organizations, the human resource department is not staffed with a lawyer, and hence, the persons attached to the HR department must serve that need. Lack of education and practical experience cannot be cited as an excuse for a bad opinion.

THE ALPHABET SOUP OF THE LAWS

It is without a doubt that there are numerous laws associated with businesses, the workplace, and human resources. The following section provides a brief review of some of these legal standards that HR practitioners need to understand and may be asked to apply during the course of a day's employment in the workplace. Consideration needs to be given to the varying applicability of these laws to organizations as well as employees within the organization. Bottom line, when asked, *Does this law apply to an organization?*—the answer would be, *It depends.* This does not mean one is trying to circumvent the question. Simply stated, it means that the applicability of the law to an organization depends on the nature of the law and the operational context of the organization (i.e., number of employees, type of business engaged in, etc.).

Civil Rights

Let's start this section with a discussion of the Emancipation Proclamation. So what does the Emancipation Proclamation by Lincoln in 1863 have to do with human resources? This proclamation laid the foundation for freedom for all within our country and brings into light that all human beings should be treated equally (Emancipation Proclamation 1863, 2013). Certainly this applies to the workplace as consideration is given with all of the facets of the human resources infrastructure from hiring practices, to training initiatives, to promotions and other types of rewards given within an organization.

This led the way to establishment of the Civil Rights Act, Title VII, of 1964 which serves as the foundation for equal treatment of individuals within organizations that "employ at least 15 individuals for 20 weeks of the year. The employer's business must have some connection with interstate commerce for Title VII to be applicable" (Moran, 2008, p. 173). The essential tenets of this act demonstrate that it is unlawful for an employer to discriminate against candidates or employees in fulfillment of the human resources infrastructure practices because they are different. What does it mean to be different? Moran (2008) noted that these differences could be in "religion, race, color, sex, or national origin" (p. 174).

Further, the Equal Employment Opportunity Act (1972) amended the 1964 Civil Rights Act of 1964 and established the Equal Employment Opportunity Commission (EEOC) (Moran, 2008). Through establishment of this agency, employees who feel that their rights have been violated can file a complaint with the EEOC within a prescribed fashion and timeframe and set into motion a review of the complaint and HR business practices of the organization. The 1964 act was further amended by the Civil Rights Act of 1991 wherein jury trials were permitted for violations (Moran, 2008).

The bottom line is summed up eloquently by Moran (2008) in the following passage:

> In hindsight, the Civil Rights Act of 1964, along with subsequent amendments, has had the most profound impact on employment since the proliferation of unions.... The Civil Rights Act, although not a panacea, provided an area of opportunity for those on the lowest levels of society.... Raising the bottom up is its underlying purpose. (p. 189)

ADA, Pregnancy Discrimination, and FMLA

Beyond legal aspects of discrimination based on the tenets of Title VII, there are also other forms of discrimination that an individual could experience in the working environment. One of these instances led to the Americans with Disability Act (ADA) of 1990. According to Phillips and Gully (2012), this law guarantees "equal opportunity for individuals with disabilities or perceived as having disabilities and grants similar protections to those provided on the basis of race, color, sex, national origin, age, and religion" (p. 58). From an HR perspective in providing advice and guidance to the organization regarding this act, one should understand the basic tenets of the act and that treatment of workers with disabilities should be the same as any other employee. An HR professional would need to understand what is covered under the ADA for impairments and if the requests for an accommodation would be considered reasonable. For example, if a candidate with poor vision applies for a position where the individual would work with a computer on a daily basis, would it be reasonable, if this candidate were hired and able to perform the essential functions of the job, to provide him or her with a large screen monitor or an amplification device to be able to see the screen to successfully complete the work? Reasonable accommodations need to be considered on an individual basis by the organization.

Another aspect of potential discrimination can be seen in the notion of the Pregnancy Discrimination Act of 1978. The HR professional must ensure that the organizational leadership is educated on the fact that women should not be asked if they plan to get pregnant or discouraged from getting pregnant. According to Moran (2008), the Pregnancy Discrimination Act is an amendment to the 1964 Civil Rights Act and stipulates that pregnant women must be treated the same as other applicants and employees. Further, management must be educated that "pregnancy, childbirth, and related medical conditions must be treated the same way as any other temporary illnesses or conditions" (Phillips & Gully, 2012, p. 58).

The Family and Medical Leave Act (FMLA) of 1991

> permits an employee in any 12-month period to take up to 12 weeks of unpaid leave for the birth or adoption of a child; for the care of a spouse, child, or parent who has a serious health condition; or because of a serious health problem that makes the employee unable to work (Moran, 2008, p. 299)

Is this law guaranteed as soon as the employee begins work? No! There are certain stipulations associated with this act that the employee must meet. Additionally, the employer practice should determine if the 12 weeks is per calendar year or on a rolling calendar basis. All of this knowledge should be possessed by the HR practitioner, and the HR practitioner should be able to competently provide advice regarding FMLA.

FLSA

The HR practitioner may ask, *What do you mean, I need to know about pay-roll? Isn't there a separate department to handle that function?* Well, that depends. It depends on the organizational size, structure, and needs, as well as other potential factors. The Fair Labor Standards Act of 1938 establishes the foundation for wages and employer conduct associated with working hours. According to Moran (2008), the FLSA regulates "the minimum compensation that could be given to a worker on an hourly basis and the maximum number of hours an employee could be required to work before being compensated at an overtime rate" (p. 433).

The HR practitioner needs to be able to provide competent guidance to the organization about the implications of minimum wage and application of overtime for hourly employees. Therefore, the HR practitioner needs to be well versed on the rate of minimum wage at any given point in time and ensure the accuracy of this information with current federal mandates. Also, while not mandated that overtime be paid for hours worked in excess of eight hours per day, the HR professional does need to understand when overtime stipulations are applicable and to which types of workers this would apply. For example, if a position in the organization is classified as an exempt position, but it is really nonexempt in the definition of the basic unit of work—the job—then the HR practitioner could be held liable for not appropriately classifying the position. Further, the employee could pursue back wages if this were the case and that employee should have been paid hourly and compensated for overtime. This example also shows the importance of defining the job in accordance with the exemption statuses mandated by the FLSA.

OSHA

Safety within the workplace is paramount! Workplace safety is the responsibility of the employer as well as the employee. In certain environments, there can be many risks associated with the safety of workers in the organization. Should the HR practitioner be responsible for knowing the OSHA laws and regulations and providing competent advice? This sounds like a rather tall order!

The early safety movement started back before the Industrial Revolution with the Code of Hammurabi (Goetsch, 2010). According to Goetsch

(2010), the code provided "clauses for dealing with injuries, allowable fees for physicians, and monetary damages assessed against those who injured others" (p. 2). Further concerns for safety, particularly given public outcry given various tragedies experienced in the U.S. workplaces, prompted legislation. Thus, the Occupational Safety and Health Act of 1970 set forth the standards for safety and health of employees in the workplace (Moran, 2008).

What does the OSHA mean to employers? Employers are expected to maintain safe, clean, and healthy working environments for the employees. Leadership within the organization should actively look for possible OSHA violations and proactively correct these items. Thus, the HR practitioner should be knowledgeable about what these issues would be. However, some of these items would be common sense while others would need more depth of knowledge and understanding about processes and procedures such as lockout/tagout of equipment. It seems implausible to ask an HR practitioner to understand how to lockout/tagout a piece of equipment unless there are extenuating circumstances associated with this request.

Additionally, this does not mean that the employee is absolved of all responsibility for safety within the workplace. The employer should educate the employees about the safety aspects within the organization, but more importantly as applicable directly to their job. For example, at Anheuser Busch, employees were trained on the overall safety aspects of working in a manufacturing environment such as slips and falls that could occur within the plant. However, there was also specific training for brewers on deadly dust and the implications of working with some of the raw materials (such as rice, grains, and hops). This example shows the importance of safety training associated with each job/position in the organization. Yet this leads to the issue that the HR practitioner may not be cognizant of all of the details associated with safety for all of the jobs.

CONCLUSION

Overall, it is easy to see how the organization must rely on the guidance of subject-matter experts to navigate the murky legal waters. The questions remain: Where should this guidance come from, and what are the risks associated with acting on the guidance provided? Are the HR professionals providing informed guidance based on their understanding of the legal implications? Or should this come from a lawyer who lives in the legal world? There are a variety of reasons the organization would position itself in one fashion or the other. Bottom line—the organization must determine what the tolerance is for risk and act accordingly.

As previously discussed, the manager does have a right to hold the HR practitioner accountable for ensuring adherence to the standards as he or she provides the opinion. In the same vein, the practitioner must approach the task with steadfastness. An organization is a system within the larger context of the environmental system. The legal landscape associated with the HR infrastructure of the organization is constantly changing. It is incumbent upon HR professionals to ensure that they are up to speed on the most recent laws and regulations. The HR practitioner must be carefully trained and educated in the laws and the interpretation of the applicable law by the courts. This is an extremely critical element, particularly if the organization does not have a lawyer on staff. We must remember the known or should-have-known arguments of employer liability, and that lack of education and practical experience cannot be cited as an excuse for a bad opinion.

REFERENCES

Adjibolosoo, S. (2011). The evolution and implications of human resources regulations and policies: A critical human factor analysis. *Review of Human Factor Studies, 17*(1), 90–134.

Ayers, A. (2011). The lawyer's perspective: The gap between individual decisions and collective consequences in legal ethics. *The Journal of the Legal Profession, 36*(1), 77–136.

Betsch, T., & Glockner, A. (2010). Intuition in judgment and decision making: Extensive thinking without effort. *Psychological Inquiry, 21,* 279–294.

Calvasina, G., Calvasina, R., & Calvasina, E. (2009). Recent United States Supreme Court decisions and human resource management decision making: The 2007/2008 term. *Journal of Legal, Ethical, and Regulatory Issues, 12*(1), 27–40.

Ferrary, M. (2009). A stakeholder's perspective on human resource management. *Journal of Business Ethics, 87*(1), 31–43

Freeman, R. (1984). *Strategic management: A stakeholder approach.* New York, NY: Harper Collins.

Goetsch, D. (2010). *The basics of occupational safety.* Englewood Cliffs, NJ: Pearson.

Lee, M., & Dry, M. (2006). Decision making and confidence given uncertain advice. *Cognitive Science, 30*(6), 1081–1095.

Massey, K., & Campbell, N. (2013) Human resources management: Big problem for small business? *Entrepreneurial Executive, 18*(2), 77–88.

McDowell, A., & Leavitt, W. (2011). Human resources issues in local government: Yesterday's headlines remain today's "hot topics." *Public Personnel Management, 40*(3), 239–249.

Moran, J. (2008). *Employment law: New challenges in the business environment.* Englewood Cliffs, NJ: Pearson.

Nielsen. J. (2005). Human resources management comes of age in the courtroom: California formally enshrines the importance of human resources expert

testimony for employment litigation. *The Psychologist-Manager Journal, 8(*2),
157–164.

Paul, R., & Elder, L. (2009). *The miniature guide to critical thinking—Concepts and tools.*
Dillon Beach, CA: Foundation for Critical Thinking.

Phillips, J., & Gully, S. (2012). *Strategic staffing.* Englewood Cliffs, NJ: Pearson.

Roehling, M., & Wright, P. (2006). Organizationally sensible versus legal-centric
approaches to employment decisions. *Human Resource Management, 45*(4),
605–627.

ALIGNING RESPECT AND DIGNITY WITH ORGANIZATIONAL INFRASTRUCTURE AND EXTERNAL REGULATION

George Denninghoff and Sheri Bias

INTRODUCTION

It is commonly understood that in a knowledge-based workplace, no company can retain a competitive advantage by engaging in arbitrary or illegal discrimination. The dignity of employment, however, can be lost when an organization begins to view employees as potential lawsuits. So how can the organization minimize the risk of these potential lawsuits based on its HR policies, practices, and procedures? This chapter examines compliance and the regulatory environment in three interrelated areas. First, we examine how values and operating principles may set the stage for values conflict and resulting compliance issues. Second, recognizing the job, the basic unit of human production, as a system that incorporates key competencies

Legal and Regulatory Issues in Human Resources Management, pages 73–95
Copyright © 2015 by Information Age Publishing

provides both compliance and performance benefits. Third, to better manage risk, the organization must assess, not audit, its processes and systems.

The regulatory environment can be examined as an element of the intersection of compliance, culture, and change. This intersection sets the context for internal and external regulation. External regulation is a floor, and not an aspiration, with compliance as the desired outcome. This type of regulation demands an understanding of legal requirements set out by the various rule-making bodies of local, state, and federal government. Obviously these are integral components that set the expectations of conduct within society and within organizations. Further, internal regulation is a more complex interaction and one that has the potential to rise above what is required by law and aspires to increased creativity and productivity as a desired outcome. This internal regulation stems from many factors including the policies established in alignment with the mission, vision, and values of the organization in pursuit of the fulfillment of the organization's goals. These factors operate in concert with each other in an internal system in operation within the external environment.

EXTERNAL REGULATION

Compliance is often viewed as a checklist of dos and don'ts. The focus is on what *must* be done not what should be done. While this may be satisfactory for some organizations, it is often insufficient to regulate behavior that is consistent with what the organization is actually attempting to achieve in pursuit of its mission and vision. Simply put, you can have the best lawyers, the best human resources staff, the best consultants and still end up in the news in a not so flattering light! Often the lack of clearly defined and implemented values within the culture exposes the company to unnecessary risk and especially so in a society of rapid change. We spend hours of training and administrative rule-making on diversity, harassment, hiring practices, and on and on. This can be looked at as the t-shirt management of change which in essence means been there, did that, got the t-shirt. After the Supreme Court rulings on sexual harassment, organizations attempted to train their way out of risk, but without underlying culture change, risk often was not avoided. Below are examples of organizations that were amiss in confusing compliance with the need for internal change.

Three organizations that had a misalignment with external regulatory compliance and confused compliance with the need for internal change were Texaco, Denny's, and U-Haul. All three of these organizations have had their time in the spotlight, and unfortunately, this was not a favorable spotlight. Texaco's Jelly Bean fable is a classic example of the conflict between internal and external regulation. On the surface, Texaco's operation seemed solid. This organization had the right policies in place, the right values being espoused, and the right people moving the operation forward. Interestingly, further examination of Texaco's equal opportunity statement was a common recital of the equal employment statement of many corporations: "Each person deserves to be treated with respect and dignity in appropriate work environments without regard to race, religion, sex, national origin, disability or position in the company. Each employee has the responsibility to demonstrate respect for others" (Issues of Race: Texaco-Race Relations, 1996).

This statement sounds aligned with ensuring that the organization is in compliance. However, what was happening behind the scenes in the organization was less than compliant as noted in the "jelly bean" situation. Texaco was the subject of an EEOC investigation that concluded it had discriminated against African Americans in promotions and other opportunities. The company defended itself from the millions in damages sought by the complainants until a tape was released. The tape was surreptitiously recorded at a meeting of Texaco senior management. In discussing "that diversity thing," they complained that African American workers were like black jelly beans. They got stuck on the bottom of the jar. Texaco settled once this information was divulged. What seems like common sense was not so common in this situation (Issues of Race: Texaco-Race Relations, 1996). Even though the guiding principles were in alignment, the behaviors of the leadership were not conducive for equality or compliance.

Another example is that of Denny's restaurants. It was purported that Denny's had a policy for discrimination; however, the organization's management repetitively denied an official policy. Documents filed by the plaintiffs of the lawsuit gave cause for concern regarding discriminatory practices being carried out within the purview of at least some of the upper-level managers at Denny's ("On Denny's Menu," 1994).

Robert Norton, formerly a manager of a Denny's restaurant in San Jose, Calif., says managers to whom he reported regularly used the word "blackout" to refer to situations where "too many black customers were in a restaurant." Mr. Norton said he and his colleagues were taught to avoid "blackouts" by requiring black customers to pay in advance or by closing the restaurants when too many blacks were present.

Black customers sued, asserting that Denny's had violated their civil rights. Denny's agreed to pay $54 million to settle the lawsuits out of court. The company also hired an outside lawyer to monitor practices throughout the chain.

Jerome J. Richardson, the chairman of Denny's parent corporation, Flagstar Companies of Spartanburg, SC, undermined these efforts by suggesting that the lawsuits originated with touchy customers. "We serve a million customers a day" he said. "... It would be naive on my part to say that customers were always satisfied." Evasions like that bode ill for the cleanup process. Denny's race problem would only continue to grow unless the leadership showed some intention of correcting it!

Another example to demonstrate this point is that of the case of U-Haul. In January 2008, the EEOC settled a race and national origin discrimination case against a Nevada U-Haul company for $153,000. The EEOC had charged that the company subjected Hispanic and Asian/Filipino employees to derogatory comments and slurs based on their race and/or national origin. Hispanic employees also were subjected to comments such as "go back to Mexico." In addition, Filipino mechanics were denied promotions while less qualified Caucasian employees were promoted. The EEOC also charged that Hispanic and Filipino employees were told they had to be "White to get ahead" at the company. As part of the injunctive relief, U-Haul further agreed to provide training to all employees in its Nevada locations, and provide annual reports to the EEOC regarding its employment practices in its Nevada branches. (*EEOC v. U-Haul Company of Nevada*, 2008).

Could liability have been minimized and/or avoided in the examples above using a standard checklist approach? There is not a simple answer to this question. On one hand, surely a checklist approach, such as that often used in an audit, would have revealed a number of these issues. However, what about a Denny's situation where the company was attempting to recover its brand through advertisements that stressed its commitment to change? Yet, literally at the same time those efforts were airing, additional charges were being made. So what is an organization to do to minimize the risk potentially associated with such situation? One key way to avoid risk is by assessing the organizational infrastructure. For our purposes, an audit will be described as an administrative review of practices focusing on documents and the processes they support and an assessment as examining those processes in the context of the culture of the organization.

The more holistic assessment provides a deeper look into the relationship of internal and external compliance. When the human resource (HR) infrastructure is viewed as driven by legal issues rather than issues of human dignity and productivity, the organization is poorly served. So how can HR professionals support the mission, vision, and values of our organization in a manner that will appropriately manage risk? In the examples above, there were obvious cultural issues and misalignment. However, the knowing disregard for external regulation, as demonstrated above, is not always the case. It can be the result of an inability to recognize the changes within the organizational culture or the society as a whole and its impact on the workplace. Mere checklists will not disclose these areas and assist the organization in minimizing the risk. However, a more thorough assessment can produce deep understanding of organizational systems (inclusive of the external environment).

Values and the Cultural Bloom

Culture can be described as the unconscious decisions within an organization. We can think of this as any newly on-boarded employees who violate the norms of their new organization. They did not intend the violation. They simply walked into it unknowing of its existence. It did not appear anywhere in their introduction to the company. The retort: "That is not the way we do things here." Likewise, few organizations set out to violate the law or to encourage a knowing disregard of its requirements. Such disregard intuitively does not make sense. The culture of an organization is made up of differing values no matter how well defined the core values. There is not a singular value system in operation, but a more complex interaction between different professions, trades, and regional systems. The possibility of conflicting values and operating principles creates the compliance management risk. The key then is to identify the areas of common values and develop operating principles based on that overlap. To do less is to invite internal conflict and future compliance issues. The use of shared values represents a core consideration in the successful collaboration between the disparate elements of widely differing entities that exists in all organizations (Senge, 1994).

Using a Venn diagram or a cultural bloom, we have introduced clients to the concept of overlapping values systems. We have also used this example with NASA's public, private partnering efforts. The ethical requirements of a professional engineer and those of a certified public account are different. However, they are often departments within one larger organization. Finding the areas of overlap and building common operating principles from them creates the context for internal self-regulation as well as external compliance. One example of a common organizational value is integrity. Certainly organizations want employees who are honest and who operate with the utmost integrity while in the employment of the business. However, one must keep in mind that the meaning of integrity can vary by organization and individual. So how can a common understanding and embracing of important values be achieved? Reaching a commonly held definition within the organization is critical in establishing a new norm. More important is the dialogue from the efforts to develop a shared understanding during the integration of the value into a functioning entity. The diagrams presented in the cultural bloom (see Figure 4.1) represent the areas that all departments may have in common. These will serve as the foundation for developing operating principles.

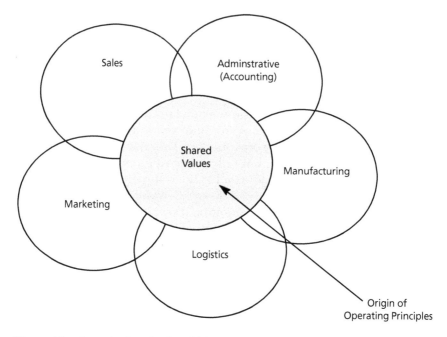

Figure 4.1 Organizational cultural bloom.

Operating principles are how we put our values into action to achieve our vision and fulfill our mission. This could be something as simple as a listing of behaviors that all members embrace and that give definition and life to our values. Each employee should know the common expectations and rules of behavior in order to be able to ensure they are in concert with internal norms. Codes of conduct fall into this area but are usually focused on identifying negative behaviors. When an organization hires, promotes, rewards, or terminates an employee, operating principles become part of the decision-making process—the better the alignment with the values of the company, the greater the validity of the decision process and the better the fit for the culture. Using the metaphor of a pallet, we can trace the alignment of values and the operating principles required to integrate them into the workplace environment.

In reconnecting to the value of integrity previously discussed, integrity appears as a straightforward value. But is it? A large manufacturing company the first author consulted with provides an interesting example. When asked how they applied quality standards to their products, the response was that it depended on the time of the month. To set the context, production occurred over a 30-day period, and all shipping was done at the end of the month. During the first two weeks of each month, the standards were applied and TQM principles governed. However, as the end of the month approached and the pressure of shipping deadlines and penalties began to set in, previously held standards became more flexible. Finally, during the last few days of the month, the unstated operating principle became one of when in doubt, ship. Let's assume that during the first part of the month a protected class supervisor had taken a shortcut that was discovered at the shipping point. The supervisor is counseled for letting the defective product move to shipping, yet if another, unprotected supervisor did the same thing during the last few days of the month, no action would be taken. The failure to act consistently with the operating principle of integrity now creates the impression of actionable discrimination when that was never the intent.

Further, let's examine alignment of a more direct operational construct for a startup in technology. How will they establish the internal validity needed in their hiring process to articulate fit? The core values of the startup were identified as integrity, initiative, and growth, and they appear on the left and in the center of Figure 4.2. The departmental values are in the center and the operating principles that applied to the organization as a whole appear in the right portion of the pallet. What the cultural bloom illustrates is that every department will have values that are in addition to those set out by the firm. It is important to realize these exist and to recognize their validity for the subject matter experts

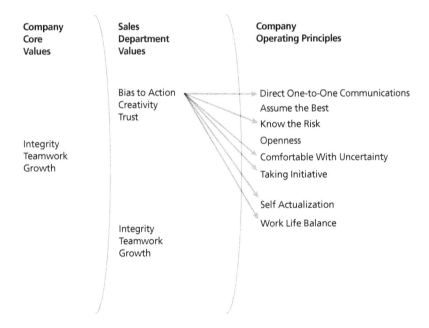

Figure 4.2   Pallet of cultural context.

that set them out. While they may have additional values, the continuity of behavior within the organization is established through shared operating principles. They describe the behaviors that will be used to create the conditions of employment. It is the alignment with the operating principles of all values that provides the consistency needed for internal control, compliance, and alignment.

Where will these principles appear in the framework of compliance? First they appear in the job analysis and its formalization in the job description. This becomes the source document for all other elements of the job continuum. The next section of this chapter discusses the job continuum, which is based on the foundational aspects of job analysis and resulting job descriptions.

THE JOB CONTINUUM

The HR infrastructure is a complex entity and should be seen as a system within the larger system of the organization. Utilizing a systems approach for understanding the HR system, we begin with the foundation using the basic unit of work—the job (See Figure 4.3). Organizations should strive to have fully integrated administrative practices that support and enhance performance rather than create constraints. Failure to do so can create unnecessary conflict and impede the natural progression of the infrastructure's foundation and human capital development.

Administrative practices need to support a systems approach to job design with fully integrated processes. The failure to use such a system adversely impact employees and can have career implications that can be linked to performance and succession/replacement planning. The effect

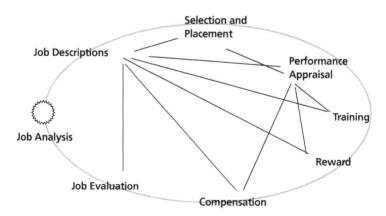

Figure 4.3   The job continuum™.

of sitting down with new team members with a clear definition of their role, the performance plan to show expectations, and a development/training plan to show how they will be prepared for the standards they must meet are powerful tools. The requirement for such a tool also helps management recognize the ambiguities and constraints facing the individual employee.

Unfortunately, this area is too often considered a formality to be complied with rather than understanding that it is the systems approach that recognizes the job as the basic unit of human production. A formal identification of a cadre is vitally important to get the right people on the bus and the wrong people off the bus (Collins, 2001). The best method is recognizing a systems approach for the identification, selection, and development of future staff. So what does all this mean? Let's dissect the job continuum to discuss how these individual pieces come together.

Job Analysis and Job Descriptions

As previously discussed, defining the job, the basic unit of work, is the essential first step of the HR infrastructure. In taking a systems view of HR, without this definition, it may not be possible for the balance of the infrastructure to be effective. How would the organization know what to recruit for without defining the job? How would managers know what training might be necessary in order to build the knowledge, skills, and abilities of an employee without understanding the expectations for the job? Is it feasible to define a pay structure for the organization if there is no understanding of the contribution of each job? These questions are difficult to answer without the clear definition and direction that is provided by the job description.

Job analysis and resulting job descriptions must be able to be used as a clear path to the roles and responsibilities of membership in the organization. Job analysis provides the organization with a systematic way to gather data to form conclusions about the unit of work. Conflict may be experienced from an organization's failure to negotiate the uncertainty created by the absence of clear roles and responsibilities. How can employees know what they should be doing and if they are performing sufficiently without the basis of job definition? It is essential that job analysis capture the essential duties of the position along with knowledge, skills, abilities, and behaviorally based competencies needed for success in a given position. These defined attributes will be used in all other components of a properly functioning HR system.

Selection and Placement

The process of selecting from the candidates those who will become employees, in order to be in legal compliance, must be free of discriminatory practices (Moran, 2008). Additionally, the process should be based on validated competency models reflected in the job descriptions. A case in November 2012 wherein Alliant Techsystems, Inc. refused to hire an African American woman because of race is an example of discriminatory practice. In this case, EEO v. Alliant Techsystems (2012), the company settled the EEOC suit by paying $100,000 to the alleged victim. The alleged victim was interviewed numerous times for a job, and she was allegedly asked to remove her braids from her hair so that she would be more professional. She did so and was told that the company did want to hire her; however, at the next meeting with the company, she had put the braids back into her hair. The next day, she was informed she would not be hired, and the company hired a white male for the position. Above and beyond the monetary penalty, the company also was required to review its workplace policies to ensure they comply with Title VII and to train its staff and the laws against discrimination.

Another case in September 2011 alleged discrimination against African Americans and Hispanics in the hiring process of a national sporting goods retailer. In the case *EEOC v. Bass Pro Outdoor World, LLC* (2011), individuals in these protected classes were denied retail positions such as cashier, sales associate, team leader, supervisor, and manager at many of the retailers nationwide locations. Additionally, management overtly made comments about the discriminatory practices including that hiring African Americans would not be a good fit for the company's persona. This lawsuit also claimed that Bass Pro would punish those employees who opposed these unlawful hiring practices up to and including forcing them to resign from employment.

Can an organization remedy these types of situations? Beyond workplace policies and adhering to the regulations with regard to this part of the HR infrastructure, organizations can use a variety of techniques to avoid these scenarios. One such mechanism would be to use behaviorally based interviews. Behaviorally based interviews and a hiring matrix that reflects the relationship skills reflected in the operating principles as well as technical skills are essential. They are made no less important when the selection process is internal. The focus on the technical skills is, of course, a core contribution, but failure to consider competencies such as emotional intelligence in the process can exact a high price on the general welfare of the organization. Human resources and human relations are complex entities within the organization, which is why the systems view is an effective model to gain understanding of what constitutes fit.

Performance Appraisal

Under the uniform guidelines, performance appraisals used for promotion, selection, or rewards must be valid. There has been a great deal written on performance appraisals, and the decision to use them has involved varying degrees of acceptance and success. Notwithstanding the rationale behind their use, we know they must be conducted in a manner that recognizes their treatment by the EEOC as a test. The connection between compliance and performance is of course most pronounced and obvious in this process. If performance is based on both how goals are achieved and what is achieved, we see again the common thread that connects behavior to the strategic objectives of the organization. Will we excuse behavior inconsistent with our values? If a department's sales were significantly higher than previous years but turnover of what had been considered your best sales folks occurred at the end of the year, was the increase in turnover appropriate to the values of the company? Will our operating principles be ignored because one member of the sales force has had a record year? The inclusion of meaningful relationship exemplars must be directly linked to our espoused values.

Compliance once again lies in the validity of the job analysis as reflected in the job description. The design of the performance instrument should reflect the desired outcomes with direct and clearly linked performance standards. The absence of the linkage has been discussed for many years. In discussing the need for proper validation of hiring tests using performance appraisal results, the Supreme Court stated in *Albemarle* that "There is no way of knowing precisely what criteria of job performance the supervisors were considering . . . were they the same criteria . . . did any supervisor actually apply any criteria of any kind" (*Albemarle Paper Co. v. Moody*, 1975).

The old saying of what gets measured, gets done is also true in behavioral outcomes. Assessment of the performance of employees should be completed based on the job description and set out as measurable outcomes to those essential duties defined on the job description. Appraisals should integrate what is done with how it was done. The behavioral aspects are often poorly defined, but if the construction of the job integrates the organization's values, this is more easily accomplished.

If positioned appropriately within the HR infrastructure, the performance appraisal/assessment program should be a meaningful exercise to provide feedback to the employee on the efforts in fulfillment of organizational, positional, and individual goals (see *EEOC v. Zia Co. and Los Alamos Constructors*, 1978). One method of insuring appropriate marks is to evaluate the managers on their execution of the program (EEOC, 2008). http://www.eeoc.gov/facts/performance-conduct.html

Compensation and Benefits

The compensation strategy of the organization must clearly align with federal statues from an external constituency, and the Civil Rights Act provides the impetus for ensuring equality regarding pay (Moran, 2008). In a July 2007 case, Walgreens settled for paying $20 million to resolve allegations of discrimination. The national drug store chain engaged in discriminatory promotion, compensation, and assignment practices within their organization. The monetary relief was estimated for approximately 10,000 impacted individuals (*EEOC v. Walgreen Co.*, 2007).

From an external focus, management does need to ensure the organization is in compliance with these laws and regulations. From an internal standpoint, management would also want to ensure that total rewards of compensation and benefits are based on definition of the unit of work and performance of the individual toward the defined goals as assessed through the performance management infrastructure. All of these items are inextricably linked within this system, and intuitively it makes sense to ensure alignment of all components in order to have an effective HR program as people are the life's blood of the organization.

Education, Training, and Development

Decisions on training and educational initiatives must be in compliance with the statutes of Title VII to ensure that the practices are in alignment with the law (Moran, 2008). From a systems perspective, additionally, it would be difficult to define what training would be needed at any level if there is no basis for understanding the basic unit of work as defined by the job description. This reinforces the necessity of the systems view of HR and the requirement to define the jobs as the foundation for the HR infrastructure. Once outcomes have been clarified and the initial performance standards examined, training and development plans should be initiated for employees. In using a competency approach, developmental plans can be easily tailored to the selected individual. Training should include experiential components to be successful.

Rewards: Recognition, Transition, or Termination—I Know What Is Expected of Me at Work

"Gallup's 12" begins with the statement "I know what is expected of me at work." In a presentation at the Hampton Roads Society of Human Resources in 2001, Buckingham described this and the second statement of "I have the materials and equipment I need to do my work right," as the most significant and indicative of the survey's twelve statements of engagement (Buckingham, 1999). Examining the job from a systems perspective as we have above creates the foundation for engagement. This is the outcome of having a systems approach. There is clarity of purpose. Rewards based on successful or exceptional performance of clearly understood linkages are easily translated and reinforced. They are also easier to defend because their stems are valid and will withstand charges of discrimination.

Change over time is a key consideration for rewards. Understanding the complexities of the present environment (trends in factors such as government regulations, economic climate, customer needs, technology, workforce, competitive issues, etc.) may not create the same competitive advantage in other phases. Most companies progress through lifecycle stages that will require new monitoring competencies to insure that behavioral values are still being met.

Removing the fear of failure will encourage the risk taking necessary in highly complex and changing environments. Transitioning workgroup members into other departments or exposing them to reduction in force can destroy trust within the group. Recognizing that competencies essential in one lifecycle stage are not the same as later stages is a crucial aspect of the staffing equation. Forecasting requirements accurately not by job per se but by skill sets identified within will allow a number of compliance issues, such as the Worker Adjustment and Retraining and Notification Act (WARN). It will also avoid the sine wave approach to staffing that creates poor morale and a fertile environment for discrimination exposure.

The creation of the performance standard "I know what is expected of me" establishes an understood floor for substandard performance and termination. But let's first examine a counseling cycle. To be able to *communicate* the difference between substandard performance and acceptable performance requires clarity in expectations. Once again, this comes from a properly executed analysis coupled with the utilization of a performance appraisal that properly incorporates both the cultural behavioral expectations and the technical expectations on the job. Insuring that the job continuum and the culture are in sync is done through the use of an assessment. Through assessments we are able to examine linkage from more than a mechanical checklist approach and begin to examine the interaction between culture, compliance, and change. The following section examines one approach to complete this task.

CONDUCTING AN ASSESSMENT

In the two previous sections, we examined why and how values and operating principles should be integrated into a systematic approach to the job. We will now examine how to insure that these efforts have indeed been integrated into the culture of the organization. We will use an assessment to examine both compliance and performance. The key to conducting an effective assessment is to take a holistic approach recognizing that it is based on a systems approach to compliance. The assessment can also be used for planning, staffing, benchmarking, training, and the future contribution to the development of a balanced scorecard.

National recognition of the high cost and scarcity of intellectual capital even in times of recession has driven a fresh look at the deliverables of an HR department. Human resources management as a discipline has undergone dramatic change. It has transitioned from the administrative demands of personnel management to the cultivation, retention, and recruitment of intellectual capital. The journey has been marked by confusion both within departments and with their internal and external customers as to how human capital should be managed. Within all of its domains, there are compliance issues that must be considered. The four domains of a full-service HR department as covered within an assessment are as follows (Ulrich, 1996):

1. Strategic management of human resources: Are new competitive models needed? How will those models be developed? How will we hire, retain, or train our people to meet the challenges? What are the human structures and strategies required for mobilizing assets to meet future demands? What are the long-term impacts of the regulatory environment on all of the above?

2. Change management: How will the needs of the workplace shift over time with new demographics and a more diverse workforce? How will HR assist in building the capacity for change? How will the department create and refine the infrastructure to insure the permanence of the desired changes?

3. Employee contribution: How will we insure the equal treatment and opportunity to insure we achieve the potential of the workforce? How do we create the environment that fosters and develops the intellectual capacity of employees? How do we insure they are free to develop the competencies needed to achieve the mission?

4. Management of infrastructure: How do we perform, measure, and develop the processes that sustain the day-to-day operation of the company? This area represents the classic approach to compliance,

but for the most part it is a lagging indicator of compliance and the impact of regulation.

APPROACH AND METHODOLOGY

Organization and internal HR assessments provide valuable insight into the operation, process, and practices of the organization. For example, these assessments can be the impetus for providing data for strategic and tactical HR planning efforts. Assessments can also equip the organization with information to evaluate the effectiveness and efficiency of the HR function. This can be important in relation to HR as a system within the larger context of the organization system.

Another noteworthy benefit of this type of deep dive into gaining understanding about organizational activities is to potentially be able to benchmark with similar companies. If there is not an understanding of where the company currently is as far as the HR infrastructure, it would be difficult to make accurate or valid comparisons with other companies. A best practice could potentially give a leading edge to an organization; however, without an assessment of the current state, how would the organizational leadership know if they are on target or missing the mark from a competitive standpoint?

Along the same lines, the impetus of change management is in knowing the current state of affairs of the organization. Once the current state is assessed, the organization can better understand the desired state of organizational effectiveness from a gap analysis perspective. This then becomes a ripe arena for promoting change and infusing creativity within organizational practices.

Positioning HR as a strategic business partner has been part of the HR evolution over the past few decades. In conducting an assessment, a systems perspective should be taken that will align HR within the departments and bring HR closer to the line functions of the organization. This can also create a clear path for implementation and integration of technology enablers, such as a Human Resource Information System (HRIS), into the organization. Additionally, building the knowledge, skills, abilities, and competencies of the HR staff can be done by identifying core areas for improvement.

External and Internal HR Assessments

- Interviews: each member of the HR Staff, all of the organization's senior staff, as well as select members of management and internal customers

- Surveys: organizational assessment, management survey, HR department members
- Focus groups: randomly selected employees on each shift and from each department

Internal HR Measurements

- Effectiveness: planning functions, employment practices, performance management (training and development, performance appraisals), and employee relations
- Efficiency: internal process mapping and measurements, recruiting, training, management development, absenteeism, turnover, staffing levels, and budget expenditures

Collecting Data

Data can be collected through multiple approaches such as interviews, surveys, and document review. The first sets of data would be used to determine alignment and employee satisfaction. There can certainly be compliance issues experienced in each of these areas, and caution should be taken to ensure that regulations and statutes are followed during this process.

Going back to the start, we discussed the impact of the operating principles on compliance. In looking at this from the system model, there is a connection with the impact of the operating principles on compliance. In checking for alignment, surveys can be used to elicit quantitative and qualitative data. Below is a survey approach to the sales example used above (Figure 4.4). The compliance aspect can be found in the hiring and performance appraisal reward aspects of the job continuum. If the company is consistent with its values, positive responses in these questions will indicate alignment. Couple these with these trust questions that reflect the response to the company values:

Value of Growth with the Operating Principle: Bias for Action

1. My group feels free to experiment with new methods to achieve higher performance.
2. When my group's assignment in terms of what we are supposed to accomplish on a daily basis is unclear, we feel free to act without further guidance.

Figure 4.4   Pallet of cultural context.

Value of trust with the accounting department operating principle of knowing the risk. Accounting department questions (see Figure 4.5):

1. Each member of the group shares a sense of individual responsibility for the group's results.
2. My department encourages development within my profession

And for all departments an open question that elicits positive input for future change:

1. If I could change one thing about working at _____, it would be to _____.

ORGANIZATIONAL AND INTERNAL HR ASSESSMENTS

Interviews

Interviews and the open questions on a survey will disclose areas not often measured in an audit. Whether systems of rewards have been used to carry out the strategic vision of the company and were actually implemented

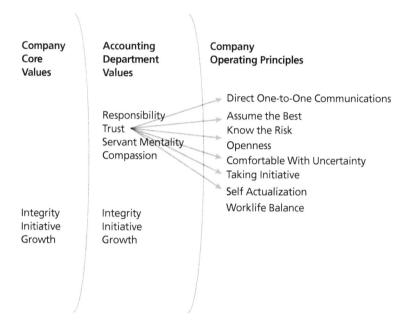

Figure 4.5 Pallet of cultural context.

in the operational and tactical world can be ascertained from these conversations. For example, the performance management, rewards systems, and processes must demonstrate clearly defined consequences for employee behaviors, positive or negative, and be measured within the performance management system. Standards of performance should be well developed. Failure to insure that rewards are aligned in a holistic manner to further the objectives of the company as a whole can be detrimental.

Interviews can also clearly define a lack of reward for the incompatible behaviors demonstrated by members of the group. In one organization we worked with, the primary concerns of those interviewed were with their careers and competencies and related only tangentially to the project's success. The focus on their particular profession and not their group members was evident from the survey as well. There has been a great deal of discussion of the future workplace as being project driven. That requires the ability to work as a team member in new and varying cultural environments. However, many organizations either do not list the competency (ability to work as a team member) or have no way to measure that competency. An exceptionally low score for internal recognition reinforces the overall negative feeling across the group. What's the compliance issue? When rewards are not established, a blank is created. "My performance justified the (raise, promotion, selection) and I would have received it if I had not been_____." Fill in the blank with the protected group of your choice. Let's now examine two facets of the job continuum on staffing and employment practices and orientation to further understand applicability.

Staffing and Employment Practices

Employment practices include the forecasting, recruiting, and placement of employees. The employment process represents the largest segment of current HR deliverables. The presence of a systematic approach to hiring will have a significant impact on the operational efficiency of the company. Processes should be flowcharted (as in Figure 4.6), a best practice, for internal and external hiring task identification.

The flow charts should be used in conjunction with spreadsheets to develop a true measurement of current processes. Managerial training for hiring is made simpler with the use of flow charts so the entirety of the process can be visualized and all the competencies associated with the process can be covered. Organizations have gone to great pains to ensure compliance with governing legislation. Those efforts demonstrate clear understanding of the requirements for protection of the company. The degree of risk the company is willing to tolerate should be discussed and explained in clear terms. Care should be taken not to create a function driven by legalism but by sound risk management.

The contrast of internal and external compliance is demonstrated by using a sample flowchart based on an actual process we worked with in a Fortune 50 company. It is not offered as an example of what should be done or what could be done in the hiring process but rather to identify the various points in the process that relate to values.

First examine the identification of the need to hire. This may have been from turnover, but for our purposes let's assume it is the outgrowth of the increased need of that job to meet the operational needs of the company as identified in the strategic plan. One of the considerations will be the need to "fit" the culture of the company. This is a compliance area but it is also an example of a performance/compliance connection as defined by the values and operating principles of the company. As we described in the job continuum, it all begins here with the context of the job being captured in the job analysis and job description. It is important to note what changes have taken place since the last strategic planning sessions occurred. If the job description predates those sessions, it must be closely examined and revised as necessary.

Let's move now to the recruiting process. Compliance issues are once again present. In our search for compliance, fit, and competence, the recruiting visit is often the first deselect in prospective candidates. Does our onsite recruitment meet the needs of the company? Have we closely

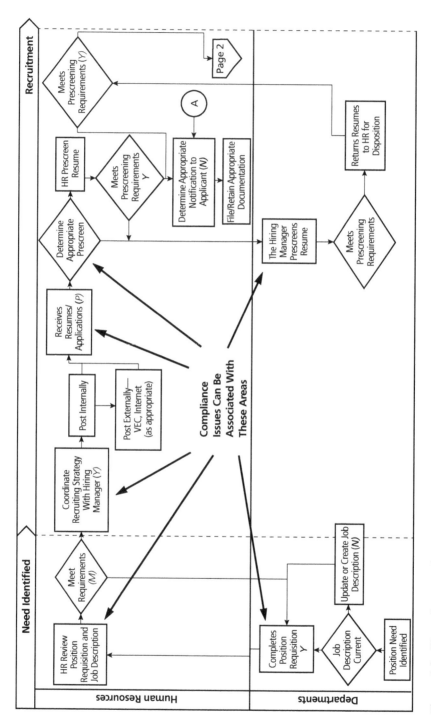

Figure 4.6 Flow of an actual process.

monitored our yield analysis to justify the methodology used in our recruitment efforts? Are we able to articulate the impact on our jobs of the operating principles and values of the company? This is an area where internal pressure on recruiters can create a numbers game whose end product is neither effective nor efficient.

Now let's look at the phone interview step in our flow chart. The process of questioning will be the same if it is either the HR department or the subject-matter expert. If we have properly analyzed the competencies required for the job we can now begin to employ what we have learned in the past in this position. If we have followed a behaviorally based approach to performance management, we should have the ability to isolate the best performance in each competency. Basing an interview on these areas increases the validity of the selection. Front loading the critical relationship skills into these questions allows for early identification of those who fit the culture and those who do not. If the competency is identified as one that must be possessed at the start of employment, it becomes a key discriminator for nonselection.

Using the checklist approach can now pay the compliance dividends we need to justify our selection process. For example, interview questions must be retained, but they also provide insight into those parts of the continuum that have been identified as key to successful hiring.

Orientation of New Hires and Why You Should Integrate, Not Indoctrinate

The handoff at the end of the selection process is to the orientation of the new employee. When the assessment process reaches an examination of the on-boarding process for new hires, we need to insure that we have covered these areas. The faster the employee is able to integrate into the new culture the quicker the path to full productivity. The orientation process:

- Is the first and best opportunity to communicate values
- Provides a description of the culture of the firm
- Begins the development of core competencies
- Introduction to how their performance will be measured

So how do we evaluate the effectiveness of our on-boarding process? One method is to conduct a mini survey at the 90- to 120-day time frame. The juxtaposition of what the new hire is told the company's values are during on-boarding with the stated values they have encountered can be measured. Of importance is asking at least one open-ended question that will allow the new hires to express their needs. The second method is to examine the number of new hires and their attrition rates both voluntary and involuntary over the next year. Assessing here gives you a look at the methodology of recruitment. In working with a large healthcare system, we discovered that recruiters were making 100% of their goal to attract graduates for one of their shortage specialties. At the end of one year, only 50% of the new hires were still in the system. The survey revealed that the informal culture within that specialty was to treat all newcomers as having to prove their value. The unwelcoming environment was atypical, and the organization was able to remedy it. Please note that the leadership in this area was approached using the integration of values and an understanding of how these measurements had an impact on evaluating their own abilities. Using the job continuum approach to their jobs, a resolution was reached.

The interviewing and selection process is open to many assessment processes that allow the close connection between culture and administrative compliance to be examined. To go further with the need for assessment at this point is beyond the scope of this chapter.

CONCLUSION

In examining the three elements set out above, committing to a set of values for the organization through its strategic planning process is the first step. While this does not need to be freshly worked and the current values may be sound, commitment to them is critical. To validate the job impact of the values and operating principles, it is helpful to create a context model of their current environment. Examining trends and their impacts and then working to uncover what is behind these factors set the stage for movement to the job design discussed in the job continuum. Too many strategic processes are completed without a clear understanding of how they will be implemented and monitored for success at the basic unit of human production, the job.

Establishing the baseline measures of performance and working them into systems for continued monitoring set the stage for assessing impact on employees of change. Organizations need to understand the implications of values and cultural norms in operation and how these align, or potentially misalign, with external guidance and regulation. By doing so, organizations should be able to stay away from the proverbial hot water that many seem to unintentionally find themselves immersed in!

REFERENCES

Albemarle Paper Co. v. Moody, 422 U.S. 405 (1975).

Buckingham, M. (1999). *First break all the rules: What the world's greatest managers do differently.* New York, NY: Simon & Schuster.

Collins, J. (2001). *Good to great: Why some companies make the leap . . . and others don't.* New York, NY: HarperBusiness.

EEO v. Alliant Techsystems, Inc. Case No. 0:11-cv-02785-DSD-JJG, (D. Minn. consent decree filed Nov. 20, 2012).

EEOC. (2008). The Americans with Disabilities Act: Applying performance and conduct standards to employees with disabilities. Retrieved from http://www.eeoc.gov/facts/performance-conduct.html

EEOC v. Bass Pro Outdoor World, LLC, Civil Action No. 4:11-cv-03425 (S.D. Tex. Sep. 21, 2011).

EEOC v. U-Haul Company of Nevada, Case No. 2:06-CV-01209-JCM-LRL (D. Nev. settled Jan. 28, 2008).

EEOC v. Walgreen Co., No. 07-CV-172-GPM; Tucker v. Walgreen Co. No. 05-CV-440-GPM (S.D. Ill. July 12, 2007).

E.E.O.C. v. Zia Co. and Los Alamos Constructors, 16 FEP Cases 1717 (D.N.M. 1976); afl"d.,582 F.2d 527 (10th Cir. 1978).

Issues of Race: Texaco-Race Relations. (1996). *PBS News Hour.* Retrieved from http://www.pbs.org/newshour/bb/business/july-dec96/texaco_11-12.html

Moran, J. (2008). *Employment law: New challenges in the business environment.* Upper Saddle River, NJ: Pearson.

On Denny's Menu: Discrimination. (1994, May 27). *New York Times* archives. Retrieved from http://www.nytimes.com/1994/05/27/opinion/on-denny-s-menu-discrimination.html

Senge, P. (1994). *The fifth discipline: The art & practice of the learning organization.* New York, NY: Doubleday Business Press.

Ulrich, D. (1996). *Human resources champions: The next agenda for adding value and delivering results.* Boston, MA: Harvard Business School Press.

CHAPTER 5

FROM IDEA
TO IMPLEMENTATION

Statutes, Regulations, and Cases

Robert A. Tufts and William I. Sauser, Jr.

INTRODUCTION

As the various chapters in this volume make abundantly clear, human resources (HR) professionals must have a working knowledge of the laws, rules, and regulations governing HR decisions if they are to be effective in fulfilling their duties. Unless an HR professional is a member of the bar, he or she should never seek to practice law; nonetheless, as Bias and Hoy point out in their chapter within this volume, HR professionals are often consulted regarding legal implications of decisions being contemplated by operating managers located throughout the organization (including top management). HR professionals are expected to provide answers within their area of expertise, and to be able to consult attorneys for guidance when necessary. Thus, the need to understand the many statutes, regulations, and court decisions that affect the practice of human resources management (HRM) is a given for HR professionals.

Legal and Regulatory Issues in Human Resources Management, pages 97–116
Copyright © 2015 by Information Age Publishing

Throughout this volume are allusions to a variety of important statutes, regulations, and court decisions about which HR professionals should be informed. This chapter is intended to provide answers to three key questions in this regard: (a) What is the source of these statutes, regulations, and court decisions? Where do they come from and who makes them? (b) How are the statutes, regulations, and court decisions interrelated? How do they come together to provide guidance to organizations seeking to comply fully with the law? (c) How can HR professionals—acting individually or through their companies or professional associations—influence the law and help to shape it?

After discussing the concept of "the law," we illustrate the interplay of *organic law, statutory law, administrative law,* and *case law* as the legislative, executive, and judicial branches of government all play their parts in shaping the law. We do so by tracing the history of one particular HR-related law, the Equal Pay Act, as it has been shaped over the past five decades. We start with the issue that led to passage of the law, and then follow legislative discussion as the statue is debated and finally passed by the U.S. Congress. We then see how the statute is considered in relation to other existing statutes as the U.S. Supreme Court interprets legislative intent. Next we follow the promulgation of administrative rules and regulations intended to guide the application of the statute in various circumstances. It is during this process that the specifics of the law are often determined, since these rules and regulations state in writing how the law will be enforced by the executive branch. Rule making is itself a complex process that involves interplay among the enforcement agency, the public, and the courts, so this too will be traced as we continue to follow the history of the Equal Pay Act. Enforcement agency decisions can be appealed to the judicial system, so the courts have yet another important role to play, as we shall see as the record of the courts' interpretation of the Equal Pay Act unfolds.

There are important roles for HR professionals to play at every step of the process. Furthermore, outcomes of each step have a considerable impact on how the law is to be interpreted and applied by HR professionals. "The law" is dynamic, not static, and it is essential for HR professionals to follow the changes in interpretation of the law as it moves through these stages. That is the only way for HR professionals to be certain they are providing valid information to the organizational decision makers who rely on their guidance. We shall return to the important roles HR professionals play in this process in the summary section of this chapter.

THE CONCEPT OF "THE LAW"

"The law" is not static; it is a very dynamic concept, and compliance advice can change as new statutes are passed, as new regulations are promulgated, and as new cases are decided in court. That is why the HR professional must stay constantly abreast of changes in the law if the best guidance is to be provided to organizational decision makers. Consultation with attorneys specializing in HR-related law, participation in professional workshops and conferences, professional reading, and other such possibilities for continuing education are readily available to HR professionals, and we advise that they avail themselves of these opportunities.

In this chapter we consider the concepts of *organic law, statutory law, administrative law* (also known as "rules and regulations"), and *case law* and the relationships among them. All of these are important and must be attended to closely by HR professionals. Together all of them comprise "the law."

Organic law refers to the most basic law of the land, the United States Constitution. Each state also has a constitution, which is the organic law of the state; the state's constitution must conform to the nation's constitution, but can vary considerably in length, style, and tone. That is why it is important to consider both federal law and state law when deciding upon the legality of a certain practice; guidance may differ from state to state. A detailed discussion of constitutional law is beyond the scope of this chapter, but suffice it to say that the constitution spells out the powers of each branch of government, as well as limitations on those powers. In the final analysis, all statutes, administrative rules and regulations, and case decisions must conform to the basic law of the land, the U.S. Constitution.

Both federal and state constitutions establish that *statutory law* is created by elected representative bodies; the details of how that is done—and the participation of the executive branch in that process—are spelled out in the constitution. Thus the U.S. Congress has the power under the U.S. Constitution to pass bills into law; state legislatures possess this power under the various state constitutions. This, then, is the origin of statutory law. The process does not end at this point, however. Frequently federal and state statutes express a clear purpose and intent, but they leave to administrative agencies (part of the executive branch under the constitution) to establish—through a process that includes input from the citizenry—to "flesh out" statutory law by establishing rules and regulations. This promulgation of rules and regulations, then, is the origin of *administrative law.*

Finally, administrative rules and regulations, as well as statutes themselves, are subject to interpretation by the courts as cases alleging violation of these rules, regulations, and statutes are brought before the courts for adjudication. The federal court system has three levels—district courts (where the trial is conducted), circuit courts (courts of appeal), and the U.S. Supreme Court (which usually settles issues decided differently in two or more Circuit Courts); states typically have a similar structure. Decisions at each level set precedents to be followed in similar cases heard by the same court; this is the origin of *case law.* Since each district court has its own jurisdiction, and each circuit court's decisions create precedents to be followed by the district courts within the specified circuit, it is possible for case law to differ across jurisdictions. Decisions by the U.S. Supreme Court set precedent for the entire nation; that is why Supreme Court decisions are watched so carefully by legal experts. Thus congress passes statutes that prescribe general norms and standards. The details of policymaking are usually left to administrative agencies that can devote time, resources, and expertise to specific policy matters. The administrative agency not only promulgates regulations, but it also interprets the regulations, adjudicates individual matters, and enforces requirements. If an administrative agency finds an individual in violation of a regulation, that individual may appeal the agency decision to the federal courts. So, to understand the total impact of a statute, one must study the legislative history as well as the statute, the administrative agency charged with implementing the statute and the accompanying regulations, and finally the precedents set by court decisions applying the statute and regulations to specific fact patterns. This chapter contains an illustration and description of this entire process.

The Equal Pay Act (EPA) is used in this chapter to illustrate the interdependence of statutes, regulations, and court decisions. Fifty years after the passage of the statute, many people, including President Obama, think women are being paid less than men (State of the Union address, 1/29/2014). The number often quoted is that women are paid 77 cents for every dollar paid to her male counterpart in 2012 (National Women's Law Center, 2013). The wage gap figure at the national level was reported by the Census Bureau and is the median earnings of women working full time, year round as a percentage of the median earnings of men working full time, year round (DeNavas-Walt, Proctor, & Smith, 2013). Is the Equal Pay Act working as planned? Let us examine this question as we illustrate the interrelated process by which the various types of law are created and interpreted.

STATUTES ARE PASSED BY CONGRESS

Article I of the U.S. Constitution states that "all legislative powers shall be vested in a Congress of the United States." Every act passed by Congress must have a constitutional basis. Because of the separation of powers, the Judiciary will determine whether a statute is constitutional and valid or unconstitutional and void, if the statute is challenged.

Many statutes find their justification in the Commerce Clause. Article I, section 8, of the U.S. Constitution states that Congress shall have the power "to regulate Commerce ... among the several States." For years the courts have interpreted the commerce clause expansively. However, the Supreme

Court struck down the Gun-Free School Zone Act of 1990, stating that the Court needed to find some judicially enforceable limit to the commerce power (*United States v. Lopez*, 1995). Five years later the Supreme Court ruled the Violence Against Women Act exceeded Congress's power under the commerce clause. The Court stated that gender-motivated crimes of violence are not, in any sense of the phrase, economic activity, and again, stated the need to impose limits on the commerce power, lest it completely obliterate the Constitution's distinction between national and local authority (*United States v. Morrison*, 2000).

Acts passed by Congress are codified into the United States Code (U.S.C.). For example, Congress passed Public Law 88-38 §2 on June 10, 1963, which has become known as the "Fair Pay Act" and it is codified at 29 U.S.C. §206(d). Congress set the general norm or standard as, "No employer . . . shall discriminate, . . . between employees on the basis of sex by paying wages . . . at a rate less than the rate at which he pays wages to employees of the opposite sex . . . for equal work." Four exceptions were provided, "where such payment is made pursuant to (i) a seniority system; (ii) a merit system; (iii) a system which measures earnings by quantity or quality of production; or (iv) a differential based on any other factor other than sex." Congress further stated that the constitutional basis for this act was its power to regulate commerce among the several states and with foreign nations (Fair Pay Act, 1963). "Congress' purpose in enacting the Equal Pay Act was to remedy what was perceived to be a serious and endemic problem of employment discrimination in private industry—the fact that the wage structure of many segments of American industry has been based on an ancient but outmoded belief that a man, because of his role in society, should be paid more than a woman even though his duties are the same. S.Rep. No. 176, 88th Cong., 1st Sess. 1 (1963)." *Corning Glass Works v. Brennan*, 1974).

The law is not static but evolving, and one statute cannot be judged in a vacuum. Although wage discrimination was the target, Congress didn't hit the bull's eye with the first try and the next year the same Congress (88th) passed Title VII of the Civil Rights Act which provides in part, "It shall be an unlawful employment practice for an employer . . . to discriminate against any individual with respect to his compensation, . . . because of such individual's race, color, religion, sex, or national origin" (Civil Rights Act, 1964).

Did Title VII of the Civil Rights Act supersede the Fair Pay Act? "First, always, is the question whether Congress has directly spoken to the precise question at issue. If the intent of Congress is clear, that is the end of the matter" (*Chevron, U.S.A., Inc. v. Natural Resources Defense Council*, 1984). Since that particular issue was not addressed in the statutes, the courts must make the determination by trying to understand the intent of Congress. The judges will study the legislative history of the statute to make that determination. There are ways for

HR professionals to influence Congress as legislative statues are written and to inform the courts as legislative intent is determined. Ways for HR professionals—individually and collectively through professional associations—to help shape the law during these early steps are discussed at the end of this chapter.

THE SUPREME COURT WEIGHS IN

The U.S. Supreme Court answered the question of legislative intent in 1981 by analyzing the legislative history.

> Any possible inconsistency between the Equal Pay Act and Title VII did not surface until late in the debate over Title VII in the House of Representatives, because, until then, Title VII extended only to discrimination based on race, color, religion, or national origin, see H.R.Rep. No. 914, 88th Cong., 1st Sess., 10 (1963), while the Equal Pay Act applied only to sex discrimination. Just two days before voting on Title VII, the House of Representatives amended the bill to proscribe sex discrimination, but did not discuss the implications of the overlapping jurisdiction of Title VII, as amended, and the Equal Pay Act. See 110 Cong.Rec. 2577-2584 (1964). The Senate took up consideration of the House version of the Civil Rights bill without reference to any committee. Thus, neither House of Congress had the opportunity to undertake formal analysis of the relation between the two statutes. (*County of Washington v. Gunter*, 1981)

The only mention in Title VII was the "Bennett Amendment," which added the following language, "It shall not be an unlawful employment practice under this subchapter for any employer to differentiate upon the basis of sex in determining the amount of wages or compensation paid or to be paid to employees of such employer if such differentiation is authorized by the provisions of section 206(d) of title 29" (*County of Washington v. Gunter, 1981*). Thus the Bennett Amendment "clarified that the standards of the Equal Pay Act would govern even those wage discrimination cases where only Title VII would otherwise apply" (*County of Washington v. Gunter*, 1981). And, "although the few references by Members of Congress to the Bennett Amendment do not explicitly confirm that its purpose was to incorporate into Title VII the four affirmative defenses of the Equal Pay Act in sex-based wage discrimination cases, they are broadly consistent with such a reading, and do not support an alternative reading" (*County of Washington v. Gunter*, 1981).

RULES AND REGULATIONS ARE PROMULGATED

Administrative agencies promulgate regulations that provide substantive and administrative guidance that is not included in the statutes. It is not practical for Congress to address the details needed to implement every piece of legislation passed.

Congress routinely delegates broad powers to administrative agencies. This is permissible as long as the legislation prescribes basic policy and contains criteria that are sufficiently clear to enable Congress, the courts, and the public to ascertain whether the agency has conformed with those standards (*Mills v. United States*, 1994). HR professionals and other members of the public can weigh in on these issues at several points in this process, as we illustrate below and discuss more fully at the end of the chapter.

The administrative agency initially charged with administering the Equal Pay Act was the Department of Labor. However, Congress created a new agency in 1978, and transferred that responsibility to it.

> There is hereby created a Commission to be known as the Equal Employment Opportunity Commission (EEOC), which shall be composed of five members, not more than three of whom shall be members of the same political party. Members of the Commission shall be appointed by the President by and with the advice and consent of the Senate for a term of five years. (42 U.S.C. §2000e-4)

> All functions related to enforcing or administering Section 6(d) of the Fair Labor Standards Act, as amended (29 U.S.C. 206(d)), are hereby transferred to the Equal Employment Opportunity Commission. Such functions include, but shall not be limited to, the functions relating to equal pay administration and enforcement now vested in the Secretary of Labor, the Administrator of the Wage and Hour Division of the Department of Labor, and the Civil Service Commission. (92 Stat 3781, 1978)

Administrative agencies make policy through rule making and adjudication under procedures specified by the Enabling Act that created the agency or the Administrative Procedures Act of 1966 sections on Rule Making (553) and Judicial Review (554). There are informal and formal procedures under both rule making and adjudication.

Most regulations are created using the informal or "notice and comment" rule making procedure as opposed to formal rule making or adjudication. Informal rule making requires that:

> General notice of proposed rule making shall be published in the Federal Register, unless persons subject thereto are named and either personally served or otherwise have actual notice thereof in accordance with law. The notice shall include—(1) a statement of the time, place, and nature of public rule making proceedings; (2) reference to the legal authority under which the rule is proposed; and (3) either the terms or substance of the proposed rule or a description of the subjects and issues involved. Except when notice or hearing is required by statute, this subsection does not apply—(A) to inter-

pretative rules, general statements of policy, or rules of agency organization, procedure, or practice; or (B) when the agency for good cause finds (and incorporates the finding and a brief statement of reasons therefor in the rules issued) that notice and public procedure thereon are impracticable, unnecessary, or contrary to the public interest. (5 U.S.C. 553(b))

After notice required by this section, the agency shall give interested persons an opportunity to participate in the rule making through submission of written data, views, or arguments with or without opportunity for oral presentation. After consideration of the relevant matter presented, the agency shall incorporate in the rules adopted a concise general statement of their basis and purpose. (5 U.S.C. 553(c))

Note that the process provides at this point a very clear way for HR professionals to involve themselves in shaping the law: comment in detail on the proposed rules and regulations! The agency must address every substantive comment and explain why it either did or did not incorporate the comment into the final rule. The final rule is then published in the Federal Register and codified in the Code of Federal Regulations.

Before a rule can take effect, the Federal agency promulgating such rule shall submit to each House of the Congress and to the Comptroller General a report containing—(i) a copy of the rule; (ii) a concise general statement relating to the rule, including whether it is a major rule; and (iii) the proposed effective date of the rule. (5 U.S.C. 801(a)(1)(A))

"A rule shall not take effect (or continue), if the Congress enacts a joint resolution of disapproval," that is not vetoed by the President (5 U.S.C. 801(b)(1)). If Congress passes a joint resolution disapproving the rule there is no opportunity for judicial review. ("No determination, finding, action, or omission under this chapter shall be subject to judicial review." 5 U.S.C. 805.) Note that here again, by informing congress of issues of substantive concern, HR professionals have an opportunity to shape the law, or even to keep a proposed rule from becoming effective.

Almost every regulation is challenged. In the case of the Equal Pay Act, either an employer group (Chamber of Commerce) or employee group (unions) will challenge the regulation, one because it went too far, the other because it did not go far enough or vice versa, depending on the effect of the rule.

If Congress does not "disapprove" the rule, then the rule may be challenged. The Equal Employment Opportunity Commission (1977) promulgated procedures for such challenges:

Any interested person may petition the Commission, in writing, for the issuance, amendment, or repeal of a rule or regulation. Such petition shall be filed with the Equal Employment Opportunity Commission ... and shall state the rule or regulation proposed to be issued, amended, or repealed, together with a statement of grounds in support of such petition. (29 C.F.R. §1601.35)

Upon the filing of such petition, the Commission shall consider the same and may thereupon either grant or deny the petition in whole or in part, conduct an appropriate proceeding thereon, or make other disposition of the petition. Should the petition be denied in whole or in part, prompt notice shall be given of the denial, accompanied by a simple statement of the grounds unless the denial be self-explanatory. (29 C.F.R. §1601.36)

Here again HR professionals may weigh in on the way the law is shaped. It is far better to object to proposed rules and regulations, or at minimum to negotiate on their wording, than it is to fight administrative law after it has been adopted.

THE COURTS HAVE ANOTHER ROLE TO PLAY

If the agency denies the petition to amend or repeal the regulation, an adversely affected individual has a right to commence an action in the federal court system. "A person suffering a legal wrong because of agency action, or adversely affected or aggrieved by agency action within the meaning of a relevant statute, is entitled to judicial review thereof" (Administrative Procedures Act, Judicial Review, 1966). This is again an opportunity for proactive HR professionals to influence the interpretation of the law: by filing for judicial relief from interpretations that appear to be professionally unsound, HR professionals in adversely affected organizations with standing (described below) can affect the way the law is interpreted. Some agency rules specify that appeals be taken to the circuit court, or even the D.C. circuit (home of most federal agencies). If a court is not specified, appeal will be filed with the federal district court.

The form of proceeding for judicial review is the special statutory review proceeding relevant to the subject matter in a court specified by statute or, in the absence or inadequacy thereof, any applicable form of legal action, including actions for declaratory judgments or writs of prohibitory or mandatory injunction or habeas corpus, in a court of competent jurisdiction. If no special statutory review proceeding is applicable, the action for judicial review may be brought against the United States, the agency by its official title, or the appropriate officer. Except to the extent that prior, adequate, and exclusive opportunity for judicial review is provided by law, agency action is subject to judicial review in civil or criminal proceedings for judicial enforcement. (5 U.S.C. §703)

When an agency finds that justice so requires, it may postpone the effective date of action taken by it, pending judicial review. On such conditions as may be required and to the extent necessary to prevent irreparable injury, the reviewing court, including the court to which a case may be taken on appeal from or on application for certiorari or other writ to a reviewing court, may issue all necessary and appropriate process to postpone the effective date of an agency action or to preserve status or rights pending conclusion of the review proceedings (5 U.S.C. §705).

Federal courts are courts of limited jurisdiction, and the plaintiff must prove to the satisfaction of the court that it will have jurisdiction. Jurisdiction is the power of a court to hear a case and render a decision. Federal courts have exclusive jurisdiction over admiralty; bankruptcy; copyrights, trademarks, and patents; claims against the U.S. government; claims arising under statutes providing exclusive federal jurisdiction; and federal criminal prosecutions. Federal courts have concurrent jurisdiction with state courts for issues that require an interpretation of the U.S. Constitution, a federal statute, or a federal treaty or cases that involves diversity of citizenship.

An aggrieved party must also have "standing" in addition to proving jurisdiction. Article III, § 2 of the U.S. Constitution limits federal judicial power to "cases and controversies." The Supreme Court has determined that there are three constitutional requirements for standing.

1. The plaintiff must have suffered an "injury-in-fact" that is concrete and particularized and actual or imminent, not conjectural or hypothetical.
2. There must be a causal connection between the injury and the conduct complained of—the injury has to be fairly traceable to the challenged action and not the result of the independent action of some third party not before the court.
3. It must be "likely," as opposed to merely "speculative," that the injury will be redressed by a favorable decision (*Lujan v. Defenders of Wildlife*, 1992, pp. 555, 559)

The reviewing court shall decide all relevant questions of law, interpret constitutional and statutory provisions, and determine the meaning or applicability of the terms of an agency action. The reviewing court will either compel agency action unlawfully withheld or unreasonably delayed, and/ or hold unlawful and set aside agency action, findings, and conclusions. The Administrative Procedures Act sets out six criteria for setting aside agency action. The reviewing court shall hold unlawful and set aside agency action, findings, and conclusions found to be:

A. arbitrary, capricious, an abuse of discretion, or otherwise not in accordance with law
B. contrary to constitutional right, power, privilege, or immunity

C. in excess of statutory jurisdiction, authority, or limitations, or short of statutory right
D. without observance of procedure required by law
E. unsupported by substantial evidence in a case subject to sections 556 and 557 of this title or otherwise reviewed on the record of an agency hearing provided by statute
F. unwarranted by the facts to the extent that the facts are subject to trial de novo by the reviewing court (Administrative Procedures Act, Judicial Review, 1966)

The substantial evidence test (E above) is applicable if the agency decision was made after a trial-type hearing on the record and the Court evaluates the reasonableness of the agency's fact finding. Unwarranted by the facts (F above) is authorized only when the action is adjudicatory and the agency fact-finding procedures are inadequate or when issues that were not before the agency are raised in a proceeding to enforce non-adjudicatory agency action (*Citizens to Preserve Overton Park v. Volpe*, 1971).

AGENCY ENFORCEMENT

A rule will become effective after it has passed Congressional review and survived the appeals process within the agency and the court system. Once the rule is effective, the agency can begin to enforce the rule.

Regulations promulgated by the EEOC are found in Title 29 of the Code of Federal Regulations (C.F.R.) Parts 1600 to 1691. Part 1620 is entitled "The Equal Pay Act" and Part 1621 is entitled "Procedures—The Equal Pay Act."

Regulations generally begin with a statement of applicability. For example, 29 C.F.R. §1620.1(a) states,

Since the Equal Pay Act, 29 U.S.C. 206(d) (hereinafter referred to as the EPA), is a part of the Fair Labor Standards Act, 29 U.S.C. 201, *et seq.* (hereinafter referred to as the FLSA), it has the same basic coverage as the FLSA with two principal exceptions: (1) The EPA applies to executive, administrative, and professional employees who are normally exempted from the FLSA for most purposes by section 13(a)(1) of that statute, and (2) The EPA covers all State and local government employees unless they are specifically exempted under section 3(e)(2)(C) of the FLSA.

However, "The EPA does not apply where the employer has no employees who are engaged in commerce or in the handling of goods that have moved in commerce and the employer is not an enterprise engaged in commerce or in the production of goods for commerce" (29 C.F.R. §1620.1(b)).

Since the Equal Pay Act is part of the Fair Labor Standards Act, activities that are exempt from FLSA are also exempt from EPA with one exception:

"any employee employed in a bona fide executive, administrative, or professional capacity . . . or in the capacity of outside salesman" 29 U.S.C. §213(a). FLSA provides for other excluded categories, such as agricultural workers, fishermen, seamen, and other categories listed in subparagraphs 1–15 of 29 U.S.C. §213(a).

The EEOC has also promulgated a rule explaining the relationship between the Equal Pay Act and Title VII of the Civil Rights Act of 1964 but it does not address the issue resolved by the Supreme Court in *County of Washington v. Gunther*, 452 U.S. 161 (1981). The rule states,

> In situations where the jurisdictional prerequisites of both the EPA and title VII of the Civil Rights Act of 1964, as amended, 42 U.S.C. 200 *et seq.*, are satisfied, any violation of the Equal Pay Act is also a violation of title VII. However, title VII covers types of wage discrimination not actionable under the EPA. Therefore, an act or practice of an employer or labor organization that is not a violation of the EPA may nevertheless be a violation of title VII. (29 C.F.R. §1620.27(a))

In addition,

> The right to equal pay under the Equal Pay Act has no relationship to whether the employee is in the lower paying job as a result of discrimination in violation of title VII. Under the EPA a *prima facie* violation is established upon a showing that an employer pays different wages to employees of opposite sexes for equal work on jobs requiring equal skill, effort and responsibility, and which are performed under similar working conditions. Thus, the availability of a remedy under title VII which would entitle the lower paid employee to be hired into, or to transfer to, the higher paid job does not defeat the right of each person employed on the lower paid job to the same wages as are paid to a member of the opposite sex who receives higher pay for equal work. (29 C.F.R. §1620.27(c))

Agencies also promulgate administrative rules to implement agency actions. For example, if an employer is concerned that he may be in violation of any of the rules under the EPA he may request an opinion letter from the EEOC. The rule explains the procedure:

> A request for an opinion letter should be submitted in writing to the Chairman, Equal Employment Opportunity Commission, 131 M Street, NE., Washington, DC 20507, and shall contain: (1) A concise statement of the issues for which an opinion is requested; (2) A full statement of the relevant facts and law; and (3) The names and addresses of the person(s) making the request and other interested persons. (29 C.F.R. §1621.3(a))

Issuance of an opinion letter by the Commission is discretionary (29 C.F.R. 1621.3(b)).

> When the Commission, at its discretion, determines that it will not issue an opinion letter as defined in §1621.4 , the Commission may provide informal advice or guidance to the requestor. An informal letter of advice does not represent the formal position of the Commission and does not commit the Commission to the views expressed therein. Any letter other than those defined in §1621.4 will be considered a letter of advice and may not be relied upon by any employer within the meaning of section 10 of the Portal to Portal Act of 1947, 29 U.S.C. 255. (29 C.F.R. §1621.3(c))

When an employee believes that an employer has violated a rule and wants to file a complaint, most agency regulations require that an aggrieved individual start with an administrative agency proceeding before taking his claim to federal court. For a Title VII sex discrimination case,

> The Commission shall receive information concerning alleged violations of title VII...from any person. Where the information discloses that a person is entitled to file a charge with the Commission, the appropriate office shall render assistance in the filing of a charge. Any person or organization may request the issuance of a Commissioner charge for an inquiry into individual or systematic discrimination. Such request, with any pertinent information, should be submitted to the nearest District, Field, Area, or Local office. (29 C.F.R. §1601.6(a))

> The investigation of a charge shall be made by the Commission, its investigators, or any other representative designated by the Commission. (29 C.F.R. §1601.15(a))

Prior to the issuance of a determination as to reasonable cause, the commission may encourage the parties to settle the charge on terms that are mutually agreeable. District directors, field directors, area directors, local directors, the director of the office of field programs, the director of field management programs, or their designees, shall have the authority to sign any settlement agreement which is agreeable to both parties (29 C.F.R. §1601.20(a)).

Where the commission completes its investigation of a charge and finds that there is not reasonable cause to believe that an unlawful employment practice has occurred or is occurring as to all issues addressed in the determination, the commission shall issue a letter of determination to all parties to the charge indicating the finding. The commission's letter of determination shall be the final determination of the commission. The letter of determination shall inform the person claiming to be aggrieved or the person on whose behalf a charge was filed of the right to sue in federal district court within 90 days of receipt of the letter of determination (29 C.F.R.

§1601.19(a)). The aggrieved person cannot file in federal court until the EEOC makes its determination.

The EPA does not require but does allow filing a complaint with the EEOC before initiating a claim in federal court:

> A complainant is authorized under section 16(b) of the Fair Labor Standards Act (29 U.S.C. 216(b)) to file a civil action in a court of competent jurisdiction within two years or, if the violation is willful, three years of the date of the alleged violation of the Equal Pay Act regardless of whether he or she pursued any administrative complaint processing. (29 C.F.R. §1614.408)

THE COURTS ADJUDICATE CASES

Even though Congress passed the Equal Pay Act and the EEOC promulgated regulations, it is almost impossible to address every situation. The courts review fact patterns and determine whether a rule has been violated when it is not clear from reading the rule. As a reminder, the Act states:

> No employer...shall discriminate,...between employees on the basis of sex by paying wages...at a rate less than the rate at which he pays wages to employees of the opposite sex...for equal work...except where such payment is made pursuant to (i) a seniority system; (ii) a merit system; (iii) a system which measures earnings by quantity or quality of production; or (iv) a differential based on any other factor other than sex. (29 U.S.C §206(d)(1))

> The most notable feature of the history of the Equal Pay Act is that Congress recognized early in the legislative process that the concept of equal pay for equal work was more readily stated in principle than reduced to statutory language which would be meaningful to employers and workable across the broad range of industries covered by the Act. (*Corning Glass Works v. Brennan, 1974, p. 198*)

Even the EEOC regulations state,

> What constitutes equal skill, equal effort, or equal responsibility cannot be precisely defined. In interpreting these key terms of the statute, the broad remedial purpose of the law must be taken into consideration. The terms constitute separate tests, each of which must be met in order for the equal pay standard to apply. It should be kept in mind that 'equal' does not mean 'identical.' Insubstantial or minor differences in the degree or amount of skill, or effort, or responsibility required for the performance of jobs will not render the equal pay standard inapplicable. (29 C.F.R. §1620.14(a))

It is also necessary to consider the degree of difference in terms of skill, effort, and responsibility. These factors are related in such a manner that a general standard to determine equality of jobs cannot be set up solely on the basis of a percentage of time (29 C.F.R. §1620.14(c)).

As an illustration of how the court system works and how courts interpret the statutes and regulations, consider the case of *Brennan v. Prince William Hospital Corporation* (1974). The plaintiff, in this case the Secretary of Labor (the EEOC had not been established at the time of trial), filed his complaint in the District Court for the Eastern District of Virginia. The location of the court where a complaint is filed is called "venue." Venue is normally proper in the district where the defendant resides or where the action complained of occurred. In the federal system, district court is where the trial is conducted. After the court sided with the hospital, the Secretary appealed the case to the circuit court and since the hospital was located in Virginia, the appeal was to the 4th Circuit.

The federal courts' structure consists of a Supreme Court, twelve circuit courts, 94 district courts and specialized courts, which won't be discussed here. The Supreme Court is the highest court in the federal Judiciary. Congress has established two levels of federal courts under the Supreme Court: the trial courts and the appellate courts. The United States district courts are the trial courts of the federal court system. Within limits set by Congress and the Constitution, the district courts have jurisdiction to hear nearly all categories of federal cases, including both civil and criminal matters. There are two special trial courts that have nationwide jurisdiction over certain types of cases. The Court of International Trade addresses cases involving international trade and customs issues. The United States Court of Federal Claims has jurisdiction over most claims for monetary damages against the United States, disputes over federal contracts, unlawful taking of private property by the federal government, and a variety of other claims against the United States. The 94 judicial districts are organized into 12 regional circuits, each of which has a United States court of appeals. A court of appeals hears appeals from the district courts located within its circuit, as well as appeals from decisions of federal administrative agencies. In addition, the Court of Appeals for the Federal Circuit has nationwide jurisdiction to hear appeals in specialized cases (United States Courts, n.d.).

In *Brennan*, the district court noted that the facts were not in dispute and that the controversy centered on the inferences to be drawn from them. It found that although aides and orderlies in hospitals do the same type of patient care work, the following differences exist between the jobs: the proportions of routine care tasks are not the same; aides do work that orderlies are neither required nor permitted to do; and, most important, orderlies do work, including extra tasks, that aides are neither required nor permitted to do, such as catheterization. It concluded, therefore, that the Secretary of Labor had failed to establish that the aides and orderlies perform substantially equal work (*Brennan v. Prince William Hospital Corporation*, 1974).

The 4th Circuit Court's opinion started with the observation:

In applying the Congressional mandate of equal pay for equal work on jobs which require equal skill, effort, and responsibility, there are two extremes of interpretation that must be avoided. Congress realized that the majority of job differentiations are made for genuine economic reasons unrelated to sex. It did not authorize the Secretary or the courts to engage in wholesale reevaluation of any employer's pay structure in order to enforce their own conceptions of economic worth.... But if courts defer to overly nice distinctions in job content, employers may evade the Act at will. (*Brennan v. Prince William Hospital Corporation*, 1974, p. 285)

One of the most common grounds for justifying different wages is the assertion that male employees perform extra tasks. These may support a wage differential if they create significant variations in skill, effort, and responsibility between otherwise equal jobs.... But the semblance of the valid job classification system may not be allowed to mask the existence of wage discrimination based on sex. (*Brennan v. Prince William Hospital Corporation*, 1974, p. 285)

Although a number of courts have applied the Equal Pay Act to hospital and nursing home aides and orderlies, varied employment practices among institutions have prevented the development of an industry-wide standard. The Act must be applied on a case by case basis to factual situations that are, for practical purposes, unique. (*Brennan v. Prince William Hospital Corporation*, 1974, p. 285)

The Court held that job descriptions and titles are not decisive, but that actual job requirements and performance are controlling. However, a mere job description without evidence of actual performance does not establish the existence of extra duties. The Court concluded that the work performed by aides and orderlies was not identical, but application of the Equal Pay Act is not restricted to identical work.

The basic routine tasks of the aides and orderlies are equal. The variations that the district court found, when tested by the Act's standard of "equal skill, effort, and responsibility," do not affect the substantial equality of their overall work. The judgment of the district court is reversed, and this case is remanded for entry of judgment for the Secretary. (*Brennan v. Prince William Hospital Corporation*, 1974, p. 285)

The opposite result was found in *Hodgson v. Golden Isles Convalescent Homes, Inc.* (1972). In that case the district court found catheterization to be a significant extra duty, and orderlies also moved heavy equipment, administered suction therapy, and did other demanding work not done by aides. (Note: This case was filed in the Middle District of Florida but the 5th Circuit was split into two circuits and Florida is now in the 11th Circuit.)

The *Hodgson* case was decided before the *Brennan* case. Does that mean that *Hodgson* set a precedent that the 4th Circuit had to follow? No. When a circuit court decides a case it sets a precedent for that circuit; however, other circuit courts are not required to follow the reasoning of another circuit court. In this situation, the *Brennan* court did cite and agree with the reasoning of the *Hodgson* court but reached a different decision. It is not until the Supreme Court makes a decision that precedent is set for the whole country.

The Supreme Court decides only a fraction of the cases that are appealed to it. For the 2012 term, 7,509 cases were filed and the Court disposed of only 76. For the 2011 term the numbers were similar, 7,713 and 73 (United States Supreme Court, 2013). Appeal to the Supreme Court is not automatic as it is in a state court system. Because of the limited time and resources, only cases the Justices deem important are heard. Three Justices must agree on the importance before the Court will hear the case.

In *Corning Glass Works v. Brennan* (1974), Corning was operating plants in Corning, NY, 2nd Circuit, and Wellsboro, PA, 3rd Circuit. Female workers filed an Equal Pay Act suit and each circuit, upon hearing the same facts, reached a different conclusion.

The Court stated,

> The principal question posed is whether Corning Glass Works violated the Act by paying a higher base wage to male night shift inspectors than it paid to female inspectors performing the same tasks on the day shift, where the higher wage was paid in addition to a separate night shift differential paid to all employees for night work.... We granted certiorari and consolidated the cases to resolve this unusually direct conflict between two circuits. 414 U.S. 1110 (1973). (*Corning Glass Works v. Brennan*, 1974)

The following excerpts describe how the Equal Pay Act and the implementing regulations should be analyzed and applied to different fact patterns.

> The Act's basic structure and operation are similarly straightforward. In order to make out a case under the Act, the Secretary must show that an employer pays different wages to employees of opposite sexes for equal work on jobs the performance of which requires equal skill, effort, and responsibility, and which are performed under similar working conditions. Although the Act is silent on this point, its legislative history makes plain that the Secretary has the burden of proof on this issue. (*Corning Glass Works v. Brennan*, 1974, p. 195)

> Again, while the Act is silent on this question, its structure and history also suggest that, once the Secretary has carried his burden of showing that the employer pays workers of one sex more than workers of the opposite sex for equal work, the burden shifts to the employer to show that the differential is justified under one of the Act's four exceptions. (*Corning Glass Works v. Brennan*, 1974, p. 196)

> Corning argues that the Secretary has failed to prove that Corning ever violated the Act because day shift work is not "performed under similar working

conditions" as night shift work. The Secretary maintains that day shift and night shift work are performed under "similar working conditions" within the meaning of the Act. Although the Secretary recognizes that higher wages may be paid for night shift work, the Secretary contends that such a shift differential would be based upon a "factor other than sex" within the catchall exception to the Act, and that Corning has failed to carry its burden of proof that its higher base wage for male night inspectors was, in fact, based on any factor other than sex. (*Corning Glass Works v. Brennan*, 1974, p. 196)

The House Report emphasized: This language recognizes that there are many factors which may be used to measure the relationships between jobs and which establish a valid basis for a difference in pay. These factors will be found in a majority of the job classification systems. Thus, it is anticipated that a bona fide job classification program that does not discriminate on the basis of sex will serve as a valid defense to a charge of discrimination. H.R.Rep. No. 309, supra, at 3. (*Corning Glass Works v. Brennan*, 1974, p. 201)

Nowhere in any of these definitions is time of day worked mentioned as a relevant criterion. The fact of the matter is that the concept of 'working conditions,' as used in the specialized language of job evaluation systems, simply does not encompass shift differentials.... [T]he company could not cure its violation except by equalizing the base wages of female day inspectors with the higher rates paid the night inspectors. This result is implicit in the Act's language, its statement of purpose, and its legislative history. (*Corning Glass Works v. Brennan*, 1974, pp. 202, 206)

SUMMARY AND RECOMMENDATIONS

As we have shown above, a vast collection of statutes, regulations, and court decisions provides the HR manager the information needed to interact with employees and to determine the rights of those employees. In this chapter we have illustrated—using the history of statutory creation, administrative enforcement, and court interpretation of the Equal Pay Act—the complex interplay among the branches of government that gives the law its dynamic nature. HR professionals must have a basic understanding of these dynamic forces and must take them into consideration when providing advice to other managers regarding the legality of decisions and actions they are contemplating. The complexity of the process described, we believe, illustrates why we advise strongly that expert attorneys be consulted any time the HR professional believes a contemplated policy or managerial action might violate the law. It is better to be safe than sorry.

In the introduction to this chapter we promised to address three key questions: (a) What is the source of the statutes, regulations, and court decisions that collectively are known as "the law"? Where do they come from and who makes them? (b) How are the statutes, regulations, and court decisions interrelated?

How do they come together to provide guidance to organizations seeking to comply fully with the law? (c) How can HR professionals—acting individually or through their companies or professional associations—influence the law and help to shape it? In the sections above we have addressed thoroughly the first and second questions in an effort to inform HR professionals and other interested readers. Now we turn our attention to the third question: How can HR professionals influence the law and help to shape it?

The material presented in previous sections suggests several important ways in which HR professionals—working individually or through their companies or professional associations—can help shape the law. The first comes during the process of legislative action to create a statute. All statutes are created by elected representative assemblies (such as the U.S. Congress), and thus the members of those bodies can be approached by the citizens they represent (including HR professionals and their employing organizations and professional associations) with advice, suggestions, and other input regarding the wisdom of the wording of statutes being considered. Lobbying for changes in statutory law is a well-accepted process in the United States, and HR professionals can take full advantage of the privileges accorded them in a democratic society to influence legislative action. Members of congress are very responsive to well-organized efforts by companies and professional associations to influence the wording of proposed statutory law. In fact, proposed statutes may be withdrawn altogether when the pressure from the electorate is strongly felt by the elected representatives of the people. Furthermore, congressional committees typically hold hearings before contemplating new laws (or substantive changes in existing laws), and expert testimony is solicited by congress from affected parties. This is an excellent opportunity for HR professionals to "gain the ear" of the legislative branch and thus to influence the shaping of the law.

A second possibility for influencing the law comes during the rule-making process. Above we described the complex process by which rules and regulations are promulgated. The process allows for input from the public (which includes HR professionals working either individually or through professional associations and other organizations) to provide ideas and suggestions regarding the wording of specific rules and regulations. Also, the process allows proposed rules to be challenged during several points along the process. This clearly is an opportunity for HR professionals to help shape the law. Proposed rules and regulations that are not professionally sound deserve to be challenged, and responsible HR professionals should not miss the opportunity to provide such challenges.

Cases heard in court provide yet another opportunity for HR professionals to shape the law, since court interpretations of statutes, rules, and regulations have far-reaching impact. (This is especially true when the U.S. Supreme Court is contemplating a case.) While it is unlikely that companies will seek to be parties to a lawsuit simply as a way to help shape the law, it is possible for professional associations and other organizations to file *amicus curia* ("friend of the court") legal briefs to be considered by the court when making its ruling. Such legal briefs—if well-reasoned—can be used to persuade the court to accept interpretations of the law favorable to the position of the organization filing the brief. Of course, if the HR professional's company should be taken to court as a party to a lawsuit, it is in that organization's best interests to mount a strong legal argument supporting its actions. A court's decision in favor of the company's position can set precedent that will shape the law and the way it is interpreted in future cases.

REFERENCES

Administrative Procedures Act, Judicial Review, 5 U.S.C. §§ 553 and 554 (1966).

Administrative Procedures Act, Rule Making, 5 U.S.C. § 702 (1966).

Brennan v. Prince William Hospital Corporation, 503 F. 2d 282 (4th Cir. 1974).

Chevron, U.S.A., Inc. v. Natural Resources Defense Council. 467 U.S. 837, 842 (1984).

Citizens to Preserve Overton Park v. Volpe, 401 U.S. 402, 413 (1971).

Civil Rights Act, 42 U.S.C. § 2000e-2 (a) (1) (1964).

Corning Glass Works v. Brennan, 417 U.S. 188, 196 (1974).

County of Washington v. Gunter, 452 U.S. 161,171 (1981).

DeNavas-Walt, C., Proctor, B. D., & Smith, J. C. (2013). *U.S. Census Bureau, Income, poverty, and health insurance coverage in the United States: 2012.* Retrieved from http://www.census.gov/prod/2013pubs/p60-245.pdf

Equal Employment Opportunity Commission, 29 C.F.R. 1600 et seq. (1977).

Fair Pay Act, P.L. 88–38 (1963).

Hodgson v. Golden Isles Convalescent Homes, Inc., 468 F.2d 1256 (5th Cir. 1972).

Lujan v. Defenders of Wildlife, 504 U.S. 555, 559.

Mills v. United States, 36 F.3d 1052 (11th Cir. 1994).

National Women's Law Center. (2013, September). *The wage gap is stagnant in the last decade.* Retrieved from http://www.nwlc.org/resource/wage-gap-stagnant-last-decade

United States Courts. (n.d.). *Federal courts' structure.* Retrieved from http://www.uscourts.gov/FederalCourts/UnderstandingtheFederalCourts/Federal-CourtsStructure.aspx

United States Supreme Court. (2013). *2013 Year-End Report on the Federal Judiciary.* Retrieved from http://www.supremecourt.gov/publicinfo/year-end/2013year-endreport.pdf

United States v. Lopez, 514 U.S. 549 (1995).

United States v. Morrison, 529 U.S. 598 (2000).

CHAPTER 6

LEGAL ISSUES IN EMPLOYEE SELECTION

Negotiating the Obstacles and Avoiding the Landmines

Brian L. Bellenger and Kenneth A. Yusko

INTRODUCTION

Decisions regarding employee selection are arguably some of the most critical and, as such, most legally vulnerable an organization can make. Certainly dynamic and visionary managers and leaders have a tremendous impact on the performance of companies and departments, and innovative products and processes will enhance an organization's fiscal success. Ultimately, however, the employees making up the workforce largely determine the long-term impact and viability of the organization. This chapter examines the legal requirements and standards for employee selection, strategies for effectively ensuring effective and legally defensible selection decisions, and the role of human resource consultants and practitioners in encouraging and guiding organizations in appropriately using and defending selection procedures.

Legal and Regulatory Issues in Human Resources Management, pages 117–135
Copyright © 2015 by Information Age Publishing

HISTORICAL PERSPECTIVES ON EMPLOYEE SELECTION

Early Efforts at Regulation

Legal issues have been impacting employment practices in the United States since the industrial revolution moved the economy from an agricultural base to a largely manufacturing base. Early efforts to regulate hiring and other employment practices were focused on children in the workforce. In the preindustrial agrarian economy, children were a natural part of the workforce in managing farming and agricultural efforts. As society became more industrialized, a family's survival depended on children working in factories and mills. This exposed children to harsh working conditions and often put even a minimal education out of reach. For several years in the early 20th century, advocates for children fought not only to improve the conditions under which children were employed, but also to make the use of children for labor below a certain age illegal. Industrial interests initially were successful in staving off regulatory actions, but ultimately, in the aftermath of the Great Depression, employment became so scarce that adults in their willingness to work for a child's wage began to replace children in the workforce (Gatewood & Feild, 2001).

The Fair Labor Standards Act, passed in 1938, became the first regulatory statute enacted by the federal government regarding employment. This act focused largely on minimum wages, work hours, and how children can be employed in the workforce. Over the next several decades, economic conditions coupled with legalized segregation in parts of the United States, particularly in the south, led to continued frustrations and social unrest surrounding the issue of employment. People of color had largely been excluded from access to jobs beyond manual labor and service industry jobs (e.g., housekeeping, cooking, lawn and garden care), and women were beginning to enter the workforce with professional degrees and intentions to move beyond the secretarial pool. The civil rights movement served as the impetus for the first of a series of federal statutes that specifically addressed issues of employment, including employee selection, Title VII of the Civil Rights Act of 1964.

TITLE VII OF THE CIVIL RIGHTS ACT OF 1964

Through Title VII, the federal government provided specific regulations regarding employment in private organizations of at least 15 employees and all government agencies and organizations. The Act prohibited such employers from discriminating in the employment process against people based on their race, color, religion, sex, or national origin. In order to ensure that employers complied with the Act, the Equal Employment Opportunity Commission (EEOC) was established to serve as the enforcement agency for the federal government in matters of employee selection. The act also outlined the procedures for filing claims of discrimination. A subsequent amendment to the act added pregnant women to the group of protected classes.

In 1978, the EEOC, in conjunction with the Civil Service Commission, the Department of Labor and the Department of Justice, published the *Uniform Guidelines on Employee Selection Procedures* (1978) to provide more technical guidance to employers regarding their hiring practices. The Uniform Guidelines serve as a resource to organizations, as well as to the court system, in determining whether selection procedures are acceptable with regard to compliance with Title VII. Several important components of the Uniform Guidelines are described below.

Definitions of Discrimination

Two forms of discrimination were defined by the Uniform Guidelines: disparate treatment and disparate impact. Disparate treatment occurs when organizations apply different standards to members of a protected class than to all other applicants in their hiring practices. For example, if an organization asked applicants to self-identify any religious affiliation, and subsequently did not hire qualified individuals self-identifying as Muslim but hired equally qualified individuals professing other faiths or no religious affiliations, then even if the organization has no specific indication that it intended to discriminate, the result would be considered disparate treatment. Disparate treatment would also include changing the test items or content depending on the class of the applicant. For example, asking women if they intend to leave the area to relocate in the future but not asking the same question of men would constitute disparate treatment.

In situations involving disparate impact, the organization treats all applicants the same (i.e., subjects them to the same testing requirements) through the selection process, but the process itself results in one or more protected classes being underrepresented in the group of new hires. In this type of situation, even if the organization has no intent to discriminate, the selection process itself becomes the means of discrimination. One example is the use of physical ability examinations for entry into public safety jobs such as police officer and firefighter. All candidates are required to meet the same standard of performance on such tests to be hired into the job, but the tests tend to include components that emphasize upper body strength and, as such, may favor men versus women. The result may be a disparate impact on women who wish to enter the public safety field.

Adverse Impact and the Four-Fifths Rule

Another tool provided by the Uniform Guidelines is a statistical measure that serves as a general guideline for determining whether protected classes are underrepresented as a result of the selection process. This tool, known as the four-fifths rule, uses a comparison of pass rates at each stage of the selection process to determine if one subgroup (based on a Title VII protected status) is more successful than another subgroup. Specifically, if the selection ratio of any group is less than eighty percent (or four-fifths) of the most favorably treated, or most successful, group, then the selection system shows evidence of adverse impact.

An example of the four-fifths rule is as follows: A police department in a large municipality wishes to hire a new group of employees to send through the police academy. The department has hired a consultant to administer a test to determine who is best equipped to become a police officer. As a first step, the department accepts applications, and it receives 800 applications: 500 from White/Caucasian individuals and 300 from Black/African-American individuals. All 800 applicants take the examination. The department wishes to send 60 employees to the training academy, so they select the top scoring 60 individuals completing the examination. If 45 of these individuals are white/Caucasian and 15 are black/African-American, then the hiring ratio for the white group is 45 out of 500 or 9% and the hiring ratio for the black group is 15 out of 300 or 5%. Using the four-fifths rule, the ratio of Black/African American individuals hired is 55.6% of the ratio of White/Caucasian individuals, indicating that the test resulted in adverse impact against the minority group.

Evidence of Validity

In addition to defining discrimination and outlining statistical measures for use in determining evidence of discrimination, the Uniform Guidelines also provide criteria for determining whether a selection system is appropriate for use. Selection systems often use a content- or criterion-related approach to demonstrate evidence of their validity. *Criterion-related validity* relies on establishing a statistical relationship between performance on the test and performance on the job. *Content validity* aims to demonstrate a relationship between the content of the test and the content (e.g., tasks and KSAs) performed on the job. It focuses on how well the test represents the job domain. The guidelines provide specific procedures for demonstrating evidence of these approaches to establishing the validity of a selection system, and it is frequently the case that when organizations fail to follow these guidelines, they introduce legal vulnerability to the selection system.

OTHER REGULATORY ACTS

Following the implementation of the Civil Rights Act of 1964, several other acts were passed by Congress to protect the rights of additional subsets of the population. The Age Discrimination in Employment Act of 1967 prohibited private and public employers from discriminating against individuals over the age of 40 years on the basis of their age. The Rehabilitation Act of 1973 was enacted to ensure people with physical and mental disabilities were not subject to discrimination by the federal government, and the Americans with Disabilities Act of 1990 expanded this to include private employers.

In addition to these acts, Congress passed the Civil Rights Act of 1991 (which amended Title VII of the Civil Rights Act of 1964), and while this act did not expand the protected classes covered by the 1964 act, it did make changes regarding litigation over selection practices. One significant change introduced by the 1991 act was the shift away from the greater burden of proof on the part of the plaintiff in cases of alleged discrimination, as introduced by the *Wards Cove Packing Co. v. Antonio* ruling. The 1991 act reversed the potential chilling effect that the Wards Cove decision would have had on potential challenges to illegal discrimination (for example, by requiring plaintiffs to hire experts in selection to review and evaluate tests, and in some cases conduct separate validity studies). A second change resulting from this act allowed victims of intentional discrimination to sue the employer for both compensatory and punitive damages. Another provision of the act made it unlawful for employers to adjust test scores for subgroups of job candidates based on a protected class category (i.e., race, sex, color, religion, national origin), or to use different cut scores for these subgroups.

This final provision of the 1991 act was a major shift in what the legislature perceived as "fair," because it meant, in effect, that race norming was now illegal. Race norming was a practice used by organizations to promote diversity by maintaining separate lists of test scores for members of each demographic group (typically Black/African-American and White/Caucasian) and selecting the top scorers on each list, often at a one-to-one relationship. By changing the standards through the passage of this act, employers had a greater burden to use selection tests that did not result in adverse impact against members of a protected class, a higher standard for employers than had previously been required under the 1964 act. This was seen as a setback by some selection experts, but ultimately, it forced employers to do a better job at developing selection systems that were not discriminatory in both intent and effect.

LEGAL LANDMINES AND STRATEGIES
FOR AVOIDING THEM

It is important to begin this section of the chapter with a disclaimer of sorts. The EEOC and its partner, the U.S. Department of Justice, are not concerned with selection procedures that result in no adverse impact against a protected class. Any public or private organization that can demonstrate through its records of employment practices that its decisions had no disparate impact will generally be safe in the eyes of the courts. As such, organizations are free to use selection systems that have no evidence of validity, as long as they do not discriminate. This can be a precarious position for many employers, but unfortunately it is a position for which some employers seem to settle. Developing valid selection systems can be seen as overly time-consuming and expensive, requiring either in-house expertise in selection or relatively expensive consultants. Organizations may determine that they would rather risk losing a long-term discrimination lawsuit than pay the shorter-terms costs for the expertise required to maintain a valid selection process.

For those many organizations that strive to use valid selection procedures, there are several key elements to designing and implementing a system of hiring or promotion which can make the difference between legal vulnerability and defensibility. There seems to be a general assumption in the field of human resources that public sector organizations are scrutinized more closely by regulatory agencies such as the EEOC than are private companies with regard to their selection practices. This may be due to the fact that public employers are largely civil service organizations in which employees have quasi-property rights to their jobs, and are therefore more likely to be the subject of legal action. It may also be the case that public sector employees are paid using public funds, and as such garner more interest from regulatory agencies who want to ensure public funds are appropriately managed. Regardless, organizations are ultimately held to the same standards regardless of the sector or nature of their work and can be subject to the same pitfalls of legal vulnerability if their selection systems.

Psychometric Issues

Selection tests are typically evaluated regarding two key properties: validity and reliability. As discussed previously, validity is the extent to which the test measures what it is supposed to measure (e.g., the ability to perform well on the job). Reliability is a measure of precision; it determines whether the test produces consistent and reliable results for all candidates. For example, a football team uses a 40-yard dash to help decide which team members should play the position of running back. The coach assumes that faster 40-yard dash times are associated with being a better running back. The consistency of the players' times in repeated dash tests is a matter of reliability. Whether faster 40-yard dash times are related to effective performance on the football field is a question of validity (i.e., is the correctness of the inference that faster dash times are associated with being a better running back).

The primary purpose of any selection system is to identify the best possible person or persons to fill vacancies in the organization. Typically, organizations have varying notions of what "best" means, because employers want not only a strong performer, but also someone who is a good fit with the culture and climate of the organization, or perhaps matches well with a particular team or project. Nonetheless, the general goal is to hire someone who will perform well, thereby making the organization more successful. The key for human resource practitioners and selection system developers is to ensure that the method used to select an employee in some way predicts how the employee might perform on the job.

So how do you establish evidence of validity? How do you ensure that selection tests predict performance? As discussed in an earlier section of this chapter, the Uniform Guidelines (1978) defined validity as it relates to selection. A criterion-related approach is used to establish a relationship between the selection tool and job performance by correlating the tool with some measure or multiple measures of performance. This is most often used to establish the validity of written tests administered to large groups of candidates, although it is certainly an appropriate strategy for validating other types of tests.

In order to understand the vulnerabilities of selection procedures from a criterion-related perspective, one must understand the various elements that comprise a validity study. The Uniform Guidelines (1978) outline the steps of a criterion study in great detail, but the general procedures are described as follows:

- To first develop a selection procedure for a specific job, one must have a well-defined description of the job, including detailed tasks or work behaviors and a comprehensive list of knowledge, skills, abilities, and other characteristics (KSAOs) needed to perform those tasks or work behaviors.
- Using this information, test developers generate test items, questions, or situations related to the job. These could be knowledge-based multiple-choice questions; questions related to experiences, preferences, dispositions, or personality; or perhaps interview questions.
- Test developers also identify appropriate and accurate measures of job performance. This might include performance appraisal instru-

ments or job evaluation information, or it might include production information, or even turnover or absenteeism records. Regardless of the form, the job performance measure or criterion used would need to be available for all employees, or a large and demographically diverse sample of employees, within the job.

- Once test items and job performance measures have been developed and identified, a relationship must be demonstrated statistically between the two, in order to show that better performers on the job either responded in certain consistent ways to test items or achieved the higher scores on the test (depending on the nature of the items). This can be done in one of two ways: either current incumbents on whom you had valid measures of job performance would take the test, and the relationship between the two would determine the scoring key for the exam, or the test would be administered and scored in order to rank candidates who would then be hired and evaluated by the job criterion after a period of time on the job.
- A key to defending tests validated using this methodology is demonstrating the degree of adverse impact of the test by showing that various protected classes performed similarly on the exam and were hired accordingly (or the test was job-related and no other reasonable test was available having equivalent validity and less adverse impact).

The other method of validation often used by organizations to ensure their selection systems are legally defensible is called content validation. Content validation can be quite useful in situations where an organization does not have sufficient numbers of incumbents in a job to effectively demonstrate a statistical relationship between the test and job performance criteria. Rather, an assumption is made that the test closely resembles tasks and duties performed on the job, and thus effectively "represents" the job domain. Therefore, the KSAs required to perform well on the test are the same KSAs that are required to perform well on the job and we conclude that better performance on the test is predictive of better performance on the job. The steps for validating a selection test using a content methodology are described below:

- As with criterion studies, validation using a content strategy is begun through a job analysis process, by which the critical work behaviors and KSAOs are identified through on-site job observations, focus groups, and work inventories. For this approach, work behaviors are often broken down into more specific tasks or duties for reference in test development.

- Once the critical components of the jobs are identified, test developers determine which are amenable to measurement and meet with job incumbents and supervisors, also known as subject matter experts (SMEs), to assist in creating job-related test exercises. While all aspects of the job are not required to be represented in the test content, a fairly significant sampling of the job duties should be present.
- SMEs also assist in determining appropriate scoring criteria for the test exercises, ensuring that these criteria mirror expectations of job performance.
- Validity is demonstrated by linking the test exercises and scoring criteria back to the components of the job.

Best Practices to Avoid Legal Vulnerability

With an understanding of the psychometric properties of tests (i.e., validity and reliability), let us now explore the ways to ensure that an organization can effectively manage a system of selection without fear of legal vulnerability. In an effort to make these strategies salient to those practitioners in human resource departments and public personnel agencies, we will use as an example a public agency that went through a significant transformation during the course of litigation from inept in employee selection to a model civil service organization. This organization (hereafter referred to as the Board), located in the southeastern United States, had been party to a consent decree for over twenty years related to discriminatory hiring practices. The consent decree had arisen from charges filed on behalf of Black/African American and female employees and citizens in a large municipal area of discrimination in its selection and promotional systems. After failing to comply with the terms of the consent decree, the organization was placed under federal receivership with a mandate to produce valid, fair selection procedures for jobs in the civil service and to transform the organization for future success.

Expertise

One of the first issues addressed by the receivership was the qualifications and expertise of the in-house staff. The staff of the Board at the beginning of the receivership, while certainly knowledgeable about the civil service system, generally lacked any training or experience related to effective employee selection techniques. An initial act to address this deficiency by the receiver was to hire a group of industrial/organizational psychologists to serve as in-house experts for the Board. Having this expertise proved to be a valuable investment in ultimately exiting the consent decree and avoiding future litigation.

Job Analysis

As the new experts were brought on board, several matters had to be addressed immediately due to a rigorous schedule imposed by the federal court regarding compliance with the consent decree. The first of these was to establish procedures for *conducting job analyses* on civil service jobs. The previous Board staff had engaged in a practice of developing for each job in the system a list of tasks/work behaviors describing the basic duties of employees, and when there was a need to develop an exam for a job, the staff would simply call a small sample of supervisors to ask if the duties had changed. If the answer was "no," then the staff proceeded with test development. There was no documentation as to the accuracy of the job description, and it was certainly not at a level of detail that would be helpful in creating a valid selection procedure.

In order to ensure the job analysis was in compliance with the Uniform Guidelines and professional standards and practice, the new staff implemented procedures for conducting a highly structured and detailed job analysis. This included researching jobs using resources such as the O*Net (National O*NET Consortium, 1999), a website developed by the U.S. Department of Labor to aid organizations in job analysis, conducting job observations (e.g., "ride-alongs") and site visits with incumbents, holding focus groups to generate detailed lists of tasks and duties and KSAOs relevant to the job, and creating and administering a job analysis questionnaire to all incumbents and supervisors in the job. Ratings of the job components regarding their importance to successful performance and whether new employees would be expected to perform duties and tasks immediately upon entry to the job were taken through the questionnaire. This allowed the staff to ensure selection procedures were based on accurate and up-to-date job information.

Test Development

For a vast majority of jobs within the civil service system, there were too few employees to utilize criterion-validation strategies in developing tests, so a content validation strategy was employed. The decision to take this approach, while seemingly simple, was essential to directing the efforts of test development. Procedures were established to ensure that tests were developed in a manner that ensured legal defensibility.

The first step in ensuring that a test is legally defensible is to develop a viable test plan. Board staff, using the results of the job analysis, would determine which aspects of the job were appropriate for inclusion in the test. This involved considering what could be measured using a content-validation strategy—in other words, what aspects of the job could be replicated or represented through test exercises. Staff members were required to consider from a variety of alternative testing formats to ensure that the most appropriate format was used in terms of reliable measurement and minimizing subgroup differences.

It is important at this point to emphasize the consideration of alternative test formats. When a test used by an organization demonstrates adverse impact, the organization is directed by the professional test standards to consider alternative forms of testing that have equal or higher levels of validity but produce less adverse impact. For example, research has shown that written mental ability tests are some of the most valid selection instruments available (Hunter & Hunter, 1984) and are very good predictors of job performance (McHenry, Hough, Toquam, Hanson, & Ashworth, 1990; Schmidt & Hunter, 1998). However, they also result in higher levels of adverse impact, particularly against Black/African-Americans, who tend to perform a full standard deviation below White/Caucasians (Bobko, Roth, & Potosky, 1999; Pulakos & Schmitt, 1996) on such tests. Conversely, structured interviews have validities equivalent to written mental ability tests (Cascio, 1998; Gatewood & Feild, 2001) but demonstrate an average difference in scores between Black and White candidates of only 0.23 standard deviation units (Bobko et al., 1999). Giving strong consideration to alternative formats and, where feasible, using different types of tests may serve to maximize the diversity of the successful candidate group and reduce legal vulnerability.

Another key element to effective test development used by the Board was to involve subject-matter experts (SMEs) in the process. While industrial/organizational psychologists understand a great deal about test construction and measurement, and they benefit from the study of jobs during job analysis, they do not possess the understanding and expertise that is derived from actually performing a job. As such, it was necessary to establish procedures that involved SMEs in the generation of test items and scenarios. The Board implemented protocols for identifying a demographically diverse sample of job incumbents and supervisors to participate in test development, and in cases where diversity was absent from the incumbent population, the Board sought this diversity by reaching out to other organizations outside the civil service system. This, too, was done in order to comply with the regulatory requirements outlined by the Uniform Guidelines (1978) and professional standards and practices (e.g., Society for Industrial and Organizational Psychology, 1987).

The mechanics of test development used by the Board prior to receivership were not in keeping with the Uniform Guidelines (1978) or with another resource, the *Principles for the Validation and Use of Personnel Selection Procedures* (1987), published by the Society for Industrial and Organizational Psychologists (SIOP) and designed to assist organizations in developing valid selection systems. As stated, test development frequently failed to include SME input, and in cases where SMEs were involved, there was often a lack of diversity in the group to ensure all demographics were represented. Additionally, there was rarely sufficient documentation to demonstrate evidence of a relationship between tests and the jobs for which they were designed. As such, another action taken by Board staff trained in employee selection was to establish a clear process for having SMEs rate test items on the extent to which they were job-related, appropriate for use to distinguish candidates, and, therefore, demonstrated evidence of validity.

Test Administration

The process used to administer selection tests has a substantial impact on the reliability of that test. In order to ensure that tests perform reliably, so that candidates of equal skill and ability receive the same test scores, the organization must ensure that candidates are exposed to the same test under the same conditions. When selection experts were hired by the Board during the receivership, they quickly determined that the Board had no structured procedures for administering tests. Since candidates have a greater probability of success in legally challenging a selection system if they can demonstrate they were treated differently than other candidates, Board staff recognized the need to provide the necessary structure to tests to protect the selection process and ensure fairness.

From the administration of the first test developed under the receivership, Board staff worked to ensure that the process was as highly standardized as possible. Strategies adopted by the Board included the use of video to convey instructions and ask questions (particularly interview questions) to all candidates, thereby ensuring that small variations in information introduced by live test administrators were eliminated. Additionally, the Board adopted the use of *structured* interviews, in which a set of predetermined questions and behaviorally based scoring guidelines are developed with SMEs so that candidates are asked the exact same questions and are evaluated according to the exact same criteria.

Other types of tests, often referred to as work samples and simulations, were utilized for jobs involving technical skills that are better assessed through a replication of job tasks than through a structured interview. These approaches are useful because they allow the candidate to demonstrate behaviorally what he or she would do in a given situation rather than saying what he or she would do. Hunter and Hunter (1984) showed that work sample tests can have criterion-related validity equal to cognitive ability tests ($r_{xy} = .53$) when current performance on the job is the criterion. In addition, work samples/simulations tend to produce positive reactions from applicants (Robertson & Kandola, 1982; Smither, Reilly, Millsap, Pearlman, & Stoffey, 1993; Steiner & Gilliland, 1996), who generally perceive them as having high face validity (Robertson & Kandola, 1982; Schmidt, Greenthal, Hunter, Berner, & Seaton, 1977; Smither et al., 1993). Furthermore, work samples provide applicants with information about the job and therefore, may serve as realistic job previews (RJP) (Downs, Farr, & Colbeck, 1978). Administering these types of tests in a highly standardized and structured manner was a key to success in defending the selection procedures by the Board to the Federal Court.

All of the actions taken by the Board in administering tests culminated in a set of procedures that are applied to all tests and that ensure each candidate has virtually the exact same experience as every other candidate throughout the examination process. This, too, is a key to success in defending selection procedures. Organizations that not only strive to standardize tests but establish clear procedures regarding how to achieve this goal will be much better prepared to defend their work in a legal challenge.

Assessment and Scoring

Other best practices have to do with the manner in which candidate performance on tests is evaluated, recorded, and scored. The Board recognized the need to ensure fairness in all scoring procedures, particularly when the manner or type of test used for a specific job called for independent assessment or rating. A first step was to remove current civil service employees and supervisors from the evaluation process. While these SMEs were valuable resources during test development, they were deemed inappropriate to fairly evaluate candidates due to preexisting biases and other inclinations that they might potentially hold regarding candidates they knew personally. Many organizations find this particular step to be extremely challenging, and many managers feel that they are best equipped to make decisions about potential hires into the organization. While we would agree that in making final decisions about hiring, managers and supervisors should have substantial input, the initial rating and ranking of candidates by these individuals can introduce bias into the process and result in legal vulnerability.

Another factor in evaluating candidates is to ensure that, where necessary, assessors possess job-related subject-matter expertise, and when not critical, assessors possess an understanding of testing. For example, with jobs in public safety or public works, in which candidates are required to complete relatively technical job simulations as part of the selection or promotion process, assessors should be experts in the target job, either through experience working in that type of job or in supervising that type of job. However, with exams for less technical jobs (e.g., clerical or administrative jobs), the content of the test is not so specialized that job-related expertise is necessary for evaluating candidates, and as such, individuals with a background in industrial/organizational psychology or human resource management are highly effective.

A third key to defending an assessment process is to ensure that the assessors are representative of the candidate population, so that demographically diverse and balanced panels of assessors can evaluate candidates. The Board established a policy that, to the extent possible, each candidate would be rated by a panel of two individuals with at least one Black/African-American and one White/Caucasian and one male and one female present. This ensured that each candidate was evaluated by at least one person who matched the candidate in terms of race and gender. In other areas, the local demographics may recommend a different type of balance, or perhaps a third assessor representing another demographic group (e.g., Hispanic, Asian). Regardless, ensuring that candidates are evaluated by demographically similar individuals helps mitigate any biases related to race or gender that might otherwise skew results from a test, and it also increases perceptions of fairness among candidates.

Another practice adopted by the Board in working through the Federal Court to end its consent decree was to electronically record candidate performance (i.e., oral responses to structured interview questions) for evaluation at a later date. This had two effects that were essential to the success of the Board. First, it allowed the Board to test more people in a single day, so multiple forms of the test (which can pollute the validity) were unnecessary and the security of the test could be maintained by allowing for single day/single session administrations. Second, it ensured that assessment could be more effectively managed and controlled, and assessors were not required to expend energy on administering a live process, but rather they could focus all their energy on making accurate ratings. This required equipment and space to manage both the administration and assessment procedures, which were initially costly, but it ultimately proved to be highly useful in defending the selection processes.

Assessor training was a practice introduced by the newly hired selection experts at the Board, and this had a significant impact on the effectiveness of the assessment process. Assessors were trained to make independent ratings of performance using the scoring guidelines developed by SMEs, compare these ratings, and reconcile discrepancies by reviewing notes or video/audio recordings of performance. Assessors were also trained on how to remove subjective impressions and inherent biases from the evaluation process and to focus on observable behaviors. Common rater errors were reviewed, and multiple practice ratings were made to ensure assessors were obtaining reliable and accurate ratings of performance.

Finally, the Board adopted procedures to manage and control test data to ensure that scores were accurate and errors were eliminated from the scoring process. Steps taken by the Board included double entry of all test data, careful checking and cleaning of data to eliminate any data-entry errors, using statistical processing software (e.g., SPSS) to calculate scores, saving syntax files so that scores could be replicated by experts for parties to the consent decree, and double checking final scores and ranks by having at least two staff members run independent scoring calculations and reconciling discrepancies until final scores were confirmed as being accurate. This again built confidence in the selection process and made the procedures much more defensible to legal challenge.

Battle for the Hearts and Minds of the Participants

In addition to using the above best practices throughout the selection process, it is critical to work to enlist the full support of the organization's employees in helping to drive the transformation to an effective selection system. The importance of such assistance cannot be underestimated, and it is manifested in many ways that underscore positive assessment results, including thoughtful subject-matter expert test design input, protecting the confidentiality of the process, employees not disparaging the process and demotivating fellow candidates, and incumbents providing their best efforts when participating in validation studies (for example, by trying hard when taking tests or taking the research appraisal process seriously and providing accurate input on ratings).

Too often, internal or external consultants believe that all they need to do is tell the incumbents what information to provide and then assume they can count on the employees to "make it so" and furnish perfect data. In fact, the organizations and their consultants must expend great effort s to actively build employee support for all stages of the testing process, for example, by sincerely "selling" the request for participation, providing abundant and accurate communication around the purpose of the initiative, modeling effective behavior for others, celebrating employee champions of the process, and keeping commitments such as only using data the way the consultant says they will be used.

In dealing with these issues at the Board, staff members recognized the need to build alliances with customers and constituents of the civil service system. One effort that proved to be quite helpful was to bring in a group of department leaders from across the merit system and hold face-to-face meetings to listen to their concerns and frustrations and to invite them to be active participants in the selection process. These leaders had been essentially placed on hold in terms of gaining access to new job candidates, and promotional tests for their departments had also be suspended while issues of the consent decree were addressed. Through a series of meetings, Board staff members were able to identify the specific concerns, acknowledge the frustrations, and explain the requirements of the federal court, as well as the legal issues described in this chapter. Ultimately, these departmental leaders became advocates for the work being done by the Board and were assets to the process rather than impediments.

RECENT COURT RULINGS RELATED TO SELECTION

Not surprisingly, despite the regulatory efforts of the federal government, litigation related to employee selection is still quite common. Many cases filed in the court system are resolved at the Circuit Court level and do not impact the practices of employee selection outside the organization subject to the lawsuit. However, there are occasionally cases that reach the higher courts and can impact the professional practices of the field above and beyond the specifics of the case.

One recent example of this is the case of Ricci v. DeStefano (2009). In this case, the New Haven Fire Department administered a promotional test in which the eighteen individuals passing were White/Caucasian or Hispanic. No Black/African American employee passed the exam. As such, the city of New Haven invalidated the test on the basis that it would otherwise have subjected itself to disparate-impact liability due to the adverse impact of the exam. The Supreme Court ultimately ruled in favor of the plaintiffs on the basis that there was demonstrated evidence of validity and that the city did not have a "strong basis in evidence" that it would have created liability by promoting the Caucasian and Hispanic candidates.

One of the reactions to this ruling was a frustration on the part of many selection practitioners that the Court failed to consider the use of alternative measures that would have been available to the department in their promotional process. While the test used did have evidence of validity, there might have been equally valid measures that might have resulted in greater diversity in the passing group, and if diversity was valued by the department they might have chosen those alternatives. Another concern rising from this ruling was the fact that the disparate treatment of Black/African American applicants was considered to be an insufficient reason to forego use of the promotional test. This, along with other recent rulings by the Court regarding affirmative action programs, is perhaps an indicator that, at least at the Supreme Court, a more colorblind viewpoint is being adopted, such that efforts designed to increase the representation of minorities in the workplace are being viewed differently than in the latter part of the 20th century.

The Board responded to this by reconsidering test weighting strategies. Prior to the Ricci case, it was the practice of the Board to consider several valid methods of weighting test items and exercises and selecting the method that produced the most diverse pool of successful candidates. This practice had been implemented during the receivership and approved by the U.S. Department of Justice to address the longstanding, institutionalized discrimination that had been practiced by the Board in the past. With the Supreme Court's ruling, the Board determined that it could no longer follow this procedure, because it essentially resulted in making a race-based decision *after* the test was scored. Practitioners in the field of selection should monitor these types of rulings to ensure that they do not put their organization at risk.

SUMMARY OF BEST PRACTICES

The following is a summary of some of the best practices described above. It is important to note that organizations that choose to adopt some or all of these strategies will not be impervious to legal challenge, but they will likely be much better positioned to defend their selection systems and avoid significant punitive damages.

- Use a detailed, thorough job analysis conducted with individuals representing key demographics to develop a test plan. Ensure that the job analysis covers all critical criteria (e.g., does not overly focus on cognitive vs. non-cognitive type KSAs).
- Use job incumbents and supervisors or other subject matter experts to build the content of tests.
- Consider a wide array of types of tests to ensure strong evidence of validity and to maximize diversity of the successful candidate pool (e.g., including "alternative" tests and newly emerging cognitive tests that aim at mitigating adverse impact).
- Document the relationship between the test and the job (including the scoring key/guidelines).
- Ensure that test administration procedures and highly structured and standardized.
- Establish appropriate test procedures in terms of timeframes and response modes (e.g., not requiring an immediate response when that doesn't happen on the job, providing a sufficient amount of time for the candidate to respond, etc.).
- Use carefully considered and thoughtful test scoring procedures (e.g., optimal test weighting procedures, cut-scores vs. top-down approaches, subject-matter expertise when appropriate).
- Provide abundant candidate support and communication (e.g., providing candidates with "how to prepare" manuals, orientation sessions, examples for practice).
- Take steps to mitigate personal biases (positive and negative) and ensure they do not impact the selection process.
- Ensure demographic diversity of assessors/evaluators involved in scoring tests and evaluating candidates for jobs.
- Train assessors on both general and content-specific ratings.
- Ensure test scores are accurate and verifiable (e.g., double check data entry procedures, scoring algorithms, etc.).
- Stay abreast of changes in the field of selection, particularly through the Court system.

CONCLUSION

It is important for human resources management professionals to recognize that employment litigation can be costly, time consuming, demoralizing, and frustrating for all parties involved. Organizations may experience crises of public opinion and are very likely to lose many of the advantages of a diverse workforce when challenged in court regarding their selection practices. Additionally, it often takes considerable time after legal action has been resolved to return to effective and efficient business operations. Even without the threat of legal action, a selection system can result in organizational issues and problems simply by the perception that it is unfair.

Given these factors, it is often astounding that many public and private organizations simply ignore the structure and standardization required when selecting employees. Unfortunately, it often takes legal action to stir organizations out of their less appropriate screening and testing practices and bring them in line with federal guidelines. Organizations that take advantage of the best practices described previously in this chapter are more likely to prevail in the event of a legal challenge and will certainly be perceived to be more unbiased and fair. Ultimately, it is in the best interest of organizations to invest in valid selection systems that are used properly to identify and acquire talent. By adopting practices that truly predict job performance and avoiding costly litigation, organizations will benefit from the return on this investment with a sound reputation, highly productive workforce, and a solid bottom line.

REFERENCES

Bobko, P., Roth, P. L., & Potosky, D. (1999). Derivation and implications of a meta-analytic matrix incorporating cognitive ability, alternative predictors, and job performance. *Personnel Psychology, 52*, 561–589.

Cascio, W. F. (1998). *Applied psychology in human resource management* (5th ed.). Upper Saddle River, NJ: Prentice Hall.

Downs, S., Farr, R. M., & Colbeck. L. (1978). Self appraisal: A convergence of selection and guidance. *Journal of Occupational Psychology, 51*(3), 271–278.

Equal Employment Opportunity Commission, Civil Service Commission, Department of Labor, & Department of Justice. (1978). Adoption by four agencies of uniform guidelines on employee selection procedures. *Federal Register, 43*, 38290–38315.

Gatewood, R. D., & Feild, H. S. (2001). *Human resource selection* (5th ed.). Mason, OH: South-Western.

Hunter, J. E., & Hunter, R. F. (1984). Validity and utility of alternative predictors of job performance. *Psychological Bulletin, 96*(1), 72–98.

McHenry, J. J., Hough, L. M., Toquam, J. L., Hanson, M. A., & Ashworth, S. (1990). Project A validity results: The relationship between predictor and criterion domains. *Personnel Psychology, 43*, 335–354.

National O*NET Consortium. (1999). *Occupational Information Network (O*NET) Online* [On-line database]. Retrieved from http://online.onetcenter.org/

Pulakos, E. D., & Schmitt, N. (1996). An evaluation of two strategies for reducing adverse impact and their effects on criterion-related validity. *Human Performance, 9*, 241–258.

Ricci v. DeStefano, 129 S. Ct. 2658 (2009).

Robertson, I. T., & Kandola, R. S. (1982). Work sample tests: Validity, adverse impact and applicant reaction. *Journal of Occupational Psychology, 55*(3), 171–183.

Schmidt, F. L., Greenthal, A. L., Hunter, J. E., Berner, J. G., & Seaton, F. W. (1977). Job sample vs. paper-and-pencil trades and technical tests: Adverse impact and examinee attitudes. *Personnel Psychology, 30*, 187–198.

Schmidt, F. L., & Hunter, J. E. (1998). The validity and utility of selection methods in personnel psychology: Practical and theoretical implications of 85 years of research findings. *Psychological Bulletin, 124*, 262–274.

Smither, J. W., Reilly, R. R., Millsap, R. E., Pearlman, K., & Stoffey, R. W. (1993). Applicant reactions to selection procedures. *Personnel Psychology, 46*, 49–76.

Society for Industrial and Organizational Psychology. (1987). *Principles for the validation and use of personnel selection procedures* (3rd ed.). College Park, MD: Author.

Steiner, D. D., & Gilliland, S. W. (1996). Fairness reactions to personnel selection techniques in France and the United States. *Journal of Applied Psychology, 81*, 134–141.

Wards Cove Packing Co. v. Atonio, 490 U.S. 642 (1989).

CHAPTER 7

NAVIGATING THE HRM RESPONSIBILITIES OF THE ADA

Christine Ledvinka Rush

INTRODUCTION

The express aim of the Americans with Disabilities Act of 1990 (ADA) is to enable persons with physical and mental disabilities to participate more fully in society (S. Rep. No. 101-116, 1989). Consistent with that expansive goal, the statute mandates inclusionary efforts in employment, in public services, in transportation, in communications, and in private-sector buildings, services, and accommodations. This examination focuses on the employment setting, highlighting employer responsibilities under the ADA. The discussion begins with a brief overview of the growth of the disability rights movement and consideration of the similarities and differences between civil rights and benefits. The analysis then turns to the technical elements of the ADA, clarifying the definitions, applications, and judicial interpretations that are essential to understanding both the original law and the 2008 amendments. The chapter concludes with an exploration of the potential penalties associated with ADA violations and practical strategies to avoid liability.

Legal and Regulatory Issues in Human Resources Management, pages 137–155
Copyright © 2015 by Information Age Publishing

THE HISTORICAL SETTING

The evolution of an American disability movement was central to the growth of disability rights as a political issue and the eventual passage of the ADA. Disability rights efforts developed during the late 1800s and early 1900s in reaction to the institutionalization and inhumane treatment of disabled persons (Pfeiffer, 1993). Those efforts expanded after the return of disabled veterans from World Wars I and II, but it was not until after the experiences of the civil rights, anti-war, and feminist movements of the 1960s that advocates for the disabled came together in a nationwide movement (Jeon & Haider-Markel, 2001; Scotch, 1988). Groups that were originally focused on advocacy for specific disabilities such as blindness and paralysis eventually coalesced into a full-fledged political and policy force with the formation of the American Coalition of Citizens with Disabilities (ACCD) in 1974.

Once disability rights advocates unified their disparate efforts, they began to pursue a political and policy agenda. The ACCD used its new status to support candidate Jimmy Carter during the 1976 presidential election. Then it employed civil disobedience techniques such as sit-ins to force the Carter administration to approve the regulations implementing the federal government's disability nondiscrimination statute, the Rehabilitation Act (Pfeiffer, 1993). Disability rights advocates built off their experiences in political activism during the Carter administration and continued to push for the changes needed to achieve greater inclusion into mainstream society during the Reagan and George H. W. Bush presidencies. As a presidential candidate, George H. W. Bush used the disability community's newfound political influence to his advantage by working to gain their backing with a promise of greater integration for disabled individuals (Pfeiffer, 1993). The resulting support from voters who favored disabled rights is considered a significant factor in Bush's victory over Massachusetts Governor Michael Dukakis (Ledvinka, 2010). Understandably, then, Bush signed the ADA into law after Congress passed it in 1990.

The eventual passage of the ADA was the result of a consolidated effort by disability advocacy groups with the collaboration of disabled individuals. During the 1970s, the composition of these advocacy groups had shifted. The leadership of the disability rights movement had evolved with parents of individuals with disabilities spearheading organizations focused on integrating disabled persons more fully into society. As disabled individuals gained greater independence, they also began to fill control positions in these advocacy organizations (Pfeiffer, 1993). These newly self-directed disability rights groups participated in the 1977 White House Conference on Handicapped Individuals, which resulted in two significant proposals. The White House conference prompted the creation of the National Council on Disability (formerly the National Council on the Handicapped) and originated the recommendation to amend the Civil Rights Act of 1964 to prohibit discrimination on the basis of disability (Ledvinka, 2010). More than a decade later, research by the National Council on Disability contributed the foundation essential to the drafting of the ADA (Jeon & Haider-Markel, 2001).

The conviction that disabled individuals deserved the same civil rights as able-bodied persons drove the development of the ADA. Advocacy groups had been motivated by civil rights groups' strategies to fight for rights for the disabled, and the philosophy of the ADA is steeped in the belief that discrimination on the basis of disability is as great a violation of our societal tenets as discrimination on the basis of race, color, sex, national origin, or religion. The ADA benefitted from bipartisan support in congress, and scholars have noted the successful efforts of these lawmakers to cast the policy discussion in civil rights terms (Jeon & Haider-Markel, 2001).

Treating the disability rights issue as a question of civil rights is more than mere semantics. Civil rights laws establish an assumption that an individual is a member of the protected class and proceed to evaluate the mechanisms for ensuring equal treatment (Cox, 2010). That contrasts with the implementation of public benefit statutes, such as the Social Security Act of 1935 (as amended), where the evaluation begins with an assessment of whether the individual qualifies as a member of the class entitled to benefits (Cox, 2010). As this chapter will describe more fully later, although supporters believed the ADA to be civil rights legislation, the judicial interpretation proceeded along the lines of a benefits statute. The judiciary's benefits law analysis cast disabled employees against their employers in a battle over who qualified as disabled rather than emphasizing what type of accommodation would enable the employee to be fully included in the workforce.

UNDERSTANDING THE LANGUAGE OF THE ADA

In order to meet their responsibilities under the ADA, human resource (HR) managers must understand the ADA's language regarding the law's application, intent, and requirements. With limited exceptions, the ADA applies to all employers with 15 or more employees working at least 20 weeks a year in the private sector, in the nonprofit sector, and in state and local governments (42 U.S.C. §12111(5)(1990) as amended).[1] In practice, the ADA applies to almost all employers outside of the federal government. The reach of the ADA ensures the law's relevance for all HR practitioners. The ADA's protection applies to prevent discrimination against not only individuals with current physical or mental disability, but also individuals who have experienced physical or mental disability in the past, and individuals who are incorrectly assumed to be disabled. Furthermore, when a disabled applicant or employee is otherwise qualified, the law requires employers to provide a reasonable accommodation to enable the individual to apply for or fulfill the requirements for employment.

Human resource managers must also be aware that the intent of the law's comprehensive protection is to ensure that disability is not the basis for employment decisions in the United States. To accomplish this substantial goal, ADA protection extends beyond individuals who are currently disabled to also cover persons who have a record of physical or mental impairment or who are regarded as having such impairment. In one of the early decisions under the ADA, the 8th Circuit Court of Appeals described the intent of the ADAs "regarded as" application by stating, "This provision is intended to combat the effects of 'archaic attitudes,' erroneous perceptions and myths that work to the disadvantage of persons with or regarded as having disabilities" (*Wooten v. Farmland Foods*, 1995, at 385).

To meet the ADA's intentions, the statute imposes expansive requirements regarding both what constitutes a disability and when an individual is protected during the employment relationship. The law encompasses almost every employer/employee interaction because it prohibits discrimination throughout the entire employment relationship. This protection from discrimination means that employers must be vigilant from the time of an individual's application for employment through the individual's testing, hiring, training, pay, promotion, benefits, discharge, and all other "terms, conditions and privileges of employment" (42 U.S.C §12112(a) (1990) as amended).

This brief overview of the ADA's requirements, application, and intent should demonstrate the breadth of responsibility that the ADA places on human resources managers. The following subsections describe the ADA's application, intent and requirements in greater detail.

Employer Requirements: Definitions in the ADA

Definitions are the foundation of every statute, and the ADA includes a broad definition of disability. The law protects any individual with "a physical or mental impairment that substantially limits one or more major life activities" (42 U.S.C. §12102(1) (1990) as amended). The inclusion of both physical and mental impairments provides for more expansive employee protections but also adds complexity for employers trying to analyze their job requirements. To provide clarification, the Equal Employment Opportunity Commission (EEOC) was required to develop regulations to assist with interpretation of the ADA. This regulatory guidance serves to illuminate the ADA's basic standards. Specifically, the EEOC's regulations provide that an impairment includes physical conditions such as physiological conditions, disfigurement and anatomical loss, as well as mental conditions such as "intellectual disability, organic brain syndrome, emotional or mental illness and specific learning disabilities" (29 CFR §1630.2(h)).

To qualify for protection under ADA, an individual's illness or injury must not only be a mental or physical impairment but also substantially limit a major life activity. This "substantially limits" element of the definition confirms that ADA protection against discrimination only applies when an individual's illness or impairment is significant enough to influence functioning in everyday life. In order to more fully describe what is considered a major life activity, the law employs a far-reaching, but not exhaustive, list. Major life activities also encompass major bodily functions. Taken as a whole, these elements

> include but are not limited to caring for oneself, performing manual tasks, seeing, hearing, eating, sleeping, walking, standing, lifting, bending, speaking, breathing, learning, reading, concentrating, thinking, communicating, and working" as well as "functions of the immune system, normal cell growth, digestive, bowel, bladder, neurological, brain, respiratory, circulatory, endocrine, and reproductive functions. (42 U.S.C. §12102(2) (1990) as amended)

While this inventory is considerable, the law is clear that the list is not exhaustive. It is possible for other injuries or ailments to qualify as affecting a major life function and afford an individual protection under the ADA. Because discrimination is also prohibited where an individual has suffered a disability in the past or is regarded as disabled, the practical effect of this protection is that HR managers must be meticulously careful not to allow almost any actual or perceived physical or mental disability to influence their actions.

When an otherwise qualified individual meets the definition of a disability, the ADA requires that employers provide a reasonable accommodation that would enable the individual to perform the essential job functions (42 U.S.C. §12112(b) (1990) as amended). EEOC regulations implementing the ADA provide for three types of reasonable accommodation: modifications to enable participation in the application process, modifications to the workplace environment, and modifications to ensure that an employee can enjoy all of the privileges and benefits of employment (29 C.F.R. § 1630.2(o)(1)(i)-(iii)). Those accommodations may take one of many forms, such as an adjustment to an employee's work schedule, a change in the physical environment, or the implementation of specialized software or technological devices.

Notably, an employer is not required to suffer undue hardship in order to provide a reasonable accommodation. The question of whether providing an accommodation would cause an employer undue hardship generally involves an analysis of the cost of the accommodation as compared with costs at the individual facility, or costs in the specific type of operation, or resources throughout the employer's holdings (Fairclough et al., 2013). An early analysis of fifty private-sector employers found that more than half of employers incurred no cost when implementing a reasonable accommodation, and 70% of employers incurred less than $500 in implementation costs (Lee & Newman, 1995).

Congressional Intent: The Purposes Motivating the ADA

Working from the momentum generated by the disability rights movement, Congress had several very specific intentions for the ADA. The broadest statement of congressional intent is the assurance that the new statute was designed to "provide a clear and comprehensive national mandate for the *elimination* of discrimination against individuals with disabilities" ((42 U.S.C. §12101(b)(1)(1990) as amended, emphasis added). With the ADA, Congress sought to completely eliminate disability discrimination, not just to enable persons with disabilities to enter the workforce. The statute's language supported this goal of "elimination" by expanding the class of protected individuals beyond the most obvious group, those with current disabilities. It also included persons who suffered discrimination based on misperceptions regarding disability. In order to completely eliminate discrimination by combating prejudice on all fronts, the statute protects persons with current and past disability as well as persons who are regarded as disabled.

The statement of purpose incorporated in the ADA also indicates that the statute is intended to have the power to force compliance, with the federal government acting as the central authority for imposing the law's anti-discrimination mandate ((42 U.S.C. §12101(b)(2)-(4)(1990) as amended). Often, federal legislation includes laudable goals without clarifying the necessary enforcement mechanism to make those goals a reality. With the ADA, Congress included the power to meet the statute's mandate, and the authority to meet the statute's high expectations. Congressional intent was tested when, more than a decade and a half after the original statute passed, judicial interpretation forced a significant limitation of the ADA's power. Congress responded with a searing rebuke and a reiteration of the original statutory intention to provide protection for a sweeping group of the American population (Public Law 110-325, S 3406, 2008).

Application: Judicial Interpretation of the ADA

The judicial branch is responsible for interpreting the application of statutes in individual situations. Consequently, once the ADA was signed into law, the courts took over to determine how it would function. The opinions that result from judicial analysis are referred to as case law.

The ADA offers expansive rights and responsibilities once a person qualifies as disabled, and the opportunity to access these rights drove many of the early cases under the new statute. Much of the initial ADA case law focused on the question of whether an individual qualified as disabled according to the statute. When the United States Supreme Court considered the question of who qualified as disabled under the ADA, the resulting decisions significantly limited the scope of protection under the law.

On June 22, 1999, The Supreme Court decided three key cases that considered the issue of how an individual qualifies as disabled under the ADA (*Albertson's v. Kirkingburg*, 1999; *Murphy v. United Parcel Services*, 1999; *Sutton v. United Airlines*, 1999). The *Sutton* case involved twin sisters who applied for positions as pilots at United Airlines and were rejected from consideration because they did not meet the employer's requirement for uncorrected vision of 20/100 or better. Although both sisters used corrective lenses that provided 20/20 or better vision, they were visually impaired without these lenses and unable to meet United's standard for uncorrected vision. The Sutton sisters filed suit against United Airlines alleging that the employer engaged in unlawful discrimination on the basis of disability or because they were regarded as having a disability in violation of the ADA (*Sutton v. United Airlines*, 1999, p. 476). In deciding the *Sutton* case, the Supreme Court determined that an individual who used a mitigating measure to ameliorate their impairment must be evaluated in light of the treatment employed. Whether the Sutton sisters were disabled had to be evaluated considering their vision when wearing their corrective lenses. Consequently, the sisters did not qualify under the ADA's definition of disability.

The *Albertson's v. Kirkingburg* case relied on the *Sutton* reasoning regarding the impact of ameliorative measures. The High Court found that Mr. Kirkingburg's monocular vision did not qualify as a disability because his brain compensated for the problem allowing his vision to function in much the same manner as a mitigating measure such as eyeglasses would. Considering his brain's compensatory actions, the Court found that Mr. Kirkingburg's ability to see was not substantially limited as required by the definition of disability contained in the ADA. Similarly, in the *Murphy v. United Parcel Services* (1999) case, the Supreme Court found that Mr. Murphy's extreme high blood pressure was so well controlled by medication that he did not meet the standards for the ADA definition of disability although his impairment disqualified him for work as a commercial truck driver with United Parcel Services. Taken in concert, the *Sutton, Albertson's,* and *Murphy* cases significantly narrowed the definition of disability under the ADA. These cases established the standard that a disabled individual had to choose between treatment to manage the impairment and receiving the ADA rights associated with being disabled. This choice substantially limited the pool of individuals who benefitted from the ADA.

Several years after the High Court decided the trio of cases that established the role of mitigating measures in determining disability under the ADA, the Court examined the extent to which an impairment must substantially limit a major life function in order to qualify an individual for protection under the ADA. In the *Toyota Motor Manufacturing v. Williams* (2003) case, Ms. Williams sought to demonstrate that the carpal tunnel syndrome and repetitive stress injuries she developed on the job entitled her to a reasonable accommodation under the ADA. One of her arguments was that these impairments substantially limited her ability to perform manual tasks. The Supreme Court determined that Ms. Williams did not successfully demonstrate that her impairments posed a substantial limitation on her ability to perform manual tasks because she was still able to care for her personal hygiene and to complete household chores. The Court stressed that the ADA requirement that an impairment must substantially limit a major life function requires evidence that an individual is "unable to perform the variety of tasks essential to most people's daily lives" (*Toyota Motor Manufacturing v. Williams*, 2003, p. 200).

Taken in concert with the Court's earlier decisions in *Sutton, Albertson's,* and *Murphy,* the *Toyota* decision made it much more challenging for individuals to qualify as disabled under the ADA in order to be entitled to a reasonable accommodation to meet a job's requirements. In a *Pepperdine Law Review* article published shortly after the *Toyota* opinion was publicized, Naef (2003) clearly identified the implications of the case stating, "The *Toyota* decision will dramatically limit the number of Americans who qualify as disabled and therefore are protected by the ADA. The decision is a landmark victory for employers, but will impose significant hardships on employees who suffer from medical conditions that limit their performance of everyday tasks" (p. 577). Other scholars suggested that the Supreme Court had made the standard for qualifying as disabled so high that no individual who qualified would also be capable of completing the essential job functions (Rozalski, Katsiyannis, Ryan, Collins, & Stewart, 2010).

While the Supreme Court's decisions in *Sutton, Albertson's, Murphy,* and *Toyota* limited the scope of who qualifies as disabled for the purposes of ADA protections, the Court's 2001 opinion in *Board of Trustees of the University of Alabama v. Garrett* (2001) also narrowed the rights of state government employees under the law. State employees are generally prohibited from suing their employer for money damages because the 11th Amendment to the United States Constitution provides states with sovereign immunity protection from such suits. In contrast, the landmark nondiscrimination statute, the Civil Rights Act of 1964 (Title VII) illustrates one significant exception to 11th Amendment sovereign immunity. Congress can nullify state sovereign immunity by first demonstrating that a state has engaged in a pattern of discrimination and then by addressing that discrimination with legislation enforcing the 14th Amendment's requirements of due process and equal protection. Title VII is one example where the Supreme Court allowed Congress to override state sovereign immunity to remedy a pattern of past discrimination by the states.

Although Congress can abrogate sovereign immunity by demonstrating pervasive discrimination by the states, the Supreme Court in the *Garrett* case decided that Congress had not demonstrated pervasive discrimination by the states against disabled persons (Kuykendall & Lindquist, 2001). Accordingly, the Court ruled that it was unconstitutional for Congress to invalidate the traditional sovereign immunity protection. In *Garrett*, the Court distinguished the ADA from Title VII and determined that Congress provided "insufficient evidence" that the states had engaged in a pattern of discrimination (Kuykendall & Lindquist, 2001, p. 66). The *Garrett* decision was only one of several cases in which the Supreme Court cited the 11th Amendment principle of sovereign immunity to limit congressional authority to address state government employment discrimination. For the ADA's application, *Garrett* represented yet another instance of judicial interpretation narrowing the group of persons who were entitled to protection under the law.

Those five cases also provided a signal that the Supreme Court interpreted the ADA as a public benefits statute rather than as a civil rights statute. The focus on whether an individual qualifies as disabled, as well as the Court's refusal to allow state employees to circumvent state sovereign immunity to seek redress for violation of the ADA, strongly suggest that the High Court saw the ADA as different from the key civil rights statute, Title VII. Recent work by Cox noted the consequences of that judicial interpretation of the ADA:

> For example, if courts regard the ADA as conferring charitable welfare benefits to persons with disabilities, courts may narrowly construe the ADA's substantive provisions to conform to a benefits framework that compensates for endogenous biological limitations. They may treat the ADA's employment provisions as a welfare benefits statute for which the paramount legal question is policing the line between those who are entitled to benefits and those who are not. By contrast, if courts regard the ADA as remedying past and current discrimination, they may be more inclined to shift the focus of ADA litigation away from the severity of the individual plaintiffs endogenous limitations to the workplace policies and practices that tend to unnecessarily exclude persons with disabilities. (2010, p. 193)

THE 2008 ADA AMENDMENTS ACT: CONVERSATION
BETWEEN CONGRESS AND THE SUPREME COURT

Our legal system may appear to be composed of a series of separate authorities with constitutional, statutory, and case law functioning independently. However, the development of a statute often occurs more like a conversation than a monologue. Congress makes the first statements through the legislative history and statutory text. The courts speak next, interpreting the statute in specific cases. In many instances, that is not the end of the dialog. Rather, Congress may choose to respond to the courts with amending legislation to clarify their initial intent and establish a clearer understanding of the legislation's goals going forward. In effect, this "conversation" shifts obligations under the law as Congress, then the courts, then Congress, each speak to the statute's true intent.

The evolution of a law through legislative and judicial interpretation can make it difficult for the HR manager to respond. The development of the ADA provides an example of the shifting obligations that can occur as Congress and the courts struggle to establish a legal standard. Because the ADA must be obeyed throughout the employment relationship, day-to-day management decisions depend on a clear understanding of an employer's responsibilities, even though those responsibilities change after the initial law is passed. Congress initially drafted legislation intended as a comprehensive protection of disabled individuals, and the Supreme Court interpreted the ADA narrowly, imposing strict requirements to qualify an individual as disabled under the law. At the time, HR managers may have been left wondering how to assess whether an applicant or employee met the ADA standard of disability in order to qualify for a reasonable accommodation.

Almost two decades after the initial passage of the ADA, Congress responded to the Supreme Court's interpretation by significantly amending the original statute (Public Law 110-325, S 3406, 2008). The Americans with Disabilities Act Amendments Act (ADAAA) begins with a direct rejection of the Supreme Court's narrow interpretation of the ADA's definition of disability, and Congress specifically named the *Sutton* and *Toyota* cases as improper explanations of the ADA's intent. To make its intent unmistakable, Congress affirmed that the definition of disability was to be read expansively. The Equal Employment Opportunity Commission (EEOC) Regulations implementing the ADAAA specified this new focus for employers by citing the congressional intent to extend broad coverage for persons with disabilities and noting that "the determination of whether an individual has a disability should not demand extensive analysis" ("Regulations to Implement the Equal Employment Provisions of the Americans With Disabilities Act, as Amended," 2011, pp. 16977–17017). Rather, the EEOC regulations make it clear that an employer should apply greater attention to the development of reasonable accommodations to enable individuals to meet the essential job requirements. A legal analysis of the new amendments asserts, "The focus under the ADA amendments shifts the emphasis to the act of discrimination rather than the subjective perception that a disability exists" (Miller, 2011, p. 56).

A Return to the ADA's Original Intent: The Text of the ADAAA

Often the "findings" that Congress includes at the start of a piece of new legislation are rather mundane. The ADAAA does not fit into that typical mold. Congress used the findings section of the new Amendments Act to directly reject the Supreme Court's repeated, limited interpretation of who qualifies as disabled under the ADA. The findings cite the original ADA goal of eliminating discrimination based on disability, highlight the "antiquated attitudes" that subject disabled persons to unequal treatment, and unambiguously reject the Supreme Court's analysis of the scope of protection under the law. Specifically, the ADAAA begins,

Congress finds that

1. in enacting the Americans with Disabilities Act of 1990 (ADA), Congress intended that the Act "provide a clear and comprehensive national mandate for the *elimination of discrimination against individuals with disabilities*" and provide broad coverage;
2. in enacting the ADA, Congress recognized that physical and mental disabilities in no way diminish a person's right to fully participate in all aspects of society, but that people with physical or mental disabilities are frequently precluded from doing so because of *prejudice, antiquated attitudes, or the failure to remove societal and institutional barriers*;
3. while Congress *expected that the definition of disability under the ADA* would be interpreted consistently with how courts had applied the definition of a handicapped individual under the Rehabilitation Act of 1973, *that expectation has not been fulfilled*;
4. the holdings of the Supreme Court in *Sutton v. United Air Lines, Inc.*, 527 U.S. 471 (1999) *and its companion cases have narrowed the broad scope of protection* intended to be afforded by the ADA, thus eliminating protection for many individuals whom Congress intended to protect;
5. the holding of the Supreme Court in *Toyota Motor Manufacturing, Kentucky, Inc. v. Williams*, 534 U.S. 184 (2002) *further narrowed the broad scope of protection* intended to be afforded by the ADA;

6. *as a result of these Supreme Court cases,* lower courts have *incorrectly* found in individual cases that people with a range of substantially limiting impairments are not people with disabilities; and

7. in particular, the Supreme Court, in the case of Toyota Motor Manufacturing, *Kentucky, Inc. v. Williams,* 534 U.S. 184 (2002), *interpreted the term "substantially limits" to require a greater degree of limitation than was intended by Congress.*

(Public Law 110-325, S 3406, 2008, emphasis added)

Although the Supreme Court is responsible for interpreting how legislation applies in individual situations, the ongoing dialog between Congress and the Supreme Court demonstrates that the legislature may respond when judicial interpretation appears inconsistent with legislative intent. One of the fundamental challenges Congress sought to remedy with the ADAAA was the lack of clarity regarding the definition of disability.

The significant judicial narrowing of the definition of disability is evidence that the original statute was vague. Recent analysis has suggested that the lack of clarity in the original ADA definition left the law open to narrow interpretation by the courts (Rush, 2012). It is disconcerting to consider that the ambiguity in the initial statute made it more likely that the courts would intervene to clarify key terms, thus resulting in the misinterpretation of the ADA's initial intent. At the time that the ADA was first implemented, human resource scholars noted the ambiguity regarding the meaning of disability in the law and suggested that determining who qualified as disabled could be a serious obstacle to applying the law (Condrey & Brudney, 1998; Percy, 2001).

The Amendments Act strengthened three elements of the definition of disability in an effort to clarify congressional intent regarding who should qualify for protection under the law. First, the ADAAA distinguished that an impairment did not need to limit more than one major life function in order for an individual to be considered disabled under the ADA (42 USC §12102(4)(C)(2008)). Second, Congress clarified that an impairment that is episodic (e.g., asthma) or in remission (e.g., cancer) would qualify for protection under the ADA as long as the same impairment qualified as a disability when active (42 USC §12102(4)(D)(2008)). Finally, the amendments also provided that an employer who is considering whether a disability substantially limits a major life function cannot take into account the beneficial effect of mitigating measures (42 USC §12102(4)(E)(2008)). In fact, ordinary contact lenses or eyeglasses are the only mitigating devices that may be regarded when assessing whether an individual is substantially impaired.

Unintended Consequences: Welfare Benefits Rather Than Civil Rights

The new legislation highlights the ADA's civil rights connections in the expressed congressional intent for a "broad scope of protection" to ensure that disabled individuals have the opportunity to fully participate in the American workforce (Public Law 110-325, S 3406, 2008). The amendments' requirement that employers focus on reasonable accommodation rather than on a restrictive definition of disability indicates that Congress regarded the legislation as a comprehensive effort to eliminate discrimination akin to other influential civil rights statutes. The repeated emphasis on an expansive reading of the term disabled also strongly suggests Congress' determination that the ADA and ADAAA were designed to remedy a societal injustice against persons with disabilities rather than to confer welfare benefits for persons who qualify as disabled. However, the legal literature examining the changes to the ADA has noted that the amendments may have some significant unintended consequences.

Judicial interpretation has significantly distinguished the ADA from prominent civil rights statutes such as Title VII, as evidenced by the Supreme Court's decision in *Board of Trustees of the University of Alabama v. Garrett.* Congress recognized that the courts' interpretation had shifted from their original intent, and accordingly the legislative history of the ADAAA includes the statement that, "the emphasis in questions of disability discrimination [should be] on the critical inquiry of whether a qualified person has been discriminated against on the basis of disability, and not unduly focused on the preliminary question of whether a particular person is even a 'person with a disability' with any protections under the Act at all" (H.R. REP. No. 110-730, pt. 1, p. 16 (2008)).

The courts' limitation in interpreting the ADA as a civil rights statute seems to lie in the application of reasonable accommodations. Cox notes that the Supreme Court views the requirement for reasonable accommodation as "preferential treatment" to compensate for the endogenous biological limitations that disabled individuals face (2010, p. 191). In contrast, many of the disability rights scholars regard these accommodations as a legislative policy response to the unintentional limitations that society imposes on disabled individuals, such as narrow doorways, small typeface, or inflexible work schedules. While the ADAAA works to clarify the breadth of coverage provided by the definition of disability, the amendments do not emphasize the goal of using reasonable accommodation to offset the effects of social barriers to full workforce inclusion. Instead, the amendments' efforts to redirect employers away from assessing whether an individual qualifies as disabled and towards development of reasonable accommodation may unintentionally reinforce the courts' assessment that the ADA is a welfare benefits statute (Cox, 2010).

The Biggest Change: New Standards for Individuals "Regarded As" Disabled

While the ADAAA changes to the definition of disability and the impact of mitigating measures are both significant, the legal literature highlights the changes in the "regarded as" standard as the most influential element in the new law (Parry & Allbright, 2008). The ADAAA both expanded and narrowed the standard for demonstrating that an employer discriminated against an individual whom it regarded as disabled. First, when an individual alleges that an employer (or prospective employer) regarded him or her as disabled, it is no longer also necessary for the individual to prove that the employer believed the impairment substantially limited a major life activity (42 USC §12102(3)(2008)). This aspect of the amendment makes it considerably easier to demonstrate that an employer violated the "regarded as" element of the ADA. However, the ADAAA also now limits the scope of protection for employees who are "regarded as" disabled to only those who are regarded as having impairments with a duration greater than six months (42 USC §12102(3)(2008)). It is important to note that the six month requirement only applies to charges of discrimination where an employee was "regarded as" disabled, not to instances of actual disability or past disability. In practice, the changes to the standard for discrimination when an employee is "regarded as" disabled to mean that fewer individuals will qualify for the ADA protection, but it will be easier to prove discrimination for those who do qualify (Parry & Allbright, 2008).

Continuing Ambiguity

While the ADAAA clarifications do address several of the concerns that arose in the efforts to implement the original statute, ambiguity still remains in the definition of disability (Rush, 2012). First, as indicated above, the amendments clearly state that an individual who is regarded as disabled does not also have to be substantially limited in a major life activity to be covered by the law. However, some see continuing ambiguity in the ADAAA's ongoing connection between a perceived and an actual disability. That connection leaves open the possibility that courts will view the definition of perceived disability as contradicting the new instruction that it is not necessary to demonstrate an individual who is regarded as disabled is also substantially limited in a major life activity (Ara, 2010). Further, the amendments also leave open the question of exactly what constitutes a substantial limitation to a major life activity (Parry & Allbright, 2008).

Those remaining ambiguities are a disappointment to the disability rights scholars who have evaluated the potential and actual impact of the ADAAA. For example, Parry and Allbright criticize,

> Curiously, Congress spends a great deal of time in the "Findings and Purposes" section of the amended act blaming the federal courts, and to a lesser extent the EEOC, for the fact that so few people with disabilities are actually covered under the original Act's disability definition. Yet, instead of correcting all the major problems it identifies with specific language changes, in a number of instances Congress has decided to compel those very courts to reinterpret the offending statutory language in new ways, which supposedly would result in expanded coverage for people with disabilities. In reinterpreting "disability" these courts will be expected to defer to the regulations issued by the three key federal agencies involved, including the EEOC. Unfortunately, these regulations may or may not be the same or as expansive in covering persons with disabilities as Congress indicates—not mandates—that they should be. (2008, p. 696)

EEOC Regulations to Implement the ADAAA

In large part, it was left to the EEOC and other federal agencies to fulfill the congressional intent to provide a wide scope of coverage in order to eliminate discrimination based on disability. On March 25, 2011, the EEOC issued the final regulations to implement the ADAAA. One evaluation of how these new regulations would affect human resource management noted that the congressional goal of greater coverage for persons with disabilities complicates EEOC efforts to clarify every instance where an individual is entitled to protection under the ADA (Rush, 2012). The EEOC's written guidance to the new regulations reveals one challenge in creating a more precise standard. The agency notes that determining whether an impairment substantially limits a major life activity "should not require extensive analysis," but also that an employer needs to engage in an "individualized assessment" to make such a determination (EEOC Questions and Answers, n.d., sec. 9). Those guidelines may not be in direct conflict, but they certainly require a careful parsing to ensure that employers meet congressional goals and regulatory standards.

When Congress left open the definition of "substantially limits" with regard to a major life activity, the lawmakers imposed partial responsibility for developing regulations to more fully define the term on the EEOC. The EEOC was not working completely without direction because Congress had provided that the term "substantially limits" should be defined accordant with findings and purposes of the ADAAA (42 U.S.C §12102 (4) (B)). This included developing the term in a manner that was compatible with the goal of broad coverage for persons with disabilities and the standard that the level of limitation should be assessed without reference to mitigating measures. The EEOC also received the delegated authority to interpret "substantially limits" under the original ADA, and Congress made it clear in the 2008 amendments that the EEOC's initial interpretation was overly restrictive. As a result, the EEOC's regulations defining "substantially limits" attempt to strike a balance that provides a clear standard that also enables broad coverage. The result is a counterintuitive definition that an individual's impairment must be a substantial limitation "compared to most people in the general population" but also that the impairment "need not prevent, or significantly or severely restrict, the individual from performing a major life activity in order to be considered substantially limiting" (76 CFR 1630.2 (j)(1)(ii))(Miller, 2011).

STRATEGIES FOR HUMAN
RESOURCE MANAGEMENT GUIDED BY THE ADA

It would not be surprising if human resource managers felt overwhelmed by the breadth of responsibility imposed by the ADA, given the shifting obligations dictated by Congress and the courts as well as the ambiguity that remains in the EEOC regulations. Managing the employment requirements of the ADA demands an understanding of both the substance of the ADA and the procedures that the statute requires. Previous research indicates that human resource managers express greater confidence regarding the substance of the ADA's protections than they do regarding the legal procedures that the statute requires (Ledvinka, 2009). For example, human resource managers respond with conviction when they are asked whether employees with mental impairments are protected by the ADA. In contrast, these same managers are much more cautious in their responses regarding how to implement a reasonable accommodation. The obligation to provide reasonable accommodation presents the greatest uncertainty for these managers. Fortunately for employers' potential liability, the managers included in this study overestimated their ADA responsibilities and were more likely to provide reasonable accommodation above and beyond that required by the statute (Ledvinka, 2009). A better option might be to find a mechanism whereby HR managers can maintain a current understanding of ADA obligations and receive continuing guidance on individual ADA analyses, difficult and costly though that might be.

Given the frequent shifts created by evolving judicial interpretation, regulations, and legislative amendments, HR managers must find a method for maintaining current knowledge of the law. Participation in regular legal training offers one solution to the challenge of staying up to date. Legal training has been demonstrated to contribute to managers' skill in responding to the specific technical responsibilities that the ADA imposes (Ledvinka, 2009). Additionally, research indicates that federal employee training contributes to an organization's ability to adapt to an environment marked by rapid change (Lee, Cayer, & Lan, 2006). The unpredictable shifts in statutes, case law, and regulations create an organizational environment that would make employee training in law a significant organizational benefit.

Human resource managers' disability rights experience could also benefit from an organizational culture that fosters appreciation for diversity. An organization's culture influences several factors related to diversity, including the practice of implementing federal disability rights policy (Spataro, 2005). Spataro describes an organizational culture of "integration" that emphasizes the new perspectives that are offered by linking employees with significant individual differences (2005, p. 33). Her research on organizational culture and disability suggests that a culture of integration "may present the greatest opportunity for managers to successfully integrate differences and maintain peak performance with a diverse workforce" (Spataro, 2005, p. 33). Recognition of the unique contributions each employee supplies makes it more likely that disabled employees will be supported and appreciated for their individual efforts.

While organizational culture develops organically from employees' beliefs and values, management may engage in several strategies to support a culture of integration. Fostering integration involves the dissemination of value statements that highlight the benefits of including disabled individuals in the workforce and ensuring that employees receive training that supports the examination of issues faced by disabled employees (Spataro, 2005). Substantively, managers can develop reward systems that are "focused on contribution by being unique or different" rather than on individual characteristics (Spataro, 2005, p. 34).

These two strategies, maintaining current competence in the law and supporting an organizational culture that rewards differences, offer distinctive approaches to meet the operational and interpersonal requirements of the ADA. Regardless of the complexities and ambiguities of disability law, human resource managers who implement strategies to maintain current expertise on the statutory, regulatory, and case law requirements of the ADA and work to cultivate an organizational culture of integration will support the broad legislative goals of the ADA. Their efforts will provide employers with the potential benefits that accompany a diverse workforce and help to avoid liability for discrimination.

NOTE

1. The ADA does not apply to 501(c) membership organizations other than labor unions or to Indian tribes. The Rehabilitation Act of 1973 prohibits employment discrimination based on disability in the federal government (42
   U.S.C. §12111(5)(B)(1990) as amended).

REFERENCES

Albertson's, Inc. v. Kirkingburg, U.S. 555 (Supreme Court 1999).

Americans with Disabilities Act, 42 U.S.C. §12101, et seq. (1990).

Americans with Disabilities Act Amendments Act, Public Law 110-325, S 3406
(2008).

Ara, A. (2010). Comment: The ADA Amendments Act of 2008: Do the amendments
cure the interpretation problems of perceived disabilities? *Santa Clara Law
Review, 50*, 255–280.

Board of Trustees of Univ. of Ala. v. Garrett, No. No. 99-1240, 531 356 (Supreme
Court 2001).

The Civil Rights Act of 1964, 42 U.S.C. §2000e, et seq. (1964).

Condrey, S. E., & Brudney, J. L. (1998). The Americans with Disabilities Act of 1990:
Assessing its implementation in America's largest cities. *The American Review
of Public Administration, 28*(1), 26–42.

Cox, J. (2010). Crossroads and signposts: The ADA Amendments Act of 2008. *Indiana Law Journal, 85*(1), 187–224.

Equal Employment Opportunity Commission. (n.d.). *Questions and Answers on the Final Rule Implementing the ADA Amendments Act of 2008.* Retrieved from http://
www.eeoc.gov/laws/regulations/ada_qa_final_rule.cfm

Fairclough, S., Robinson, R. K., Nichols, D. L., & Cousley, S. (2013). In Sickness and
in Health: Implications for Employers When Bipolar Disorders are Protected
Disabilities. *Employee Responsibilities and Rights Journal*, 1–16.

Jeon, Y., & Haider-Markel, D. P. (2001). Tracing issue definition and policy change:
An analysis of disability issue images and policy response. *Policy Studies Journal,
29*(2), 215–231. doi: 10.1111/j.1541-0072.2001.tb02087.x

Kuykendall, C. L., & Lindquist, S. A. (2001). Board of Trustees of the University of Alabama v. Garrett: Implications for public personnel management. *Review of Public Personnel Administration, 21*(1), 65–69. doi: 10.1177/0734371x0102100105

Ledvinka, C. B. (2009). *Law and professionalism in public management: An examination
of Georgia counties.* Unpublished PhD thesis, University of Georgia, Athens,
Georgia.

Ledvinka, C. B. (2010). The Americans with Disabilities Act. In S. E. Condrey (Ed.),
Handbook of human resource management in government (Vol. 3rd, pp. 491–513).
San Francisco, CA: Jossey-Bass.

Lee, B. A., & Newman, K. A. (1995). Employer responses to disability: Preliminary
evidence and a research agenda. *Employee Responsibilities & Rights Journal,
8*(3), 209–229.

Lee, H., Cayer, N. J., & Lan, G. Z. (2006). Changing federal government employee attitudes since the Civil Service Reform Act of 1978. *Review of Public Personnel Administration, 26*(1), 21–51.

Miller, C. J. (2011). EEOC reinforces broad interpretation of ADAAA disability qualification: But what does substantially limits mean. *Missouri Law Review, 76*, 43–80.

Murphy v. United Parcel Service, Inc. 527 U.S. 516 (Supreme Court 1999).

Naef, A. K. (2003). Toyota Motor Manufacturing v. Williams: A case of carpal tunnel syndrome weakens the grip of the Americans with Disabilities Act. *Pepperdine Law Review, 31*, 575.

Parry, J. W., & Allbright, A. L. (2008). The ADA Amendments Act of 2008: Analysis and commentary. *Mental & Physical Disability Law Reporter, 32*, 695–697.

Percy, S. L. (2001). Challenges and dilemmas in implementing the Americans with Disabilities Act: Lessons from the first decade. *Policy Studies Journal, 29*(4), 633–640.

Pfeiffer, D. (1993). Overview of the disability movement: History, legislative record, and political implications. *Policy Studies Journal, 21*(4), 724–734. doi: 10.1111/1541-0072.ep9501244181

Rozalski, M., Katsiyannis, A., Ryan, J., Collins, T., & Stewart, A. (2010). Americans with Disabilities Act Amendments of 2008. *Journal of Disability Policy Studies, 21*(1), 22–28. doi: 10.1177/1044207309357561

Rush, C. L. (2012). Amending the Americans with Disabilities Act: Shifting equal employment opportunity obligations in public human resource management. *Review of Public Personnel Administration, 32*(1), 75–86. doi: 10.1177/0734371x11433883

Scotch, R. K. (1988). Disability as the basis for a social movement: Advocacy and the politics of definition. *Journal of Social Issues, 44*(1), 159–172.

Spataro, S. E. (2005). Diversity in context: How organizational culture shapes reactions to workers with disabilities and others who are demographically different. *Behavioral Sciences & the Law, 23*(1), 21–38. doi: 10.1002/bsl.623

Sutton v. United Air Lines, Inc., 527 U.S. 471 (Supreme Court 1999).

Toyota Motor Mfg., Ky., Inc. v. Williams, 534 U.S.184 (Supreme Court 2002).

U.S. Senate. Committee on Labor and Human Resources. The Americans with Disabilities Act of 1989: Report Together with Additional Views (to accompany S. 933). (S. Rpt. 101–116). Washington: Government Printing Office, 1989.

Wooten v. Farmland Foods, 58 F.3d 382 (Court of Appeals, 8th Circuit 1995).

CHAPTER 8

IMMIGRATION IN A NUTSHELL

Sue Ann Balch

INTRODUCTION

As a human resources professional, you are probably already well aware of how mobile our workforce has become. With the advent of the internet as a platform for advertising jobs, you now receive applications from candidates who are down the street or on the other side of the globe. You may find yourself working for a company, a nonprofit, or an educational/research institution with offices in more than one country or, at the very least, the need to move personnel from country to country. All of this increased globalization of our economy comes at the same time as increased government scrutiny, audits, and ever-changing regulations as to whom we can hire and where and for how long.

This chapter cannot be an all-in-all information source or compendium of legal advice for you on this subject. The area of immigration law and regulations is ever changing, and sweeping immigration reform is being debated in Congress as this chapter is being written. What this chapter will do is provide you with basic terminology, a brief history behind the current law, and a short guide of where to go for more in depth information.

Legal and Regulatory Issues in Human Resources Management, pages 157–168
Copyright © 2015 by Information Age Publishing
All rights of reproduction in any form reserved.

BASIC TERMINOLOGY

Starting with the basics, a visa is a stamp placed in a passport by the government of issuance at an embassy or consulate abroad after an interview by a U.S. Department of State officer known as a Consular Affairs officer. These officers attempt to determine the person's intentions regarding why he or she wishes to come to the United States. Many visa types (and they resemble alphabet soup) are considered visas of nonimmigrant intent such as tourist (B-2), business (B-1), student (F-1 or J-1 depending on the source of their funding), and J-1 exchange visitors. Individuals trying to obtain these visas must prove to the satisfaction of the visa officer that it is NOT their intent to remain permanently in the United States. Other visas such as the H-1b specialty worker visas are considered dual intent, so their burden to prove whether or not they will stay is irrelevant in their interview. In this post-9/11 world that we live in, persons who are applying for visas are also subject to background checks prior to being issued a visa stamp in their passport.

Generally, a U.S. visa cannot be obtained inside the United States since 9/11/2001. The visa is not in most cases a work permit at all. It is a ticket that allows that person to enter the United States for a specified period of time and for either one or multiple entries. In some situations it is meaningless without other accompanying documents.

For example, an F-1 student visa would have to be accompanied by a valid I-20 and a school's admission letter for initial entry. After the first entry, if the visa permits, the student may enter again and again without the admission letter. This is not a permit to work, however, except on the specific university campus that issued the I-20 and where the student is registered in the Student Exchange Visitor Information System (SEVIS). With a letter from the school's international designated officials, the student may apply for a Social Security card, but this still only allows him or her to work on campus and only part-time (no more than 20 hours a week) except under special circumstances.

Another type of commonly issued visa that is used by employers to lawfully hire a foreign national is the H-1b visa. This is a visa that is for educated specialty workers in a specified field, for a specified employer, and for a specified length of time. The position that the individual will be working in must require a minimum of a bachelor's degree. Universities may hire an unlimited number of persons on this type of visa and yet for private industry, there are currently less than 100,000 of these visas available each year and they must be filed for on April 1 of each year for an October 1 start date because if they wait later than this, the government will run out of visas to issue. This number of visas is set by Congress. It is one of the few areas of the current immigration debate where both sides could reach an agreement. The numbers must come up. Without the numbers going up, highly skilled and highly educated persons are not able to obtain jobs here although they are trained at the best U.S. colleges and universities. They are forced to go to other countries or back to their home country to look for jobs. As a nation we lose that skill and the money that we have spent educating them. Not enough U.S.-born college students of today are choosing the science, technology, engineering, or mathematics (STEM) fields of study, and they are certainly not choosing to continue in the field into graduate school in these areas. This is the reason many U.S. college students are taught math or chemistry by professors born in another country.

The H-1b visa is not cheap. The authorization to work on an H-1b visa may be obtained inside or outside the United States. It requires that the employer who wants to hire the foreign national file a petition first with the U.S. Department of Labor (USDOL) verifying the employer's need and intent to hire the foreign national at or above the prevailing wage and that no U.S. workers will be adversely affected by this hire. A public access file must be kept showing the record of the internal and external postings that this has been done and approved by the USDOL.

After obtaining the approval of the Department of Labor, the process moves to a stage known as the labor condition application (LCA). At this point, the employer files a petition with the United States Citizen and Immigration Service (USCIS) at the service center designated for the employer's part of the country. Normal processing time for this whole visa is anywhere from three to six months, depending on the time of year, so you must plan ahead as an employer when you decide to hire a foreign national on one of these visas. If you need the person to begin working sooner, it is possible to premium process the application and obtain the approval in fifteen days from the time that it is received by the USCIS. The cost for premium processing is currently $1,225, and it is only refundable if the service center is not able to process the package within the fifteen days. There are other fees associated with the petition so that the filing fees alone for an H-1b petition could be in the neighborhood of $2,500 without premium processing. There is no requirement to hire an attorney to represent the employer (or potential employee) in these petitions, but the application and the subsequent requests for evidence that may possibly come from the government makes having an attorney who is an immigration specialist the best scenario. Fees for the attorney's services vary greatly due to the attorney's overhead costs, years of experience, and location.

For short-term visits for conferences or meetings inside the United States, people will generally need a B-1 visa for business. This visa will even allow for the individual to be paid an honorarium and travel expense reimbursement. A person on a B-1 visa is not allowed to work for earned income while on that visa type. Many companies will choose to have their employees or company officials come into the country for various lengths of time.

The L or E visa is the type of visa that is used for company transferees and for investors.

A passport is issued by the country of citizenship of the individual and is usually valid for ten years at a time. It can be obtained at any U.S. Post Office or at one's local courthouse. The applications for passports are found online. A person must have a passport before attempting to leave the country. Without a passport it will not be possible to reenter the United States. Depending on the country where one plans to travel, a U.S. citizen may or may not need to obtain a visa from that country before traveling. There is currently no need to obtain a visa to go to Canada, Mexico, most countries in the Caribbean, and most countries in the British Isles and the European Union. It is always a good idea to check whether a visa is needed well in advance of travel because it may take weeks to obtain a visa. If one is traveling to Iraq, for example, and the traveler's plane has a layover in Europe, the traveler is required to obtain a transient visa even if he or she has no plans to leave the airport during the stop. Most countries now have excellent websites where you can find most of the information that you would need for a trip to their country.

An employment authorization document (EAD card for short) is obtained from the United States Citizenship and Immigration Service (the old Immigration and Naturalization Service) after a person is inside the United States. There are several ways a person may be able to obtain one of these, and they are sometimes called temporary "green cards." A student on an F-1 or J-1 visa may obtain one when doing postdoctoral training or post-master's degree training. This card can be good for one year or up to 29 months, depending on the student's field of study. Students who have one of these cards will have applied through their school's officers who issued their other documents (I-20 or DS-2019 in the case of a J-1), and they are limited to working in their field of study but with no other limitations as to where or for how many hours per week. On the card it will be noted that the student is approved for "optional practical training." The card will have a start date and an end date. Initially the card is valid for only one year, but if students are in a STEM field that is predesignated by USCIS, then they may be eligible to extend this card for another 17 months.

Other EAD cards may be issued to persons who have applied for political asylum, refugee status, or permanent residency. These cards are usually valid for one to two years, and the individual must apply to renew in a timely fashion.

Recently, President Obama signed an executive order that allows certain persons of certain ages who were brought to the United States by their parents illegally to apply for a temporary EAD card. Stiff criteria must be met before these persons can obtain a card. This is a temporary attempt to fix our current immigration crisis for a large number of persons who but for their illegal entry as a child would be welcomed into our nation as any other immigrants have been who came here legally. This plan, known as DACA (which stands for deferred action for childhood arrivals), has seen almost one third of the estimated qualified persons receive this benefit. It is not a fix to the situation and still does not give these individuals a pathway to citizenship but it at least allows them a means to legally work while they await the outcome of immigration reform legislation.

Still other people may have a valid EAD card because they may be illegally in the United States but have been given a temporary card while they await determination by an immigration judge as to whether or not they will be deported or granted legal status for an extremely limited number of people.

Fraud is rampant in the EAD card world. Whether through lack of knowledge or deceit, persons may pay their life savings to a "coyote" or other broker to get them a false EAD card and a false Social Security card. The documents may look perfectly valid on their face and yet the Social Security number with their name may be your number or mine.

To combat this problem, the U.S. Department of Homeland Security saw the need to come up with yet another system whereby employers could have a way to verify whether or not the documents presented when they are doing a new I-9 on a new employee are valid or not. This system is known as E-Verify. For now, except in some states, it is for the most part a voluntary system. There is a less than 1% error rate in this system. There will be more information on E-Verify ahead.

Now to the "green card" or permanent residency card. Historically, it was called a "green card" because it enabled a new immigrant to be legally employed and make money, yet the card was never actually green until just recently. When a person finally is able to obtain one of these cards, there is no restriction on their working anywhere in the United States. For hiring purposes, persons who have a valid green card should be treated exactly as if they are already citizens of the United States. They cannot vote or hold elected office and certain grants or U.S. government jobs may not be available to them due to security issues. If a U.S. citizen is married to a lawful permanent resident, there may be death tax consequences for the citizen that would otherwise not happen for two citizens married to each other.

Obtaining a green card takes a long time for most people and a lot of money in filing fees alone without mentioning the attorney fees if they choose to hire someone to help with the process. There are quotas for some countries where only a certain number of immigrant visas (lawful permanent status) will be issued each year. The U.S. system of determining who gets these visas is based on family preference first, and employment and government necessity comes second.

A family-based petition, which is by far the easiest and fastest way for an individual to obtain a permanent means of working legally in the United

States, is also filed with the USCIS service centers. The filing fees, although considerable, are not as high as an employment-based petition, and this petition does not involve the U.S. Department of Labor. The petition, known as an I-130, is filed by an individual for his or her spouse, child, parents, or other close relatives. Generally when the I-130 is filed, a family member will at the same time also file for an EAD card as well as travel documents that will enable the family member to come and go from the United States with greater ease once the I-130 is approved.

A highly skilled worker such as a research faculty person with considerable experience can self-petition under a National Interest Waiver petition. This would be an appropriate avenue for anyone who has received awards, patents, or any other highly recognized acclaim that would be evidence to demonstrate that it is in the best interest of the people and government of the United States to allow the individual to be here contributing to our economy and research.

A third way to obtain permanent residency is through an employment-based process. This does involve approval by the U.S. Department of Labor as well as the USCIS. It is quite expensive. The employer is required to pay at a minimum the labor portion of the process. The remainder of the process, which begins with the filing of an I-140 petition, cannot start until the labor portion known as program electronic program review (PERM) is approved. This can take months. There is no way to premium process this action to speed up the approval. It involves a retesting of the labor market to make sure that no qualified U.S. workers are being displaced by this worker. The process for this type of green card may take between two and eight years, depending on the country of citizenship of the beneficiary (the worker) of the petition. Remember that this is a petition not just for a green card but for an immigrant visa, and there are quotas per country. Persons from the People's Republic of China or from India have a very lengthy wait time for immigrant visas.

A BRIEF HISTORY OF U.S. IMMIGRATION LAW

So how did all of this become so complex? Early in our nation's history, there were no restrictions on immigration of any kind. After the American Revolution, Congress passed the Naturalization Act of 1790, which set up the requirements for citizenship. At this time, the only restriction was that citizenship was open only to "free white persons." During the early 1800s many Catholic immigrants started to pour into the United States due to economic hardships such as the Irish Potato Famine, and a lot of local discriminatory laws were passed, but no federal regulations were adopted limiting their entry into the United States. This was followed by waves of

Chinese immigrants who came to work on the transcontinental railroad and to work in mines during the gold rush in California. In 1849, in a case that came to be known as the Passenger Cases (*Smith v. Turner*, 1849) the Supreme Court held that immigration matters were the business of the federal government and not the states. After the Civil War there were various restrictions that were passed at different times and then repealed at various times. Restrictions were placed on unaccompanied women, prostitutes, the mentally ill, criminals, and any person who might become a burden on the government. By 1882, the Chinese Exclusion Act was passed to stem the tide of Chinese persons that had poured into the United States to provide labor during the 19th century. This law was not repealed until 1943 when it was thrown out by the Court in the Chinese Exclusion Case (*Chae Ching Ping v. United States*, 1889).

In the late 1800s there were two primary ports of entry into the United States: Ellis Island in New York and Angel Island in California. Persons entering through these gates were questioned, medically examined for disease, and quarantined in some cases prior to being allowed entry into the country.

As is always the case with the constant worldwide migration of people, the economic problems of the Great Depression naturally curtailed the massive flow of immigrants into the United States for a time. After World War II, the federal government temporarily lifted the quotas to allow over 650,000 immigrant refugees in from Europe. In 1952, the McCarran–Walter Act was passed, which is also known as the INA or Immigration and Naturalization Act. This legislation retained quotas, set the entry procedures, set the deportation and exclusion procedures, and established the family-based preference for all immigration petitions. Not until 1965 under President Johnson did the U.S. Department of Labor become involved in the process when that department was required to certify that no U.S. workers were being adversely affected by the new immigrants.

In 1986, shortly after the bombing of the Marine barracks in Lebanon, Congress passed the Immigration Reform and Control Act. This was the first blanket amnesty for all persons who were then inside the United States illegally whether by having entered illegally across a border or by having legally entered but illegally overstayed. This was passed during the Reagan administration but did not go into effect until the George H. W. Bush administration. This did not just give illegal immigrants to the United States a pathway to legalization but also set up the first sanctions for employers who illegally hired people. This led to the creation of the I-9 as a means for employers to verify whether a person being hired was legally in the United States. All employers beginning with this act and until today with the new I-9 (which is required effective May 7, 2013) must complete and hold for inspection an I-9 form as well as the supporting documentation on all new hires. On the instructions for the form are lists of documents that can be used to complete the I-9. The new I-9 appears more complicated than the previous I-9, and the instructions are lengthy. The penalties to the employer for not properly completing and storing these documents are high. Many immigration law firms as well as some CPAs are qualified to do a self-audit of an employer's I-9s prior to any potential government audit.

The next major change in immigration law began during the Clinton administration and shortly after the first World Trade Center bombing. This is known as the Illegal Immigration Reform and Immigrant Responsibility Act of 1996. This act eliminated many of the loopholes that allowed convicted felons to remain in the country and created mandatory detention for many with criminal convictions. It was the first major act to attempt to deal with the threat of terrorism. The act had many other provisions that greatly effected how illegal immigrants are processed in this country. It promoted the previously mentioned student and exchange visitor tracking system that we now know as SEVIS-Student Exchange Visitor Information System.

Many of the provisions of the above act, which I will call IIRAIRA for short, were not yet completed, enforced, or implemented when on September 11, 2001, our world made a dramatic shift in favor of enforcement. The terrorists who attacked us that day had legally entered the United States on tourist or B-2 visas, and many had changed to F-1 student visas in order to be able to remain legally in the United States and "off the grid" in terms of detection while they put their plan into motion. In response to the attacks of that day, Congress passed the USA Patriot Act. It made the proposed tracking system mandatory. It tripled the number of border and port immigration inspectors. It created a system of greater information sharing between the various government agencies including the U.S. Department of State, the soon to be created Department of Homeland Security, and the Department of Justice. After 2002 and the passage of the Homeland Security Act, the old INS would be a part of the newly created Department of Homeland Security. The main divisions of Homeland Security would be USCIS (immigration services), Customs and Border Protection, and Immigration and Customs Enforcement, better known as ICE.

Today the debate is hot and getting hotter. Few people do not have an opinion. People who have an opinion as to what direction the law should go from here have a tendency to change that opinion in the face of the reality of specific situations of people they may know in their workplace or their community. Comprehensive immigration reform is needed. This is a fact that all sides agree on. As the current economic recession hit, the need for construction workers, landscapers, and other laborers took a nose dive, and many of the workers who were illegally here went home. Increased enforcement concerns caused many chicken processing centers and other agricultural-related or forest products businesses to curtail the hiring of foreign workers with questionable or no paperwork. Many states such as

Arizona, Georgia, and Alabama passed state legislation that would seek to put additional requirements on employers and additional penalties in place for those who hire persons who are illegally in the country. Most of the provisions of these state laws have been struck down, yet some remain such as the requirement for E-Verify, which was held to be constitutional and appears to be here to stay in some form.

Prior to 2005, all persons in the United States could apply for a Social Security number, although with restrictions, just by being able to provide the proper ID. As of the spring of 2005, only foreign persons legally inside the United States who have a bona fide job offer letter of employment from an employer may apply for a Social Security card. Social Security document fraud has been as rampant as EAD card fraud. Identity theft is everywhere. Persons who have otherwise taxable income in the United States not by employment (such as scholarships and investment income) must apply for a taxpayer ID number (which looks like a Social Security number but is not the same).

SOURCES FOR FURTHER INFORMATION

The complexity of these laws, regulations, and forms may leave the reader's head spinning or at least in need of pain medication. So where should you turn for more information? If employers or HRM professionals want to read more and/or attempt to process petitions for potential foreign national employees or to apply for green cards for family members, the Internet has a wealth of information. But proceed with caution. Many websites are bogus, and many websites have inaccurate or out-of-date information. To protect yourself or your company, finding a lawyer who is a member of the American Immigration Lawyers Association (www.aila.org), and seeking their advice is a terrific start. The AILA website is also a reliable source of information, and through it you can locate an attorney in your area. Because immigration is such a rapidly expanding area of the law, there may not yet be a trained attorney in your area. Immigration law is primarily a federal law practice, so as long as the lawyer is licensed in the state court of their residence and admitted to practice in the federal courts, he or she can help you no matter your location. Beware the lawyer who does immigration as a sideline to other areas of the law. This is, in this author's opinion, the legal equivalent of using a heart surgeon who occasionally does brain surgery to take out your tumor.

Thankfully, the latest and most accurate information can be found for free on the United States government websites. The forms that are needed to file most any petition are found online. Some forms can even be submitted online in order to get the petition in the queue to be processed. If one files online, then one must also send in the supporting documentation via regular or express mail. In some cases, people can apply for a waiver of the fees but it is hard to obtain a waiver in most cases. The major government websites from which to obtain more information and greater detail are listed as follows:

- For immigration forms and procedures and the latest news on changes in this area go to the United States Citizenship and Immigration Service site: www.uscis.gov. Here you will also find the fee amounts, the addresses where petitions should be filed and links to other sites that will provide information. You will also see links to the E-Verify site as well as the latest I-9 developments and the new mandatory form.
- For United States Department of Labor information on the role that they play and their requirements in these processes, including foreign labor certification, prevailing wage information, and foreign labor statistics, see www.dol.gov/dol/topic/hiring/foreign.htm. Here you can even sign up to be able to do your own labor certification applications.
- The law itself can be found in the following volumes of the Code of Federal Regulations, which can be found online or at most libraries: 8CFR, 20CFR, and 22CFR.
- There are a number of law firms that provide free to the public a wealth of good information. The ones that this author turns to for information include the following firms: Fisher and Phillips, LLP (www.laborlawyers.com), Baker Donelson (www.immigration.bakerdonelson.com), the Fragomen Law Firm (www.fragomen.com), and Miller Martin (www.millermartin.com). This is not an endorsement of these firms or the attorneys who practice there, but the counsel of some of these people and their instruction has been invaluable to the author.
- Many professional organizations exist to help employers seeking information about US immigration laws. These organizations provide expert training on immigration issues to human resource professionals. Among these are the American Council on International Personnel and the Society of Human Resource Management. Their 2013 primer, *Navigating the U.S. Employment-Based Immigration System,* emphasizes that immigration is a critical component to build a competitive workforce. The primer points out, "Despite a high national unemployment rate, U.S. employers today have open jobs across many skill levels that they cannot fill because there are not available workers with the special skill sets to hire" (p. 6). Human capital talent recruitment and selection are critical HRM functions that are linked to navigating the complexity of an employment based immigration system.
- Employment-based immigration is governed by complex laws, regulations, policy, and court decisions that have human resource

management implications. The complexity involves the need for HRM professionals to deal with a maze of federal, state, and local agencies. It is clear that an employment-based immigration system is a strategic HRM concern for today's and tomorrow's organizations. Linking employment-based immigration to organizational goals is essential to organizational competitiveness and profitability. This is the HRM strategic implication of immigration reform.

The following books are excellent resources and are updated regularly: First is *Essentials of Immigration Law* by Richard A. Boswell (2009), published by the American Immigration Lawyers Association. It is a terrific basic overall view of immigration. Mr. Boswell is a professor of immigration law at the University of California, Hastings College of Law.

Secondly, for a more in-depth analysis, *Immigration Practice* by Robert Divine assisted by Blake Chisam (2012) is for the highly skilled yet written in a style that is easy to follow and understand. Mr. Divine was the first chief counsel of the newly formed United States Citizenship and Immigration Service during its first days under the Bush administration. His insight is invaluable. He has been assisted in his later editions by Blake Chisam who was the former Chief Counsel to the Ethics Committee of the U.S. House of Representatives and former Senior Counsel to the Immigration Subcommittee of the Judiciary Committee of the U.S. House of Representatives.

Third is *Kurzban's Immigration Law Source Book, 13th Edition* by Ira Kurzban (2012–2013). This work is considered by most immigration attorneys as the first "go to" resource for case updates and highly specific technical sources. Mr. Kurzban is one of the most experienced immigration attorneys in the nation. He practices in his own firm in south Florida and is a highly sought after expert in the field. This volume was first published in 1990 and is updated on a regular basis.

HRM professionals should ask their in-house or retained legal counsel to create standard form questionnaires with lists of documents required, so that they can get all the information and documents for immigration issues required from the start. It really helps if the questionnaires are available electronically, so that they and current or prospective employees can download, complete, and return them without faxing or mailing. This enables the HRM professional to work quickly and helps to avoid the necessity to request further information or documents, which creates delays and sometimes embarrassment or dissatisfaction. HRM professionals should also ask their legal counsel to create desk references to which they can refer on an ongoing basis to deal with issues as they arise. Examples of desk references might include one for I-9 procedures, one for labor condition application procedures, and one for labor certification application procedures.

HRM professionals should also work with their legal counsel to create handouts to give to alien employees to answer frequently asked questions or to prevent frequently recurring problems. For example, it is helpful to have prepared form letters that HRM professionals can give to alien employees regarding travel in and out of the United States, covering issues such as visa issuance, airport inspections, and proper dates on I-94 cards.

HRM professionals should have their legal counsel create status report forms so that they can be constantly updated on the status of all alien employees. These forms should include the myriad of expiration dates that allow for advance planning, such as expiration dates of passports, visas, I-94 cards, I-797s, and labor condition applications. These forms should also include the same dates for spouses and children. These status reports should be accessible electronically through an agreed-upon web page.

Finally, HRM professionals, with the help of their legal counsel, should develop a corporate policy manual for immigration-related matters. Such a manual could include coverage of issues such as when the organization will apply for permanent residence status for an employee, what questions are appropriate to ask at interviews, when a company will apply for H-1B status for a foreign student, and when and by whom I-9s will be completed.

In conclusion, don't go it alone! When in doubt, seek wise counsel of an experienced professional immigration attorney. Keep your I-9s up to date and attend training on the new I-9 form available. Do a self-audit or hire someone who is trained to do one for you. Be ready for a government auditor to show up at your door and sleep easy at night.

REFERENCES

American Council on International Personnel (ACIP) and the Society for Human Resource Management (SHRM). (2013). *Navigating the U.S. employment-based immigration system: Your guide to understanding why reform matters to America's future.* Alexandria, VA: Author.

Boswell, R. A. (2009). *Essentials of immigration law* (2nd ed.). Washington, DC: American Immigration Lawyers Association.

Chae Ching Ping v. United States, 130 U.S. 581 (1889).

Divine, R., & Chisam, B. (2012). *Immigration practice.* Huntington, NY: Juris Publishing.

Homeland Security Act, 6 U.S.C. 101 (2002).

Illegal Immigration Reform and Immigrant Responsibility Act, 8 U.S.C. Ch. 2 Subch. I and II (1996).

Immigration Reform and Control Act, 8 U.S.C. 1101 (1986).

Kurzban, I. (2012–2013). *Kurzban's immigration law source book* (13th ed.). Washington, DC: American Immigration Council.

McCarron-Walter Act, I.N.A. Sec. 101 (1952).

Smith v. Turner, 48 U.S. 283 (1849).

USA Patriot Act, Pub. L. No. 107-56, 115 Stat. 272 (2001).

CHAPTER 9

COMBATING AGE DISCRIMINATION

Legal and Regulatory Issues, Challenges, and Opportunities

Jonathan P. West

INTRODUCTION

The age profile of the American workforce is profoundly changing. Between 2012 and 2060, the working age population (18 to 64) is expected to increase by 42 million from 197 million to 239 million (U.S. Bureau of the Census, 2012). What has been vividly termed the demographic "tsunami" or "time bomb" poses major challenges to society, and more specifically to human resource managers in public, private, and nonprofit organizations, who must respond by designing and implementing strategies to meet the needs of an aging workforce.

There is a burgeoning literature about the impact of the aging baby boomers, those born between 1946 and 1964, the oldest of whom turned 65 in 2011 and the youngest turned 49 in 2013. The workplace has been transformed in many ways as 76 million boomers joined the ranks of older workers, defined

Legal and Regulatory Issues in Human Resources Management, pages 169–205
Copyright © 2015 by Information Age Publishing
169

by the Bureau of Labor Statistics as those aged 55 and older. About half of employees ages 45–70 have plans to work into their 70s and beyond (Jackson, 2010). Despite legislative initiatives, court decisions, regulatory enforcement, and educational efforts, there are numerous age-related stereotypes surrounding the effects of the aging process and the competencies of mature workers, and too few efforts to effectively combat these erroneous perceptions and egregious behaviors. While some innovative organizations have successfully attacked this human resource challenge, ageism and workplace age discrimination continue to pose barriers to aging workers.

There is evidence that human resource professionals recognize the challenge of changing workforce demographics. Over the past decade, the Society for Human Resource Management (2013, p. 13) has identified the top demographic and societal trends confronting the human resource field. Five items on the 2013 list are related to aging workers: the increased proportion of older workers in the workplace, large numbers of baby boomers leaving the workforce at around the same time, reduced career opportunities for younger workers, growth in response to generational differences among employees, and increase in the legal retirement age. These items are listed among those that will have a major or minor impact on the U.S. workplace over the next five years. Yet SHRM/AARP surveys find that almost half of organizations polled have not engaged in strategic planning analyzing the impact of boomer retirements on their workforce (Jackson, 2010). To be effective talent managers, concerted planning and action are needed. This chapter begins by briefly highlighting demographic trends and economic restructuring initiatives that compel interest in the issue of mature workers. It then focuses on the extent and nature of discrimination complaints, ageism, and negative age-related stereotypes. The bulk of the chapter considers the relevant laws, court decisions, and regulatory actions surrounding aging workers and assessments of legal scholars regarding their effectiveness. Human resource management strategies for creatively coping with aging workers' special needs are then examined together with several practical examples and profiles of best organizational practices in meeting the needs of older workers. The chapter ends with a summary and concluding comments.

TRENDS

Demographic Developments

Key demographic facts highlight the graying of America.[1] U.S. Census Bureau (2012) projections are that the numbers of Americans over 65 will more than double by 2060 (from 43.1 million in 2012 to 92.0 million). Just over one in five U.S. residents will be 65 and over by 2060, up from one in seven today. Even more dramatic, those aged 85 and older are expected to more than triple from 5.9 million to 18.2 million, or 4.3% of the U.S. population.

The number of Americans over 65 has increased since 1900 (from 2.1 million to 43.1 million), and the percentage of Americans over 65 has more than tripled (4.1% in 1900, 13.7% percent in 2012). Population projections portend continued increases in the future, with the biggest blip to occur as the boomer generation turns 65.

These population trends are reflected in the U.S. workforce. The civilian labor force participation rate of male workers age 55–64 in 2010 was 70%, and in 2018 it is projected to be 71%. Comparable rates for similarly aged female workers in 2010 was 60.2%, and it is projected to be 65.3% in 2018 (U.S. Bureau of the Census, 2012).

In 1990 12.1% of the age 65 and over population was in the labor force; by 2010 this increased to 16.1 (while over the same period the labor force participation rate of the 16–64 year old population decreased from 75.6 to 74.0%). Within the 65 and older population, 65–69-year-olds underwent the greatest change (21.8 to 30.8% from 1990–2010), in comparison to a 5.0% change for those aged 70–74 and a 1.0% change for those 75 and older (Kromer &Howard, 2013). Many older workers occupy higher level positions: in 2011, 43.1% of workers 55 and over are in management, professional, and related occupations; 24.3% are in sales and office occupations (U.S. Census Bureau, Current Population Survey, Annual Social and Economic Supplement, 2011)

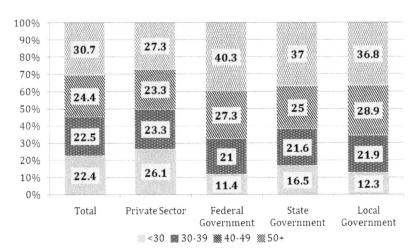

Figure 9.1 Age distribution of workers in private and government sector 2012. *Source:* Bureau of Census, Current Population Survey (CPS), March 2012 (Annual Social and Economic Supplement)

Figure 9.1 shows the percentage of workers aged 40 and over, which is substantially greater in the public sector than in the private sector. According to the census for 2012, 50.6% of private sector workers were over 40 years of age, while 67.6% of the federal workforce was over 40. The percentages for state and local governments were 62 and 65.7, respectively. Because it is not unusual for workers to be in the 40 and older age group, especially in the public sector, it is crucial for management to give careful consideration to developing strategies that address the needs of this critical workforce segment. Older worker needs change partly in response to contextual factors in the macro-socioeconomic environment, a topic deserving our attention next.

Economic Restructuring

It used to be that many workers nearing the later phases of their work life could expect relative employment stability and the possibility of early retirement with a relatively comfortable pension. These secure late employment careers with relatively low unemployment risks have changed in recent years as a result of macroeconomic and demographic shifts. Globalization has accelerated the pace of change, and today older workers face greater unemployment risks, precarious work, and uncertain pension benefits, especially those in traditional industries hard hit by economic restructuring, technological change, and increased competition for jobs, markets, and talents. Jobs in service industries are expected to continue increasing, while those in manufacturing will continue to shrink. In many industries, exit options for older workers are no longer available; early retirement programs have been cut; and pensions, where they existed, have been increasingly converted from defined benefits to riskier defined contribution plans (West & Bowman, 2008). Absent the exit option, many older workers will find the later years of their working life are less stable with lower pay and uncertain pensions.

Kurz, Buchholz, Veira-Ramos, Rinklake, and Blossfeld (2011) identify four general trends affecting older workers in the United States and Europe: (a) a rise in the risks of unemployment and downward mobility; (b) cutbacks in early retirement options; (c) reduced pensions resulting from unstable employment, declining wages and reformed pensions; and (d) increased inequalities among occupational classes with regard to labor market risks and pension guarantees. The risky economic changes are known to adversely impact those in the millennial generation who are entering the labor market (see West, 2012), but it is becoming increasingly clear that those in the later phases of their work life are encountering higher risks as well.

Older workers also confront the impact of change when they are forced to move out of one job situation into another because the job characteristics chosen near the start of employment may no longer be suitable later on. The possibility of reducing hours as a smooth transition toward retirement may not be available. Mature employees may be threatened by technological change resulting from global competition and find that their skills acquired years earlier are no longer sufficient to meet today's work requirements. Employers might be unwilling to invest in retraining of such workers because they may conclude it is an inefficient use of funds given that they have only a few more years of employment. As a result, older workers systematically receive less training (Booth, Chen, & Zoega, 2002). Furthermore, the absence of the opportunity for part-time and flexible-hours work in many organizations may be a disincentive for aging workers to keep working, leading to labor market withdrawal (Gielen, 2009; Blau & Shvydko, 2007). The lifelong career process increasingly consists of transitions between jobs and jobless states. Once withdrawn from the labor market, reentry is difficult and it takes longer for older workers than their younger counterparts to rejoin the workforce (Bureau of Labor Statistics, 2009). Difficulties seeking employment are magnified by job seekers after age 65 (Rothenberg & Gardner, 2011).

Given market trends it is not surprising that more and more adults are postponing plans to retire. This is confirmed by results from an American Association of Retired Persons survey (AARP, 2009) of adults 45 and older showing 22% of those aged 45–54 and 27% aged 55–64 postponed plans to retire, a trend that is likely to continue (Johnson, 2009; Rothenberg & Gardner, 2011). The recent recession deeply eroded 401(k) accounts, forcing many to postpone retirement. It is not surprising, then, that SHRM/AARP surveys show "financial reasons such as the need for money or health insurance" as the primary reason given for workers ages 50+ to continue working or looking for work (Brown, 2012, p. 1). Delayed retirements will result in a "gray ceiling" limiting career opportunities for younger workers.

Coupled with these demographic and macroeconomic shifts that have negative impacts on aging workers is the persistence of widespread age-based discrimination.

Age Discrimination

Even though surveys find that most American workers agree that a more diverse workforce equals a more successful organization, discrimination at the office continues to be a problem. A recent Adecco USA (2008) survey of 2,206 adults age 18 and over finds that half of employees (47%) have felt discriminated against at the office, with age cited as the top form of discrimination. Of that group of American workers who experienced discrimination at work, age (52%) was the most often cited form, followed by gender (43%), race (32%), religion (9%), and disability (7%).

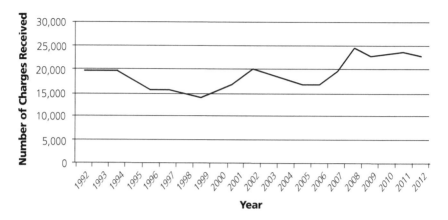

Figure 9.2   Charges filed under ADEA, 1992–2012.

Annually, an estimated 15,000 to 25,000 age discrimination charges are filed with the Equal Employment Opportunity Commission, as shown in Figure 9.2. It is widely understood that the number of actual incidents greatly exceeds the number of filed complaints (Rothenberg & Gardner, 2011), and the 20-year trend line shows an increase over the past 15 years. The fewest number of complaints during this two decade period was in 1999 (14,672) and the largest number was in 2008 with 24,582, an increase of 40.3%. According to the EEOC (2013a, 2013b), of the 27,335 resolutions issued in ADEA cases (including concurrent charges with Title II, ADA and EPA) in FY2012, 19,239 (70.4%) were found to have "no reasonable cause" and 4,045 (14.8%) were closed for administrative reasons. Excluding charges withdrawn or resolved without EEOC intervention, only 770 (2.8%) resolutions were deemed to be reasonable claims of age-based discrimination and progressed to the conciliation phase, where only 343 (1%) were successfully mediated (i.e., sufficient compensation to claimant) by the EEOC. The EEOC can bring a suit in federal court if mediation is unsuccessful, but it does so very infrequently. In FY 2012, the EEOC only filed 155 suits under ADEA, .6% of all age discrimination cases resolved that year. Clearly, while age discrimination is widespread, it is often subtle and hard to prove, in part because underlying it are attitudes reflecting ageism, stereotyping, and bias—the next topic for brief consideration.

AGEISM, STEREOTYPING, AND AGE BIAS

Among the challenges facing older workers are the negative perceptions and stereotypes that are pervasive and perverse in their consequences, often resulting in discriminatory behavior.[2] Research reflects conflicting perceptions about older workers, with some managers viewing such employees positively because of their experience, knowledge, work ethic, attitudes, loyalty, respect for authority, steadiness, and even-temperedness (Tishman, Van Looy, & Bruyere, 2012). Other positive perceptions praise aging workers for their judgment, commitment, reliability, low turnover, high attendance, and punctuality (Butler & Barret, 2012; Cappelli, 2009). Studies also indicate that managers have negative perceptions of mature workers, stressing inflexibility, lack of aggressiveness, reluctance to change, difficulty adapting to new technology, complacency, costliness, low energy, and poor health (Cavico & Mujtaba, 2012; Jackson, 2013; Roscigno, 2010). Negative perceptions sometimes refer to skill deficits, low productivity, unfamiliarity with social media, inability to keep up with their work, and lack of mobility (Rothenberg & Gardner, 2011; Billett, Dymock, Johnson, & Martin, 2011). While many of these ageist stereotypes have been challenged and refuted by empirical research, employers may continue to believe they are accurate. Indeed, as Gregory (2001, p. 29) observes, "Although negative age stereotypes abound and employers continue to view age, not in terms of experience and stability, but as mental and physical deterioration as well as inflexibility and lack of enthusiasm, data supporting these stereotypes are nonexistent."

Ageism or age bias can be defined as referring to prejudice and discrimination against any age group, including bias and unfairness toward employees because they are too young or too old (Snape & Redman, 2003). Further distinctions refer to a "tripartite view of bias" (Fiske, 2004), later refined by Finkelstein and Farrell (2007) to categorize "'stereotyping' as the cognitive component, 'prejudice' as the affective component and 'discrimination' as the behavioral component" (quoted in Kunze, Boehm, & Bruch, 2011, p. 265). Discrimination against mature workers is often based on such systemic stereotyping and prejudice. This poses what Jackson (2013) refers to as the "stereotype threat," referring to expectations that a person will be evaluated based on a negative stereotype about group membership instead of actual or potential performance.

The stereotype threat can lead to a variety of responses by (in this case) the older worker including, according to Jackson (2013), fending off the stereotype threat, discouragement by the stereotype, or resilience to the stereotype. The "fending off" approach might lead the person being stereotyped to either act against the stereotype by showing that it does not apply to them and that they are not typical of their group or to overcompensate by working harder to fend off the stereotype. Those discouraged by the stereotype might psychologically disengage their self-image from their work performance, become angry, attribute their work failures to the discrimination of others, or withdraw from work. The resilient response involves use of coping strategies, such as the ability to acknowledge but recover from the stereotype or to challenge and confront negative group perceptions. Negative stereotypes can not only reduce opportunities for hiring, training, promotion, and retention of mature workers, but they can also take a psychological toll on the object of the stereotype.

Yeatts, Folts, and Knapp (2000) have identified two contrasting models of employer perceptions regarding older workers: the depreciation model—workers' value to the organization declines as they near retirement age, and the conservation model—employees are viewed as organizational assets worthy of investment. The depreciation model receives more extensive treatment by many authors, but some researchers find more positive accounts of experiences with older workers (e.g., Billett et al., 2011; Billett, 2011; Duncan, 2003). Nonetheless, employer views often reflect assumptions of the depreciation model that worker productivity diminishes as they age, a view sometimes advanced by economists who subscribe to a life-cycle model of career development. This model presumes that worker salaries typically exceed employee productivity at both the start and end of an employee's work life, but salaries are usually lower and productivity higher closer to the midpoint of the work cycle (Butler & Berret, 2012; Gregory, 2001). Acting on this questionable assumption, employers might engage in subtle and not so subtle forms of discrimination.

Age stereotypes can take many forms and have serious consequences. Two forms are important for HR professionals to keep in mind: first, age stereotyping refers to the misconceptions people may hold about age and worker competency (e.g., inability to learn about new forms of technology); second, age norming establishes a correlation between job tasks and the "typical" age of the employee who completes these tasks (e.g., younger workers in construction jobs) (see Woolever, 2012, p. 121). Age norming poses the danger of bias leading to assumptions that certain jobs exceed the capabilities of workers just because they are older. Both forms can result in discrimination at either the institutional level (e.g., in hiring, training, promotion, firing decisions) or the interpersonal level (e.g., prejudicial attitudes or discriminatory actions in daily interactions).

Actions at the institutional level might include rejecting mature job applicants as overqualified, requiring years of experience on job applications and then screening out candidates by inferring age from their response, using age limits as a proxy for health and fitness, refusing to hire the long-term unemployed or to consider mature employees for training and development opportunities, making unfair work assignments based on age, monitoring older workers more closely on the job than others, and providing them less favorable feedback. Actions at the interpersonal level might involve ageist remarks such as insulting jokes, disrespect, patronizing behavior, or assumptions about frailty or ailments (Chou & Choi, 2011). HR professionals need to not only be aware of all forms of bias and discrimination, whether explicit or implicit, but also act when necessary to correct such prejudicial beliefs or actions. It is also crucial that they have up-to-date knowledge of the legal and regulatory issues that affect mature workers.

LEGAL AND REGULATORY ISSUES

Federal and State Laws

The Age Discrimination in Employment Act (ADEA) of 1967 and its amendments in 1986 provided managers with another reason to critically examine their attitudes, policies, and practices regarding mature workers. Originally, the legislation prohibited age-related discrimination for persons aged 40 to 65, but in 1978 amendments increased the upper age limit to 70 and in 1986 upper limits were eliminated altogether. The purpose of the ADEA is to get employers to make decisions based on employee or applicant qualifications and to discourage the use of ageist assumptions. The ADEA is designed to protect workers aged forty and over from workplace discrimination in hiring, promotion, training, and retirement and from unfavorable actions with regard to pay, working conditions, or terms of employment. The ADEA applies to private sector firms with 20 or more employees and labor unions with 25 or more members as well as federal, state, and local government employers. In 1990, further protection was provided with the passage of the Older Workers Benefit Protection Act, which amended the ADEA and prohibited employers from denying benefits to older workers. Most states also have their own laws protecting older workers from age discrimination.

Enforcement of the ADEA was initially handled by the Wage and Hour Division of the Department of Labor but subsequently shifted, as mentioned previously, to the Equal Employment Opportunity Commission (EEOC). Excellent guides are available to assist older workers who wish to take informal or formal action against age discrimination (see, e.g., AARP, 2002). In assessing the potential impact of the ADEA, demographics once again become important. With significant numbers of employees aged 40 and up (see Figure 9.1) and discrimination charges rising (see Figure 9.2), the antidiscrimination provisions of the ADEA that stress the continued employment of qualified workers over 40 become especially relevant to human resource and other public managers.

Managers should not only keep abreast of statutory law but also be mindful of court decisions in this area. For example, in the Supreme Court case *Kimel v. Florida Board of Regents* (2000), Daniel Kimel, an elderly employee, faced age discrimination and sued the Florida university system under the ADEA. The Florida Board of Regents argued that citizens could not sue states in federal court because it violated the state's sovereign immunity. The Supreme Court agreed, holding that Congress cannot force the states to abide by the ADEA and potentially other civil rights statutes. Although thorny legal issues remain, this case calls into question the ability of federal law to curb discriminatory actions by state governments. However, states often pass their own legislation to protect against discrimination based on age.

Figure 9.3 shows a map of the 50 states and differentiates those with stronger remedies, weaker remedies, and those with no legislation. Twenty-nine states are classified as having stronger remedies, which means they allow for compensatory and/or punitive damages (or, in a few cases, civil penalties/damages) either with or without proof of intent. These state age discrimination laws are stronger than federal laws. Eighteen states are classified as having weaker remedies. In the three states that have no laws, only the ADEA applies. Surprisingly, recent research by Neumark and Button (2013) for the National Bureau of Economic Research finds that stronger state age protections are associated with more adverse effects of the Great

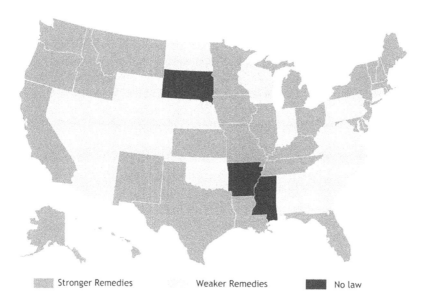

Stronger Remedies   Weaker Remedies   No law

Figure 9.3 Strength of remedies under state age discrimination laws, 2011. *Source:* Adapted from Neumark & Button (2013); Neumark & Song (2011). *Note:* States classified as having stronger remedies allow for compensatory and/or punitive damages (or, in a few cases, civil penalties/damages) either with or without proof of intent, classified as having weaker remedies do not. In the three states that have no laws only the ADEA applies.

Recession on older workers: jobless rates for older workers are higher in states with strong age discrimination protections.

Notwithstanding the *Kimel* case, managers need to be vigilant to avoid potential liability under the ADEA or state law and to conform to both the letter and the spirit of such legislation. Age-related discrimination has been detected in the areas of hiring (for example, rejecting applicants for age-related reasons), promotion (advancing younger candidates over older or more qualified ones), training (excluding older workers from training or retraining), reductions in force (terminating or forcing retirement of older workers exclusively or disproportionately), termination (linking firing decisions to declining performance or medical problems tied to age), and other aspects of personnel management. Managers must take care not only in what they do but also in what they say. As shown in Figure 9.2, age discrimination charges by employees have been rising over the past two decades. Thus, in addition to myriad demographic, social, and economic challenges, managers of older workers must be aware of the legal requirements and tread cautiously to avoid lawsuits arising from age-related missteps. This involves not only having familiarity with constitutional and statutory law, but, as the Kimmel case shows, also having an awareness of significant court decisions. Selected court decisions discussed below reinforce this point.

Age Discrimination Supreme Court Cases

Six Supreme Court cases on or related to age discrimination deserve special attention. The cases were decided during the time period 1993 to 2009 and each will be briefly considered in turn. The first case is *Price Waterhouse v. Hopkins* (1989). This sex discrimination case is significant for the present discussion because the Supreme Court departed from its *Waterhouse* decision 16 years later in its landmark decision in *Gross v. FBI Financial Services, Inc.* in 2009. While the Court recognized in the Title VII *Price Waterhouse* case that "mixed-motive" claims involve employer actions based on both discriminatory and nondiscriminatory rationales, in *Gross* it assessed the kinds of evidence the parties must present as well as who must bear the burden of proof in mixed-motive ADEA cases. In *Gross* the court rejected *Price Waterhouse* as a controlling precedent for ADEA cases. Whereas in *Price Waterhouse* the court "held that 'because of' language in Title VII of the Civil Rights Act of 1964 prohibits employment decisions based in whole *or* in part on a protected characteristic," in *Gross* the Court interpreted similar language in the ADEA in terms of 'but for' causation (Bisom-Rapp & Sargeant, 2013, p. 755). Thus, in ADEA actions, unlike those brought under Title VII, liability requires establishing that age was a necessary, or but-for, cause of the decision being challenged.

Lower courts applied the *Price Waterhouse* framework to ADEA mixed-motive cases up until *Gross*. In 1991, Congress amended Title VII of the Civil Rights Act specifying the *Price Waterhouse* framework as the guide courts should follow in disparate treatment discrimination cases involving mixed motives. The three-step process briefly involves: (a) the plaintiff demonstrating that the employer acted illegitimately, causing an adverse employment action; (b) if discrimination based on a protected characteristic is successfully established, the burden of proof shifts from the plaintiff to the employer; and (c) if the employer proves it would have made the same decision even if the protected characteristics played no role, the burden of proof shifts back to the plaintiff who must show the employer's defense was a mere pretext for discrimination (see Tishman, Van Looy, & Bruyere, 2012, pp. 31–32). The above framework applied to Title VII cases (e.g., those dealing with race, sex, religion), but the 1991 amendment did not affect the ADEA. Nonetheless, until *Gross* the courts were uncertain about the applicability of the *Price Waterhouse* framework to ADEA disparate-treatment mixed-motive cases.

The second case is *Hazen Paper Co. v. Biggins* (1993). This case, according to Bisom-Rapp and Sargeant (2013), offers "the first inkling of differentiation between age discrimination and other forms of discrimination" (p. 757) and "demonstrates that age discrimination law privileges economic concerns over civil rights" (pp. 760–761). In *Biggins*, the court addressed the distinction between seniority and age, indicating that while they are correlated, they are analytically distinct, meaning employers can make work-related decisions based on seniority without it being based on age (see Rothenberg & Gardner, 2011). Bisom-Rapp and Sargeant (2013, p. 758) see significance in the case because "the Court significantly restricted the type of circumstantial evidence available to prove age discrimination," with the result that "employers are free to use salary and length of service—factors commonly associated with age and higher costs—as the rationale for economically devastating employment actions, such as reductions in force."

Smith v. City of Jackson (2005) is the third case of special relevance. The case is important because it represents the first time the Supreme Court recognized disparate impact claims under the ADEA as well as under Title VII (Wilson, 2012, p. 22). Azel Smith and his coworkers brought suit against the Jackson, Mississippi police department, objecting to a new salary plan. They contended that the plan resulted in bigger raises to officers with tenure of less than five years and maintained that the plan had a disparate impact on older workers, a protected class, the majority of whom had tenure for more than five years. While the court ruled in favor of the city because they thought the plan was based on valid material unrelated to age, it opened the door to disparate impact claims under the ADEA and established that a reasonable factor other than age (RFOA) is a legitimate defense (Elkins, 2012).

Various legal scholars have analyzed the case, showing how the "reasonableness" standard is a very "employer friendly one." Bisom-Rapp, Frazer, and Sargeant (2011) point out how RFOA is an easier burden for employers to meet than the "business necessity defense available in disparate impact claims brought on grounds apart from age" (p. 109). Harper (2012) discusses *Smith* in the context of ADEA v. Title VII on disparate impact and observes that RFOA is an affirmative defense and that therefore "the burden of proving a reasonable justification is on employers" (p. 31). Rothenberg and Gardner (2011) explain how the RFOA defense blunted the impact of the Supreme Court's decision to allow disparate impact claims under the ADEA. Finally, Cavico and Mujtaba (2012, p. 171) stress that the court's reasonableness standard is indeed "employer friendly" by recognizing that "necessary and legitimate job requirements" may adversely affect older workers to a greater extent than younger ones.

In the fourth case, *Kentucky Retirement Systems v. EEOC* (2008), the Supreme Court further established that "employers may, without violating the ADEA, make employment decisions based on cost factors that are highly correlated with age, such as pensions or high salaries, as long as their actions are not actually based on age" (Feder, 2010, p. 5). (For factual details on the case see Tishman et al., 2012, Appendix B.) Commenting on the significance of this case, Bisom-Rapp et al. (2011) point out that to prove age discrimination, the plaintiff would be required to show "animus" beyond the issue of age as a factor in disability retirement benefit determination. This requirement poses an additional burden, which is not required of plaintiffs proving other forms of disparate treatment discrimination. In the view of these authors, this "may doom many ADEA claims because it is rare to find direct evidence of discriminatory animus" (Bisom-Rapp et al., 2011, p. 108). Bisom-Rapp and Sargeant (2013, p. 760, emphasis in original) further explain elsewhere that "it is especially difficult to find animus in the context of age discrimination because . . . age bias typically operates *without the hostility* present in other forms of employment discrimination." One specific takeaway from this case is that discrimination based on pension status does not violate ADEA.

The fifth case, *Meacham v. Knolls Atomic Power Laboratory* (2008), was decided during the same year as *Kentucky Retirement Systems*. Here the Supreme Court further clarified "whether it is the employee or employer who bears the burden of demonstrating that the challenged employment practice is reasonable or unreasonable," holding that "the employer is responsible for proving that its action was in fact reasonable" (Feder, 2010, p. 10). As a result, the case would seem to be a win for the plaintiff, making it easier for them to prevail in disparate impact claims; however, subsequent case law suggests that the RFOA defense typically defeats disparate impact cases (see Bisom-Rapp & Sargeant, 2013, pp. 762–763). The court implied that it was easy for employers to establish a broad RFOA defense to charges of disparate impact treatment under ADEA. In the years following the Supreme Court's recognition of the RFOA defense, many factors correlated with age have been considered reasonable, including high salary, healthcare costs, and benefits; advantages in attracting new recruits; desire to minimize loss of employees during a reduction in force; and retirement status (see Tishman et al., 2012). The ease with which employers can use the RFOA defense makes the proffer of reasonableness "virtually impenetrable" (Tracey, 2009).

Finally, the sixth, and arguably most important, case is the aforementioned *Gross v. FBL Financial Services, Inc.* (2009), decided by a 5–4 margin the year after *Kentucky Retirement Services* and *Meacham*. This case has sparked substantial commentary and some confusion. As noted previously, the court held that the plaintiff in a mixed-motive case bears the burden of establishing that age was the "but-for" cause, or deciding factor, of the challenged adverse employment action, and not just one of several factors motivating the employer's action. According to several observers, the standard established in this case is likely to make it more difficult for plaintiffs to succeed in age discrimination cases when age is just one of several factors behind the adverse employment decision (see Cavico & Mujtaba, 2012; Feder, 2010; Tishman et al., 2012). Indeed Diana Johnson, EEOC assistant legal counsel, sees this case as a "startling departure" from decades of past precedents developed in the federal courts that "erected a new, higher (and potentially insurmountable) legal hurdle for victims of age-based employment decisions" (cited in Bisom-Rapp et al., 2011, pp. 107–108).

Prior to the *Gross* decision, an employee had to prove age was a *key* factor for an adverse action. Now, unlike plaintiffs challenging other types of discrimination, plaintiffs in age bias cases charging disparate treatment have to demonstrate that age was a *decisive* cause of the employer's action, even when employers admit that age partially motivated the decision (see Cavico & Mujtaba, 2012; Tishman et al., 2012; Woolever, 2012). Currently, the employee must show by a preponderance of the evidence that but-for the illegal age discrimination the adverse action would not have occurred, a higher standard than showing that discrimination was a "motivating or substantial factor" (see Cavico & Mujtaba, 2012; Fleischer, 2009). The *Gross* ruling takes away the possibility of shifting the burden of proof to the employer in disparate treatment cases and, in the opinion of Bisom-Rapp and Sargeant (2013, pp. 754–757), it "allows some age-biased employers to escape liability without consequence, under-deters illegal employment decision-making, and provides a windfall to discriminating employers who relied on factors in addition to age."

Taken together these six cases show the Supreme Court's evolving view of the ADEA, with its provisions prohibiting employment discrimination against individuals over age 40 and its purpose of promoting employment of older persons based on their ability rather than age. As noted in the review of six cases, the court's interpretations have created numerous exceptions and clarifications in the areas of disparate treatment, disparate impact, mixed-motive cases, and the standards to be followed in determining the legality and reasonableness of employer actions vis-à-vis older workers. Many legal scholars have concluded that proving age discrimination has become more and more difficult with the increasingly "employer friendly" rulings of the court since the passage of the ADEA. Employers in an age discrimination lawsuit can, among other approaches, defend themselves by demonstrating that the alleged discrimination is based on "reasonable factors other than age." The legal burden on the plaintiffs has become more difficult now that they must prove that age was the decisive factor motivating employers' adverse action against them. While complaints about age discrimination have increased over the past decade, the likelihood of proving the case in court has decreased, with the standard of proof much higher now than a decade ago.

CRITIQUES OF THE ADEA

Critics and reformers of the ADEA allude to it as "weak" and "largely ineffective" in addressing issues confronting older workers (Bisom-Rapp et al., 2011; Harper, 2012; Neumark, 2008; Rothenberg & Gardner, 2011). They view the law as a "well intentioned" but "inherently flawed" or "failed" policy, in large measure due to a combination of factors beyond the content of the legislation itself. Among the factors undermining the effectiveness of the ADEA are a downturn in economic conditions; pervasive ageism; negative age-related stereotypes; age-based workplace discrimination; under-funded, understaffed, and overworked regulatory agencies; inefficient processing of complaint charges; unbalanced enforcement strategies; and judicial decisions favoring the employer and the market-based economy. Rothenberg and Gardner (2011, p. 19), in assessing the nearly five-decade experience under the ADEA, conclude that "at best, it does not provide sufficient protection to 'older workers as a group,' and at worst is seemingly used to rationalize discriminatory practices, as in . . . RFOA arguments." These two authors conclude that, given the failure of the ADEA to resolve negative stereotyping, it is the responsibility of employers to prevent or combat such assumptions about the competencies of older workers.

Focusing on the ADEA itself, Michael Harper (2012) has a specific set of policy reform proposals that would strengthen the law by reducing the

ADEA

- Provide for compensation and punitive damages
- Provide for Rule 23 ADEA class actions
- Provide equivalent disparate impact cause of action
- Provide equivalent causation test for disparate treatment liability

TITLE VII

Figure 9.4 Closing the gap between ADEA and Title VII protections. *Source:* Adapted from Harper (2012).

gap between protections provided for age discrimination victims and those afforded to other protected groups under Title VII of the Civil Rights Act of 1964. Figure 9.4 illustrates the reforms he is suggesting. First is providing for equitable compensatory and punitive damage remedies for victims of age discrimination similar to those available under Title VII and in most states. Second is allowing private plaintiffs charging age discrimination the same assistance for class action procedures (Rule 23 of the Federal Rules of Civil Procedure) available to plaintiffs challenging discrimination (e.g., race, sex, national origin, disability) under Title VII. Third is authorizing an equivalent disparate impact cause of action to that available under Title VII, which would allow victims of age discrimination to challenge employer justifications by offering alternative practices that do not result in disparate impact. Fourth is allowing an equivalent causation test for disparate treatment liability so that liability turns not on establishing that age was a necessary or but-for cause of the challenge decision, but instead on demonstrating that it was a "motivating factor." Harper advocates Congressional action to reduce the gap between ADEA and Title VII protections, but he is not optimistic that such reforms will occur.

David Neumark (2008), under contract with AARP, performed a critical literature review of research on age discrimination and assessed the success of the ADEA in meeting its objectives. He notes that enforcement activity under the ADEA has focused on terminations of older workers and that there has been a lack of activity on hiring, in part because hiring discrimination cases are harder to prove than termination cases. Neumark's report highlights the economic benefits of high employment rates among mature workers: "lower dependency ratios, greater income, more tax revenues and decreased public expenditures on health insurance, retirement benefits, and income support" (p. vii). He also stresses the diminished economic well-being of older persons that can result from policies that reduce retirement incentives, increase retirement age by fiat, and lower the value of pensions (particularly once retirement decisions have been made).

These issues are especially important for persons aged 45–64, about 75% of whom are currently employed, and two thirds of this group claim to have experienced age discrimination in the workplace. Further, with projections that those aged 65 and over will increase markedly in future years, reducing age discrimination will be important for that portion of the workforce as well. To the extent that such discrimination plays a role in suppressing employment of older workers, determining how the ADEA can contribute to combating discrimination is a highly salient policy issue. For the 65 and older age group wishing to remain in the workforce, "short-term jobs," "partial retirement," or "bridge jobs" are recommended, but with the caution that rooting out hiring discrimination will be necessary for these strategies to succeed. Neumark also points to the link between aging and work-limiting disabilities. This may deter employers from hiring aging workers because of fear that they could become disabled and impose firing costs related to discrimination claims under either the ADEA or the Americans with Disabilities Act. Attention now turns to the pivotal role of HR professionals in managing older workers.

HRM STRATEGIES

Given the issues surrounding demographic developments, age discrimination, ageist stereotypes, statutory requirements, court rulings, and critiques of the ADEA, what strategies can HR managers pursue to address problems confronting older workers? HR professionals must help develop and implement such strategies because they are increasingly expected to be both compliance officers and ethics officers (West, forthcoming) upholding the legal rights of employees and insuring that workers are free of mistreatment or discrimination. As compliance officers they focus on what *must* be done; as ethics officers they are concerned with what *should* be done (Woolever, 2012, p. 116). Consideration of managerial strategies—directed to both the must-do and the should-do obligations—will be grouped into four categories: demographic understanding, combating negative stereotypes, legal compliance, and performance enhancement.

Demographic Understanding

It is imperative that HR managers be aware of the increasing age diversity of their workforce and the potential of increased perceptions of age discrimination. As Florian Kunze and colleagues (2011, p. 282) found in their research, "organizations may experience poor performance when employees perceive discriminatory treatment." It is crucial to prepare for an aging workforce; failure to do so, especially when combined with negative perceptions of younger employees regarding their older coworkers, can alter workplace dynamics and may lead to age discrimination lawsuits (Bjelland, Bruyère, von Schrader, Houtenville, Ruiz-Quintanilla, & Webber, 2010). Such preparation should include an "age audit" of the number of employees nearing retirement age and the likely impact of loss of their skills, knowledge, and abilities (Hursh, Lui, & Pransky, 2006). An audit can also provide the age composition of the organization, enabling creation of an aging profile analysis and projection. Audits can help HR officers understand the distribution of employee ages across positions in the organization and enable them to insure there is an ample distribution of older workers throughout the workplace. In combination with other data collection tools such as employee surveys, focus groups, exit interviews, and grievances filed, an audit can increase awareness of perceived age discrimination (Ensher, Grant-Vallone, & Donaldson, 2001; Jonker & Ziekemeyer, 2005; Kunze et al., 2011).

AARP provides a useful workforce assessment tool (see http://www.aarp-workforceassement.org) for HR managers that helps them to determine how retiring employees will affect their organization, the resulting skill shortages, ways to create an attractive work environment for qualified workers of all ages, tools for managing a multigenerational workforce, and branding strategies to recruit and retain first-rate talent (see also Brown, 2012).

The changing age structure of the workforce makes succession planning especially important. Such planning, if successful, enables an organization to prepare for and replace key personnel who leave their positions. As older workers retire or transition to short-term employment arrangements, their successors need to be ready to step in as replacements. Succession planning is key to an organization's continued and future success. Three brief case examples are provided below as models of successful succession planning.

First, a private-sector example is Johnson and Johnson Company, a manufacturer and distributor of consumer goods with over 114,000 employees operating in different parts of the world. The company's succession planning program, as described by Cantoria (2010), is organized around two committees: the nominating and corporate governance committee (NCGC), composed of the CEO and an oversight group, and a selection committee. The selection committee identifies, evaluates and selects candidates with potential who are then presented to the higher-level NCGC for review. The NCGC then reviews the employees with the greatest potential as future managers. In making distinctions among candidates, two groups of employees are selected: one for future top management positions and the other as "change drivers" to provide leadership for current or future business initiatives. Each selected candidate is helped to map out a personal development plan including both individual and managerial training. The curriculum is different for the "change drivers," who are groomed for both business sector or departmental responsibilities and more general exposure to the company's overall operations and manufacturing processes. As a consequence of Johnson and Johnson's succession planning program, half of the company's CEO's have been promoted from within the organization's staff. This two-pronged strategy has helped to ensure a smooth leadership transition within the company (Cantoria, 2010).

A second successful approach to succession planning is at IBM. A distinctive feature of people management at IBM is the use of a personal business contract (PBC) and an individual development plan (IDP). As summarized by Bilmes and Gould (2009), the contract and the plan together enable top management to prepare for effective leadership transition. The PBC aids in succession planning because each employee draws up a contract showing his or her performance plans and how they fit with overall corporate goals. The contracts are used in performance assessments with grading across a range of performance achievements and links to the pay structure. The IDP is separate from the PBC and designed to aid employees in their short- and long-term career and training needs. This plan also links to company goals and tracks competency mastery and certifications over time. Careful review by top executives helps in plotting career moves aligned to employee needs and company requirements.

The Oklahoma Department of Corrections (DOC) provides a public sector example of succession planning. As is the case at Johnson and Johnson and IBM, leadership transitions are critical to individual and organizational success and growth. Key features of the Oklahoma DOC's succession planning model, according to Wilkerson (2007), involve (a) recruitment of candidates for leadership positions both formally and informally, ensuring that upcoming openings are known to all potential candidates; (b) rigorous interviews of the candidate with top management confirming selections; (c) performance feedback to both successful and unsuccessful candidates with reasons behind selection or rejection decisions; (d) provision of training and development experience to prepare for advancement; (e) managing transitions as a "learning journey" with ample opportunities for dialogue in preparation for increased responsibilities; and (f) a hands-on role for the department director in training and transition to assure top management commitment.

In each of these cases there was an organizational strategy to make sure that the transition would occur smoothly and that the successor would be well trained and qualified to assume top-level responsibilities. In anticipation of the retirement of aging managers, organizations are well advised to prepare for leadership transition well in advance of the exodus. A weak bench or pipeline of likely successors to leadership can greatly impede future performance.

Three actions broader HR professionals can consider when confronting changing age demographics in their workforce are identified by Pitt-Catsouphes, Smyer, Matz-Costa, and Kane (2007), including recruitment (selecting people from diverse age groups, hiring retirees, customizing benefit plans for older workers), engagement (employee participation in decision-making regarding their work, skill/competency development opportunities for workers of all ages, flexible work options), and retention (incentives to work beyond traditional retirement age, appreciate the benefits of a multigenerational workforce, supervisory training to manage in a diverse setting). A range of strategies can be adopted around these three focal functions. Beyond understanding the changing demography of the workplace, HR managers need to think strategically about how to deal with barriers facing mature workers, including age-related stereotypes.

Combating Age Stereotypes

HR professionals must be vigilant to ensure that age discrimination and age stereotyping—direct or covert—are avoided in the workplace. Respecting the experience and contribution of aging workers, recognizing and rewarding their contributions, and treating them with respect will show that they are valued by the organization. Providing opportunities for development, treating them fairly, and insuring a good fit between their job and skills will help them to stay engaged in their work. Access to training programs for managers, supervisors, and older workers is especially important. Managerial and supervisory awareness training can sensitize them to issues of an aging workforce, a first step in keeping age discrimination from gaining a foothold. As noted by James Woolover (2012, p. 115), "Organizations often adopt a parochial mindset that views older workers as durable goods with a limited life-span." Leadership training can address these issues and provide an arena for building a commitment to anti-age-discriminatory behavior and a positive view of diverse work climates on the part of managers and supervisors. Trainees should become aware that their explicit and implicit behaviors can affect older workers' attitudes, satisfaction, and performance at work. They should be helped to identify myths and stereotypes regarding the aging process, to recognize age stereotyping, and to appreciate the contributions of older workers. HR professionals could then monitor managerial and supervisory behaviors toward older employees, acknowledging and rewarding positive behaviors. Leaders need to be clear regarding their expectations about continuous learning and employee training, especially in the area of new technology. HR managers must be sure employees are aware of the consequences of not availing themselves of opportunities for ongoing training, particularly if it is a necessary condition for retention.

Eight strategies have been identified by Klatt (1999) and Woolever (2012) to be successful in training an aging workforce:

- Encourage older workers to engage in training and learning activities (e.g., job rotation, coaching).
- Apply the same training standards and evaluation instruments to older workers as well as young employees.
- Make sure trainees are in a comfortable setting with good lighting and acoustics.
- Provide personal attention from the trainer (e.g., small class size).
- Stress concrete concepts over abstract ideas, using simple, straightforward language.
- Offer practice-based, low-stress learning, especially in computer-based training.
- Create an open, self-paced environment allowing freedom for self-discovery.
- Respect trainees at all times and give continuous reinforcement.

For older workers, training programs can be customized to their needs, focus on renewing their critical skills, and provide them with new developmental challenges (modified tasks and roles). Training should stress that one is never too old to learn. Topics such as financial planning and investment, computer skills, and retirement planning are helpful. Refresher courses for older workers, using mature workers to train others, and offering tuition reimbursement are among best practices adopted by savvy employers.

To avoid age discrimination complaints and to create a positive work environment, employers should not collect unnecessary information about age and stereotype employees based on age. Job descriptions should contain factual descriptions of the work to be done with measurable expectations for performance. Regular performance evaluations should be conducted and documented. Actions such as layoffs, terminations, reduced pay/benefits, or discipline should be grounded in objective evidence and avoid, where possible, differential adverse effects on older workers as compared to younger workers. Woolever (2012) suggests that, to avoid age-discrimination practices or age-based stereotyping, it is important for older workers to have a "point person" or contact on the ethics committee with whom they can discuss their ethical concerns. Obviously, to prevent age discrimination, HR managers must be conversant with both the statutory and common law regarding the rights of older workers.

Legal Compliance

As compliance officers, HR managers need to guarantee that those in the organization are observing criminal and regulatory laws protecting older workers. Preventing illegal behavior and minimizing inappropriate behavior requires development of workplace standards and procedures as well as norms and cultures of workplace etiquette.

It is important that HR professionals be aware that disparate impact theory is more narrowly interpreted under the ADEA than interpretations of Title VII of the Civil Rights Act. This means that coverage under the ADEA and an employer's liability are more limited in age discrimination cases than they are in cases brought under Title VII. Further narrowing the application is the "reasonable factor other than age" (RFOA) provision in the ADEA, meaning that employers may be using criteria and practices routinely that are legitimate even though they adversely impact older workers as a group (Cavico & Mujtaba, 2012). The employer must provide a "reasonable rationale" for such action (e.g., recruiting or reputation concerns, retaining high-skill employees, budgeting or performance-related considerations) with evidence that these factors other than age were "reasonable."

However, where it is clear that these rationales are used as ploys or subterfuge to remove older workers, it would be deemed unreasonable and illegal since age-related factors were the basis for action taken (Wood, Wood, Wood, & Asbury, 2010). One preventive approach employers can use to avoid or defend age discrimination lawsuits alleging disparate impact is to collect statistical data (e.g., prior to a reduction in force) providing evidence that the impact would not disproportionately have an adverse impact on older vs. younger employees. Used properly, such analysis could reduce the employer's risk of age-related litigation (Birk, 2008).

Other preventive approaches linked to age-related disabilities have been identified by Tishman and her colleagues (2012), including ergonomic design for older workers to avoid injuries, job analysis of functions that can put people at risk, assistive technology, job accommodations, and training, as well as wellness and integrated health promotion. Providing a supportive work environment is an important step in making mature workers comfortable, satisfied, and productive.

Performance Enhancement

Employers can take actions to capitalize on the contributions of older workers. Some ways to do so include targeting and recruiting older workers, welcoming older workers back to the workforce, and offering customized training for aging workers that is sensitive to adult learning styles and taught at an appropriate pace. The knowledge, skills, and experience of older workers can be helpful when they are put in roles such as mentors, coaches, mediators, and educators. Where necessary, making adaptations like assistive technology can improve the performance of older workers who require such aids (e.g., magnifiers, amplifiers). Failure to provide reasonable accommodations to older workers is second only to termination as a cause cited in discrimination charges filed under ADEA and ADA (Bjelland et al., 2009; Tishman et al., 2012). Providing phased retirement programs, educational benefits, part-time options, telecommuting and flexible work schedules can be valuable perks for aging workers. Indeed, a survey in 2012 of workers aged 50+ reports that 62% of respondents rated flextime as "very important" or "somewhat" important (Brown, 2012, p. 2). Customized benefits, financial advice, and competitive compensation are important as well (see Cavico & Mujtaba, 2012; Mujtaba & Cavico, 2010; Wood et al., 2010).

Workplace flexibility can take many forms, as discussed by Tishman and colleagues (2012), including work hours (reduced hours, job sharing, part time), work schedule options (flex schedule, compressed workweek), career flexibility (occupational shift, phased retirement), flexi-place, flexible employment relationships (contracting, project assignments, temporary work, deferred retirement), task flexibility, and flexible benefits (cafeteria style). The federal government's Partnership for Public Service program provides an example of efforts to assist older workers by helping to:

> promote job opportunities for older workers at federal agencies; match skill sets and experience; streamline the hiring processes, when possible; provide career transition resources, such as how-to guides and networking events; encourage flexible work arrangements; and help establish mentoring programs and other friendly on-boarding practices. (quoted in Tishman et al., 2012, p. 17)

Hiring practices targeting mature workers could involve recruiting materials designed to reflect an age-diverse workforce, creating alumni programs whereby mature or retired workers help train younger employees, stressing that "retirees are welcome" when recruiting, establishing partnerships with RetirementJobs.com and Operation A.B.L.E., capitalizing on senior groups when recruiting, and establishing a database of retirees who may want part-time work (see AARP, 2008). Many age-sensitive organizations implement phased retirement programs that allow employees to transition from full- to part-time work; others institute "work-to-retire" programs that encourage retirement over a phased-in period (e.g., 3 years); still others let older workers test their readiness for retirement by allowing them to try it with the option of returning to full-time employment if the trial proves unsuccessful.

Competitive compensation, solid benefits, and tailored financial advice are especially important, as indicated in research by Brown (2012, p. 1), who found that "financial reasons such as the need for money or health insurance" was the main reason workers over age 50 are working or seeking employment, while only one in five work or seek employment for "non-financial reasons such as enjoyment or the desire to be productive." Eight in ten respondents to the survey indicated that employer-provided health-care, a retirement plan, and paid time off were critical to their decision of whether to remain on the job or accept a job offer. Attention to such matters by HR professionals should pay dividends in retention of older workers.

Towers Perrin (2007, pp. 17–19) has identified eight useful strategies for administrators to use in creating an age-friendly workplace, including:

- Offer workers maximum work flexibility to respond to the changing needs of the workforce in all stages of the employment lifecycle.
- Create healthier work environments, ergonomic working conditions, and additional access to health promotion programs.
- Promote visible leadership related to aging workforce issues.
- Provide management training that enables leaders to recognize the unique needs of various employee groups while teaching them how to manage and lead a multigenerational workforce.
- Conduct research related to employees to aid in the understanding of employee behavior, changes in employee perceptions and needs, and the effectiveness of organizational investments and workplace programs.
- Eliminate age-related stereotypes and empower innovative thinking throughout the workforce.
- Focus performance requirements on job-related and not age-related characteristics for hiring, promotion, and/or retention.
- Devote careful attention to strategic talent deployment issues through ensuring equality of opportunity training and development and providing lifelong learning and growth to employees of all ages to maximize individual and organizational performance.

Fortunately, many organizations are following these guidelines; some have received special recognition for their exemplary policies and practices related to mature workers.

BEST PRACTICE EXEMPLARS

Many of the HRM strategies previously mentioned are currently in use by public, private, and nonprofit organizations. In 2011 the AARP recognized the Best Employers for Workers Over 50 in non-U.S. settings. These award-winning employers and their best practices are shown in Table 9.1. In addition to practices already mentioned, these organizations also stress

TABLE 9.1 AARP 2011 Best Employers for Workers Over 50

Best Practice	1*	2	3	4	5	6	7	8	9	10	11	12	13	14	15
Flexible Work Schedules, pensions and/or Accounts		X		X				X	X		X				X
Personalized Retirement Models	X								X	X					
Well-Balanced Age Structure	X		X												
Health Promotion and Diversity Management	X	X	X							X	X		X	X	X
Employability Training	X														
Family Care-Giving Leaves		X		X											
Reintegration to Return to Work		X		X	X										
Strategic Plan for Aging Workforce			X												
Individual Capacity Building Options				X											
Training/Life Long Learning Targeting Older Workers					X		X							X	X
Alternate Position Options						X					X	X			
Work Ability and Risk Assessment Profiles							X						X		
Mixed Age Work Teams								X							
Age-Sensitive Work Atmosphere								X							
Work-Life Balance										X		X			
Mentor Programs for Older Workers												X			

Source: Chart adapted from Ciampa and Chernesky (2011)

* 2011 Award Winning Organizations
  1. BMW Group: Munich, Germany
  2. Bundesagentur Fur Arbeit: Nurnberg, Germany
  3. Centrica plc: Windsor, United Kingdom
  4. Daikin Industries: Osaka, Japan
  5. DB Services: Berlin, Germany
  6. DSW 21: Dortmund, Germany
  7. Elkerliek Hospital: Helmond, Netherlands
  8. Jena-Optronik, Gmbh: Jena, Germany
  9. Lam Soon Edible Oils: Shah Alam, Malaysia
  10. Marks and Spencer plc: London, England
  11. National Australia Bank Limited: Melbourne
  12. National Environment Agency: Singapore
  13. Raffles Institution: Singapore
  14. Salzburg AG for Energie, Verkehr und Telekommunikation: Salzburg, Austria
  15. The Cooperative Group: Manchester, United Kingdom

mixed-age work teams, family care-giving leaves, and risk assessment profiles. Several organizations incorporate multiple strategies simultaneously, and some strategies are used widely across organizations (e.g., flexible work schedules, pensions and/or accounts, and health promotion and diversity management).

Three U.S.-based organizations, in particular, have been singled out for special recognition for their efforts on behalf of older workers (AARP, 2013). The top three-ranked organizations profiled in Table 9.2 have repeatedly won awards in recent years: National Institutes of Health (Bethesda, MD), Scripps Health (San Diego, CA), and Atlantic Health Systems (Morristown, NJ). As noted, they have won AARP awards numerous times and have substantial numbers of workers age 50 and over, who have on average spent 15 to 18 years with their employer. Each of the organizations engages in extensive recruitment efforts for older workers, has a workplace culture with opportunities for continuous employee development, offers generous benefits and workplace flexibilities, and provides retirees opportunities to remain engaged with the organization. These best practices provide positive models of what can and should be done to create an employee-friendly environment for older workers.

CONCLUSIONS

The changing age structure of the American workforce requires creative responses from policymakers, organizational executives, and HR professionals. The role of HR professionals is pivotal if attitudes, policies, and procedures are to be adopted or adapted to meet the needs of a graying workforce. The barriers to fair and equitable treatment are formidable where negative stereotypes, prejudice, and discrimination are widespread. The ADEA, though well intentioned, has fallen short in achieving its purpose of rooting out discrimination so that older workers and job applicants can be judged on their abilities and not just their age. Judicial interpretations have further weakened the impact of the law, and regulatory enforcement has been narrowly focused and marginally successful. State laws, while generally stronger than the ADEA, vary considerably from state to state, and the strength of the laws has had little impact on reducing negative effects on older workers of the economic downturn.

In combination, these developments raise the stakes for employers and HR managers who must confront the results of the changing age structure of the workforce on a daily basis. If the implications of age-related demographic shifts are to be understood, legal compliance is to be assured, age stereotypes are to be effectively combated, and organizational performance is to be enhanced, it will be up to the employers working with their HR professionals who will be in the forefront of such efforts. As John F. Kennedy said, "There are risks and costs to a program of action, but they are far less than the long-term risks and costs of comfortable inaction" (quoted in Bowden, 2011, p. 271). Table 9.3 provides

TABLE 9.2 Profile of Three Exemplary Organizations Responding to Older Workers

Employer	2013 Rank	Number of Years Won	Percent of Workforce Age 50+	Average Tenure of Employees Age 50+	Best Practices			
					Recruiting	Workplace Culture and Opportunities	Benefits	Retiree Opportunities
National Institutes of Health (Bethesda, MD)	1	4	47%	18.4 years	• Participates in annual 50+ job fair • Notifies recent NIH retirees of current job openings	• Tuition reimbursement, in-house classroom training, online training, certification classes, reimbursement for professional dues • Average of 8 hours of training per year • Formal job rotation and mentoring programs • Free on-site, low-impact exercise classes	• Health benefits for retirees: individual and spouse medical, drug, dental, long-term care, and death benefit coverage; Employee Assistance Program • Wellness benefits including flu shots, health screenings, health club discounts, weight loss programs, and stress management training • "Fit Plus Program" that supports the needs of employees age 50+ on fitness regimens • Regular financial planning seminars	• Website with employment opportunities exclusively for retired federal employees • Invitations to organization events • Ongoing access to retirement planning workshops • Temporary work assignments • Consulting/contract work • Telecommuting • Full- and part-time work

continued

TABLE 9.2 Profile of Three Exemplary Organizations Responding to Older Workers (continued)

Employer	2013 Rank	Number of Years Won	Percent of Workforce Age 50+	Average Tenure of Employees Age 50+	Best Practices			
					Recruiting	Workplace Culture and Opportunities	Benefits	Retiree Opportunities
							• Pre-retirement classes • Lifecycle funds • Flextime, compressed work schedules, job sharing, telecommuting, formal phased retirement	
Scripps Health (San Diego, CA)	2	8	36%	15 years	• Uses senior placement agencies • Posts positions on career websites intended for seniors • Hires former experienced employees through the	• Tuition reimbursement, in-house classroom training, online training, certification classes, department-based training, new leader orientation, reimbursement for professional dues	• Health benefits for retirees: individual and spouse medical, drug, vision, dental long-term care, and death benefit coverage; Employee Assistance Program • Wellness benefits including flu shots, health screenings, health club discounts, weight	• Dedicated retiree relations officer • Invitations to organization events • Ongoing access to retirement planning workshops • Temporary work assignments • Consulting/contract work • Telecommuting

continued

TABLE 9.2 Profile of Three Exemplary Organizations Responding to Older Workers (continued)

Employer	2013 Rank	Number of Years Won	Percent of Workforce Age 50+	Average Tenure of Employees Age 50+	Best Practices			
					Recruiting	Workplace Culture and Opportunities	Benefits	Retiree Opportunities
					Scripps Alumni Program	• Average of 40 hours of training per year • Formal job rotation and mentoring programs • PSD Incentive program recognizes and rewards long service and strong attendance (and was established in response to feedback from employee surveys) • College Fund 529 plan • Return to Work program offers individualized managed care by on-site nurse	loss programs, and stress management training • Staged retirement programs for employees age 55+ that allow employees to collect full-time benefits and to dip into retirement funds while working part-time • Financial hardship benefits: salary advances, PTO hardship withdrawals, financial hardship assistance with paid time off • Scripps Financial Fairs and Retirement/	• Full- and part-time work

continued

TABLE 9.2 Profile of Three Exemplary Organizations Responding to Older Workers (continued)

Employer	2013 Rank	Number of Years Won	Percent of Workforce Age 50+	Average Tenure of Employees Age 50+	Best Practices			
					Recruiting	Workplace Culture and Opportunities	Benefits	Retiree Opportunities
						to employees returning to work after illness or injury • On-site Employee Care Clinic	Financial Planning Seminars • Lifecycle funds • Flextime, compressed work schedules, job sharing, telecommuting, formal phased retirement	
Atlantic Health System (Morristown, NJ)	3	6	38%	15.9 years	• Uses senior placement agencies • Posts positions on career websites intended for seniors	• Tuition reimbursement, in-house classroom training, online training, certification classes, reimbursement of professional dues • Average of 75 hours of training per year	• Health benefits for retirees: individual and spouse medical, drug, vision, and death benefit coverage; Employee Assistance Program; free hospital/ facility coverage and lab and radiology services • On-site nurse	• Retirees in the 1000 Hour club can return to work either on a part-time or per diem basis three months after retirement—can work up to 999 hours annually and continue to collect retirement benefits

continued

TABLE 9.2 Profile of Three Exemplary Organizations Responding to Older Workers (continued)

Employer	2013 Rank	Number of Years Won	Percent of Workforce Age 50+	Average Tenure of Employees Age 50+	Best Practices			
					Recruiting	Workplace Culture and Opportunities	Benefits	Retiree Opportunities
						• Formal job rotation and mentoring programs • Free shuttle service from train stations and for employees attending wellness programs offsite • Working environment improvements for older employees (e.g., ergonomic evaluations, transitional duty program for those returning to work after illness or injury)	• practitioner for nonacute illnesses • Wellness benefits including flu shots, health screenings, health club discounts, weight loss programs, cancer prevention programs, and stress management training • Free Focus on Your Financial Future Workshops • Lifecycle funds • Flextime, compressed work schedules, job sharing, formal phased retirement	• Health fairs with free screenings • Dedicated retiree relations officer • Invitations to organization events • Ongoing access to retirement planning workshops • Lifetime discounted meals at the hospital cafeterias • Temporary work assignments • Consulting/contract work • Telecommuting • Part-time work

TABLE 9.3 Selected HR Strategies to Manage an Aging Workforce

Demographic Understanding

- Age audits
- Aging profile analysis
- Workforce projections
- Succession management
- Conduct research to better understand employee behavior and changing employee needs
- Discuss with employees implications of
- population projections and graying workforce
- Show employees that older workers are important to the current and future economic health of the nation and organization
- Promote awareness that not all older workers wish to retire at normal retirement age
- Undertake studies to determine projected future retirement dates

Combating Age Stereotypes

- Diversity training (including an age awareness module)
- Mentoring opportunities for older workers
- Employee opinion surveys and focus groups
- Exit interviews
- Analyze patterns of employee grievances
- Support local diversity groups
- Promote open communication
- Gain senior management commitment
- Focus performance requirements on job-related and not age-related characteristics
- Include older workers on ethics committees
- Identify myths and inaccurate generalizations about the aging process
- Emphasize developing retention strategies

Legal Compliance

- Statutory requirements (ADEA, OWBPA, and state statutes)
- Court precedents
- Review HR policies and practices for actual or potential instances of disparate impact (e.g., benefit and retirement plans, layoffs, compensation schemes, hiring and promotion policies)
- Identify and document reasonable factors other than age for borderline policies and practices
- Establish data collection policies that exclude age-related information
- Keep detailed records of factors considered in the employment decision making process
- Change employment practices to avoid age
- Discrimination charges

Performance Enhancement

- Take advantage of and cultivate the skills and experience of older workers
- Acknowledge and reward loyalty
- Lower turnover
- Supervisor support
- Provide life-long learning opportunities
- Work flexibility (e.g., flextime, flexlocation, job sharing, part-time work, phased retirement)
- Personnel alignment
- Integrate training into recruitment
- Provide customized benefits
- Adopt assistive technologies
- Provide tailored financial advice
- Competitive compensation
- Implement wellness programs
- Offer employment options to older workers

a summary of selected HR strategies to manage an aging workforce. In summary, this chapter has examined background on the demographic trends, legal developments, barriers, and some practical strategies and exemplary practices that can help those in organizations to understand and act to prevent age-based discrimination.

ACKNOWLEDGMENTS

Special thanks to Alexander Ades whose valuable research assistance contributed to this chapter.

NOTES

1. Portions of this subsection are adapted from West (2010).
2. Portions of this subsection are adpated from West (2010).

REFERENCES

AARP. (2002). Recognizing age discrimination in employment. Retrieved from http://www.aarp.org/careers-tools/Articles/a2002-11-11-agediscrimination.html

AARP. (2008, December 30). Recruiting practices. Washington, DC: Author. Retrieved from http://www.aarp.org/work/employee-benefits/info/12-2008/recruiting_practices

AARP. (2009). *AARP bulletin survey on employment status of the 45+ population.* Retrieved from http://www.aarp.org/research

AARP. (2013). *Search AARP best employers for workers over 50.* Retrieved from http://www.aarp.org/work/2013-aarp-best-employers

Adecco USA. (2008, July 12). Survey: Age discrimination leading form of workplace discrimination. *Aging workforce news.* Retrieved from http://www.agingworkforcenews.com/2008/07.html

Billett, S. (2011). Promoting lifelong employability for workforce aged over 45: Singaporean workers' perspectives. *International Journal of Continuing Education and Lifelong Learning, 3*(2), 57–73.

Billett, S., Dymock, D., Johnson, G., & Martin, G. (2011). Last resort employees: Older workers' perceptions of workplace discrimination. *Human Resource Development International, 14*(4), 375–389.

Bilmes, L., & Gould, W. (2009). *The people factor.* Washington, DC: Brookings Institution.

Birk, M. (2008, April). RIFs: Use statistical analysis to avoid disparate impact based on age. *Legal Report (SHRM),* 5–8.

Bisom-Rapp, S., Frazer, A., & Sargeant, M. (2011). Decent work, older workers and vulnerability in the economic recession: A comparative study of Australia, the

United Kingdom, and the United States. *Employee Rights & Employment Policy Journal, 15*, 43–121.

Bisom-Rapp, S., & Sargeant, M. (2013). Diverging doctrine, converging outcomes: Evaluating age discrimination law in the United Kingdom and the United States. *Loyola University Chicago Law Journal, 44*, 717.

Bjelland, M. J., Bruyère, S. M., von Schrader, S., Houtenville, A. J., Ruiz-Quintanilla, A., & Webber, D. A. (2010). Age and disability employment discrimination: Occupational rehabilitation implications. *Journal of Occupational Rehabilitation, 20*(4), 456–471.

Blau, D., & Shvydko, T. (2007, August). *Labor market rigidities and the employment behavior of older workers.* Discussion Paper No. 2996.

Booth, A., Chen, Y., & Zoega, G. (2002). Hiring and firing: A tale of two thresholds. *Journal of Labor Economics 20*(2), 1–32.

Bowden, P. (2011). *Telling it like it is.* Seattle, WA: CreateSpace/Author.

Brown, S. K. (2012). *What are older workers seeking? An AARP/SHRM survey of 50+ workers.* Retrieved from http://www.aarp.org/content/dam/aarp/research/surveys_statistics/econ/2012/What-Are-Older-Workers-Seeking-An-AARP-SHRM-Survey-of-50-Plus-Workers-AARP.pdf

Bureau of Labor Statistics. (2009). *Labor force statistics from the current population survey.* Retrieved from http://www.bls.gov

Butler, T. H., & Berret, B. A. (2012). A generation lost: The reality of age discrimination in today's hiring practices. *Journal of Management and Marketing Research, 9*, 1–11.

Cantoria, C. (2010). Actual examples of succession planning in entrepreneurship. Retrieved from http://www.brighthub.com/office/human-resources/articles/98380.aspx

Cappelli, P. (2009, April 12). Qualified. Yes. Expensive? No. *New York Times.* Retrieved from http://www.nytimes.com/2009/04/12

Cavico, F. J., & Mujtaba, B. (2012). Age discrimination in the American workplace: Legal analysis and recommendations for employers and employees. *International Review of Social Sciences and Humanities, 3*(2), 161–185.

Chou, R. J.-A., & Choi, N. G. (2011). Prevalence and correlates of perceived workplace discrimination among older workers in the United States of America. *Ageing & Society, 31*(6), 1051–1070.

Ciampa, E., & Chernesky, R. (2011). Creating supportive workplace environments for older workers. In P. Brownell & J. Kelly (Eds.), *Ageism and mistreatment of older workers: Current realities, future solutions* (pp. 93–112). Dordrecht, The Netherlands: Springer.

Duncan, C. (2003). Assessing anti-ageism routes to older worker re-engagement. *Work, Employment & Society, 17*(1), 101–120.

Elkins, T. J. (2012). New HR challenges in the dynamic environment of legal compliance. In S. Werner (Ed.), *Managing human resources in North America: Current issues and perspectives* (pp. 44–59). New York, NY: Routledge.

Ensher, E. A., Grant-Vallone, E. J., & Donaldson, S. I. (2001). Effects of perceived discrimination on job satisfaction, organizational commitment, organizational citizenship behavior, and grievances. *Human Resource Development Quarterly, 12*(1), 53–72.

Feder, J. (2010). *The Age Discrimination in Employment Act (ADEA): A legal overview* (No. RL34652). Washington, DC: Congressional Research Service.

Finkelstein, L. M., & Farrell, S. K. (2007). An expanded view of age bas in the workplace. In K. S. Shultz & G. A. Adams (Eds.), *Aging and work in the 21st century*. Mahwah, NJ: Lawrence Erlbaum.

Fiske, S. T. (2004). *Social beings: Core motives in social psychology*. Hoboken, NJ: John Wiley & Sons.

Fleischer, R. A. (2009, July 13). Another bad right turn by the Supreme Court. *The Miami Herald*, p. 7G.

Gielen, A. (2009). Working hours flexibility and older workers' labor supply. *Oxford economic papers. 61*(2), 240–274.

Gregory, R. F. (2001). *Age discrimination in the American workplace: Old at a young age*. Piscataway, NJ: Rutgers University Press.

Gross v. FBL Financial Services, 129 S. Ct. 2343 (2005).

Harper, M. C. (2012). Reforming the Age Discrimination in Employment Act: Proposals and prospects. *Employee Rights & Employment Policy Journal, 16*(1), 13–49.

Hazen Paper v. Biggins, 507 U.S. 604, 611 (1993).

Hursh, N., Lui, J., & Pransky, G. (2006). Maintaining and enhancing older worker productivity. *Journal of Vocational Rehabilitation, 25*, 45–55.

Jackson, H. (2010). HR and the aging workforce: Two CEO points of view. *HR Magazine, 55*(10), 11–14.

Jackson, M. A. (2013). Counseling older workers confronting ageist stereotypes and discrimination. In P. J. Brownell & J. J. Kelly (Eds.), *Ageism and mistreatment of older workers: Current reality, future solutions* (pp. 135–144). Dordrecht, The Netherlands: Springer.

Johnson, R. (2009). Employment opportunities at older ages: Introduction to the special issue. *Research on Aging, 31*(1), 3–16.

Jonker, B., & Ziekemeyer, M. (2005). Wake up call—Human Resource Management (HRM): An orientation on company models anticipating ageing. *International Congress Series, 1280*, 371–376.

Kentucky Retirement Systems v. EEOC, 128 S. Ct. 2361 (2008).

Kimel v. Florida Board of Regents 528 U.S. 62 (2000) Klatt, B. (1999). *The ultimate training workshop handbook: A comprehensive guide to leading successful workshops and training programs*. New York, NY: McGraw-Hill.

Kromer, B., & Howard, D. (2013). Labor force participation and work status of people 65 years and older. *American Community Survey Briefs*. Washington, DC: U.S. Census Bureau.

Kunze, F., Boehm, S. A., & Bruch, H. (2011). Age diversity, age discrimination climate and performance consequences—A cross organizational study. *Journal of Organizational Behavior, 32*(2), 264–290.

Kurz, K., Buchholz, S., Veira-Ramos, A., Rinklake, A., & Blossfeld, H. (2011). Comparing late working life in Europe and the U.S.: The development of social inequalities in times of globalization and aging societies. In H. Blossfeld, S. Buchholz, & K. Kurz (Eds.), *Aging populations, globalization, and labor market* (pp. 311–325). Northampton, MA: Edward Elgar.

Meacham v. Knolls Atomic Power Laboratory, 128 S. Ct. 2395 (2008).

Mujtaba, B., & Cavico, F. J. (2010). *The aging workforce: Challenges and opportunities for human resource professionals.* Davie, FL: ILEAD Academy.

Neumark, D. (2008). *Reassessing the age discrimination in employment act.* Washington, DC: AARP.

Neumark, D., & Button, P. (2013). *Did age discrimination protections help older workers weather the Great Recession?* (No. Working Paper 19216). National Bureau of Economic Research. Retrieved from http://www.nber.org/papers/w19216.pdf?new_window=1

Neumark, D., & Song, J. (2011). *Do stronger age discrimination laws make Social Security reforms more effective?* (No. Working Paper 17467). National Bureau of Economic Research. Retrieved from http://www.nber.org/papers/w17467.pdf?new_window=1

Perrin, T. (2007). *AARP profit from experience: Perspectives of employers, workers, and policy-makers in the G7 countries on the new demographic realities.* Washington, DC: AARP.

Pitt-Catsouphes, M., Smyer, M., Matz-Costa, C., & Kane, K. (2007). *National study of business strategy and workforce development.* Boston, MA: Sloan Center on Aging and Work, Boston College. Retrieved from http://www.bc.edu/content/dam/files/research_sites/agingandwork/pdf/publications/RH04_National-Study.pdf

Price Waterhouse v. Hopkins 490 U.S. 228, 250 (1989).

Roscigno, V. J. (2010). Ageism in the American workplace. *Contexts, 9*(1), 16–21.

Rothenberg, J. Z., & Gardner, D. S. (2011). Protecting older workers: The failure of the Age Discrimination in Employment Act of 1967. *Journal of Sociology & Social Welfare, 38*(1), 9–30.

Smith v. City of Jackson, 544 U.S. 228 (2005).

Snape, E., & Redman, T. (2003). Too old or too young? The impact of perceived age discrimination. *Human Resource Management Journal, 13*(1), 78–89. doi:10.1111/j.1748-8583.2003.tb00085.x

Society for Human Resource Management. (2013). *SHRM workplace forecast.* Alexandria, VA: Author.

Tishman, F. M., Van Looy, S., & Bruyere, S. M. (2012). *Employer strategies for responding to an aging workforce.* New Brunswick, NJ: NTAR Leadership Center.

Tracey, A. M. (2009). Still crazy after all these years? The ADEA, the Roberts Court, and reclaiming age discrimination as differential treatment. *American Business Law Journal, 46*(4), 607–661.

U.S. Bureau of the Census (2012, March). Age distribution on workers in private and government sector. 2012. Current Population Survey (CPS). (Annual Social and Economic Supplement). www.census.gov

U.S. Bureau of the Census. (2012, December 12). U.S. census bureau projections show a slower growing, older, more diverse nation a half century from now. Retrieved from http:www.census.gov/newsroom/releases/archives/population/cb12-243.html

U.S. Equal Employment Opportunity Commission. (2013a). ADEA (includes concurrent charges with Title V11, ADA and EPA) FY 1997-FY 2012. Retrieved from www1.eeoc.gov//eeoc/statistics/enforcement/adea.cfm?

U.S. Equal Employment Opportunity Commission. (2013b). EEOC Litigation Statistics, FY 1997 through FY 2012. Retrieved from http://www1.eeoc.gov//eeoc/enforcement/litigation.cfm?

West, J. (2010). Managing an aging workforce: Trends, issues and strategies. In S. Condrey (Ed.), *Handbook of human resource management in government* (3rd ed., pp. 171–197). San Francisco, CA: Jossey-Bass.

West, J. (2012). Employee-friendly policies and development benefits for millennials. In W. Sauser & R. Sims (Eds.), *Managing human resources for the millennial generation* (pp. 201–228). Charlotte, NC: Information Age Publishing.

West, J. (forthcoming). Ethics and human resource management. In S. Hays, R. Kearney, & J. Coggburn (Eds.), *Public human resource management: Problems and prospects* (6th ed.).

West, J., & Bowman, J. (2008). Employee benefits: Weighing ethical principles and economic imperatives. In C. Reddick & J. Coggburn (Ed.), *Handbook of employee benefits and administration* (pp. 29–54). Boca Raton, FL: CRC Press.

Wilkerson, B. (2007). Effective succession planning in the public sector. *Watson-Wyatt Worldwide.* Retrieved from http://www.4cleanair.org/chicago/EffectiveSuccessionPlanningforPublic.pdf

Wilson, K. L. (2012). Age Discrimination in Employment Act of 1967 (ADEA). In R. K. Prescott (Ed.), *Encyclopedia of human resource management: Key topics and issues* (Vol. 1, pp. 17–23). San Francisco, CA: Pfeiffer.

Wood, S. G., Wood, M. A. Q., Wood, S. Q., & Asbury, R. A. (2010). Section III.C: Labor law: Prohibition on age discrimination in labor relations. *American Journal of Comparative Law, 58*(1), 377–412.

Woolever, J. (2012). Human resource departments and older adults in the workplace. In P. J. Brownell & J. J. Kelly (Eds.), *Ageism and mistreatment of older workers: Current reality, future solutions* (pp. 111–134). Dordrecht, The Netherlands: Springer.

Yeatts, D. E., Folts, W. E., & Knapp, J. (2000). Older workers' adaptation to a changing workplace: Employment issues for the 21st century. *Educational Gerontology, 26*(6), 565–582.

CHAPTER 10

THE CONTINUING DEVELOPMENT OF THE LAW ON SEXUAL HARASSMENT

William J. Woska

INTRODUCTION

Title VII of the Civil Rights Act of 1964 (Title VII) makes it "an unlawful employment practice for an employer...to discriminate against any individual with respect to his compensation, terms, conditions, or privileges of employment, because of such individual's race, color, religion, sex, or national origin" (Civil Rights Act of 1964). The use of the term "sex" was not included in Title VII legislation first proposed to Congress. It was not until the legislation was being debated on the House floor that "sex" was added to prevent discrimination against another minority group—women (Freeman, 2008). Initially only intended to provide protection for women from discrimination, the prohibition of sex discrimination applied to both males and females.

The term "sexual harassment" did not originate until several years later. The term was used by women's groups in Massachusetts in the early 1970s. The term was further used in a report to the president and chancellor of

Legal and Regulatory Issues in Human Resources Management, pages 207–227
Copyright © 2015 by Information Age Publishing
All rights of reproduction in any form reserved.

the Massachusetts Institute of Technology in 1973 addressing various forms of gender issues (Rowe, 1973).

In the years immediately following the passage of Title VII, sexual harassment claims were rarely brought under the statute, and when they were, courts dismissed them, reasoning that Title VII was not applicable. Finally, in the mid 1970s, courts began to accept sexual harassment as a form of gender discrimination under Title VII.

The Early Years

There are many stories that led to the development of the law on sexual harassment. For example, consider the librarian who worked as a waitress while pursuing her master's degree who was regularly "patted on the butt" by the restaurant manager as she waited on tables. When she asked him to stop he informed her that it was a way of indicating that she was doing a good job and she could either "like it or leave," meaning that she could either continue working or quit. When she complained to the owner of the restaurant, he laughed and asked if "it felt good." Then there is the young nurse who was continuously propositioned by several doctors. The bus driver who was continuously called "honey" or "sweetheart" by her supervisor, and the office worker who was told that if she wants a promotion, working hard is not as important as being cooperative and having fun.

Are these examples of sexual harassment? Sometimes the line is fuzzy and you stay quiet. Other times it is obvious and you are forced to act. The common denominator in the several stories is that all the individuals who were placed in uncomfortable positions were in the workplace, and all were women. Furthermore, they were placed in these situations by men who were in positions of authority.

The significance of the workplace is important with respect to sexual harassment. The offensive conduct in the workplace is often not all that dissimilar from conduct that is acceptable, or even desirable, outside of the work environment. This distinction between work and leisure is one of the reasons that understanding sexual harassment law continues to be an enigma today (Lindeman & Kadue, 1992).

The general misunderstanding of sexual harassment may be considered generational in nature. It is not unusual today that many men and women still refer to individuals of the opposite sex as "honey" or "sweetheart." A waitress in a restaurant refers to a customer as "honey." A man refers to a younger woman as "sweetheart." Other terms such as "babe," "hunk," and "doll" are also commonly used. Terms such as these were regularly used prior to the 1990s. Today they are offensive to many members of each sex and referred to as example of "environmental" sexual harassment in the workplace. The generations of individuals previously exposed to these terms sometimes have difficulty understanding and/or adjusting to the current environment with respect to the workplace.

The Beginning of Change

Some states have had laws addressing employment discrimination dating back to the 1940s. New York led the way in 1945, and within two years was followed by New Jersey, Massachusetts, and Connecticut. By the time Congress passed the Civil Rights Act of 1964, 22 states had already adopted administratively enforced "fair employment" legislation that prohibited labor market discrimination on the basis of race, color, creed, and national origin. The state laws laid the institutional and political groundwork for the federal legislation that eventually followed (Collins, 2000).

Title VII of the Civil Rights Act of 1964 (Title VII) covers private employers with 15 or more employees. Title VII prohibits discrimination on the basis of race, color, religion, national origin, or sex. The legislation was amended in 1972 by the Equal Employment Opportunity Act to provide coverage for local, state, and federal government employees (42 U.S.C. §2000e *et seq*). In 1978, Title VII's coverage was extended to enhance protection for pregnancy (42 U.S.C. §2000e *et seq*). In 1991, Congress again amended Title VII in an effort to strengthen federal civil rights laws, to provide for damages in employment discrimination cases, and to clarify provisions of the 1964 act relating to disparate impact actions (42 U.S.C. §1981a, §§2000e-2(k)–(n)). The Equal Employment Opportunity Commission (EEOC) is charged with administration and enforcement.

Although state legislation prohibiting discrimination in employment laws dates back to the 1940s and 1964 at the federal level, it was not until the 1970s that the area of harassment law began to develop (Gregg, 1989). The early cases were met with resistance by the courts. Initially, federal courts held that no cause of action existed under Title VII for sexually harassing conduct. Unwilling to deem the personal proclivities of employment discrimination by supervisors, the courts rendered decisions that lacked consistency without the benefit of legislative history or statutory guidance (Conte, 1992).

It is significant that the case that opened the door with respect to sexual harassment being recognized under Title VII was not a case involving sex, but rather national origin. In 1969 a charge of employment discrimination was filed by Josephine Chavez in the federal court in the Eastern District of Texas claiming that she was terminated because her employer created an offensive work environment for employees by segregating Hispanic clients (*Rogers v. Equal Employment Opportunity Commission*, 1970/1971). Since Mrs. Sanchez was an employee, the lower court found that she was not aggrieved and could not claim that she was terminated because of her national origin. Frustrated by unsuccessful efforts to secure voluntary production of materials considered relevant to its investigation, the EEOC invoked its statutory authority and issued upon the defendants a Demand for Access to Evidence (42 U.S.C. §2000e-8(a)). The district court granted partial enforcement of the demand, denying the EEOC's request for full access. The EEOC appealed to the Fifth Circuit.

The United States Court of Appeals, Fifth Circuit, considered the several issues. With respect to the connection between the defendant's discrimination against its patients and Mrs. Chavez's sensibilities, the court found "that the relationship between an employee and his working environment is of such significance as to be entitled to statutory protection." Title VII provides that it shall be an unlawful employment practice for an employer "to fail or refuse to hire or to discharge any individual, or otherwise to discriminate against any individual with respect to his compensation, terms, conditions, or privileges of employment, because of such individual's race, color, religion, sex, or national origin" (*Rogers v. Equal Employment Opportunity Commission*, 1971, pp. 234, 238). The majority opinion of the Fifth Circuit found that the Title VII "language evinces a Congressional intention to define discrimination in the broadest possible terms. Congress chose neither to enumerate specific discriminatory practices, nor to elucidate in extenso the parameter of such nefarious activities. Rather, it pursued the path of wisdom by being unconstrictive (sic), knowing that constant change is the order of our day and that seemingly reasonable practices of the present can easily become the injustices of the morrow" (*Rogers v. Equal Employment Opportunity Commission*, 1971, pp. 234–238). Furthermore, the court held that Title VII should be accorded a liberal interpretation in order to effectuate the purpose of Congress to eliminate the inconvenience, unfairness, and humiliation of ethnic discrimination.

The defendants further argued that Mrs. Chavez could not relate to an unlawful employment practice because the complaint alleges discrimination directed toward the patients of the defendant and not toward any employee. Therefore, Mrs. Chavez cannot complain that she is treated differently than any other employee. The Fifth Circuit held that the defendant's argument was not consistent with the interpretation recently accorded Title VII by the United States Supreme Court. In *Griggs v. Duke Power Co.* (1971), the Court held that the absence of discriminatory intent by an employer does not redeem an otherwise unlawful employment practice and that the thrust of Title VII's proscriptions is aimed at the consequences or effects of an employment practice and not at the employer's motivation. Hence, the defendant's failure to direct intentionally any discriminatory treatment toward Mrs. Chavez is simply not material to the finding of an unlawful employment practice.

The Fifth Circuit's decision in *Rogers* was important with respect to Title VII and defining discrimination in the broadest possible terms. "Knowing that constant change is the order of our day and that seemingly reasonable practices of the present can easily become the injustices of the morrow" (*Rogers v. Equal Employment Opportunity Commission,* 1971, p. 238) laid the foundation for the sexual harassment cases that followed.

SEX DISCRIMINATION AND TITLE VII

Ten years after the enactment of Title VII, the federal judiciary confronted its first Title VII case in which sexual harassment was the primary allegation. In *Barnes v. Train* (1974/1977), the court held that the complainant's refusal to have sexual relations with her supervisor, and the subsequent elimination of her job, was not discrimination. Rather, it was due to "the subtleties of an inharmonious personal relationship." The "alleged retaliatory actions of (appellant's) supervisor taken because (appellant) refused his request for an after hour affair are not the type of discriminatory conduct contemplated by the 1972 Act" (*Barnes,* 1974, memorandum opinion p. 2).

Upon appeal under a different name, *Barnes v. Costle,* the United States Court of Appeals, District of Columbia Circuit, reversed *Barnes v. Train* finding sex discrimination in violation of Title VII (*Barnes,* 1977). The court reviewed the legislative history of Title VII and noted that it provided no assistance in defining discrimination because of sex. It was not until Title VII was amended by the Equal Employment Opportunity Act of 1972 that discrimination because of sex was formally recognized as employment discrimination (42 U.S.C. §2000e *et seq*). Citing *Rogers,* the court recognized that Title VII must be construed liberally to achieve its objectives in addition to the need to recognize the continuing change that occurs in the workplace.

GUIDELINES ON SEXUAL HARASSMENT

Although all federal courts eventually recognized sexual harassment as a form of sex discrimination under Title VII, confusion surrounding the issue prompted the EEOC to develop the Guidelines on Discrimination Because of Sex (Guidelines). In 1980, the EEOC issued guidelines declaring sexual harassment as a form of sex discrimination (29 C.F.R. §1604). The guidelines established criteria for determining when unwelcome conduct of a sexual nature constitutes sexual harassment, defining the circumstances under which an employer may be held liable, and suggesting affirmative steps an employer should take to prevent sexual harassment (29 C.F.R.

§1604). The EEOC has applied the guidelines in its enforcement litigation, and these guidelines have been relied upon by the lower courts. The guidelines define sexual harassment as:

> Unwelcome sexual advances, requests for sexual favors, and other verbal or physical conduct of a sexual nature constitute sexual harassment when (1) submission to such conduct is made either explicitly or implicitly a term or condition of an individual's employment, (2) submission to or rejection of such conduct by an individual is used as the basis of employment decisions affecting such individual, or (3) such conduct has the purpose or effect of unreasonably interfering with an individual's work performance or creating an intimidating, hostile, or offensive working environment. (29 C.F.R. §1604.11)

The guidelines define two types of sexual harassment: "quid pro quo" and "hostile environment." The guidelines provide that "unwelcome" sexual conduct constitutes sexual harassment when "submission to such conduct is made either explicitly or implicitly a term or condition of an individual's employment" (29 C.F.R. §1604.11 (a) (1). "Quid pro quo harassment" occurs when "submission to or rejection of such conduct by an individual is used as the basis for employment decisions affecting such individual" (29 C.F.R. §1604.11 (a) (2). This could include a pay increase, a promotion, or some other benefit. A "hostile working environment" is found in situations when a supervisor, coworker, or client repeatedly acts in an intimidating or hostile manner creating an environment that causes an employee much anxiety. The hostile environment may include verbal comments such as referring to a woman as "babe, doll, or honey," pictures of a sexual nature, flirting, unwelcome touching, invading a person's space, unwelcome gifts, and other actions causing the individual discomfort and anxiety.

Meritor Savings Bank v. Vinson (1986)

Although courts are not required to follow the guidelines, they received significant recognition when the United States Supreme Court accepted it first sexual harassment case, *Meritor Savings Bank v. Vinson* in 1986. The primary question before the court was whether a hostile working environment created by unwelcome sexual behavior is a form of employment discrimination prohibited under Title VII when no economic loss or quid pro quo harassment exists.

Mechelle Vinson was employed as a teller at a Meritor Savings Bank. After being fired from her job, she sued Sidney Taylor, the vice president of the bank. Vinson charged that Taylor had coerced her to have sexual relations with him and made demands for sexual favors while at work. Vinson stated that she had sexual relations with Taylor 40 or 50 times. Additionally she testified that Taylor had touched her in public, exposed himself to her, and forcibly raped her multiple times. She argued that such harassment created a hostile working environment and a form of unlawful discrimination under Title VII. She sought injunctive relief in addition to compensatory and punitive damages against Taylor and the bank. The District Court for the District of Columbia denied relief (*Meritor Savings Bank v. Vinson,* 1980/1985/1986). The District of Columbia Circuit reversed (*Meritor Savings Bank,* 1985).

In a unanimous decision, the court found that Vinson's charges were sufficient to claim hostile environment sexual harassment, which must be severe or pervasive to support a claim. Additionally, the court established the standards for analyzing whether conduct was unlawful and employer liability. This case became the cornerstone for answering sexual harassment questions under Title VII. The court also provided credence to the guidelines and that hostile environment sexual harassment is a form of sexual harassment even when the victim suffers no economic loss (*Meritor,* 1986).

The *Meritor* decision was important in finding that Title VII was "not limited to 'economic' or 'tangible' discrimination," and that the intention of Congress was to "strike at the entire spectrum of disparate treatment of men and women in employment" (p. 64). The court pointed out that the guidelines specified that sexual harassment leading to non-economic injury was a form of sex discrimination prohibited by Title VII and that plaintiffs could establish a violation "by proving that discrimination based on sex has created a hostile or abusive work environment" (p. 65). For sexual harassment to be actionable, it must be sufficiently severe or pervasive "to alter the conditions of [the victim's] employment and create an abusive working environment" (p. 67).

Meritor was the beginning of several decisions by the court clarifying sexual harassment law under Title VII. Seven years after *Meritor,* a case addressing the issue of psychological damage was accepted by the Supreme Court.

Harris v. Forklift Systems, Inc. (1993)

In 1993 the United States Supreme Court accepted its second sexual harassment case, *Harris v. Forklift Systems, Inc.* (1993). The question before the court in *Harris* was whether sexual harassment must seriously affect the employee's psychological well-being in order to create an "offensive work environment" that violates Title VII.

The plaintiff, Teresa Harris, worked for two years as a rental manager for Forklift Systems, Inc., before resigning. Two months before her resignation she filed a complaint alleging that the company's president had created a hostile environment by, among other things, calling her a "dumb-ass woman" and asking her and other employees to retrieve coins from his front pants pockets (p. 19). The district court for the Middle District of Tennessee found that she was not protected by Title VII since she had not suffered any psychological injury on the job. The Court of Appeals for the Sixth Circuit affirmed the decision (*Harris,* 1992/1993).

The Supreme Court unanimously reversed the decision and remanded the case back to the lower court. Justice Sandra Day O'Connor's opinion made two important contributions to the law surrounding sexual harassment. First, O'Connor held that a person need not be damaged psychologically to demonstrate the presence of sexual harassment and a hostile work environment. The court did not reject that standard but instead found that a person deserved the protection of federal law before she suffered a nervous breakdown. However, it was not necessary for a plaintiff to show that her job performance had suffered as a result of the harassment. Instead, courts were expected to examine all workplace conditions including the frequency of discriminatory conduct, the severity of such conduct, and whether it was physically threatening or humiliating. In order to be actionable under Title VII, a sexually objectionable environment must be both objectively and subjectively offensive, one that a reasonable person would find abusive, and one that the victim in fact did perceive to be so (*Harris,* 1993).

Oncale v. Sundowner Offshore Services, Inc. (1996/1998)

Oncale was the first case addressing same-sex sexual harassment before the Supreme Court. The question before the court was whether same-sex sexual harassment claims were actionable under Title VII.

Joseph Oncale was a male oil rig worker who claimed that he was repeatedly subjected to sexual harassment by his male coworkers. Oncale was apparently harassed simply because he did not fit the stereotype his peers had of what he should be like. He complained to supervisory personnel but no remedial action was taken. Oncale filed a Title VII action in the district court for the Eastern District of Louisiana. The district court granted summary judgment to the defendants relying on a 1994 Fifth Circuit decision that harassment by a male supervisor of a male subordinate does not state a Title VII claim (*Oncale v. Sundowner Offshore Services, Inc.,* 1995/1996/1998). On appeal, the Fifth Circuit affirmed (1996).

The United States Supreme Court, in a unanimous decision, held that Title VII, banning on-the-job sexual harassment, applies when the harasser and the victim are the same sex. Justice Scalia, delivering the opinion for the Court stated: "We see no justification in the statutory language or our precedents for a categorical rule excluding same-sex harassment claims from the coverage of Title VII...merely because the plaintiff and defendant (or the person charged with acting on behalf of the defendant) are of the same sex" (*Oncale*, 1998, pp. 75, 79).

The court drew on its previous holding in *Meritor* to emphasize that Title VII "evinces a congressional intent to strike at the entire spectrum of disparate treatment of men and women in employment" (p. 78). The court rejected the notion that the harassing conduct should be motivated by sexual desire to support an inference of discrimination on the basis of sex (p. 80). The plaintiff must show, however, that the harasser's conduct was not "merely tinged with offensive sexual connotations, but actually constituted discrimination because of...sex" (p. 81). Conduct that is not severe or pervasive enough to create an objectively hostile work environment is beyond the reach of Title VII.

Faragher v. City of Boca Raton (1998)

The issue before the court in *Faragher* was whether an employer can be held liable under Title VII for the acts of an employee whose sexual harassment of subordinates has created a hostile work environment amounting to employment discrimination. Between 1985 and 1990, Beth Ann Faragher worked part time during the summer as a lifeguard for the City of Boca Raton. During this time she alleged that two of her supervisors created a "sexually hostile atmosphere" at the beach by repeatedly subjecting female lifeguards to "uninvited and offensive touching" by making lewd remarks and by speaking of women in offensive terms. Asserting that her supervisors were agents of the city, and that their conduct amounted to discrimination in the "terms, conditions, and privileges" of her employment, Faragher sought a judgment against the city for nominal damages, costs, and attorney's fees.

The district court for the Southern District of Florida found that the conduct of Faragher's supervisors was discriminatory harassment sufficiently serious to alter the conditions of her employment and constituted an abusive working environment. The court noted that the harassment was pervasive enough to support an inference that the city had "knowledge or constructive knowledge" (pp. 1552–1564) of it (*Faragher v. City of Boca Ratan*, 1994/1997/1998). The district court awarded Faragher one dollar in nominal damages on her Title VII claim. The Eleventh Circuit Court of Appeals reversed (*Faragher*, 1997).

The Supreme Court held that an employer is vicariously liable under Title VII for an actionable hostile environment caused by a supervisor. Additionally, such liability is subject to an affirmative defense looking to the reasonableness of the employer's conduct as well as that of the plaintiff victim. If no tangible employment action is taken, the employer may escape liability by establishing that (a) the employer exercised reasonable care to prevent and correct any harassing behavior and (b) that the plaintiff unreasonably failed to take advantage of the preventive or corrective opportunities that the employer provided (*Faragher*, 1998).

Burlington Industries, Inc. v. Ellerth (1996/1997/1998)

The issue before the Court in the *Ellerth* case was whether an employer should be liable for a supervisor's sexual harassment of an employee if the employee did not acquiesce to her supervisor's threats and suffered no adverse employment actions. The case is significant with respect to establishing an employer's liability for sexual harassment by a supervisor. Imposing liability on employers would shift the risk and burdens associated with sexual harassment from the employee to the employer. Shifting the burden would encourage employers to establish and disseminate policies and procedures against sexual harassment and to develop and implement training programs accordingly.

Kimberly Ellerth quit her job after 15 months as a salesperson in one of the defendant's worksites claiming that she had been subjected to constant sexual harassment by one of her supervisors consisting of offensive remarks and gestures. Ellerth placed particular emphasis on three incidents where her supervisor's comments could be construed as threats to deny her tangible job benefits. Ellerth refused all of her supervisor's advances, suffered no tangible retaliation, and was, in fact, promoted once. Moreover, she did not inform anyone in authority about her supervisor's conduct although she knew that the defendant had a policy against sexual harassment. In filing her lawsuit, Ellerth alleged that Burlington engaged in sexual harassment and forced her constructive discharge in violation of Title VII. The United States District Court, Northern District Illinois, Eastern Division, granted Burlington summary judgment (*Burlington Industries, Inc. v. Ellerth*, 1996/1997/1998). The Seventh Circuit Court of Appeals reversed (*Ellerth*, 1997).

The Supreme Court held that an employee who refuses the unwelcome and threatening sexual advances of a supervisor, but suffers no adverse, tangible job consequences, can recover against the employer without showing that the employer is negligent or otherwise at fault for the supervisor's actions. Furthermore, the employer is strictly liable (*Ellerth*, 1998). However, unfulfilled threats must meet the "severe or pervasive" test for sexual harassment (p. 754).

The *Ellerth* and *Faragher* cases were filed and argued separately before the Court. Both cases involved Title VII and were handed down by the Court on

June 26, 1998, each by a vote of 7 to 2. The effect of the two decisions was to make some lawsuits against employers easier to win while rewarding companies with effective anti-harassment policies by limiting their legal exposure.

Vance v. Ball State University, et al. (2008/2013)

Although *Vance* involves racial discrimination, the issue before the Court was: "who qualifies as a 'supervisor' when an employee asserts a Title VII claim for workplace harassment?" The question to be decided was left open from the Court's 1998 *Ellerth* and *Faragher* decisions.

The Court held in *Ellerth* that if the harasser is a supervisor and his/her harassment culminates in a tangible employment action (i.e., a significant change in employment status such as hiring, firing, failing to promote, reassignment with significantly different responsibilities, or a decision causing a significant change in benefits), the employer is strictly liable. But if no tangible employment action is taken, the employer may escape liability by establishing an affirmative defense as set forth in *Faragher*.

Maetta Vance was the only African American working in her department at Ball State University (BSU). In 2005 Vance began filing complaints with BSU alleging that a fellow employee, Saundra Davis, created a racially hostile work environment in violation of Title VII. The alleged hostile environment created by Davis included the use of racial epithets, references to the Klu Klux Klan, veiled threats of physical harm, and other troublesome comments. In 2006 she filed two complaints with the EEOC for race discrimination and, later, retaliation. After receiving her right-to-sue letter, she subsequently filed this action in the district court for the Southern District of Indiana alleging a range of federal and state discrimination claims. The district court granted summary judgment to BSU and dismissed the case. It held that BSU could not be held vicariously liable for Davis' alleged racial harassment against Vance because Davis could not "hire, fire, demote, promote, transfer, or discipline" Vance because she was not a supervisor (*Vance v. Ball State University, et al*, 2008/11/13). The Seventh Circuit Court of Appeals affirmed (*Vance*, 2011).

The Supreme Court ruled 5–4 in favor of upholding the judgment of the Seventh Circuit. The majority decision rejected the more expansive definition of "supervisor" adopted by EEOC and several circuit courts as someone authorized to either take tangible employment actions or direct the employee's daily work activities. Instead, the Court ruled that the term "supervisor" should be limited to one who is authorized by the employer to take tangible actions like hiring, firing, promoting, demoting, or reassigning employees to significantly different responsibilities (*Vance*, 2013).

The Supreme Court's decision in *Vance* not only impacts employment discrimination and harassment litigation, it also requires employers to proactively reexamine policies, training, and job descriptions to ensure the *Faragher/Ellerth* defense is available if litigation arises. Since the meaning of a "supervisor" for purposes of vicarious liability under Title VII is limited to individuals who are empowered by the employer to take tangible employment actions (to hire, fire, demote, promote, transfer, or discipline) against other employees, an employer may find its exposure to Title VII litigation has been reduced.

SEXUAL HARASSMENT—THE CONTINUING CHALLENGE

Women in Positions of Authority

Sexual harassment is a legal term created for the purpose of ending harassment and discrimination against women in the workplace. Although the term is constantly being redefined and extended in legislation and court decisions, the basic definition comes from the EEOC guidelines.

Sexual harassment may occur at all levels within an organization in relationships categorized as male-to-female, male-to-male, female-to-male, and female-to-female. Harassment often occurs because the harasser is in a position of leadership or authority that provides the necessary power to facilitate the harassing behavior. This type of harassment is considered quid pro quo harassment. Heather Hemming defined the power approach to sexual harassment as "a product of power differences between men and women in society and the workplace" (Hemming, 1985, pp. 67–79). Since the workplace is dominated by men in positions of authority, combined sexual harassment charges filed with the EEOC and state Fair Employment Practice Agencies (FEPAs) confirm that a large percentage of the complaints are predominately female against male (U.S. Equal Employment Opportunity Commission, 1997–2011). During the 2011 fiscal year, 83.7% of sexual harassment complaints were filed by women. However, the number of complaints filed by men has increased by almost 41% since 1997.

Since the turn of the century, women have made progress into positions of authority in the private and public sectors. Education is a major factor in preparing women for management positions in the workplace. Women now earn a majority of diplomas in fields men used to dominate, from biology to business (National Center for Educational Statistics, n.d., tables 27–31). Women account for about half of the enrollment in professional programs such as law, medicine, and optometry (National Center for Educational Statistics, n.d., tables 27–31). During the 2009–2010 academic year, women received 57% of baccalaureate degrees, 63% of master's degrees, and 53% of doctorate degrees from major colleges and universities (U.S. Department of Education, 2012, table A-47-2). Women make up more than 57% of both professional and related and service occupations (U.S. Department of Labor, 2010, table 11), the occupations expected to grow most rapidly from 2008 to 2018 (Lacey & Wright, 2009).

During the last decade the number of women in Congress has increased by 32%, from 60 to 78 in the House of Representatives, and from 14 to 20 in the United States Senate (Center for American Women and Politics, 2013). A woman became the Speaker of the House of Representatives in addition to a woman appointed as the chairwoman of the world's most powerful economic post, the Federal Reserve System. With the appointments of Sonia Sotomayer in 2009 and Elena Kagan in 2010 to the United States Supreme Court, the Court has three women justices, more than any other time in history.

Without question, women are obtaining a more influential role in business, education, law, and politics in the United States. It is unknown whether there will be a correlation between women in positions of authority and sexual harassment consistent with the historical trend of men in positions of authority. However, it is interesting to note that in 2010 the first sexual harassment cased filed by a man against a woman was decided by a federal circuit court of appeals. The Ninth Circuit found that a male employee was subjected to verbal or physical conduct of a sexual nature by a female co-worker that was unwelcome and was sufficiently severe or pervasive to alter the condition of the plaintiff's employment and created an abusive work environment (*Equal Employment Opportunity Commission v. Prospect Airport Services, Inc.*, 2010). The Ninth Circuit emphasized that the law requires employers to treat complaints of sexual harassment made by men with the same seriousness they apply to complaints by women (p. 1,001).

Nontraditional Sexual Harassment

While male-female sexual harassment cases have historically predominated, the reality is that same-sex and other forms of harassment are a growing trend. Workplace harassment includes out-of-office scenarios including business trips, offsite meetings, the internet, and other settings. In terms of the internet, federal and state governments have enacted laws to protect individuals from online sexual harassment, which falls under the umbrella of "cyberstalking" (see, e.g., California Civil Code 1708.7).

Cyberstalking or "cyberharassment" laws explicitly include electronic forms of communication within more traditional stalking or harassment laws. In addition, recent concerns about protecting minors from online bullying or harassment have led states to enact "cyberbullying" laws. Cyberstalking is the use of the internet, email or other electronic communications to stalk, and generally refers to a pattern of threatening or malicious behaviors.

Cyberstalking may be considered the most dangerous of the three types of internet harassment, based on posing a credible threat of harm.

Cyberharassment differs from cyberstalking in that it may generally be defined as not involving a credible threat. The term usually pertains to threatening or harassing email messages, instant messages, or to blog entries or websites dedicated solely to tormenting an individual. Some states approach cyberharassment by including language addressing electronic communications in general harassment statutes, while others have created stand-alone cyberharassment statutes.

Educating the General Public

During the last 25 years, employers have acquired considerable insight about the law of sexual harassment following a number of cases handed down by the United States Supreme Court. The State of California and several other states now have legislation requiring mandatory sexual harassment training for supervisors, managers, and other employees in positions of authority (see, e.g., California Government Code §12950.1). The media regularly report sexual harassment cases handed down by the courts. However, the law of sexual harassment continues to be confusing for many.

Unless there is a significant newsworthy event involving sexual harassment, the general public may not otherwise follow developments involving this area of law. Even today, more than a quarter century after the Supreme Court's *Meritor* decision, it is not unusual for women to refer to a man as a "hunk," or men referring to women as "chicks, babes, or dolls." A driving incident involving a woman may result in criticism by a man referring to the situation as involving a "woman driver." Many individuals have difficulty understanding that the use of derogatory terms specifically referring to an individual's sex may in fact be sexual harassment. A 2011 report addressing sexual harassment in middle and high schools makes reference to

> incidents that appear 'minor' such as sexual comments and jokes or being called gay or lesbian, may have a profound impact on the emotional well-being of some students. Feeling sick to one's stomach or being unable to concentrate at school may not be sufficiently severe, persistent, or pervasive for legal action, but it can certainly affect the educational experience. Sexual harassment in middle and high schools can be a problem long before it reaches the level of legal action. (Hill & Kearl, 2011)

In 1991 Clarence Thomas was nominated by President George H. W. Bush to a seat on the United States Supreme Court. During Thomas's confirmation hearings before the Senate Judiciary Committee, he was accused of sexual harassment by Anita Hill, a former employee. The allegation of sexual harassment was widely reported by the press. Although Thomas was subsequently confirmed by the full senate and seated as a justice on the Court, the publicity from the confirmation hearing was significant in educating the American public about sexual harassment in the workplace. In 1991 there were 6,886 charges of discrimination with EEOC involving sexual harassment. In 1992, the number increased to 10,577, a 53% increase that can be attributed to some extent to the Clarence Thomas confirmation hearings (U.S. Equal Employment Opportunity Commission, 1993–1994).

PREVENTING SEXUAL HARASSMENT: SOME BASIC STEPS FOR EMPLOYERS[1]

Prevention is the best tool for eliminating sexual harassment in the workplace. The EEOC (see 29 CFR 1604.11[f]) requires employers to "take all steps necessary to prevent sexual harassment from occurring," including raising the subject, expressing strong disapproval of harassment, developing appropriate sanctions against it, informing employees of their rights under Title VII, and developing methods to sensitize all concerned (Bradbery & Lally, 1998). Employers must clearly communicate to employees that sexual harassment will not be tolerated. The surest way to do this is by establishing an effective complaint or grievance procedure and taking immediate and appropriate action in response to every employee complaint. Some states, such as California, require employers to post sexual harassment policies in the workplace and communicate them to employees.

Employers should take these basic steps to discourage sexual harassment:

1. Develop a policy prohibiting sexual harassment. A written policy that expressly prohibits sexual harassment by all employees and nonemployees in the workplace is a critical component of prevention. The policy should include:
   a. A statement that sexual harassment will not be tolerated in the workplace.
   b. A definition of sexual harassment, including these elements:
      i. unwelcome sexual advances
      ii. requests for sexual favors
      iii. other verbal or physical conduct of a sexual nature directed toward an employee when submission or rejection of this conduct explicitly or implicitly affects an individual's employment, unreasonably interferes with an individual's work performance, or creates an intimidating, hostile or offensive work environment.

c. A procedure telling employees how and to whom to make a complaint. The most important element of a sexual harassment complaint procedure is identifying specific individuals to receive harassment complaints. These can be supervisors, human resources professionals, or other managers. More than one person should be designated to handle complaints to ensure that workers have a place to turn if the designated person is the harasser.

d. A statement that complaints will be investigated promptly and that appropriate actions will be taken against individuals found to have engaged in harassing conduct.

e. A statement indicating that the employer will maintain information in as confidential manner as possible. (Note: Avoid promising *absolute* confidentiality since employers need to investigate complaints, and this may necessitate telling those accused of harassment the names of their accusers so they can properly defend themselves.)

f. A statement promising that the employer will not retaliate against an individual for lodging a complaint nor allow any other employee to engage in retaliatory behavior toward a complainant. The employer should, however, retain the right to discipline or fire employees who knowingly lodge false complaints.

2. Effective communication of the policy statement to employees is essential. Workers have won cases against employers by showing, in part, that their harassment policies were tucked in a handbook, never discussed, and virtually unknown to employees. Employers should make sure all new and existing employees receive a copy of their organization's sexual harassment policy. Employees' signatures should be obtained on forms acknowledging receipt of the policy and promising to comply with it. To further ensure broad dissemination of its policy, an employer should:

   a. Post the policy on bulletin boards within each company facility
   b. Re-disseminate its sexual harassment policy at least annually
   c. Include the policy in personnel manuals or employee handbooks
   d. Discuss the policy at employee orientation meetings
   e. Discuss the policy during training programs.

Employee training on a company-wide basis is crucial to implementing an effective sexual harassment policy. The primary emphasis of sexual harassment training is on changing workers' behavior; the secondary emphasis is on changing their attitudes. Attitudinal changes are beneficial but optional; behavioral changes are essential.

Training most often consists of a series of presentations and workshops designed for three groups: (a) executive-level management, (b) supervisors and other managers, and (c) other employees. All workers should be included in the training programs, and attendance should be mandatory. Employers should keep a record of those employees who have attended the training.

In announcing the training program, it is important to indicate management's strong and positive support for it. Workers will not buy into the training if they see that managers do not.

In addition to the general training, supervisors and managers should be told how to receive, refer, and investigate complaints. This specialized training should include a detailed discussion of

- appropriate procedures for responding to complaints;
- appropriate procedures for reporting complaints to management and conducting prompt and fair investigations;
- management's obligations regarding harassment of which it knew or should have known;
- procedures for promoting confidentiality in the investigation process;
- procedures for balancing the interests of all parties, bearing in mind the potential damage to the reputations of the involved parties; and
- recordkeeping requirements

Supervisors and managers should attend periodic refresher courses on sexual harassment prevention and complaint procedures. Some states require mandatory sexual harassment training for supervisors and managers on a continuing basis (see e.g., California Government Code 12950 *et seq*).

ESTABLISHING A COMPLAINT PROCEDURE

An effective complaint procedure helps employers minimize or avoid liability. Employees who are aware of their organization's procedures usually are more inclined to file complaints or raise concerns within the organization than to turn to outside agencies or the courts. Further, employers may reduce their liability even when employees directly pursue external legal remedies if effective complaint procedures are in place and the employer has a track record of dealing effectively and fairly with employees.

Even if no one lodges a complaint, a company can be liable for a sexually charged environment if managers become aware of it through other channels. Tip-offs include pictures on cubicles, writing on bathroom stalls, rumors flying through the e-mail system, and gossip that sets the lunchroom abuzz. If managers see the pictures and read the writing, the company is considered to be "on notice," and it must respond. Likewise, if the chit-chat is pervasive and managers hear it, they cannot later feign ignorance or say they didn't try to stop the behavior because nobody complained.

Employers should make it easy for workers to bring forward harassment complaints. Employees should be assured that their complaints will be handled promptly and discreetly. They also should be assured that managers will not permit retaliation to be taken against workers who file sexual harassment complaints.

These elements should be a part of any employer complaint procedure:

- Training for all employees on how to lodge a complaint
- Training for supervisors and managers on how to spot and report potential problems
- Procedures for ensuring prompt investigations
- Procedures for documenting complaints
- Instructions for communicating with complainants
- Instructions for maintaining confidentiality as much as possible
- Procedures for submitting a written report detailing the investigator's conclusions and recommended corrective action

An employer must act immediately to stop harassment. Failure to take prompt remedial action to address harassment will result in employer liability.

Human resource management (HRM) professionals can more effectively help their organizations combat sexual harassment behavior through knowledge and prevention. It is important that those in leadership and management positions recognize the different types of harassment and the scenarios in which they occur. In situations where sexual harassment has already taken place, HRM professionals and others in positions of authority should be equipped with the tools to mitigate and meditate the issue. Furthermore, all HRM professionals and other supervisors and managers should have sexual harassment training in order to respond to complaints in the best possible way.

CONCLUSION

Although significant progress has been made in the courtroom and the workplace since the early cases in resolving sexual harassment issues, new issues will continue to surface. For example, claims of third-party sexual harassment are becoming more common. Third-party sexual harassment may consist of either an employee being harassed by a nonemployee, such as a client, or someone other than the employee receiving a benefit because of a sexual relationship with a person in a position of authority. The nonemployee sexual harassment may include any nonemployee such as a delivery person, customer, or other third party who sexually harasses an employee. An example of third-party harassment involving an employee who was not sexually harassed would be a situation where the supervisor provides his or her subordinate extra benefits because of a sexual relationship but the benefits were not available to another employee without acquiescing to a sexual relationship with the supervisor. This is a classic form of third-party quid pro quo sexual harassment. Third-party hostile environment sexual harassment would involve a supervisor providing extra benefits to a subordinate because of receiving sexual favors, impacting the motivation and work performance of other employees who are negatively affected. In either case, if the employer knew or should have known about the problem and failed to take immediate and appropriate corrective action, the employer may be liable (*Meritor,* p. 72).

"Unwelcomed behavior of a sexual nature" becomes "zero tolerance" for employers with respect to sexual harassment. Examples of sexual harassment may include calendars, posters, a one-time joke, an e-mail message, unwelcome touching, openly viewing sexually explicit websites, invading a person's space, sexual comments about a person's body, looking a person up and down (elevator eyes), or repeatedly asking a person out who is not interested. Sexual harassment is a sensitive subject. It is difficult to discuss, especially between people of different sexes. Many consider the subject imprecise, and perceptions and comfort levels differ regarding sexual harassment and the roles of men and women in society and at work. The continuing challenge requires that we understand that society is in a constant state of evolution. In a world of instant communication, changes tend to occur rapidly. As gays, lesbians, and transsexuals acquire equal rights, sexual harassment by persons of different sexual preferences will require our attention. Similarly, dealing with sexual harassment in the information age requires increased attention by organizations. Employers will have to handle such situations with tact and understanding, and with a full recognition of (a) the rights of all involved, (b) the need for fair and equal treatment for persons thought by some to be "different," and (c) the morale problem that can arise from improper handling of explosive sexual situations (Reinhardt, 1992). We must learn to treat all persons with courtesy, respect, and dignity, in the workplace or elsewhere, on a continuing basis.

NOTES

1. From *Investigating Sexual Harassment: A Practical Guide to Resolving Complaints,* Second Edition (pp. 14–16), by Angela Bradbery and Rosemarie Lally, 1998, Washington, D.C., Thompson Publishing Group. Copyright 1998, 1999, by Thompson Publishing Group. Reprinted with permission. http://hr.complianceexpert.com/charm/chapter=1/1-2.

REFERENCES

Barnes v. Train (Costle), 13 Fair Empl. Prac. Cas. (BNA), 123 (D.D.C. 1974); *reversed Barnes v. Costle*, 561 F.2d 983 (D.C. Cir. 1977).

Bradbery, A., & Lally, R. (1998). *Investigating sexual harassment: A practical guide to resolving complaints (2nd ed.).* Washington, DC: Thompson Publishing Group.

Burlington Industries, Inc. v. Ellerth, 912 F. Supp. 1101, 1124 (1996); reversed 123 F.3d 1530 (7th Cir. 1997); affirmed, 524 U.S. 742, 761 (1998).

California Civil Code Sec. 1708.7.

California Government Code Sec. 12950 et seq.

Center for American Women and Politics (CAWP), Eagleton Institute of Politics, Rutgers University (2013). *Women in the U.S. Congress 2013.*

Civil Rights Act, Pub. L. 88-352; §7, 42 U.S.C., §2000e, et seq (1964).

Collins, W. J. (2000). *The political economy of race, 1940–1964; The adoption of state-level fair employment legislation.* Cambridge, MA: National Bureau of Economic Research.

Conte, A. (1992). *Sexual harassment in the workplace: Law and practice* (4th ed.). Frederick, MD: Aspen Publishers.

Equal Employment Opportunity Act, Pub. L. 92-261 (1972).

Equal Employment Opportunity Commission v. Prospect Airport Services, Inc., 621 F.3d 991 (9th Cir. 2010)

Faragher v. City of Boca Ratan, 864 F. Supp. 1552, 1563–64 (1998).

Freeman, J. (2008). *We will be heard: Women's struggles for political power in the United States.* Lanham, MD: Rowman & Littlefield.

Gregg, R. E. (1989). Harassment in the workplace. *Journal of Aboriculture, 15*(12), 303–308.

Griggs v. Duke Power Co., 401 U.S. 424 (1971).

Harris v. Forklift Systems, Inc., 976 F.2d 733 (6th Cir. 1992). Unpublished; reversed 510 U.S. 17 (1993).

Hemming, H. (1985). *Women in a man's world: Sexual harassment.* Thousand Oaks, CA: Sage Publications.

Hill, C., & Kearl, H. (2011). *Crossing the line: Sexual harassment at school.* Washington, DC: American Association of University Women.

Lacey, T. A., & Wright, B. (2009). *Occupational employment projections to 2018.* Washington, DC: U.S. Department of Labor, Bureau of Labor Statistics.

Lindeman, B., & Kadue, D. D. (1992). *Sexual harassment in employment law.* Washington, DC: Bureau of National Affairs.

Meritor Savings Bank v. Vinson, 23 Fair Empl. Prac. Cas. (BNA), 37, 42, (D.C. 1980); reversed 753 F.2d 141 (D.C. Cir. 1985); *affirmed* 477 U.S. 57 (1986).

National Center for Education Statistics (n.d.), Projections of education statistics by 2016, Tables 27–31.

Oncale v. Sundowner Offshore Services, Inc., 1995 WL 133349 (E.D. La.); affirmed 83 F.3d 118, 120 (5th Cir. 1996); reversed 523 U.S. 75, 79 (1998).

Reinhardt, S., Judge. (1992). United States Court of Appeals for the Ninth Circuit, foreword. In Lindeman & Kadue (Eds.), *Sexual harassment in employment Law* (pp. v–xxi). Washington, DC: Bureau of National Affairs, Inc.

Rogers v. Equal Employment Opportunity Commission, E.D. Tex. (1970), 316 F. Supp. 422; reversed 454 F.2d 234 (1971).

Rowe, M. (1973). *Barriers to equality: The power of subtle discrimination to maintain unequal opportunity.* Report to the President and Chancellor of the Massachusetts Institute of Technology, Cambridge, MA.

U.S. Department of Education, National Center for Education Statistics, The condition of education 2012. (NCES 2012-045). Table A-47-2.

U.S. Department of Labor, Bureau of Labor Statistics, Current Population Survey, Table 11, *Employed persons by detailed occupation, sex, race, and Hispanic or Latino ethnicity,* 2010.

U.S. Equal Employment Opportunity Commission, *Sexual harassment charges EEOC & FEPAs combined: FY 1997–FY 2011.*

U.S. Equal Employment Opportunity Commission, 1993–94 Sexual Harassment Statistics.

Vance v. Ball State University, et al, WL 4247836, S.D. Ind. (2008). Unpublished; affirmed 646 F.3d 461 (2011); affirmed 570 U.S. (2013).

CHAPTER 11

THE USE OF TECHNOLOGY IN EMPLOYEE SELECTION AND DEVELOPMENT

Advantages and Pitfalls

Martinique Alber

INTRODUCTION

Talent management has become one of the most important, yet one of the most difficult tasks an organization faces. Developing an effective employee selection process is critical to ensure your company is able to hire the best talent available with the right skill set. Hiring and retaining the right people can make a huge difference in your organization's competitiveness and ultimate level of success. Using technology in the selection process can lead to significant improvements in time to fill vacancies, increased metrics, decreased cost, and so on. If done incorrectly, however, it can also lead to an organization's downfall. The following chapter explores some of the latest technological advances and how they have been used throughout human resource management (HRM) processes, citing their advantages as well as their potential legal pitfalls.

Legal and Regulatory Issues in Human Resources Management, pages 229–246
Copyright © 2015 by Information Age Publishing
All rights of reproduction in any form reserved.

DEFINING THE APPLICANT

In general, the first phase of the selection process is recruitment. As such, it is important that it is done correctly in order to select the "right" candidate and to avoid certain legal issues in the future. One of the first questions organizations should ask themselves is, "Who are my potential applicants?" The Office of Federal Contract Compliance Programs (OFCCP) (2013) broadly defines an *applicant* as anyone who expresses interest in a position (http://www.dol.gov/ofccp/regs/compliance/faqs/iappfaqs.htm). This would include individuals applying via electronic resumes, Internet applications, paper applications and resumes, or even simply an oral statement of interest—despite an individual's qualifications. For example, a person with a background in customer service or sales who applies for a nursing position would need to be maintained as a valid applicant for the nursing position. This is in conflict with what human resources professionals have typically maintained, which is that an *applicant* is someone who meets all job qualifications (or possibly only those interviewed for a position). These conflicting definitions are important with regard to two employment law issues:

1. Only *applicants* may establish a prima facie case of unlawful discrimination regarding hiring decisions under state and federal discrimination statutes.
2. Employers must determine who qualifies as an *applicant* in order to ascertain whether hiring practices, policies, or procedures have an *adverse impact* on protected classes (e.g., minorities, women).

In the past, defining the applicant pool was easy; however, with today's technological advances, organizations do not rely on "traditional" resources (e.g., newspaper advertisements). Instead, they have turned to fast, easy, and inexpensive recruiting sources (e.g., organizational websites, television, internet sites, social media, radio) and thus receive feedback online (e.g., internet applications) or via email (e.g., resumes). This makes the process of determining applicants harder as it opens up the potential applicant pool from a few local and regional applicants to hundreds and thousands of national and international applicants. Anyone, anywhere, can now apply for a job.

Due to the confusion, the OFCCP issued their definition of an "internet applicant." An internet applicant, under the definition in the final rule, is an individual who meets the following four criteria:

1. The individual submits an expression of interest in employment through the internet or related electronic data technologies.

2. The contractor considers the individual for employment in a particular position.
3. The individual's expression of interest indicates the individual possesses the basic objective qualifications for the position.
4. The individual, at no point in the contractor's selection process prior to receiving an offer of employment from the contractor, removes himself or herself from further consideration or otherwise indicates that he or she is no longer interested in the position.

If the above criteria are met, the organization must retain all application or resume responses for two years. To minimize record retention, organizations do not have to consider job posting responses that are not submitted in accordance with the organization's standard procedures (e.g., if the organization considers expressions of interest through both the internet and traditional means, the internet applicant regulations apply to both types of submissions; if the contractor does not accept electronic submissions for a position, the internet definition of an applicant does not apply).

Now that the applicants have been clearly defined, what about "adverse impact"? Employers must be able to show that their selection processes do not adversely affect individuals with regard to classes protected under Title VII of the Civil Rights Act of 1964 (Section 703(b); U.S. Equal Employment Opportunity Commission, 2013b). Adverse impact is typically determined by comparing the pass/fail rates of individuals from protected groups (Adverse Impact, n.d.).

In order to determine if a selection process has adverse impact, you need to know the race and sex of each applicant. This demographic information is voluntary information on most applications, both paper and electronic. Collecting this data becomes increasingly difficult if an employer accepts emailed resumes and letters. Generally, applicants are advised not to and therefore rarely include race and sex data on their resumes or letters of interest. As such, if an organization accepts and considers these types of applications, they must be included in adverse impact calculated scores.

At this point, all forms of applicants discussed are those actively seeking employment. While highly qualified applicants are in this pool, many organizations also see value in focusing recruitment efforts on the passive job seeker as well. Where does the passive job seeker lie among these applicants? Passive job seekers can be defined as those who are comfortable in their current job and are not actively seeking other employment. These are the individuals that some organizations are attempting to attract or "poach" from another organization. Since these job seekers did not indicate an interest in the job, when do they become a viable applicant?

The best advice would be to use a standardized process with a strict definition of who an organization considers an applicant. For example, sending all applicants to your Internet site to apply using your own application process, as well as gathering race and sex data via this means, would be preferable. In this way, the organization should be able to easily determine "basic qualifications" and adverse impact. However, please be aware that the OFCCP retains the ability to assess whether selection criteria used by federal contractors are discriminatory. The use of an application blank provides a standard structure where all potential applicants can provide required information using the same questions. In addition, this type of standardization allows consistency among all the individuals. A resume, on the other hand, may highlight areas that are of interest to a potential employer, but there is no guarantee that everyone will present the same experience in a favorable light. This could lead potential employers to make biased judgments and lead to unfair hiring decisions.

RECRUITING QUALIFIED APPLICANTS

Online recruiting and advertising efforts typically yield larger response rates than traditional recruiting methods. In these situations, many applicants are not willing to invest additional time and effort to test or interview for a given position. This lack of interest from applicants wastes the time and money of the potential employers that screened their applications. Recruiters often wonder why an applicant would apply for a job if the individual is not truly interested in accepting employment. One reason may be higher unemployment rates. Many states require individuals collecting unemployment benefits to apply to a minimum of three jobs a week. The ease of electronic application submission may be a contributing factor to higher numbers of unqualified applicants. The process in a sense has become too easy since a majority of jobs are accessible online and there is no longer a need to "pound the pavement" to find someone hiring. Internet recruiting is advantageous, though, in that it can allow you to do more targeted recruiting. For more specialized areas such as nursing, potential employers can send recruiting emails or advertisements to list serves, schools with nursing programs, and professional organizations regionally or from across the nation.

Since the Internet is so expansive, there is a level of amenity between the applicant and organization. With online applications, an organization does not know if the individual completing the application is the person who is actually applying for the job. We have all asked for help tweaking our resume to present ourselves in the best light possible, but at what point does this assistance become misrepresentation? It is a challenge for any organization to manage reference checks for hundreds of potential applicants, so the information included in an application is typically taken at face value until the potential applicant pool can be narrowed down by the use of required qualifications or through testing. With this in mind, many organizations have begun using an application blank rather than relying on submitted resumes.

Another concern that an organization may have regarding online applications is the access potential applicants have to email-capable technologies. Almost all online application processes require applicants to have an email address to apply. If an applicant does not have a computer, tablet, or smartphone, what is the point of having an email address? An online application process could potentially have a disparate impact on applicants with a low socioeconomic status (SES) because they may not have easy access to email or the Internet or may lack basic computer skills required to complete an online application. These applicants may rely on the help of friends to assist them in the application process. On occasion in this situation, applicants may use the email addresses of friends or relatives, which poses a problem. These applicants may not receive direct correspondence regarding the status of their application or future testing or interview information. This communication is time sensitive, so in some instances it may be too late when these applicants finally receive critical information. Some businesses have attempted to resolve this problem by providing computer assistance or kiosks on-site. This allows applicants to come in and complete their own applications with support provided by an employee who is available to assist if needed.

SELECTING THE "RIGHT" EMPLOYEE

As stated earlier, the use of recruiting in this day and age of technology can create an overwhelming number of applicants for a single job. Many online application processes are setup in order to automatically screen individuals' applications. For example, some entry-level positions may require a driver's license. An online application blank can be programmed so that those answering "No" to the question, "do you have a valid driver's license?" are automatically screened out. Many other general skill sets that are requirements of a particular job can easily be set up as auto-screens. For example: *Do you have experience in accounting? Do you have experience supervising? Are you able to work on-call any hour of the day or night?* These questions can be presented to individuals online as simple yes or no questions. This allows applicants to opt out of the selection process, assuming they answer the questions honestly.

Recruiting for the most qualified applicant is not just a matter of posting qualifications for a position; recruiting online per se may have adverse impact, so it often comes down to whether organizations can show that their selection tools are valid predictors of success on the job. When an organization decides to use a published test, there are many precautions the organization must take to ensure the test is appropriate. Organizations are liable for whatever violations result from the techniques used by test publishers and vendors. Caution must be taken as few of the tests or screening criteria used by the online industry have been validated or shown to actually predict job performance for global jobs. Even if the vendor has validated the tests and criteria with their own data, the employer still has to demonstrate that the tests accurately predict performance in the employer's own organization. Further, some tests can only be used if they can be shown to be necessary for performing the particular job in question, whether or not they have adverse impact. An example of an employment screen that has questionable utility is credit checks. Credit checks are now easily and affordably performed by online vendors, but they are illegal to perform on applicants under most state laws unless the employer can show that good credit is necessary for performing the job in question.

Other tests appear to be legal at their face value, but may not be depending on their use. Personality tests, for example, have become a very popular source for screening employees online for entry-level jobs, especially for sites that match applicants to jobs. If they delve into the psychological characteristics of the employees, personality tests can be seen as medical tests, which cannot be administered to applicants under the Americans with Disabilities Act (ADA).

For higher-level positions, the requirements for a job are more intricate and require an individual to manually screen applications to ensure that only the qualified individuals are moving on to the next phase of the selection process. This step typically involves a more in-depth review of applicants' work experience to ensure that they meet the qualifications of the job and are weeding out more individuals who are clearly not qualified. Having a standardized and uniform application for a given position also places all candidates on a level playing field with regards to the forum in which they are providing their information. The use of these various techniques and the streamlining of the online process have significantly reduced the amount of time that human resource employees have to invest in administrative paperwork. This now frees up their time to focus on other aspects of their job.

One challenge with the entire process is verification of work experience. Many organizations typically have a disclaimer stating that all references and work experiences may be verified and therefore the applicant must provide contact information for the individual's previous employers. Most organizations cannot verify this type of information on their own for the overwhelming numbers of applicants they receive, so in some cases this portion of the application process is outsourced to companies that have capitalized on this portion of the market. These companies do all the legwork and verify employment and work experience of the applicant. Because this service does require money, most organizations rely on this type of service when their list of potential applicants has dwindled down to a select few.

Some organizations have even used "headhunters" to find and lure passive job seekers from their current jobs with something bigger and better than what they currently have. By using this technique, one is assured that the individual is qualified, therefore justifying the extra time and expense in recruiting. The use of social media has impacted how passive job seekers are recruited and treated. LinkedIn is a resource through which prospective employers can get connected to individuals already in the field with desired skill sets. Attempting to engage a passive job seeker is much more time consuming and takes more effort than recruiting an active job seeker; however, the payoffs can be well worth it.

PROS AND CONS WITH THE USE OF TECHNOLOGY IN RECRUITING

Social media have drastically impacted the sharing of job posting and potential employment opportunities. With all the pros to the use of social media, there are still some major cons. The application and selection process has changed drastically from employers recruiting by simply placing a help wanted sign in their window front with exposure to the limited individuals in that town or city, to merely posting a job listing on the internet that could reach thousands of individuals. Organizations are still using resumes and applicants' work experiences to determine if they are qualified for a position; however, now, with the pervasiveness of social media, do employers have the right to look at a potential hire's Facebook page and make a judgment based on what they see? There are several questions to ask: Is what a person places on his or her personal social media site going to be a direct reflection of that individual's work ethic? Should employers let a potential hire's social media site influence their selection decision? And finally, is this even legal?

There is no doubt that social media are changing the way business is conducted, from recruiting to applicant screening. A majority of individuals have a Facebook, Twitter, or LinkedIn account. If the use and review of social media is done incorrectly, this leaves employers open to litigation. As of right now, most of the court cases involve the termination of current employees based on comments that are being made on their own personal social media pages about managers, policies at work, or even customers. Once employers obtain this information, these employees are being terminated. The National Labor Relations Board (NLRB) is the body of government that is attempting to protect employees from discriminatory or unfair practices by an employer.

The NLRB is constantly revising its policies of protection based on developments in social media. Technology is progressing so rapidly that social media law is constantly evolving and often playing catch-up.

Some employers are requesting applicants provide information regarding their social media pages upon submission of an application. Think about what people post—their likes, dislikes, what they have been doing (legal or illegal activity), information about their family and friends, and so on. With this type of information, an applicant is no longer "blind" regarding race and sex to a potential employer, and therein lies the legal challenge. The person is no longer being evaluated based on work experience alone, but possibly selected or not selected on something that may fall within a protected class. A recruiter can identify an applicant's race, sex, sexual orientation, familial status, and/or age. Most of the categories named are protected classes according to the Equal Employment Opportunity Commission (EEOC), and any hiring decisions made on this information can be deemed discriminatory.

Now if a potential applicant's social media activity is public, then shame on that individual for posting defamatory information that might turn off a potential employer; however, if the applicant's passwords have been solicited by an organization and the applicant is attempting to keep information private, then the individual may have some protection. Maryland was one of the first states to make it illegal for employers or potential employers to require individuals to provide their passwords to their personal social media sites. There may also be no retribution by the employer or potential employer for individuals who refuse to provide that information. This has become such a large issue today that an act has been introduced on the federal level called the Social Networking Online Protection Act. Another act has been proposed to the Senate, the Password Protection Act of 2012, which would make it illegal for employers or potential employers to require passwords from individuals (Guerin, n.d.).

As quick as it is to advertise or share a job posting using the Internet and social media, these advances in technology have also created an environment where information may be shared too easily. A potential employee's resume or application can be forwarded to anyone in an organization for review, but with that comes a certain level of responsibility to ensure that only the appropriate individuals are receiving this personal information. Certain safeguards may need to be put in place by prospective employers to ensure that applicants' information is secure and not being exploited.

APPLICANT TESTING

The next step in the process is testing applicants once they have successfully passed the required qualifications. Many organizations, especially civil service agencies, give pencil-and-paper tests for a majority of their exams. Other types of selection tests that are used are interviews (structured and unstructured) and work samples, to name a few. With the use of technology, the testing of candidates has practically no limit. There are so many advantages to introducing technology into testing; however, there are some obstacles that come with it too.

Video-based testing in essence means that the testing material delivered is in video form. It can range from structured interviews to multiple-choice questions. The flexibility and diversity of the use of technology is almost limitless. For example, if the test material (e.g., structured interview) is narrated and recorded, then all applicants are being exposed to the same material in the identical manner. By having this type of standardization, you can ensure the fairest possible testing. When applicants are given a live interview, there are nonverbal cues that applicants read and respond to, and in some instances test readers are not reading the same questions or follow-up questions to all applicants. Video-based testing also allows an organization to be creative in how the tests are administered. For example, if you have a position that does not require a high reading level, test developers can convert a written test to pictures with a narration. This allows individuals to hear the test questions and see on the video monitor what their answer options are. An advantage of this is that it does not require a higher reading level to take the test than would be required to be successful in the job, leading to a more fair selection process. As long as an individual has the imagination to produce something via video, it can be used for testing.

Another advantage of using technology in testing is the capability to record the responses of individuals for scoring at a later date or for archiving or record keeping. In this day and age, it is practically obsolete to record anything to a tape or disc anymore; everything is being recorded digitally and kept on servers or memory cards. This can be as simple as recording with a digital camcorder or having an intricate system of digital cameras, streaming into digital recorders and media servers. The price for both systems is drastically different, but in effect they maintain the same function. Also, by having the recorded responses of an individual, an organization has verifiable documentation of everything that happened in the interview or test in the event of any type of legal challenge. Using video and audio enables evaluators to have an exact record of each candidate's responses, thus increasing the legal defensibility of the method. It also enables decision makers to review the interviews if questions arise or when there are disagreements between raters. The hiring body no longer has to contend with a "he said, she said" case; now all that needs to be said is "let's go to the recording." Using video and audio can help maximize the number of interviewers who can evaluate interviewees, thus enhancing the validity and reliability of selection decisions.

For many higher-level positions and jobs in public safety, the trend has been to conduct oral boards. This involves live assessors reading interview questions to candidates and then scoring the candidates as they are giving their responses. This requires multiple assessors to be available for each applicant on test days. These live assessments not only lead to issues in the testing process, but it is also costly because of the need for live assessors. With a video-based testing process, candidate responses can be recorded and then evaluated when feasible. This has the potential to reduce costs (e.g., transportation associated with conducting face-to-face interviews), reduce the human resources necessary for assessment (e.g., when several individuals have a stake in the selection decision), and reduce assessor fatigue (e.g., assessors may evaluate candidates at any convenient time) (Miller & Alber, 2012). This may result in the video assessment process being more reliable by reducing assessor errors so that better hiring decisions are made. Logistics can be planned out in order to save money and enable the ability to host an assessment days if not weeks later. When raters score a recording of a candidate's responses, it takes the stress off the rater. They do not have to worry about capturing every little detail that is stated because at any time raters can rewind and review what they just saw or heard. Videos can even be sent securely to people in other states to review, practically eliminating the cost of having to bring individuals onsite to rate. Allowing interviewers in geographically dispersed locations to evaluate candidates without having to travel not only saves money but also increases utility.

Obviously, there are many advantages to using video and audio delivery and recording. However, it should be noted that there are a few disadvantages as well. For instance, using video and audio may seem "impersonal" to candidates. They may not like speaking to a computer, video camera, or audio recorder. While some may consider it impersonal, it is for the protection and fair treatment of each applicant. It is human nature to make mistakes and have biased judgments. Even the best trained test administrators can give off nonverbal cues that may lead candidates in a different direction with their responses.

Furthermore, startup costs and production costs—like equipment and recording materials—can be quite expensive. As stated earlier, the use of technology is very expensive and the initial set up is time consuming. The payoff, however, is priceless. If an organization were to put the time and effort into an updated system, the money invested is nominal compared to the money an organization could spend on potential lawsuits. The documentation and the standardization of the execution of the test material (as long as done properly) can significantly reduce the likelihood of an organization having litigation brought against them.

An important consideration for organizations wanting to use digital recording is to make sure that there is some type of redundancy. An organization does not want to lose everything if a camera goes down or if the digital recording fails. After testing, there needs to be some kind of quality assurance check to verify that the recording is good before allowing the test candidate to leave the premises. A tester should avoid a situation where a candidate has to be retested, but it would be much worse to allow the applicant to leave only to be brought back another time to retest, as this may compromise the integrity of the test and perceived fairness of the process. Other issues may be encountered when trying to retrieve videos. Organizations need to account for the potential of the following: the network may go down, the server may not want to communicate with outside computers, or a computer simply may not cooperate.

As organizations continue to move towards paperless applications and digital test material, questions arise concerning how long organizations are required to keep this material. Many states' archival standards require agencies to retain their records anywhere from three to five years. That means any paper, DVDs, and audio recordings could legally be destroyed once that legal timeframe is exceeded, but what happens if an organization no longer has physical recordings and paper documents to retain and instead everything is electronic? There is a school of thought that everything needs to be kept indefinitely. All of this material is no longer taking up physical space, but now it is taking up server space. Although digital storage is less expensive than it used to be, it still costs money, especially for organizations that are testing thousands of candidates annually over several years. Video files are large and require large amounts of space in order to archive years of testing. Organizations also need to consider whether simply deleting these records is equal to destroying them. The use of technology right now in this manner is too new for these issues to become a problem, but five years from now organizations will be running into major dilemmas.

Another great function of the advances in technology is online testing. Applicants no longer have to come to a physical location to take an exam; they can take it in the comfort of their own home. There are many pros to this technique: First you are not constrained regionally, especially if it is for an entry-level job. The candidate is not constricted to a certain time and date to take the exam. Allowing some flexibility may result in a better applicant pool since it may be difficult for applicants who currently have a job to take time off of work. Scoring would be fairly quick since the test can be autoscored as the applicant is taking it and the organization can choose to reveal the score immediately to the applicant or at a later date. Online testing is also very economical, especially if you have created your own test and are not using a vendor.

There are many cons, however, to using online testing. One of the major issues is verifying the identity of the applicant to make sure the individual taking the test is truly the applicant. Also, an employer wants to ensure the security of the environment in which the applicant is taking the test to be certain no one else is in the room helping the applicant. Another issue is verifying the security of the test itself to be sure that the test material is not being shared. These are all issues that may impact the integrity of any test and the entire testing process. Many organizations conduct phone interviews when an individual cannot travel, but an increasing number of organizations are using SKYPE in order to conduct interviews face to face—or rather, computer to computer. This allows organizations to be able not only to test the candidate, but to get a feel of the candidate to see if the individual would be a good organizational fit. Obviously there is a drastic difference between online written testing and structured interviews, but in essence both have the same challenges. For online entry-level testing, an organization needs to consider whether or not to require applicants to have webcams, so they can be monitored during the entire testing process. Suddenly online testing does not seem as grand and easy as previously thought, but it is manageable, and there are many great benefits if implemented and managed correctly.

The invention of the smartphone has brought its own unique challenges to testing. From the beginning, cell phones were not allowed in testing facilities because they were more of a disruption to the process because some people would not turn them off. When they did go off, they were a disturbance to everyone in the test, opening up the test to challenges from individuals who were ambitious enough to claim that the disruption caused them to lose focus or not test as well as they could have without the disruption. Today, smartphones are capable of taking pictures, making videos, and making voice recordings, and in an instant anything can be distributed to hundreds, if not thousands of people. It is critical that in any testing environment where any portion of information is confidential and/or proprietary that cell phones are strictly prohibited. Depending on the testing environment no one can have eyes on everyone all of the time. Some organizations ban any type of communication device completely, such as cell phones, iPads, and tablets, since even the most basic tablet or e-reader can surf the web and connect to email.

Many organizations are not going to invest the time and energy to search every test taker to verify that they do not have a cell phone, but some organizations implement a rule that if a cell phone is found on an individual, that person is immediately disqualified from the testing process. As long as this rule is communicated to the applicants prior to testing, there is no legal retribution. It tends to help if it is presented to the applicants in several different forms, in several different locations, and even as they enter the testing area.

HUMAN RESOURCE APPLICANT TRACKING SYSTEMS

Many government agencies, especially local governments, are just beginning to embrace the use of technology and going paperless with just about everything. Individuals are so used to submitting paper forms that it is a hard transition for them to make. When going to a paperless process, there is a significant amount of training involved for those that are within the system. As usual, you will have the individuals who are reluctant to change and do not understand computers and do not understand the new processes. In cases where an entire new system is being implemented, the cost of training all the users of the system must be considered. With any new system, there will be a range of users, from individuals who only use one particular function to those who will use almost every aspect of the system. These employees will get up to speed very quickly, while there will be others who will struggle to learn a new system.

Paperless HRM solutions include electronic applicant tracking systems or talent management systems. These systems are designed to handle applications for an organization including applicants' personal information and resumes. There are many companies that can offer an off-the-shelf product that is tweaked for the customer, but each customer is unique and what is marketed to work does not necessarily function in an ideal manner for all organizations. It is impractical for a company to specifically customize their product to meet every little demand of a customer because of the time and, therefore, cost required for this level of customization. In many organizations, a second electronic system tracks current employees' longevity, leave, pay rate, and so on. In some cases, an organization may be advanced enough to have performance appraisals paperless also. Consequently, as the technology advances, it is possible to build a system that integrates everything from the application process to finalizing one's retirement paperwork. This type of system can be referred to as a "cradle to grave" paperless applicant tracking system.

There are several different areas within HRM that currently use an online system or could greatly benefit from transferring its functions to an online system. Some organizations in this day and age are still using a mainframe system. There are many organizations that would greatly benefit from an integrated system or a customizable system.

INTEGRATED SYSTEM

A major part of any organization is keeping track of all current and past employees. This includes employees' personal information, job title, pay grade, department, and longevity in the position, for any and all positions that they have held within an organization. Regardless of how long an employee has been with the organization, this tracking process would start from the beginning when the individual first submitted an application for a job. A challenge to all online systems is the user. Organizations frequently run into the issue of potential applicants not knowing how to properly submit their applications or not entering valid email addresses. A quick solution to this problem is to require email confirmations. Using this method, potential applicants cannot successfully submit a job application without confirming their email address by clicking a link that is sent to the email address entered by the applicant. This technique is often used for online registrations of various kinds.

Once an application is successfully submitted, the applicant can be screened, tested, and then be eligible for hire by a department. The system would capture every job for which the individual applied or tested. This part of the system would be visible to both the applicant and the hiring agency's personnel department. Once hired, the system would record the hire date, location, and starting pay rate for the individual. At this point, all information going forward would be made private, accessible only by the personnel department.

Once a person has been consistently working in the organization for a period of time, a performance appraisal would need to be completed on that employee, which could also be tracked in the system. Instead of having a paper-and-pencil appraisal that is scanned in and attached to the file, it could be an online form. Having an online form for all employees would help standardize and provide consistency amongst everyone in the organization that is being evaluated in order to maintain fairness for everyone. These evaluations could ultimately be tied into raises, promotions, demotions, or even terminations. The more that is documented, the more an organization can be protected from or in the event of litigation.

BUILDING AN ELECTRONIC APPLICANT TRACKING SYSTEM

For any organization starting from the ground up, a solid job analysis would need to be performed on many, if not all, positions in the organization. These could be placed in an online format, allowing for quick and easy completion of the job study questionnaire by incumbents and supervisors. Having an online format makes it very easy for individuals to access the questionnaire (e.g., not having to travel anywhere), but it can also allow them to complete it at their leisure. One of the major pitfalls of allowing access to the questionnaire without guidance is that if people do not understand what they are rating, the resulting data may not be good. Remember "garbage in, garbage out"—if individuals do not understand or do not care about what they are rating, your entire process could be compromised. It is always good to ensure that an employee filling out a job study survey has access to a person that can help the person navigate the process.

Once that basic domain of the job is established, including the work behaviors and knowledge, skills, and abilities (KSAs), qualifications for the position can be created. Once created and validated, all this information could be automatically synchronized into an application posting, creating a seamless line from start to end. This process would save tens if not hundreds of hours of staff time, especially if jobs are being constantly studied and announced, as in many civil service organizations. This also establishes the validity of the process when almost everything is documented and calculated electronically, minimizing how much the data is touched, therefore reducing the likelihood of errors. Human judgment should never be taken out of the process completely, but having online systems to manage the data may prove to be beneficial.

Once this type of database is built, it would be easy to then integrate classification and compensation processes. If employees complain they are working out of class or not being paid appropriately for the work they are doing, they can simply fill out a job survey blank or compare what they currently do to an established job description for the job they are claiming they are or are not performing. Comparisons to other jobs can either be automatically completed by the system, or an employee can pull relevant job descriptions for manual comparison. The great thing about having so much information in one system is that everything is indexed. This means any and every bit of information can be organized into categories and pulled, allowing for a wide array of uses for the employees and departments that would be using the system. Another benefit is that by having everything built together and synchronized with each other, an organization does not have to worry about compatibility issues between separate electronic software. The more you can standardize a process, the higher the likelihood that you can protect yourself from potential lawsuits.

Because an HRM system like this would be so rich in data, it could easily be a target for hackers. A successful hacker could access all the information one would need in order to wreak havoc on an individual or an organization by bringing down the entire system. With that in mind, additional heightened security measures would need to be put into place to ensure the protection of all applicants' and employees' personal information. No organization wants to be held liable for a breach in security, as we have already seen a few times in the media (e.g., Advocate Medical Group, BP, and AT&T).

EMPLOYEE DEVELOPMENT

Another major contribution of the advances in technology is how it impacts the training and development of current employees. Technology can be used during a training class to poll attendees about the training content to get "real time" feedback. It has also impacted how training content can be distributed—for example, via video blogs posted to recap training classes, webinars, distance learning, and video conferencing. One clear benefit is that individuals could potentially participate in training at their leisure. Several different classes and training portals are available online, which provides an opportunity for individuals to train at any location such as their home, office, or while traveling. It also allows individuals to work at their own pace. Training can be customized; not everyone learns in the same manner, so having flexibility in being able to customize training may allow the maximum benefit for the learner (Ensher, Nielson, & Grant-Vallone, 2002). Another advantage of the use of technology is that it can bring people from different geographical locations together through videoconferencing. This in turn saves the time and money spent on travel for the participants and the trainer. The ability to post training content for a large audience has also shaped training techniques themselves. Instead of a four-hour webinar being posted online, individuals have modularized their training into relevant segments. Now individuals can search for the "nugget" of information that they need right then and there. Society works in such a fast-paced environment that many people operate on a "just in time" process. For example, if someone needs to get disciplinary feedback to an employee they may watch that 5–10 minute segment before having to address the employee.

The use of technology can be maximized with compliance trainings, such as safety, diversity, and workplace harassment training. More specifically, any mandatory training programs that are "nondiscussion-based trainings" can be documented by human resource departments and retained to provide evidence to state and federal oversight agencies that their employees have complied with policies. Creating a webinar class for core trainings that all employees need to participate in, such as sexual harassment training, gives employees the flexibility to participate in those trainings on their own schedule. This may significantly reduce the burden of training (time and money) on staff, depending on the size of the workforce. Trainings such as this can require participation once a year that can be tracked online, and an evaluation of the content of the training can be provided, allowing for immediate feedback.

Technology has also been used in the creation of mechanical simulations, language acquisition, computer programming, and so much more. This type of training has allowed individuals to hone their skills without risking their safety, machinery, or capital. It allows for training in real-life situations without real-life consequences.

While there are numerous benefits to online training, there are some drawbacks to e-learning. Soft skills are still the focus of many training programs, and these benefit from a more interactive training environment that allows for discussion and a flow of information. Technology will be, for the most part, only an enhancer rather than a replacement for this type of training. Also, if individuals are training off-site or even at their computer, their attention may be divided (e.g., phone ringing, emails, etc.); therefore, you cannot guarantee that the individuals have learned what they were supposed to learn (Ensher et al., 2002). Outside individuals who are participating may not have the proper equipment. Another question to pose is, are the employees actively learning the content of the material or just going through the motions? Having a traditional in-class setting cannot guarantee that an employee is retaining the content, but there is a level of interaction to ensure that something is ascertained.

Almost anyone can create an online training seminar for internal or external use; however, that training is a direct reflection of the organization's branding. Organizations need to ensure that there is not a bad product out there with their name on it because they are liable for the content of the training in addition to the trainer (Warning, 2010). When training, one will want to keep in mind the confidentiality of the material being trained and to also make sure that all appropriate individuals have access to those training sessions or classes; otherwise an organization can find itself in violation of the Age Discrimination in Employment Act or other sections of the Equal Employment Opportunity Commission regulations (U.S. Equal Employment Opportunity Commission, 2013a).

CONCLUSION

As stated throughout the chapter, the use of technology in human resource processes such as recruiting, testing, development, and applicant tracking can have huge benefits, including saving time, money, and resources. However, the things that make the use of technology so great are also what can cripple an organization if not implemented properly. Many organizations need to focus their searches for prospective employees in order to recruit high-quality candidates rather than anyone and everyone looking at the job posting. In addition, there needs to be an emphasis on the security and responsibility of applicant and current employee personal information. Today, electronic information can be easily shared, moved, and distributed. There is a false sense of privacy and security—any system is only as good as the least honest or reliable individual working on it. There have been several situations where it has not been hackers accessing information but employees being negligent and irresponsible about the protection of personal information (e.g., leaving a laptop with employee information in a public place). The ways in which current employees can be developed using technology is near limitless, from language acquisition to realistic simulations.

Online tracking of risk management trainings can ensure an organization's legal compliance.

The benefits of these technological systems used throughout human resource processes certainly outweigh the costs and maximize the contribution of the workforce. One of the greatest challenges is that a system needs to be put in place that serves the functions of the entire organization. Whoever is going to integrate the use of technology not only needs to understand how to integrate processes and procedures but to also have an intimate understanding of how the current organization or system operates. If there is any disconnect between those two processes, one can be certain to run into major legal pitfalls that can open an entity to litigation that may destroy a free-standing organization.

REFERENCES

Adverse Impact. (n.d.). Retrieved from http://www.adverseimpact.org/

The Civil Rights Act of 1964, 42 U.S.C. §2000e, et seq. (1964).

Ensher, E. A., Nielson, T. R., & Grant-Vallone, E. (2002). Tales from the hiring line: Effects of the interest and technology on HR processes. *Organizational Dynamics, 31*(3), 224–244.

Guerin, L. (n.d.). Can potential employers check your Facebook page? Nolo Law for All. Retrieved from http://www.nolo.com/legal-encyclopedia/can-potential-employers-check-your-facebook-page.html

Miller, L., & Alber, M. (2012, April). *Live versus video assessment.* Poster session presented at the annual meeting of the Society of Industrial/Organization Psychology, San Diego, CA.

Office of Federal Contract Compliance Programs. (2013). *Internet Applicant Recordkeeping Rule.* Retrieved from http://www.dol.gov/ofccp/regs/compliance/faqs/iappfaqs.htm

U.S. Equal Employment Opportunity Commission. (2013). *The Age Discrimination in Employment Act of 1967.* Retrieved from http://www.eeoc.gov/laws/statutes/adea.cfm

U.S. Equal Employment Opportunity Commission. (2013). *Title VII of the Civil Rights Act of 1964* (Section 703(b)). Retrieved from http://www.eeoc.gov/laws/statutes/titlevii.cfm

Warning, R. (2010). *Special Issues in Training and Employee Development.* Retrieved from http://busn.uco.edu/rwarning/PowerPoints/Ethical...Legal/Chapter%2010.ppt

CHAPTER 12

TECHNOLOGY AND EMPLOYEE PRIVACY CHALLENGES

Sheri K. Bias and Karin L. Bogue

INTRODUCTION

The increased use of cell phones, iPads, and laptops for business purposes presents a variety of privacy issues for employers and employees that deserve special attention from HRM professionals. When computers arrived in the office, employees were warned through employee handbooks and other communications that the computers belonged to the company and employees had no expectation of privacy when using company-owned equipment. Employers developed security features that were installed on computers and cell phones to protect company information. The use of technology continued to grow and employers sought increased security measures. Seeking additional availability and productivity from employees, employers provided employees with a company cell phone and/or laptop, which allowed the employee to work from home and check mail and messages when away from the physical office environment. Both parties may view these devices as useful technology tools because they provide the employee with a little flexibility and the opportunity for more productivity for the employer.

Legal and Regulatory Issues in Human Resources Management, pages 247–266

However, there is a catch to technology. When equipped with GPS and similar devices, laptops and cell phones are capable of the same type of tracking from remote locations as computers found in the office (Barker, 2009; Ciocchetti, 2011). While employers often use GPS to track employees' locations in the workplace, the same tools allow them to track cell phones outside the workplace during nonworking hours. Does the employer have a legitimate business need or right to know where an employee is during the nonworking hours? RFID chips have proved to be great tools for retailers to track merchandise and reduce theft of merchandise (Barker, 2009). Transportation companies use RFIDs to track and increase the security of the cargo to satisfy government security concerns as well as monitoring their employees (Barker, 2009). What is next? Will employers require employees to be implanted with RFID chips to track their actions? At least three states, Wisconsin, North Dakota, and California, have enacted laws that prohibit employers from mandating RFID implants for employees (Ciocchetti, 2011).

Another challenge to employee privacy is the monitoring of social media and the implications within the workplace. More private sector businesses are intruding into the personal lives of employees. One of the most controversial situations in the news recently is requiring job applicants to turn over passwords to social media accounts.

This chapter explores the history and development of private and public employer/employee workplace privacy laws and provides guidance for HRM professionals to use in creating sound policies. In this chapter we review the history of employee privacy to lay the foundation for our discussion. We then explore current issues and case law surrounding technology such as cell phones and laptops; additionally, we focus on other legal areas that have impacts such as credit reports. An important facet of this exploration is employer and employee rights associated with these areas and what employers are doing with policy creation. We conclude by sharing insights and perspectives on the future, and where technology and employee privacy challenges may be headed.

HISTORY OF EMPLOYEE PRIVACY

It is well known that employees do not have a reasonable expectation of privacy when using equipment owned by private employers because employers have a legitimate need to monitor employee email and computers. Concerns about monitoring what employees are doing in the workplace have surged to the forefront of attention for business owners given the evolution of technology coupled with the litigious society in which we live. Monitoring in some industries such as healthcare and finance may be necessary to ensure compliance with regulations. Monitoring of Internet usage may be necessary to ensure productivity. Additionally, monitoring of emails and other communication may also help employers avoid potential discrimination, harassment, and intellectual property violations (Sprague, 2007). Given that more and more employees are being provided with company-paid tools and resources with which to work, it would seem prudent that this would come with increased monitoring. Or should it?

As time and technology have evolved, it has become more and more prudent for employers to ensure that employees are using company-provided tools to execute the necessary actions to fulfill business strategy. This is a double-edged sword as far as monitoring. In fact, in 1994, George Webster noted:

> The U.S. Constitution's First Amendment free-speech clause and the Fourth Amendment protection against unreasonable searches and seizures apply only to action by the government, not to private-sector employers. . . . By and large, employees leave their constitutional rights at the workplace door. A few state constitutions do extend speech and search protection to private-sector employees.
>
> The key legal issue in privacy cases is this: Did the employer, by what it did or failed to do, create a reasonable expectation of privacy by the employee? If the answer is yes and the employer did not meet that expectation, then it may be held liable for invasion of privacy. (p. 1)

Do employees fully understand how their rights to privacy may be altered when they enter the work environment? In the text *The Naked Employee: How Technology is Compromising Workplace Privacy* by Frederick Lane (2003), the analogy of clothing and personal privacy is deftly made. Lane describes this phenomenon as everyone being naked at some point in the day and our choice of clothing is often dictated by the events planned for the day:

> The clothing choices we make . . . mirror the way our society treats personal privacy. When we stand naked before the mirror in the morning, our cloak of personal privacy is wrapped most tightly around us, and it takes extraordinary circumstances to strip it away. From the moment we cross our property line onto public property, however, the cloak of privacy begins to flap and flutter, and offers us only sporadic protection. And once we cross the line onto someone else's property, particularly as an employee, our cloak is at its thinnest and most revealing.
>
> . . . the nation's legislatures and courts have made occasional efforts to reweave some threads of the privacy cloak for employees, but there is little more than a patchwork of protection. (pp. 3–4)

What is a reasonable expectation of search and monitoring, and have the expectations changed over time? According to Dana Hawkins (1997), many workers have been the target of organizational monitoring efforts without even knowing. Hawkins noted that many organizations have increased scrutiny of both candidate and employee behaviors and that more and more out-of-workplace activities that were once thought private are being monitored. Why is this increase occurring? Hawkins (1997) noted, "Employers say they feel intense pressure from lawsuits of every sort. The number of sex, race, disability, and age-discrimination suits brought by workers has more than doubled from over 10,700 in 1992 to 23,000 in 1996" (p. 1). While monitoring may be necessary to ward off potential liability, employers should only use monitoring for business purposes (Ciocchetti, 2011).

As employers, urged by HRM experts, began including appropriate use policies in employee handbooks and requiring employees to sign privacy agreements, employees started to understand that their privacy in the workplace was limited. In June of 2010 there was a landmark ruling by the U.S. Supreme Court in the case *City of Ontario, California v. Quon*. In this case, it was contended that:

> police department did not violate an officer's Fourth Amendment rights when the officer's supervisor reviewed personal text messages the officer sent using a work-issued pager. The Court held that the search of the messages was reasonable, and did not resolve the question of whether the officer had "a reasonable expectation of privacy" in the text messages. The Court stated that it was reluctant to wade into employee privacy debate in light of the novelty of the issue, the implications of opining on emerging technology before its role in the society has become clear, and the risk of making a ruling that is not fully informed.
>
> ... The Court observed that in *Quon* a finding of an expectation of privacy in text messages could have been supported by the ubiquity of mobile communications that makes the communications essential or necessary instruments for self-expression, even self-identification. On the other hand, the Court suggested that the ubiquity of messaging devices also made them generally affordable, so that employees who need mobile devices for personal use can purchase and pay for their own. The Court observed that employee communications policies shape the reasonable expectations of their employees, especially when such policies are clearly communicated to the employees. (Segalis, 2011, p. 2)

CURRENT ISSUES IN HR PRACTICE

As new technologies are developed, human resource professionals and legal counsel must anticipate the potential legal and ethical issues of how the technology is used. The Electronic Communications Privacy Act (ECPA) has been around since 1986 and still has application to the monitoring of email. Amended to the Federal Wiretap Act that prohibited the interception of wire and oral communications, the ECPA added the prohibition to intercept electronic communications (see Electronic Communications Privacy Act, 1986). The Stored Communications Act (SCA) was included under the ECPA and makes the unlawful and unauthorized access of electronically stored communications a crime. The ECPA prohibits access of electronic communications or stored communication; however, employers can read employees' emails without violating the ECPA as long as the emails accessed have already been sent (SEE *Fraser v. Nationwide Mut. Ins. Co.*, 2003).

Email Privacy—Private Employers

Employees should be aware that emails sent using company-owned equipment using a company-assigned email account are not subject to privacy, but what about emails sent from the employees' personal email accounts while using the employer's network? The courts have ruled variously in favor of both the employer and the employee in these situations. In *Stengart v. Loving Care Agency, Inc*, decided in 2010, the New Jersey Supreme Court ruled in favor of the employee noting that the employees' privacy rights had been violated by her former employer. Ms. Stengart exchanged emails on a private matter through her private email system with her attorney. However, Ms. Stengart used the organization's computer infrastructure for this exchange, which is where the organization deemed it acceptable to review these exchanges. The employer's case was that Ms. Stengart violated the company's electronic communications policy by using their computers for such communications. However, the New Jersey Supreme Court found the organization's electronic communications policy to be ambiguous, and this was held against the employer. The policy was deemed ambiguous because there was lack of disclosure of the monitoring of private web-based emails even though these communications took place on company resources. The court held that Ms. Stengart should have had a reasonable expectation of privacy given these circumstances in that these communications with her attorney were from a personal email account versus the company-sponsored email system. Additionally, the court acknowledged that employers should consider adopting and enforcing policies as guidance to organizational computer resources and protecting the assets and productivity of the business. (This is an observation by the court that we heartily recommend for adoption by HRM professionals.) However, given the circumstances that these attorney–client communications were sent and received from the employee's personal web-based email system, a policy that allows the employer to review these communications is not enforceable.

The courts went the other way in favor of the employer in *Holmes v. Petrovich*. Holmes claimed invasion of privacy, wrongful termination, intentional infliction of emotional distress, and other causes of action. Normally, communications between the client and attorney are protected by the attorney–client privilege; however, Holmes had been warned that the company's computers were for company business only and not for personal email. Additionally, the employer warned the employees that all emails were subject to review. If an employee has been advised that the electronic communications may be monitored and should be used for business purposes and proceeds to use the employer's computer system to send emails to the attorney, then the employee should not have any reasonable expectation of privacy in those communications (see *Holmes v. Petrovich Development Co.*, 2011).

Email Privacy—Public Employers

The Fourth Amendment provides a little more reasonable expectation of privacy for government employees; however, that expectation must be balanced by the defining elements in *O'Connor v. Ortega*, which include exclusive work space, nature of employment, and notice of privacy policy. The police chief for the City of Ontario was trying to determine if the city needed to increase the amount of characters used in the text feature after several officers exceeded the limit for several months. A police officer claimed that a review of the officer's texts by the police chief violated the Fourth Amendment and also filed a claim against the wireless provider for violation of the SCA. While government employees are protected against unreasonable searches by the government, retrieval of work-related information that could be classified as a search is considered reasonable similar to the private employer searches. While the officer had a reasonable expectation of privacy in the text messages, the court ruled that the retrieval of information was motivated by a valid work-related purpose and was therefore a reasonable search. The court was careful to note that these issues should be decided carefully, as the law would continue to develop as technologies continued to evolve (see *City of Ontario, Cal. v. Quon*, 2010).

Balancing Expectations in Personal Communications

While it seems more reasonable for employers to monitor activities that occur while using company-owned equipment, how much of an employee's online activity can the employer monitor and control? More private sector businesses are starting to intrude into the personal lives of employees by monitoring personal blogs and social media sites. How much of a person's life belongs to the employer and how much should remain private beyond the purview of the employer? The answers are still unclear, as laws are still developing to contend with these new issues. A recent controversial situation involving intrusion into personal privacy occurred when an employer required job applicants to turn over passwords to social media accounts (*Pietrylo v. Hillstone*, 2009). In Pietrylo, the plaintiff felt coerced into providing her MySpace chatroom log-in information to her manager and had not actually authorized access. The managers accessed the chat area several times; however, the evidence was clear that the chat room was based on invitation only. The jury ruled that the managers unlawfully accessed the chat room (*Pietrylo v. Hillstone*, 2009). Even though the courts struggle to keep up with rapid changes in technology, they have shown preference to employers by following three general principles, which include the workplace exists for the purpose of work, employers pay the employee in return for work, and employer liability overrides enhancing employee privacy protections (Ciocchetti, 2011).

When a person logs into his or her personal Web-based accounts on a work computer, even a company laptop, this creates a temporary file that—along with the password—is then stored in that computer. Employers are then able to view those files and access those accounts. Web-based accounts that are separate from the employer's internal computer system are protected from access by the SCA (Peerce & Shapiro, 2010).

Case law instructs that employers can review temporary Internet files on a company computer; however, the employer cannot access an employee's personal web-based email account, which is protected by the SCA. The SCA prohibits intentional access without authorization and applies to personal Web-based email; however, it does not apply to company email that is owned by the employer (Peerce & Shapiro, 2010). In *Van Alstyne v. Electronic Scriptorium Ltd* (2009), the defendant admitted to logging into the plaintiff's AOL account that had been used with her company account to conduct business. The court ruled in favor of the plaintiff and awarded damages. The ruling in *Van Alstyne* puts employers on notice about the potential consequences of accessing employee Web-based accounts. It is important to note that even though an employer cannot access employee Web-based accounts, the government can as long as they follow proper rules and procedures that are outlined in SCA, many times requiring a search warrant in order to obtain (Peerce & Shapiro, 2010).

Computer-Monitoring Programs

Programs can be installed directly and remotely to record every keystroke the user makes. While keystroke monitoring might be a reasonable expectation on company-owned equipment, should an employer be able to place the logger on an employee's personal devices through the delivery of the logger through a "Trojan horse" email attachment that the employee might open while checking email remotely? Similarly, employers can employ software programs that track the content of email, including an employee's personal accounts such as AOL or Yahoo (Ciocchetti, 2011; Konrad & Ames, 2000).

Using keyloggers can be risky, as determined in the California case of *Brahmana v. Lembo* (2009), where a company's former employee sued the employer for violation of the ECPA. The former employee alleged that the company intercepted a password with a keylogger and logged into his personal email account without permission. As previously decided in *Konop v. Hawaiian Airlines* (2002), simply gaining access to stored electronic information is not a violation of the ECPA; however, the use of an intercepted password provides a clearer violation of §2511(1)(d) of the ECPA. In the initial ruling, the *Brahmana* court found that the act of keylogging was acceptable, but to use the device to access personal information borders on violation, depending on the court's interpretation of whether a keylogger is integrated with the computer connected to a system that affects interstate commerce.

Keylogger programs can record computer use as well as smartphone use. Companies make apps that work with smartphones to record text messages, contacts, call logs, photos, and even GPS location (Komando, 2012). Keyloggers are almost impossible to detect and even more difficult to eliminate. Running afoul of the law is not the only consideration for employers using keyloggers. What message does the use of keyloggers and similar snooping software send to employees about trust, and how will the knowledge the programs are being used affect employee morale?

Hiring and Firing

Technology provides the means for employers to obtain information that would be prohibited in an actual interview. All an employer has to do is conduct a Google search on a potential employee to find out his or her age, marital status, names of children, home ownership, and anything the applicant may have posted on the Internet. Are employers required to inform applicants that they conduct this type of detective work? If information about an applicant is readily available by conducting a search, should employers be able to use these tools to learn more about applicants? Is there a difference between an employer who searches the applicant's Facebook page and learns information about children and religious views and the employer who finds a criminal conviction on another applicant?

With so much information online about applicants available to employers, what are the limits in using this information during the hiring process? In some situations, job applicants complained that employers requested passwords to social media accounts, which resulted in state lawmakers from over 30 states introducing legislation to prevent employers from requesting passwords to personal email and social media sites as a requirement to obtain or maintain employment (National Conference of State Legislatures [NCSL], 2014). Maryland was the first state to prohibit employers from requesting that applicants provide passwords for social networking accounts (Electronic Privacy Information Center, 2012). Similar legislation is pending in at least 36 states (NCSL, 2014). On the employer's side is the ability to ask. An employer can ask for information that seems to invade privacy, but candidates and employees also have the right to refuse. As organizations embrace differences among employee groups in the workplace, there needs to be an understanding of the implications on workplace infrastructure. For example, the use of social networking and social media has become more and more commonplace. Interestingly, Microsoft, Starbucks, Goldman Sachs, and Deloitte are just a few large U.S. companies who admit to using searches on social networking sites, including LinkedIn to evaluate applicants (Roberts & Roach, 2009).

Even more alarming than the fact that employers are looking at social networks of applicants to begin with is that 63% of employers viewing online social networking profiles have actually rejected prospective employees based on the information in those profiles (Genova, 2009). One of the most popular examples of a social media-related interception involved a young woman who used Twitter to communicate that she had been offered a job at Cisco and was faced with considering the utility of a fat paycheck against the commute and hating the work. Someone from Cisco saw the post and suggested that the hiring manager might be interested in knowing that the Tweeter would hate the work (Comstock, 2011).

Background Investigations

What information does a business legitimately need to collect in pre-employment screening? After the events of September 11, 2001, employers either implemented or expanded their background investigations for potential employees. Employers conduct background checks on potential employees for a number of reasons such as avoiding negligent hiring lawsuits, complying with security requirements, and hiring responsible employees; however, applicants must provide consent for the background investigations. Because employers may face potential liability in the form of negligent hiring lawsuits, there needs to be a balance in place so that the information collected is suitable for the position being filled. For example, employers need a more thorough background check on employees working with children than employees working in a customer service call center.

First, employers are concerned about negligent hiring lawsuits, which hold the employer liable when an employee causes injuries and the employer failed to conduct a background investigation. The negligent hiring situation usually occurs when an employee commits an intentional tort against a customer or a member of the public and the employer would have been aware that the employee had posed a risk to others in the course of completing the job responsibilities if a background check had been completed.

In *Grover v. Augustine* (2007), Pamela Grover was attacked by an elevator operator in the office building where she worked. Grover filed a negligent hiring suit against the operator's employer. Even though the employer was aware the defendant had a criminal record, they failed to do a background check, which would have revealed that the employee had a lengthy criminal record, including convictions for sexual abuse and that he was a registered sex offender. Grover claims negligent hiring because the operator presented an unreasonable risk to the safety of individuals accessing the elevators in the building.

In *Rockwell v. Sun Harbor Budget Suites* (1996), Vernon, Londa, and Andrew Rockwell lived in an apartment at Sun Harbor where Londa was killed by a Sun Harbor security guard. Londa became involved with the security guard in 1992 and when she tried to end the affair in 1993, she was killed when the guard shot her eighteen times. The guard was terminated from other security jobs for alleged aggressive behavior. The guard was also a convicted sex offender and had not properly registered with the authorities in accordance with Nevada laws. The court ruled that the guard was an employee of Sun Harbor and that the employer should have conducted a background investigation that would have alerted them that the employee had previous incidents of violent behavior, along with his criminal convictions.

The second area of interest is related to responsible behavior of employees. For example, employers check credit as a measure of applicant responsibility. When employers use third parties to conduct a background check of credit, criminal and employment history, the employer must notify the applicant in writing and obtain the applicant's written consent (FCRA 15 U.S.C. § 1681 *et seq.*). Employers conducting their own investigations through use of government agency information and conducting searches of online resources are not subject to the FCRA; however, they may be liable under other laws, depending on how the information is used. "A 2010 poll of the Society of Human Resource Management shows that approximately 60 percent of employers use credit checks and approximately 92 percent use criminal histories in screening job applicants" (Lawyers Committee for Civil Rights Under Law, 2010. p. 2).

The Equal Employment Opportunity Commission (EEOC) has been on the warpath to catch employers abusing the background check for discriminatory purposes. In the case of *EEOC v. Freeman* (2013), the EEOC filed suit against an employer that indicated the employer used background checks that had a discriminatory effect on African American male applicants. Like many employers, Freeman experienced issues with theft, drug use, and workplace violence; therefore, the company implemented a background check to better evaluate trustworthiness and reliability of potential employees. After the background checks were initiated, Katrina Vaugn filed a discrimination lawsuit claiming that Freeman illegally denied her employment based on the poor credit history. Some specific uses of criminal and credit investigations may be discriminatory and a violation of Title VII and the EEOC bears the burden of supplying reliable expert testimony and statistical analysis that supports disparate impact stemming from a specific employment practice before such a violation can be found. The court ruled the EEOC had not met this burden; therefore, summary judgment was granted to Freeman. (See also *Singleton v. Domino's Pizza*, 2012.)

With the rise in use and popularity of Facebook, Twitter, and other electronic media, employers frequently turn to Internet tools and social media to uncover information about applicants that go beyond what an employer could normally ask in an interview. For example, the employer could not ask about religion in the interview, but by viewing the candidate's Facebook page could discover a religious affiliation. In some instances, even if the applicants have set their profile to "private," employers have enlisted the help of a friend of the applicant to gain access to the profile (Smith & Kidder, 2010). Employers must be careful, though, viewing profiles over social networking sites, as they cannot use this information to discriminate against groups that are protected under Title VII.

Employers also need to consider the source and validity of the information they access. Some websites collect information about individuals from a variety of sources, and the information may no longer be valid or verified by the individual (MyLife, 2013). Spokeo, a data provider that compiles and sells profiles on consumers, entered into a settlement agreement with the FTC in June of 2012 to pay $800,000 in civil penalties because the company provided incorrect information about individuals and did not take steps to validate the information or provide notice (Federal Trade Commission, 2012). A person could even create a fake profile on Facebook or another social media site and post information as if they were that person. In *Blue Mountain School District v. J.S. ex rel. Snyder* a student created and posted a fictitious Facebook account using the name of the principal. The information posted to Facebook suggests the principal is a sex addict and a pedophile.

Confidentiality Agreements

As previously discussed, employers frequently inform employees of their monitoring practices and privacy expectations in employee handbooks. Employees often sign confidentiality agreements that prohibit employees from discussion certain topics outside of the office. One employee ran afoul of what the employer felt was within the confidentiality agreement when posting an image of his paycheck on Instagram (Hagen & Green, 2013). The National Labor Relations Act (NLRA) protects discussion of pay and working conditions with colleagues, but does posting the information on social media take it too far? On the other hand, employers have a duty to protect certain information. Consider the examples of employees who posted copies of credit card receipts containing inappropriate comments. A CVS customer filed a civil complaint in the United States District Court in New Jersey, alleging violations of federal and state discrimination and intentional and negligent infliction of emotional distress resulting from a receipt showed her name as "Ching Chong" Lee, when the customer had actually provided her real name when placing the order. The complaint names the employee as a "John Doe" and the employer, CVS, as a party through theories of respondeat superior and agency. See *Lee v. CVS, New Jersey District Court*, 2013).

Does the confidentiality agreement work both ways? If employees are not allowed to discuss the company on their social media sites, should the employer be able to publish employee information on the Internet? Some companies have resolved that issue by encouraging employees to sign releases, yet there still appears to be a gap in expectations and actual practice in this area (Knapp & Soylu, 2013).

Global Positioning Systems

Global positioning systems (GPS) provide real-time location of the devices (Ciochetti, 2011). Although the use of GPS for monitoring company vehicles and cellular phones is on the rise, employers need to consider the reason for tracking. The use of GPS for tracking employer vehicles to monitor compliance with government regulations, safety, and company policy seems reasonable; however, prolonged tracking, method of tracking, and sophistication of the device may eventually cross the line.

Currently, there are no federal laws that regulate the employer's use of GPS devices; however, California, Connecticut, Delaware, and Texas have enacted laws that regulate the use of electronic tracking (Blish & Stiller, 2009; Rosenberg, 2010). In earlier cases, the courts favored the employer's use of GPS on company-owned equipment because employees should not have any expectation of privacy in company-owned equipment (see *Elgin v. St. Louis Coca-Cola Bottling Company*, 2005). But what about the expectation of privacy in one's personal vehicles? In *Matter of Cunningham v. New York State Dept. of Labor* (2011), a state employee was suspected of taking time off that had not been authorized and falsifying his time sheets. The employer hired an investigator to follow the employee; however, when the employee became aware someone was following him, the employer then placed a GPS on the employee's personal vehicle. The court found that using the GPS on the personal vehicle was not unreasonable since the employee had a history of disciplinary actions. The ruling in *Cunningham* appears to leave the door open for employers to use GPS on the employee's personal equipment; however, employers should approach that open door carefully and be able to document a legitimate reason for the tracking. In a more recent decision, the Supreme Court ruled that the use of a GPS on a suspected drug dealer's vehicle without a warrant was unconstitutional under the 4th Amendment (see *U.S. v. Jones*, 2012). Although the *Jones* case involved government action under the 4th Amendment, which does not apply to a private employer, the case provides a reminder to private employers to define a legitimate business purpose and provide employees with a policy that notifies them of potential use of GPS devices. Justice Scalia's opinion could result in claims against employers under common-law trespass if the employer places a tracking device on an employee's personal property. Additionally, the court noted that the length of time the tracking device was used may have some bearing, as short-term monitoring of a person's movements is considered more reasonable than longer-term monitoring.

Similar to a GPS are the infrared sensors that track the location of employees. Sensors can be implanted in employee identification badges. In the healthcare field, the sensors are used by hospitals to track the location of nurses via their badges so that they can be dispatched to patients in the most efficient and expedient manner (Hawkins, 1997). While on the job, use of the infrared system to track the employee's whereabouts should not be a problem, but should the employer be able to continue to track the employee after working hours?

Web Cams

Similar to GPS monitoring, employers may want to conduct workplace monitoring by video cameras or webcams for safety and observation of productivity. What appeared to be a tool to facilitate communication may actually be a spying device, depending on how it is used. Consider the employer-owned laptop that travels home with the employee. Some devices have the ability to be activated remotely so that the employer could ultimately view the location of the computer, which might include the employee's bedroom, if the employee was working at home. In 2008, the Lower Merion School District distributed laptops to almost 2,300 students and did not inform the students that lost computers could be tracked remotely through the use of webcams (Martin, 2010). One student discovered that hundreds of images of him were taken, including one while he was sleeping, and the student had not reported his laptop missing. The student filed a lawsuit; however, the school system entered into a settlement in the case (Martin, 2010). Although the school district was cleared of criminal charges, private employers should consider whether the reasons for monitoring outweigh the potential ramifications if monitoring is not properly administered. In *M.E. v. St. Louis Medical Clinic* (Your Missouri Courts, 2013), a case filed in the St. Louis County Circuit Court, the plaintiff claims that the camera on her laptop was secretly activated and tapes of some of the patients at the office, as well as pictures of her at home, were shared (Patrick, 2013). The ownership of the laptop was not determinable from the initial court documents; however, employers should monitor this case and create official policies for the use of webcams.

Role of Human Resources

While information technology may be responsible for the actual monitoring of email and computer use, human resources is the guardian of all that is considered private. If in doubt, just ask yourself who is responsible for personnel files, background checks, drug tests, compensation data, credit reports, and insurance information (Sumser, 2012). As improvements are made in monitoring technologies and the laws regulating the appropriate use of these technologies continues to evolve, human resources managers, legal departments, and key executives should review current policies to ensure they adequately explain the company's view on technology. The remaining part of this chapter provides suggestions for potential best practices that companies can customize to fit their organizations.

POTENTIAL BEST PRACTICES
FOR HR MANAGERS TO CONSIDER

Trust and Management Perspective

Does it simply come down to trusting employees and considering that they will conduct themselves in ways that are in the best interest of the organization? According to Wakefield (2004), trust is not the issue for organizations. The main point is security of organizational information and privacy, which has been elevated due to federal statutes and requirements. Trusting employees is not at issue here; however, the importance of securing organizational information and unique competitive advantages is!

One could argue that the organization's philosophy can be related back to management style and techniques. If a leader or supervisor takes the stance that employees generally do not want to be at work or will do whatever it takes to get out of working, Theory X, then the organization's monitoring efforts may be more stringent. If the general view of employees as being willing to work and wanting to do their best is embraced, Theory Y, then the monitoring efforts may not be as rigorous. Further research should be conducted to ascertain the parallels of management philosophy and the connection with monitoring efforts.

Policy Creation

Since technology evolves faster than laws to regulate it, the job of human resources and legal professionals tends to focus on risk management when it comes to creating policies related to technology. The key to making sure employees understand the rules for using technology is to create strong, clear policies for employees' use of email, Internet, blogs, instant messaging, social media, and texting, as well as use of company-owned equipment such as cellular phones and computers. Providing a clear message promotes transparency in management. Informing employees of the specifics related to monitoring may also deter inappropriate activities. Including specific prohibitions such as using company equipment to send offensive or defamatory comments is also important. Organizations should also consider alternatives to monitoring such as blocking access to certain websites that are known for inappropriate content such as pornography and discriminatory sites that might create issues related to a hostile work environment. Human resources departments should also create guidelines for the hiring process to avoid the pitfall of invading the privacy of potential employees, as well as intentionally or unintentionally violating federal and state laws on discrimination.

The National Workrights Institute (2010) provides a Model Policy on Electronic Monitoring that we recommend be studied carefully by HRM professionals. When possible, organizational leaders and HR professionals should strive to create a culture of trust. Trust is not just related to technology issues, but to the information as a whole. If employees feel that Big Brother is watching every move they make during work and possibly nonworking hours, they will not be as eager to share knowledge with the company. Remote employees present additional concerns because they do not perform work in the office. Courts usually "uphold an expectation of privacy much more in the home than in the office" (Koster, 2012. p. 8). Therefore, it is even more important for the employer to provide a detailed and very specific policy regarding electronic monitoring, equipment use, and privacy when working with remote employees.

As with other employment policies, employers must be prepared to enforce their rules. If the employer creates a procedure for addressing violations of the electronic use and privacy policies but does not follow through or enforces the policies inconsistently, the employee may be maintain a reasonable expectation of privacy (Smith & Burg, 2012). For example, consider a written policy that prohibits the use of the company's email system for personal use, but the company does not enforce the policy or does not enforce it equally. Failure to enforce and/or apply the policy equally could lead employees to assume they still have some expectation of privacy.

THE FUTURE

What does the future hold? With the increase of technologically savvy employees in the workplace, employers certainly need to be vigilant about assessing the performance of employees and potentially crossing the line of privacy and the law. Current efforts toward maximizing employee productivity include implementing policies as previously discussed, as well as IT business solutions such as management surveillance products (MSPs) (Gurnee, 2013). The foundation of these efforts begins with a sound policy regarding employee conduct, privacy, and monitoring.

Since employers are ultimately responsible for the productivity of the employees, ensuring that employees are fully contributing in pursuit of fulfillment of the mission and vision of the organization is essential. A recent advance is to install an app on the iPhone that will allow employers to track employees; the app is called StealthGenie (Jacobs, 2013). This app allows employers to track the whereabouts and activities of employees during the workday on their smart devices. The individual controlling the system can log into the account from anywhere in the world and monitor activities. StealthGenie will allow the controller to read emails of an employee, see appointments and schedules, review SMS messages, and view videos and photographs stored on the smart device. However, how much is too much tracking? This seems to lend itself to Theory X management style in not believing that employees will do their best to meet their goals. Certainly, this type of monitoring could only be done on an employer-owned device. A key question would be if the employer would tell the employee of such monitoring tactics.

Legislation does not currently address the privacy of employee information found on social media; however, increased use of the information by employers will likely lead to court cases that will set the stage for legislation (Smith & Burg, 2012). For now, employee information that is posted on a social media site—but unavailable to the public without permission from the employee—should continue to be private, which means employers should not be allowed to request access. On the other hand, information that is posted for the public to view should not carry any expectation of privacy.

Some employers have created private social networks for use by employees, vendors, and customers. Additionally, some employers have considered the using social networking for performance reviews. Have you noticed how social media sites encourage users to rate certain things, such as the ability to "like" posts on Facebook and "endorse" skills on Linkedin? Should organizations use the same type of rating tools to encourage employees to "like" or "endorse" the work performance of their colleagues? If so, should employees who keep to themselves, follow the rules, and produce quality work *but avoid social media* receive a lower score on their review than an employee who has more online social interaction on a company social network? The use of an internal social network creates additional questions on whether employees will use it and how the time spent on the network impacts work performance.

With the increased use of smartphones, tablets, and other devices, it is likely that the courts will hear more cases of this nature and that the result will provide new legal guidelines explaining the employees' expectation of privacy on social networking sites. Employers should monitor court cases and proposed legislation for guidance on the expectations of privacy of both employers and employees. HRM professionals are advised to seek current advice from legal counsel before producing or revising privacy standards because we believe future cases (or legislation) will have much to say about these matters.

CONCLUSION

The evolving area of human resources and the application of the law are but the tip of the iceberg at this time as more and additional avenues of communication open through technological advances. Consideration must be given to what is a fair expectation to protect both the employer and the employee. The organization wants to ensure that there is reasonable protection of its assets, resources, and unique organizational capabilities. This can be accomplished through multiple avenues of security, one of which is employee monitoring. Yet the methods of monitoring should not intrude into areas in which employees should have a reasonable expectation of privacy, such as their personal social media accounts that are password protected.

Organizations need to give consideration to the full lifecycle of human resources activities. Policy formulation surrounding the HR infrastructure will be critical to stay in tune with the technological advances. With regard to recruiting, employers will want to understand the past actions of their potential employees before making a solid determination if this individual would be a good hire. For an employee of an organization, discretion needs to be exercised regarding the information posted on social media. Even if activities conducted on social media are done outside of company time, the employee can still be held liable for any damages that occur to the organization. It is of utmost importance to remember that once information is posted on social media, no matter how private an individual thinks it may be, it becomes public domain. Finally, the topics discussed here have implications for multinational employers. While the laws of the United States may be slow to catch up with technology, organizations must be careful to abide by privacy regulations in all countries in which they operate.

REFERENCES

Barker, J. (2009, January 14). Businesses use RFID to track workers, pay for fewer hours. *Medill Reports*. Retrieved from http://news.medill.northwestern.edu/chicago/news.aspx?id=111561

Blish, N. A., & Stiller, S. P. (2009). Tracking employees using technology. *ACC Docket*, 84–92. Retrieved from http://www.abramslaw.com/Articles/Tracking-Employees-Using-Technology-pdf.pdf

Blue Mountain School Dist. v. J.S. ex rel. Snyder, 132 S.Ct. 1097 (Mem) U.S., 2012.

Brahmana v. Lembo, No. 09-106, 2009 WL 1424438 (N.D. Cal. May 20, 2009).

Ciocchetti, C. (2011). The eavesdropping employer: A twenty-first century framework for employee monitoring. *American Business Law Journal, 48*(2), 285–369. doi:10.1111/j.1744-1714.2011.01116.x

City of Ontario, Cal. v. Quon, 130 S.Ct. 269 (2010).

Comstock, C. (2011). Morgan Stanley uses the "CiscoFatty" story to teach its new hires how not to use Twitter and Facebook. *Business Insider*. Retrieved from http://www.businessinsider.com/morgan-stanley-uses-the-ciscofatty-story-to-teach-its-new-hires-how-to-use-twitter-and-facebook-2011-1

EEOC v. Freeman 2013 WL 4464553 (D.Md., 2013).

Electronic Communications Privacy Act of 1986, Pub.L. No. 99-508. 100 Stat. 1848 (1986).

Electronic Privacy Information Center. (2012). Following Maryland, Congress and California consider bills banning employers from asking for Facebook passwords. Retrieved from http://epic.org/2012/05/following-maryland-congress-an.html

Elgin v. St. Louis Coca-Cola Bottling Company, No. 4:05-cv-970-DJS, 2005 WL 3050633 (E.D. Mo. Nov. 14, 2005).

Federal Credit Reporting Act 15 U.S.C. § 1681 *et seq.*

Federal Trade Commission. (2012). Spokeo to pay $800,000 to settle FTC charges company allegedly marketed information to employers and recruiters in violation of the FCRA. Retrieved from http://www.ftc.gov/news-events/press-releases/2012/06/spokeo-pay-800000-settle-ftc-charges-company-allegedly-marketed

Fraser v. Nationwide Mut. Ins. Co., 352 F.3d 107 (3d Cir. 2003).

Genova, G. (2009). No place to play: Current employee privacy rights in social networking sites. *Business Communication Quarterly, 72*(1), 97–101.

Grover v. Augustine, 38 A.D. 3d 364 (N.Y. App. Div. 2007).

Gurnee, F. (2013). Could employee surveillance, monitoring, and tracking be the next IT service trend? Retrieved from http://www.lookscloudy.com/2013/04/could-employee-surveillance-monitoring-and-tracking-be-the-next-it-service-trend/

Hagen, L., & Greene, L. (2013, August 7). Pic 'coste' guy his job. *New York Post,* 9. Retrieved from http://search.proquest.com

Hawkins, D. (1997, September 15). Who's watching now? *U.S. News & World Report, 123*(10), 56–58.

Holmes v. Petrovich Development Co., 191 Cal. App. 4th 1047 (3d Dist. 2011).

Jacobs, N. (2013, October 14). Employee monitoring policies to make sure your business does not suffer. Retrieved from http://www.stealthgenie.com/blog/employee-monitoring-policies-to-make-sure-your-business-does-not-suffer/

Knapp, K. R., & Soylu, A. (2013). Technology: The good, the bad, and the ugly. *Mustang Journal of Management & Marketing, 2,* 69–81.

Komando, K. (2012). Can your employer monitor your smartphone? *USA Today.* Retrieved from http://usatoday30.usatoday.com/tech/columnist/kimkomando/story/2012-02-24/work-monitor-smartphone/53221804/1

Konop v. Hawaiian Airlines, Inc., 302 F.3d 868 (9th Cir. 2002).

Konrad, K., & Ames, S. (2000). Web-based email services offer employees little privacy. *CNET.* Retrieved from http://news.cnet.com/2100-1017-246543.html

Koster, K. (2012). Employee privacy: Tattle-tale technology. *Employee Benefit News, 26*(5), 8.

Lane, F. (2003). *The naked employee: How technology is compromising workplace privacy.* New York, NY: American Management Association.

Lawyers Committee for Civil Rights Under Law. (2010). Employers guide to best practices for use of background checks in employment decisions. Retrieved from http://www.lawyerscommittee.org/admin/employment_discrimination/documents/files/Employers-Best-Practices-Background-Checks-Guide.pdf

Lee v. CVS, New Jersey District Court (No. 1:2013cv02432). Retrieved from www.appellate-brief.com/images/stories/PDF/Lee/cmpl1.pdf

Martin, J. P. (2010). Lower Merion district's laptop saga ends with $610,000 settlement. Retrieved from http://articles.philly.com/2010-10-12/news/24981536_1_laptop-students-district-several-million-dollars

Matter of Cunningham v. New York State Dept. of Labor, 89 A.D. 3d 1347 (N.Y. Ap. Div. 2011).

MyLife. (2011). Privacy policy. Retrieved from http://www.mylife.com/privacy-policy/

National Conference of State Legislatures [NCSL]. (2014). Employer access to social medial usernames and passwords. Retrieved from http://www.ncsl.org/research/telecommunications-and-information-technology/employer-access-to-social-media-passwords-2013.aspx

National Workrights Institute. (2010). Model policy on electronic monitoring. Retrieved from http://workrights.us/?products=model-policy-on-electronic-monitoring

O'Connor v. Ortega, 480 U.S. 709 (1987).

Patrick, R. (2013, Mar 28). Clinic secretly taped employee with webcam, St. Louis County lawsuit claims. *St. Louis Post–Dispatch*, A.2. Retrieved from http://search.proquest.com

Peerce, M. J., & Shapiro, D. V. (2010). The increasing privacy expectations in employees' personal email. *Journal of Internet Law, 13*(8), 1–21.

Pietrylo v. Hillstone Restaurant Group, WL 3128420 (D.N.J. 2090).

Roberts, S. J., & Roach, T. (2009). Social networking web sites and human resource personnel: Suggestions for job searches. *Business Communication Quarterly, 72*(1), 110–114. doi: 10.1177/1080569908330380

Rockwell v. Sun Harbor Budget Suites, 925 P.2d 1175 (Nev. 1996).

Rosenberg, K. (2010). Location surveillance by GPS: Balancing an employer's business interest with employee privacy. *Washington Journal of Law, Technology & Arts, 6*(2), 143–154. Retrieved from https://digital.lib.washington.edu/dspace-law/bitstream/handle/1773.1/479/6wjlta143Rosenberg.pdf?sequence=4

Segalis, B. (2011). Employee privacy gains in the United States. Retrieved from http://www.infolawgroup.com/2011/01/articles/enforcement/employee-privacy-gains-in-the-united-states

Singleton v. Domino's Pizza, LLC, 2012 U.S. Dist. Lexis 8626 (D. Md. Jan 25, 2012).

Smith, D. V., & Burg, J. (2012). What are the limits of employee privacy? *GPSolo, 29*(6), 9-11.

Smith, W. P., & Kidder, D. L. (2010). You've been tagged! (then again, maybe not): Employers and Facebook. *Business Horizons, 53*(5), 491–499.

Sprague, R. (2007). From Taylorism to the omnipticon: Expanding employee surveillance beyond the workplace. *John Marshall Journal of Computer and Computer & Information Law, 25*(1), 1–37.

Stengart v. Loving Care Agency, Inc. 201 N.J. 300, 900 A.2d 650 N.J. 2010.

Sumser, J. (2012). Information privacy 5: Futures and issues in HR. *HR Examiner.* Retrieved from http://www.hrexaminer.com/information-privacy-5-futures-and-issues-in-hr/

U.S. v. Jones, 132 S.Ct. 945 U.S., 2012.

Van Alstyne v. Electronic Scriptorium Ltd. 560 F.3d 199 (4th Cir. 2009)

Wakefield, R. L. (2004). Employee monitoring and surveillance: The growing trend. *Information Systems Audit and Control Journal,1. Retrieved from http://www.isaca.org/Journal/Past-Issues/2004/Volume-1/Pages/Employee-Monitoring-and-Surveillance-The-Growing-Trend.aspx*

Webster, G. D. (1994). Respecting employee privacy. *Association Management, 46*(1), 142.

Your Missouri Courts. (2013). *M.E. v. St. Louis Medical Clinic PC ETAL.* Retrieved from https://www.courts.mo.gov/casenet/cases/parties.do

CHAPTER 13

NEGOTIATING CONTRACT MANAGEMENT AND PERSONNEL IN HIGH-TECHNOLOGY, HIGH-COMPLEXITY DOMAINS

Issues of Inherently Governmental and Critical Functions in Big Data Analytics Teams

Sara R. Jordan

INTRODUCTION

The "Big Data" revolution in private and public business has outpaced regulatory and human resource planning initiatives, constituting a clear problem domain for human resource managers. Vis-à-vis workforce planning, it is not clear what measures can or should be taken at the firm level to build analytics professionals. Vis-à-vis regulations, it is not clear whether

Legal and Regulatory Issues in Human Resources Management, pages 267–284
Copyright © 2015 by Information Age Publishing

Big Data sets can be constructed or managed by contractors if contractors' efforts must not constrain federal employees' decision-making capabilities.

Finding workers to fill the needs of Big Data analytics is likely to trouble human resources and contract managers in the coming years. According to surveys of human resource professionals in information technology, "63 percent of respondents said it's somewhat or very challenging to find skilled IT professionals, particularly talent in the functional areas of networking, security and help desk/technical support. Fifty-seven percent of those surveyed said network administration is among the skill sets in greatest demand within their IT department" (Minton-Eversole, 2013). But, in a tongue-in-cheek bit of Big Data analytics, technology blogger Vincent Granville noted up to 400 varieties of job titles associated with skills deemed relevant to the role of "data scientist," which is a role also blessed (or cursed) with the title "The Sexiest Job of the 21st Century" (Granville, 2013). These two bits of analysis of the future of analytics and IT staffing point out just one of the many potential issues confronting government organizations as they attempt to manage the Big Data Revolution.

In addition to "ordinary" problems of staffing, such as finding and funding qualified workers in high-technology fields, as I will outline in this chapter, there are two major and unique problems associated with Big Data management: nondiscriminate staffing and contracting that abides by relevant regulations. The problems with staffing relate to issues of compliance with relevant antidiscrimination policies in the federal government while the problems related to contracting relate to issues of compliance with office of management and budget requirements for contract management under conditions where contractors may perform "inherently governmental" tasks.

This chapter is divided into four sections: (a) an introduction to Big Data in government; (b) the demographic challenges of hiring for Big Data; (c) an exploration of the meaning of "inherently governmental," "critical," and "closely associated" functions in government; and (d) an argument that Big Data analytics are inherently governmental activities. In the conclusion, I will elaborate on some key workforce planning strategies that government agencies ought to pursue to manage a recentralization of Big Data into the hands of federal employees.

BIG DATA IN GOVERNMENT

What is Big Data? What is Big Data in Government?

Big Data is a phenomenon currently taking public, private, and nonprofit organizations by storm. Oracle sells analytics solutions; Google gathers data on its three billion search queries per day; international relations scholars mine the "global database of events, language and tone" to identify trends in conflicts;

the Centers for Disease Control and Prevention predicts influenza strains and severity through its aggregated databases; and countless businesses small and large ponder whether to introduce Big Data analysis into their marketing strategies. Everyone is talking about Big Data, but few professionals seem to be able to articulate a meaningful definition of Big Data that applies to their genuine needs. In this section, I outline the definition and meaning of Big Data in simple terms, and then show what the U.S. government, particularly the Executive Office of the President and the U.S. National Science Foundation, mean when they discuss the meaning and importance of Big Data.

Quite simply put, Big Data is the for-purpose analysis of large, complex, disaggregated databases by tools purposefully designed to effectively mine through masses of noisy, dynamic, rapidly evolving data. When speaking of Big Data, the inputs into Big Data aggregates can include traditional quantified statements of a phenomenon (e.g., representation of a "strongly agree" survey answer as 5 on a Likert scale) or can be the "datified" representation of any number of images, texts, phrases, transactions, locations, actions, or even bodies. Database use can be fixed or relational, and the data put into Big Data analysis can be structured or unstructured. But the term also refers to the analytical tools (e.g., machine learning algorithms) that capture and "use" these bytes to produce an end product, such as through data visualization. Furthermore, the personnel who make the decisions that establish the purposive nature of a Big Data exercise must also be considered as part of the definition of the concept of Big Data.

Big Data is an object, processes, and personnel. Big Data does not exist without a database somewhere (although that location is likely virtual). It also does not exist as a static entity. Big Data databases are a managed amalgamation of multiple preexisting and simultaneously updated databases. Like cloud computing analysis, which uses the analysis capacities of multiple servers to perform large-scale analyses that cannot be done on a single server bank, or which clients prefer to be performed or available in multiple disaggregated locations, Big Data is a managed unity of parts. Big Data is also different from traditional information technology (IT). While traditional IT services include design, implementation and oversight of operating systems (OS), hardware, applications, databases, and information technology development, Big Data processes are tools and techniques for "capturing, curating, maintaining, storing, searching, sharing, analyzing, and presenting" databases, analysis, and reports (Balci, 2013, p. 1).

Big Data only "exists" insofar as it is the product of discrete actions on the part of integrated technical and managerial processes. Technically, Big Data exists when the architecture to support a unification of disaggregated data sources is constructed and maintained. Big Data architecture includes data capture and curation programs that synchronize with long-term (archival), medium-term (infrequent analysis), and immediate-term (frequent analysis) storage units. Big Data architecture also includes the utilities designed to search, analyze, present, and visualize the disaggregated data sources captured and maintained. One example of a component of Big Data architecture is "Hadoop." As Krihely neatly summarizes it, "Hadoop … is an open source data platform which performs a very neat trick. Simply put, Hadoop is a tool for tying together multiple servers into single, easily-scalable clusters, ideal for distributed data storage and processing" (2013, p. 1). But, while Hadoop makes capturing and storing data from multiple, formerly "siloed" databases much easier, it is, alas, only software. Behind the decision to implement an open-source data aggregation plan, or to outsource the development of architecture into a single entity, there must be an individual or group of individuals making those critical decisions.

The technical or process architecture of Big Data is only half the body of Big Data. The other half is the personnel who make essential decisions for determining what to capture, search, share, analyze, or present. The body of persons who make up the managerial structure of Big Data—those individuals responsible for building, cleaning, maintaining, and analyzing the data gathered—play an essential role in shaping the technical and object body of Big Data. That is, data architects determine how, when, and why variables are imported, cleaned, and presented; the individuals behind the data are essential to determine the "Bigness" and usefulness of the data object. Consequently, the selection of individuals—the resolution of the problems of human resources and Big Data—is an essential component of Big Data management.

"Transforming Data to Knowledge to Action" Big Data in Government

In March of 2012, well before the explosion of concerns about Big Data analytics and the privacy violations of the National Security Administration (NSA), the Obama White House unveiled a "$200 Million in New R&D Investments" initiative to "make the most of the fast-growing volume of digital data" (Office of Science and Technology Policy, 2012). This "Big Data Research and Development Initiative" was designed to help catalyze use of Big Data architecture and analytics in six key areas of government. Importantly for this chapter, this initiative helped the agencies and programs selected (described in Figure 13.1, Big Data Initiatives in the U.S. government) to "expand the workforce needed to develop and use Big Data technologies." Following this announcement and the disbursement of funding, a notable increase in positions for "data scientists," "data engineers," and other titles encompassing analytics and database software could be found on a query of usajobs.gov.

National Science Foundation and the National Institutes of Health—Core Techniques and Technologies for Advancing Big Data Science & Engineering
"'Big Data' is a new joint solicitation supported by the National Science Foundation (NSF) and the National Institutes of Health (NIH) that will advance the core scientific and technological means of managing, analyzing, visualizing, and extracting useful information from large and diverse data sets."

National Science Foundation
"NSF is implementing a comprehensive, long-term strategy that includes new methods to derive knowledge from data; infrastructure to manage, curate, and serve data to communities; and new approaches to education and workforce development." Selected projects include "Funding a $10 million 'Expeditions in Computing' project based at the University of California, Berkeley that will integrate… machine learning, cloud computing, and crowd sourcing"; "Issuing a $2 million award for a research training group to support training for undergraduates to use a graphical and visualization technique for complex data"; and "Providing $1.4 million in support for a focused research group of statisticians and biologists to determine protein structures and biological pathways."

Department of Defense—Data to Decisions:
"The Department of Defense (DoD) is "placing a big bet on big data" investing approximately $250 million annually (with $60 million available for new research projects) across the Military Departments in a series of programs" to "harness and utilize massive data… to bring together sensing, perception and decision support to make truly autonomous systems that can maneuver and make decisions on their own." "In addition, the Defense Advanced Research Projects Agency (DARPA) is beginning the XDATA program, which intends to invest approximately $25 million annually for four years to develop computational techniques and software tools for analyzing large volumes of data, both semi-structured (e.g., tabular, relational, categorical, meta-data) and unstructured (e.g., text documents, message traffic)."

National Institutes of Health—1000 Genomes Project Data Available on Cloud
To make the 200 terabytes, "1000 Genomes Project data set" publicly available for free.

Department of Energy—Scientific Discovery through Advanced Computing
"The Department of Energy will provide $25 million in funding to establish the Scalable Data Management, Analysis and Visualization (SDAV) Institute. Led by the Energy Department's Lawrence Berkeley National Laboratory, the SDAV Institute will bring together the expertise of six national laboratories and seven universities to develop new tools to help scientists manage and visualize data on the Department's supercomputers, which will further streamline the processes that lead to discoveries made by scientists using the Department's research facilities."

US Geological Survey- Big Data for Earth System Science:
"through its John Wesley Powell Center for Analysis and Synthesis. The Center catalyzes innovative thinking in Earth system science by providing scientists a place and time for in-depth analysis, state-of-the-art computing capabilities, and collaborative tools invaluable for making sense of huge data sets."

Figure 13.1 Big Data initiatives in the U.S. government. *Source:* Excerpted from "Obama Administration Unveils 'Big Data' Initiative: Announces $200 Million in New R&D Investments," Press Release from March 29, 2012.

BIG DATA HIRING DEMOGRAPHICS

Understanding Positions in Big Data Analytics Teams

As suggested in the introduction to this chapter, one of the problems of Big Data is whether or not human resources management (HRM) is up for the task. Specifically, Big Data, like many other high-technology professions, has a demographic skew that does not fit the overall demographic profile of the United States. That Big Data professionals also come from a variety of discrete professions, such as software developers, database managers, mathematical modelers, and statisticians also compounds the problem of hiring analytics teams that are demographically representative of the individuals from whom they curate or analyze data. In this section, I first outline the known problems of staffing in Big Data analytics, then identify demographic trends in five of the professional categories that may come together to make a Big Data analytics team: business analyst, data scientist, database engineer, mathematician, and software engineer. At the close of the section, I discuss how the general staffing and demographic representation issues may create problems for building Big Data analytics teams in the United States and state and local governments. A review of the information in Figures 13.2 and 13.3 at this point will help the reader follow this discussion.

Database Administrator. This is by far the most commonly used database-related job title. A database administrator (DBA) is a person responsible for the daily care and feeding of a database. A DBA's primary responsibility is to ensure that the database is available, is performing properly and is kept safe. This includes such tasks as software installation, upgrades and patching, backup and recovery, performance tuning, security, monitoring, problem solving, etc.

Database Architect. Often referred to as a Data Architect, a DA is responsible for gathering business requirements, designing a logical model and ultimately building the physical database. The DA is expected to analyze business needs and create a database solution to meet them. Tasks include requirements definition, business analysis, data modeling, database design; E-R (Entity Relationship) models, database programming, business report generation, ETL procedure development, database performance optimization, etc.

Database Engineer. This term is not really that commonly used and can often just be referring to one or both of the above definitions. One example job description that I found describes the Database Engineer as someone who is expected to "design, implement and maintain database systems," (serving as both DB and DBA). http://searchoracle.techtarget.com/answer/What-is-the-difference-between-a-database-engineer-architect-and-administrator

---

Figure 13.2 Defining database workers. *Source:* Adapted from Hillenbrand, n.d., "What is the difference between a database engineer, architect, and administrator?"

Typical Education Qualifications:
Bachelors or Master degree in either computer science, statistics, epidemiology, or other mathematics or computing related field

Some Typical Skills Include:
Software Programming languages:
  NoSQL
  Python
  Perl
  Java
  Linux
  C++

Database Skills:
  Microsoft Excel
  QlikView BI apps
  SQL and NoSQL

Data Visualization Skills:
  Tableau Software
  Flare
  Google Visualization

Machine Learning Skills:
  Predictive statistics and forecasting
  Text and data mining

Mathematical and Statistical Skills:
  Statistical software packages (e.g., R, STATA, SAS)
  Statistics (econometrics, linear models, classification and regression models)
  Bayesian analysis

Data Engineering Skills:
  Hadoop
  MapReduce
  Cassandra

Communication:
  Microsoft Powerpoint
  Prezzie
  Web-meeting platforms (e.g., WebEx)

Figure 13.3   Skills for Big Data architecture and analysis. *Source:* Excerpted and adapted from: "Data Scientist Core Skills," Sanders, 2013.

Business Analyst

As described in the sections above, Big Data analytics is about more than just the data itself. Big Data analysis is about the decisions that lead to capturing, storing, analyzing and ultimately using the mass of information that can be compiled by database and software engineers, modeled by mathematicians, and compiled and structured by data scientists. The oversight of this analysis may be done by a business analyst, formerly known as Systems Analysts.

The consulting firm BusinessAnalystSolutions (2012) defines simply the relationship between systems analysis, business analysts, and the purpose and responsibilities of business analysts today.

While the systems analyst belonged to the IT department, business analysts can now be found throughout the organization, such as in the IT fields or within individual units or departments. But wherever they sit, business analysts must be great communicators, tactful diplomats, problem solvers, thinkers, and analyzers—with the ability to understand and respond to user needs in rapidly changing business environments.

> We define the purpose of the role of the Business Analyst as being ultimately responsible for ensuring that organizations get the most from their limited IT and change management resource.
>
> Business Analysts are responsible for identifying change needs, assessing the impact of the change, capturing and documenting requirements and then ensuring that those requirements are delivered by IT whilst supporting the business through the implementation process. Business Analysts should not just write specifications and then leave them to be delivered. The development lifecycle is an iterative one and the Business Analyst must be involved from initial concept through to final implementation. (BusinessAnalystSolutions, 2012)

Ultimately, business analysts serve a critical function to bridge the business or firm purpose and the firm technology.

While certification programs for business analysts such as the CBAP (Certified Business Analysis Professional) suggest that certification may increase salaries and career tenure for business analysts, there are few demographic indicators available for this field. A review of LinkedIn profiles for the CBAP, however, suggests some representation of women, but not minorities, among certified individuals.

Database Engineer

The first problem of describing the demographic characteristics of an average database engineer is to identify what a database engineer is. Hillenbrand differentiates a database engineer as someone who functions as both a database architect and a database administrator.

In creating the industry profile for the position of "database administrators," the Bureau of Labor Statistics (BLS) defines the role as to "administer, test, and implement computer databases, applying knowledge of database management systems. Coordinate changes to computer databases.

May plan, coordinate, and implement security measures to safeguard computer databases" (Bureau of Labor Statistics, 2012). The Bureau of Labor Statistics shows that a substantial number of database administrators, who likely make up the population of individuals from whom the role "database engineer" may come, live on the east coast of the United States (e.g., Virginia 6,090) or in California (10,510) and earn a mean wage of around $79,102 per year. In blogs and other posts associated with database administration, bloggers note the "vanishingly small" number of women in database administration roles (SQLservercentral.com, 2007). Other bloggers also note that "minority underrepresentation and racism appears to be especially prevalent in Information Technology, lurking just under the covers, hidden and well-disguised behind rigorous education requirements and institutional barriers" (Burleson, n.d., p. 1).

Data Scientist

A query for jobs and "data scientist" run through Google during 2013 would have turned up the line "data scientist: the sexiest job no one has" for multiple queries. The sexiness of the job of data scientist can be attributed to three factors: the scarcity of individuals who could be called "data scientists" as such, the expected pay for and expected return-on-investment for a company that selects the right data scientist, and the anticipation that data scientists are "universal problem solvers" or "unicorns" that can solve multiple Big Data conundrums for companies trying to harness the Big Data revolution (Bertolucci, 2013a). An often-quoted study from the McKinsey Global Institute, published in 2011, called up the alarming statistic that "the US could face a shortage of up to 190,000 data scientists by 2018" (Bertolucci 2012).

What is meant by "data scientist" varies according to the person or organization using the term. One chief data scientist of an existing Big Data analytics firm describes the role of data scientist as "really several different roles. . . . When people say there's a shortage of data scientists, [they mean] there is a shortage of people with all of these different skills . . . business analyst, machine learning expert, and data engineer" (Bertolucci, 2013b). In many cases, position advertisements for data scientists require substantial analytical skills, but also creativity, self-pacing, and strong communication skills that allow data scientists to design and present cutting-edge analyses to nontechnical and business experts.

The newness of the job category of data scientist means that reliable demographic data on this position are not available. However, given the requirements for exceptional mathematical and statistical skills, we can expect that demographic characteristics of mathematicians may overlap with those of data scientists.

Mathematicians

One of the key professional categories for Big Data teams is that of mathematical modelers. There are two functions for modelers in the Big Data environment: modeling as design and modeling for analysis. While mathematicians and statisticians may work as designers for relating components of databases to one another or to relate components of a database to the external environment (e.g., users and feeds), their skills may be used for creating models for analysis. Analysis modelers have the task of creating the equations that help to communicate the relationships between data that users request. Modelers create expected formulas that take the real-world problem of a user query and apply it to a database (possibly created on the spot for the user based on relationships between data fields crafted by design modelers) that presents users with a mathematical solution to help the user identify a real-world solution. Analysis modelers, also possibly called machine learning experts, may use a variety of mathematical tools to achieve the end goal of providing a mathematical output for use in solution generation, such as differential equations, weighted analyses, or simple statistical procedures, such as chi-square analysis. Irrespective of the tools used, mathematicians with extensive modeling skills are an integral component to a Big Data analysis team.

Mathematicians, like software engineers and database professionals, tend to be overwhelmingly male in gender and, according to data from the Annual Survey of the Mathematical Sciences from the American Mathematical Society (2013), are increasingly from outside of the United States. According to the 2011–2012 annual survey of doctoral degree recipients, 1,149 were male, while only 495 were female. Of that, however, the number of U.S. and non-U.S. males was roughly equal. For women, there were almost 20% more women receiving doctoral degrees in mathematics from U.S. institutions who came from outside of the United States. This finding suggests that one of the key human resource challenges for Big Data teams may be attending to immigration and visa requirements.

Software Engineers

As Garvin (2013) points out, the stereotype of a software engineer suggest a lonely, probably divorced, middle-aged male. These outdated stereotypes, however, are increasingly shown to be wrong by workplace surveys. Instead, "the typical developer is a married, middle-aged male, who has two to three children.... [T]he median age of software developers is now 36 and ... 85% of them have college degrees, about 4 in ten have Master's and another 5% have doctoral degrees" (Gavin, 2013, p. 1). But the typical developer as a male is an increasingly incorrect stereotype, as the National Center for Women and Information Technology (NCWIT) shows. Instead, "Women comprise 34% of web developers; 23% of programmers; 37% of database administrators; 20% of software developers; and 15% of information security analysts" and "of the approximately 903,000 women holding computing and mathematical occupations in the United States, about a quarter million are between the ages of 25 and 34, and another quarter million are between the ages of 35 and 44" (NCWIT, 2013, p. 1).

Data Scientists and Data Engineers: Analytics Decision Makers

As discussed below, directives from the Office of Management and Budget and the Office of Federal Procurement Policy suggest that decision making is an inherently governmental task. In an analytics team, decision-making tasks are known as DADs. These DADs tasks, which are "Discover/Access/Distill" are key tasks for data base development and management. DADs tasks are not divorced from ETL tasks, such as to "Extract/Load/Transform" data, which is the province of data engineers, but there are qualitative—value laden— choices made by data scientists that may not be performed by data engineers.

Briefly, as Granville deftly summarizes in nontechnical language:

> Data science is at the intersection of computer science, business engineering, statistics, data mining, machine learning, operations research, six sigma, automation, and domain expertise. It brings together a number of techniques, processes, and methodologies from different fields, together with business vision and action. Data science is about bridging the different components that contribute to business optimization at large, and eliminating the silos that slow down business efficiency. (Granville, 2014, p. 12)

When we look to the two "D" dimensions of the tasks of data scientists, it becomes clear that data science is truly about decision making. Discovery of data sets and evaluative models is an exercise not dissimilar to the research task of designing an inquiry. As social scientists in particular have documented well, the construction of a project often leads to its outcomes. If form follows function, then the functions chosen by a data scientist weigh heavily upon the outcomes of the apparently neutral projects of extraction and so forth. Further, distillation of data, or to "extract essence from data, the stuff that leads to decisions, increased ROI (return on investment) and actions" involves such non-neutral tasks as cleaning and refining data or determining what goes and what stays in the framework (Granville, 2014). Such chores have an effect on outcomes of analytics that are far from neutral and are, as I show in the final section of this chapter, *not* something that should be outsourced under the terms of the guidance related to determination of inherently governmental tasks.

DECISION MAKING AS AN INHERENTLY GOVERNMENTAL ACTIVITY

What Is Inherently Governmental Activity?

For individuals accustomed to being data users, databases may seem to be an inert, value-free space of numbers and bytes. However, as was pointed to above and is outlined at greater length below, construction, maintenance, and analysis of data, *even in the case of user-guided relational databases*, is an activity fraught with complex and high-consequence decision making. It is the consequential decision making that lends Big Data development and analysis its "inherently governmental" character.

The Office of Federal Procurement Policy (OFPP, a part of the Office of Management and Budget) struggled to carve out definitions of inherently governmental functions that are "so intimately related to the public interest as to mandate performance by Federal employees" (OFPP, 2011, p. 56227). These functions are supposed to be distinct from those that are "critical" to or closely associated with the performance of agency missions and can be performed by government contractors. In some government domains, these distinctions can be made readily. In others, such as in the construction and analysis of material stored in "Data Lakes" and other "Big Data" repositories, it is far less clear what can be contracted and what must be performed by Federal employees.

The OFPP (2011) defines that either federal employees or contractors may perform "support for policy development, such as drafting policy documents and regulations, performing analyses, feasibility studies, and strategy options" (p. 56,234). Only federal employees can ultimately make a "determination of the content and application of policies and regulations" (p. 56,234). The final policy letter outlines that "a function is not appropriately performed by a contractor where the contractor's involvement is or would be so extensive, or the contractor's work product so close to a final agency product, as to effectively preempt the Federal officials' decision-making process, discretion or authority" (p. 56,238). In the case of aggregation or analysis of large, complex datasets it is not clear how this instruction could be applied. Aggregation of data is more than a merger of databases; compilation of required metadata requires professional judgment calls with significance for the subsequent use of the data. Analysis of data also requires judgments that are so significant as to define the uses of the data. If aggregation and analysis produce substantive changes to the raw material of Big Data archives, then the tool has, I argue, been so extensively altered that the contractor's work is intermeshed with the final product. In the case of Big Data initiatives with a public health purpose, such as the CDC's "FluView," it is even murkier whether contract data analytics professionals are or are not performing functions that meet the definition of "inherently governmental."

WHAT CONTRACTING PROBLEMS DOES BIG DATA PRESENT FOR GOVERNMENT DEPARTMENTS?

The primary problem facing government agencies as they address the Big Data future is that the required architecture and personnel necessary to build that future are not currently at hand. Big Data must be built, whether by the hands of internal experts, by internal trainees working under repurposed job functions, or through procurement of services through contractors. As government departments work to stay abreast of the Big Data wave, they may find that turning to contracted services represents an "easier" solution to hiring data scientists or placing Big Data tasks into the hands of currently stretched employees. In this section, I address the problem of procurements of Big Data services from three perspectives: purchasing "turnkey" services through contracts with external vendors, outsourcing modeling, and using outside vendors for in-house training.

External Vendors

What services might government departments be interested to find vendors to provide? Or, for building what competencies might an agency be interested to find outside training vendors? The essential skills of Big Data are computer programming, mathematical skills, statistical know-how, modeling capability, database management, data mining, data storage, machine learning, and communication skills.

Externally sourcing services to fill the drive to build Big Data architecture,, whether in whole or in part, on a temporary or long-term basis, means making careful decisions about which tasks are outsourced. First, it is essential to point out that outsourcing or contracting employment does not free the agency completely from the requirements to comply with relevant antidiscrimination and employment law. For example, while applicability of other antidiscrimination laws has not been decided by the courts, Houseman (1999) notes that "the ADA specifically prohibits a business from participating in an arrangement that results in the discrimination against a disabled applicant or worker; thus, both the client and the staffing firm are legally liable for discrimination under ADA" (p. 1). Even this determination, however, may not apply to independent contractors, of which data analytics individuals may be an important population.

Second, if agencies intend to outsource to external vendors those tasks described above as either (a) DADs tasks or (b) business analysis, then they are cautioned to revisit the distinction between inherently governmental and critical functions. The following set of critical questions may help to organize this decision making. See Figure 13.4 for some guidance in making these decisions.

In-House Human Resource Development

To solve the problem of meeting the expectations of the office of management and budget to keep inherently governmental activities "in house" and to establish a personnel system that avoids the problems of data-securitization against internal threats (e.g., leaks), government departments must undertake a focused hiring effort to find or train data architects, programmers, data scientists, and analytics professionals. However, in doing so, there is a probability that human resource managers hiring Big Data professionals will run into problems complying with applicable federal hiring laws. Specifically, the demographic composition of the Big Data workforce, like the cloud computing workforce, places government departments at risk of appearing to or actually running afoul of Equal Employment Opportunity and similar programs and laws (see Figure 13.5 for a list of these laws). To circumvent this, training programs may be brought into the organization to train existing government employees how to construct and use Big Data analytics.

In the event that in-house job development is selected, considerations of the accessibility of sensitive data to external vendors must be considered.

Sample questions for Department, Agency or Office human resources or contract managers to ask when determining whether to out-source Big Data technical staffing to an external vendor:

- Is this employee meant to decide on the content or modeling tools used to construct or create output protocols for a fixed or relational database use to determine eligibility, allocation, application, or implementation of a policy or regulation?
- Is this employee meant to either 1) extract value from data sources, 2) decide upon data sources to be used, 3) decide upon a strategy for refinement of data sources that meaningfully changes the data from what is input to what is used, or 4) decide upon strategies for data integration that mean that the data input is meaningfully different than data used in analysis?
- Is this employee meant to decide on the value-added strategy for presentation of the data to in-house or external decision-makers, including the public?

Figure 13.4 Is it a government function?

- Title VII of the Civil Rights Act of 1964: Prohibits employment discrimination based on race, color, religion, sex, or national origin
- The Equal Pay Act of 1963: Protects men and women who perform substantially equal work in the same establishment from sex-based wage discrimination
- The Age Discrimination in Employment Act of 1967: Protects individuals who are 40 years of age or older from employment discrimination
- Title I and Title V of the Americans with Disabilities Act of 1990: Prohibits employment discrimination against qualified individuals with disabilities in the private sector and in state and local governments
- Section 510 and 505 of the Rehabilitation Act of 1973: Prohibits discrimination against qualified individuals with disabilities who work in the federal government
- Title II of the Genetic Information Non-discrimination Act of 2008: Prohibits employment discrimination based on genetic information about an applicant, employee or former employee
- The Civil Rights Act of 1991: Provides monetary damages in cases of intentional employment discrimination

Figure 13.5　Federal laws prohibiting job discrimination. *Source:* Adapted from "Federal Laws Prohibiting Job Discrimination Questions and Answers"; http://www.eeoc.gov/facts/qanda.html (Last accessed January 2, 2014).

Although the Personal Data Privacy and Security Act of 2009 did not make it to law in the United States, the attention garnered by the bill and subsequent data breaches and leaks, ultimately resulting in issuance of Executive Orders 12968, 13526, and 13587, makes inclusion of contracted training programs that use "live" data, even for training purposes, potentially problematic.

Executive Order 13597 directed the Office of the National Counterintelligence Executive to establish the National Insider Threat Task Force to "prevent, deter and detect compromises of classified information by malicious insiders" (NCIX, 2014). What counts as "classified information" and levels of classification were outlined in EO 13526. Importantly, given the initiatives for Big Data incentivized by the White House, classified information will include data relevant to implementation of Big Data initiatives in the Department of Defense and may include those in other programs, since "scientific, technological or economic matters relating to the national security" or "U.S. government programs for safeguarding nuclear materials or facilities" or programs assessing "vulnerabilities or capabilities of systems, installations, infrastructures, projects, plans, or protection services relating to the national security" may be part of Big Data resources used by the National Science Foundation, National Institutes of Health, or Department of Energy. Finally, who may access classified information is outlined in EO 12968, which restricts access based upon determination of eligibility of access to classified information.

In the event that training programs for analytics or Big Data decision making are planned using live data, there should be extensive conversations beforehand with data scientists who have determined the content of databases and data engineers who may incorporate potentially classified data into relational databases. Alternatives to use of live data abound, such as the use of Monte Carlo simulated data, but these may be of limited utility for individuals whose intended training is to upgrade their skills to those of data scientists.

In-House Science, Outsourced Extraction, but What About Models?

One alternative to limitations on the number of data scientists is to outsource some functions of Big Data architecture construction and Big Data analysis. In general, federal agencies, departments and offices are advised to restrict outsourcing to ETL or "extract/load/transform" functions as these have less to do with critical decision-making skills. If DADs (discover/access/distill) skills are restricted to in-house services, but mathematical modeling skills are in limited supply (a concern particularly as the number of qualified mathematicians able to pass required security clearances dwindles), some model construction (and access) skill could be outsourced. However, the outsourcing of modeling skills should be restricted to the construction of analytical models that will be used on a variety of data types to achieve departmental purposes. With sufficient foreknowledge of the purpose of Big Data analysis, department leaders should be able to lead modeling teams through the necessary information to build analytic models and even to instruct staff on general interpretation of results.

CONCLUDING REMARKS

The U.S. government holds Big Data up as a solution to problems of information gathering and analysis related to solving public problems. While Big Data initiatives in some federal departments hold out great potential for enhancing the lives of Americans and others globally, other Big Data initiatives may threaten the privacy or even lives of Americans and others globally. For example, in the recent debate about the use of data by the National Security Administration (through the PRISM or Dishfire programs), a central question has been about the purpose of data access, extent of data access, and breadth of data access to contractors. As is brought to the fore in broad relief by the disclosure of documents by contractor Edward Snowden, access to models, results, and even sources of data by contractors or even government employees poses a legitimate threat to the security of the public and the government at large.

Attempts by the executive office to constrain access to information by contractors and attempts by the office of management and budget to define appropriate contracting relationships go some distance towards prevention of future leaks. However, these orders and definitions have implications for the staffing of Big Data teams in any other departments. What these implications are may only be revealed fully as human resources and contract management professionals grapple with staffing the new analytics teams incentivized by White House and other initiatives.

REFERENCES

American Mathematical Society. (2013). Data in the profession. Retrieved from http://www.ams.org/profession/data/emp-survey

Balci, T. (2013). Bid data #3: Impact on the data center. Retrieved from http://http://webhostinggeeks.com/blog/big-data-3-impact-on-the-data-center/

Bertolucci, J. (2012). Wanted: Qualified data scientists, people skills a plus. *Information Week*. Retrieved from http://www.informationweek.com/big-data/big-data-analytics/wanted-qualified-data-scientist-people-skills-a-plus/d/d-id/1107324

Bertolucci, J. (2013a). Are you recruiting a data scientist, or unicorn? *Information Week*. Retrieved from http://www.informationweek.com/big-data/big-data-analytics/are-you-recruiting-a-data-scientist-or-unicorn/d/d-id/899843?ngAction=register

Bertolucci, J. (2013b). How to build a successful data science team. *Information Week*. Retrieved from http://www.informationweek.com/big-data/big-data-analytics/how-to-build-a-successful-data-science-team-/d/d-id/1113234

Bureau of Labor Statistics, United States Department of Labor. (2012). Occupational employment and wages, May 2012: Data base administrators. Retrieved from http://www.bls.gov/oes/current/oes151141.htm

Burleson, D. (n.d.). U.S. information technology racism. Retrieved from http://www.dba-oracle.com/oracle_news/news_technology_racism.htm

BusinessAnalystSolutions. (2012). What is a business analyst? Retrieved from http://www.businessanalystsolutions.com/what_is_a_business_analyst.html

EEOC. (n.d.). Federal laws prohibiting job discrimination questions and answers. Retrieved from http://www.eeoc.gov/facts/qanda.html

Garvin, J. (2013). Who are software developers? Retrieved from http://www.drdobbs.com/architecture-and-design/who-are-software-developers/240162014

Granville, V. (2013). Job titles for data scientists. *Data Science Central*. Retrieved from http://www.datasciencecentral.com/profiles/blogs/job-titles-for-data-scientists

Granville, V. (2014). Data scientist versus data engineer. *Data Science Central*. Retrieved from http://www.datasciencecentral.com/profiles/blogs/data-scientist-versus-data-engineer

Hillenbrand, M. (n.d.). What is the difference between a database engineer, architect and administrator? TechTarget/Search Oracle. Retrieved from http://searchoracle.techtarget.com/answer/What-is-the-difference-between-a-database-engineer-architect-and-administrator

Houseman, S. N. (1999). Flexible staffing arrangements—A report on temporary help, on-call, direct-hire temporary, leased, contract company, and independent contractor employment in the United States: Anti-discrimination laws. Retrieved from http://www.dol.gov/oasam/programs/history/herman/reports/futurework/conference/staffing/9.7_discrimination.htm

Krihely, F. (2013). Hadoop: What it is and why it's such a big deal. *Hadoop360*. Retrieved from http://www.hadoop360.com/blog/hadoop-what-it-is-and-why-it-s-such-a-big-deal

Minton-Eversole, T. (2013, December 11). IT hiring to continue into 2014 at slower pace, experts predict. *Society for Human Resource Management*. Retrieved from http://www.shrm.org/hrdisciplines/staffingmanagement/Articles/Pages/IT-Hiring-in-2014.aspx

NCIX.gov. (2014). Our mission: National Insider Threat Task Force. Retrieved from http://www.ncix.gov/nittf/index.php

National Center for Women & Information Technology. (2013, June 30). Did you know: Demographics on technical women. Retrieved from http://www.ncwit.org/blog/did-you-know-demographics-technical-women

Office of Federal Procurement Policy. (2011). Work reserved for performance by federal government employees. Retrieved from http://http://www.whitehouse.gov/omb/procurement_work_performance

Office of Science and Technology Policy, Executive Office of the President. (2012, March 29). Obama administration unveils 'Big Data Initiative': Announces $200Million in new R&D investments. Retrieved from http://www.whitehouse.gov/sites/default/files/microsites/ostp/big_data_press_release_final_2.pdf

Sanders, M. A. (2013). Data scientist core skills. *Data Science Central*. Retrieved from http://www.datasciencecentral.com/profiles/blogs/data-scientist-core-skills

SQLservercentral.com. (2007). Where did the women go? Retrieved from http://www.sqlservercentral.com/Forums/Topic345008-263-1.aspx

CHAPTER 14

ELECTRONIC SURVEILLANCE IN THE WORKPLACE

Legal, Ethical, and Management Issues

Jonathan P. West, James S. Bowman, and Sally Gertz

INTRODUCTION

Surveillance at work refers to the use of electronic technology to instantaneously and continuously collect, store, and report the behavior of employees. The issue currently is not whether technology will be used to monitor workers (it already is), but rather how it will evolve and what safeguards are needed to control it. Several trends have converged to raise these questions now. First, people primarily rely on electronic technology to communicate with others about work and to access work-related information. Face-to-face meetings and file cabinets are rarer than ever. Since electronic communication and retrieval of data can be done at any time and place, people regularly perform work at places not owned by employers, and they often do so during "personal" time. As a tradeoff, they handle private matters at work, often using their employer's equipment. Along with this increased reliance on technology, and the blurring of boundaries between work and personal life, has come the enhanced

Legal and Regulatory Issues in Human Resources Management, pages 285–314
Copyright © 2015 by Information Age Publishing

capability of employers to monitor. Like Orwell's "Big Brother," today's employers seemingly have the ability always to be watching. Yet it is useful to recall that electronic monitoring, like any other organizational practice, is socially constructed: Technology can be an enabler of ends, both constructive and destructive (Schmidt & Cohen, 2013; Vorvoreanu & Botan, 2000).

The paradox is that electronic surveillance is more widely used than understood. Accordingly, the purpose of the present chapter is to examine this phenomenon. The background section reviews the extent, form, and goal of workplace surveillance, followed by an examination of differing perceptions of monitoring. The core of the chapter explores relevant legal, ethical, and management issues: The legal section analyzes pertinent law; the ethics section assesses a case study; and the management section considers notification, performance, leadership, and ethical practices. The conclusion discusses implications of the analysis and charts future developments.

BACKGROUND: SURVEILLANCE EXTENT, FORM, PURPOSE, AND PERSPECTIVES

Extent

Surveillance is pervasive and a critical part of modern information systems and work environments. Like the assembly lines of an earlier era, and consistent with Taylorism and the tenets of scientific management, it allows management to monitor worker activities and productivity—but without the need of direct supervisory observation.

From 1997 to 2000 the percentage of major U.S. corporations that recorded and monitored employee communications and activities at work (e.g., phone calls, email, internet connections, and computer files) doubled to 73.5% (Sarpong & Rees, 2013). More recent surveys by the American Management Association (AMA), US News, and the ePolicy Institute found that there was an increase in surveillance practices from 2001 to 2007 (the latest year available from these sources): an expansion in the percentage of employers who monitored website connections (from 62% to 66%), reviewed and stored employee computer files (36% to 43%), and blocked connections to inappropriate sites (38% to 65%). By 2007, 43% of organizations monitored emails, 12% reviewed the blogosphere for company-related posts and 10% checked social networking sites for company-related content (e.g., text, photos, videos) (AMA, U.S. News, & ePolicy Institute, 2001; AMA & ePolicy Institute, 2007). Productive and unproductive use of the internet and networks can be determined and the cost of improper use calculated (Bupp, 2001; Sarpong & Rees, 2013). This daily trail of "digital footprints" may be easily applied to evaluate employee conduct; recall, for example, that former CIA Director David Petraeus' affair likely would have remained secret had the FBI been unable to access his emails. In short, monitoring personnel is not new, but the advent of sophisticated technology at low cost and small size (enabling concealment) has made it more attractive (Kizza & Ssanyu, 2005).

Forms

Surveillance technologies can take many forms, including door swipes, computer log-in and activity reports, printer and photocopy details, and video recordings of staff comings and goings. Fingerprint, facial, and iris scans, as well as smart cards, are available to control access to facilities. Programs check computers for activities such as keystrokes, start dates, and down times. Software can be utilized to take frequent screen snapshots. Connections between terminals can be monitored to produce logs of the type and frequency of interactions. Apps surveil use of company-provided smartphones, and GPS devices can track employees in employer-owned vehicles.

At call centers, software records call volume, duration of calls, and idle time for quality control purposes. The content of cyberspace dialogue, instant message usage, personal blog activity, and public postings can be retrieved. Deleting and encrypting messages does not insure privacy. Together these monitoring strategies create the "electronic equivalent of DNA evidence" (Flynn, 2009, p. 196). It is estimated that 66% of employers track employee internet usage and 43% monitor employee email accounts (American Management Association & ePolicy Institute, 2007), giving some credence to the "Big Brother" and "electronic sweatshop" descriptions of the contemporary workplace.

Purpose

Increased reliance on the internet and email at work and their link to productivity, along with the desire to deter "cyber-loafing," are spurs to monitoring. Organizations have legitimate concerns such as protecting secrets, curtailing theft, controlling costs, reducing absenteeism, ensuring security, maintaining workplace safety, and avoiding information leaks (Mujtaba, 2003; Sarpong & Rees, 2013). Employers can detect whether workers are visiting sexually explicit sites, games, sports, social networking, or shopping or entertainment sites (Privacy Rights Clearinghouse, 2013).

The costs of leaving such concerns unaddressed are substantial: Employee theft and fraud alone account for more than $200 billion in losses annually (Pierce, Snow, & McAfee, 2013). With renewed emphasis on results-oriented management, it is not surprising to see greater scrutiny given to productivity measurement and performance review, both of which are made easier by electronic surveillance. Further, managers have a longstanding interest in reducing liability and ensuring legal compliance, objectives also served by monitoring (Mujtaba, 2003).

By and large, organizations have the right to oversee employee internet usage, assuming that their motivation is to detect inappropriate behavior and cultivate a safe and respectful work environment. Numerous methods are available to reduce internet abuse. Mirchandani and Motwani (2003) surveyed 66 companies to see which approaches were used with greatest frequency:

- a written policy specifying that the Internet use for work-related purposes only
- use of software to detect websites visited by subordinates
- limiting Internet access after obtaining supervisor's consent
- reprimanding those who abuse internet use
- removal of privileges from those who misuse internet privileges

Utilization of these strategies ranged from 24% (removal of privileges) to 42% (policy manual), with 1 in 4 (or more) of the firms using the other policies. The more recent, and more extensive, AMA and ePolicy Institute survey (2007) provides additional insight into these employer practices. That survey indicates that 83% of employers inform their workers of keystroke monitoring and 74% notify employees of email monitoring, with the vast majority of employers (70%) using policy handbooks to inform employees and only 27% incorporating monitoring policies into on-site training: one of the more effective mechanisms for ensuring compliance. The survey also reveals that employers are willing to go beyond reprimanding workers and revoking their computer privileges, as 30% and 28% of employers have fired workers for internet and email misuse, respectively.

Best practices suggest the need to notify users that computers and email should be primarily for business reasons.[1] Transparency, publicity, and employee participation (discussed below) are keynotes in policy development and deployment. To be effective, however, monitoring should be for mutual benefit; managers are well-advised to "balance surveillance needs with employee quality of life" (Fazekas, 2004, para. 31). Given the scope, types, and rationale of monitoring, differing attitudes about it are to be expected.

Perceptions

Proponents contend that monitoring increases organizational control, facilitates in managing resources and workload planning, and aids in designing training programs. It enables frequent and timely performance feedback and helps to enforce work standards to detect problems and assess employee behavior (Bates & Holton, 1995). Fazekas (2004) believes that if it is done properly, there are few incentives to abuse surveillance and, for liability reasons, real disincentives.

Opponents, nonetheless, fear that information obtained from such programs may be used in detrimental ways. Such data, for example,

- may not be made available to personnel,
- may be linked to work speed-ups,
- may emphasize quantity over quality of work,
- may reduce employee discretion,
- may erode procedural fairness, and
- may be employed for disciplinary instead of developmental purposes (Bates & Holton, 1995, p. 269).

On the latter point, the 2007 AMA/ePolicy Institute survey revealed that "more than a quarter of companies have fired employees for misuse of email and one third have fired employees for misusing the internet" (PCWorld, 2008). Fazekas (2004) suggests that such concerns may be justified in light of the asymmetric power relationship between employers and workers. In the "at-will" work setting, people may be terminated for any reason—for example, because of email comments about a superior, or a log showing too frequent bathroom use, or a program revealing excessive chair "wiggling." Critics believe that "Big Brother" technologies are a weapon to control and spy on workers (Lee, 2007).

Further, some psychological studies have documented the link between monitoring and fatigue, anxiety, stress, depression, nervous disorders, and adverse impacts on health and productivity (Blackman & Franklin, 1993). Other effects can include increased suspicion, fear, distrust, resentment, and hostility in the workplace (Lim, 2002; Sarpong & Rees, 2013; Schulman, 2001).

To summarize, surveillance monitoring is common, takes many forms, and is growing. It is practiced for a variety of legitimate and dubious reasons and is likely to be most efficacious when employer and employee rights are carefully weighted. The focus now shifts to consideration of legal, ethical, and management issues surrounding electronic surveillance at work.

LEGAL ISSUES

In the vast majority of circumstances, employer monitoring is lawful. One reason is that the area is virtually unregulated, a situation not entirely surprising considering that privacy rights historically have received little protection in the American law. The national Constitution does not mention the word "privacy," and only ten state constitutions do. To the extent an individual's personal information and activities are protected, it usually is done by sector—for example, via financial, health, or education regulations. To date, no legislation comprehensively addresses employee privacy rights and employer monitoring rights.[2] Instead, the United States approach is piecemeal. An array of common law claims, constitutional provisions, and state and federal statutes guards privacy. Many apply narrowly to specific populations and protect specific communications. Most were enacted years ago with different technologies in mind and must be adapted continually for contemporary use. The main legal provisions that apply to electronic surveillance of employees are discussed below.

Laws That Protect Privacy Generally

Two legal provisions provide individuals with a general right to privacy in the work setting (and elsewhere): The common law claim for "unlawful intrusion upon seclusion" (applicable to private and public employees) and the Fourth Amendment's prohibition on unreasonable searches (applicable to civil servants). The analysis is similar under both provisions: to be entitled to the protection of the law, an employee must have a reasonable expectation of privacy—which means an actual expectation in his own mind, *and* one that society recognizes as reasonable.

The Common Law Action of Intrusion Upon Seclusion (Private and Public Employers)
Under their common law, almost all states allow a few civil claims for damages for invasion of privacy. "Intrusion upon seclusion" is the theory most likely to be used for a claim alleging intrusive monitoring by an employer. It applies to both private and public employers and to any type of physical or electronic invasion. Two elements must be proven: (a) an *intrusion* into a private place or matter, (b) that occurs in a manner *highly offensive* to a reasonable person ("Restatement," 1977).

As to the "intrusion" element, an individual must show that the employer penetrated some zone of privacy. The California Supreme Court explained that this could be "informational privacy," which refers to a person's interest in precluding the dissemination or misuse of sensitive and confidential information, or "autonomy privacy," which encompasses a person's interest in making intimate personal decisions or conducting personal activities without observation, intrusion, or interference (*Pioneer Electronics (USA), Inc. v. Superior Court,* 2007).

For an intrusion to be unlawful the employee must have an actual, subjective expectation of privacy. He must genuinely believe that the matter is not subject to the employer's inspection. While a person may insist he held such a belief, a judge will examine all the surrounding facts to ascertain someone's true mindset, including

- written and verbal communications he received from the employer on the subject;
- ownership of the equipment used;
- circumstances suggesting the employer had given the employee permission or authority to use the equipment for personal reasons;
- the individual's ability to protect the information from others by using a password or personal folder on a computer, or by using security settings on a social media site;
- the access that fellow employees, supervisors, and the public had to the space; and
- whether the data were stored on a stand-alone hard drive or other media, or on a network.

In addition to this subjective expectation of the employee, society as a whole must recognize the employee's expectation of privacy as reasonable, which is closely related to whether it is "highly offensive," the second element that an employee must prove.

A "highly offensive" intrusion should be sufficiently serious in nature, scope, and actual or potential impact to constitute an egregious breach of social norms. Circumstances that are important to this determination include

- the location (a bathroom versus an office),
- the type of information accessed (medical records versus items sold on EBay),
- the openness of the surveillance (a hidden camera versus one in plain sight),
- the data captured (a word-for-word audio recording versus URL addresses visited),
- the time contours (office hours versus non-office hours, a day versus a month),
- the employer's motivation (safety versus nosiness), and

- the availability of safeguards and alternatives (24-hour GPS tracking versus disabling the device during nonworking hours).

What is considered objectively reasonable changes as society's expectations change. What provoked outrage yesterday may evoke a shrug today. In 2013, when stories were published about Edward Snowden's revealing of the National Security Agency's mass covert surveillance methods, some commentators expressed surprise at the public's apathy. But according to a survey conducted just days before the stories appeared, 85% of Americans already thought it was likely that their "communications history, like phone calls, emails and Internet use" was "available for businesses, government, individuals and other groups to access" without their consent (Rich, 2013). If, as these data suggest, citizens are inured to having their electronic communications monitored, then courts increasingly may determine such intrusions to be culturally acceptable in the workplace and elsewhere.

The Fourth Amendment (Public Employers)

This amendment to the U.S. Constitution protects people from "unreasonable searches and seizures" by government agents, including public employers, without a warrant. It does not apply to private employers.[3] In 1987, in *O'Connor v. Ortega,* a doctor objected to a hospital administrator's search of his filing cabinet and a plurality of the Supreme Court announced that, to prove that the right has been violated, a person must show that (a) he had a reasonable expectation of privacy, and (b) that the search was unreasonable (*O'Connor v. Ortega*, 1987). These elements closely resemble the ones required for a common law intrusion upon seclusion claim and courts examine similar facts to determine if a violation occurred.[4]

The Fourth Amendment can be used defensively, by a defendant in a criminal case to prevent the government from using evidence obtained through an overly intrusive search, or offensively, to assert a civil claim for damages. Most state constitutions have provisions similar to the Fourth Amendment. California's constitution is conspicuously different: privacy expressly is an inalienable right, and the right is enforceable against public and private encroachers.

Courts have applied the Fourth Amendment two-part test in a variety of electronic surveillance contexts. In *City of Ontario v. Quon*, decided in 2010, the Supreme Court held that a city did not violate the amendment when it obtained (from its wireless provider) a transcript of text messages, some of them personal, sent by a swat team member on a city-provided pager. The court sidestepped the first part of the test, whether Quon had a legitimate expectation of privacy in his communications, and concluded that the search was reasonable. It gave significant weight to the city's legitimate work-related motive, which was to audit work usage to determine if it needed to pay for more, and to its finding that the city's method was not excessive in relation to its purpose (*City of Ontario v. Quon*, 2010).

Email monitoring has been challenged using the Fourth Amendment and other laws with little success. Overwhelmingly, courts have found employers' access legal, particularly when a policy authorized it and the email was sent over the office network or using office-issued equipment. A contradictory assurance from a supervisor that email would not be intercepted did not change the outcome, nor did the employee storing the email in a password-protected personal folder. When the messages were sent from a personal account (e.g., Gmail), but were stored on the employer's network, or were stored on a laptop the employer owned, access also was lawful. Text messaging shares characteristics of email and likely will be treated similarly. Not all scenarios have been tested, but it is clear that if an organization has adopted a policy to monitor these communications, courts will give it wide latitude to do so (Crowther, 2012).

Location tracking of vehicles, identification cards, and phones using global positioning satellite (GPS) and radio frequency identification (RFID) technology has incited claims of Fourth Amendment violation and "intrusion upon seclusion." In 2012, the Supreme Court held in *U.S. v. Jones*, a criminal case, that when government agents secretly attached a GPS device to a car without a valid warrant and tracked its movement for 28 days, it conducted a "search" (*U.S. v. Jones*, 2012). The court was not asked to determine if the search was reasonable, and did not answer that question, but a lower federal court soon did. In *U.S. v. Katzin*, another criminal case, the Third Circuit Court of Appeal held that secretly attaching a GPS tracking device to a suspect's car without a warrant was an unreasonable search that violated the Fourth Amendment (*U.S. v. Katzin*, 2013).

In the employment context, two federal trial courts have held that employers who covertly installed GPS devices on employer-owned vehicles and tracked employees during work and nonwork hours did not commit "intrusion upon seclusion" because the vehicles' locations were public information (*Elgin v. St. Louis Coca-Cola Bottling Co.*, 2005; *Tubbs v. Wayne Transportation Services*, 2007). The judges in *U.S. v. Jones* and *U.S. v. Katzin* rejected that reasoning, and employers should be wary of relying on it. The prudent strategy, legally speaking, is to notify employees of tracking and to confine it to work time.

Federal and State Statutes That Protect Privacy for Specific Activities

"Intrusion upon seclusion" and the Fourth Amendment protect individuals from invasions in any area where there is a reasonable expectation of privacy. An assortment of statutes more narrowly targets and protects specific types of communications and activities.

National Labor Relations Act and State Public-Sector Labor Laws

The National Labor Relations Act (NLRA) safeguards private-sector employees' right to organize and join a union (and many states protect public employees' right to organize). To prevent intimidation, the act prohibits videotaping (or pretending to videotape) employee attendance at union activities. It also protects the right to discuss work conditions with coworkers, verbally and in writing, for example, on social media sites. An organization may not enact a policy that chills this protected speech, or discipline a worker for expressing it. Employees at nonunionized and unionized worksites are covered by these speech protections. If a work rule would reasonably tend to chill employees in the exercise of these speech rights, it is unlawfully broad. For example, a Costco rule that prohibited statements "that damage the Company, defame any individual or damage any person's reputation" violated the act because employees reasonably would construe the rule to prohibit their right to discuss working conditions, especially since Costco's rule did not specifically exclude NLRA-protected communications (*Costco v. Wholesale Corp.*, 2012).

Once a workplace is unionized, the NLRA protects employees' right to bargain over work conditions. Surveillance is a mandatory subject of bargaining, which means a business cannot unilaterally begin monitoring without first bargaining with the union over the parameters of the surveillance and how the information collected will be utilized.

The Electronic Communications Privacy Act

The Electronic Communications Privacy Act of 1986 is a federal statute, violation of which is a crime and creates a civil action for damages. Title I of the ECPA, The Wiretap Act, prohibits an employer from monitoring a wire, oral, and electronic communication if (a) it is an *interception* and (b) it does not fall within an *exception* to the act. To be an interception, the communication must be obtained in transit, as opposed to when it is stored. In the 1980s, when the act was passed, phones and telegraphs were the main forms of wire communication, and it was easy to determine when a communication was in transit. Now, the inquiry is more complex. Email and text messages pass from sender to receiver in under a second and they are stored simultaneously while they are being received. Wiretapping a phone and keystroke logging are interceptions. Most other monitoring today is not, but for guidance a manager should consult IT professionals and look for precedent addressing use of the specific technology (Ciochetti, 2011). If it is an interception, the next step is checking for an exception.

The Wiretap Act has three exceptions that give employers wide latitude to monitor: consent, ordinary course of business, and provider. If an employee has given prior consent to the monitoring, then no violation occurs. Only one party must consent, either the sender or the recipient. The employee need not expressly declare "I consent to you monitoring me." Instead, the facts must show that the individual knew she was being monitored and proceeded in the face of that knowledge. Depending on the jurisdiction, the "ordinary course of business" exception may require a legitimate business reason, and/or surveillance in the ordinary course of business as a routine practice, and/or notice to the employee. Last, the "provider" exception applies when an agent of the provider monitors to protect the rights or property of the provider. A provider is someone who supplies the communication service. "Rights or property" is construed broadly. An information technology employee who was routinely performing his job was protecting the employer's property, as was a manager who read the business email of a former worker suspected of violating a covenant not to compete (Levinson, 2011a).

The Stored Communications Act, Title II of the ECPA, prohibits (a) intentional unauthorized access to a *stored communication* that (b) does not fall within an *exception*. A "stored communication" generally is one held by an internet service provider. Unopened email in an inbox, deleted email on a server, and most social media postings are stored. "Unauthorized access" means without a legitimate business reason or through circumvention of a code-based restriction (for instance, by guessing a password). In one case, a manager who obtained access to a MySpace group being used by employees to complain about managers and customers may have obtained "unauthorized access" because she asked a subordinate employee for her log-in information and the person felt coerced to give it (Wugmerster & Lyon, 2011).[5]

The act has two exceptions: provider, and user authorization. The provider exception in the Stored Communications Act is expansive. It allows anyone to access a stored communication if the service provider authorizes it. As a result, if an employer offers its own electronic communications service, it can access any of its own stored communications. When a third party provider is used, the analysis is more complicated, and a manager should seek guidance directly on point. For the user authorization exception to apply, the employee must have notice of the particular type of monitoring being conducted and must assent to it.

Law enforcement officials regularly ask employers to cooperate with criminal investigations of employees, but the ECPA limits the access that a service provider voluntarily may give. If the search will involve electronic communications, the organization should ask for a subpoena, warrant, wiretap order, or other legal order to avoid violating the ECPA.

State Privacy Statutes

Most states have electronic surveillance statutes, or "mini-ECPAs," that prohibit some interceptions and retrievals of digital communications. A minority make it harder for an interception to fit within the consent exception by requiring two-party consent, as opposed to the one-party consent the federal act allows. Many states, including New York and Rhode Island, have statutes that protect privacy in places where employees remove their clothing, such as restrooms and changing rooms. Several states, such as Connecticut and Delaware, have laws that require notice of monitoring, modeled after the proposed federal Notice of Electronic Monitoring Act that failed to pass in 2000.[6] In Michigan and Illinois, state legislation governs the integrity of personnel records. While not specifically geared towards electronic monitoring, they prohibit information gathering about people's nonemployment-related communications. If an employee consents to such prying, the employer must keep a record of the contents and allow the employee to review it.

Lifestyle discrimination statutes in a handful of states, including New York, North Dakota, and Colorado, allow employees to engage in lawful off-duty conduct without adverse work consequences. Someone disciplined for social media postings might fall within the protections of one of these statutes. Table 14.1 below summarizes these state privacy statutes (Levinson, 2011b). The focus thus far has been on laws limiting an employer's ability to surveil, but occasionally, as the next section explains, the law requires it.

TABLE 14.1   State Workplace Privacy Legislation

Subject of State Legislation	Proposed In	Enacted In	
Constitutional Right to Privacy(applies broadly)		California	
Constitutional Right to Privacy (applies to state action only)		Alaska Arizona Florida Hawaii Illinois	Louisiana Montana South Carolina Washington
Notice of Electronic Monitoring Required	California (vetoed) Massachusetts New York Pennsylvania Arkansas Oklahoma	Colorado[a] Connecticut Delaware	
Required Email Monitoring Policy		Colorado[b] Tennessee[b]	
Interceptions of Electronic Communications (only one party need consent to monitoring)		Alabama Alaska Arizona Arkansas Colorado Delaware	Georgia Hawaii Idaho Indiana Iowa Kansas

(continued)

TABLE 14.1   State Workplace Privacy Legislation (continued)

Subject of State Legislation	Proposed In	Enacted In	
		Kentucky	North Carolina
		Louisiana	North Dakota
		Maine	Ohio
		Minnesota	Oklahoma
		Mississippi	Oregon
		Missouri	Rhode Island
		Nebraska	South Carolina
		New Jersey	South Dakota
		New Mexico	Tennessee
		New York	Texas
Interceptions of Electronic Communications (all parties must consent to monitoring)		California Connecticut Florida[c] Illinois Maryland Massachusetts	Michigan Montana Nevada New Hampshire Pennsylvania Washington
Surveillance in areas employees remove their clothing prohibited by state legislation		California Connecticut Delaware New York	Rhode Island Utah West Virginia
Employers cannot take adverse action based on employee off-duty activities or employee off-duty use of lawful products	Michigan	California Colorado Connecticut Illinois Minnesota	Missouri[d] Nevada North Carolina Tennessee[e]
Prohibition on information-gathering about people's non-employment-related communications		Illinois Michigan	
Prohibition on requiring employee or applicant to provide access to personal social media account		Illinois Nevada New Jersey	Oregon Utah Washington
Prohibition on employers embedding radio frequency identification chips in employees.		California Missouri	North Dakota Wisconsin

[a] Applies to wiretapping/eavesdropping devices only
[b] Applicable to state employers only
[c] One-party consent required for interceptions in the ordinary course of business
[d] Alcohol and Tobacco only
[e] No discrimination against employee use of any legal agricultural product
Sources: Ciochetti (2011), Finkin (2013), Levinson (2010, 2011b)

An Employer's Duty to Monitor and Follow Up on Information Gathered

Employers often justify their intrusions as necessary to avoid liability to third persons, which sometimes is true. In the financial sector, companies that fail to keep customer records safe face fines from regulatory agencies like the Federal Trade Commission and Securities Exchange Commission. In late 2013, when Target's system was hacked and 40 million customers' credit and debit card information were compromised, customers filed class action suits against the corporation. To avoid liability, employers must safeguard clients' confidential data, and surveillance of employees may need to be part of a security system to do that.

Fear of liability for sexual harassment is frequently raised as a concern, but the risk may be overstated. Currently, no law requires an employer to monitor employees' computer use to prevent harassment, just as no law requires an employer to record conversations in the break room. A duty to monitor might arise if an employer suspected abuse—for example, if someone reported that an employee was using an online forum to harass a coworker. As well, if an employer suspected a staff member of using its technology to harm the public, it might have a duty to investigate because failure to do so may create liability for negligent supervision (Fazekas, 2004).

If an organization does monitor, it must react reasonably to the information it uncovers. In one case, a company discovered that an employee was sending pornographic pictures of his ten-year old stepdaughter on his work computer; the firm did not report it to authorities or effectively stop it and was sued for damages to the child.[7] An employer that adopts a policy to monitor also should develop policies to ensure that the information obtained is effectively followed up on.

In sum, solely from a legal perspective, an employer has a strong incentive to adopt a policy of comprehensive, regular surveillance and zero privacy. Doing so destroys any legally recognized expectation of privacy and undercuts a claim for an intrusion upon seclusion or a Fourth Amendment violation. It also brings an employer within the consent and user authorization exceptions to the ECPA. A few laws protect employees' privacy in specific situations, such as when they are engaging in union-related activities or changing clothes, and those rights cannot be destroyed by notice, but those protections are minimal. In general, so long as they give notice, employers have wide latitude to monitor. If an employee objects to an organization's announced policy, his recourse ultimately is to leave.[8] If he stays, the law deems him to have consented.

When legal problems arise, it typically is because the employer did not give notice, the employee did not receive it, it was contradicted by other employer communications, or it was not sufficiently clear or specific. In particular, as technology changes notices become outdated and gaps in coverage develop (Determann & Sprague, 2011). Legal problems also may result when a surveillance policy is not enforced consistently or even-handedly. Finally, in a few situations, employers have a duty to monitor, and any time surveillance reveals harmful behavior occurring, the employer should take steps to stop it.

Understanding the law—both statutory and common law, federal and state—is crucial, but private, public, and nonprofit sector managers must pay attention to ethical issues surrounding performance monitoring as well.

ETHICAL ISSUES:
ELECTRONIC SURVEILLANCE CASE STUDY

When it comes to surveillance, even good intentions, such as the desire to detect and correct unproductive or unethical work behavior, can pave the way to unwise decisions. The case below illustrates how using monitoring software and videotaping to deal with "cyberlollygagging" (wasting time on nonwork-related websites) and low productivity can have positive and negative consequences.

> Marisol Sanchez is the director of productivity improvement a metropolitan county government. After surveying the performance of the major departments, and benchmarking productivity indicators from comparable jurisdictions, she is convinced that changes are needed. She is considering installing monitoring software on all office computers because of concerns about "cyberlollygagging."

> The technology will allow her to examine employee browsing patterns and determine whether they are visiting web sites that the program categorizes as "productive," "unproductive," or "neutral." The software makes it possible to grade staff according to their browsing habits, singling out the most frequent users and the most commonly visited websites. Marisol could also apply it to search emails and close access to websites. She has been assured by general counsel that this strategy is legally acceptable. While Marisol has some ethical reservations about proceeding, she decides to buy the monitoring software. She also secretly installs videotaping equipment in all offices to further observe employee performance. It does not take long for Marisol to get feedback about these initiatives. Bonnie Albright was furious to discover that, because of concern about performance in her department, her office had been videotaped 24/7—Bonnie often changed clothes in her office before leaving for the day. Burt Christianson also complained when he saw his supervisor printing and distributing emails he had sent to fellow employees.

Marisol's decision is examined below, first by using the traditional philosophical approach to decision making, then by applying a behavioral ethics analysis to the case.

While various frameworks shed light on how ethical issues might be considered, one is particularly helpful because its broad scope reduces the chances of an incomplete—and therefore potentially flawed—decision.[9] This tool, the ethics "triad," recognizes the value and utility of the imperatives in three philosophical schools of thought based on results of an action (consequentialism or teleology); pertinent rules (duty ethics or deontology); and personal rectitude, integrity, or character (virtue ethics).

When considering results in decision making, the question is, "Which policy produces the greatest good for the greatest number?" (e.g., "What is right is that which creates the greatest amount of human happiness."). In contemplating rules, the issue is, "Would I want everyone else to make the same decision that I did?" (e.g., "What is good for one is good for all."). From the virtue ethics vantage point, one might ask, "Does the decision enhance my character and that of the community?" (e.g., seek the "golden mean" between the extremes of excess and deficiency). The ethics triad, comprehensive yet succinct, can help provide a defensible decision derived from evaluation of consequences, rules, and virtues. It offers a conscious attempt to reconcile conflicting values, accomplishing a key function of policymaking: generating alternative viewpoints, systemically evaluating them, and crafting a considered assessment. It cannot, of course, produce a final, definitive judgment.

From a *results* perspective, Marisol believes the program will improve productivity, reduce wasted time, and keep people honest. She thinks it will help employees as well as employers—workers will be supported in their career goals free of distractions, and employers can reward high performers. The initiative can foster a positive, task-focused professional work environment. It will advance government's core purpose: cost-effective service. Protecting government property from misuse is an obligation of management. Surveillance is a way to hold everyone accountable. Those not violating policy should not mind, and abusers deserve to be caught. The policy, in short, is the greatest good for the greatest number.

The workforce, however, could resent the intrusion and feel the employer–employee psychological contract—shared perceptions of expectations and obligations—has been broken by an invasion of privacy. People may object that their rights are being compromised by an overly aggressive, intrusive management. They could believe that surveillance disrupts the power balance between managers and workers and fear the misuse of information. Individuals will question the program, especially if the organization's motives are suspect or if they think the severity of the problem is insufficient to warrant management's overreaching. Personnel may find the program to be unfair, likely to result in fewer rewards or undeserved punishment, and will believe that it has a "chilling effect" on the work environment. It may increase competition and stress, while simultaneously lowering morale and eroding trust. Some will try to "work around" the policy (using their personal iPad or cell phone). Performance could suffer if the worry, concern, and dislike by employees alter the organizational culture. If so, in the short term and probably in the long term, the policy is not, at least for the county's workforce, the greatest good for the greatest number.

When *rules* become the focus, it is the agency's prerogative to make and implement policies. Marisol, as noted, has been assured that the policy has been tailored to comply with existing legal provisions. Although the county does not have a code of ethics, Marisol—as a member of the International City/County Management Association—has an obligation to follow its code. She carefully examined its most relevant tenet (i.e., "to improve the members' professional ability and to develop the competence of associates"), and is satisfied that she is in compliance. It is Marisol's duty, after all, to work responsibly to improve employee performance and public service. By implementing surveillance in all departments, it is applied fairly: What is good for one is good for all. As stewards of government resources, administrators can be confident that government property is being used for legitimate purposes. In short, monitoring helps managers to manage.

The workforce, however, may feel that its privacy expectations are being violated. They also likely will resent not being included in the formulation of the policy and will object to the secrecy of its implementation. Because they have been excluded, they may question whether adequate procedures are in place to ensure the information collected will be accessed and used fairly. And without information about the scope of the problem, they may feel the means (privacy invasion) do not justify the ends (a speculative increase in productivity).

Virtue ethics provides a third lens to assess the program. Aristotle argued for prudence—to avoid both excesses and deficiencies in an effort to build character. Marisol feels that the monitoring strategy is a reasonable middle ground, one that respects the county's interests and employees' rights. Surveillance is reasonable measure to take for a government that genuinely cares about its public service function. She believes it is necessary and that the data will not be misused. Overall, she expects this program will make her and her community better. In comparison, employees may reject the idea that the initiative enhances the character of the community and the health of its institutions. Rather, employees may believe that privacy fosters self-discipline and collective social responsibility, and that the employer should nurture these virtuous habits to develop the moral fiber of the workforce. Excellence in the individual and community is nourished by building trust. In addition, the "golden mean" would be to strive for a prudent course of action that lies between accepting and rejecting the plan "as is." Instead, the county should use a participatory and transparent approach to create an exemplary program.

The ethics triad has been criticized for its failure to link moral theorizing and ethical action. As Gazzaniga (2008, p. 148) observes, "It has been hard to find any correlation between moral reasoning and proactive moral behavior. In fact, in most studies, none has been found." This suggests that other factors—unconscious biases, moral emotions, personal intuitions—are likely to affect behavior (Shao, Aquino, & Freedman, 2008).

Those who focus on behavioral ethics believe that to increase ethical decision making, one must understand the psychological factors that lead to unethical decision making. By examining psychological tendencies to explain human conduct, behavioral ethics introduces considerations like

- bounded rationality (human rationality is bounded by the situation and cognitive limits),
- decision framing (the manner in which a situation is defined can affect the outcome),
- action bias (the felt pressure to do something),
- naïve idealism (the belief that one's own view reflects reality and is shared by others),
- over-confidence (overestimating one's ability to make good decisions), and
- ethical fading (visceral responses become dominant in a decision and exclude ethical implications)

Marisol's bounded rationality, her mono-focus on curbing "cyberloafing" and improving productivity, may have led her to downplay privacy concerns. Decision framing, as well as action bias and ethical fading, can lead to unintentional minimization of legitimate moral concerns. It may be that the initial introduction of monitoring software was implemented with few objections and resulted in limited legal exposure, but the videotaping and distribution of emails raised more serious legal and ethical concerns. Naïve idealism and over-confidence biases meant the failure to involve employees in designing the policy, to inform them of the videotaping, and to develop guidelines on use of information technology and protection of privacy rights.

The heroic assumptions made by the traditional philosophical approach—that individuals are ostensibly and universally logical, possess full information, have the willpower to use it, and act in their self-interest—often do not hold in real life. For Bazerman and Tenbrunsel (2011), the goal is to be prepared for the unconscious psychological forces that routinely occur during decision making. By anticipating these forces and deliberately considering their influence, a manager may ensure that selfishness does not smother personal integrity. If Marisol had applied the prescriptions of the philosophical decision-making model and the descriptions of conduct in the behavioral model as two complementary approaches, she would have gained a more complete understanding of workplace dynamics. In essence, both ask decision-makers to think about thinking. Organizations that incorporate a synthesis of these two models into their organizational cultures and ethics training will improve the quality of decision-making.

Given the extent of electronic monitoring and its continued growth, as well as the legal and ethical issues involved, it is important to consider selected management practices. Four topics in particular are briefly discussed in the next section—notification, performance, leadership, and ethical practices. To provide practical guidance, Table 14.2 summarizes key actions when dealing with performance monitoring concerns.

TABLE 14.2 Selected Practices to Manage Electronic Surveillance

Notification	Performance
Awareness of pertinent provisions of: • U.S. Constitution (4th Amendment) • State constitutions • Common law (intrusion upon seclusion) • Case law (Ortega and Quon) • Federal statutes (ECPA—particularly Wiretap Act and SCA) • State statutes	• Utilize attendance and time monitoring systems • Weigh the value of the projected increase in productivity against the projected cost of increased stress and decreased morale • Be wary of backlash—monitoring perceived to be excessive may trigger declines in productivity, resistance, sabotage, and noncompliance • Recognize that culture of monitoring can decrease employees' intrinsic motivation
Leadership	**Ethics**
• Choose surveillance techniques that minimize invasiveness and maximize enterprise protection (i.e., productivity, liability, and the security of proprietary information) • Disclose surveillance policies in plain language and prior to any instance of monitoring (e.g., automatic screen warnings) • Conduct an in-house assessment prior to establishing an electronic surveillance regime • Solicit employee opinions on productivity problems before instituting electronic surveillance	• Training programs will help ensure ethical use of surveillance techniques • Electronic surveillance constitutes an objective, unbiased method of employee monitoring—but difficult-to-measure qualities (e.g., effort, quality) are also significant • Gathering too much personal information may erode trust and violate employee dignity and autonomy • A pervasive surveillance culture can negatively affect employee behavior and character

MANAGEMENT PRACTICES

Notification

Office-issued equipment and office-provided computer systems are the employer's property and employees have no reasonable expectation of privacy when transmitting email, surfing the web, or using other electronic means of communication. Computer activity is apt to be monitored, regardless of whether or not personnel have been notified (most states, as shown in Table 14.1, do not require formal notification). Even when employees are told their email transmissions will not be monitored, people should not expect privacy when communicating on organization-owned electronic systems (Flynn, 2009).

Even though notice may not always be required by law, surveillance policies and procedures should be clearly explained to help ensure employee understanding of company policy. Onsite orientation of new hires, periodic staff meetings, and inservice training are among the occasions to discuss the reasons for and advantages of monitoring. Memos, employee handbooks, and union contracts can also communicate relevant information.

Best practices suggest the need for a carefully crafted Internet and email use policy to protect employer interests, prevent litigation, and comply with privacy laws. Such policies help to curb misuse of employer-owned computers, reduce the likelihood that inappropriate materials will be accessed, and alert employees that Internet and email use is authorized for business purposes. Where Internet and email use is allowed for certain non-business purposes, the policy should clearly specify restrictions on such use including definitions of inappropriate mail and Web sites (e.g., pornography). To reduce the risk of litigation claims, employees should receive written notice that Internet and email use is monitored and be required to sign that they received such notification. Additional precautions might include pre-login procedures on employee computers requiring employees to acknowledge the Internet and email use policy before proceeding. Further, permission could be required prior to downloading and installing software or other items, if downloading any materials is allowed.

Performance

Is there a link between surveillance and performance? Pierce and colleagues (2013) examined the impact of software monitoring on theft, prior to and after program installation, at 392 restaurants in 39 states, and found positive effects of surveillance. They concluded that "when management implements increased monitoring under a pay-for-performance scheme, employees will redirect effort toward productivity because their incentives have been realigned" (Pierce et al., 2013, p. 19). Other authors, however, are more cautious about the surveillance–productivity link. Stanton and Julian (2002) found that implementing a monitoring system "that emphasizes one aspect of work at the expense of another appears to be a bad idea both for organizational effectiveness and for humanitarian reasons" (p. 98). Systems that are "lopsided" by capturing the quantity of work may neglect other equally valued dimensions of performance. If employees believe that the system fails to capture important aspects of the job, then conflict could occur and impact productivity.

Bates and Holton (1995) also point out the shortcomings of surveillance when used to the exclusion of other factors. Organizations consist of people, policies, technology, supplies, and the sociopolitical environment within which all operate. Accordingly, the causes of good and bad performance are spread throughout the organization and its processes. Performance evaluation is a function of the system within which employees work, yet many of the results of the workplace are outside the power of employees; nevertheless, they are usually made responsible for those consequences. Surveillance, for instance, often yields measures of outcome productivity (units produced) or behavioral performance (clerical errors) that can be substantially influenced by system characteristics. Using such data understates other organizational elements that need to be taken into account. A fair performance appraisal would ensure that all relevant data are included. Best practices include an assessment of organizational-level performance as well as regular individual developmental feedback using 360-degree appraisal techniques.

Leadership

Officials should be fully conversant with surveillance policies and their effects, including physical and psychological health effects such as high blood pressure and employee alienation. Certain forms of monitoring, in addition, are more risky than others (e.g., filters, firewalls, key logging, internet and clickstream data monitoring, and social network and search engine monitoring) because they are more invasive and produce negative perceptions of the workplace (Ciochetti, 2011).

It is not difficult to imagine that some executives might be tempted to use surveillance data in undesirable ways. Ariss (2002, p. 557), for instance, observes: "Managers who have a negative, 'Theory X,' style of managing may use electronic monitoring to micromanage the company." Because monitoring can result in improvements or impediments to performance, administrators should strive to anticipate the human effects of technological applications by considering such things as the need for social connectedness, meaningful work, and effective participation (Ottensmeyer &

Heroux, 1991). Best practices require balancing employee and employer interests, weighing both the promise and pitfalls of surveillance. The case study portrayed in Exhibit 14.1 is an example of one organization's implementation of electronic monitoring using best practices.

EXHIBIT 14.1. THE WELSH AMBULANCE SERVICE TRUST CASE: ELECTRONIC PERFORMANCE MONITORING

Welsh Ambulance Services Trust (WAST) provides emergency service for the population of Wales in the United Kingdom. As a major employer, and part of the National Health Service, WAST uses performance monitoring at call centers. The centers rely on technology to supply a variety of services, including nurse triage, dental assessment, and health information. Intranet, internet, and emails are accessible to all staff. They may use the internet for personal reasons but are limited to 60 minutes per day; email use for other-than-official-purposes is also allowed.

Sarpong and Rees (2013) assessed the effects of electronic monitoring of staff and management. The authors were interested in the type of systems used, the extent to which people were conscious of them, the frequency with which they thought about the system or had concerns about their use, and any negative experiences. Questionnaires, interviews, and direct observation were used to gather data. In general, they found that electronic surveillance was viewed as a win-win situation for both rank-and-file and administrators, confirming the idea that when employees know they are watched they will perform better.

More specifically, personnel did not express concern about being monitored, reported no negative experiences, and felt surveillance of personal email and internet use was fair. Most managers did not feel that use of technology was a weapon of control. They used monitoring daily and unanimously agreed that it improved performance, although they reported receiving complaints from staff about being monitored.

What accounts for this seeming success? Why do administrators and employees view monitoring favorably? Sarpong and Rees (2013, pp. 3, 5) attribute this to:

- personal access to email and internet, which was viewed as a perk or entitlement
- the perceived need and right of employers to monitor employees to ensure no misuse and to create a secure work environment
- policies that made clear liability issues, specified acceptable and appropriate behavior, and outlined results of misuse of monitoring (which reduced fear and anxiety)

- requiring staff to sign policies prior to accessing systems
- a code of conduct agreed to by management and unions ensuring ethical conduct when using IT facilities at work
- training to promote awareness of surveillance policies prior to involvement in WAST's system

The researchers recommend: (a) periodically updating and discussing with employees IT policies and practices; (b) training managers to avoid micromanaging and pressuring staff; (c) being transparent about monitoring systems, their purpose, and significance; and (d) reinforcing the point that as long as employees are doing what they are supposed to do, they should not be concerned. Results from this study, then, suggest the importance of letting people know the rationale for surveillance systems and how such systems provide employee protection, while potentially enhancing productivity.

Ethics

At a minimum, to be ethical surveillance must be lawful. Employers are permitted by law to engage in surveillance to meet legitimate business objectives, but when it becomes unduly intrusive, overly controlling, or used for questionable purposes, it may be unlawful and unethical (Riedy & Wen, 2010). For example, courts probably will side with employees when monitoring includes hidden cameras in bathrooms or locker rooms. Because monitoring data can be objective, employees may see advantages to surveillance. But, as noted earlier, they also might regard such practices as invasions of privacy. Other cherished values may be considered at risk as well. Ethical questions may arise about fairness, autonomy, human dignity, and health impacts (Office of Technology Assessment, 1987). Neither the law nor the collective bargaining agreement is likely to provide adequate guidance for how to navigate all of these ethical concerns.

As discussed, considering the ethics of surveillance from multiple perspectives—employing tools such as the ethics triangle and insights from behavioral ethics—can improve decision making. Other strategies can also be utilized to inform decisions, including the principles of necessity (e.g., to prevent illegal or defamatory acts), finality (confining monitoring to specific, explicit, legitimate purposes), proportionality (appropriate, relevant and proportionate monitoring), and transparency (disclosure of reasons for monitoring) (see Mitrou & Karyda, 2006). Furthermore, as Mujtaba (2003) points out, it is crucial to provide "practical support to employees for handling ethical issues when it comes to the use of company properties such as computers" (pp. 15–16). This can include careful review of the code of conduct, appointment of ethics officers or ombudspersons, and ethics audits.

Such policy decisions and support mechanisms involve dialogue and deliberation, rather than capitulation to technological determinism. Yet managers may not frame decisions about electronic surveillance as ethical issues; they more likely are influenced by their responsibilities to shareholders to protect and make use of available assets (Ottensmeyer & Heroux, 1991). In this environment, the unconscious, and sometimes conscious, minimization of ethical implications occurs when ethics is reduced to, or subsumed by, nonethical considerations.

The promise of performance enhancement can be undermined by an unbalanced program. Leaders need to be aware of surveillance risks and rewards. Management policies and practices for notification, performance, leadership, and ethical decision making especially merit attention.

CONCLUSION

HR professionals are well aware that employees expect to be monitored, reviewed, and evaluated in some manner as a part of good management and the social contract at work. Goal setting, structural design, and conflict management are central to an effective surveillance program. Controversies arise when surveillance is intrusive and unnecessary, and these conflicts compromise work productivity and erode trust. Acceptability depends upon what is measured, how it is measured, how information is utilized, and the amount of employee participation in program development and implementation. It is critical for management to ensure rank-and-file support for work standards. That is, the policy should be empowering, not debilitating. Monitoring should be seen as beneficial to both the employer and the employees. HR professionals should keep these key points in mind when recommending and/or enforcing any monitoring policies and practices.

The centuries-old dividing line between work life and personal life no longer exists: Technology has made it possible to blend work time and personal time. Rather than causing conflict and discontent, is it possible to meld these two domains in a complementary way? One approach, known as results-only-work environment (ROWE), promises to do just that (Kidwell, 2010). It provides the opportunity for people to do what they want, when they want, and where they want so long as work is done. This new paradigm recognizes that a "working vacation" need not be a cynical oxymoron. It also acknowledges that some activities, such as participating in social networking, may be both personally important and job-related. For example, an employee might use it to identify other prospective employees or to develop "out-of-the-box" ideas and insights. Monitoring is largely self-directed, even unnecessary, provided that tasks are completed.

Pioneered at Best Buy's 4,000-employee corporate headquarters, the ROWE approach has been implemented by Gap, Inc.; Minnesota Department of Transportation; and the City of Minneapolis, as well as pilot initiatives in the federal government. ROWE's transformational strategy redefines work from a place to go to something people do. The result: Morale and productivity go up, and absenteeism and turnover go down (Ressler & Thompson, 2010). As might be expected, however, not all initiatives have been successful, and future experimentation and research are needed.[10]

The same technology that enables socially constructive workplace solutions like ROWE could also facilitate socially destructive practices of Orwellian proportions. Electronic surveillance could allow an institution to exercise complete control over individuals, as illustrated by the best-selling novel *The Circle* (Eggers, 2013).

The Circle, the world's most admired and powerful internet company, links personal emails, social media, and ecommerce, resulting in one online identity for users. In this future of complete transparency, full disclosure, and ubiquitous surveillance, the corporation can accomplish much for both its employees and society (e.g., openness produces a dramatic drop in crime). As the story progresses, the enterprise seeks to "close the Circle" and monitor every detail of everyone's life. In successive stages, people willingly give up privacy for sheer convenience, economic gain, and social acceptance, untroubled by massive centralization of information, video monitoring, and corporate invasion of personal life. Chilling questions about freedom, democracy, and the limits of human knowledge either go unasked or, when necessary, are suppressed.

The book, in the end, is less about technological advances and more about the nature of people. Stated differently, surveillance technology itself is value neutral, a tool that can be used and abused. But its rise should be an occasion for careful examination to ensure protection of humanitarian values. The challenge ahead—for HR professionals and other corporate leaders—is to retain the benefits surveillance technology provides while fully confronting its dangers.

NOTES

1. Indeed, a U.S. court ruled in a California case that, "Employers can diminish an individual employee's expectation of privacy by clearly stating...that electronic communications are to be used solely for company business, and the company reserves the right to monitor or access all employee Internet or email usage" (Flynn, 2009, p. 81).

2. Two proposals for federal legislation to provide privacy protection from employer technological monitoring have failed to pass: The Privacy for Consumers and Workers Act, introduced first in 1990, and the more modest Notice of Electronic Monitoring Act, introduced initially in 2000 (Levinson, 2010).

3. Although the Fourth Amendment does not apply directly to private employers, it may apply when a private employer acts as an agent of the government—for example, when it gives the government permission to search an employee's computer without a court order.

4. A judge may observe that a government employer has "special needs" and "operational realities," but courts weigh private employers' interests heavily in intrusion upon seclusion cases and private companies perform many functions essential to society, so the distinction largely seems rhetorical.

5. The court denied the employer's motion for summary judgment because there were disputed issues for the jury to decide about whether the employee who provided the manager with her password did so voluntarily (*Pietrylo v. Hillstone Restaurant Group*, 2008).

6. The law purportedly failed to pass because employers opposed it, predicting it would increase the workload for human resources employees and increase litigation (Watson, 2001).

7. The court held that the company breached its duty of care, but denied summary judgment because there were disputed issues for the jury to decide about whether the harm to the child would have occurred anyway (*Doe v. XYC Corp.*, 2005).

8. Numerous commentators have observed that, in America, the job market, not the law, is the primary check on employer excesses. Determan and Sprague (2011, p. 1005), for example, note that "during periods of economic growth or in industries with limited access to talent, employees gain market power.... In such circumstances, employers tend to keep notices and policies friendlier to employees."

9. This section draws upon Bowman and West (2014).

10. The Best Buy program lasted nearly a decade, but in 2013 its new CEO found it to be too radical; participation in ROWE is no longer a right, as now employees must ask their supervisor if they can participate. The federal government's pilot programs, while showing some promise, were terminated after one year due to management's concerns about control.

REFERENCES

American Management Association & ePolicy Institute. (2007). *2007 Electronic Monitoring & Surveillance Survey*. Retrieved from http://www.plattgroupllc.com/jun08/2007ElectronicMonitoringSurveillanceSurvey.pdf

American Management Association, U.S. News, & ePolicy Institute. (2001). *2001 AMA, U.S. News, ePolicy Institute Survey: Electronic Policies and Practices Summary of Key Findings*. Retrieved from http://www.epolicyinstitute.com/survey2001Summary.pdf

Ariss, S. S. (2002). Computer monitoring: Benefits and pitfalls facing management. *Information & Management, 39*(7), 553–558.

Bates, R. A., & Holton, E. F., III (1995). Computerized performance monitoring: A review of human resource issues. *Human Resource Management Review, 5*(4), 267–288.

Bazerman, M., & Tenbrunsel, A. (2011). *Blind spots: Why we fail to do what's right and what to do about it.* Princeton, NJ: Princeton University Press.

Blackman, P., & Franklin, B. (1993, August 19). Blocking Big Brother: Proposed law limits employer's right to snoop. *New York Law Journal,* p. 5.

Bowman, J., & West, J. (2014). *Public service ethics: Individual and institutional responsibilities.* Thousand Oaks, CA: Sage.

Bupp, N. (2001). Big Brother and Big Boss are watching you. *WorkingUSA, 5*(2), 69–81.

City of Ontario v. Quon, 560 U.S. 746 (2010).

Ciochetti, C. A. (2011). The eavesdropping employer: A twenty-first century framework for employee monitoring. *American Business Law Journal, 48*(2), 285–369.

Costco v. Wholesale Corp., 358 N.L.R.B. No. 106 (2012).

Crowther, B. (2012). (Un)reasonable expectation of digital privacy. *Brigham Young University Law Review, 2012,* 343–369.

Determann, L., & Sprague, R. (2011). Intrusive monitoring: Employee privacy expectations are reasonable in Europe, destroyed in the United States. *Berkeley Technology Law Journal, 26,* 979–1036.

Doe v. XYC Corp., 382 N.J. Super. 122 (N.J. Super. Ct. App. Div. 2005).

Elgin v. St. Louis Coca-Cola Bottling Co., 2005 WL 4755007 (E.D. Mo. 2005).

Eggers, D. (2013). *The circle.* New York, NY: Knopf.

Fazekas, C. P. (2004). 1984 is still fiction: Electronic monitoring in the workplace and U.S. privacy law. *Duke Law & Technology Review, 15,* 1–17.

Finkin, M. W. (2013). *Privacy in employment law* (4th ed.). Arlington, VA: Bureau of National Affairs.

Flynn, N. (2009). *The e-policy handbook* (2nd ed.). New York, NY: American Management Association.

Gazzaniga, M. (2008). *Human: The science behind what makes us unique.* New York, NY: Harper Perennial.

Kidwell, R. E. (2010). Loafing in the 21st century: Enhanced opportunities—and remedies—for withholding job effort in the new workplace. *Business Horizons, 53,* 543–552.

Kizza, J., & Ssanyu, J. (2005). Workplace surveillance. In J. Weckert (Ed.), *Electronic monitoring in the workplace. Controversies and solutions* (pp. 1–18). London, UK: Idea Group Publishing.

Lee, Ji-Y. (2007, June 23). There is big brother: Workplace control and workforce surveillance. *Union Review.* Retrieved from http://unionreview.com/there-big-brother-workplace-control-and-workforce-surveillance.

Levinson, A. R. (2010). Carpe diem: Privacy protection in employment act. *Akron Law Review, 43,* 331–433.

Levinson, A. R. (2011a). Toward a cohesive interpretation of the Electronic Communications Privacy Act for the electronic monitoring of employees. *West Virginia Law Review, 114,* 461.

Levinson, A. R. (2011b). Workplace privacy and monitoring: The quest for balanced interests. *Cleveland State Law Review, 59,* 377–398.

Lim, V. K. G. (2002). The IT way of loafing on the job: Cyberloafing, neutralizing and organizational justice. *Journal of Organizational Behaviour, 23*(5), 675–694.

Mirchandani, D., & Motwani, J., (2003). Reducing internet abuse in the workplace. *SAM Advanced Management Journal, 68*(1), 22–26.

Mitrou, L., & Karyda, M. (2006). Employees' privacy vs. employers' security: Can they be balanced? *Telematics and Informatics, 23*(3), 164–178.

Mujtaba, B. G. (2003). Ethical implications of employee monitoring: What leaders should consider. *Journal of Applied Management and Entrepreneurship, 8*(3), 22–47.

O'Brien, C. N. (2013). The top ten NLRB cases on Facebook firings and employer social media policies. *Oregon Law Review, 92*(2), 337–380.

O'Connor v. Ortega, 480 U.S. 709 (1987).

Office of Technology Assessment, U.S. Congress. (1987, September). *The electronic supervisor: New technology, new tensions.* (OTA Publication No. OTA-CIT-333). Washington, DC: U.S. Government Printing Office. Retrieved from http://www.princeton.edu/~ota/disk2/1987/8708/870801.PDF.

Ottensmeyer, E. J., & Heroux, M. A. (1991). Ethics, public policy, and managing advanced technologies: The case of electronic surveillance. *Journal of Business Ethics, 10*(7), 519–526.

PCWorld. (2008, February 29). Email, 'Net abuse is likely to get you fired. *ABC News.* Retrieved from http://abcnews.go.com/Technology/PCWorld/story?id=4362433.

Pierce, L., Snow, D., & McAfee, A. (2013). *Cleaning house: The impact of information technology monitoring on employee theft and productivity.* St. Louis, MO: Washington University.

Pietrylo v. Hillstone Restaurant Group, 2008 WL 6085437 (D. N.J 2008).

Pioneer Electronics (USA), Inc. v. Superior Court, 150 P.3d 198 (Cal. 2007).

Privacy Rights Clearinghouse. (2013). Fact sheet 7: Workplace privacy and employee monitoring. Retrieved from https://www.privacyrights.org/workplace-privacy-and-employee-monitoring.

Ressler, C., & Thompson, J. (2010). *Why work sucks and how to fix it.* New York, NY: Portfolio.

Restatement (Second) of Torts §652B (1977). American Law Institute.

Rich, F. (2013, June 30). When privacy jumped the shark. *New York Magazine.* Retrieved from http://nymag.com/news/frank-rich/domestic-surveillance-2013-7/.

Riedy, M. K., & Wen, J. H. (2010). Electronic surveillance of Internet access in the American workplace: Implications for management. *Information & Communications Technology Law, 19,* 87–99.

Sarpong, S., & Rees, D. (2013). Assessing the effects of "big brother" in a workplace: The case of WAST. *European Management Journal.* Retrieved from http://www.sciencedirect.com/science/article/pii/S0263237313000868#

Schmidt, E., & Cohen, J. (2013). *The new digital age: Reshaping the future of people, nations and business.* New York, NY: Knopf.

Schulman, A. (2001). *The extent of systematic monitoring of employee email and internet use.* Retrieved from http://www.sonic.net/~undoc/extent.htm

Shao, R., Aquino, K., & Freeman, D. (2008). Beyond moral reasoning: A review of moral identity research and its implications for business research. *Business Ethics Quarterly, 18,* 513–540.

Stanton, J. M., & Julian, A. L. (2002). The impact of electronic monitoring on quality and quantity of performance. *Computers in Human Behavior, 18*(1), 85–101.

Tubbs v. Wayne Transportation Services, 2007 WL 1189640 (S.D. Tex. 2007).

U.S. v. Jones, 132 S. Ct. 945 (2012).

U.S. v. Katzin, 732 F.3d 187(3rd Cir. 2013). Judgment vacated and rehearing en banc granted, 2013 (WL 7033666).

Vorvoreanu, M., & Botan, C. H. (2000, June). *Examining electronic surveillance in the workplace: A review of theoretical perspectives and research findings.* Paper presented to the Conference of the International Communication Association, Acapulco, Mexico. http://www.cerias.purdue.edu/assets/pdf/bibtex_archive/2001-32.pdf.

Watson, N. (2001). The private workplace and the proposed "Notice of Electronic Monitoring Act": Is "notice" enough? *Federal Communications Law Journal, 54*(1), 79–102.

Wugmerster, M., & Lyon, D. (Eds.). (2011). *Global employee privacy and data security law.* Arlington, VA: BNA Books.

FOR FURTHER READING

Ball, K. (2010). Workplace surveillance: An overview. *Labor History, 51,* 87–106.

Ball, K., & Margulis, S. T. (2011). Electronic monitoring and surveillance in call centers: A framework for investigation. *New Technology, Work, and Employment, 26,* 113–126.

Berkowitz, A. D., Downes, J. I., & Burdick, J. L. (2012). National Labor Relations Act update. *Employee Relations Law Journal, 37*(4), 39–66.

Carroll, W. R. (2008). The effects of electronic performance monitoring on performance outcomes: A review and meta-analysis. *Employee Rights & Employment Policy Journal, 12,* 29–47.

Collinson, D. L. (2003). Identities and insecurities: Selves at work. *Organization, 10,* 527–547.

Coultrup, S., & Fountain, P. D. (2012). Effects of electronic surveillance on the psychological contract of employees: An exploratory study. *Proceedings of ASBBS, 19*(1), 219–235.

Halpern, D., Reville, P. J., & Grunewald, D. (2008). Management and legal issues regarding electronic surveillance of employees in the workplace. *Journal of Business Ethics, 80,* 175–180.

Herbert, W. A. (2008). The electronic workplace, to live outside the law you must be honest, *Employee Rights & Employment Policy Journal, 12,* 49–104.

Knapp, K. R., & Soylu, A. (2013). Technology: The good, the bad, and the ugly: How technology is affecting employee privacy, work life balance, and workplace relationships. *Mustang Journal of Management & Marketing, 2,* 69–80.

Koen, C. M. J., & Mitchell, M. S. (2012). Guidelines for conducting bulletproof workplace investigations: Part II–searches, surveillance, and other legal issues. *The Health Care Manager, 31*(3), 221–229.

Koops, B. (2010). Law technology and shifting power relations. *Berkeley Technology Journal, 25,* 973–1036.

Lalli, M. A. (2011). Spicy little conversations: Technology in the workplace and a call for a new cross-doctrinal jurisprudence. *American Criminal Law Review, 48,* 243–283.

Levinson, A. R. (2009). Industrial justice: Privacy protection for the Employed. *Cornell Journal of Law and Public Policy, 18,* 609–688.

Martin, K., & Freeman, R.E. (2003). Some problems with employee monitoring. *Journal of Business Ethics, 43*, 353–361.

Naito, A. (2012). A Fourth Amendment status update: Applying constitutional privacy protection to employees' social media use. *Journal of Constitutional law, 14*(3), 849–883.

National Workrights Institute. (2011). *Privacy under siege: Electronic monitoring in the workplace.* Retrieved from http://workrights.us/wp-content/uploads/2011/02/NWI_EM_Report.pdf

O'Donnell, A. T., Ryan, M. K., & Jetten, J. (2013). The hidden costs of surveillance for performance and helping behaviour. *Group Processes & Intergroup Relations, 16*(2), 246–256.

Palm, E. (2009a). Privacy expectations at work—What is reasonable and why? *Ethical Theory and Moral Practice, 12*, 201–215.

Palm, E. (2009b). Securing privacy at work: The importance of contextualized consent. *Ethics and Information Technology, 11*, 233–241.

Rosenberg, K. (2008). Location surveillance by GPS: Balancing employer's business interest with employee privacy. *Washington Journal of Law, Technology & Arts, 6*, 145–154.

Sewell, G., Barker, J. R., & Nyberg, D. (2012). Working under intensive surveillance: When does "measuring everything that moves" become intolerable? *Human Relations, 65*(2), 189–215.

Sheriff, A. M., & Ravishankar, G. (2012). The techniques and rationale of e-surveillance practices in organizations. *Zenith: International Journal of Multidisciplinary Research, 2*(2), 281–290.

Sprague, R. (2008). Orwell was an optimist: The evolution of privacy in the United States and its de-evolution for American employees. *John Marshall Law Review, 42*, 83–133.

Taylor, R. E. (2012). A cross-cultural view towards the ethical dimensions of electronic monitoring of employees: Does gender make a difference? *International Business & Economics Research Journal, 11*(5), 529–534.

What privacy rights do I have in the workplace? (2013, April 8). *Los Angeles Times.* Retrieved from http://articles.latimes.com/2013/apr/08/business/la-fi-mo-what-privacy-rights-in-workplace-20130408.

CHAPTER 15

PERSON–ORGANIZATION FIT AND ITS IMPLICATIONS FOR HUMAN RESOURCE MANAGEMENT PRACTICES

Daniel J. Svyantek, Kristin L. Cullen, & Alexa Doerr

INTRODUCTION

Person–environment fit is a concept that impacts organizational behavior and organizational performance. There are two primary forms of person–environment fit (Kristof, 1996) to be considered in human resource practices that may have legal implications for a company. These are person–job fit and person–organization fit.

Person–job (PJ) fit is concerned with the degree to which there is a match between an employee's skills and abilities and the requirements of the job the employee holds (Kristof, 1996). The better the match, the more likely the employee is to be a successful employee. As this match decreases and employees do not have the needed skills and abilities to perform the job, employees tend to be frustrated and dissatisfied. This leads to decreases in both individual and organizational performance. This concept of fit is consistent with traditional approaches to human resource practices

Legal and Regulatory Issues in Human Resources Management, pages 315–340
315

(e.g., selection and performance evaluation). Defining person–job fit is done in traditional ways by matching the needs of job analyses to the knowledge, skills, and abilities of applicants.

Person–organization (PO) fit is concerned with the degree to which there is a match between employee characteristics and the characteristics of the organization (e.g., organizational culture) in which the employee works (Kristoff, 1996). The better the match, the more likely the employee is to be a successful employee. For example, some organizations value teamwork, and some organizations value individual accomplishment. Individuals with a high need for individual accomplishment will have good fit with an organization valuing individual accomplishment. However, their fit will be poor in an organization valuing teamwork. As this match decreases and employee characteristics and values do not reflect organizational characteristics, employees tend to be frustrated and dissatisfied. This leads to decreases in both individual and organizational performance. This concept of fit may impact traditional human resource practices; however, this impact is much more complex. Defining person–organization fit is complex, and linking this construct to legal issues is more difficult for both researchers and practitioners.

Research on the effects of person–organization fit on organizational and individual effectiveness continues to mount, and we believe increasing PO fit may eventually become as important a concern for human resources (HR) professionals as increasing PJ fit has been over the past several decades. Thus, it is important for the successful HR practitioner of the future to have a good understanding of the PO fit construct and its implications for the practice of HR management. The relationship between the work environment and the employee is increasing in importance. For example, consideration of the determination of what defines a hostile work environment (cf., Robinson, Franklin, & Wayland, 2002) to a reasonable person (cf., Gutman, 2000) may be helped by consideration of the issue of PO fit. Accordingly, the goals of this chapter are (a) to review the literature on person–organization fit; (b) discuss the role of organizational culture as the variable defining the organization component of the fit construct; (c) describe the attraction-selection-attrition (ASA) model (Schneider, 1987b) and how this model describes person–organization fit; and (d) review the potential legal issues facing organizations that use person–organization fit in human resource practices.

PERSON–ORGANIZATION FIT

The operational definition of fit varied greatly throughout its history. An early conceptualization was Tom's (1971) operationalization of fit as personality–climate congruence. It proposed that an employee's fit is a match between his or her own self-construct and the representative image of the organization, consisting of a conglomeration of its knowledge, beliefs, and feelings. These antecedents of fit represent a very broad notion that has narrowed and divided over time. Tom's definition of fit leads directly to newer conceptions of PO fit.

PO fit is "the compatibility between people and organizations that occurs when at least one entity provides what the other needs, they share similar fundamental characteristics, or both" (Kristof, 1996, pp. 4–5). The research and literature available only begin to delve into the questions surrounding this conceptualization. Determining the operationalization of PO fit requires distinguishing between actual PO fit and perceptions of PO fit, measurement techniques, and underlying construct relationships. A clear conception of PO fit is difficult to obtain, as many different theories have surfaced attempting to address these issues. Verquer, Beehr, and Wagner (2003) completed a meta-analysis in which they considered four different operational definition differences that may moderate the PO fit relationship with various work outcomes. These moderators included (a) the dimensions measured: values, goals, personality, or needs-structure fit; (b) the choice between subjective fit, perceived fit, or objective fit; (c) scores calculated as differences between PO fit measures or using polynomial regression and intra-individual correlation; and (d) the questionnaire used. The mostly commonly used questionnaire, the Organizational Culture Profile (OCP), is discussed in relation to the other moderators.

Kristof (1996) defines PO fit as the fit of the person not with any specific subgroup, job, or vocation, but with the organization as a whole. Cable and DeRue (2002) describe PO fit as the judgment of value congruence between the organization and the employee. The important thing to note, however, is that, even when controlling for PJ fit, PO fit results in positive work outcomes (Bretz & Judge, 1994; O'Reilly, Chatman, & Caldwell, 1991). When Lauver and Kristof-Brown (2000) investigated the distinction between PJ and PO fit, they found that the two constructs weakly related to each other ($r = .18$), implying that employees distinguish between the types of fit in the work environment. The findings of Kristof-Brown, Zimmerman, and Johnson (2005) support the idea that job-related constructs are most strongly associated with attitudes about the job, while organization-related constructs are related to organizational attitudes (Shore & Martin, 1989). This is evident in job satisfaction's high correlation to PJ fit and organizational commitment's relationship with PO fit.

These findings support Chatman's (1989) claim that PJ and PO fit are similar, but distinct constructs. PJ fit predicted job satisfaction and turnover intention, but not organizational commitment. The findings of Cable and Judge (1996) further support this argument. They again found that PO fit and PJ fit were weakly related ($r = .18$), suggesting that employees discern the difference between these forms of fit. Furthermore, they found that job seekers place far less emphasis on PJ fit than PO fit when they make job decisions regarding accepting a job offer. This seems intuitive if we assume that applicants are choosing between similar jobs at different companies. Thus, if the organization is the differentiating factor, then it only makes sense that job seekers would place more emphasis on PO fit. Employment interviews are an opportunity for the company and the applicant to assess their respective fit with each other. Specifically, this gives the applicant an opportunity to learn more about the culture and values of the organization after having previously received preliminary job information. PO fit research implies that job satisfaction develops through self-selection based on fit with the company (e.g., Bowen, Ledford & Nathan, 1991; Schneider, 1987b). Based on these findings, vocational counseling and recruitment should emphasize job selection based on knowledge, skills, and abilities (KSAs) and the culture of the organization. Positive outcomes of person–organization fit include more commitment, more satisfaction, and less intention to quit (Bretz & Judge, 1994; Chatman, 1989; Meglino, Ravlin, & Adkins, 1989; O'Reilly et al., 1991).

The concept of PO fit has implications for both organizations and employees. The primary organizational variable impacting PO fit is organizational culture, in our opinion. We describe our logic for this in the following section.

ORGANIZATIONAL CULTURE

There are four primary organization-level variables that help define the context of workplace behavior. These are organizational structure, organizational culture, organizational climate, and organizational design. *Organizational structure* refers to the formal system of task and authority relationships within an organization (Morgan, 1998). This variable is often defined as the "organizational chart," although it should be recognized that power relationships, political structures, and so on are often not reflected in an organizational chart. Organizational structure is concerned with how organizational members coordinate their actions and use resources to achieve organizational goals. *Organizational culture* may be defined by a set of shared values and norms, held by employees, that guide employees' interactions with peers, management, and clients/customers (Morgan, 1998). *Organizational climate* is more behaviorally oriented in that climates for safety or service, for example, may be found in the workplace (Schneider, 2000). These climates represent the specific patterns of interactions and behaviors that support safety or service in the organization. *Organizational design* is the process through which an organization's administration manages organizational structure, organizational culture, and organizational climate to control the activities necessary to meet the organization's goals (Morgan, 1998).

Taken together, these variables help define the context in which workplace behavior occurs. Organizational culture is proposed as the antecedent, causal element for organizational structure, organizational climate, and organizational design. A major reason for the formation of organizational culture is the creation of social order (Trice & Beyer, 1993). Organizational culture allows recurrent behavior patterns among people to develop within organizations. These patterns form the basis of predictable interactions within an organization.

Organizational culture provides employees with the contextual information necessary to be successful members of the company to which they belong. Namenwirth and Weber (1987) propose that culture serves four purposes for any social group. These purposes define (a) what it means to be a member of the group, (b) social and economic justice within the group, (c) how the elements of the group are organized to produce a socially "good" group, and (d) how the group makes the materials or services it was formed to produce.

Namenwirth and Weber's (1987) first three purposes are closely linked to how a social group integrates individual members in the social system. These three purposes provide group members with information on what are the valued behaviors within a social situation. The last purpose of the cultural system is concerned with adaptation of the social group to its external environment. The integration function and adaptation function of the culture may not be directly related (Svyantek, 1997; Svyantek & Brown, 2000). Organizational cultures may be (a) integrated in a satisfying manner for employees and be productive, (b) integrated in a satisfying manner for employees and be nonproductive, (c) integrated in a nonsatisfying manner for employees and be productive, or (d) integrated in a nonsatisfying manner and be nonproductive. We propose that, for purposes of predicting the impact of PO fit on behavior related to human resource practices within an organization, that the integration function is most critical.

Schein's (1985) model of the three levels of organizational culture is a multidimensional, multilevel definition of culture. First, the most superficial or visible level of culture is artifacts and creations: These represent the physical and social environment of the social situation. The second level of culture is values, norms, and attitudes, or a sense of what "ought to be." Finally, at the deepest level lie the unconscious assumptions uniformly held by all members of the culture. It is these unconscious assumptions that make up the true culture of an organization.

Organizational culture, therefore, is the antecedent of other organization-level variables. Organizational culture is maintained over time through organizational socialization practices to assimilate newcomers into the organization. Therefore, organizational culture may be highly resistant to change and "frozen" in a sense that the assumptions and beliefs established by the founder(s) are maintained although change may be required to improve organizational effectiveness. Organizational culture may be so embedded in the people, processes, and relationships that change is resisted even as the organizational culture ceases to be relevant in a changing environment (Schein, 1985).

Organizational culture affects behaviors within an organization. Organizational culture defines a *strong situation* (Mischel, 1977) for individuals residing within it. A strong situation provides people with generally accepted rules and guidelines for appropriate behavior. The rules that are present in strong situations constrain people from acting in a manner inconsistent with accepted conduct and behavior. Organizations develop values and norms to set parameters on the behaviors exhibited within an organization.

For example, organizations possess norms and values regarding proper decision making practices (Ott, 1989). These have been shown to effect choice of decision-making strategies through the creation of organizational decision making styles (Furlong & Svyantek, 1998; Svyantek, Jones, & Rozelle 1991; Svyantek & Kolz, 1996). Such a collection of norms and values can be labeled an organizational decision climate. The policies and practices of an organization supporting such styles are hypothesized to create a specific decision-making climate for that organization.

The effects of organizational climate are particularly strong when the individual is motivated to adapt (Showers & Cantor, 1985). The ability to recognize and correctly adapt to the reality of organizational life is a critical component of career success (Sathe, 1985) where managers are very motivated to understand the behaviors that are supported in their environment (Hannaway, 1989). Managers rely heavily on the information they receive from their social structure to infer behaviors that are appropriate and use this information to balance organizational goals and their personal career interests when making a decision (Hannaway, 1989; Svyantek et al., 1991; Svyantek & Kolz, 1996). They must, in effect, analyze and interpret their organization's decision-making climate and use these interpretations to guide their decision behavior. This maximizes individual rewards and minimizes individual punishments for the decision maker. Thus, the appropriateness of a decision will be contingent upon the organizational culture within which the decision maker operates.

The constraints on the accepted range of behaviors within an organization create multiple organizational climates supporting responses for organizational criteria (e.g., customer service or decision making). These constraints are created by, and reflect, the values and assumptions that comprise an organizational culture.

Person–organization fit has been defined as "the congruence between patterns of organizational values and patterns of individual values, defined here as what an individual values in an organization, such as being team-oriented or innovative" (Chatman, 1991, p. 459). The emphasis here is on the match of an individual's values, when considered along with the value system in a specific organizational culture, and the potential effects that this match (or lack of match) has on that individual's subsequent behavior and attitudes in the company. The model we use for understanding these effects is the ASA model (Schneider, 1987b).

THE ATTRACTION-SELECTION-ATTRITION MODEL

Person–organization fit has been shown to be related to a number of organizational variables including (a) job choice decisions by organizational applicants (Cable & Judge, 1996); (b) organizational attraction of applicants (Judge & Cable, 1997); (c) selection decisions made by recruitment interviewers (Cable & Judge, 1997); (d) employee job satisfaction, job tenure, and career success (Bretz & Judge, 1994); and (e) employee's level of task and organizational citizenship performance (Goodman & Svyantek, 1999).

The process by which person–organization fit may come to maintain an organizational climate across time, influence organizational human resource practices, and affect employee behavior is illustrated in the ASA model (Schneider, 1987a, 1987b; Schneider, Goldstein, & Smith, 1995). Schneider proposed that "attributes of people, not the nature of the external environment, or organizational technology, or organizational structure, are the fundamental determinants of organizational behavior" (i.e., "the people make the place") (Schneider, 1987b, p. 437). The attraction–selection–attrition (ASA) framework is a mechanism for explaining homogeneity of organizational level variables such as organizational culture found in organizations. Schneider (1987a) stated that this homogeneity is due to three main processes. First, it occurs because people are attracted to places that they prefer (attraction). People will seek out organizational environments in which they are comfortable being a member. The primary human resource practice affected by this is recruitment, and there are potential legal implications for organizations here. Second, homogeneity results from people being selected into settings to which they are perceived to be compatible (selection). Organizations tend to select certain individuals who appear to fit with those already there. The primary human resource practice affected by this is selection, and there are potential legal implications for organizations here. Third, if people manage to enter an environment that is not a fit for them, they will tend to leave it (attrition) or the organization may terminate them. The behaviors exhibited by individuals with lack of fit may come to be dysfunctional (Svyantek & Brown, 2002). The primary human resource practice affected by this is termination, and there are potential legal implications for organizations here.

This model been supported empirically. For example, Schein and Diamonte (1988) found a relationship between three different personality variables and organizational characteristics. People who rated themselves as high on a personality characteristic were more likely to be attracted to an organization that was described as reflecting that characteristic. Similarly, it was found that organizational climate information and personality variables interact in a recruitment situation (Furlong & Svyantek, 1998). Personality variables were found to prime individuals to perceive and select organizational climates in which they will have a high probability of succeeding.

Schneider's ASA (attraction–selection–attrition) framework indicates that particular kinds of people are attracted to certain settings, and those who fit are not as likely to leave the organization. Thus, the ASA framework suggests there will be a restriction in range of individual differences in organizations (i.e., as compared with the general population). This restriction of range results in an organization of people who will also be very similar in behavior, experiences, orientations, feelings, and reactions and creates a relatively homogenous group of individuals. This homogeneity, in turn, helps maintain the organizational culture across time. However, it also means that, for those employees joining the organization and exhibiting different patterns of behavior, there may be negative human resources consequences for the employee. This in turn means that there will be potential legal implications for the organization using PO fit in their human resource practices.

PERSON–ORGANIZATION FIT
AND HUMAN RESOURCE PRACTICE

Bowen, Ledford, and Nathan (1991) proposed that there is a "new model of selection" in which employees are hired to fit the characteristics of an organization, not just the requirements of a particular job. This notion is based on the idea of hiring a "whole" person who will fit well into the specific organization's culture. This model of person–organization fit changes the nature of decisions made during the selection process. Now the selection process should achieve two types of fit (Bowen et al., 1991). First, the selection process must match the KSAs of the individual and the task demands of the job (i.e., person–job fit). Second, the selection process must match individual dispositional variables and the culture of the organization (i.e., person–organization fit).

There is an interesting conundrum in studying PO fit. This construct is recognized as important in predicting employee well-being and performance criteria. However, there is a paucity of work on PO fit's legal standing and legal implications for human resource management practice. We seek to provide a logical argument for the use of PO fit in human resource practice that might address this paucity. The remainder of the chapter will (a) review important employee well-being and performance criteria predicted by PO fit, (b) show how the ASA model provides a framework for understanding how PO fit operates in organizations, and (c) discuss a potential model for understanding the implications of PO fit for organizations using this construct in making human resource decisions.

PERSON–ORGANIZATION FIT
AND ORGANIZATIONAL CRITERIA

Person–organization fit is recognized as a critical component of basic human resource practices. There is a large body of research describing the effects of PO fit on important organizational criteria. The largest correlations between PO fit and dependent measures occur with job satisfaction, organizational citizenship behaviors (OCB), commitment, turnover, and job search and choice. Performance outcomes are less related as there are many other mediating factors, including the job type, limitations of technology, and factors present in the external environment. Even with these moderators, Bretz and Judge (1994) still found that PO fit relates to job promotions and salary level, which are indicators of performance. The following section discusses the personal outcomes most related to PO fit.

Job Satisfaction

Job satisfaction is the individual worker's subjective evaluation of the degree to which his or her needs are meet by the organization. Bretz and Judge (1994) proposed the theory of work adjustment (TWA), which is a need–supply explanation of person–organization fit. They state that job satisfaction, tenure, and rewards moderate the relationship between person–environment fit. If there is congruence between an employee's needs and what the organization provides, then both job satisfaction and job tenure will follow. Given that person–organization and person–job fit are weakly related (Cable & Judge, 1996, r = .18), it is not surprising that when controlling for the other each has a unique impact on job satisfaction and intentions to quit. Job satisfaction correlates with person–organization fit r = .40 and person–job fit r = .39, while intentions to quit correlate with each at r = -.47 and r = -.22, respectively (Lauver & Kristof-Brown, 2001). These findings imply that each of the types of fit measured contribute equally to job satisfaction; however, employees' perceptions of their person–organization fit has the largest impact on their intention to quit. Tett and Meyer (1993) hoped to address the issue of predictive direction between commitment and satisfaction and eventual turnover intentions. They found satisfaction and commitment to be distinguishable, yet moderately related constructs that contribute uniquely to turnover intentions.

Intentions to Quit and Actual Turnover

PO fit is a more likely predictor of intentions to quit than actual turnover. Turnover is a more distal outcome; thus, other factors may prevent employees from exercising their intentions. Those who do not fit will often leave, as predicted by the ASA framework (Schneider, 1987a, 1987b). Westerman and Cyr (2004) found that employee satisfaction and commitment further mediate the relationship between PO fit and employee's intentions to leave an organization.

Organizational Citizenship Behavior

OCBs are extra-role behaviors that benefit the company. Bateman and Organ (1983) propose that these behaviors are valued by supervisors because they cannot require OCBs; however, when employees perform them of their own volition, the manager's job is now easier, and the manager is able to devote time and resources elsewhere. The relationship between satisfaction and OCBs is much stronger than the relationship between satisfaction and job performance (Bateman & Organ, 1983). These behaviors may be more controllable by employees, while the satisfaction/job performance relationship may hinge on other factors. To obtain the benefits of increased OCBs in the workplace, the selection process should match not only the KSAs of the individual and the task demands of the job, but also the dispositions of the applicants and the culture of the organization. Goodman and Svyantek (1999) found further support for the relationship between person–organization fit and organizational citizenship behavior. They measured both perceived and actual culture on many dimensions, and after assessing the congruence of the measures, they found that the employee's perceptions of the organization's warmth and competence were the strongest predictors of OCBs.

Task Performance

Goodman and Svyantek (1999) also studied the influence of person–organization fit on employees' task performance. It was hypothesized that the fit between employees' desired organizational culture and their actual organizational cultures would predict task performance. It was found that (a) perceptions of the organizational culture and (b) the discrepancy between employees' ideal organizational culture and their perceptions of the actual organizational culture were important in predicting task performance. Bright (2007) also investigated the role of PO fit in job performance. This research looked at whether person–organization fit mediates the relationship between public service motivation (PSM) and performance of public employees. Results also yielded a strong relationship between respondents who reported being highly congruent with their organization and those who reported receiving higher performance ratings from their managers when compared to the ratings reported by their counterparts with lower congruence with their organization. Furthermore, findings indicated that PSM had no significant direct impact on the self-reported performance of public employees, when PO fit was taken into account, which supports the posed hypothesis that the influence of PSM on job performance is completely mediated by PO fit.

USING THE ASA MODEL TO UNDERSTAND PO FIT

Schneider's (1987a, 1987b) ASA model is used to frame the research on PO fit's effects on human resource practices in organizations. This model's three components—attraction, selection, and attrition—are used to organize existing work on PO fit.

Attraction

The effects of PO fit on the attraction and recruitment of employees into organizations is probably the best researched component of the ASA model. Exposure to business during everyday life is likely to influence potential applicant's perceptions of the company before they even summit an application. Organizations must be aware of anticipatory socialization and approach recruitment with knowledge that an image exists of their company that may or may not be in line with the picture they are trying to present to potential employees.

Judge and Cable (1997) found during their study of applicant attraction and personality congruence that applicants gather information prior to interviewing for a job, including visiting a career placement office and attending information sessions in an attempt to learn, among other things, about the company's organizational values. During recruitment, employers must balance their desire to attract candidates with their need to present an accurate picture of not only the job, but the culture of their company. Cable, Animan-Smith, Mulvey, and Edwards (2000) found that companies could influence applicants' beliefs about organizational culture during anticipatory socialization.

A company's reward system is one mechanism that shows cultural aspects of the organizational value systems (Cable & Judge, 1997). Bretz, Ash, and Dreher (1989) showed that organizations that used individually based reward systems attracted applicants that scored highly on need for achievement. Thus, a company that values individual achievement attracted those that had a similar need. Turban and Keon (1993) also found that although applicants are more attracted to decentralized firms that distribute decision-making responsibility and use individual performance-based reward pay systems, self-esteem (SE) and need for achievement (nAch) moderate the effects of attraction. Their findings imply that a match based on individual differences in SE and nAch results in attraction to the firm. These findings suggest that companies can target ideal employees based on their pay preferences. They found that individual characteristics were associated with stable preferences in pay systems. With level of pay being equal, flexible benefits, individual-based pay, fixed-pay, and job-based pay were differentially attractive. Furthermore, dispositional risk aversion led to less emphasis on pay in favor of stability and that taking risks may require and incentive premium.

Cable and Judge (1996) concluded that congruence between job seekers' values and their perceptions of recruiting organizations' values predicts their assessment of PO fit, not their demographic similarity with the organizational representatives. Person–organization fit predicts both job choice intentions and work attitudes, even after controlling for the attractiveness of job attributes. The recruiter may be the only source of information that the applicant has about the company, and thus it is necessary for the applicant to make inferences about the rest of the organization based on his or her interaction with the recruiter. These inferences are valid to the extent that the company sends a recruiter that is representative of the successful and dominant organizational cohort (Rynes & Gerhart, 1990).

Coldwell, Billsberry, and Van Meurs (2008) propose that an ethical dimension of organizational culture and personal values and the fit between them may explain differences in attraction to specific organizations. They discuss potential consequences of corporate social responsibility and of corporate reputation regarding an organization's ability to acquire and retain employees based on individual perceptions of ethical–organizational fit.

Internet technology gives companies the ability to provide information about values to potential applicants before actually beginning the screening process; furthermore, companies can provide feedback to applicants regarding their level of fit with the organization. Applicants' perceptions of the organization may change after viewing a company website with a statement of the company's values. Dineen, Ash, and Noe (2002) explored the relationship between feedback, applicant attraction, and other organizational outcomes. They found that both the level of feedback and the applicant's objective PO fit were related to attraction; however, this relationship was mediated by the applicant's agreement with the feedback (agreement based on their own evaluation of their subjective person–organization fit) and the applicant's self-esteem. Positive objective person–organization fit related to attraction, commitment, and decreased turnover. Agreement with fit feedback affects the degree to which an employee internalizes the company values. When agreement is high, feedback and attraction are more related. PO fit feedback influences individuals low in self-esteem more; when determining attraction, they are more likely to believe that the feedback is valid or diagnostic (Dineen et al., 2002). Even when objective feedback is high, low-self-esteem individuals report lower attraction when they received low feedback. Level of fit feedback relates more strongly to attraction among higher rather than lower self-esteem individuals. A company's ability to influence the attraction levels of their applicants by making tailored feedback regarding potential fit available to job seekers will most likely narrow the applicant pool with positive and negative consequences.

During recruiting and selection, the use of realistic job previews shares positive and negative aspects of the job with applicants, reducing unrealistic expectations and allowing applicants to assess their fit with the organization and self-select out if necessary. Cable et al. (2000) further found that the short-term benefits that companies see from presenting an overly positive picture of the organization are lost in later turnover. Allowing candidates to self-select out of the hiring process appears beneficial to both the employee and the company.

The primary potential legal issue for organizations in the attraction phase is following accepted recruitment practices that ensure that all potential applicants have equal access to the information used to attract and recruit employees. For example, there might be potential biases in the degree to which certain employment advertisement sites differentially are visited by protected groups. An interesting possibility, as companies increase the use of Internet technology, is whether or not different groups of individuals have equal access necessary to find out about companies.

Selection

The second phase, selection, is where organizations need to be especially careful when using PO fit to make hiring decisions. This is because the fit is often "in the eye of the beholder," and the actual measurement of PO fit is more complex than it is for standard tests (e.g., work performance or personality tests) used singly or in test batteries.

Kristof-Brown (2000) showed that interviewers rely on KSAs to assess PJ fit, and use values and personality traits to assess PO fit. She found that 100% of recruiters mentioned KSAs as an element in their assessment of both fit constructs; however, they mentioned KSAs much more frequently in relation to PJ fit. Both factors uniquely accounted for variance in selection to hire despite being highly correlated (r = .72), suggesting that while PJ fit is essentially a requirement, PO fit represents an ideal and thus is sought after as well.

Cable and Judge (1997) found that recruiters' (generally inaccurate) perceptions of PO fit are more indicative of hiring decisions than actual PO fit. Adkins, Russel, and Werbel (1994) explained that recruiters assess applicants separately on their employability and their fit with the organization. General employability rests on the applicant possessing the relevant KSAs for the job while PO fit involves a more specific match, most often between the values of an employee and the organization. Interestingly, applicant–organization work value congruence was unrelated to both employability and PO fit. This difference was demonstrated by showing that assessment of PO fit was significantly lower than assessment of general employability and PO fit was more variable (Adkins et al., 1994; Rynes & Gerhart, 1990).

This implies that recruiters share a general opinion of the necessary qualifications to perform the job, but they differ in perceptions of which individuals will fit within the company. Rynes and Gerhart (1990) reported that interviewers also respond differently to requests for general employment and firm-specific ratings of fit. They found that interviewers were more stringent on their ratings of fit than general employability.

Adkins et al. (1994) also found that recruiters are more like to fall into a "similar-to-me" bias when assessing applicant's person–organization fit. They base their assessment of fit on the fit between themselves and the applicant (idiosyncratic fit) when assessing an applicant's general employability; recruiters rely on a "similar-to-ideal" bias by comparing the applicant to an ideal standard. The effect of recruiter person–organization judgment variability appears to occur later in the two-step process of selection: first assessing an applicant's employability and then their PO fit. Applying the findings to the workplace, an organization may promote the selection of individuals with high person–organization fit by ensuring that their recruiters embody the values and culture of the company.

McCulloch and Turban (2007) examined whether a measure of PO fit as a selection tool yields incremental value above and beyond cognitive ability for predicting continued length of service and performance. The sample consists of 228 call center agents. This position was selected because it is considered a job with historically high turnover. PO fit was measured using the correlation between managers' descriptions of the work culture and participants' work preferences. Results indicated that PO fit contributed significant incremental variance in predicting employee retention. The authors recommended that firms consider using measures of PO fit for selection purposes, especially when turnover is a significant problem.

Using PO fit to select employees is, however, potentially problematic from a legal standpoint, and this is an important point for HR professionals to realize. Arthur, Bell, Villado, and Doverspike (2006) noted that the use of measures of person–organization (PO) fit are liable to the same psychometric and legal standards as other employment tests when used to guide personnel decision making. The authors utilized meta-analytic procedures to assess the criterion-related validity of PO fit as a predictor of job performance and turnover. Results estimated true criterion-related validities of .15 ($k = 36$, $N = 5,377$) for PO fit as a predictor of job performance and .24 ($k = 8$, $N = 2,476$) as a predictor of turnover. A stronger effect of .31 ($k = 109$, $N = 108,328$) was found for the relationship between PO fit and work attitudes. Furthermore, the relationship between PO fit and both job performance and turnover were partially mediated by work attitudes. As work attitudes contribute to these relationships, there is even less of a direct effect of PO fit on these two factors. However, the relations between PO fit and attitudinal outcomes including job satisfaction, organizational commitment, and turnover intentions were relatively strong and generalizable. These findings, according to the authors, should caution organizations about the appropriateness of using PO fit in selection decisions without having conducted local validation studies that demonstrate its criterion-related validity. The authors also noted that this logic is appropriate for other human resource decisions where PO fit might be used (e.g., promotions, selections for leadership positions, transfers, terminations, and the formation of work teams).

Defining PO Fit for Employment Decisions

Arthur et al. (2006) proposed that the use of PO fit requires local validation studies demonstrating criterion-related validity. These validation studies are complex and require the use of organizational and employee measures that are combined somehow in one measure describing the unique relationship between the two sources.

Person–organization fit's emphasis here is on the match of an individual's values with the value system in a specific organizational context, and the potential effects that this match (or lack of this match) has on that individual's subsequent behavior and attitudes. Therefore, both situational and dispositional aspects are combined into one measure that, conceptually, represents an interaction between the two classes of situational and dispositional variables. There are two related methods of doing this.

Person–organization fit assessment involves collapsing two constructs into one measure as a predictor of some outcome. The vast majority of person–organization fit studies have operationalized congruency by collapsing two or more measures into a single index. These profile similarity indices (PSIs) combine two sets of measures, or profiles, from corresponding entities (e.g., the ideal state and organization) into a single score intended to represent overall congruence (Cronbach & Glesser, 1953). Examples of this include the use of discrepancy scores and the use of correlations between observed culture and personal values (cf. O'Reilly et al., 1991).

Edwards (1993, 1994, 1995), however, suggests that PSIs should no longer be used in congruence research, such as person–organization fit. Instead, researchers should use polynomial equations containing measures of both entities (here the actual and ideal culture measurements) that typically are collapsed in PSIs (cf. Edwards, 1993, 1994; Edwards & Cooper, 1990; Edwards & Harrison, 1993; Edwards & Parry, 1993). The general approach suggested by Edwards (1993, 1994) offers several advantages over congruence indices currently in use. First, polynomial regression maintains the interpretability of the original component measures. Second, polynomial regression yields separate estimates of the relationships between component measures and the outcome. Third, polynomial regression provides a complete test of models underlying congruence indices, focusing not only on the overall magnitude of the relationship, but also on the significance of individual effects, the validity of implied constraints, and the significance of higher-order terms. Finally, the approach proposed by Edwards (1993, 1994) may yield considerable increases in explained variance.

Goodman and Svyantek's (1999) findings were based on the use of Edwards' (1993, 1994) approach. The use of this method allowed interpretable patterns of results using actual and ideal measure of organizational cultural dimensions. The actual measure reflects the organization's current state while the ideal measures reflect the employees' values in this approach. It was found that PO fit measured this way was predictive of employee task and organizational citizenship performance.

Therefore, we recommend that Edward's approach be used when addressing issues of person–organization fit when investigating the interaction of situational and dispositional factors as defined by the construct of person–organization fit. The key thing for organizations seeking to use PO fit is that, as Arthur et al. (2006) noted, the use of PO fit is context-specific. We believe that the use of PO fit may also be decision-specific (e.g., the use of PO fit measures for hiring new employees and the use of PO fit measures for promoting individuals may require two separate validation studies). HR professionals should take note of this recommendation.

Attrition

The final phase of the ASA model, attrition, is another area where PO fit may become relevant in human resource practice. This is traditionally seen, from the organization's perspective, as the impact of turnover on the organization based on employee decisions.

Autry and Wheeler (2005), for example, examined PO fit during the initial phases of actual employment when socialization and training are taking place. This research examines the lasting influence of formal organizational socialization and training practices on PO fit. Formal socialization was found to relate to fit with supervisors and firm procedures, but not with coworkers. Duration of formal training was found to relate to cognitive PO fit with supervisors and firm procedures, but not with coworkers. The authors drew implications from their results. If formal socialization and formal training duration is increased, this may influence employees' perceptions and feelings of fit with their supervisor and with the firm and may contribute to employees' belief that they belong with the organization for the long term.

Moynihan and Pandey (2008) proposed that a strong and positive intraorganizational social network, characterized by good relations with and a sense of obligation toward other staff, establishes a situation in which employees are more likely to stay. The authors hypothesized that PO fit shapes turnover intention, in that those who experience a strong PO fit with regard to value congruence are more likely to offer a long-term commitment.

Finally, organizational cultural dimensions influence turnover. Sims and Kroeck (1994) found that PO fit related to the ethical culture of an organization was related with turnover intentions, continuance commitment, and affective commitment. McCulloch and Turban (2007) also found that PO fit contributed significant incremental variance in predicting employee retention. The authors recommended that firms consider using measures of PO fit for selection purposes, especially when turnover is a significant problem.

Taken together, these results provide organizations with ways to change and influence employees' voluntary decisions to leave the organization. Organizations have ways to influence employees' perceived lack of fit and retain valuable employees.

PO Fit and Organizational Decisions to Force Attrition

However, as Arthur et al. (2006) stated, PO fit may also be used to make decisions about the termination of employees. The question remains whether or not such termination decisions are legally defensible. We believe they are. We will describe our logic by (a) discussing the relationship between PO fit and undesirable organizational behavior and (b) providing an example of how PO fit might affect decisions to terminate an employee and how an organization might defend itself after making such a decision.

The organization behavior literature has shown a disproportionate emphasis on desirable phenomena (such as improved productivity or organizational citizenship behaviors) as topics of research (Robinson & Bennett, 1995). Dysfunctional employee behavior, however, may be responsible for millions, if not billions, of dollars in losses to organizations and are potentially dangerous to employees within the organization (Robinson & Bennett, 1995).

This has led to a growth in research on dysfunctional behavior in the workplace (Griffin, O'Leary-Kelly, & Collins, 1998). Much of this research has focused on how individual differences in employees relate to dysfunctional behavior. Griffin et al. (1998), for example, have developed a model of the dynamics of dysfunctional behaviors in organizations that is concerned with individual differences and individual pathologies as antecedents of behavior. This model, however, also includes organizational characteristics (e.g., norms, culture, reward and control systems) as potential influences on employee behavior in general. Clearer understanding of how organization-level variables affect dysfunctional behavior in the workplace, however, is needed.

Robinson and Bennett (1995) have defined a typology with four types of dysfunctional work behaviors. Robinson and Bennett (1995) proposed that two dimensions may be used to define dysfunctional behaviors. These dimensions are (a) the seriousness or harmfulness of the dysfunctional acts and (b) the degree to which the dysfunctional behaviors are harmful to individuals within the organization or directed at the organizations. These two dimensions define four types of dysfunctional behavior. *Production deviance* includes acts that are less serious and directed at the organization. Examples of these include employees leaving early, taking excessive breaks, intentionally working slowly, and wasting organizational resources. *Property deviance* includes acts that are more serious but still directed at the organization. Examples of these acts include employees sabotaging equipment, accepting kickbacks, lying about the number of hours worked, and stealing from the company. *Political deviance* includes acts that are less serious and directed at individuals in the organization. Examples of these acts include showing favoritism, gossiping about coworkers, blaming coworkers, and excessive competition against others in the organization. *Personal aggression* includes acts that are more serious and directed at individuals in the organization. Examples of these acts include sexual harassment, verbal abuse, stealing from coworkers, and endangering coworkers.

Person–organization fit is a critical variable in understanding the relationship between organizational culture and dysfunctional behavior. Not all individuals are equally suited to all organizations. The performance of dysfunctional behavior may be a matter of misfit between the individual and the situation and not just a set of individual and/or organizational variables considered in isolation from each other. For example, Sperry (1998) proposes that good fit is related to higher job performance; higher job satisfaction; increased self-esteem, and less stress for employees. Dysfunctional responses to poor fit, however, include increased stress, burnout, cynicism, role ambiguity, and role conflict among employees.

Poor fit is not necessarily a deficit of either the person or the organization. Rather, *misfit* occurs when there is a mismatch between employee value systems and organizational culture. This misfit, however, leads to issues that the organization may be required to address because decrements in performance may be found.

The higher in the organizational hierarchy, the more likely that misfit will have a negative effect on organizational performance. We will provide an example below to illustrate this. This example assumes that a manager has been hired from outside the organization. The manager is experienced and has been successful in other organizations. However, in this organization, the manager is having a detrimental influence on the performance of the organization. This type of example is at likely situation in which PO fit may be grounds for termination of an employee.

First, we believe a lack of PO fit is potential grounds for termination based on the nature of managerial positions. Managerial and executive jobs operate in a context (Cascio, 1998). This context involves interaction with superiors, peers, and subordinates and interactions with the organizational values represented by the specific organizational culture in which the manager resides. Different organizations have different cultural values: These differences in values manifest themselves as unique approaches to organizational behaviors such as communication, decision making, and problem solving. Different organizations will have different methods of generating solutions to problems. The ability to take on the perspective of the organization may be critical to organizational efficiency and effectiveness criteria.

Person–organization fit is concerned with the degree to which there is a match between employee characteristics and the characteristics of the organization (e.g., organizational culture) in which the employee works. The better the match, the more likely the employee is to be a successful employee. For example, some organizations value teamwork and some organizations value individual accomplishment. Individuals with a high need for individual accomplishment will have good fit with an organization valuing individual accomplishment: However, their fit will be poor in an organization valuing teamwork. As this match decreases and employee characteristics and values do not reflect organizational characteristics, employees tend to be frustrated and dissatisfied. This leads to decreases in both individual and organizational performance.

Second, we believe performance at the managerial level may be linked more closely to lack of PO fit as well. This is because the behaviors at this level are more visible, so their effects on the organization may be linked to observed performance issues, and these deficits may be linked to PO fit. These behaviors may be seen as politically deviant, for example, by the organization in which the manager currently resides. Such behaviors may have been normal in the other organizations in which the manager has been successful. The key here for the decision to terminate is not necessarily that the behaviors are simply observed. Rather, the decision to terminate should be based on the response of the manager to feedback about the appropriateness of the behavior in the current context. If the manager responds to feedback and changes the behaviors exhibited, the issue of lack of fit goes away. However, if the manager refuses to change such behaviors, then the effects of this misfit on performance will increase.

Finally, we propose that the reason misfit often leads to decreased employee and organizational performance has been well described by Steiner (1972). Steiner proposed that, for any job in which groups are involved:

$$\text{Actual Productivity} = \text{Potential Productivity} - \text{Process Loss}$$

Process involves the humans in an organization. Therefore, the human element in this model is a source of error. Process loss involves communication, interpersonal dealings with others, and discussing and making decisions for situations where there is no clearly superior solution. Individuals who lack person–organization fit will cause disruption and process loss. This decreases the performance of the organization in which they reside: the greater the misfit, the greater the process loss. The effects of lack of PO fit will be magnified as the job held by an employee rises through the organizational hierarchy. The disruptions caused by an hourly employee will probably be minor. The disruptions by individuals in executive positions have the potential to be catastrophic for an organization.

We believe that organizations have the right to terminate employees based on misfit. These decisions reflect a need to improve organizational performance. Such decisions, however, are decisions that must typically be made on an individual basis. Each employee's misfit may be unique and have differential effects on the performance of the organization. We believe that organizations seeking to use misfit as a reason for termination must follow procedures similar to those laid down for progressive discipline for any negative employee behavior. Organizations must provide documentation showing a series of attempts to provide the employee with feedback about (a) the behaviors being exhibited that do not fit the cultural values of the organization (e.g., how information is communicated to subordinates or superiors here); (b) provide information on how these behaviors are affecting the organization (e.g., meetings are taking too long or decisions are being made without taking all pertinent information into account); and (c) provide the employee with corrective behaviors based on the way this organization operates (e.g., we like to get subordinate input on all such decisions here). If these procedures are followed, we believe that lack of PO fit becomes a defensible reason for termination.

SUMMARY

Research about PO fit and its resultant outcomes is important for organizations to understand; this literature provides valuable information when creating appropriate human resource practices for today. Today, with the onset of the Information Age, there may be a revolutionary change occurring in the human resource management principles that guide business organizations as economic forces in the world change models of organizations emphasizing long-term employment and employee loyalty to those emphasizing short-term employment and rapid turnover of employees. In addition, with the growing divide between skilled and unskilled positions in the labor force, PO fit may become critical to organizations seeking to attract and retain individuals with valued skill sets.

Person–organization fit issues will become more important as these new human resource practices are developed. Our chapter has used Schneider's (1987a, 1987b) attraction–selection–attrition model for providing a framework for the role PO fit in human resource practices. Our conclusions follow.

First, PO fit may be used to inform recruitment practices (attraction). Organizations should make sure that prospective employees have a realistic preview of the organizational values so that applicants may make informed decisions on whether or not they wish to be a member of the organization. Organizations should ensure that prospective applicants from all groups have the same information and that these individuals have access to the information in some manner.

Second, there are things that organizations may do in their hiring practices based on PO fit research (selection). Organizations should take steps to ensure that all individuals assessing PO fit have a common framework and understanding of the culture and of the complex set of characteristics that makeup the employees in the culture. Recruiters and interviewers should have knowledge of the values and culture of the company. In addition, organizations using PO fit must understand that selection based on traditional testing methods (e.g., paper-and-pencil instruments) is complex. PO fit requires that measures of both employee and organizational variables (e.g., personality and organizational culture) are required. These measures must be combined into a single PO fit variable. We agree entirely with Arthur et al. (2006), who proposed that the use of PO fit requires local validation studies demonstrating criterion-related validity. We believe that the use of PO fit may also be decision-specific (e.g., the use of PO fit measures for hiring new employees and the use of PO fit measures for promoting individuals after time in the organization will require two separate validation studies).

Third, lack of fit may be enough of an issue for an organization to decide to terminate employees (attrition). Organizations have the right to eliminate low performers based on PO misfit. However, these decisions should be made on an individual basis and follow the tenets of progressive discipline.

It will be interesting to see how the courts treat PO fit in future cases regarding selection, promotion, and dismissal. PO fit appears to be an important and promising predictor in these important HR decisions, but the courts have not yet pronounced a verdict that may be used in HR practice. As noted earlier, consideration of the determination of what defines a hostile work environment (cf. Robinson et al., 2002) to a reasonable person (cf. Gutman, 2000) might be helped by consideration of the issue of PO fit, and we believe that the same holds for more traditional HR decisions..

REFERENCES

Adkins, C. L., Russell, C. J., & Werbel, J. D. (1994). Judgments of fit in the selection process: The role of work value congruence. *Personnel Psychology, 47,* 605–623.

Arthur, W. R., Bell, S. T., Villado, A. J., & Doverspike, D. (2006). The use of person–organization fit in employment decision making: An assessment of its criterion-related validity. *Journal of Applied Psychology, 91,* 786–801.

Autry, C. W., & Wheeler, A. R. (2005). Post-hire human resource management practices and person-organization fit: A study of blue-collar employees. *Journal of Managerial Issues, 17,* 58–75.

Bateman, T. S., & Organ, D. W. (1983). Job satisfaction and the good soldier: The relationship between affect and employee "citizenship." *Academy of Management Journal,* 26, 587–595.

Bowen, D. E., Ledford, G. E., & Nathan, B. R. (1991). Hiring for the organization, not the job. *Academy of Management Executive, 4,* 35–51.

Bretz, R. D., Ash, R. A., & Dreher, G. F. (1989). Do people make the place? An examination of the attraction–selection–attrition hypothesis. *Personnel Psychology, 42,* 561–581.

Bretz, R. D., & Judge, T. A. (1994). Person-organization fit and the theory of work adjustment: Implications for satisfaction, tenure, and career success. *Journal of Vocational Behavior, 44,* 32–54.

Bright, L. (2007). Does person–organization fit mediate the relationship between public service motivation and the job performance of public employees? *Review of Public Personnel Administration, 27,* 361–379.

Cable, D. M., Animan-Smith, L., Mulvey, P. W., & Edwards, J. R. (2000). The sources and accuracy of job applicants' beliefs about organizational culture. *Academy of Management Journal, 43,* 1076–1085.

Cable, D. M., & DeRue, D. S. (2002). The convergent and discriminant validity of subjective fit perceptions. *Journal of Applied Psychology, 87,* 1–17.

Cable, D. M., & Judge, T. A. (1996). Person-organization fit, job choice decisions, and organizational entry. *Organizational Behavior and Human Decision Processes, 67,* 294–331.

Cable, D. M., & Judge, T. A. (1997). Interviewer's perceptions of person-organization fit and organizational selection decisions. *Journal of Applied Psychology, 82,* 546–561.

Cascio, W. F. (1998). *Applied psychology in human resource management* (5th ed.). Upper Saddle River, NJ: Prentice-Hall.

Chatman, J. A. (1989). Improving interactional organizational research: A model of person–organization fit. *Academy of Management Review, 14,* 333–349.

Coldwell, D., Billsberry, J., & Van Meurs, N. (2008). The effects of person–organization ethical fit on employee attraction and retention: Towards a testable explanatory model. *Journal of Business Ethics, 78,* 611–622.

Cronbach, L. J., & Glesser, G .C. (1953). Assessing the similarity between profiles. *Psychological Bulletin, 50,* 456–473.

Dineen, B. R., Ash, S. R., & Noe, R. A. (2002). A web of applicant attraction: Person–organization fit in the context of web-based recruitment. *Journal of Applied Psychology, 87,* 723–734.

Edwards, J. R. (1993). Problems with the use of profile similarity indices in the study of congruence in organizational research. *Personnel Psychology, 46,* 641–665.

Edwards, J. R. (1994). The study of congruence in organizational behavior research: Critique and a proposed alternative. *Organizational Behavior and Human Decision Processes, 58,* 51–100.

Edwards, J. R. (1995). Alternatives to difference scores as dependent variables in the study of congruence in organizational research. *Personnel Psychology, 64,* 307–324.

Edwards, J. R., & Cooper, C. L. (1990). The person-environment fit approach to stress: Recurring problems and some suggested solutions. *Journal of Organizational Behavior, 11,* 293–307.

Edwards, J. R., & Harrison, R. V. (1993). Job demands and worker health: Three-dimensional reexamination of the relationship between person-environment fit and strain. *Journal of Applied Psychology, 78,* 628–648.

Edwards, J. R., & Parry, M. E. (1993). On the use of polynomial regression equations as alternatives to difference scores in organizational research. *Academy of Management Journal, 36,* 1577–1613.

Furlong, M. A., & Svyantek, D. J. (1998). The relationship between organizational climate and personality: A contextualist perspective. *Journal of Psychology and Behavioral Sciences, 12,* 43–53.

Gutman, A. (2000). *EEO law and personnel practices* (2nd Ed.). Thousand Oaks, CA: Sage.

Griffin, R. W., O'Leary-Kelly, A., & Collins, J. (1998). Dysfunctional work behaviors in organizations. In C. L. Cooper & D. M. Rousseau (Eds.), *Trends in organizational behavior* (Vol. 5, pp. 65–82). New York, NY: Wiley.

Goodman, S. A., & Svyantek, D. J. (1999). Person–organization fit and conceptual performance: Do shared values matter? *Journal of Vocational Behavior, 55,* 254–275.

Hannaway, J. (1989). *Managers managing: The workings of an administrative system.* New York, NY: Oxford Press.

Judge, T. A., & Cable, D. M. (1997). Applicant personality, organizational culture and organizational attraction. *Personnel Psychology, 50,* 359–394.

Kristof, A. L. (1996). Person–organization fit: An integrative review of its conceptualization, measurement, and implications. *Personnel Psychology, 49,* 1–49.

Kristof-Brown, A. L. (2000). Perceived applicant fit: Distinguishing between recruiter's perceptions of person-job and person-organization fit. *Personnel Psychology, 53,* 643–671.

Kristof-Brown, A. L., Zimmerman, R. D., & Johnson, E. C. (2005). Consequences of individuals' fit at work: A meta-analysis of person-job, person organization, person-group and person-supervisor fit. *Personnel Psychology, 58,* 281–342.

Lauver, K. J., & Kristof-Brown, A. (2001). Distinguishing between employees' perceptions of person-job and person-organization fit. *Journal of Vocational Behavior, 59,* 454–470.

McCulloch, M. C., & Turban, D. B. (2007). Using person–organization fit to select employees for high-turnover jobs. *International Journal of Selection & Assessment, 15,* 63–71.

Meglino, B. M., Ravlin, E. C., & Adkins, C. L. (1989) A work values approach to corporate culture: A field test of the values congruence process and its relationship to individual outcomes. *Journal of Applied Psychology, 74,* 424–432.

Mischel, W. (1977). The interaction of person and situation. In D. Magnusson & N. S. Endler (Eds.), *Personality at the crossroads: Current issues in interactional psychology* (pp. 333–352). Hillsdale, NJ: Lawrence Erlbaum.

Morgan, G. R. (1998). *Organizational theory* (2nd ed.). Reading, MA: Addison-Wesley.

Moynihan, D. P., & Pandey, S. K. (2008). The ties that bind: Social networks, person–organization value fit, and turnover intention. *Journal of Public Administration Research & Theory, 18,* 205–227.

Namenwirth, J. Z., & Weber, R. P. (1987). *Dynamics of culture.* Boston: Allen & Irwin.

O'Reilly, C. A., III, Chatman, J., & Caldwell, D. F. (1991). People and organizational culture: A profile comparison approach to assessing person-organization fit. *Academy of Management Journal, 34,* 487–516.

Ott, J. S. (1989). *The organizational culture perspective.* Pacific Grove, CA: Brooks/ Cole Publishing.

Robinson, R. H, Franklin, G. M., & Wayland, R. (2002). *The regulatory environment of human resource management.* Fort Worth, TX: Harcourt College Publishers.

Robinson, S. L., & Bennett, R. J. (1995). A typology of deviant workplace behaviors: A multidimensional scaling study. *Academy of Management Journal, 38,* 555–572.

Rynes, S., & Gerhart, B. (1990). Interviewer assessment of applicant "fit": An exploratory investigation. *Personnel Psychology, 43,* 13–22.

Sathe, V. (1985). *Culture and related corporate realities.* Homewood, IL: Richard D. Irwin.

Schein, E. H. (1985). *Organizational culture and leadership.* San Francisco, CA: Jossey-Bass.

Schein, V. E., & Diamonte, T. (1988). Organizational attraction and the person-environment fit. *Psychological Reports, 62,* 167–173.

Schneider, B. (1987a). E=f(P,B): The road to a radical approach to person–environment fit. *Journal of Vocational Behavior, 31,* 353–361.

Schneider, B. (1987b). The people make the place. *Personnel Psychology, 40,* 437–453.

Schneider, B. (2000). The psychological life of organizations. In N. M. Ashkanasy, C. P. M. Wilderon, & M. F. Peterson (Eds.), *Handbook of organizational culture and climate* (pp. xvii–xxi). Thousand Oaks, CA: Sage.

Schneider, B., Goldstein, H. W., & Smith, D. B. (1995). The ASA framework: An update. *Personnel Psychology, 48,* 747–773.

Shore, L. M., & Martin, H.J. (1989). Job satisfaction an organizational commitment in relation to work performance and turnover intentions. *Human Relations, 42,* 625–638.

Showers, C., & Cantor, N. (1985). Social cognitions: A look at motivated strategies. *Annual Review of Psychology, 36,* 275–305.

Sims, R., & Kroeck, K. (1994). The influence of ethical fit on employee satisfaction, commitment, and turnover. *Journal of Business Ethics, 13,* 939–947.

Sperry, L. (1998). Organizations that foster inappropriate aggression. *Psychiatric Annals, 28,* 279–284.

Steiner, I. D. (1972). *Group process and productivity.* New York, NY: Academic Press.

Svyantek, D. J. (1997). Order out of chaos: Non-linear systems and organizational change. *Current Topics in Management, 2,* 167–188.

Svyantek, D. J., & Brown, L. L. (2000). A complex systems approach to organizations. *Current Directions in Psychological Science, 9*(2), 69–74.

Svyantek, D. J. & Brown, L. L. (2002). Mental health and organizational design, climate and culture. In M. Hersen & J. Thomas (Eds.), *Handbook of mental health in the workplace* (pp. 477–500). Thousand Oaks: Sage.

Svyantek, D. J., Jones A. P., & Rozelle, R. (1991). The relative influence of organizational decision frames on decision making. *Advances in Information Processing in Organizations, 4,* 127–145.

Svyantek, D. J., & Kolz, A.R. (1996). The effects of organizational frames and problem ambiguity on decision-making. *Journal of Business and Psychology, 11*(2), 131–150.

Tett, R. P., & Meyer, J. P. (1993). Job satisfaction, organizational commitment, turnover intention, and turnover: Path analyses based on meta-analytic findings. *Personnel Psychology, 46,* 259–293.

Tom, V. R. (1971). The role of personality and organizational images in the recruiting process. *Organizational Behavior and Human Performance, 6*, 573–592.

Trice, H. M., & Beyer, J. M. (1993). *The cultures of organizations.* Englewood Cliffs, NJ: Prentice-Hall.

Turban, D. B., and Keon, T. L. (1993). Organizational attractiveness: An interactionist perspective. *Journal of Applied Psychology, 78*, 184–193.

Verquer, M. L., Beehr, T. A., & Wagner, S. H. (2003). A meta-analysis of relations between person-organization fit and work attitudes. *Journal of Vocational Behavior, 63*, 473–489.

Westerman, J. W., & Cyr, L. A. (2004). An integrative analysis of person-organization fit theories. *International Journal of Selection and Assessment, 12*, 252–261.

CHAPTER 16

TOWARD A BETTER UNDERSTANDING OF INTERNATIONAL HUMAN RESOURCES MANAGEMENT LAWS AND LEGAL ISSUES

Ronald R. Sims

INTRODUCTION

The environment in which business competes has rapidly become global. More and more firms are entering international markets by exporting their products overseas, building plants in other countries, and entering into alliances with foreign companies. Indeed, most organizations function in the global economy. U.S.-based businesses (i.e., McDonald's, Google, Procter & Gamble, Coca Cola, and others) have long had extensive overseas operations, of course, and as more U.S. businesses enter international markets, foreign companies (i.e., Novo Nordisk, Diageo, Toyota, Deutsche Bank) are entering the U.S. market.

It is clear that the global corporation is playing an increasingly major role in the world economy, and globalization is a dominant driving force in the

Legal and Regulatory Issues in Human Resources Management, pages 341–373
Copyright © 2015 by Information Age Publishing
All rights of reproduction in any form reserved.

world economy, reshaping societies and politics as it changes lives. There is every indication that the trend towards expansion in global markets will continue as companies attempt to gain a competitive advantage, which can be provided by international expansion in a number of ways. First, as U.S. and foreign-based companies look for new markets with large numbers of potential customers, it is logical for them to look to other countries or international markets. For companies that are producing below their capacity, foreign markets provide a means of increasing sales and profits. Second, in an effort to capitalize on other countries' lower labor costs for relatively unskilled jobs, many companies are continuing to build production facilities in other countries. For example, many of the *maquiladora* plants (foreign-owned plans located in Mexico that employ Mexican laborers) and facilities in other countries like Bangladesh continue to provide low-skilled labor at considerably lower costs than the United States. Third, rapid increases in information technology and telecommunications enable a customer service or support network work to be established and maintained more rapidly, efficiently, and effectively around the world. With the best college graduates available for much lower hourly rates in India versus hourly rates in the United States, organizations can hire the best talent (resulting in better work) at a lower cost. And because their day is our night, work done in the United States can be handed off to those in India or other southeastern Asian countries for a 24/7 work process.

Deciding whether to enter foreign markets and whether to develop plants or other business or service facilities in other countries is no simple matter, and many contemporary human resource management (HRM) issues, challenges, and opportunities surface as HRM professionals have to help their host organizations navigate the differing HRM laws, regulations, or legislation. Ensuring legal and regulatory compliance can be very challenging in a foreign environment where laws and business practices may be different. HRM professionals must make sure that their companies take note of local laws impacting not only how their business is run, but also how their employees are managed. More specifically, this means ensuring that their organizations comply with a wide range of labor and employment laws by developing and maintaining related policies for their organizations. HRM professionals seek to minimize the risk of going afoul of a host nation's laws or regulations while at the same time avoiding employee lawsuits and audits by federal or state governments, for example, in the United States. In short, HRM professionals need profound knowledge of workplace laws and regulations no matter where their organization does business in the world.

The chapter first takes a look at managing organizations and human resources across borders. Next, the discussion turns to the internationalization of business and factors affecting HRM in global markets before focusing on domestic versus international human resources management (IHRM). The chapter then considers some specific HRM activities and laws within an international business before concluding with a comparison of HRM laws in China and the United States and antidiscrimination laws around the world.

MANAGING ORGANIZATIONS
AND HUMAN RESOURCES ACROSS BORDERS

International business operations can take several different forms. A large percentage of these operations carry on their international business with only limited facilities and minimal representation in foreign countries. Others have extensive facilities and personnel in various countries of the world. Managing these resources effectively and integrating their activities to achieve global advantage is a challenge to the leadership of these firms. However, before focusing on these challenges, it is important for HRM professionals to first understand what is meant by international human resources management (IHRM) and the different levels of participation in international markets. This is especially important because, as a firm becomes more involved in international trade, different types of HRM problems arise.

Broadly defined, IHRM is the process of procuring, allocating, and effectively utilizing human resources in an international business. More specifically, global or international human resource management (IHRM) is the process of employing, developing, and rewarding people in international or global organizations. It involves the worldwide management of people, not just the management of expatriates. An international organization or firm is one in which operations take place in subsidiaries overseas that rely on the business expertise or manufacturing capacity of the parent company. Such companies or organizations bring with them their own management attitudes and business styles. HRM professionals of such organizations cannot afford to ignore the international influences on their work.

IHRM involves a number of issues not present when the activities of the company or organization are confined to one country. For example:

- The variety of international organizational models that exist
- The extent to which HRM policy and practice should vary in different countries (This is also known as the issue of convergence and divergence.)
- The problem of managing people in different cultures and environments
- The approaches used to select, deploy, develop, and reward expatriates who could be nationals of the parent company or "third-country nationals" (TCNs)—nationals of countries other than the parent company who work abroad in subsidiaries of that organization

INTERNATIONAL ORGANIZATIONAL MODELS

Bartlett and Ghoshal (1991) identified the following four international organizational models:

- Decentralized federation in which each national unit is managed as a separate entity that seeks to optimize its performance in the local environment (This is the traditional multinational corporation.)
- Coordinated federation in which the center develops sophisticated management systems enabling it to maintain overall control, although scope is given to local management to adopt practices that recognize local market conditions
- Centralized hub in which the focus is on the global market rather than on local markets. Such organizations are truly global rather than multinational.
- Transnational in which the corporation develops multidimensional strategic capacities directed towards competing globally but also allows local responsiveness to market requirements

Convergence and Divergence

Another issue facing international organizations is the extent to which their HRM practices should either *converge* worldwide to be basically the same in each location, or *diverge* to be differentiated in response to local requirements. There is a natural tendency for managerial traditions in the parent company to shape to the nature of key decisions, but there are strong arguments for giving as much local autonomy as possible in order to ensure that local requirements are sufficiently taken into account. (This is known as the global/local dilemma.) Convergence may be increasing as a result of the following factors:

- The power of markets
- The importance of cost
- Quality and productivity pressures
- The development of like-minded international cadres
- The widespread practice of benchmarking "best practices"

Adler (2008) offers another categorization of the various levels of international participation from which a company may choose and includes the following levels of involvement: domestic, international, multinational, global/transnational.

Domestic

Most organizations begin by operating within a domestic marketplace. For example, a business that starts in the U.S. marketplace must recruit, hire, train, and compensate their employees who are usually drawn from the local labor market. The focus of the selection and training programs is often on the employees' technical competence to perform job-related duties and to some extent on interpersonal skills. In addition, because the company is usually involved in only one labor market, determining the market rate of pay for various jobs is relatively easy.

As the company grows, it might choose to build additional facilities in different parts of the country to reduce the costs of transporting the products over large distances. In deciding where to locate these facilities, the company must consider the attractiveness of the local labor markets. Various parts of the country may have different cultures that make those areas more or less attractive according to the work ethics of the potential employees. Similarly, the potential employees in the different areas may vary greatly because of differences in educational systems. Finally, local pay rates may differ.

International

As more competitors enter the domestic market, companies face the possibility of losing market share; thus they often seek other markets for their products. This usually means entering international markets, initially by exporting products but ultimately by building production facilities in other countries. Essentially, these companies build on their existing capabilities to penetrate overseas markets. Companies such as General Electric, Procter & Gamble, and Honda all used this approach to gain access to Europe.

The decision to participate in international competition raises a host of HRM issues. All the problems regarding locating facilities are magnified. For example, HRM professionals must consider whether a particular location provides an environment where human resources can be successfully acquired and managed.

Multinational

A multinational corporation (MNC) is a more complex form that usually has fully autonomous units operating in multiple countries. Whereas international companies build one or a few facilities in another country, they become multinational when they build facilities in a number of different countries, attempting to capitalize on lower production and distribution costs in different locations. The lower production costs are gained by shifting production from higher-cost locations to lower-cost locations. For example, some of the major U.S. (and non-U.S.) automakers have plants all over the world. They continue to shift their production from the United States, where labor unions have gained high wages for their members, to maquiladora facilities in Mexico, where the wages are substantially lower. Similarly, these companies minimize distribution costs by locating facilities in Europe for manufacturing and assembling automobiles to sell in the European market. And over the past decade or so they have expanded into some of the former Soviet bloc countries to produce automobiles for the European market.

MNCs have traditionally given their foreign subsidiaries a great deal of latitude to address local issues such as consumer preferences, political pressures, and economic trends in different regions of the world. Frequently, these subsidiaries are run as independent companies, without much integration.

Global

The global corporation can be viewed as a multinational firm that maintains control of operations back in the home office. Global organizations compete on state-of-the-art, top-quality products and services and do so with the lowest cost possible. Whereas MNCs attempt to develop identical products distributed worldwide, global companies increasingly emphasize flexibility and mass customization of products to meet the needs of particular clients. MNCs are usually driven to locate facilities in a country as a means of reaching that country's market or lowering production costs, and the company must deal with the differences across the countries. Global organizations, on the other hand, choose to locate a facility based on the ability to effectively, efficiently, and flexibly produce a product or service and attempt to create synergy through the cultural differences.

Japanese companies such as Matsushita and NEC, for example, have tended to treat the world market as a unified whole and try to combine activities in each country to maximize efficiency on a global scale. These companies operate much like a domestic firm, except that they view the whole world as their marketplace.

Transnational

A transnational corporation attempts to achieve the local responsiveness of an MNC while also achieving the efficiencies of a global firm. To balance this "global/local" dilemma, a transnational uses a network structure that coordinates specialized facilities positioned around the world. More specifically, transnational corporations use geodiversity to great advantage, placing their top executives and core corporate functions in different countries to gain a competitive edge through the availability of talent or capital, low costs, or proximity to their most important customers. Of course, it is all made possible by the Internet, as improved communication facilitates an integrated global network of operations ("Borders are so 20th century," 2003).

By using this flexible structure, a transnational provides autonomy to independent country operations but brings these separate activities together into an integrated whole. For most companies, the transnational form represents an ideal rather than a reality. However, companies such as British Petroleum, Unilever, and Ford have made good progress in restructuring operations to function more transnationally. Also, consider Logitech International, for instance. Its manufacturing headquarters are in Taiwan to capitalize on low-cost Asian manufacturing. Meanwhile, its business development headquarters in Switzerland has lined up strategic partnerships that have kept the company at the cutting edge of peripherals design, particularly for optical pens and mice, which has helped Logitech hold its own against mighty Microsoft in worldwide markets for peripherals ("Borders are so 20th century," 2003).

The development of transnationals has led to a fundamental rethinking about the nature of a multinational company. Does it have a home country? What does headquarters mean? Is it possible to fragment corporate functions like HRM globally? To be sure, organizational structure directly affects all HRM functions from recruitment through retirement because to be effective, HRM must be integrated into the overall strategy of the organization. Indeed, from the perspective of strategic management, the fundamental problem is to keep the strategy, structure, and HRM dimensions of the organization in direct alignment (Briscoe & Schuler, 2012) while being respectful of local country laws or regulations.

THE INTERNATIONALIZATION OF BUSINESS AND FACTORS AFFECTING HRM IN GLOBAL MARKETS

Although various forms of organizations exist, this chapter generally refers to any company that conducts business outside its home country as an international business. Clearly, the United States has no monopoly on international business. In fact, some Pacific Rim and European companies have been conducting business on an international basis much longer than their U.S. counterparts.

International business is not a new phenomenon. Indeed, its origins can be traced back literally thousands of years as merchants plied their wares along ancient trade routes linking southern Europe, the Middle East, and the Orient. Silks, spices, grains, jade, ivory, and textiles were among the most popular goods forming the basis for early trade. Wars have been fought over issues arising from international commerce, and the British Empire was built around the financial and business interests of the British nobility.

In the 1950s and 1960s, most large multinational corporations (MNCs) operating in the world were American (Phatak, 1989). These organizations operated in a world economy relatively safe from competition from firms of other nationalities. The world of international business became far more complex and competitive in the 1970s and particularly in the 1980s. Beginning in the 1990s and even more so since the beginning of the 21st century, the nature of international business has truly become global in nature as firms from many countries are competing for their share of an ever-increasing world market of goods and services. International business and global competitiveness have become almost commonplace for most large organizations in the past two decades, and more and more medium-size and smaller businesses are engaged in international business as well.

Today, an expanding high-tech, information-based economy increasingly defines globalization and shapes the business cycles within it. Much of the flow of capital, labor, services, and goods among the United States, Europe, and Asia is technology based. As new markets and new sources of technology and labor are opened, the increase in international competition accentuates the need to manage human resources effectively to gain competitive advantage in a global marketplace. This requires understanding some of the factors that can determine the effectiveness of various HRM practices and approaches.

Firms that enter global markets must recognize that these markets are not simply mirror images of their home country. Countries differ along a number of dimensions that influence the attractiveness of direct foreign investment in each country. These differences determine the economic viability of building an operation in a foreign location, and they have a particularly strong impact on HRM professionals and HRM in that operation. Among a number of factors that can affect HRM in global organizations are: culture, education–human capital, the political–legal system, and the economic system.

Culture

Perhaps the most important factor influencing IHRM is the culture of the country in which a facility is located. Culture is a society's set of assumptions, values, and rules about social interaction. A country's culture can be defined as the set of values, symbols, beliefs, and languages that guide behavior within that culture. The culture in which one is raised programs the mind to react to the environment in certain ways. In essence, culture provides people with a mental road map and traffic signals (Black, Gergersen, & Mendenhall, 1992). The road map depicts the goals to be reached and the ways to get there; the traffic signals indicate who has the right of way, when to stop, and so on.

Culture is composed of the societal forces affecting the values, beliefs, and actions of a distinct group of people. Cultural differences certainly exist among nations, but significant cultural differences exist within countries also. One only has to look at the conflicts caused by religion or ethnicity in Central Europe and other parts of the world to see the importance of culture on international organizations. Getting individuals from different ethnic or tribal backgrounds working together may be difficult in some parts of the world. Culture can lead to ethical differences among countries as well.

Culture is important to HRM for two reasons. First, it often determines the other factors affecting HRM in the global marketplace. For example, culture can greatly affect a country's laws, in that laws are often the codification of right and wrong as defined by the culture. Second, culture is also important to HRM because it often determines the effectiveness of various HRM practices. Practices found to be effective in the United States may not be effective in a culture that has different beliefs and values. Simply put, cultural differences from country to country necessitate corresponding differences in management and HRM practices among a company's subsidiaries.

It is obvious that national cultures differ and that such differences cannot be ignored by HRM professionals and their organizations. A key issue however is: what does this mean for HRM professionals and their organization's HRM practices? Research by Stiles (2009) on MNCs has suggested that the answer seems to be: not very much, and this point is worth HRM professionals paying attention to. Stiles has noted that there is a great deal of similarity in how these companies approach and manage their human resources; however, bigger differences exist, and are more salient, in terms of their organizational cultures. Further, there was local variation and adaptation of global standards to country-level operation, but this was often to do with regulatory practices, labor market issues, and stage of economic development, rather than national cultural values. The important point for HRM professionals to understand is that to think there is one best way of managing human resources is simplistic and wrong, but the variation and the contextualization of HRM, for companies at least, may not have as much to do with national culture but rather with issues like local laws and regulatory practices.

Education–Human Capital

An organization's potential to find and maintain a qualified workforce is an important consideration in any decision to expand into a foreign market. Thus, a country's human capital resources can be an important HRM issue. Human capital refers to the productive capabilities of individuals— that is, the knowledge, skills, abilities (KSAs) and experience that have economic value (Snell & Dean, 1992).

Countries differ in their levels of human capital. For example, the United States suffers from a human capital shortage because the jobs being created require skills beyond those of most new entrants into the workforce. A company opening subsidiaries in Europe faces a much different HRM challenge than one opening subsidiaries in a country in western Africa. In Europe, the available work force is likely to be well educated and have considerable technical and management experience, while this is less likely to be the case in western Africa at present.

A country's human capital is determined by a number of variables. A major variable is the educational opportunities available to the labor force. In the Netherlands, for instance, government funding of school systems allows students to go all the way through graduate school without paying (Adler & Bartholomew, 1992). Some Third World countries, such as Haiti and Nicaragua, have relatively low levels of human capital because of a lack of investment in education.

A country's human capital may profoundly affect a foreign company's desire to locate there or enter that country's market. Countries with low human capital attract facilities that require low skills and low wage levels. This explains why U.S. companies desire to move their currently unionized low-skill–high-wage manufacturing and assembly jobs to Mexico or similar countries, where they can obtain low-skilled workers for substantially lower wages.

Economic Factors

Different countries have different economic systems. Differences in economic systems also translate into differences in HRM practices. For one thing, some countries are more wedded to the ideals of free enterprise. For instance, France—though a capitalist society—imposed tight restrictions on employers' rights to discharge workers and limited the number of hours an employee could legally work each week. The need for efficiency tends to favor HRM policies that value productivity, efficient workers, and staff cutting where market forces dictate. For example, in China where communism is still prevalent, the government is using unemployment and layoffs to reduce government enterprises bloated with too many workers. However, moving along the scale toward more socialist systems, HRM practices tend to shift toward preventing unemployment, even at the expense of sacrificing efficiency.

Differences in labor costs are also substantial. Hourly compensation costs in U.S. dollars for production workers differ very drastically say than those of Mexico or Taiwan, in the United Kingdom, and Germany, for instance. There are other labor costs to consider. For example, there are wide gaps in hours worked, as evident by differences in the average hours worked annually from country to country (e.g., Portuguese workers average about 1,940 hours of work annually, while German workers average 1,648 hours). There are also differences in requirements for severance pay to departing employees and vacation days allowed to workers.

Many lesser-developed nations are receptive to foreign investment in order to create jobs for their growing populations. Global organizations often obtain significantly cheaper labor rates in these countries than they do in Western Europe, Japan, and the United States. However, whether firms can realize significant profits in developing nations may be determined by currency fluctuations and restrictions on transfer of earnings.

Economic conditions vary greatly. Cost of living is a major economic consideration for global corporations. In many developed countries, especially in Europe, unemployment has grown, but employment restrictions and wage levels remain high. Consequently, over the past decade or so, many European companies have transferred jobs to lower-wage countries, as Mercedes-Benz did at its Alabama plant. In addition, both personal and corporate tax rates are quite high. These factors all must be evaluated along with a country's prevailing HRM laws or regulations as part of the process of deciding whether to begin or purchase operations in foreign countries.

Political–Legal Factors/Systems

The nature and stability of political and legal systems vary from country to country. U.S. organizations are accustomed to a relatively stable political system, and the same is true in many of the other developed countries in Europe. Although presidents, prime ministers, premiers, governors, senators, and representatives may change, the legal systems are well established, and global firms can depend on continuity and consistency.

The reality is that in many other nations, the political and legal systems are turbulent. Some governments regularly are overthrown by military coups. Others are ruled by dictators and despots who use their power to require international firms to buy goods and services from host-country firms owned or controlled by the rulers or the rulers' families. Political instability can lead to situations in which the assets of foreign companies are seized.

In addition, nations with weak economies may not be able to invest in maintaining and upgrading the necessary elements of their infrastructures, such as roads, electric power, schools, and telecommunications. The absence of good infrastructures may make it more difficult to convince managers from the United States or Japan to take assignments overseas.

As noted earlier, legal factors also vary from country to country. The rules and regulations imposed by a country's legal system can strongly affect HRM. The political–legal system often dictates the requirements for certain HRM practices, such as hiring, training, compensation, firing, and layoffs. In large part, the legal system is an outgrowth of the culture in which it exists. Thus, the laws of a particular country often reflect societal norms about what constitutes legitimate behaviors (Ledvinka & Scardello, 1991).

For example, in the United States we have strong beliefs regarding the equity of pay systems: thus the Fair Labor Standards Act, among other laws and regulations, sets the minimum wage for a variety of jobs. We have regulations that dictate much of the process for negotiation between unions and management. These regulations profoundly affect the ways human resources are managed in the United States.

Codetermination is the rule in Germany and several other countries. Codetermination means employees have the legal right to a voice in setting company policies. Workers elect their own representatives to the supervisory board of the employer, and there is a vice president for labor at the top management level (Castillo, 2000; Gaugler, 1998). In the United States, HRM policies on most matters such as wages and benefits are set by the employer, or by the employer in negotiations with its labor unions. The codetermination laws, including the Works Constitution Act, largely determine the nature of HRM policies in many German firms.

HRM professionals must understand that their international organizations may have to decide strategically when to comply with certain laws and regulations and when to ignore them because of operational or political reasons. Another issue involves ethics. Because of restrictions imposed on U.S.-based firms through the Foreign Corrupt Practices Act (FCPA), a fine line exists between paying "agent fees," which is legal, and bribery, which is illegal.

HRM regulations and laws vary among countries in character and detail. In many Western European countries, laws on labor unions and employment make it difficult to reduce the number of workers because required payments to former employees can be very high. Further, in some countries, laws address issues such as employment discrimination and sexual harassment. In others, because of religious or ethical differences, employment discrimination may be an accepted practice.

The points highlighted above reveal that it is crucial for HRM professionals and the organization's senior leaders to conduct a comprehensive review of the political environment and employment-related laws before beginning operations in a country. The role and nature of labor unions should be a part of that review, as will be discussed later.

In conclusion, every country differs in terms of its culture, human capital, legal system, and economic systems. These variations directly influence the types of HRM systems that must be developed to accommodate the particular situation. The extent to which these differences affect an organization depends on how involved the organization is in global markets.

DOMESTIC VERSUS INTERNATIONAL HUMAN RESOURCE MANAGEMENT (IHRM)

People are unique assets and, therefore, today's and tomorrow's companies cannot continue to treat them in the age-old way as profit centers by just paying them without understanding their specific needs, wants, and desires. An insight for managing human resources in the context of today's globalized world is of utmost importance for all organizations, and this is even more important for those international organizations. IHRM continues to rapidly change and draw the attention of all multinational companies (MNCs) who must navigate the very different HRM laws and legislation that exists within those countries in which they do business.

One of the central questions related to MNCs is the extent to which their subsidiaries act and behave as local firms (local isomorphism) versus the extent to which their practices resemble those of the parent company or some other global standard (internal consistency). In the light of globalization, HRM continues to evolve from being a mere support function to one of strategic importance as HRM policies and practices are increasingly crucial because they can act as mechanisms for the successful coordination and control of international operations. At the same time, it is important to acknowledge that HRM can constitute a major constraint when MNCs try to implement global strategies, mainly because of the different cultural and institutional frameworks of each country in which the MNC operates.

HRM professionals are most often charged with the responsibility of helping their organizations understand the importance of suitable strategies for managing their human resources along with the different HRM laws and approaches to IHRM adopted by different countries. And this must be done given the reality that all major MNCs employ strategic planning that drives their IHRM efforts, a plan that should result from a careful analysis of both the external and internal environment.

HRM professionals in international businesses must achieve two somewhat conflicting strategic objectives. First, they must integrate HRM policies and practices across a number of subsidiaries in different countries with often very different laws and regulations so that overall corporate objectives can be achieved. At the same time, the approach to HRM must be sufficiently flexible to allow for significant differences in the types of HRM policies and practices that are most effective in different business and cultural settings. This problem of balancing integration (control and coordination from headquarters) and differentiation (flexibility in policies and practices at the local subsidiary level given the prevailing laws, legislation, or regulations) has long been acknowledged as a common dilemma facing HRM and other functional managers in multinational corporations (Bartlett & Ghoshal, 1989).

Although some argue that IHRM is not unlike HRM in domestic settings, others suggest that IHRM differs from a domestic HRM in several ways. In broad terms, IHRM involves the same activities as domestic HRM (e.g., procurement refers to HRM planning and staffing); however, domestic HRM is involved with employees within only one national boundary. For example, IHRM necessarily places a greater emphasis on functions and activities such as relocation, orientation, and translation services to help employees adapt to a new and different environment outside their own country. Many larger organizations have a full-time staff of HRM professionals devoted solely to assisting globalization efforts. McDonald's, for example, has a team of HRM directors who travel around the world to help country managers stay updated in international concerns, policies, and programs (Sims, 2002, 2007).

Others suggest that there are more significant differences between IHRM and domestic HRM. Specifically, compared with domestic HRM, IHRM (a) encompasses more functions, (b) has more heterogeneous functions, (c) involves constantly changing perspectives, (d) requires more involvement in employees' personal lives, (e) is influenced by more external sources, and finally (f) involves a greater level of risk than typical domestic HRM (Schuler, Dowling, & DeCieri, 1991, p. 430).

When compared to domestic HRM, IHRM requires a much broader perspective on even the most common HRM activities. This is particularly so for HRM professionals operating from the global companies' headquarters location. The number and variety of IHRM activities are daunting: for example, government regulations about staffing practices in foreign locations, local codes of conduct, influence of local religious groups, and so on. If an American organization is sanctioned license by the Indian government to set up its subsidiary in India, the American company is under legal obligations to provide employment to local residents. Further, IHRM staff must deal with issues as varied as international taxation; international relocation and orientation; various other administrative services for expatriates; selecting, training, and appraising local and international employees; and managing host–government relations in a number of countries around the world. Even when dealing with a particular HRM activity like compensation, IHRM professionals are faced with a great variety of national and international pay issues. For example, when dealing with pay issues, the headquarters-based HRM professionals must coordinate pay systems in different countries with different currencies that may change in relative value to one another over time.

In the case of fringe benefits provided to host country employees, some interesting complications might arise. For example, it is common in the United States for companies to provide health insurance benefits to the employee and the employee's family, which usually meant spouse and children until June 26, 2013, when the U.S. Supreme Court issued its decision in *United States v. Windsor* and struck down the section of DOMA (the federal Defense of Marriage Act) that defined marriage as a "union between a man and a woman." As a result, if you're in a valid marriage, you will qualify for immigration status and federal employee benefits (if either of you works for the federal government), even if you live in a nonrecognition state now by the U.S. Citizenship and Immigration Services (USCIS) and the U.S. Office of Personnel & Management. The same goes for the IRS and eligibility for federal tax benefits. In August 2013, the U.S. Department of Treasury ruled that all same-sex couples who are legally married in any U.S. state, the District of Columbia, a U.S. territory, or a foreign country will be recognized as married under all federal tax provisions where marriage is a factor. The Treasury Department further clarified that federal recognition for tax purposes applies whether a same-sex married couple lives in a jurisdiction that recognizes same-sex marriage (such as California) or a nonrecognition jurisdiction (such as Texas) (Nolo Law for All, n.d.). In the end, there are over one thousand federal laws in which marriage status is a factor. These laws confer rights, protections, and benefits to married couples—from Social Security survivor benefits to federal tax benefits to federal employee health and retirement benefits. In some countries, however, the term "family" may encompass a more extended group of relatives—multiple spouses, aunts, uncles, grandparents, nephews, and nieces. It is important for HRM professionals to understand how an organization's benefit plan deals with these different definitions of family and differences in international HRM laws and regulations as they relate to other issues. For example, consider the case of same-sex married gay and lesbian couples who can now take advantage of federal tax benefits in the United States, but this will surely not be the case in other countries that international business organizations operate in—for example, Russia or middle-eastern countries like Saudi Arabia.

There is heightened exposure to risks in international assignments. These risks include the health and safety of the employee and family. A major aspect of risk relevant to IHRM today is possible terrorism. Several MNCs must now consider this factor when deciding on international assignments for their employees. Moreover, human and financial consequences of mistakes in IHRM are much more severe than in domestic business. For example, if an executive posted abroad returns prematurely, it results in high direct costs as well as indirect costs.

A final aspect of the broader scope of HRM is that headquarters-based HRM professionals deal with employee groups that have very different cultural backgrounds, which, as suggested earlier, is a major factor that complicates HRM. The headquarters HRM professionals must coordinate policies and procedures to manage expatriates from the firm's home country (parent country national, PCN—such a person is also referred to as an expatriate), host country nationals (HCNs), as well as third country nationals (TCNs, e.g., a German manager working for an American MNC in the firm's Chilean subsidiary) in subsidiaries around the world. Although such issues are important for the headquarters-based manager, they are also especially relevant to the HRM professionals located in the subsidiary. The HRM professionals must develop HRM systems that are not only acceptable in the host country but also compatible with the company-wide systems being developed by his or her headquarters-based counterpart. These policies and practices must effectively balance the needs and desires of local employees, PCNs, and TCNs as well.

It is at the subsidiary level that the increased involvement of IHRM in the personal lives of employees becomes particularly apparent. Often subsidiary HRM professionals are involved in arranging housing, healthcare, transportation, education, and recreational activities for expatriate and local staff. Subsidiary HRM professionals may even find themselves dealing with expatriates who have marital and/or alcohol problems, acting as counselor and legal advisor (Solomon, 1995).

IHRM activities are also influenced by a greater number of external forces than are domestic HRM activities. The headquarters-based HRM professionals may have to set EEO policies that meet the legal requirements of both the home country and a number of host countries. Because of the visibility that global organizations tend to have in foreign countries (especially in developing countries), subsidiary HRM personnel may have to deal with government ministers, other political figures, and a greater variety of social and economic interest groups than would normally be encountered in purely domestic HRM.

The final difference between domestic and IHRM concerns the levels of risks and consequences associated with HRM decisions. There certainly are major risks associated with HRM in domestic situations. Unfair hiring practices may result in a firm being charged with violation of EEO laws and subjected to financial penalties. The failure to establish constructive relationships with domestic unions can lead to strikes and other forms of labor actions. However, IHRM personnel face these same risks, as well as some additional ones that are unique and more threatening. Depending on the countries where the international company operates, headquarters and subsidiary HRM professionals may have to worry about the physical safety of employees (i.e., in some countries kidnapping and terrorism are of concern to IHRM personnel). More will be said about international labor relations and safety issues later in this chapter.

Frequently, the human and financial consequences of failure in the international arena are more severe than in domestic business. For example, expatriate failure (the premature return of an expatriate from an international assignment) is a potentially high-cost problem for international companies. Direct costs (salary, training costs, and travel and relocation expenses) per failure to the parent firm may be as high as three times the domestic salary plus relocation expenses, depending on currency exchange rates and location of assignments. Indirect costs such as loss of market share and damage to international customer relationships may be considerable. Clearly, if managers do not perform well and must be recalled to the home country, their failure represents a huge financial loss for the company.

A final risk is that of expropriation or seizure of the international business's assets in a foreign country. If HRM policies antagonize host country unions or important political groups, the international business may be asked to leave the country, have its assets seized, or find the local government taking majority control of its operation. Again, this is not the sort of risk that most domestic HRM personnel face.

Increasingly, domestic HRM is taking on some of the flavor of IHRM as it deals more and more with a multicultural workforce given the changing demographics in the United States. Thus, some of the current focus of domestic HRM on issues of managing workforce diversity will undoubtedly prove to be beneficial to the practice of IHRM. While not necessarily transferable to a multinational context, the management of diversity within a single national context at least lays the foundation for appreciating the challenges of being an international business.

INTERNATIONAL RECRUITMENT
AND SELECTION PROCEDURES

As noted earlier, international businesses can approach the management of IHRM in a number of ways: ethnocentric, polycentric, and geocentric. These approaches to IHRM are translated from an organization's corporate values. For example, in the ethnocentric corporation, "the prevailing attitude is that home country attitudes, management style, knowledge, evaluation criteria, and managers are superior to anything the host country might have to offer" (Perlmutter, 1989, as discussed in Phatak, 1989, p. 129). In the polycentric corporation, there is a conscious belief that only host country managers can ever really understand the culture and behavior of the host country market; therefore, the foreign subsidiary should be managed by local people (Sims, 2007). Geocentrism assumes that management candidates must be searched for on a global basis, on the assumption that the best manager (or other employee) for any specific position anywhere on the globe may be found in any of the countries in which the organization operates. (Other approaches also exist, but this chapter focuses only on these three approaches.)

These three sets of international values translate into three broad international selection policies or sources for staffing international operations. First, the company can send people from its home country to manage operations in the host country. These employees are often referred to as expatriates, or home-country nationals. Second, it can hire host-country nationals, natives of the host country to do the managing. Third, it can hire third-country nationals, natives of a country other than the home country or the host country.

Each of these sources of overseas workers provides certain advantages and certain disadvantages. Some of the more important advantages are as follows: (a) host-country nationals—less cost, preference of host-country governments, intimate knowledge of environment and culture, and language facility; (b) home-country nationals (expatriates)—talent available within company, greater control, company experience, mobility, and experience provided to corporate executives; and (c) third-country nationals—broad experience, international outlook, and multilingualism. Most companies use all these sources for staffing their multinational operations, although some companies exhibit a distinct bias for one or another of the three sources (Tung, 1998).

At early stages of international expansion organizations often send home-country expatriates to establish activities (particularly in less-developed countries) and to work with local governments. At later stages of internationalization, there is typically a steady shift toward the use of host-country nationals. There are three reasons for this trend:

1. Hiring local citizens is less costly because the organization does not have to worry about the costs of home leaves, transportation, and special schooling allowances.
2. Since local governments usually want good jobs for their citizens, foreign employers may be required to hire them.
3. Using local talent avoids the problem of employees having to adjust to the culture.

Subsidiary HRM personnel should use a hiring process that fits the local labor market and takes into consideration the prevailing labor or employment laws. For example, an international business may need the services of a local HRM selection agency to identify the sources of skilled employees.

INTERNATIONAL RECRUITMENT

In general, employee recruitment in other countries is subject to more government regulation than it is in the United States. Regulations range from those that cover procedures for recruiting employees to those that govern the employment of foreign labor or require the employment of the physically disabled, war veterans, or displaced persons. Many Central American countries, for example, have stringent regulations about the number of foreigners that can be employed as a percentage of the total workforce. Virtually all countries have work-permit or visa restrictions that apply to foreigners. A work permit or work certificate is a document issued by a government granting authority to a foreign individual to seek employment in that government's country.

As in the United States, various methods are used to recruit employees from internal and external sources. In any country, but particularly in the developing countries, a disadvantage of using current employees as recruiters is that considerations of family, similar social status, culture, or language are usually more important than qualifications for the vacant position. More than one manager depending on employees as recruiters has filled a plant with relatives or people from the same hometown. In small towns much of the recruiting is done by word of mouth. Thus, having locals involved is critical. Churches, unions, and community groups also play a role.

MNCs tend to use the same kinds of external recruitment sources as are used in their home countries. While unskilled labor is readily available in the developing countries, recruitment of skilled workers is more difficult. Many employers have learned that the best way to find workers in these countries is through radio announcements because many people lack sufficient reading or writing skills. The solution is to have a recruiter who uses local methods within the context of the corporation's culture and needs or to put an expatriate in charge of recruiting.

The laws of almost all countries require the employment of local people if adequate numbers of skilled people are available. Thus, recruiting is limited to a restricted population. Specific exceptions are granted (officially or unofficially) for contrary cases, as for Mexican farmworkers in the United States and for Italian, Spanish, Greek, and Turkish workers in Germany and the Benelux countries (i.e., Belgium, Netherlands, Luxembourg). Foreign workers invited to come to perform needed labor are usually referred to as guest workers. The employment of non-nationals may involve lower direct labor costs, but indirect costs—language training, health services, recruitment, transportation, and so on—may be substantial.

Just like local employment laws must be adhered to, premium salaries may have to be offered to lure highly qualified individuals away from local firms. Additionally, in some countries, hiring may require using a government-controlled labor bureau. This may be particularly prevalent in hierarchical cultures with high power distance. In Vietnam, for example, local labor bureaus are heavily involved in the hiring process. Thus, while top managers may have preferences for one source of employees over another, the host country may place pressures on them to restrict their choices. Such pressure takes the form of sophisticated government persuasion through administrative or legislative decrees to employ host-country individuals. In short, important selection issues may have to be approved by very high government officials.

Clearly, selection practices vary around the world. In the United States, managers tend to emphasize merit, with the best-qualified person getting the job. In other countries, however, organizations tend to hire on the basis of family ties, social status, language, and common origin. The candidate who satisfies these criteria may get the job even if otherwise unqualified. While much of this is changing as a result of the growing realization among some organizations in other nations that greater attention must be given to hiring those most qualified, there still exists a number of challenges that subsidiary HRM professionals must be cognizant of in their international selection efforts.

COMPENSATION

One of the most complex areas of IHRM is compensation. The whole area of international compensation presents some tricky problems. On the one hand, there is a certain logic in maintaining companywide pay scales and policies so that, for instance, divisional marketing directors throughout the world are all paid within the same narrow range. This reduces the risk of perceived inequities and dramatically simplifies the job of keeping track of disparate country-by-country wage rates.

Yet adapting pay scales to local markets can present the HRM professionals with more problems than it solves. The fact is that it can be enormously more expensive to live in some countries (like Japan) than others (like Greece); if these cost-of-living differences aren't considered, it may be almost impossible to get managers to take "high-cost" assignments.

However, the answer is usually not just to pay, say, marketing directors more in one country than in another. For one thing, you could thereby elicit resistance when telling a marketing director in Tokyo who's earning

$3,000 per week to move to your division in Spain, where his or her pay for the same job will drop by half (cost of living notwithstanding). One way to handle the problem is to pay a similar base salary companywide and then add on various allowances according to individual market conditions.

Determining equitable wage rates or, for that matter, compensation systems in many countries is no simple matter. There are a variety of factors that affect compensation systems within international businesses. International business compensation systems are influenced by internal business factors such as varying wage costs, levels of job security, and differing business strategies. Compensation is affected by differences in prosperity and spending power related to the strength of national economies and currencies. Social factors such as the extent to which pay differences are considered acceptable; the appreciation of different forms of pay, and the acceptance of different forms of compensation and appraisal (e.g., stock options, incentive pay based on performance) also affect international business compensation systems within a particular country. Wage and other legislation, along with the influence of unions, has an impact on compensation systems as well.

It is beyond the scope of this chapter to discuss the myriad influences on international business compensation practices around the world. Suffice it to say that the subsidiary HRM professionals must know or have access to information about these issues. Regulations concerning pensions, social security, medical insurance, and other benefits are critically important and vary greatly. In some countries, benefits such as housing, transportation, and year-end bonuses are common; in others they are not.

Issues relating to gender-based or racially based wage differentials are of particular concern for subsidiaries of U.S. organizations. Even though such differentials may be acceptable in countries where U.S. international businesses operate, they are certainly not consistent with U.S. HRM policies. U.S. HRM specialists in foreign subsidiaries must make decisions as to whether it is ethical to have discrimination in one part of the international business but not in another. Union influences may play an important role in determining wage policies in some countries but not in others. For example, Australia has had for some years now a national wage setting system in which the government and unions negotiate pay rates for workers that apply countrywide. In Hong Kong, by contrast, labor unions are extremely weak, and wage rates are determined by the free market.

Compensating host-country employees is another basic managerial or administrative issue that must be addressed by HRM professionals when an organization establishes operations overseas. More specifically, host-country employees are generally paid on the basis of productivity, time spent on the job, or a combination of these factors. In industrialized countries, pay is generally by the hour; in developing countries, by the day. The piece-rate method is quite common. In some countries, including Japan, seniority is an important element in determining employees' pay rates. When companies commence operations in a foreign country, they usually set their wage rates at or slightly higher than the prevailing wage for local companies. Eventually, though, they are urged to conform to local practices to avoid "upsetting" local compensation practices.

Compensation of expatriate managers is another issue that international businesses must address. Compensation plans for expatriate managers must be competitive, cost-effective, motivating, fair and easy to understand, consistent with international financial management, easy to administer, and simple to communicate. To be effective, an international compensation program must:

- Provide an incentive to leave the United States
- Allow for maintaining an American standard of living
- Facilitate reentry into the United States
- Provide for the education of children
- Allow for maintaining relationships with family, friends, and business associates (Gould, 1999)

Other compensation issues HRM professionals should be aware of, which will vary greatly from country to country, might include the following:

1. *The cost of benefits in another country.* Many countries offer universal healthcare (offset by higher taxes), and therefore the employee would have health benefits covered while working and paying taxes in that country. Canada, Finland, and Japan are examples of countries that have this type of coverage. In countries such as Singapore, all residents receive a catastrophic healthcare policy from the government, but they need to purchase additional insurance for routine care. A number of organizations offer healthcare for expatriates relocating to another country in which healthcare is not already provided.

2. *Legally mandated (or culturally accepted) amount of vacation days.* For example, in Australia, twenty paid vacation days are required, ten in Canada, thirty in Finland, and five in the Philippines. The average number of U.S. worker vacation days is fifteen, although the number of days is not federally mandated by the government.

3. *Legal requirements of profit sharing.* For example, in France, the government heavily regulates profit sharing programs.

4. *Pay system that works with the country culture, such as pay systems based on seniority.* For example, Chinese culture focuses heavily on seniority, and pay scales should be developed according to seniority.

5. In Italy, Japan, and some other countries, it is customary to add semi-annual or annual lump-sum payments equal to one or two months' pay. These payments are not considered profit sharing but an integral part of the basic pay package. Profit sharing is legally required for certain categories of industry in Mexico, Peru, Pakistan, India, and Egypt among the developing countries and in France among the industrialized countries. Compensation patterns in Eastern Europe are in flux as these countries experiment with more capitalistic systems.

In the end, it is important for international businesses and their HRM professionals to understand that the "trick" in designing compensation systems in global environments is to understand what motivates employees in each culture and to design the system around those motivations. Money, praise, or external symbols (a corner office, a personal parking space), while attractive to U.S. employees, may not hold the same attraction for members of other cultures. Simply superimposing American compensation and reward systems onto a foreign subsidiary oftentimes will not only fail to work, but may actually damage the productivity of the workers in that subsidiary and go against the host country's HRM laws and regulations.

GLOBAL LABOR–MANAGEMENT RELATIONS

The strength and nature of unions differ from country to country. In some countries, unions either do not exist at all or are relatively weak. Such is the case in China and a number of African countries. In other countries, unions are extremely strong and are closely tied to political parties. This is the case in some European countries. In still other countries, such as the United States and Great Britain, unions have declined in influence and membership during the last decade.

Differences from country to country in how collective bargaining occurs also are quite noticeable. In the United States, local unions bargain with individual employers to set wages and working conditions. In Australia, unions argue their cases before arbitration tribunals. In Scandinavia, national agreements with associations of employers are the norm. In France and Germany, industry-wide or region-wide agreements are common. In Japan, local unions do the bargaining but combine at some point to determine national wage patterns. In spite of these differences, unions appear to have somewhat similar effects internationally in most situations regarding employment and provision of benefits.

Labor relations structures, laws, and practices vary considerably among countries (Budd, 2005). Clearly, companies opening subsidiaries abroad will find substantial differences in labor relations practices among the world's countries and regions. First, unions may or may not exist. Second, each country has a different history of unionism. Third, each government has its own view of its role in the labor relations process and labor agreements may or may not be contractual obligations. Fourth, management may conclude agreements with unions that have little or no membership in a plant or with nonunion groups that wield more bargaining power than the established unions. Fifth, government's role is often reflected in the types and nature of the regulations in force. While the U.S. government generally takes a "hands-off" approach toward intervention in labor–management matters, the Australian government, to which the labor movement has very strong ties, is inclined to be more involved. Thus, not only must the international business's industrial relations office and HRM personnel be familiar with the separate laws of each country, they also must be familiar with the environment in which those statues are implemented. Understanding international labor relations is vital to for HRM professionals as they work with other organizational leaders in their strategic planning efforts and potential success in the global arena.

In general, unions may constrain the choices of international businesses in three ways: (a) influencing wage levels to the extent that cost structures may become noncompetitive, (b) limiting the ability of companies to vary employment levels at their own discretion, and (c) hindering or preventing global integration of such companies (i.e., by forcing them to develop parallel operations in different countries) (Movassaghi, 1996; Sims, 2007).

Since labor relations can affect the strategic planning initiatives of international businesses, it is important to consider the issue of headquarters' involvement in host-country international union relations. The organization must assess if the labor relations function should be controlled globally from the parent company, or if it would be more advantageous for each host country to administer its own operation. There is no simple means of making this assessment, however; international businesses must decide whether or not to keep labor relations centrally located at corporate headquarters or to adapt to host-country standards and have the labor relations function decentralized. Many European countries have opted for decentralization of labor relations while American organizations are more inclined to centralization of labor relations.

The national attitude toward unions is another divergence among international businesses in labor relations. Generally, Europeans have had greater experience with unions, are accustomed to a larger proportion of the work force being unionized, and are more accepting of the unionization of their own workers. American global companies, on the other hand, view unions negatively at home and try to avoid unionization of the work force. In Japan, as in other parts of Asia, unions are often closely identified with an organization.

There are also significant differences in countries outside the United States in the collective bargaining process. The collective bargaining process is typically carried out in companies operating in the United States. When we look at other countries, we find that the whole process can vary widely, especially with regard to the role that government plays. In the United Kingdom and France, for example, government intervenes in all aspects of collective bargaining. Government involvement is only natural where parts of industry are nationalized. Also, in countries where there is heavy nationalization, there is more likely to be acceptance of government involvement, even in the non-nationalized companies. In developing countries it is common for the government to have representatives present during bargaining sessions to make sure that unions with relatively uneducated leaders are not disadvantaged in bargaining with skilled management representatives.

Overall, unions have found international businesses particularly difficult to deal with in terms of union power and difficult to penetrate in terms of union representation (Katz & Kochan, 2004; Levine, 1988). Some of the problems that international businesses present to unions are as follows:

1. While national unions tend to follow the development of national companies, union expansion typically cannot follow the expansion of a company across national boundaries, with the exception of Canada. Legal differences, feelings of nationalism, and differences in union structure and industrial relations practices are effective barriers to such expansion.

2. The nature of foreign investment by international businesses has changed. In the past, they tended to invest in foreign sources of raw materials. As a result, the number of processing and manufacturing jobs in the home country may actually have increased. However, there continues to be a shift toward the development of parallel, or nearly parallel, operations in other countries. Foreign investment of this type threatens union members in the home country with loss of jobs or with a slower rate of job growth, especially if their wages are higher than those of workers in the host country. This threat is very real in some countries where labor rates are higher than in many others.

3. When an international business has parallel operations in other locations, the firm's ability to switch production from one location shut down by a labor dispute to another location is increased. This, of course, assumes that the same union does not represent workers at each plant, or that, if different unions are involved, they do not coordinate their efforts and strike at the same time. Another assumption is that the various plants are sufficiently parallel that their products are interchangeable (Cascio, 2012).

Clearly, some important differences exist in the area of labor relations between countries. Any company that wants to be successful in the international arena must be aware of what is happening and pending in labor legislation and fully understand and comply with the host country's laws and customs.

SAFETY AND HEALTH ENVIRONMENTS

Safety and health laws and regulations vary from country to country, ranging from virtually nonexistent to more stringent than in the United States. The importance placed on workplace safety varies among different countries. As a result, it is important for HRM professionals to know the safety and health environments of each country in which an organization operates. Generally, companies in Western Europe, Japan, Canada, and the United States put great emphasis on the health and welfare of their employees. However, most businesses in less-developed countries have limited resources and thus cannot establish health and safety awareness or protection programs.

Most countries have laws and regulatory agencies that protect workers from hazardous work environments. As noted earlier, it is important for international businesses to learn the often complex regulations that exist, as well as the cultural expectations of the local labor force. Manufacturers, in particular, where there are myriad potentially hazardous situations, must design and establish facilities that meet the expectations of the local employees—not necessarily those of their host countries.

IHRM provides an organized framework for developing and managing people who are comfortable with the strategic and operational paradoxes embedded in global or international organizations and who are capable of managing cultural diversity. Because of cultural diversities and issues of convergence and divergence, it is impractical for HRM professionals and their organizations to develop a truly international approach to global human resource management. This means that organization structures, management styles, organization cultures, and change management programs have to be adapted to the various host country cultural and legal attributes or HRM laws of the host nation just as a careful balancing act is sought between being global and local needs. In short, HRM professionals must not lose sight of the fact that differences in HRM laws and regulations will always exist for the truly international organization. Such differences are most evident when one considers many of the key differences in employment law between countries around the world and more specifically, for example, between China's employment laws and those of the United States and among the varying various antidiscrimination laws found around the world.

CHINESE VERSUS AMERICAN EMPLOYMENT SYSTEM

The Chinese employment system is based on Asian socialist and Northern European models (Harris, 2010; Zhang, n.d.). China's employment law system is quite different from the U.S system. The main difference is that the United States is an employment at will system, which means employees can be terminated at any time for pretty much any reason. China's system is the opposite. The Chinese system is a contract employment system. This means all employees must be engaged pursuant to a written employment contract, and during the term of that contract, it is very difficult to terminate an employee. An employee can only be terminated for cause, and cause must be clearly proved. This means the employer must maintain a detailed set of rules and regulations and must maintain careful discipline records to be able to establish grounds for dismissal. This whole situation makes the employment relationship and the employment documents much more adversarial than is customary in the U.S. HRM professionals should recognize that such an approach is not consistent with the normal "team" approach that might be used in dealing with employment issues in the United States.

HRM professionals should also know that China does not really have the concept of a "salaried" employee. The Chinese work week is 40 hours, and overtime must be paid for work exceeding the 40-hour limit. This approach may be very foreign to HRM professionals in the United States. However, there are no exceptions to this rule. Table 16.1 provides a more detailed comparison of HRM-related law differences between the United States and China.

ANTIDISCRIMINATION LAWS AROUND THE WORLD

Antidiscrimination law refers to the law on people's rights to be treated equally. Some countries mandate that in employment, in consumer transactions, and in political participation, people may be dealt with on an equal basis regardless of sex, race, ethnicity, nationality, sexuality, and sometimes religious and political views. Table 16.2 provides a list of antidiscrimination acts (often called discrimination acts), which are laws designed to prevent discrimination in different countries.

CONCLUSION

International HRM efforts will continue to present particular issues, challenges, and opportunities for HRM professionals. There are a number of best practices available to HRM professionals and other organizational leaders for managing an organization's most valuable resource—its people

TABLE 16.1   Examples of HRM-Related Law Differences Between the United States and China

	United States	China*
Employment Contracts	Most states have at-will employment	Contract employment system. All employees must have a written contract
Layoffs	No severance required. Two years of service required to pay severance; more than five years of experience requires a long service payment	Company must be on verge of bankruptcy before it can lay off employees
Termination	Employment at will	Employees can only be terminated for cause, and cause must be clearly proved. They must be given 30 days' notice, except in the case of extreme circumstances, like theft.
Overtime	None required for salaried employees	Employees who work more than 40 hours must be paid overtime
Salary	Up to individual company	A 13-month bonus is customary, but not required, right before the Chinese New Year
Vacation	No governmental requirement	Mandated by government: • First year: no vacation • Year 2–9: 5 days • Year 10–19: 10 days • 20 years or more: 15 days
Paid Holidays	None required by law	3 total: Chinese New Year, International Labor Day, and National Day. However, workers must "make up" the days by working a day on the previous weekend
Social Security	Required by law for employer and employee to pay into social security	Greater percentages are paid by employer: 22% of salary paid by employer; 8% paid by employee
Discrimination Laws	Per EEOC, cannot discriminate based on race, sex, age, genetic information, or other protected groups	Laws are in place but not enforced
Maternity Leave	Family and Medical Leave Act allows 12 weeks	90 days' maternity leave

* In China, all employees are covered by the Labor Contract Law.

Sources: Harris, 2010; Zhang, n. d.)

TABLE 16.2   International Antidiscrimination Laws

India

- The Caste Disabilities Removal Act, 1850
- Hindu Succession Act, 1956—Abolished the "limited owner" status of women who owned property, amended in 2004 to give daughters equal inheritance rights with sons.
- Scheduled Caste and Scheduled Tribe (Prevention of Atrocities) Act, 1989

As there was Equal Opportunity Commission (EOC) in countries like United States, United Kingdom, Australia, Brazil, Canada, France, Hong Kong, and South Africa for the purpose of providing equal opportunity in employment and education for deprived people, India Union Ministry of Minority resolved to constitute an Equal Opportunity Commission (EOC) during the 12th plan.

United States

- Lilly Ledbetter Fair Pay Act of 2009
- Age Discrimination Act of 1975
- Age Discrimination in Employment Act of 1967
- Americans with Disabilities Act of 1990
- California Fair Employment and Housing Act
- Civil Rights Act of 1871
- Civil Rights Act of 1964
- Civil Rights Act of 1968
- Civil Rights Act of 1991
- Employment Non-Discrimination Act
- Equal Pay Act of 1963
- Executive Order 11478
- Executive Order 13166—"Improving Access to Services for Persons with Limited English Proficiency"
- Fair Employment Act of 1941
- Family and Medical Leave Act of 1993—enables qualified employees to take prolonged unpaid leave for family and health-related reasons without fear of losing their jobs; for private employers with 15 or more employers
- Fourteenth Amendment to the United States Constitution
- Genetic Information Nondiscrimination Act
- Immigration and Nationality Services Act of 1965
- Lloyd–La Follette Act (1912)
- No-FEAR Act
- Pregnancy Discrimination Act of 1978
- Rehabilitation Act of 1973

Australia

- Anti-Discrimination Act 1977 (NSW)
- Australian Human Rights Commission Act 1986
- Disability Discrimination Act 1992
- Racial and Religious Tolerance Act 2001 (Victoria)
- Racial Discrimination Act 1975
- Sex Discrimination Act 1984

Canada

- Canadian Charter of Rights and Freedoms
- Canadian Employment Equity Act
- Canadian Human Rights Act
- Ontarians with Disabilities Act
- Quebec Charter of Human Rights and Freedoms

(continued)

TABLE 16.2   International Antidiscrimination Laws (continued)

European Union

- Directive 76/207/EEC on the implementation of the principle of equal treatment for men and women as regards access to employment, vocational training and promotion, and working conditions
- Directive 2000/43/EC on Antidiscrimination
- Directive 2004/113/EC implementing the principle of equal treatment between men and women in the access to and supply of goods and services
- Directive 2006/54/EC on the implementation of the principle of equal opportunities and equal treatment of men and women in matters of employment and occupation

France

- Edict of Nantes 1598
- Germany
- General Equal Treatment Act of 2006
- Hong Kong
- Disability Discrimination Ordinance
- Family Status Discrimination Ordinance
- Hong Kong Bill of Rights Ordinance
- Race Discrimination Ordinance
- Sex Discrimination Ordinance
- International
- Equality of Treatment (Accident Compensation) Convention, 1925
- Convention against Discrimination in Education, 1960
- Equality of Treatment (Social Security) Convention, 1962
- Convention concerning Migrations in Abusive Conditions and the Promotion of Equality of Opportunity and Treatment of Migrant Workers, 1975
- Convention on the Elimination of All Forms of Discrimination Against Women, 1979
- Convention on the Elimination of All Forms of Racial Discrimination, 1965
- Convention on the Rights of Persons with Disabilities
- Discrimination (Employment and Occupation) Convention, 1958
- Equal Remuneration Convention, 1951
- Protocol No. 12 to the European Convention on Human Rights, 2000

South Africa

- Chapter 2 of the Constitution of South Africa
- Employment Equity Act, 1998
- Promotion of Equality and Prevention of Unfair Discrimination Act, 2000
- United Kingdom
- Disability Discrimination Act 1995
- Disability Discrimination Act 2005
- Equal Pay Act 1970
- Equality Act 2006
- Equality Act 2010
- Race Relations Act 1965
- Race Relations Act 1968 and Race Relations Act 1976 amended by the Race Relations Amendment Act 2000
- Representation of the People Act 1918
- Representation of the People (Equal Franchise) Act 1928
- Sex Discrimination Act 1975, amended by the Sex Discrimination (Election Candidates) Act 2002
- See also the Employment Equality Regulations covering sexual orientation, religion or belief, and age.

Source: www.whatishumanresource.com

at work. Much of what has been discussed throughout this chapter and others in this book on HRM laws can be applied to both domestic and internationally successful organizations that are able to sustain and prolong their success through the way they manage their human resources.

While there are many similarities, IHRM is distinct from domestic HRM because of its broader perspective, the greater scope of activities included in IHRM, and the higher level of risk associated with IHRM activities. Today's and tomorrow's global organizations will continue to take any one of a number of different approaches to HRM, with the choice depending on political and legal regulations; the managerial, educational, and technological development in the host country; and differences between the home and host cultures.

HRM professionals will need to increase their skill and competence in working with other organizational members to successfully coordinate IHRM operations in a variety of countries, each with its own local cultural, legal, and traditional influences. HRM professionals must ensure that their organization's policies are flexible enough to allow for these local variations while not losing sight of the fact that such policies also must be developed to help achieve the overall strategic global objectives of the MNC.

Increased care must be taken by HRM professionals in developing the various HRM activities to ensure that they take into consideration each local country's cultural and legal nuances. Staffing, training and development, performance appraisal, compensation, workplace safety, management of labor relations, and the use of expatriates versus locals are of paramount concern to successful IHRM.

Like all of the other HRM activities discussed in this chapter and throughout this book, HRM professionals and their organizations must recognize the important role that an understanding of HRM laws has on the effective management of human resources in their organization's success be it in the national or international arena. The collective HRM activities all play important roles in developing and sustaining competitive advantages for an organization. Today and in the future, the organization's ability to attract, develop, and retain a talented workforce will be a critical factor in developing a high-performance, successful organization.

In the end, it is important for HRM professionals to recognize that the legal system practiced in a country has a great effect on compensation programs; union issues; how people are hired, fired, and laid off; and safety issues. Rules on discrimination, for example, are set by the country. In China, for example, it is acceptable to ask candidates for employment their age, marital status, and other questions that would be considered illegal in the United States. In another legal example, in Costa Rica, "aguinaldos," also known as a thirteenth month salary, is required in December. This is a legal requirement for all companies operating in Costa Rica.

The "universalistic" approach to HRM must be rejected by HRM professionals as the basic functions of HRM are given different weights among countries and are carried out differently. In addition, the cultural differences (and for our purposes differences in HRM laws) among countries have produced the slogan in international human resource management: "Think GLOBALLY and act LOCALLY." This means that an international balancing act is required by HRM professionals and their organizations, which leads to the fundamental assumption made by Bartlett and Ghoshal (1989, 1991) that balancing the needs of coordination, control, and autonomy is critical to the success of the multinational company. To achieve this balancing act, there are six capabilities that enable HRM professionals and their organizations to integrate and concentrate international HRM laws and activities and also separate and adopt local HRM activities:

- Being able to determine core activities and noncore activities
- Achieving consistency while allowing flexibility
- Building global brand equity while honoring local customs and laws
- Obtaining leverage (bigger is better) while achieving focus (smaller is better)
- Sharing learning and creating new knowledge
- Engendering a global perspective while ensuring local accountability

REFERENCES

Adler, N. (2008). *International dimensions of organizational behavior* (5th ed.). Boston, MA: PWS-Kent.

Adler, N., & Bartholomew, S. (1992). Managing globally competent people. *The Executive, 6,* 52–65.

Bartlett, C. A., & Ghoshal, S. (1989). *Managing across borders: The transnational solution.* London, UK: Century Business.

Bartlett, C. A., & Ghoshal, S. (1991). *Managing across borders: The transnational solution.* London, UK: London Business School.

Black, J. S., Gergersen, H. B., & Mendenhall, M. E. (1992). *Global assignments: Successfully expatriating and repatriating international managers.* San Francisco, CA: Jossey-Bass.

"Borders are so 20th century." (2003, September 22). *Business Week,* pp. 68–79.

Briscoe, D. R., & Schuler, R. S. (2012). *International human resource management* (4th ed.). London, UK: Routledge.

Budd, J. W. (2005). *Labor relations: Striking a balance.* Burr Ridge, IL: McGraw-Hill/Irwin.

Cascio, W. F. (2012). *Managing human resources* (12th ed.). Burr-Ridge, IL: McGraw-Hill.

Castillo, C. R. (2000). Collective labour rights in Latin America and Mexico. *Relations Industrielles/Industrial Relations, 55*(1), 59–79.

Gaugler, E. (1998). HR management: An international comparison. *Personnel, 65*(8), 24–30.

Gould, C. (1999, September). Expat pay plans suffer cutbacks. *Workforce,* 40–46.

Harris, D. (2010, April). China employment contracts. Ten things to consider. Retrieved from http://www.chinalawblog.com/2010/04/china_employment_contracts_ten.html

Katz, H. C., & Kochan, T. A. (2004). *Collective bargaining and industrial relations* (3rd ed.). Burr Ridge, IL: McGraw-Hill/Irwin.

Ledvinka, J., & Scardello, V. (1991). *Federal employment regulation in human resource management.* Boston, MA: PWS-Kent.

Levine, M. J. (1988). Labor movement and the multinational corporation: A future for collective bargaining? *Employee Relations Law Journal, 13,* 382–403.

Movassaghi, H. (1996). The workers of nations: Industrial relations in a global economy. *Compensation & Benefits Management, 12*(2), 75–77.

Nolo Law for All. (n.d.). Federal marriage benefits available to same-sex couples. Retrieved from http://www.nolo.com/legal-encyclopedia/same-sex-couples-federal-marriage-benefits-30326.html

Perlmutter, H. V. (1989, January-February). The tortuous evolution of the multinational corporation. *Columbia Journal of World Business,* 11–14.

Phatak, A. V. (1989). *International dimension of management.* Boston, MA: PWS-Kent.

Schuler, R. S., Dowling, P. J., & DeCieri, H. (1991). An integrative framework of strategic international human resource management. *Journal of Management, 19*(2), 419–459.

Sims, R. R. (2002). *Organizational success through effective human resources management.* Westport, CT: Quorum Books.

Sims, R. R. (2007). Toward successful international human resources management. In R. R. Sims (Ed.), *Human resources management: Contemporary issues, challenges, and opportunities* (pp. 69–108). Charlotte, NC: Information Age Publishing.

Snell, S., & Dean, J. (1992). Integrated manufacturing and human resource management: A human capital perspective. *Academy of Management Journal, 35,* 467–504.

Solomon, C. M. (1995). Danger below! Spot failing global assignments. *Personnel Journal, 76*(11), 78–85.

Stiles, P. (2009, January). *CIHRM opinion: What's the difference? Managing people across borders.* Cambridge, UK: Center for International Human Resource Management.

Tung, R. L. (1998). American expatriates abroad: From neophytes to cosmopolitans. *Journal of World Business, 33*(2),125–144.

whatishumanresource.com. (n.d.). Anti-discrimination laws. Retrieved from http://www.whatishumanresource.com/anti-discrimination-laws

Zhang, C. (n.d.). Employment law in China. Retrieved from http://www.attorneycz.com/

CHAPTER 17

THE ROLE AND FUNCTION OF THE ORGANIZATIONAL OMBUDSPERSON

C. Kevin Coonrod

INTRODUCTION

The organizational ombudsperson[1] assists people in conflict within their particular organization. This assistance is supplemental to such offices as human resources management and legal departments, and it is distinguished by its confidentiality, neutrality, informality, and the ombuds' independence from direction or control by others. The purpose of the ombudsperson is to provide a more harmonious, just, and efficient environment within the organizational community. The organizational ombudsperson can be a source of guidance for employees, managers, and HR professionals seeking an unbiased understanding of organizational policies, codes of ethics, applicable human resource-related laws and regulations, and their interpretation and application. That is why more and more organizations are adding professional ombudspersons to their staff.

In that pursuit, the organizational ombudsperson helps community members navigate institutional policies and problems; coaches them in ways to deal with conflict, intervening as a facilitator when appropriate;

Legal and Regulatory Issues in Human Resources Management, pages 375–402
Copyright © 2015 by Information Age Publishing

and provides unbiased data to the administration for consideration when discussing systemic change. This chapter provides an overview of the role and functions of the organizational ombudsperson, the benefits to the organization for maintaining an ombuds office, the relationship with human resources departments, and legal issues facing the ombuds practitioner.

ORIGINS OF THE MODERN OMBUDSPERSON

Although this chapter deals primarily with the organizational ombudsperson in the United States of America, the foundation for the modern practice of ombudsing is found in eighteenth century Sweden. There, King Charles XII appointed a watchdog to prevent and respond to governmental abuses of citizens while he was away from the country.

King Charles had been absent from Sweden for over a decade, battling Peter the Great in Russia. After a disastrous defeat at Pultava, Charles found refuge in what is now Moldova, between Romania and the Ukraine. While traveling in Turkey, in 1713, he signed a Swedish ordinance instituting the King's Highest Ombudsman. This ordinance charged the ombudsman with the directive to oversee the actions of government officials, to ensure compliance with the country's laws (Orton, 2001). The inspiration came to King Charles after learning of a centuries-old Ottoman tradition of a similar institution, also referred to in the Koran. Nearly one hundred years later, in 1809, the Swedish Parliament established an independent office of Parliament, known as the Parliamentary Ombudsman of Sweden.

Under Swedish nomenclature, the Ombudsman was known as the *umboðsmaðr*, meaning "representative of the people," or "agent of the folk." From this Swedish word, which has no gender-based attributions, comes our own "ombudsman." Like the different forms of modern-day ombudsing, this name has been modified to reflect our culture and needs of the present. The ombudsman is thus now also known in North America as "the ombudsperson" and "the ombuds."

The origin of the American organizational ombudsperson arose during the political and cultural discord of the 1960s. Ombuds in both higher education and corporate organizations were installed to help work with the strife of the time. Simon Fraser University in British Columbia, Canada established a student ombuds in 1965, and Eastern Montana College opened the first American educational ombudsman office in 1966. Shortly after, in 1967, Michigan State University followed with an ombuds office, and the practice began to spread (Conway, 2013).

THE DIFFERENT OMBUDS MODELS

Classical Ombuds

The original North American outgrowth of the Swedish *umboðsmaðr* was the classical ombudsman. Befitting its name, the classical model followed the Swedish practice of watching over government officials for the benefit of a country's citizenry. Classical ombuds receive and investigate citizen and employee complaints against government employees and officers.

Fortified with subpoena power, the classical ombuds conducts inquiries, draws conclusions, and makes recommendations to the appropriate governing body. Although the classical ombudsman has no authority to make binding decisions or judgments, the ombuds can make her or his recommendations public. Notwithstanding this lack of decision-making authority, the classical ombudsman's power to approach the press can have great influence over those who govern. The classical ombuds is usually established and authorized by a constitution, the appropriate legislative body, or via an executive order. Different types of classical ombuds are thus known as legislative ombuds and executive ombuds.

Advocate Ombuds

An advocate ombuds typically addresses complaints from a narrow and defined sector of the population. Operating independently, these ombuds advocate for a designated constituency. For example, specialized ombudspersons work with issues concerning long-term care residents. Similarly, medical ombuds work in hospitals to assist patients and even employees to work better with doctors and administrators. There are educational ombuds who help students and parents navigate issues within a school system, and ombuds who assist injured workers of self-insured businesses. Banking ombuds serve both internal and external clients of an organization. Advocate ombuds in the public sector are typically established by statute, although private medical ombuds normally derive their authority from an executive order or a charter. Advocate ombuds normally have authority to investigate and make recommendations to the relevant governing authority.

Media Ombuds

Media ombuds are reader, listener, and viewer advocates who are employed by a particular media company. These ombuds are publically critical of their employer and the manner in which news is investigated and reported by that organization. Media ombuds are not behind-the-scenes ombudspersons, but instead individuals who publish their thoughts and concerns for consideration by the public.

Organizational Ombuds

The organizational ombudsperson serves within a specific entity and works informally to help institutional citizens interact amicably and efficiently. The organizational ombudsman seeks to help parties come to fair resolutions of their own creation, advises them on policy questions, and provides anonymous data to the administration that may result in systemic change. This type of ombuds is typically found in universities, colleges, and corporations. The organizational ombudsperson's authority and foundation normally come from a charter or executive order.

Canadian Model

The Canadian model incorporates elements from the classical and organizational models and is often characterized as advocacy for fairness. The Canadian ombudspersons perform investigations impartially and objectively and write opinions based upon their findings.

The lines between these different types of ombuds are often blurred, depending upon the needs of the ombudsperson's constituency and the particular ombuds' ability and willingness to adapt to those demands.

CORNERSTONE PRINCIPLES
OF THE ORGANIZATIONAL OMBUDSPERSON

The organizational ombudsperson is a neutral resource available to help persons discuss conflict and resolutions, facilitate productive communications, explore options, and assist them in understanding organizational policies. He or she operates nonjudgmentally and does not advocate for any party. The role of the office is informal and the ombuds does not participate in formal grievance procedures. Users of the office are not referred to as "clients" or "parties," but instead, "visitors" or "office visitors."

The organizational ombudsperson's purpose is to help the organization's stakeholders work well together to the betterment of their experience in the organization. Joint use of the process is voluntary—each party to an issue must agree to become involved if the ombuds is to facilitate conversations between them. The ombudsman is an alternative to other types of conflict resolution, such as at the human resources department or through legal avenues.

The ombudsperson is not an adjudicator and therefore does not make decisions or come to judgments regarding whether one party is right and the other party wrong. Rather, the organizational ombuds attempts to help all parties understand each other better and to possibly see the matter at hand from a perspective that has not been previously considered or comprehended. By helping his or her constituents identify their underlying interests and needs, the ombuds assists the disputants to resolve problems on their own terms and with their own creativity.

Although the power of an organizational ombuds is usually derived from a charter, bylaw, executive order or statute, the office must have the respect and confidence of its community in order to operate effectively. To this end, the ombuds individually must enjoy a superlative moral authority engendered through her or his actions and reputation for integrity and fairness. Maintaining one's independence and neutrality and strictly abiding by the promise of confidentiality to a visitor—except in cases of imminent risk of serious harm or resolutely fought court order—is critical to establishing and maintaining that moral authority.

The majority of organizational ombuds operate under four foundational principles. These principles are promoted within the International Ombudsman Association's ("IOA") Standards of Practice (International Ombudsman Association, n.d. b) as: (a) independence; (b) neutrality and impartiality; (c) confidentiality; and (d) informality. The interrelationship of these precepts assists the ombudsperson to establish and maintain the attribute most necessary for the effective operation of the ombuds office: the trust of the members comprising the organization.

In this section, the four standards of the practice of organizational ombudsing, independence, neutrality, confidentiality and informality, are enunciated as set forth in the IOA Code of Ethics. Note, however, that not all organizational ombuds subscribe to the four standards articulated by the IOA, nor do all ombuds belong to the IOA. There is no legal requirement that a person belong to a professional organization to practice as an ombuds, such as attorneys and doctors are mandated to do through state bar and medical associations. In the United States, ombudsing is not a governmentally regulated occupation.[2]

Independence

"Solitary trees, if they grow at all, grow strong" (Churchill, 1933, p. 21). The strength of the ombudsman lies in her or his ability to operate unfettered by direction or pressure from management or influence by others. The ombudsman is not answerable to any person but does report, on a limited and well-defined basis, to the highest office or employee of the organization. The ombudsman is independent in structure, function, and appearance to the highest degree possible within the organization (International Ombudsman Association, n.d. a).

Unlike the marionette, the ombudsperson has no attached strings to guide or control his or her actions. Office visitors must have confidence that the organizational ombudsman has no agenda that might conflict with their concerns or issue. The ombuds thus does not aspire to assume any employment position within the organization other than the office of the ombudsperson. Additionally, the ombuds maintains sole discretion over how she or he assists an office visitor or reports on trends discovered while listening to complaints and observing organizational practices. Moreover, the ombuds has authority to act on issues directly observed, as an advocate for fairness, without having first heard a complaint from a community member.

The ombuds is responsible for office budgetary expenditures and is thus answerable for those. She cannot assume managerial authority in any part of the organization other than within her own ombuds office. In the course of her work, the ombudsperson will likely spot trends related to community members' concerns over institutional policies or actions repeated by specific individuals. The ombuds may submit unbiased reports concerning those trends and also provide statistical data on the types of complaints being brought to the ombudsperson's office and demographic data relating to the office visitors. These reports and data should be submitted to the highest person or office within the organization.

For those purposes, the ombudsperson typically reports to the board of directors or president of a corporation, or the board of trustees or president or provost of a university. On an organizational chart, the ombuds' office should be in a self-contained rectangle, with only one connecting line—to the rectangle housing the highest office in the organization. More than one connecting line dilutes the independence of the ombudsperson and possibly will place the office in a political situation between the two offices with which it is connected. If so, the ombud's independence and neutrality is compromised and thus in jeopardy of being destroyed.

Neutrality and Impartiality

"Neutrality is the ultimate standard of practice for an ombuds, demanding fairness, objectivity, impartiality, and even-handedness despite personal preferences, partisan commitments, previous experiences, and individual subjectivities" (Gadlin & Pino, 1997 p. 19). The ombudsperson stands alone, aloof from the interests and rights projected by the parties into a dispute. From this neutrality comes the respect and trust afforded by those parties that enables the ombuds to guide them to their resolution of the conflict. The ombudsman, as a designated neutral, remains unaligned and impartial. The ombudsman does not engage in any situation that could create a conflict of interest (International Ombudsman Association, n.d. a).

Often called the loneliest person in his organization, the ombudsperson eschews personal and professional relationships with members of the organizational community. An essential imperative of the ombuds is to provide a level playing field for all parties to a dispute, with equal opportunity to express their concerns and voice proposed resolutions. If an ombuds prefers one party over another, or is perceived to have a bias for or against one party, her effectiveness is diminished, if not extinguished.

The ombudsperson must therefore avoid any entanglement that may cause others to question her neutrality or impartiality. Ideally, the ombuds should have no relationship with the organization prior to becoming employed as the ombudsperson. As an insider, the ombudsperson will have developed relationships with some community members and likely will either have animosity toward others or be associated with persons who have such animosity toward other members of the community.

The belief that an ombuds hired from the inside is wholly neutral is thus doomed from the outset of her new organizational role as ombudsperson. An outsider with no previous ties with the organization or any of its members, however, will not bring any preferred relationships, biases, or personal encumbrances to the position of ombudsperson. Neutrality, as well as the appearance of neutrality, is fundamental to the ombuds' ability to safeguard and advocate for principles of fairness. Stepping into the role without the detritus acquired through previous relationships allows the ombuds to be perceived as a representative of equality and fairness for all members of the organizational populace.

Once employed, the ombuds must work to maintain her appearance of neutrality and impartiality.

> Acting neutral in order that clients perceive the ombudsman to be fair and impartial is critical to the job. Whether the work of an informal or formal ombudsman is officially designated as a "neutral" is almost irrelevant. Perceived and real neutrality is essential to the successful carrying out of the job. (Ziegenfuss & O'Rourke, 2011, pp. 58–59)

For logistical and metaphorical purposes, the office of the ombudsperson should not be located near the organization's human resources or legal departments, nor company administrative offices. Although all four of these offices have the common goal of creating a stronger, more efficient and amicable organization, the latter three often possess coercive power to punish or terminate employees or otherwise affect legal rights. The ombudsperson office should be situated in a location that is accessible to all, but which will discreetly protect the anonymity of persons entering and exiting.

Since the organizational ombudsperson does not have such authority, and is indeed neutral, the employee is more likely to relate transparently and fully to the ombuds in an effort to voice and confront her problem. A respected ombuds thus enjoys the power of trust and rapport that, in many cases, can be far more productive than the use of fear or negative consequences.

Confidentiality

"Confidentiality is the bedrock on which virtually all ombuds programs are built. In order to serve as the 'conscience' of an organization—someone to whom its members may turn with problems of a sensitive or ethical nature—an ombuds frequently needs to be able to discuss matters in confidence" (Howard & Gulluni, 1996, p. 1). The ombudsperson's promise of confidentiality is a solemn invitation for the office visitor to truthfully and completely reveal the facts and emotions underlying the visitor's concern.

The ombudsman holds all communications with those seeking assistance in strict confidence and does not disclose confidential communications unless given permission to do so. The only exception to this privilege of confidentiality is where there appears to be imminent risk of serious harm (International Ombudsman Association, n.d. a). The essence of the ombuds office is to "encourage the airing and resolution of disputes and issues" (Howard & Gulluni, 1996, p. 1). Honest discussions are difficult to hold without the availability of all relevant facts. Legitimate fears of reprisal, termination, or reprimand make it difficult for some organizational members to air a grievance. The ombuds office provides the one safe institutional venue where complaints can be discussed without discovery by others and possible subsequent retaliatory action.

The effectiveness of the ombuds office is defined by the trust the community has in the ombuds' willingness and ability to uphold his or her promise to maintain the office visitor's statements in confidence. Unfortunately, the state of the law does not always support the ombudsperson's commitment to keep the visitor's statements confidential.

The "ombuds' promise to maintain confidentiality... is only as good as the legal recognition given to such a promise. Without legal protection, an ombuds' commitment to confidentiality would be irrelevant, because he or she could be compelled [by a court] to reveal confidences" (Howard & Gullini, 1996, p. 1).

The willingness of courts to recognize an ombudsperson's assertion of confidentiality and testimonial privilege is the main legal challenge to the American organizational ombudsman and is discussed later in this chapter. Fortunately for the ombuds and his visitor, many courts have recognized the validity of the confidential nature of ombuds and office visitor communications under various legal arguments. These include common law privilege, implied contact theories, evidentiary rules and statutes in support of mediation privilege and confidentiality, and a constitutional right to privacy.

In order to avail themselves of these arguments, the ombudsperson must hold herself or himself out as a confidential resource. In her literature and promotional materials, the ombuds should state the office is not an agent of notice to the organization and that it follows the practice of independence, neutrality, confidentiality, and informality. Consistently practicing to those standards will lay the groundwork to make the above referenced legal arguments if summoned to court.

Per the IOA Code of Ethics, the only exception to the maintenance of confidentiality is an "imminent risk of serious harm." Pursuant to IOA Standards of Practice 3.1, it is within the ombuds' discretion to determine what constitutes an imminent risk of serious harm. SOP 3.1 further provides that the exception only applies if there is no other reasonable option. If the information is available from another source, the exception may thus not be applicable (International Ombudsman Association, n.d. b). Undefined is whether the "risk of harm" pertains to a person, to property, or both.

To practice confidentially, the ombudsperson must do more than refuse to repeat others' statements. The ombuds does not keep records on behalf of the organization. The ombuds' own records are shredded when they are no longer of use to the ombuds' participation in the particular matter. Some ombuds shred their notes and any documents given or generated during the course of their involvement when the matter is resolved or otherwise concluded. Others wait for a specified period of time to elapse after that conclusion before destroying the documents. Some shred them in front of the office visitor at the end of a session, and others do not take notes at all. Whatever the ombuds' practice, it should be set forth as an office policy and performed consistently.

Organizational ombuds practicing under the IOA Standards of Practice will not reveal the identity of any person contacting the ombudsperson office. The ombuds treats communications between herself and others as privileged—she will not testify in formal organizational hearings and will resist testifying in legal proceedings even if permission is given and a request is made to do so (National Ombudsman Association, n.d. b, Standards 3.2 & 3.3). The ombudsperson owns her own privilege and thus cannot be directed to waive it by any person within the organization, including her office visitor (National Ombudsman Association, n.d. b, Standard 3.2; Howard, 2010, p. 244).

The ombuds does report generic information to upper administration, as she should have a pipeline to the highest level within the organization. When making those reports, she must maintain the confidentiality of individuals unless she has been given permission by her visitors to reveal names. The same is true when publishing annual reports. The ombuds can compile statistics and information but must report them in a manner to safeguard the identity of sources.

The ombudsperson's stock in trade is trust. When the ombuds invites a person—often one whom she has never met—to reveal emotional, personal, and closely held information, she is promising to keep that information confidential in return. If she fails in that endeavor, the trust of that person and possibly of the community may break. If she succeeds, her ability to help that person and others in the future will flourish.

Informality

"Informality" provides the ombuds the flexibility she needs to assist each person according to his or her specific circumstances. The organizational ombudsman works behind the scenes in an effort to help persons communicate and understand each other better. The ombuds is not empowered with authority to make decisions or judgments, or to punish, promote, or give orders to any individual.

The ombudsman, as an informal resource, does not participate in any formal adjudicative or administrative procedure related to concerns brought to his or her attention (International Ombudsman Association, n.d. a). The ombudsperson's role in an organization is in addition to all else that is available to an organizational member. Organizational members may avail themselves of formal resources, such as through the human resources department, compliance or ethics offices, binding arbitration, or through legal process in the courts. Use of the ombuds is an alternative to those avenues, and it is voluntary. Through this voluntariness and informality, persons are able to craft resolutions of their own without imposition of ideas, preferences, or opinions by any person in authority.

When visitors are given the freedom and encouragement to think for himself or herself, fertile opportunity for empowerment is presented. Tapping into courage previously unknown to the visitor can produce an element of positivism that radiates toward others in the organization, thus enhancing the health of both the institution and the individual. Conversely, decisions imposed by a third-party decision maker, but disagreed with or deemed unfair by the participant, can engender bitterness and a lack of compliance with the end result.

As an informal conflict resolution practitioner and guide, the ombudsperson uses such skills as active listening, coaching, reality testing, and identifying issues and obstacles to help his office visitor consider options and formulate a plan to approach her problem. The ombuds may also intervene, with the permission of the office visitor, by speaking directly to the person against whom the visitor complains, or that person's superiors. Additionally, the ombuds may mediate disputes, either by shuttle or with all relevant people together in the room.

All of these methods are informal in nature and not mandated or restricted by rules or formal process. Because of the confidential nature of the organizational ombudsperson's work, with limited exceptions statements made to the ombuds will not be passed on to any other member or office of the organization. The ombuds thus cannot be considered an agent of notice for the institution. By design, the ombuds is in a position to listen to grievances but, since the office visitor's statements cannot be repeated to those in authority without that person's permission, knowledge given to the ombuds cannot be acted upon by administrative officials because they are not aware.

Moreover, the ombuds is neither an official of the organization nor an agent with speaking authority to bind the organization. The organizational ombuds has no official authority to make decisions or direct others to act or cease actions. The ombuds does have inherent power derived from intangible sources such as rapport, respect, ability to persuade, and observance or application of principles of fairness to assist participants to a dispute resolve their issues.

The organizational ombudsman works behind the scenes and off-the-record. He does not conduct formal investigations or make judgments. However, the ombuds can "look into" matters for the purpose of gathering "multiple perspectives, exploring motivations, and examining interpersonal and group dynamics and providing feedback, in a balanced and unbiased way" (Gadlin, 2012, p. 36). Facts learned from such forays can be included in reports to the administration and may then factor into effecting systemic change for the organization. Although the organizational ombuds does not have the subpoena power granted to the classical ombudsman, the organizational ombuds usually has authority via charter or other originating document or bylaw to access personnel files if relevant and necessary to an inquiry.

Not all organizational ombuds practitioners regard "informality" as a foundational practice standard. In relative terms, organizational ombudsing is a recently developed occupation. Although organizational ombudsing arose from the foundations of the classical ombuds, the two practices serve somewhat different purposes with sometimes dissimilar methods. As such, the art of organizational ombudsing is advancing and there remain differences of opinion among its practitioners regarding approaches and boundaries.

The establishment of "informality" as a tenet of organizational ombudsing is one of those that has sparked convivial debate among some ombuds. Long-time ombudsperson Howard Gadlin has asserted that "[i]nformality is not a principle, it is a style" (Gadlin, 2012, p. 32). Since it is not a principle, he argues "informality should not be considered a Standard of Practice with the IOA" (Gadlin, 2012, p. 32). In contrast, Carolyn Noorbakhsh writes, "I find informality so inextricably woven with the other SOPs that we have to practice informally in order to be confidential, neutral and independent" (Noorbakhsh, 2012, p. 28). Mary Rowe agrees, stating that informality is one of the "four tenets of ombuds practice" which, when "taken together, help to build the image of a (near) zero barrier office that can offer many options" (Rowe, 2012, p. 8). These three respected, experienced ombuds find consensus in the great value of informality, however, regardless of its designation as a cornerstone of the profession.

THE ROLE, PRACTICES AND FUNCTIONS OF THE ORGANIZATIONAL OMBUDSPERSON

The organizational ombudsperson promotes and supports the emotional, psychological, and economic health within the organization. She does so by working with individuals who make up the organization, in an effort to help them better their environment and be satisfied, happy parts of the whole. The ombudsperson's "purpose is to foster values and decent behavior—fairness, equity, justice, equality of opportunity, and respect" (Rowe, 1995, p. 103).

As the roles performed by the ombudsperson are discussed, it is important to note the activities in which the ombuds does not engage. The ombudsperson does not:

- Adjudicate
- Set policy
- Draft reports at the direction of management
- Give legal advice
- Act as an agent of notice for the organization
- Participate in formal grievances or other formal processes
- Offer therapy
- Keep records
- Advocate for any party to a conflict

Principally, the organizational ombudsman participates in three broad activities: (a) conflict resolution, (b) providing guidance regarding organizational policy, and (c) discovering and reporting on organizational trends.

Conflict Resolution

The majority of the ombudsperson's time is spent working with people in conflict with others in the organization. Office visitors typically approach the ombuds with a complaint about a superior or coworker. They may perceive unfair or unequal treatment, or they may feel they are a target of mobbing or bullying. In many cases, they are hopeful the ombuds will solve their problem for them.

The role of the organizational ombudsman is to help the office visitor help herself (Rowe, 1995). Rather than instructing the visitor how to handle a problem, the ombudsman asks questions to assist her to arrive at her own solution. By doing so, the visitor will hopefully arrive at a solution that fits her needs and values. The ombudsman's personal ideas may be founded upon his own values, which may or may not reflect the needs of the visitor. The ombudsman's ideals are therefore irrelevant when discussing another person's issues. Moreover, advice interposed by the ombuds may invest him in the resolution and possibly affect his neutrality.

Many ombuds will thus use an interests-based approach to assist the visitor understand and address her needs in the context of the particular conflict. Underlying interests such as fairness, boundaries, security, integrity, respect, trust, or loyalty may be central to the visitor's conflict and may hold the keys to a resolution. The ombuds will help the visitor analyze her problem, consider options, and formulate a plan to resolve the situation.

The ombuds has many tools in his toolkit. One of the most important is the ability to listen intently and openly to the visitor's story, while asking open-ended questions to help the tale unfold. The need to be heard and understood is vastly important to most office visitors who are experiencing conflict. Using active listening techniques such as restating and reframing the visitor's words and positions and identifying and acknowledging the importance of the visitor's underlying interests can sometimes be all that is needed. The ombuds will act as a sounding board and offer genuine empathy as he listens. At times, this may assist the visitor in finding the courage to empower herself and set out to confront the issue on her own.

Once the ombudsperson has assessed the needs of the visitor, he may make referrals to such professionals as attorneys, experts in other areas, or counselors. Although the ombuds does not give legal advice, he can provide information on germane laws to the visitor in the form of pamphlets, books, or links to pertinent websites.

Another technique is to help the visitor write a letter, expressing her viewpoint on the situation and offering proposals to resolve the issue. This letter may not even be intended to be read by the other person in the conflict, but it may help the writer organize her thoughts and give her a cathartic opportunity to vent. If the visitor decides to send the letter, the ombuds can help her craft the message diplomatically.

Coaching the visitor on how to approach the other party and have what are known as "crucial" or "difficult" conversations can be helpful (Patterson, Grenny, McMillan, & Switzler, 2002; Stone, Patton, & Heen, 1999). The ombuds may introduce techniques to the visitor to help her make the responder feel safe and therefore nondefensive at the beginning of a crucial conversation. Through use of role playing or other teaching devices, the ombuds may then coach the visitor to have a frank yet respectful conversation with the other party to her conflict.

When coaching a visitor, the ombuds will want to discover and discuss the visitor's goal. The ombuds will listen and ask curious questions about the facts that gave rise to the particular conflict and then help the visitor analyze the conflict to increase her self-awareness and to consider the other party's perspective. After considering other insights and alternatives, the ombuds may ask the visitor to reassess her goal and then consider other options for resolution. They may then discuss what obstacles may arise and formulate an action plan to achieve the visitor's refined goal (Noble, 2012, p. 111).

The ombuds may decide to speak with the other party to the conflict, to listen to that person's perspective. Rarely will there be an instance where both parties agree completely on either the facts or the philosophy behind a certain course of action. Permission from the office visitor to approach this person, the responder, will be needed so as not to violate the ombudsperson's promise of confidentiality to the visitor. The office visitor may not wish for the ombudsperson to speak directly with the responder, for fear of repercussions. In that event, the ombuds may consider speaking with the responder's manager, that person's supervisor, or a person involved in the conflict dynamic who is trusted by the office visitor. Again, permission from the office visitor will be required to approach any of those persons.

Ombuds neutrality can become a challenge when the ombuds makes contact with the responder or the responder's supervisor. Calling on or communicating with a person who is not expecting a contact from the ombuds can engender defensiveness. When the ombuds states that she is contacting the responder (or responder's supervisor) in regards to a certain person, usually one who has a complaint, easy assumptions can be made that the ombuds is representing the person who has made the complaint. The ombuds must take care to explain, preferably in writing, that she does not represent the complainant (office visitor), that she is a neutral party to the dispute, and that she is operating informally.

Maintaining neutrality, and the appearance of neutrality, can be a challenge to the ombuds if she learns of facts that support the office visitor's contention that she has been wronged. Since it is not the ombudsman's role to make judgments or binding decisions, she should check in with herself with a reminder that she will be unable to operate effectively if one of the parties perceives ombuds bias. If she does not have a trusting rapport with that person, then she will be unable to efficiently assist the parties resolve the conflict on their own.

In the situation described above, it was suggested that the office visitor may not want the ombuds to speak with her supervisor, but instead may consent to the ombuds approaching the supervisor's manager. To avoid appearing as an advocate, the ombuds might inform the manager that the facts relayed from the office visitor are anecdotal and not scientific. Additionally, the ombuds might suggest performing 360 degree evaluations or exit interviews of other employees to obtain a more objective or balanced viewpoint regarding the supervisor's practices (Erbe & Sebok, 2008).

Assuming the office visitor consents to the ombudsman speaking with the responding party, the ombuds will also need to obtain the responding party's agreement to engage in a conversation. As an informal participant in the conflict resolution dynamic, the ombuds has no authority to order the responder to speak with her. Once the responder understands that the ombuds is not an advocate, but a neutral party attempting to help both parties, she may be inclined to speak with the ombuds. After all, if the office visitor has stated there is a problem between her and the responder, the responder may possess her own difficulties with the office visitor. Or, she may simply wish to attempt constructive action to alleviate the conflict and may welcome the assistance of the third-party ombudsperson.

In attempting to facilitate a resolution to the parties' problem, the ombuds will encourage the parties to speak with each other. This can be done via shuttle conferences or with all parties speaking together in the same room.

Shuttle facilitation may appear safer or more comfortable to the parties, as they will not be facing each other. In this process, the ombudsman speaks with each party separately and then relays information between the two. During her separate meetings with the parties, the ombuds will help them brainstorm options and develop proposals for consideration by the other. This process can be cumbersome and lends itself to the possibility of information being misinterpreted or relayed inaccurately. Additionally, the ombuds will not be able to deliver information with the same heart and voice as the person who experienced the impact of whatever gave rise to the conflict. That person is the only expert on how that impact affected her, a role neither the ombuds nor any other person can fill.

The use of a skilled conflict resolution expert, such as a mediator, can help the parties speak to each other productively, face to face. In a mediation, all relevant parties to the conflict will meet in the same room to recount their particular viewpoint on what has transpired, relate how that history impacts and continues to impact them at present, and then move forward to discuss how they wish to resolve the conflict and interact in the future.

The ombudsperson may serve as the mediator if she has the education and experience, or she may wish to contract with an external mediator to facilitate the meeting. Organizational ombudspersons normally engage in facilitative mediation techniques, which are designed to help the parties address their interests and come up with their own solutions to the conflict. This is consistent with the neutral and informal nature of the organizational ombuds profession, where there is no authority to arrive at a judgment and the ombuds does not treat any party more favorably than another. The purpose of the mediator is to assist the parties to have a discussion on a level field.

The mediation may span several sessions, and private meetings with each party may be held during any one of the mediation sessions. If the mediator is also the ombudsperson, she will promise to hold statements made during the joint session and the private sessions confidential. If the parties wish for their own mediation statements to be confidential, they must agree among themselves to keep their conversation confidential or mediate in a state where mediation statements are legislated as confidential by statute.

In addition to helping the parties help themselves, the ombuds may informally "look into" matters. The ombudsman may make inquiries at another person's request or at her own discretion if she sees activity that she believes is not just or fair. The ombuds does not enjoy subpoena power as the classical ombudsman does, but she should have access to personnel files pursuant to the ombuds charter or other document giving authority to the office. The organizational ombudsman may relay nonconfidential facts obtained during these inquiries to the top administrative person to whom she reports, but she does not make the results public. Permission from the parties to the conflict is not needed when the ombudsman looks into an issue; however, the identity of the parties must be concealed by the ombuds. Finally, the administration is under no obligation to act on the ombuds findings.

The ombuds may also facilitate discussions with stakeholders of various groups within the organization. The purpose of group facilitations is to help different factions focus on common interests and discuss how to proceed on topics that affect them all. These group discussions are not normally confidential, and the ombuds should make clear that the members know she has no duty to keep their conversations private. The ombuds will act as a neutral during the group facilitation and must take care not to be perceived as taking sides. The ombuds must not participate in the discussion other than as an impartial facilitator.

Finally, some ombudspersons engage in conflict resolution training. This may consist of staging seminars or workshops, or simply coaching individuals or small groups how to interact when conflict appears in the workplace or elsewhere within the organization.

Providing Guidance Regarding Institutional Policy

The ombudsperson provides guidance concerning the organization's policies to the office visitor. An expert on company manuals and policies, the ombuds can discuss the visitor's rights and responsibilities, as well as company grievance procedures in the comfort of a confidential setting. By virtue of the independent, confidential, and neutral services offered by the ombuds, a visitor can brainstorm scenarios to discover what is and is not acceptable conduct within the parameters of organizational rules. The ombuds does not warrant that particular conduct will be acceptable, but does provide guidance regarding the efficacy of a visitor's action plan.

Trend Reporting for Purposes of Systemic Change

The organizational ombudsman is in a different position to learn about organizational members' desires and dislikes than the administration. Due to the ombudsperson's promise of confidentiality, visitors have the security to speak freely about their issues without fear of reprisal. As a result, the ombuds will hear raw data that may never be conveyed by the visitors to institutional decision-makers.

As the ombuds hears similar stories from different visitors, important trends may emerge. If enough members voice a concern over a particular matter, it may be impossible to identify individuals when the concern is voiced to the administration. Their anonymity will be protected by the existence of the crowd. In this way, the ombuds can safely give a voice to those who otherwise would not report transgressions or other issues to their superiors.

The information reported by the ombudsperson should be viewed as credible by top administration. Since the ombuds has no professional aspirations within the organization other than to be an excellent ombudsman, there is no need to slant the information in her favor. The ombuds thus provides unvarnished information to the administration—data without an agenda that has not percolated up through the filters of middle management.

Additionally, as an independent neutral, the ombudsperson may see the information in a different light than viewed by others. She may thus be able to connect the dots and present an alternative perspective concerning the issue that had not been contemplated by the administration. Suggestions or recommendations may be made by the ombuds, but she has no vote in setting policy.

This upward feedback can effect systemic change by the decision-makers of the organization, and provide early warnings of matters that may grow to be of serious consequence if not addressed immediately. From her unique perch, the ombuds can be of tremendous benefit to the organization by surfacing hidden complaints, data, and desires of the members of the institution.

RELATIONSHIP WITH HUMAN RESOURCES

Due to its independent nature, the ombuds office is separate and distinct from the human resources department, company administration, and the organization's legal department. All of these offices, however, have the common goal of promoting and effecting a healthy and productive organization. Different tools are used by each, and all of the offices have their own constructs within which they work.

There are many distinctions between the roles and functions of the ombuds and human resource departments. For instance, HR personnel keep detailed records and make recommendations. They have authority to formally investigate, sanction, demote, promote, hire, and terminate employees. Statements made to HR workers by an employee can be disseminated to administrative personnel and others, including law enforcement officers. The HR employee will produce documents pursuant to *subpoenas duces tecum* and testify in depositions, hearings and trials.

Such actions are incongruous with the role of the ombudsperson, who shreds documents and has no authority to alter a person's employment status or otherwise order an employee to cease or perform an act. The ombuds will resist subpoenas and assert legal privilege to avoid testifying in legal proceedings. The organizational ombudsperson does not pass judgment or recommend disciplinary action to an employee's superior. Rather, the ombudsman works behind the scenes, confidentially and neutrally, in an effort to assist the employee or supervisor in developing options to help herself or himself.

Ideally, the ombuds and human resources offices will complement each other in their attempts to benefit those they serve. When they work together within their established boundaries, they can offer different but helpful aid to those who seek their services. When the offices distrust or compete with each other, alternatives for the members of the organization can unfortunately narrow.

In contrast to the informal, neutral, independent, and confidential ombudsman, human resources personnel are directed by management and are involved in formulating and enforcing company policies. Complaints brought to human resources can be investigated formally and binding decisions are made at the conclusion of the investigation or after a hearing. Reporting actions to human resources can also trigger legal mechanisms that would not be set in motion if the same grievance were brought to the ombuds.

For example, the human resources department is an agent of legal notice for the organization. If an employee were to bring a claim alleging violation of Equal Employment Opportunity laws to human resources, the organization would be deemed to have immediately been placed on notice of that claim. Organizational responsibilities to investigate, mitigate, or otherwise act may commence upon receipt of that notice. Conversely, the ombudsperson is a confidential resource who has promised not to speak about anything his visitor says to him without permission. The ombuds thus cannot fill the role of notice agent for the organization.

If the office visitor shares the grievance with the ombuds, there are many alternatives available. The ombuds can listen, empathize, brainstorm, and offer resource referrals for counseling, legal knowledge, or assistance; look informally into the matter; or encourage the visitor to meet with the appropriate HR representative. Coaching the aggrieved person in handling the matter himself or herself may be helpful or, if appropriate, the ombuds may facilitate a conversation between the principals to the issue.

The ombudsman can also help the office visitor prepare an EEO complaint form and assist that person to timely file it in the appropriate venue, often the human resource department. Once that is done, the matter might be referred back to the ombuds for mediation if all parties and representatives of both offices agree. In the event the mediation fails to produce an agreeable result to the parties, then human resources' formal handling of the claim will continue.

Claims made to the human resource department that do not rise to the level of a meritorious EEO claim or any other dismissed complaint may be referred by the HR person to the ombuds. Even though a claim may not be legally actionable, invariably there is an issue present that is keeping the parties to the conflict from working well together. Conflict is not always defined by boundaries set forth in law books. The ombuds may be able to help those parties work out a resolution for themselves, and the complaining party may be grateful for this alternative avenue after having his voice silenced at the conclusion of the original complaint.

This type of collaboration between human resources and the ombudsman should be encouraged in all organizations. A good working relationship and knowledge of what each office offers can lead to more options for the parties in conflict, and likely enhanced morale within the organization.

The ability to complement, rather than compete, will therefore heighten alternatives available for amicable human relations within the organization. A trusting and respectful dynamic between the two offices will foster that desired and productive goal.

BENEFITS BROUGHT TO THE ORGANIZATION BY THE ORGANIZATIONAL OMBUDSPERSON

An organizational ombuds office is an institutional asset that produces both intangible and tangible benefits. Overall, effective ombuds' work should increase a prosperous spirit within the organization as well as identifiable economic savings.

Some of those economic savings can be assessed through a cost-benefit analysis. Perhaps just as importantly, the impact of an ombuds office can promote an enhanced sense of workplace comfort and security within individuals who have been able to resolve their problems through the office, who have gained or regained trust or respect for their fellow workers or supervisors, or who come to understand how to communicate more productively and respectfully with those persons.

An ombudsman equipped with conflict resolution skills can help identify patterns of bullying and assist targets to confront and work through the problem. By keeping her ear to the ground, the ombuds surfaces negative issues and either reports them to top administration or works with the individuals involved—or both—to prevent the problem from becoming more destructive.

By helping persons work through their issues early in the conflict, the ombuds can help stem feelings of bitterness, jealousy, trespass, or anger. Unchecked, the pain associated with those sensitivities can fester into a much larger and destructive problem. This can lead to lessened productivity, absenteeism, employee turnover, violence in the workplace, sabotage, crimes of dishonesty, and substance abuse (Newcomb, 2010).

Of course, the ombuds can become involved at any time during the conflict, provided all relevant parties agree that the boundaries of formal process are not being intruded upon. As a mediator or facilitator, the ombudsperson may be able to help parties resolve affirmative action or workplace grievances before a complaint is filed. With permission, efforts to resolve those matters may commence or continue after a formal grievance process has begun. The ombuds must make clear that she or he is not involved—and will not become involved—with the formal process and cannot be looked upon to make a report, testify, or render a decision. The scope of the ombudsperson's activity will be to informally help the parties come to a resolution on their own, thus avoiding a third party making a decision for them.

By gaining their office visitors' trust, the ombuds may help them avoid destructive behavior that may harm the visitor, organization, or other person. Specific examples of ombudspersons persuading others to cease threats or the actual commission of pernicious behavior include:

- Relinquishment of deadly arms
- Threats of self-harm or violence to others
- An arsonist surrendering to authorities at the urging of the ombuds
- Early warnings of environmental hazards
- Assisting office visitors to understand they may have an emergency medical problem in time to obtain treatment
- Uncovering plans to sabotage tangible and intellectual property (Rowe, 2010)

Table 17.1 presents Martin Freres' (2013) different types of costs of conflict in the workplace. Under a cost-benefit analysis, perhaps the most easily quantifiable savings an ombudsman can bring to an organization is the amelioration or outright avoidance of the last entry in Mr. Freres' chart: legal and dispute costs. As stated earlier in this chapter, many disputes arise from personality conflicts that grow into deeply divisive disputes. Often, those disputes fester and ultimately form the basis of a legal claim one or more parties believe is valid. Whether or not the claim has merit, it will

TABLE 17.1 Typology of Organizational Costs of Workplace Conflict

Theme	Content
Medical Health	Sick Leave, Health Insurance Premium, Accident Likelihood, Physical or Psychological Disability (including Depression)
Individual Psyche	Lower Job Motivation, Satisfaction, Commitment, and Diligence
Wasted Time	Absenteeism, Presenteeism, Pretending to Work, Time Spent Resolving Conflict
Counterproductive Work Behavior	Sabotage, Theft (including Intellectual Property), Vandalism, Violence, Incivility
Team Behavior	Quality and Frequency of Decision-Making, Morale, Less Organizational Citizenship Behavior
Customer Relationship	Customer Service, Customer Complaint Handling
Human Resources and Organizational Development	Turnover, Employer Reputation, Relationship- instead of Task-Driven Assignment of People, Distrust, and Change Resistance
Legal and Dispute Costs	Grievances, Litigation, Discrimination Claims, Compensation/ Settlement

certainly occupy a great deal of the worker's, supervisor's, administration's, and legal counsel's time.

Not only will this affect the ability of those individuals to direct their attention to more productive tasks, but actual costs to the organization can be exorbitant. In conjunction with attorney fees, the court costs for discovery, expert witnesses, travel, and preparation of expensive exhibits can eclipse the principal amount originally claimed in the legal complaint. If the matter can be resolved in the germination stages of the dispute with the help of the ombudsperson, none of those costs will be incurred. Instead, a more harmonious workplace likely will have been nourished by parties coming to their own resolution, using personal creativity and values to address the interests they felt were intruded upon in the conflict.

If the matter remains unresolved during the course of the conflict, it will still be capable of settlement at any time up to the moment a judgment is rendered in court. Any such settlement will likely be more rights-based than interest-based at that point, and it will follow a risk-benefit analysis by both sides. When calculating the human time occupied during the court process, together with the actual expenses of the litigation and the amount of the settlement itself, a monetary settlement may be excessively high.

Worse for the institution, a judgment entered against it can be exceedingly costly and detrimental to the organization's reputation. The judgment will include principal, postjudgment interest, court costs, and possibly, if allowable by law, attorney fees, prejudgment interest, and punitive damages. If the organization prevails in the lawsuit, it may realize it has stumbled into a pyrrhic victory when a review of its own attorney fees, court costs, time lost from work, and the expenditure of other resources is undertaken.

This costly result may have been avoided if the organizational ombudsman was involved early in the conflict. By listening to the parties, letting them know they are being heard, brainstorming with them, and helping them discover and address their underlying interests, the litigants may have been able to settle the matter amicably and constructively. Perhaps an apology would have ended the dispute, or an agreed upon alteration or cessation of certain behavior, or, simply, a truer understanding of the intent behind one of the parties' words or actions.

Such a resolution not only would render costly litigation unnecessary, but will likely contribute to a more efficient and congenial work environment. Both of these positive outcomes articulate the value of the ombuds to an organization. Indeed, an effective ombudsman office will not only pay for itself but add to the revenues of the organization by contributing to the productivity of the workforce and mitigating the amount of monies paid out in settlements, judgments, and lost time. As was once sagely enunciated by Benjamin Franklin, "A penny saved is a penny earned."

Finally, certain federal statutes encourage the establishment and maintenance of an ombudsperson office. The mere presence of an ombuds within an organization can help diminish criminal penalties under the United States Sentencing Guidelines. Under that statute, sentencing penalties can be reduced if the organization has installed a program to discover and protect against legal violations.

The benefits of a well-organized ombudsperson office to an entity are numerous. From helping the people who make up the organization work more efficiently and amicably together to enhance productivity to helping resolve expensive legal claims and their attendant costs to reduce loss, the ombuds brings significant cost-effectiveness to the group.

LEGAL ISSUES FACING
THE ORGANIZATIONAL OMBUDSPERSON

The fundamental nature of the ombudsperson's practice, working with those in conflict, continuously places him in the midst of rancor, competitive positioning, and enmity. Lawsuits are threatened and sometimes filed. The greatest legal challenges facing the organizational ombudsperson are protecting himself from being called to testify in a matter in which he has promised confidentiality and being deemed an official of the organization capable of receiving legal notice.

Imputed Notice

The organizational ombudsperson is not an agent of notice for his institution. Regardless, people with serious issues visit the ombuds in hope of finding a resolution to their conflict. They are not typically concerned that the ombudsman is outside of the normal organizational hierarchy, nor do they usually care that the ombuds is an informal resource. They are seeking assistance for a matter of significance to them, and that is the purpose of their visit.

Unless they are informed otherwise at the outset of the visit, many office visitors will believe they are speaking to the organization when they are talking with the organization's ombudsperson. Therefore, when they are asked on a later date if they gave notice to the organization of their claim by a specific deadline, they will remember they brought up the issue with the ombuds before that date elapsed. Unfortunately, since the ombuds kept their conversations confidential, those in the organization with authority to act never received notice that the office visitor had a claim. If the failure to file the claim or complaint by the particular deadline time barred the filing of the grievance, the visitor's rights to assert the claim legally may have vanished.

In an attempt to revive her claim, the office visitor may argue in court that the organization had "imputed notice" of the claim when she brought the issue to the ombuds. She would argue that the organization had constructive notice of an issue because an organizational agent had been made aware of her facts and circumstances, and that such notice should be imputed to the organization.

Pursuant to the *Restatement (Second) of the Law of Agency,* § 268 (1)(a) and (b) (1958) (cited in Howard, 2010), notification given to an organization's agent will constitute notice to the organization if the agent was either authorized or apparently authorized to receive the notice. Moreover, notice will not be effective if it is given to an agent authorized to conduct a particular transaction but who is known by the person giving the notice as a person who is not authorized to receive the notice.

A purpose of the ombuds' consistent insistence on noting that he is not an agent of notice to the institution, that he is independent and has no managerial authority other than within his own office, and that he is an alternative and off-the-record form of conflict resolution, is to avoid successful claims that notice to him constituted legal notice to the organization. If he were authorized to accept claims, then he would have a duty to report them to the organization, rendering the promise of confidentiality farcically inapposite.

Challenges to Ombuds Maintenance of Confidentiality

Attempts have been and are being made to pass legislation creating a legal privilege for ombuds conversations, but as of the date of this publication, no statutes have been enacted that directly grant that protection. The ombuds should operate his office in a manner that will assist in resisting efforts to compel his testimony in judicial proceedings.

When subpoenaed to testify in a legal proceeding, the organizational ombudsperson asserts he has a legal privilege keeping him from being compelled to testify. "Privilege" is distinguished from an agreement to keep matters "confidential" in that it relates to sworn testimony. Therefore, a person asserts privilege to avoid testifying in court, during a deposition or other legal proceeding. Agreeing to keep something confidential is much broader and extends to an agreement not to speak with anyone, at any place, and in any context, about the matter discussed.

Although there is not a strict statutory "ombudsperson/office visitor" privilege, such as physicians, attorneys, and priests enjoy, other legal theories have been approved by courts in support of the notion that ombuds cannot be compelled to testify about matters they have promised to keep confidential.

Attorney, author, and organizational ombudsman legal expert Charles Howard (2010) has summarized these theories in his book, *The Organizational Ombudsman: Origins, Roles, and Operations, A Legal Guide*, already referenced in this chapter. One of these theories is a common law privilege, first reported in a federal case originating in Iowa, *Shabazz v. Scurr, 662 F. Supp. 90 (S.D. Iowa 1987)*.

In the *Shabazz* case, a prison ombuds asserted a state immunity statute to prevent a former employee from testifying about events arising during a prison riot. The state statute was not binding on the federal court, but the court utilized the federal evidentiary rule on privilege, Federal Rule of Evidence 501, to "apply the state testimonial immunity law to recognize a privilege in federal court" (Howard, 2010, p. 227). The court noted policy arguments that (a) confidentiality was necessary to the prison ombuds so that prisoners would bring complaints to him, (b) public policy supporting plea bargains and other settlement of disputes rendered informal negotiations a necessary tool, and (c) the privilege applied only to statements made to the ombuds, not to statements made through other channels.

Those same public policy arguments were instrumental in finding a common-law privilege in *In Re Doe*, 711 F.2d 1187 (2d Cir. 1983). In that case, the United State Court of Appeals articulated four factors that may establish a common-law privilege:

1. The communication must be made in the belief that it will not be disclosed.
2. Confidentiality must be essential to the maintenance of the relationship between the parties.
3. The relationship is one that society considers worthy of being fostered.
4. The injury to the relationship incurred by the disclosure must be greater than the benefit gained in the correct disposal of the litigation (*In re Doe*, at 1193 cited in Howard & Gullini, 1996).

A district court judge's decision in the unpublished *Roy v. United Technologies Corp.*, CIVIL H-89-680 (JAC) has become the "seminal case recognizing both a federal common-law privilege for ombuds and as authority for an implied contract basis for protecting the confidentiality of ombuds' communication" (cited in Howard, 2010, p. 227). Not only did the judge in *Roy* approve a federal common-law privilege, but he ruled that since the ombuds had taken such care to publicize and practice confidentiality, the visitor's acceptance of the ombuds' services constituted an implied agreement that their conversations would be confidential, not to be repeated by the ombuds.

Ombudspersons in California enjoy a qualified state constitutional privilege for statements made during mediation sessions pursuant to the Court of Appeals decision in *Garstang v. Superior Court of Los Angeles County and California Institute of Technology, (1995),* 39 Cal. App. 4th 526 [46 Cal. Rptr. 2d 84]. In *Garstang,* the court ruled that the state's constitutional right of privacy prohibited the compulsion of an ombud's testimony about communications made during a mediation.

State mediation confidentiality statutes have been recognized in some courts as support for the assertion by an ombuds of the privilege not to testify. Some, like the Texas statute, are broad enough to cover alternative dispute resolution activities in addition to mediation (Howard, 2010). Additionally, states which have adopted the Uniform Mediation Act have specific language regarding privilege that may be used by ombuds under the UMA's broad mediation-related definitions.

Finally, courts have invoked their own rules concerning discovery processes to rule that the value of the ombuds' testimony to the court case is outweighed by the damage that can be done to the publicly favored promise of confidentiality. *Miller v. Regents of the University of Colorado,* 1999 U.S. App. LEXIS 16712 (10th Cir 1999).

Although these arguments have proven successful in many courts, the ombudsperson must perform the background work well before a case makes its way to a court to establish the foundation for issuance of a court order precluding his testimony. The ombuds should not only publicize that he adheres to certain ethical guidelines and standards of practice, but he should make them a habit and follow them scrupulously in actual practice. These practices include operating independently, neutrally, confidentially and informally, per IOA Standards and Practices, and only relating confidential information with the permission of the visitor or in those cases where the ombuds deems there is an imminent threat of serious harm (International Ombudsman Association, 2009).[3]

CONCLUSION

The organizational ombudsperson occupies a unique position within an organization. She works for the benefit of workers and administration alike yet is neutral for all. She doesn't set policy but she can hear and see unknown factors that can be of great importance in effecting systemic change. From her vantage point she sees the underbelly of the organization on a daily basis, while at the same time her work assists the organization and its people in reaching their optimal potential. As a person whose noble and unselfish mission is to help others help themselves, the organizational ombudsperson brings out the vitality, ethics, justice, and pride inherent in the organization and all those that comprise its soul.

NOTES

1. Derivations of the word "ombudsman" are "ombudsperson," "ombuds," and "ombud." These terms are used interchangeably in this chapter.
2. The IOA does certify organizational ombudspersons and awards a credential known as Certified Organizational Ombudsman Practitioner, or "CO-OP®." To acquire this credential, the ombuds must possess a bachelor's degree or equivalent, pass a certification examination, and practice as an organizational ombudsperson for the equivalent of one full year. The examination must be taken and passed within the three years leading up to the application. The full year of experience must be compiled within four years of applying, with credit for part-time employment being given over the course of more than one year. The CO-OP credential does not require membership in the IOA, although the applicant must demonstrate that he or she practices in accordance with the IOA Code of Ethics and Standards of Practices. Possession of this credential is not a prerequisite for employment as an ombuds practitioner, unless it is made a requirement within the discretion of the prospective employer.
3. Not all organizational ombudspersons practice to such a strict standard. Although the principal of confidentiality is respected, many offices make exceptions for statutes requiring disclosure, compliance issues, and organization-specific expectations. International Ombudsman Association (2009, Ch. 3).

REFERENCES

Churchill, W. (1933). *The River War: An account of the reconquest of the Soudan.* New York, NY: Charles Scribner's Sons.

Conway, M. (2013). Celebrating ombuds in higher education: ACCUO 1983–2013. Association of Canadian College and University Ombudspersons. Retrieved from http://www.uwo.ca/ombuds/student/ACCUO30En.pdf

Erbe, N., & Sebok, T. (2008). Shared global interest in skillfully applying IOA standards of practice. *Journal of the International Ombudsman Association, 1*(1), 28–41.

Freres, M. (2013). Financial costs of workplace conflict. *Journal of the International Ombudsman Association, 6*(2), 83–94.

Gadlin, H. (2012). Some thoughts on informality. *Journal of the International Ombudsman Association, 5*(1), 31–36.

Gadlin, H., & Pino, E. (1997). Neutrality: A guide for the organizational ombudsperson. *Negotiation Journal, 19*(1), 17–37.

Howard, C. (2010). *The organizational ombudsman, origins, roles and operation: A legal guide.* Chicago, IL: ABA Publishing.

Howard, C., & Gulluni, M. (1996). *The ombuds confidentiality privilege, theory and mechanics.* Hillsborough, NJ: International Ombudsman Association.

International Ombudsman Association. (2009). *Ombudsman 101: An introductory program for new ombudsman or those seeking information about the organizational ombudsman role.* Hillsborough, NJ: Author.

International Ombudsman Association. (n.d. a). IOA code of ethics. Retrieved from http://www.ombudsassociation.org/about-us/code-ethics

International Ombudsman Association. (n.d. b). IOA standards of practice and IOA best practices. Retrieved from http://www.ombudsassociation.org/about-us/mission-vision-and-values/ioa-best-practices-standards-practice

Newcomb, J. (2010). Assessing the cost-effectiveness of an ombudsman: A corporate case study. *Journal of the International Ombudsman Association, 3*(1), 40–42.

Noble, C. (2012). *Conflict management coaching: The CINERGY model.* Toronto, Canada: Cinergy.

Noorbakhsh, C. (2012). I was just thinking: Musings on ombudsman informality from the perspective of an organizational ombudsman. *Journal of the International Ombudsman Association, 5*(1), 27–30.

Orton, F. (2001). The birth of the ombudsman. Retrieved from europeandcis.undp.org/files/uploads/John/OMBUDS_HISTORY.doc

Patterson, K., Grenny J., McMillan R., & Switzler, A. (2002). *Crucial conversations: Tools for talking when stakes are high.* New York, NY: McGraw Hill.

Rowe, M. (1995). Options, functions and skills: What an organizational ombudsperson might want to know. *Negotiation Journal, 11*(2), 103–114.

Rowe, M. (2010). Identifying and communicating the usefulness of organizational ombuds with ideas about OO effectiveness and cost-effectiveness. *Journal of the International Ombudsman Association, 3*(1), 19–23.

Rowe, M. (2012). Informality: The fourth standard of practice. *Journal of the International Ombudsman Association, 5*(1), 8–17.

Stone, D., Patton, B., & Heen, S. H. (1999). *Difficult conversations: How to discuss what matters most.* New York, NY: Penguin Group.

Ziegenfuss, J., Jr., & O'Rourke, P. (2011). *The ombudsman handbook: Designing and managing an effective problem-solving program.* Jefferson, NC: McFarland & Company.

CHAPTER 18

PRACTICAL ADVICE FOR HRM PROFESSIONALS WHEN FACING A FEDERAL LAWSUIT

William I. Sauser, Jr., Ronald R. Sims, and John G. Veres, III

INTRODUCTION

The three authors, all of whom are academics with considerable consulting experience in human resources management (HRM), served in various capacities as consultants to a federal judge in a complex and lengthy class-action federal lawsuit with multiple plaintiffs, intervenors, and defendants. During their service in these capacities they had considerable opportunities to observe the strategies and tactics of all parties involved in the case. On the basis of these observations, they offer in this chapter practical advice to HRM professionals facing a federal lawsuit. The authors are not attorneys and are not offering legal advice. Instead, they are commenting on actions HRM professionals might take that could potentially weaken or strengthen their efforts to help their organizations make any necessary changes resulting from their case in federal court. We hope that all HRM professionals can learn from the experience—the frequently painful experience—of the plaintiff organization referred to extensively in this chapter.

Legal and Regulatory Issues in Human Resources Management, pages 403–434

The chapter first offers a brief discussion of the roles of (and differences among) three types of court-appointed agents (i.e., special masters, receivers, and monitors). Next, some background on the class-action federal lawsuit the authors were involved in is offered before we recommend some specific actions HRM professionals can take to help their organizations better respond to the challenges accompanying a federal lawsuit and the needs for change that may result from such a lawsuit. The chapter concludes with a list of recommendations HRM professionals should consider when confronted with legal issues or a federal lawsuit that may well require changes for them, their HRM department, and the organization as a whole.

COURT-APPOINTED AGENTS: SPECIAL MASTERS, MONITORS AND RECEIVERS

Ray Fitzpatrick, a Birmingham lawyer who specializes in employment reform cases, has commented that a huge amount of money can be spent in a federal lawsuit if the case is not properly managed, and that does not help anyone. "The goal is not to just hire a lot of consultants," he continued. "The goal here is to insure compliance with federal law" (quoted in Wright, 2013). And that is where court-appointed agents like special masters (SMs), monitors, and receivers come into play. Because the functions performed by SMs, monitors, and receivers vary in their intrusiveness into a defendant's operations, these agents occupy places along a spectrum that lacks bright-line boundaries.[1] A court's aim in any reference is to enlist aid in ensuring that defendants comply with statutes or the common law, or to structure the substantive changes that the court feels are equitable or necessary (Feldman, 1991).

Special Master

In law, a special master (SM) is an authority appointed by a judge to make sure that judicial orders are actually followed. According to the Academy of Court Appointed Masters (ACAM) (2009a), the role of the special master is to supervise those falling under the order of the court to make sure that the court order is being followed and to report on the activities of the entity being supervised in a timely matter to the judge or the judge's designated representatives.

The Legal Information Institute (2013a) notes that a "special master" is appointed by a court to carry out some sort of action on its behalf. Theoretically, a "special master" is distinguished from a "master." A master's function is essentially investigative, compiling evidence or documents to inform some future action by the court, whereas a special master carries out some direct action on the part of the court. It appears, however, that the "special master" designation is often used for people doing purely investigative work, and that the simple "master" designation is falling out of use (Special Masters.biz, 2013).

Johnson (2014) notes that SMs, or referees as they are called under Rule 53 of the North Carolina rules of Civil Procedures, are appointed by judges to oversee one or more aspects of litigation. SMs can help the court with time-consuming and very involved tasks such as discovery production, discovery disputes, and complicated accounting matters. They can be an effective tool for both the parties and the court in sifting through difficult issues and helping facilitate resolutions.

Activities carried out by SMs are as diverse as the actions taken by courts. SMs perform a variety of judicial duties, including pretrial case management,[2] fact-finding,[3] and the development of equitable remedies both before and after liability has been established.[4] Historically, the special master was a frequently employed agent of the equity courts.[5] Further, they are often appointed as facilitators in child custody cases, for example, but the term "special master" was also used to describe the person appointed by Congress to administer compensation for the victims of the 9/11 terrorist attacks in New York (Department of Justice, 2013; ACAM, 2009a). The term often appears in *original jurisdiction* disputes (cases such as disputes between states that are first heard at the Supreme Court level) decided by the Supreme Court; these are often cases involving boundary disputes between the states, with an SM appointed to resolve questions of geography or historical claims. The SM conducts what amounts to a trial court (the taking of evidence and a ruling). The Supreme Court can then assess the master's ruling much as a normal appeals court would, rather than conduct the trial itself. This is necessary as trials in the United States almost always involve live testimony and it would be too unwieldy for nine justices to rule on evidentiary objections in real time. See, for example, New Jersey v. New York (1998; see also Legal Information Institute, 2013b).

In *U.S. v. Microsoft*, Judge Jackson appointed a SM to advise the court about technical issues and to investigate certain claims, such as Microsoft's assertion that removing Internet Explorer from the Windows operating system would make the system slower (Legal Information Institute, 2013a). Infrequently, attorneys taking a deposition in a distant, non-courthouse location may anticipate that a witness will refuse to testify, or that some other problem will come up. For good cause shown, judges may appoint an SM to appear at the deposition to make evidentiary rulings on the spot.

The usage of special masters in matters involving complex electronic discovery (or "eDiscovery") has been promulgated by the Academy of Court Appointed Masters (ACAM). The United States Court of Federal Claims operates an Office of Special Masters to resolve claims under the National Childhood Vaccine Inquiry Act, which is popularly known as the vaccine court (U.S. Court of Federal Claims, 2013).

Cases involving SMs also often involve situations where it has been shown that governmental entities are violating civil rights. High-profile cases where SMs have been utilized include some in which states have been ordered to upgrade their prison facilities that were held to violate the United States Constitution, which bars cruel and unusual punishment, and state mental hospitals that have been found so substandard as to violate the rights of their inmates (Academy of Court Appointed Masters, 2009b).[6] Summaries of cases involving special masters are published at *Cohen's Special Master Case Reporter* (Special Masters.biz, 2013).

In *"What's the Big Deal? Federal Receiver or Special Master?"* (University of California Hastings College of Law, 2009), the authors note that SMs often monitor the activities of other parties. They lack, however, direct executive authority and must rely on the federal courts to order changes when they discover problems in compliance with court orders. Receivers, on the other hand, do have direct executive authority. More will be said about this distinction later.

Monitors

Monitors can be helpful towards the end or after a federal lawsuit case is resolved to ensure that a court's order or settlement agreement is implemented properly and complied with over time (Academy of Court Appointed Masters, 2009a). In civil cases, monitors are often appointed to monitor compliance with structural injunctions, especially those involving employment or other organizational change, those involving facilities assisting the disabled, or those requiring reform in government agencies. By surveying the defendant's remedial efforts, the monitor can facilitate judicial evaluation of the defendant's capability, willingness, and compliance with equitable relief or with a decree.[7]

Monitorship is a means to elicit the defendant's cooperation in determining curative measures,[8] to accomplish nonadversarial resolution of potential disputes concerning the remedy, and importantly, to provide the plaintiffs and the court with a way to ascertain the defendant's good faith (Feldman, 1991). To further these ends, the court may order a neutral observer placed with the defendant's entity[9] or approve a monitoring committee chosen by the parties and representing their respective interests. Feldman (1991) notes that due to intra-board disagreements and self-interested evaluation of defendants' compliance, monitoring committees composed of the adversaries' representatives may be less effective at exposing and resolving disputes or in helping the court to forge a remedial strategy than nonpartisan court-selected agents.[10]

A monitor's presence acts as a reminder of the court's authority and of public concern that the defendant's organization or government facility operates in a responsible fashion. The monitor may inform the defendant's employees and the community of the dispute, or, if the defendant is a public agency, even invite community participation in implementing the decree.[11]

A monitor's mandate also may extend beyond surveillance for the court. A court may instruct a monitor to recommend compliance techniques to the defendant.[12] A reference to a monitor to gather information that is important to the court for adjusting the remedial plan may allow the monitor to consult specialists, perform inspections, and conduct ex parte investigations.[13]

Monitors lack independent enforcement powers and cannot direct a defendant's conduct (Academy of Court Appointed Masters, 2009a; Feldman, 1991; Legal Information Institute, 2013a). It is the monitor's role neither to create policy nor to assume operational control of an organization. A monitor's reports may lead a court to apply sanctions or lift restrictions, but monitors are judicial agents, not judges (Academy of Court Appointed Masters, 2009b; Feldman, 1991).

Given their restricted coercive powers, monitors have a measured exercise of equitable authority causing limited intrusion into a defendant's internal affairs. In the end, monitors serve an important role in overseeing court-ordered change and in gathering information from those who are affected by the court's decree, even if those individuals are not parties to the suit. In accomplishing their task, monitors generally play a less intrusive role than special masters or receivers.

Receivers

Receivers are neutral agents of the court often recommended by various parties to the federal lawsuit (Sims, 2010). Receivership represents a judicial determination that the operator of an organization may be unwilling or incapable of acting in good faith toward compliance with a judgment.[14] Receivership is used to denote a situation in which an institution or enterprise is being held by a receiver. In law, a receiver is a person "placed in the custodial responsibility for the property of others, including tangible and intangible assets and rights" (Philip & Kaminski, 2007, p. 30). Various types of receiver appointments exist:

1. a receiver appointed by a (government) regulatory agency pursuant to a statute

2. a privately appointed receiver
3. a court-appointed receiver

The receiver's powers flow from the document(s) underlying his or her appointment—a statute, financing agreement, or court order. A receiver can be given quite extensive responsibilities. In some cases, they have been appointed to run parts of governments or businesses (Satori Alternative Dispute Resolution, 2014).

Special masters and monitors aid the court in the adjudication of a suit. Courts charge receivers, in contrast, with the active custody and management of an entity.[15] Thus, unlike special masters and monitors, the receivers completely displace the defendants: The receiver makes large and small decisions, spends the organization's funds, and controls hiring and firing determinations (Bradley, 2007; United States General Accounting Office, 2004).

A receiver is a disinterested person or organization whom the court appoints to safeguard property that is the subject of diverse claims. In the 1970s, federal courts began to assign receivers to temporarily take over the function of administrative bodies that violated constitutional standards. Throughout the 1970s and 1980s, courts used receivers to mandate sweeping reforms in prison conditions. One observer commented:

> Court orders had an enormous impact on the nation's jails and prisons by direct regulation, their indirect effects, and the shadow they cast. Among the areas affected were staffing, the amount of space per inmate, medical and mental health care, food, hygiene, sanitation, disciplinary procedures, conditions in disciplinary segregation, exercise, fire safety, inmate classification, grievance policies, race discrimination, sex discrimination, religious discrimination and accommodations, and disability discrimination and accommodations—in short, nearly all aspects of prison and jail life. (Schlanger, 2006, p. 550)

More recent examples of court-appointed receivers include:

- In the District of Columbia, the jail's medical care facility was placed under court-ordered receivership in August 1995, after the District was held in contempt for repeatedly failing to implement court orders intended to ensure adequate medical services to jail inmates (Ekstrand, 2000). The receivership ended in September 2000 (United States General Accounting Office, 2004).
- An insolvent fuel company has been managed by a court-appointed receiver (Evans, 2007).
- A U.S. District Judge appointed a receiver for the multilevel marketing company Equinox International in August 1999 (Geer, 1999). The receiver was authorized to distribute settlement funds from the now-defunct company to approved claimants (Evans, 2007).

- In February 2007, a judge in Florida appointed a receiver for companies owned by Lou Perlman that defrauded investors (Huntley, 2007).

After placing the California state prison health care system into receivership in June 2005 (United States General Accounting Office, 2004), U.S. District Judge Thelton Henderson appointed a receiver for it in February 2006 (Moore, 2007). In this case, the court appointed an administrator to prevent imminent or irreparable harm to the parties' rights and interests. The receiver's charge in these situations is to ensure certainty in the execution of a court's order (CWP Advisors, 2014; Feldman, 1991). After months of consent decrees, hearings, expert testimony, and negotiation, Judge Henderson commented on the California prison healthcare system's "depravity" and ruled that it violated the Constitution's Eighth Amendment prohibition against cruel and unusual punishment (California Health Care Services, 2014). Henderson estimated that on average, an inmate in one of California's prisons needlessly died every six to seven days. He ordered a receiver to take over the healthcare functions of the California Department of Corrections (CDC) as soon as possible.[16]

The California Receivers Forum is a nonprofit organization formed by interested receivers, attorneys, accountants, and property managers, with support from the Los Angeles Superior Court, to address the needs and concerns of receivers, to facilitate communication between the receivership community and the courts, and to assist in raising the level of professionalism of receivers throughout the state. Court-appointed receivers are the most powerful and independent of the judicially appointed managers (Bradley, 2007). It is important to recognize that because receiverships consume a large portion of a court's time and shift the court from its traditional role as passive arbiter of the facts into a role as an active supervisor through its appointed agent, courts hesitate to impose receivership unless other remedies are clearly inadequate. There is no compelling reason, however, for a court to wait until severe noncompliance has transpired or a defendant has flouted statutes and consent decrees before the court exercises the full scope of its equitable power.

POST-RECEIVER/SPECIAL MASTER/MONITOR

Once a receivership (or SM or monitorship) is completed, the court-appointed agent should be discharged from her or his duties. Depending on the type of receivership, for example, this is accomplished either by a letter from the appointing creditor or by petition to and order of the court. The next step for the organization is to determine its best course of action relative to continuing operations. With respect to these continuing operations, the organization can benefit considerably from the efforts of the SM, receiver, or monitor by demonstrating that it can fulfill the court's mandates following the departure of the SM, receiver, or monitor. Long-term, it is in the organization's best interests to demonstrate the institutionalization of the expected behaviors or actions by the organization and its leader (i.e., new norms or behaviors are infused throughout the organization—resulting in significant culture change).

SMs, monitors, and receivers can evaluate the situation, devise a plan of action, and execute that plan. It is imperative that HRM professionals and other organizational leaders ensure that their organization have legal counsel who are experienced with court-appointed agents and who have an understanding of the realities surrounding federal lawsuits. In summary, HRM professionals must recognize that the appointment of a SM, receiver, or monitor is a demonstrated value-adding tool that should not be overlooked when their organizations are faced with a federal lawsuit.

In the end, regardless of whether it is a special master, receiver, or monitor appointed by the court, HRM professionals must understand that each offers a mechanism through which the courts can assume oversight and supervision of those who fail to comply with the requirements of a federal lawsuit. Each court-appointed agent can prove to be a cost-effective means by which to limit the parties' dispute and provide a means by which a case can more easily be resolved. The next section of this chapter provides a brief look at the federal lawsuit the authors were involved in as they served in the roles of court-appointed special master (Veres), receiver (Sims), and monitor (Sauser). More specifically, the section focuses on the background events leading up to and the imposition of the receivership. It should be noted that the special master had been engaged as a court-appointed agent in July 1998 and, clearly, prior to the imposition of the receivership and appointment of the monitor.

BACKGROUND EVENTS LEADING UP TO AND THE IMPOSITION OF THE RECEIVERSHIP AT THE PERSONNEL BOARD OF JEFFERSON COUNTY, ALABAMA

On January 4, 1974, the Personnel Board of Jefferson County, Alabama was sued for maintaining discriminatory hiring and promotion practices in violation of the Fourteenth Amendment, Title VII of the Civil Rights Act of 1964, and other federal statutes. Several similar lawsuits followed, with similar claims. In 1981, the Personnel Board entered into a binding consent decree, which required the elimination of longstanding discriminatory employment practices. As amended in 1995, the consent decree required the Personnel Board to establish and maintain job selection procedures that complied with the *Uniform Guidelines on Employee Selection Procedures*—a highly technical set of test specifications and standards promulgated by the U.S. Equal Employment Opportunity Commission (Department of Labor, 1978).

The United States District Court gave the Personnel Board more than two decades to comply with its obligations under the consent decree and applicable state and federal laws. During this time, untold millions of dollars were wasted by a mismanaged Personnel Board that achieved little toward complying with the consent decree (*Receiver's Final Report*, 2006).

As noted in the *Memorandum Opinion* (2002), from December of 1995 until mid-1998, the Personnel Board abjectly failed to comply with the requirements of the 1995 Modification Order, *missing every deadline set by the court* in the face of repeated objections by the other parties. By June of 1998, the Personnel Board had not developed lawful selection procedures for any of the public safety positions, even though it was obligated to have completed all of them by that time. As further noted in the *Memorandum Opinion* (2002):

> Pursuant to its equity jurisdiction, a federal court has power to take broad remedial action to effectuate compliance with its orders. This equitable power includes the power to appoint a receiver.

> The appointment of a person to carry out functions the court deems necessary to provide full and complete relief is not a novelty in American jurisprudence. Receivers have been appointed to coerce public officials to comply with legal mandates in a number of factual settings, including public schools, housing, highways, nursing homes, and prisons.

> The mechanisms at work in the creation of . . . a receivership of a public institution, are fairly clear. The political process has failed to produce an institution conforming to law and those subjected to the illegality, who are usually politically powerless, turn to the courts for the vindication of their rights. Injunctive remedies are called for, but the judge lacks expertness in the particular field, and lacks time even when he chances to have the knowledge. Hence the appointment of adjunct officers who supply expert knowledge and sometimes implicitly encourage acceptance by the parties and the general public of the results of the judicial intervention. (p. 6)

Factors Considered

HRM professionals must understand that the appointment of a receiver to act in the place of elected and appointed officials is an extraordinary step warranted only by the most compelling circumstances. Essentially it is the remedy of last resort, and therefore, should be undertaken only when absolutely necessary. An important consideration is whether any other remedy is likely to be successful. Where more traditional remedies, such as contempt proceedings or injunctions, are inadequate under the circumstances, a court acting within its equitable powers is justified, particularly in aid of an outstanding injunction, in implementing less common remedies, such as a receivership, so as to achieve compliance with a constitutional mandate. Since appointing a receiver is typically viewed as a remedy of last resort, a court will not usually appoint a receiver if a less drastic remedy exists. Appointing a receiver is appropriate only when other approaches have failed to bring about compliance with a court's orders, whether through intransigence or incompetence (*Memorandum Opinion*, 2002; Philip & Kaminski, 2007).

At the time of the imposition of the receivership in this particular case, courts in the District of Columbia (where most of the reported receiverships had been imposed on public institutions) had identified six nonexhaustive factors to consider when determining whether other remedies were inadequate and the imposition of a receivership remained the only viable option for securing compliance with court orders. These included:

1. whether there were repeated failures to comply with the court's orders
2. whether further efforts to secure compliance would only lead to confrontation and delay
3. whether leadership is available that can turn the tide within a reasonable time period
4. whether there was bad faith
5. whether resources are being wasted
6. whether a receiver can provide a quick and efficient remedy (*Memorandum Opinion*, 2002, p. 7)

The next section provides a brief look at some of the litigation and factors related to the decision by the court to impose a receivership at the Personnel Board.

Relevant Historical Litigation

In making its determination on whether to impose a receivership or not the court reviewed the procedural and evidentiary record to determine, first, whether the Personnel Board should be held in civil contempt and, if so, whether application of the factors enumerated above lead to the conclusion that the appointment of a receiver was warranted (see *Memorandum Opinion*, 2002; *Receiver's 90 Day Report*, 2002; *Receiver's Final Report*, 2006). In order to facilitate the comprehensive factual review necessary to an examination of these issues, the court drew upon prior court opinions and the uncontested factual statements contained in the parties' briefs.[17]

The history of the case involving the Personnel Board was very long and consisted of an amalgam of three consolidated and two intervening class actions. Clearly it is beyond the scope of this short chapter to tell the whole story; interested readers can examine the hundreds of pages of history contained in the documents cited above and listed in note 17. As stated in the court's *Memorandum Opinion* (2002), the "case already [is] older than the average college student; January 4, 2003 will mark its 29th 'birthday,' if such a thing were cause for celebration" (p. 9). Over the life of litigation related to the Personnel Board, various court orders had been addressed on appeal eight times: once by the former Fifth Circuit, six times by the present Eleventh Circuit, and once by the Supreme Court.

Board Members' Failure to Understand and Enforce the Consent Decree

An important factor in the court's consideration to impose a receivership was the recognition of the lack of awareness and understanding of the requirements of the 1981 consent decree, 1995 modification order, and other court orders manifested by the three persons who controlled the Personnel Board as an entity. It appeared that the three board members had shirked their responsibilities under the consent decree and modification orders largely because they had no idea what those obligations were.

During evidentiary hearings, it was noted that the board members were not familiar with either the 1981 consent decree or the 1995 modification order. Nor had they read (or were familiar with) the Eleventh Circuit's *Ensley II* decision, met with Personnel Board staff to discuss the decision, developed a strategic plan, or hired new staff in response to that decision. For the court, such evidence unmistakably demonstrated that the board members failed to apprehend their legal obligations, or take any steps—much less meaningful steps—to ensure compliance.

The Personnel Board repeatedly had failed to disclose its noncompliance to the court and the parties until the deadline for compliance had passed. Faced with the Personnel Board's noncompliance, it was determined that either the court or the parties had to confront the Personnel Board, thereby frustrating the efforts of the court and parties to effectuate compliance with the consent decree, wasting the court's and the parties' time and resources, and unnecessarily delaying the development and implementation of lawful selection procedures.

The court noted that in *Ensley II*, the Eleventh Circuit saw through the Board's attempts to obfuscate its slothful efforts to comply with the 1981 consent decree, and directed the district court to issue an order with "teeth," to force the Personnel Board to develop and implement lawful race- and gender-neutral selection procedures (*Memorandum Opinion*, 2002). Despite the order, from December of 1995 until mid-1998, the Personnel Board failed to comply with the 1995 modification order, missing every court-imposed deadline, despite the parties' objections (*Receiver's Final Report*, 2006). At some point, the Personnel Board certainly must have realized that it could not meet each of those deadlines but chose not to disclose its inability to do so until the deadlines had passed. By June of 1998, the Personnel Board had not developed lawful selection procedures for *even one* public safety position, let alone *all*, as it was required to have done.

The Lack of Viable Leadership

Based on the facts above, the court concluded that neither the Personnel Board's staff nor the individual board members had competently discharged their duties. The individual board members lacked knowledge about their responsibilities under the 1981 consent decree or 1995 modification order. It was noted by the court that "Such ignorance is shocking, when one considers the Board members were deposed in connection with the present proceedings almost one year after they had been subjected to criminal contempt proceedings" (*Memorandum Opinion*, 2002, p. 77). Further, the Personnel Board's staff had been chronically deficient in size, qualifications, organization, training, and ability. Moreover, poor interpersonal relations among staff constituted a further impediment to progress.

Board Members Lacked an Understanding of Its Legal Obligations

In addition to the individual board members' ignorance of court orders, they also lacked basic knowledge of employee selection procedures, the requirements of Title VII, or the *Uniform Guidelines*, and never undertook any real effort to educate themselves about those subjects. Not only had board members failed to undertake these important actions, but—due to their failure to acquire even the most basic knowledge of federal requirements—they had been forced to defer to Personnel Board staff and counsel as to all facets of compliance with the court's decrees.

It was noted by the court, "Instead of assuming responsibility for the Personnel Board's compliance, the individual board members, because they lacked relevant knowledge, skills, and abilities, simply acted as rubber stamps" (*Memorandum Opinion*, 2002, p. 79). Based on this record, it was determined by the court that the three board members lacked the leadership to discharge their duties under the consent decrees and, ultimately, the United States Constitution.

Staff Lacked Sufficient Competence to Discharge Its Obligations

In the years prior to the imposition of the receivership the Personnel Board had relied heavily on various outside consultants. This could be interpreted as a tacit admission that the board staff lacked the in-house competence to develop lawful selection procedures. Further, even those employees hired specifically by the Personnel Board to assist with its efforts to comply with the 1995 modification order lacked experience in the development of selection procedures for a government employer, and with selection procedures challenged in litigation.

The Personnel Board's ineffective "hit or miss" efforts to develop selection procedures for the job classifications remaining under court scrutiny clearly demonstrated the lack of internal staff competence (*Memorandum Opinion*, 2002). For example, consider that in an attempt to comply with the court's May 24, 2001 order, the Personnel Board or its retained consultants created selection procedures and provided validation reports for 56 classifications. The Personnel Board's staff failed to recognize (or admit) that any of the newly developed procedures had problems of any sort. When, finally, the Personnel Board retained a competent outside consulting firm to conduct a review of the selection procedures developed for 33 of the 56 classifications, the firm identified at least 15 needing total redevelopment, with the remainder requiring varying degrees of revision. For each of those procedures, a Personnel Board staff member was responsible for supervision of the consultant's efforts, yet no Personnel Board staff member ever identified, or advised the parties or the court, that any selection procedure actually was inadequate.

Personnel Board's Structure: Impediment to Development of Staff Competence

By segregating its consent decree efforts from the development of non-consent decree selection procedures, the Personnel Board had created a situation in which the institutionalization of competence in the development of lawful selection procedures—whether by contact with outside consultants, the parties, experts, or the special master—remained cabined within the consent decree team (*Memorandum Opinion*, 2002; *Receiver's Final Report*, 2006). The inappropriate structural design was further evidence that the Personnel Board's staff suffered from a lack of internal leadership (*Receiver's 90-Day Report*, 2002; *Receiver's Second Transition Plan*, 2006).

The transcripts of depositions conducted by the parties during May of 2002 revealed a longstanding "poisoned" work environment in which the staff members regarded one another with varying degrees of suspicion and distrust and appeared to be more focused on such issues than in accomplishing their day-to-day duties and responsibilities. While the divisions among staff did not appear to be solely based on race, there were some staff members who believed that management decisions were motivated by such considerations.

Based on the factors and history above, the court found that there was indeed clear and convincing evidence for a *prima facie* case of civil contempt. Thus, the burden shifted to the Personnel Board to show either that it had not violated the court's orders or that it should be excused for noncompliance. In such a situation, a defendant like the Personnel Board could be excused from complying only where it had made in good faith *all* reasonable efforts to comply (*Memorandum Opinion*, 2002).

The Personnel Board did not deny that it violated the court orders; rather, the Personnel Board argued that it made "good faith attempts to perform [its] professional and constitutional duties." The Personnel Board professes that its "'willingness and desire' to develop lawful selection procedures had ripened into a realization that competent leadership, reorganization of the entity, and significant investment in developing and maintaining technical competence among the staff were requisites for completing the Personnel Board's obligations under the consent decree." The Personnel Board pointed to "the thousands of pages of technical materials created by" the Personnel Board as evidence of its efforts to comply with the decrees (*Memorandum Opinion*, 2002, p. 88).

Unfortunately for the Personnel Board, the court was not convinced that the Personnel Board made all reasonable efforts to comply with the decrees. The record had established that the Personnel Board was unwilling to comply with the consent decree and subsequent modification orders, failed to devote sufficient resources to its compliance efforts, failed to coordinate consent decree related activities, failed to hire and train sufficient qualified staff or otherwise provide sufficient resources, and inadequately supervised its consent decree-related projects. The Personnel Board had not designated any staff to oversee compliance efforts until June of 1999 and did not formulate a plan to comply with the decrees until November of 2000. In addition, the Personnel Board did not adequately monitor the work of the consultants it hired to develop the remaining selection procedures. Apart from hiring one industrial/organizational psychologist during 1999, the Personnel Board took no other steps to ensure that its staff possessed the technical competence necessary to bring the Personnel Board into compliance with the requirements of federal law. Throughout, the three board members remained quite ignorant of the Personnel Board's obligations.

Accordingly, despite the Personnel Board's protestations that it "tried its best" (Memorandum of Opinion, 2002, p. 89), the court found that the Personnel Board did not make all reasonable efforts to comply with the decree and that it did not act with reasonable diligence to seek relief from the decree when compliance became difficult. As noted in the *Memorandum Opinion* (2002), the court—based on the consideration of precedent cases—determined that other remedies were inadequate and that the imposition of a receivership remained the only viable option for securing compliance with court orders. In making this determination, the court had focused on the following factors: whether there were repeated failures to comply with the court's orders, whether further efforts to secure compliance would only lead to confrontation and delay, whether leadership is available that can turn the tide within a reasonable time period, whether there was bad faith, whether resources were being wasted, and whether a receiver could provide a quick and efficient remedy. The court carefully examined each of those factors in the context of the Personnel Board case.

Based on the review of the procedural history of the Personnel Board litigation and factors considered in the imposition of a receiver, the court determined that there was no question that the Personnel Board repeatedly had failed to comply with the court's orders since the consent decree was entered in 1981. In addition, the Personnel Board had continually earned the criticism of the parties, the district court, and the Eleventh Circuit for its failure to accomplish the goals established by the 1981 consent decree, the 1995 modification order, and subsequent orders of the court.

The court had become convinced that further efforts to secure compliance would lead only to more confrontation, frustration, and delay. Furthermore, the court already had done all it could to ensure compliance through less drastic means than appointing a receiver. For example, despite his hard work, the special master (Veres) appointed in July of 1998 had been, at best, only moderately successful in spurring the Personnel Board to fulfill its responsibilities under the consent decree; he *was* successful in assisting the parties' efforts to narrow the scope of those job classifications subject to additional litigation to four police, five fire, and 57 nonpublic safety positions. However, despite the court's December 18, 2000, order imposing a more generous schedule than the one proposed by the Personnel Board for the completion of its remaining tasks, the special master's efforts (a) to encourage the Personnel Board's adherence to that schedule and (b) to facilitate the development of lawful selection procedures met with markedly less success *because the Personnel Board refused to follow many of the recommendations provided by the special master,* who had no authority to intervene in the day-to-day decision making and operations of the Personnel Board.

The special master reported that his efforts had been frustrated by defensiveness on the part of the Personnel Board's staff. For example, the special master had reported that the parties' pre-monthly status conference meetings—designed, in part, to resolve issues of testing methodology—were characterized by evasiveness and defensiveness on the part of the Personnel Board's staff.

Perhaps the most striking aspect of the Personnel Board's failure to meet deadlines imposed by paragraph 19 of the December 18, 2000, order may be these facts: The Personnel Board was intimately involved in the determination of those milestones by which the pace of its progress would be measured and consented to the imposition of each. As a result of this and other factors, it appeared to the court that the Personnel Board was habituated to the "casual pace" condemned by the Eleventh Circuit almost seven years ago. A further illustration of the Personnel Board's lethargy was contained in its most recent monthly status report, wherein the Personnel Board "only now, some twenty years after the fact, asks for 'clarification' of language contained in its 1981 *consent* decree" (*Memorandum Opinion,* 2002, p. 48).

Therefore, to comply with the mandate of the Eleventh Circuit, "to bring [the] truth home" (p. 30) to the Personnel Board, the court determined that it was left with no choice but that of putting "teeth" into its orders through the initiation of criminal contempt proceedings, to compel the Personnel Board to discharge duties which it had neglected for more than two decades. The court considered civil contempt proceedings but determined that a civil remedy would be inappropriate and ineffective.

It was determined by the court that further monetary sanctions, in the form of a fine, would be impotent as a motivational tool, because of the vast sums of money that already had been expended in the Personnel Board case, to no avail. More importantly, the cost of monetary sanctions ultimately would be borne by the taxpaying citizens of those governmental entities served by the Personnel Board, and thus would not have the "teeth" necessary to spur compliance.

The most compelling basis for the court's conclusion that other sanctions were inadequate, however, was the fact that even the threat of criminal contempt sanctions against the three individual Personnel Board members did not inspire those individuals to ascertain their constitutional obligations. The court found the total abdication of responsibility to be shocking and agreed with the blunt assessment of one of the parties: "The board members have done nothing because they have not bothered to find out what the courts have ordered them to do" (*Memorandum Opinion,* 2002, p. 94).

The Personnel Board lacked the leadership to turn the tide toward compliance within a reasonable period of time. In addition, the Personnel

Board's former personnel director was on administrative leave pending retirement. Further, those employees who had training and experience in the development of selection procedures had either resigned or been terminated. Two of the three board members had resigned their appointments. As a result of this leadership void, the Personnel Board's staff was not functioning productively. There did not appear to be anyone employed by the Personnel Board who could successfully lead the organization to fulfill its professional and constitutional obligations.

Given events noted above, the court also was concerned about the good faith of the Personnel Board to accomplish its constitutionally mandated goals of developing lawful, race- and gender-neutral employee selection procedures. The court noted the following: When discussing "good faith" as a defense to a motion for imposition of civil contempt sanctions in *LaShawn A. v. Kelly*, the District Court for the District of Columbia wrote (*Memorandum Opinion*, 2002, p. 94):

> [D]efendant's [sic] good faith is arguable at best. The remedial history outlined above demonstrates that the defendants have repeatedly attempted last-minute adjustments or compromises in an attempt to avoid sanctions. Because this pattern has persistently recurred since 1991, the Court must question whether the defendants truly intend to cooperate in the remedial efforts. Additionally, the defendants' recent actions cast an extremely bad light on their alleged good intentions.

Time and again, the court had observed similar last-minute adjustments or compromises in an attempt to avoid sanctions. It was time for the court to take more drastic action and appoint a receiver to oversee directly the Personnel Board's work to achieve compliance with its professional and constitutional obligations.

IMPOSITION OF RECEIVERSHIP AS REMEDY FOR CIVIL CONTEMPT

As evidenced by the discussion in the previous section, the members of the Personnel Board, the jurisdictions served by the Personnel Board, and the public at large had established a clear pattern of accepting inferior performance from the Personnel Board. Unfortunately, ongoing oversight and supervision by the federal court had come to be viewed as a normal and acceptable part of doing business at the Personnel Board. While the pre-receiver leadership of the Personnel Board may have viewed this situation as tolerable, the federal court clearly did not.

On July 8, 2002, the federal judge overseeing the case appointed one of the authors (Sims) to serve as the receiver at the pleasure of the federal district court (Battaglio & Condrey, 2006; *United States of America v. Jefferson County, Alabama, et al.*, 2002, p. 20). Battaglio and Condrey refer to the imposition of the receivership at the Personnel Board as "the unique chapter in the history of civil service reform in the United States. The federal court-ordered reforms imposed on the board are the only such instance of its kind that could be determined by the authors" (2006, p. 131; see also, Sims, 2010). In a sense one could say that the federal court-ordered reform was both an effort at modernization while at the same time an effort to avoid the complete abolition of the Personnel Board as called for by a number of politicians and municipalities in Jefferson County.

In describing his rationale for appointment of a receiver, the federal judge noted the following:

- "Pursuant to its equity jurisdiction, a federal court has power to take broad remedial action to effectuate compliance with its orders. This equitable power includes the power to appoint a receiver."
- "The appointment of a person to carry out functions the court deems necessary to provide full and complete relief is not a novelty in American jurisprudence."
- "The court has the power, pursuant to its equity jurisdiction, to take broad remedial action to secure compliance with its orders, including the power to appoint a receiver."
- "Public officials who fail to abide by legal standards are not immune to these remedies. . . . A court with equity jurisdiction has the discretion to appoint a receiver to take over the main functions of public officials" (*Memorandum Opinion*, 2002, pp. 5–6; Sims, 2010).
- Receivers have been appointed "to coerce public officials to comply with legal mandates in a number of factual settings, including public schools, housing, highways, nursing homes, and prisons."

The mechanisms at work in the creation of . . . a receivership of a public institution, are fairly clear. The political process has failed to produce an institution conforming to law and those subjected to the illegality, who are usually politically powerless, turn to the courts for the vindication of their rights. Injunctive remedies are called for, but the judge lacks expertness in the particular field, and lacks time even when he chances to have the knowledge. Hence the appointment of adjunct officers who supply expert knowledge and sometimes implicitly encourage acceptance by the parties and the general public of the results of the judicial intervention. (*Memorandum Opinion*, 2002, p. 6)

In conclusion, the court found that the extraordinary step of imposing a receivership on the Personnel Board was the only means of providing a quick and efficient remedy. The court noted that while the terms "quick" and "efficient" were foreign in the context of this litigation, due to its tortured history, the court was persuaded that, with the proper receiver in place, the Personnel Board's obligations under the consent decree, at long last, would be fulfilled. Moreover, appointing a receiver appeared to the court the most expedient way of ending federal judicial oversight of the Personnel Board, and returning it to local authority in full compliance with its constitutional mandate. This mandate clearly had been disrupted over the years as the Personnel Board muddled along doing little to reform itself despite the court's and several other federal judges' efforts over several decades.

RECEIVER'S POWER AND CHARGES

The court-appointed receiver was ordered by the federal judge to "manage and control property and employees, and perform contractual, financial, legal and personnel duties" of the Personnel Board (*United States of America v. Jefferson County, Alabama, et al.*, 2002, p. 2). In short, Dr. Sims was appointed to take over and completely reform the operations of the Personnel Board. The factual history giving rise to the appointment of a receiver of the Personnel Board was partially described earlier in this chapter and is thoroughly set out in the lengthy and extraordinarily detailed July 2002 opinion of the federal judge (see *Memorandum Opinion*, 2002). As detailed in the judge's findings, the Personnel Board had become ineffective as an organization. Too often, the Personnel Board had failed in its mission to provide Jefferson County, the City of Birmingham, and numerous other employers with highly qualified candidates for public service. Even worse, the Personnel Board had failed to develop job selection procedures that complied with the requirements of federal law.

As ordered by the U.S. District Court, the ultimate mission of the receiver was to:

> transform the Board into a strong and competent civil service agency with a clearly defined mission, the infrastructure, systems, and skills to support that mission, and an agency that discharged all functions in an efficient, professional, and cost-effective manner in substantial compliance with all applicable federal and state laws. (Memorandum Opinion, 2002, p. 6)

Ultimately, the purpose of the Personnel Board was to deliver efficient, professional, and cost-effective service to local governments, their employees, applicants for employment, and the public at large. Central to the work of the receiver, therefore, was the task of refocusing the Personnel Board and its employees on the potential satisfaction of working in an organization that not only fulfilled its mission, but did so in an exemplary manner. Otherwise, the task of sustaining "valid selection criteria" would prove impossible, if not meaningless.

Accordingly, the overriding goal of the receivership imposed by the court was that of creating an instructive collaboration among the receiver and Personnel Board employees, with the advice of consultants, so that authority and responsibility were progressively assumed by the Personnel Board and its employees during the course of the process, resulting in the legacy of a strong and competent Personnel Board team with a clearly defined mission, and the systems and skills to support that mission in a manner that met the requirements of the Constitution and federal law in all respects.

It was clear to the receiver and the court that the accomplishment of those goals sketched above would require more skills than just those of devising valid selection procedures. The receiver and his consultants had to be able to gain the confidence of Personnel Board's employees and other stakeholders across the political spectrum. This would require conflict resolution skills and sensitivity to (and concomitant ability to communicate with) diverse groups with deeply held positions. Any effective resolution of the Personnel Board's difficulties also would depend, at least in part, on establishing communications systems and conflict resolution procedures in a climate in which diversity is respected. Further, the longstanding failure of the Personnel Board to meet its obligations under the 1981 consent decree and 1995 modification order argued for a receiver with demonstrated expertise in changing dysfunctional organizational cultures. The details of the work of the receiver are documented in detail in Sims' (2010) volume, and are not repeated here. These efforts to reform/transform the Personnel Board took the better part of three years of hard work on the part of the receiver and his team.

THE FINAL RESULTS OF THE RECEIVERSHIP

After decades of stagnation, political resistance, incompetence, and expensive court proceedings, the work of a federally appointed receiver finally accomplished the following objectives:

Focused the Organization on Its Critical Mission

One of the major outcomes of the receivership was that the reform effort confronted ingrained political and organizational resistance to catalyze the thawing of systemic gridlock/inertia and to effectuate strategic investments in qualified human talent, infrastructure, and technology. Today, the strategic investments pushed by the receiver are being leveraged to effectively perform mission critical work at significant cost savings to Jefferson County taxpayers. Essentially, the receiver forced the necessary strategic investments to build solid internal capacity. Merit system employees and the taxpayers of Jefferson County are realizing significant returns from the strategic investments. This is in sharp contrast to the abysmal return on investment and abject dysfunction (e.g., inability to provide qualified talent for the merit system jobs, legal entanglement, employment discrimination, court condemnation, employee distrust, poor public organizational image) that resulted from the millions spent over decades on consultant and attorneys' fees to preserve the status quo of the Personnel Board's operations. These prior (significant) expenditures of public resources did not produce the necessary changes to correct the problems in the system or build organizational accountability and capacity to effectively deliver on the agency's mission. Sadly, much of the substantial money spent prior to the court's imposition of the receivership represent squandered public resources!

Instituted Regulations, Procedures, and Methodologies

The receiver instituted regulations, procedures, and methodologies to ensure that the Personnel Board's activities were focused on adherence to the applicable laws (state and federal) and consistent with best practices in the field of human resource management. Reforms during the receivership also provided *fair access to public employment* within Jefferson County by establishing nondiscriminatory and job related testing procedures for the county.

Leveraged Technology

Technology was leveraged to:

1. *expand access to employment opportunities* (e.g., allowing individuals to search job listings and apply for merit system positions 24/7 from anywhere in the world) within the Jefferson County merit system
2. *increase efficiency* (e.g., significant cycle time improvements in high-impact areas; reduction in manual and labor intensive-data entry; improved management reporting, analysis, and accountability)
3. *improve cost-effectiveness* of the system

Improved Service Quality and Innovation

The receivership also led to *improved service quality and innovation.* Before the receivership, the jurisdictions served by the Personnel Board suffered tremendously from the dysfunction and paralysis in the Personnel Board's operations. Critical jobs went unfilled because of the Personnel Board's inability to formulate qualified pools of competent individuals for hire in a timely manner. This resulted in secondary problems such as increased overtime costs, poor service delivery to the public due to inadequate staffing of functions, and poor worker morale. All of this occurred while the operating costs of the merit system increased steadily. Since the time of the receivership, the critical service metrics of the agency have improved continuously (e.g., availability of quality candidates, turn-around time on business processes), and operating costs have declined every year for the past four years. The current Personnel Board has stripped its badge of dishonor (duly awarded for decades of malaise, dysfunction, and discrimination) and has evolved as a transparent example of best practices and innovation in the public sector human resource operations. Merit system employees now have a system with restored integrity, and the taxpayers of Jefferson County can now see tangible returns on their substantial investment in the system. The Personnel Board has in recent years been recognized for innovation in the areas of employee selection and training and for the application of technology in the public sector.

COURT-APPOINTED MONITOR

In the spring of 2005, the receiver and the three-member board worked together to ensure a smooth transition of power from the receiver back to the three-member board. On July 11, 2005, full authority for the Personnel Board's operations officially returned to the three-member board. This included authority over the Personnel Board's day-to-day operations, finances, contracts, budget, staff, and overall management. Would the three-member board be able to operate in a manner that would keep the receiver's reforms underway? That critical question had to be answered in the affirmative before the court would release the board from its supervision. Although the court had not yet released or discharged the receiver, he was no longer onsite and had no operational responsibilities. The court indicated, however, that a monitor would likely be appointed to observe and report on the Personnel Board's progress in fully complying with the consent decree. The monitor would be an agent of the court and be completely independent of the parties.

On November 15, 2005, the court issued an order appointing a court monitor (Sauser) to oversee the efforts of the Personnel Board to comply with its obligations under its 1981 consent decree, as modified in 1995, and extended in December of 2000, and to assist the court and the parties in determining the Personnel Board's ability and commitment to function in compliance with Federal law absent judicial supervision. The court further specified in part that:

- The monitor, as an agent of the court, is independent of the parties and under the direct control and supervision of the court.
- The monitor has no authority to intervene in the administrative management of the Personnel Board.
- The monitor has the responsibility of investigating facts that may bear on the Personnel Board's compliance with its obligations under the consent decree, or on the Personnel Board's ability and commitment to function in compliance with federal law absent judicial supervision.

As one would expect with any reform effort like that at the Personnel Board of Jefferson County, the change did not end with the receiver no longer being physically onsite at the agency after August 26, 2005. Under the leadership of the new personnel director, the reform momentum continued at the Personnel Board, although not without a number of twists and turns that perplexed the court, the special master, and the monitor.

As noted above, the monitor had no power to make decisions about the Personnel Board; instead, his role was to observe meetings and actions of the Personnel Board, stay in contact with legal counsel for all the parties involved, report his findings to the court on a frequent (at least monthly) basis, and advise the court on possible actions that the judge might order. The monitor thus functioned in a complex role that included being a careful observer, a mediator among the parties to the suit, and a consultant to the court and the parties on how to meet the obligations of the consent decree. The work was intense and demanding and drew on all the monitor's skills as an industrial/organizational psychologist and management consultant.

After many twists and turns (including additional contempt-of-court hearings, a breach of test security, and elections of new public officials), the Personnel Board succeeded in convincing the court on November 20, 2009 (three years after the monitor became involved in the case) that the Personnel Board had had met all its obligations, and the Personnel Board was at last released from federal court supervision.

SUMMARY OF THE EXPERIENCE

What can be learned from this lengthy case? An important lesson for HRM professionals to learn from these efforts to reform the Personnel Board of Jefferson County is that reforming a public HRM function, let alone a public HRM agency, cannot be accomplished overnight, even when the force of a federal court is behind the reform; it requires making reform the norm and increasing its velocity. As such, in order for public HRM professionals (and their organizations) to fulfill their role when confronted with a federal lawsuit, the organization and its leaders must continually reform (and some would say transform) within the bounds of local, state, and federal mandates to deliver on the organization's promises. The organization must be focused on its mission, regardless of the methods (i.e., traditional, reformation, privatization, or outsourcing) it uses to deliver its services (Condrey, 2005).

HRM professionals seeking to reform a public HRM entity that is part of a federal lawsuit should not look for a "magic change pill" or look to the latest change management fad or quick fix, but rather, they should concentrate on the three components of holistic organization transformation (Sims, 2010; Walker, 2002): people, process, and technology. In particular, everything that has been presented regarding public HRM professionals and reform as part of a federal lawsuit or consent decree has as its most significant linchpin—*people*. Nothing gets done without people. And in the end, it is the people served by a public HRM function or agency that are the ultimate beneficiaries of these reformation/transformation efforts.

All the theories, modeling techniques, analysis, and technology will mean nothing if adequate attention is not given to the real authors and benefactors of public HRM reform—HRM professionals and other people in the organization. HRM professionals must understand that regardless of the legal issues, mutual *trust* must be established. Trust must be *earned*. In order to establish a *trust organization*, HRM professionals and other organizational leaders responsible for leading reform must first be *trustworthy*. Public HRM professionals when confronted with the legal issues or challenges that come with a federal lawsuit must work to help create an environment that embraces open communication. This openness means that critics and supporters have equal voice in any public HRM reform initiative.

The efforts to reform the Personnel Board also illustrate how important it is for HRM professionals to understand what radical reform in public HRM means versus process improvements, which only creates more efficient execution of *existing* processes. Such reform is an ongoing process that permeates the entire public HRM function or agency and represents a sharp break with the past. This break is a major difference between holistic public HRM reform and a simple or more narrow reform. The kind of public HRM reform as that accomplished by the Personnel Board may be viewed as an attempt to go down the same path more efficiently, yet such reform involves HRM professionals understanding the importance of the development or discovery of entirely new paths. This example supports the idea of the value of public HRM reform when conducted by HRM professionals, and in most contexts the work of reform is tied closely to *innovation*.

Another lesson for HRM professionals from the effort to reform the Personnel Board focuses on what Kotter (1996) refers to as the necessity for creating a crisis (or sense of urgency) without creating panic. The importance of this is presented by Burke, Wilson, and Salas (2005) in their study of *highly reliable organizations* (HROs). In their research, they call this step "unfreezing," and it is characterized as a precipitory *jolt* to the organization. Something must occur to convince the organization that *business as usual is not working*. In this case, it was the imposition of a receivership. Reforms have a greater chance of succeeding if something is done by HRM professionals and other organizational leaders to create a sense of urgency and to convince the organization that the status quo is no longer acceptable.

As has been reported in many sources, the biggest barrier to change or reform is the *organizational culture* (Smith, 2003). Kotter (1996) and others (see for example, Smith, 2003; Schraeder, Tears, & Jordan, 2005) discuss the challenges and approaches for changing culture. According to Kotter (1996), culture is *very hard to change*. Organizational culture at agencies like the Personnel Board and other organizational entities has been *reinforced* through incentives, human resource policy, and management style. However, in reality, the strengths and capabilities that have made a public HRM entity successful in the past may become irrelevant or even *inhibitive* to future success. In any case, reform requires new organizational models that better serve the public HRM customers. Successful public HRM reform demonstrates the success of new approaches that are superior to old methods or more appropriate given a new agency or government context. The fact remains: Culture does not change easily.

It is important for HRM professionals to understand that changing a culture must begin with *policies and incentives* that *drive behavior*. Incentives and HRM policy must align with new approaches that comprise a reform initiative. One of the greatest challenges and tools for HRM professionals in implementing reform, whether in a public HRM entity or other organization, is changing HRM policy. For example, establishing new job titles for new types of jobs can be so difficult that those leading civil service reform might be tempted just to give up. The best situation is where HRM professionals and other organizational leaders responsible for reform encounter public personnel who are also change or reform leaders who are not content with the status quo. Public HRM professionals should and must be enablers, not barriers, even when it means reforming their own function or agency.

Battaglio and Condrey (2006) recently noted, "The Personnel Board of Jefferson County, Alabama, illustrates a unique chapter in the history of civil service reform in the United States. The federal court-ordered reforms imposed on the board are the only such instance of its kind that could be determined by the authors" (2006, p. 131). While the experience described herein may indeed be unique, we hope this chapter adds to the growing body of knowledge related to legal issues, federal lawsuits, consent decrees, and civil service reform. We also hope it fosters a continuing effort to systematically analyze this and other civil service systems. Unlike change in the private industry sector—which is typically driven by the need to secure market share in an increasingly competitive global economy—change in public sector organizations is often a reaction to political, regulatory, and (in our situation) legal pressures.

LESSONS LEARNED AND RECOMMENDATIONS FOR HRM PROFESSIONALS

While reform in a government agency is always difficult, it is especially difficult when one considers the challenge of undertaking transformational reform (if there is such a thing) related to the development of a practice of administering lawful selection procedures. Developing lawful selection procedures is difficult enough on its own without the involvement of a federal court and multiple stakeholders or parties who have their own and most often conflicting expectations, demands, and agendas! But such was the case at the Personnel Board during the imposition of the receivership. In the end, HRM professionals must understand that administering lawful selection procedures requires simply following some of the employer best practices for testing and selection (Equal Employment Opportunity Commission, 2007) as advocated by the EEOC and the use of some agreed upon steps as follows:

- HRM professionals and their organizations should monitor selection procedures' results for evidence of adverse impact—substantially different rates of selection in hiring or promotion decisions that work to the disadvantage of a particular subgroup based upon race, gender, or ethnicity.
- HRM professionals and their organizations should ensure that employment tests and other selection procedures are properly validated for the positions and purposes for which they are used. If a selection procedure produces adverse impact, the test or selection procedure must be job-related, and this job-relatedness must be documented.
- HRM professionals and their organizations should ensure that tests and selection procedures are not adopted casually by managers who know little about these processes. A test or selection procedure can be an effective management tool, but no test or selection procedure should be implemented without an understanding of its effectiveness and limitations and its appropriateness for a specific job.
- If a selection procedure screens out a protected group, HRM professionals and their organizations should determine whether there

is an equally effective alternative selection procedure that has less adverse impact and, if so, adopt the alternative procedure.

- To ensure that a test or selection procedure remains predictive of success in a job, HRM professionals and their organizations should keep abreast of changes in job requirements and should update the test specifications or selection procedures accordingly.

In addition to the recommendations above, we suggest the following:

- Whatever processes are used to exclude people from further consideration or to select people to interview must meet EEOC guidelines as job-related selection procedures.
- When taking any action that excludes some applicants from further consideration, it is important that HRM professionals and their organizations use procedures that are structured, job-related, and as objective as possible.
- One way to make selection procedures more job-related is for HRM professionals and their organizations to do a job profile on the position to determine competencies and requirements.
- Employment tests, when well developed by HRM professionals and their organizations, should provide a consistent and fair basis on which to make employment decisions, making them less subject to intentional or unintentional bias.
- Professionally developed selection procedures serve a legitimate business purpose: They allow HRM professionals and their organizations to base hiring and promotional decisions on solid, job-related information.
- The evidence that a selection procedure measures behavior consistently (i.e., its reliability) and is an accurate measure of job performance (i.e., its validity) is the basis on which a selection procedure is shown to be job-related.
- Job-related procedures ensure that employees possess the necessary skills to perform the job; such procedures can be used by employers to predict which candidates will be able to successfully perform the job. In short, good selection procedures are fair to candidates (i.e., standardized and objective in their administration and scoring) and useful to organizations (i.e., result in gains in overall productivity).

HRM professionals involved in federal lawsuits like the one experienced by the Personnel Board that required the development of good selection procedures or tests should consider including the following suggestions (Lundquist, 2007):

1. Determine the need and appropriateness of testing.
2. Determine the necessary job requirements.
3. Develop tests to measure the job's requirements.
4. Collect data to evaluate test quality.
5. Collect data to evaluate job-relatedness.
6. Establish administrative procedures and controls.
7. Implement and monitor on a continuous basis the effectiveness of the test.

In concluding this chapter, we offer the following advice for HRM professionals who find themselves and their organizations confronted by legal issues, or more specifically federal lawsuits in the form of consent decrees:

1. Retain a competent and experienced legal counsel.
2. Never underestimate the intelligence of a federal judge and especially one who has retained a competent and experienced special master.
3. Be careful whom you choose as expert witnesses.
4. Do not undermine your case with ill-advised statements to the press.
5. Never withhold important information from your own legal counsel.
6. Don't depend on political contacts to shield you from the justice system.
7. Assemble your facts and organize your evidence carefully.
8. Make certain you have a clear, accurate, and current job description for every position.
9. Carefully document the job-relatedness of every test, interview process, application blank, or other device you use to make employment-related decisions.
10. If your past actions are indefensible, seek a settlement.
11. Communicate to all of the organization's employees the seriousness of a court order resulting in receivership.
12. Encourage senior leaders (and all employees) to cooperate with the parties and especially the special master, receiver, or monitor, as they are there to help. The sooner you partner with them, the sooner they will leave!
13. Understand what needs to be done to get out from under a court order or receivership—focus on the future by fixing things, not on the past.
14. Be proactive when you are able to have a voice and contribute to an agreement or settlement with the parties. Once a receivership is imposed, such an agreement will not likely be possible.
15. Institute regulations, procedures, and methodologies to ensure that the organization's activities are focused on adherence to applicable laws (state and federal) and are consistent with the best practices in the field of human resources management.

16. Commit to holistic HRM versus a simple or narrow reform or transformation of the organization's HRM areas.
17. Create an environment that embraces open communication and trust within the organization and among the various parties.

NOTES

1. *See* Halderman v. Pennhurst State School & Hosp., 446 F. Supp. 1295, 1326-1327 (e.D. Pa. 1978), aff'd, 612, F. 2s 84 (3d Cir. 1979).
2. *See* United States v. Hardage, 750 F. sup. 1460, 1471-72 (W.D. Okla. 1990) reviewing role played by special master during suit's liability phase); United States v. Hardage, 7 Fed. R. Serv. 3d 266, 272 (W.D. Okla. 1987) (court's reference order to master at the suit's outset).
3. *See* United States v. Moss-American, 78 F.R.D. 214. 215 (E.D. Wis. 1978).
4. City of Quincy v. Metropolitan Dist. Comm'n, Civ. No. 138, 477 (Mass. Super. Ct., Norfolk City, filed Dec. 17, 1982).
5. Silberman, *Masters and Magistrates Part II: The American Analogue*, 50 N.Y.U. L. REV. 1297, 1322 (1975); *see also* W.D. Brazil, *Authority to Refer Discovery Tasks to Special Masters: Limitations on Existing Sources and the Need for a New Federal Rule*, in Managing Complex Litigation: A Practical Guide to the Use of Special Masters 305, 337-64 (W. Brazil, G. Hazard & P. Rice eds., 1983).
6. See Coleman v. Schwarzenegger, 2:90-cv-00520-LKK-JFM (E.D. Cal.),
7. See. E.g., Morgan v. Kerrigan, 401 F. Supp. 216, 248, 265-67 (D. Mass. 1975), aff'd, 580 F.2d 401 (1st Cir.), cert. denied, 426 U.S. 935 (1976).
8. Note, Monitors: A New Equitable Remedy?. 70 YALE L.J. 108, 113 (1960).
9. Newman v. Alabama, 559 F. 2d 288, 290 (5th Cir.), reh'd denied, 504 F. 2d 97 (5th Cir. 1977), rev'd in part 438 U.S. 781 (1978).
10. Note, Implementation Problems in Institutional Reform Litigation, 91 HARV. L. REV. 428, 442 (1977).
11. Morgan v. Kerrigan, 401 F. Supp. 216, 248, 265-67 (D. Mass. 1975), aff'd, 580 F.2d 401 (1st Cir.), cert. denied, 426 U.S. 935 (1976).
12. Morales v. Turman, 364 F. Suppp. 166, 179 (E.D. Tex. 1973, *rev'd*, 535 F.2d 864 (5th Cir.), *reh'g denied*, 539 F. 2d 710 (5th Cir. 1976), *rev'd*, 430 U.S. 322 (1977). In *Morgan*, the court charged a 40-member monitoring council to "foster public awareness" and delegated to it the primary responsibility for monitoring implementation of the court's school desegregation order. 401 F. Supp. At 265-67. The court granted the council authority to hold public meetings, make recommendation to the court and the defendant Boston School Committee, and identify "unresolved problems" for consideration by the parties, the court, and "other appropriate persons." *Id.* The council, though, was not given managerial duties. *Id.*
13. *Morgan*, 401 F. Supp. At 266; Wyatt v. Stickney, 344 F. Supp. 387, 392 (M.D. Ala. 1972), *aff'd in part*, *remanded in part sub nom.* Wyatt v. Aderholt, 503 F.2d 1305 (5th Cir. 1974).

14. Johnson, *Equitable Remedies: An Analysis of Judicial Neoreceiverships to Implement Large Scale Fundamental Change,* 1976 Wis. L. Rev. 1166-67.
15. *See* 75 C.J.S. Receivers § 151, at 794 (1952).
16. *See* Madrid v. Gomez 889 F. Supp. 1146 (N.D. Cal. 1995)
17. *See* Personnel Board of Jefferson County's Response to Show Cause Order (*Memorandum Opinion,* 2002); United States' Reply to Personnel Board of Jefferson County's Response to Order to Show Cause Why it Should Not be Held in Civil Contempt (*Memorandum Opinion,* 2002); Wilks Class' Response to Court's Order Dated April 5, 2002 (*Memorandum Opinion, 2002*); Jefferson County's Memorandum Brief (doc. no. 916); Martin Plaintiffs' and Bryant Intervenors' Memorandum in Support of Their Order to Show Cause (*Memorandum Opinion,* 2002).

REFERENCES

Academy of Court Appointed Masters. (2009a). *Appointing special masters and other judicial adjuncts: A handbook for judges and lawyers.* Retrieved from http://www.fjc.gov/public/pdf.nsf/lookup/ACAM2009.pdf/$file/ACAM2009.pdf

Academy of Court Appointed Masters. (2009b). Appointed masters. Retrieved from http://www.courtappointedmasters.org/

Battaglio, R. P., & Condrey, S. E. (2006). Civil service reform: Examining state and local government cases. *Review of Public Personnel Administration, 26*(2), 116–118.

Bradley, C. M. (2007). Old remedies are new again: Deliberate indifference and the receivership in Plata v. Schwarzenegger. *New York University Annual Survey of American Law, 62,* 703–744.

Burke, C. S., Wilson, K. A., & Salas, E. (2005). The use of team-based strategy for organizational transformation: Guidance for moving toward a high reliability organization. *Theoretical Issues in Ergonomics Science, 6*(6), 509–530.

California Health Care Services. (2014). About us. Retrieved from http://www.cphcs.ca.gov/about.aspx

Condrey, S. E. (2005). Toward strategic human resource management. In S. E. Condrey (Ed.), *Handbook of human resource management* (2nd ed., pp. 1–14). San Francisco, CA: Jossey-Bass.

CWP Advisors. (2014). Why install a receiver? Retrieved from http://cwpadvisors.com/view_resource.php?id=103

Department of Justice. (2013). Final report of the special master for the September 11th victim's compensation fund of 2001. Retrieved from http://www.justice.gov/final_report.pdf

Department of Labor. (1978). *Uniform guidelines on employee selection procedures.* Washington, DC: Department of Labor.

Equal Employment Opportunity Commission. (2007). Employer best practices for testing and selection. Retrieved from http://www.eeoc.gov/policy/docs/factemployment_procedures.html

Ekstrand, L. E. (2000). District of Columbia receivership: Selected issues related to medical services at the D.C. jail. United States General Accounting Office (30 June. Testimony GAO/T-GGD-00-173).

Evans, R. (2007). Receiver of Equinox International Corp. Retrieved from http://www.robbevans.com/

Feldman, S. P. (1991). Curbing the recalcitrant polluter: Post-decree judicial agents in environmental litigation. *Boston College Environmental Affairs Law Review, 18*(4), 809–840.

Geer, C. (1999, August). Court-appointed receiver to retain control of Equinox Corp. for now. *Las Vegas Review-Journal, 18*, 1–2.

Huntley, H. (2007, February 3). Regulators call Pearlman saving plan a fraud. *St. Petersburg Times*. Retrieved from http://www.sptimes.com/2007/02/03/Business/Regulators_call_Pearl.shtml

Johnson, A. A. (2014). The role of special masters in complex commercial litigation before the North Carolina business court. Retrieved from http://www.hedrick-gardner.com/wp-content/uploads/2012/12/Role-of-Special-Masters-in-Complex-Commercial-Litigation-before-the-North-Carolina-Business-Court.pdf

Kotter, J. P. (1996). *Leading change*. Boston, MA: Harvard Business School Press.

Legal Information Institute. (2013a). Special master. Retrieved from http://www.law.cornell.edu/wex/special_master

Legal Information Institute. (2013b). State of NEW JERSEY, Plaintiff, v. State of NEW YORK. Retrieved from http://www.law.cornell.edu/supremecourt/text/523/767

Lundquist, K. (2007). *Employment testing and screening testimony*. Retrieved from http://www.eeoc.gov/abouteeoc/meetings/5-16-07/lundquist.html

Memorandum Opinion. (2002). United States of America v. Jefferson County, Alabama, et al., Civil Action No. CV-75-S-666-S.

Moore, S. (2007, August 27). Using muscle to improve health care for prisoners. *New York Times*. Retrieved from http://www.nytimes.com/2007/08/27/us/27prisons.html?_r=0

New Jersey v. New York, 523 US 767 (1998).

Philip, K., & Kaminski, K. (2007). Receivership: A value-adding tool. *Secured Lender, 63*(1), 30, 34, 36.

Receiver's Final Report. (2006). United States of America v. Jefferson County, Alabama, et al., Civil Action No. CV-75-S-666-S.

Receiver's 90 Day Report. (2002). United States of America v. Jefferson County, Alabama, et al., Civil Action No. CV-75-S-666-S.

Receiver's Second Transition Plan. (2006). United States of America v. Jefferson County, Alabama, et al., Civil Action No. CV-75-S-666-S.

Satori Alternative Dispute Resolution. (2014). Special master services. Retrieved from http://www.satoriadr.com/PageDisplay.asp?p1=2370

Schlanger, M. (2006). *Civil rights injunctions over time: A case study of jail and prison court orders*. Retrieved from http://www.nyulawreview.org/sites/default/files/pdf/2_2.pdf

Sims, R. R. (2010). *Reforming (transforming) a public human resource management agency: The case of the Personnel Board of Jefferson County, Alabama*. Charlotte, NC: Information Age.

Schraeder, M., Tears, R. S., & Jordan, M. H. (2005). Organizational culture in public sector organizations: Promoting change through training and leading by example. *Leadership & Organization Development Journal, 26*(5/6), 492–502.

Smith, M. E. (2003). Changing an organization's culture: Correlates of success and failure. *Leadership & Organization Development Journal, 24*(5/6), 249–261.

Special Masters.biz. (2013). Cohen's special master case reporter. Retrieved from http://specialmaster.biz/reporter.php

United States General Accounting Office. (2004, June). *District of Columbia jail: Medical services generally met requirements and costs decreased, but oversight is incomplete.* Report GAO-04-750. Washington, DC: Author.

United States Court of Federal Claims. (2013). Special masters. Retrieved December 31, 2013 from: http://www.uscfc.uscourts.gov/special-masters-biographies

United States of America v. Jefferson County, Alabama, et al. (2002) Civil Action No. CV-75-S-666-S.

University of California Hastings College of Law. (2009). What's the big deal? Federal receiver or special master? Retrieved from http://californiacorrection-scrisis.blogspot.com/2009/03/whats-big-deal-federal-receiver-or.html

Walker, D. (2002, January). *Transformation in government.* Presentation to Association of Government Accountants 13th Annual Leadership Conference, Washington, D.C. Retrieved from http://www.gao.gov/cghome.htm

Wright, B. (2013, August 26). See how much previous court appointed receivers have cost Jefferson County. Retrieved from http://blog.al.com/spot-news/2013/08/court_appointed_receivers_can.html

CHAPTER 19

HUMAN RESOURCES MANAGEMENT, THE LAW, AND ORGANIZATIONAL CHANGE

Ronald R. Sims and William I. Sauser, Jr.

INTRODUCTION

One thing that should be crystal clear to the reader after examining the other chapters in this book is that human resources management (HRM) laws continue to have a major impact on organizations. Clearly, laws and regulations at the federal, state, and local levels regulate how companies conduct such critical strategic operations as, for example, staffing. Title VII of the 1964 Civil Rights Act banned most discriminatory hiring practices in the United States, and there are three sensitive areas of legal concern that HRM professionals (and other organizational leaders) must make sure their organizations comply with: equal opportunity, affirmative action, and sexual harassment. These areas, as well as other laws and regulations, impact organizations and all HRM practices within them.

The main purpose of the Equal Employment Opportunity (EEO) laws is to ensure that everyone has an equal opportunity of getting a job or being

Legal and Regulatory Issues in Human Resources Management, pages 435–456
Copyright © 2015 by Information Age Publishing
435

promoted at work, and that such employment or promotion is based on ability to perform the job. While EEO laws aim to ensure equal treatment at work, affirmative action requires the employer to make an extra effort to hire and promote people who belong to a protected group. Affirmative action includes taking specific actions designed to eliminate the present effects of past discriminations. Few workplace topics have received more attention in recent years than that of sexual harassment. Since Professor Anita Hill confronted Supreme Court nominee Clarence Thomas on national television over two decades ago, the number of sexual harassment claims filed annually in the United States has continued to rise. Since 1980, U.S. courts generally have used guidelines from the Equal Employment Opportunity Commission (EEOC) to define sexual harassment. *Sexual harassment* is defined as "unwelcome sexual advances for sexual favors, and other verbal or physical conduct of a sexual nature" (BNA Communications, 1992) Sexual harassment may include sexually suggestive remarks, unwanted touching, sexual advances, requests for sexual favors, and other verbal and physical conduct of a sexual nature. Since the passage of this law, there have been substantial efforts to change the culture and practices of most U.S. organizations to eliminate such behavior in the workplace. In many cases, HRM professionals have been at the forefront of guiding this change.

Several other laws impact staffing practices as well. The Fair Labor Standards Act specifies the minimum wage, overtime pay rules, and child labor regulations. The Employee Polygraph Protection Act outlaws almost all uses of the polygraph machine for employment purposes. Privacy laws provide legal rights regarding who has access to information about work history and job performance for employees in certain jurisdictions. Under the Whistleblower Protection Act, some employees who publicize dangerous employer practices are entitled to legal protection. And, as noted earlier, the previous chapters highlight the reality for today's and tomorrow's HRM professionals: local, state, federal, and international laws and regulations will continue to shape their organizations and their HRM practices. And in many cases, we believe, HRM professionals will be called upon to shape strategies and lead organizational change efforts to ensure that the organization complies fully with the law.

A second thing should also be clear to the reader: HRM laws and regulations are not static; they are very *dynamic* as new legislative statutes, administrative regulations, and court decisions change the law on a continuous basis in response to changing societal norms and expectations. This means that HRM professionals must keep themselves continually aware of changing laws and regulations affecting HRM policies and practices, and must also be ready at any time to plan and implement organizational change processes to keep the organization in compliance with the changing legal and regulatory context. This means that, now more than ever, effective HRM professionals must be well versed in such topics as organizational culture, strategy, and change management.

The intent of the chapter is to emphasize to HRM professionals how important it is that they prepare themselves to be effective leaders of change. As HRM continues to grow in importance as a global strategic factor for organizations, and as HRM laws continue to be dynamic and to differ among nations, those HRM professionals who will be well prepared to lead their organizations into the future must understand and be able to guide effective organizational change. This chapter discusses the important role that HRM professionals can play in helping to set the tone and direction their organizations take in response to HRM laws and regulations. The chapter first discusses HRM departments and professionals and how they can and do help shape the organization's culture. Next, the focus is on several cultural responses organizations might take in response to HRM laws and regulations. The discussion then focuses on how HRM professionals can use traditional HRM practices to help their organizations best introduce and institutionalize HRM laws in the organization. The chapter then describes a number of things HRM professionals can do to help their organizations adapt or change in response to the introduction of new HRM laws and regulations.

HUMAN RESOURCE MANAGEMENT PROFESSIONALS, RECEIVED WISDOM, AND ORGANIZATIONAL CULTURE

Not only will HRM professionals need to have knowledge of the various HRM laws and regulations, but they must also both educate and help others in the organization implement these laws and regulations. Thus, when necessary, this means they must be ready to help the organization change or make reforms to comply with the new or changing laws and regulations. As suggested above, laws and regulations that include compliance include those in areas like employment discrimination and equal employment opportunity, affirmative action, workplace safety and health, employee benefits, legally required insurance protection, personal rights of employees, labor relations and collective bargaining, and the employment-at-will doctrine. The HRM professional will need to be able to work with others in the organization to recognize HRM issues, analyze situations in the workplace, develop strategies to avoid legal liability, and help to set the tone and direction and make organizational changes when needed.

HRM is an active participant in setting the tone and direction the organization takes in responding to or incorporating HRM laws in the organization—and thus affects the entire organizational culture. When new laws or regulations must be adhered to by the organization, its leaders, and other employees, HRM has a critical leadership push role to play. HRM departments or functions and HRM professionals serve as consultants to those in the organization, monitor progress, provide advice and direction, and work closely with organizational leaders at all levels.

HRM professionals must understand the relationship between HRM and related laws, strategic organizational change, and organizational culture. More specifically, to what extent can HRM laws influence and change an organization, and subsequently the organization's culture? HRM professionals must be willing to accept the responsibility of being an agent of change in working with others in the organization to successfully introduce, implement, and institutionalize HRM laws within the organization. And this often means change for the organization and its culture.

The culture of an organization is so pervasive that it must have a strong influence on performance and general behavior of the organization. Organizational culture not only affects what the organization does, but it also affects how it does it, to whom, and when. Culture is thus a significant part of the bedrock foundation that determines the design, structure, system components, and functions of an organization. Consider, for example, the design and implementation of an organizational change initiative. Today, many organizational leaders turn to the HRM department or function for guidance and assistance when planning, implementing, and evaluating organizational changes (i.e., the introduction of new policies and practices to respond effectively to a new HRM law). Thus, HRM professionals must have change agent skills or competencies. This means that they must have the ability to build trust with other organizational members and thereby minimize resistance and overcome negative reactions from various members of the organization. For example, when organizational leaders or others are unwilling or unable to provide the leadership necessary to implement or get the organization to adhere to a new HRM law, HRM professionals should be prepared to take on both a more assertive and an educating role.

The reality is that most HRM departments or professionals actually influence and shape organizational culture on a regular basis. The extent and nature of the HRM influence, however, depends on the role the HRM department plays in an organization and the expectations of HRM that exist in the organization. For example, in an organization with a more centralized strategic HRM role or model, HRM most often has strong influence on the organizational culture. In the more traditional and some might say consultative or organizational development model, HRM most likely will participate in the formulation and implementation of organizational change and development initiatives. And with this, while HRM will influence the organizational culture, its influence will be more difficult to identify.

In either role, HRM professionals and their departments or functions given their charges can help unfreeze the status quo—to help organizations to improve such things as performance, productivity, flexibility, innovation, effectiveness, or introduction or implementation of a new HRM law. The introduction and implementation of new HRM laws is no different than the HRM professional's role in managing any other internal organizational change initiative. HRM professionals develop implementation strategies and collaborate with others in the organization in coordinating and executing changes that result from HRM laws—using, one hopes, systematic and necessary processes that maintain organizational trust while also effecting the changes. When change resulting from HRM laws is collaborative and strategic, the experience crystallizes organizational practices into norms, which become part of the organizational culture.

RECEIVED WISDOM AND ORGANIZATIONAL CULTURE

No matter whether an HRM law or regulation is local, state, federal, or international in its origination, the HRM department will usually have responsibility for developing a plan to implement or coordinate its roll-out and to monitor activities and outcomes. Thus HRM professionals have a central voice in the design of specific activities or interventions that are consciously intended to change or alter aspects of the belief and value systems of the organization's employees—core elements of the organizational culture—which most often results in newly expected behaviors. Before offering more discussion on how and what HRM professionals can do to help bring about changes central to the introduction and institutionalization of policies, procedures, and behaviors resulting from a new HRM law, it is important to take a closer look at received wisdom and organizational culture, two concepts that will impact any HRM change efforts. And in doing so, it is our premise that HRM professionals need a more thorough understanding of received wisdom and especially organizational culture if they wish to have an effective impact.

Received Wisdom

"Received wisdom" simply means the normative "folk wisdom" that everyone has come to accept in society in general and—more specifically for purposes of this chapter—in an organization. In other words, it is the set of beliefs and standards (norms) that people have come to accept as true in a given organization. Dibbs (2012) has defined received wisdom as the knowledge or information that people generally believe is true, although in fact it is often false knowledge.

According to Svyantek and Bott (2004), received wisdom is knowledge imparted to people by others. The epistemological derivation of received wisdom seems to be based on two sources of knowledge used by humans—tenacity and authority. Tenacity refers to the continued presentation of a particular bit of information to an individual until it is accepted as true (Smith & Davis, 2003). Authority refers to the acceptance of knowledge as truth because of the position and credibility of the source. Neither of these sources of knowledge, however, is considered scientific (Svyantek & Bott, 2004).

Received wisdom is often believed and used by individuals in the absence of confirming evidence and, in some cases, is held to be true although contradictory evidence exists. For example, Ptolemy of Alexandria developed a theory of solar and planetary motion in 150 A.D. that guided the science of astronomy for 1,500 years until it was replaced by Kepler's theory. Ptolemy's theory has been described as "beautiful, complex, and wrong" ("Things fall apart," 2004, p. 1). Why do we blindly accept widespread theories and their widely employed practices as valid, assuming (without questioning the evidence) that they are well substantiated? Consider the amount of received wisdom that:

- as it turns out, is the result of either a person or group's obsession or viewpoint, and
- despite the fact that it has been disproved, has not been discarded.

This point has been stressed recently by Jonah Lehrer, a writer for *The New Yorker*, whose two articles (2012a, 2012b), although separated by several months and covering vastly different subject matter, sound similar themes. Cases in point: brainstorming and casino design as discussed briefly below.

Brainstorming is the brainchild of John Osborn. Osborn popularized his approach to creativity in one of several books that spread the word about his brainstorming methodology back in the 1940s (Osborn, 1963). Not long thereafter, brainstorming theory was subjected to research at Yale University, and that was only the beginning of "[d]ecades of research [that] have consistently shown brainstorming groups think of far fewer ideas than the same number of people who work alone and later pool their ideas" (Taylor, Berry, & Block, 1958, p. 46).

Apparently the central tenets of brainstorming, considered essential for generating truly breakthrough insights, were soundly debunked almost as soon as brainstorming was popularized, but that hasn't stopped anyone from adhering to these principles or the practice. In fact, many organizations have been founded on them, embracing them with near religious fervor.

The Friedman International Standards of Casino Design developed 13 principles on how to design casinos. Who is Friedman, and how did he arrive at these principles? Friedman was a former gambling addict who became a student of the environments in which he had lost so much money. He went on to manage a few casinos and teach some of the first university courses in casino management. Distilling what made him tick when he gambled and what he observed about other gamblers into solid granite principles, Friedman exerted huge influence, and his rules dominated casino design for an amazing run of almost 30 years.

But then Roger Thomas, a commercial interior designer, went to work for Steve Wynn, and his design principles, sumptuously expressed at The Bellagio, were diametrically opposed to Friedman's. Spending upwards of $1.6 billion on lavish interior design from the casino floor to the guest rooms to the iconic fountain show, Thomas violated all 13 principles. The result was a property where the guests spent four times as much per room as the average property in Las Vegas. Research into gambling behavior followed and, lo and behold, it turns out that people spend more money when they feel they are winners (a feeling that is reinforced by a luxurious, relaxing environment). Even people who don't gamble are softened up by the environment and are more likely to give it a go.

So, if incorrect "received wisdom" on brainstorming and casino design have been so thoroughly trashed, why are they still being practiced as faithfully as if they had not? How far back must someone have to step to detach sufficiently from the received wisdom of any given frame of reference to gain enough perspective to become aware that they are holding beliefs that have been absorbed without due diligence? Perhaps brainstorming and casino design are the exception rather than the rule? Not true!

Many beliefs in psychology and organizational studies seem to be based on received wisdom. These beliefs, however, do not hold up to close examination using basic scientific methods. In psychology, for example, William James's purported view on unconscious processes has been shown to be based on a misreading of a passage in James's work by an early writer (Weinberger, 2000), and the espoused view that experts and lay people evaluate risk differently does not hold up to close scrutiny (Rowe & Wright, 2001). In organizational studies, there has been growing evaluation of the received wisdom pertaining to the value of current strategies in the airline industry (Kangis & O'Reilly, 2003); the belief that employee satisfaction and loyalty are related to service profitability (Silvestro, 2002); the advantages of economies of scale (Pil & Holweg, 2003); the belief that organization-wide incentives and capable subordinates make top-level oversight of a company less valuable (Rivkin & Siggelkow, 2003); the importance of organizational control mechanisms based on autocratic, hierarchical assumptions (Romme, 1999); the belief that downsizing leads to a better and swifter responding organization (Majumdar, 2000); and the relationship of diversity and organizational performance (Svyantek & Bott, 2004). In each case, the received wisdom has not stood up to research based on the scientific method.

Received wisdom comes to serve as the unquestioned assumptions guiding one's interpretation of the world and the decisions we make in the world. This unquestioned acceptance leads to organizational practices that, at a minimum, waste organizational resources for no benefit, and in some cases—like unethical or unlawful behavior—have a negative effect on the organization.

Received wisdom is based on two primary sources (Svyantek & Bott, 2004). First, received wisdom may be derived from old empirical results or experiences that create a lasting legacy long after these results or experiences should be replaced by new findings. Second, received wisdom may be derived by the need to justify certain individuals', groups', or organizations' important goals. The acceptance of such received wisdom is often crucial to being accepted as a member of a group. Such "received wisdom" forms the "vital lies" that define group beliefs (Goffman, 1997) and groupthink (Janis, 1982). So, received wisdom is the belief, principle, or set standard that people have come to believe is true.

Received wisdom is an important aspect of organizational culture and—in many cases—is a primary vehicle (along with group-administered sanctions) for transmitting organizational culture. Unfortunately, received wisdom may not always be wise and it may not always be the truth, even if the general or critical masses of the organization believe it to be. This is certainly the case when one considers the failed introduction of a new HRM law or the continued noncompliance with HRM laws or regulations and its possible implications for an organization. More will be said about this later in the chapter.

Organization Culture

Culture permeates all aspects of any society. It acts as the basic fabric that binds people together. Culture dictates tastes in music, clothes, and even the political and philosophical views of a group of people. Culture is not only shared, but it is deep and stable (Schein, 1992, 1999). However, culture does not exist simply as a societal phenomenon. Organizations, both large and small, adhere to a culture. Organizational culture determines how an organization operates and how its members frame events both inside and outside the organization.

A plethora of definitions exist for organizational culture. Various scholars define culture as how an organization goes about meeting its goals and missions, how an organization solves problems, or as a deeply rooted value that shapes the behavior of the individuals within the group (Sanchez, 2004). In reality, organizational culture is all of these things. In its entirety, organizational culture consists of an organization's shared values, symbols, behaviors, and assumptions (Goffee & Jones, 1998). Simply put, organizational culture is "the way we do things around here" (Martin, 2006, p. 1).

It is the way wisdom is received or the cornerstone of normative "folk wisdom" that everyone has come to accept about how the organization functions or how individuals are expected to behave in an organization.

Stories and legends can stay with an organization and become part of the established way of doing things. Perhaps the founder's views about the importance of education and training will stay current; on the other hand, in the course of time there may be a "culture shift" as new managers and leaders move into the organization and change the old ways. However, stories and legends continue to be important determinants of "the way we do things around here" and—as in the past—over time the organization will develop new "norms," that is, established (normal) expected behavior patterns within the organization.

A norm is an established behavior pattern that is part of a culture. And culture encompasses moral, social, and behavioral norms of an organization. The norms serve to establish the new or evolving normative "folk wisdom" within an organization (e.g., interpretations of acceptable and unacceptable behavior, understanding, guidance, and priorities for members). There are many elements that fall under the concept of organizational culture and the subsequent established behavior patterns that are part of a culture. And employees receive their wisdom from all these aspects of the organization's culture. For example, these elements often include:

- The way people dress
- The way people act (both on and off the job)
- The way people present themselves
- The way people conduct their work
- The way supervisors are encouraged to manage units or departments
- The way customers are treated and served
- The way employees interact with their immediate supervisors
- The way employees interact with each other
- The way people interact across departments
- The way people interact with the public
- The way business is conducted and done
- The way decisions are made
- The way employees are recruited, selected, rewarded, promoted, and dismissed
- The way people prioritize and manage time

Individually and collectively, these and other factors serve as the vehicle for received wisdom within an organization. Wisdom received through organizational culture is the source of the beliefs and standards that are accepted as true if one is to survive and thrive in the organization or comply or not comply with an HRM law, for example. When a new HR law or regulation conflicts with "received wisdom" based on longstanding organizational culture (as did the sexual harassment law mentioned earlier), it is imperative that the HR professional take steps to change the prevailing culture if the organization's efforts to comply with the new law are to succeed.

Given the reality of factors like those above it is clear that every organization has a unique culture. Each has its own business philosophy and principles, its own way of approaching problems and making decisions, its own work climate, its own embedded patterns of "how we do things around here," its own lore (stories told over and over to illustrate company values and what they mean to stakeholders), its own taboos and political don'ts—in other words, its own ingrained beliefs, behavior, and thought patterns; business practices; and personality that defines its organizational culture. For example, the bedrock of Wal-Mart's culture is dedication to customer satisfaction; zealous pursuit of low costs; a strong work ethic; Sam Walton's legendary frugality; the ritualistic Saturday-morning headquarters meetings to exchange ideas and review problems; and company executives' commitment to visiting stores, talking to customers, and soliciting suggestions from employees. New entrants into the Wal-Mart family receive wisdom on how and what is important in the organization beginning with their first experience and throughout their tenure with the organization. This is how they come to believe what is true, what is important, and what is and is not expected of them as employees of Wal-Mart.

At Microsoft, there are stories of the long hours programmers put in, the emotional peaks and valleys in encountering and overcoming coding problems, the exhilaration of completing a complex program on schedule, the satisfaction of working on cutting-edge projects, the rewards of being part of a team responsible for a popular new software program, and the tradition of competing aggressively. At McDonald's, the constant message from management is the overriding importance of quality, service, cleanliness, and value; employees are drilled over and over on the need for attention to detail and perfection in every fundamental of the business. The organizational culture at American Express Company stresses that employees help customers out of difficult situations whenever possible. This attitude is reinforced through numerous company legends of employees who have gone above and beyond the call of duty to help customers. This strong tradition of customer loyalty might encourage an American Express employee to take unorthodox steps to help a customer who encounters a problem while travelling overseas. Such strong traditions and values have become a driving force and the basis for received wisdom in many other companies—for example, Procter & Gamble Co. and Southwest Airlines.

Cultural Responses to HRM Laws and Regulations

Unfortunately, the received wisdom for employees in some organizational cultures is, for example, to scorn HRM laws and other regulations and seek to resist or defy them wherever possible. That is, the received wisdom is one of "bending" the law, cutting ethical corners, or breaking the law when the likelihood of detection is perceived to be low (or reward for breaking the law is gauged to be high enough to risk the consequences). These and other such tactics would be rewarded and encouraged in this type of culture. Top management would model the way with questionable behaviors and messages indicating to other organizational members that defiance of the law is acceptable when necessary to meet or exceed economic goals (Sims & Sauser, 2010). "Achieve economic success at any cost; just don't get caught" would be the theme and received wisdom for organizational members in an organization embracing a culture of defiance. Denial of guilt would be expected if noncompliance by members of such an organization were detected and made public. Consider, for example, the situation where an employer is found guilty of violations of the Federal Family Medical Leave Act (FMLA) and the Americans with Disabilities Act (ADA). Upon further review of the facts, it is found that senior organizational leaders and other lower-level managers were aware that they were violating the law and had also engaged in retaliatory acts against several employees for "bringing their concerns to management's attention." Clearly, such behavior is a blatant case of noncompliance and seeking to resist or defy the laws all together.

Some organizations have developed cultures (through unwise "received wisdom") that do not promote compliance; these cultures are appropriately classified as cultures of *defiance* (Schermerhorn, 2005; Sauser, 2008) aligned with an *obstructionist strategy* towards, for example, HRM laws or regulations. This unfortunate form of organizational culture tends to lead employees to behave accordingly and actually defy the law. Consider the situation where an organization pays women less than their male counterparts performing the same jobs and managers and other leaders have no disincentive to do otherwise. In such a case, individuals who join the ranks of management will have a hard time surviving unless they follow suit (the received wisdom on the acceptable behavior for these individuals—i.e., not following the guidelines set by the Equal Pay Act of 1963—is expected and accepted).

There are also organizations characterized by a *culture of compliance* where it would be expected to exhibit behaviors associated with the *defensive* and *accommodative* strategies described by Schermerhorn (2005; Sauser, 2008). Their leaders and members may not *agree* with the legal HRM standards they are forced to operate within, but they would take actions designed to meet (at least minimally) their legal obligations. In fact, this is an important distinction between *compliant* organizations and those with *character* as defined below. In psychological terms, the received wisdom of compliance means yielding to standards one does not necessarily accept (McGuire, 1969, p. 190). It is only when one *internalizes* (accepts and incorporates within one's value system) the principles underlying "the letter of the law" that *character* can be inferred as the underlying cause of behavior aligned with laws and regulations. In other words, the received wisdom of *compliance* implies a grudging sort of acceptance of laws, not a true incorporation of the "spirit" of those standards within one's individual personality or corporate culture (Krech, Crutchfield, & Ballachey, 1962). Here are a few examples of "mixed messages" one might find in a culture of compliance, where the letter—but not the spirit—of laws and regulations may be embraced. The first three examples are provided by Murphy (1988); the other three are drawn from Sauser (2010):

- I don't care what the HRM law says, just hire her/him.
- Find a way to fire that person.
- Don't bother me with the details, you know what to do.
- No one gets injured on this worksite . . . period. Understand?
- I'm the boss; just do what I say and you'll be okay.

In these cases, the supervisor could be expected to deny ever having given permission to break the rules, and in fact may express shock that the order or received wisdom was perceived in that manner. Nonetheless, these messages from supervisors often actually provide a distinct signal to employees that the organization may go through the motions to do what is right but does not really value what is right. This is the culture of compliance, a reluctant acknowledgment of laws and regulations and a grudging attempt to abide by them.

The *culture of neglect* is all too often a tragic case. The leaders of the organization may be seeking to follow Schermerhorn's (2005; Sauser, 2008) strategy of *accommodation* or even *proaction*, but one or more flaws in the culture lead to a failure to achieve the goals of this strategy. Such shortcomings might include a failure to know or understand the HRM laws and regulations governing the organization, a failure adequately to communicate those laws and regulations, a failure to detect and/or punish wrongdoers within the organization, or even blindness within the culture—caused by one or more tragic flaws—that leads to unintentional noncompliance. While leaders of cultures of character are constantly vigilant to detect and correct legal or regulatory compliance shortcomings on the part of themselves or their employees, leaders of cultures of neglect fail in their responsibility of due diligence. The consequences of this failure of diligence can be as devastating as the consequences of the deliberate defiance of the law taken by organizations with cultures of the first type.

The final type of organizational culture is the *culture of character* (Sauser, 2008). This is the organizational culture whose leaders and members are truly committed to making compliance with HRM laws and regulations a fundamental component of their every action. They put a stake in the ground, explicitly stating what the organization intends and expects. Value statements and codes of compliance or expectations are used as a benchmark for judging both organizational policies and every individual's conduct. They do not forget that trust, integrity, and fairness do matter, and they are crucial to [everyone] in the organization.

Here is an important statement made by Carl Skoogland, the former ethics director of Texas Instruments, in a speech he made on October 16, 2003, that can directly apply to compliance or noncompliance with HRM laws: "Ethical managers must *know* what's right, *value* what's right, and *do* what's right" (Skoogland, 2003, emphasis in original). These three key principles are essential in the practical and successful compliance with HRM laws at the organizational level. With respect to Skoogland's (2003) three key principles, the received wisdom of organizational members of *cultures of defiance* may (or may not) include knowing what's right, but it certainly includes neither valuing what's right nor doing what's right. The received wisdom of organizational members of *cultures of compliance*, from this same perspective, includes knowing what's right and even doing what's right, but not really valuing what's right. Consequently, as a result of this received wisdom, members of these organizations may be tempted to bend or break the HRM laws, regulations, and rules when opportunities occur, and may even be surreptitiously rewarded by their supervisors and peers for doing so. In *cultures of neglect*, there may be a conscious effort because of received wisdom to know what's right, value what's right, and do what's right, but—through some (often unconscious) flaw in the culture—this effort flags through lack of diligence, resulting in a breach of HRM compliance. Finally, in *cultures of character*, compliance with HRM laws are ingrained throughout the organization such that all of its members strive without fail as a result of the received wisdom to know what's right, value what's right, and do what's right.

HRM, more than any other organizational function, plays a key role in shaping, reinforcing, and changing organizational culture. Thus, HR professionals are critical in helping to determine whether an organization—when confronted with HRM laws or regulations—takes on a culture of defiance, compliance, neglect, or character. The fact is that culture directly contributes to the bottom-line performance of any organization as well as impacts the organization's very survival. Given the importance of culture to an organization's success, it will serve the HRM department or function well to increase its ability to close the gap or bring about changes when they exist between HRM compliance requirements and actual organizational compliance.

HOW HRM PROFESSIONALS IMPACT ORGANIZATIONAL CULTURE AND CHANGE

A great strategy is no guarantee of long-term organization success. Clearly, many other factors impact organizational performance and especially in the case of compliance or noncompliance with HRM laws and regulations. As emphasized in our discussion in the previous section, one such factor is organizational culture, which helps an organization create a highly responsive and compliant environment that supports an organization's efforts to not just survive but thrive in the world of HRM laws and regulations. Because culture is so important to the success of an organization, HRM professionals need to increase their proficiency at impacting culture and bringing about the requisite organizational changes.

It might not be surprising that HRM professionals, if asked to describe their organization's culture, might respond "family atmosphere," "team oriented," and "performance-driven." On the other hand, it would be curious to see whether or not the same HRM professionals would as confidently describe their role in shaping organizational culture. The reason is that few terms have been more ignored or misunderstood by HRM professionals (and others) who apparently fail to understand just how much HRM professionals and practices impact an organization's culture.

Culture defines the proper way to think, act, and behave in regards to HRM laws and regulations within an organization. Those who do things in the "proper" way in regards to HRM laws and regulations will fit-in and do well. Those who choose not to do things in the proper way regarding HRM laws and regulations will most likely not last long with the organization. They must be told, "We don't do things like that here."

Organizational leaders define what is considered proper within the organization. Leaders create cultures that they believe will provide them with a competitive advantage and more specifically keep them from being sued or feeling the wrath of noncompliance from enforcement agencies like the EEOC. If the organization competes in the international arena where adherence to HRM laws and regulations in an industry or country is important, organizational leaders and HRM professionals must create cultures where adherence to HRM laws and regulations is nonnegotiable and is considered the proper way to think, act, and behave. This is because culture helps an organization adapt to its external environment and drives internal integration and adherence to HRM laws and regulations.

Educating Organizational Members

For HRM professionals, the implications are clear. To impact culture, they must work with organizational leaders to help define what the organization considers proper with regards to how people think, act and behave with respect to HRM laws and regulations. This is not simply a "feel-good" exercise. The ultimate goal should be to improve the organization's adherence to HRM laws and regulations, both for the organization and for the employee. HRM professionals must never lose sight of the fact that they need to help organizational leaders perceive that if they do not accurately understand the strengths and weaknesses of the cultures they create, they will have a much harder time achieving their organizational objectives, because these are in turn dependent upon leveraging the various HRM laws and regulations. For example, one could cite the cultures of some of the organizations that are before federal courts today in employment-related disputes or in state court cases where there are allegations of discriminatory acts in employment. And for some of those complaints, there are managers and others who carried out those actions under the guise of an organizational culture that failed to dissuade such behavior. Also, organizational leaders often do not have an accurate understanding of the cultures that they create. Because they are removed from the front lines, organizational leaders tend to believe that the espoused culture they intended to create as it relates to HRM laws and regulations actually exists throughout the organization. However, often this is not the case, and these organizational leaders end up with an inaccurate perception of their organizational culture and thus with failures to successfully implement or adhere to HRM laws and regulations. Here is where HRM professionals can provide tremendous value by helping to keep a pulse on the organizational culture.

Human Resources Management Cultural Levers

HRM professionals have at their disposal many of the necessary levers to create, sustain, and change organization culture, in general, and more specifically when it comes to HRM laws and regulations. The challenge is for HRM professionals to make choices about the use of these levers and to where to focus their energy.

Pay Systems

Compensation and reward systems are one of the most important mechanisms HRM professionals can use to adhere to HRM laws and regulations. Quite simply, those employees who think, act and behave in the proper way should be rewarded. Those who do not should not receive rewards because doing so will send a mixed message to employees. Remember the mixed messages referred to earlier!

HRM professionals must be careful when designing such pay for performance reward programs. To effectively impact organizational culture, pay systems should reward not only job outcomes, but also behavioral expectations when it comes to, for example, HRM laws and regulations. For example, it is quite common for HRM to design a pay system that rewards based simply on productivity. However, such narrowly defined expectations could be creating a culture that is counter to adherence to HRM laws and regulations. That is, negative behaviors may be exhibited and rewarded that are counter to the desired culture of the organization. Yet, based on the pay system designed by HRM and approved by the organizational leader, such negative behavior is rewarded as though it is actually desired. Such a pay system does not support the organizational culture of adherence to HRM laws and regulations, and this will no doubt result in some legal implications down the road.

Performance Management

As one would expect, performance management (PM) programs can greatly impact organizational culture because they clearly articulate to an organization's employees what is expected from them as well as provides a feedback mechanism to inform them if they are being "proper" as defined by the organization's culture. To impact culture, PM systems need also to address employee behaviors and not just work objectives. Doing so helps to eliminate mistakes, for example, where employees are rewarded even though they demonstrated behaviors counter to the culture. So even though organizational objectives may be met, if behavioral expectations related to HRM laws and regulations are not met, the PM process will point out this discrepancy to an employee so that his or her behaviors can be realigned with the organization's culture.

Also, culturally aligned PM systems have a strong element of differentiation. This means that those who think, act, and behave in the proper way as it relates to HRM laws and regulations according to the culture should be given higher ratings, increases, and/or promotions than those who do not. If the PM process simply gives every employee the same rating and/or pay increase regardless of whether they are thinking, acting, or behaving properly as it relates to HRM laws and regulations (and of course any other critical areas), the PM management process then does *not* impact the organization's culture in the way the organizational leaders and HRM professionals desire.

Recruiting and Selection

Talent acquisition efforts impact culture by determining the types of employees who are brought into the organization. HRM professionals must look for more than just the right skills and capabilities in a potential employee; they should also determine if the candidate will be a good cultural fit for the organization. To do this effectively, HRM professionals must have a solid understanding of the culture of the organization if they wish to determine if someone will fit into the culture. Questions focused on determining cultural fit should be a part of every new employee interview.

One organization recently hired a division manager for their international operations and failed to ask cultural fit questions. This particular division manager consistently failed to follow host country HRM laws and preferred to ignore the advice of his designated HRM representative. Employees within the division soon began to resign because the new division manager did not display actions or behaviors that were in alignment with a culture that had always valued fairness, nondiscrimination, and an emphasis on respecting and adhering to local HRM laws and regulations. The division manager was soon let go because he did not fit into the culture (i.e., accepted norms, expectations, and behaviors around HRM laws and regulations) desired by the organization even though he possessed the proper skills, education, and experience. This is a very powerful lever for change.

Training & Development

By focusing on training and development efforts that help employees to think, act, and behave in the proper way, HRM can impact the culture. Training programs on HRM laws and regulations can be designed to help employees demonstrate the behaviors desired by the organization's culture. Also, HRM professionals and other organizational leaders must ensure that those who are successful within a culture should be given additional development opportunities so that they can assume positions of greater responsibility. By developing and promoting those who support the organization's culture, HRM professionals (and the HRM practices they establish) again have the opportunity to impact the way things are done in the organization when it comes to HRM laws and regulations.

Also, HRM professionals and other organizational leaders who promote employee development as part of their organizational culture must ensure that enough resources are allocated to the HRM department's training and development budget for it to have a real impact. The allocation of scarce resources is another sign that employees look for when determining if an organization is serious about creating the culture they espouse.

To see how this all works together, let's look at a situation where organizational leaders want an HRM department to help create an organizational culture that focuses on adherence to HRM laws and regulations. First, HRM can establish reward programs that focus on employee compliance or adherence with HRM laws and regulations. Next, they can create a PM management process that evaluates employees on their adherence to the HRM laws and regulations. HRM can then help shape training programs (hopefully beginning during new employee orientation or the organization's onboarding process) designed to improve employees' adherence to HRM laws and regulations. Lastly, the HRM professionals can look to hire individuals who recognize or have demonstrated their willingness to abide by HRM laws and regulations. By leveraging just these core HRM elements alone, HRM professionals can continue to have a tremendous impact on shaping adherence to HRM laws and regulations and institutionalizing behaviors based on an organizational culture that goes beyond sheer compliance.

Clearly, HRM professionals have many levers at their disposal to impact organizational culture. Other HRM levers that can be used include organizational design, organizational values, and even the physical work environment. The truth is that the ability to perceive the limitations of one's culture and to develop that culture's adaptability is the essence and ultimate challenge for HRM professionals as they continue to help their organizations be more responsive to local, state, federal, and international HRM laws and regulations. HRM professionals can add a great deal of value to their organization by understanding how much they can impact organizational culture and whether it is one based on *defiance, compliance, neglect,* or *character* when it comes to HRM laws and regulations.

INTRODUCING AND INSTITUTIONALIZING HRM LAWS AND REGULATIONS: SIMPLY MANAGING CHANGE EFFECTIVELY?

There is every indication that new HRM laws and regulations will continue to have a substantial impact on organizations, HRM practices, and HRM professionals. In short, change will continue to be the mantra for organizations and HRM professionals, especially if one accepts the reality of the continuing emergence of, for example, employment litigation. HRM laws and regulations or employment litigation are not necessarily a new development, of course, but the legal context in which they arise has imparted a new urgency for organizations to effectively adapt and change.

For organizations to change, and to do it effectively, as is required by most HRM laws and regulations, HRM professionals must help in moving the organization from its current state to a future desired state at minimal cost to the organization. Bateman and Zeithaml (1990) identified three steps HRM professionals and others in the organization should follow when implementing organizational change:

1. Diagnose the current state of the organization. This involves identifying problems or issues the organization faces regarding HRM laws and regulation, assigning a level of importance to each one, and assessing the kinds of changes needed to solve the problems or issues.
2. Design the desired future state of the organization. This involves picturing the ideal situation for the organization after the change (i.e., introduction and institutionalization of the HRM law or regulation) is implemented, conveying this vision clearly to everyone involved in the change effort, and designing a means of transition to the new state. HRM professionals must remember that an important part of the transition should be maintaining some sort of stability; some things—such as

the organization's overall mission—should remain constant in the midst of the introduction of the new HRM law or regulation.

3. Implement the change. This involves managing the transition effectively from the old way of doing things to the new way of doing things as a result of the new HRM law or regulation. HRM professionals increase the likelihood of a more successful introduction of a new HRM law or regulation when they and others in the organization take the time to draw up a plan, allocate resources, and appoint a key person to take charge of the change process. HRM professionals and other organizational leaders should do everything possible to generate acceptance and even enthusiasm for the change (i.e., new HRM law or regulation) by sharing their goals and vision and acting as role models, as noted earlier in this chapter. In some cases, it may be useful to try for small victories first in order to pave the way for later successes.

While there are indeed many other things that must be done under each of the three steps above to effectively introduce and institutionalize new HRM laws and regulations into an organization, HRM professionals at a minimum should start out with such a framework or model. Effectively changing or transitioning to new HRM laws or regulations and when necessary changing the organization's culture requires wisdom, prescience, energy, persistence, communication, education, training, resources, patience, timing, and the right incentives (Answers.com, 2014).

CONCLUSION

There is no doubt that HRM professionals and their organizations will continue to be greatly influenced and shaped by state, federal, and international HRM laws and regulations. Indeed, regulations and laws govern all aspects of HRM, including recruitment, placement, development, and compensation areas, to name a few. Much of the growth in the HRM function over the past three decades is the result of the increasing trend toward viewing organizations as vehicles for achieving social and political objectives. Most organizations continue to be deeply concerned with potential liability resulting from HRM decisions that may violate laws enacted by local governments, state legislatures, the U.S. Congress, and international governments. Legislation like the 1964 Civil Rights Act requires organizations to respond to larger social, political, and legal issues. Other legislation requires organizations to provide reasonable accommodations for the disabled and for employees with HIV virus. And the Patient Protection and Affordable Care Act (PPACA) will undoubtedly result in major impact and required changes for organizations, HRM professionals, and other employees.

How successfully an organization manages the introduction and institutionalization of HRM laws and regulations depends to a large extent on its ability to deal effectively with subsequent and necessary organizational changes. Operating within the HRM laws and regulations requires keeping track of the external legal and social environments and developing internal systems (for example, supervisory training on the new HRM laws or regulations or new policies and procedures that serve as the received wisdom vehicles) to ensure compliance and minimize complaints.

Organizational responses to legislative requirements today in the United States, for example, generally follow a realization that important issues need national attention. As entities within the larger society, organizations can't help but be influenced by the ideology and culture around them. As changes occur in the larger society, organizations must adapt and change. Just like the 1960s and 1970s, the results of today's and tomorrow's HRM laws and regulations are added pressures on organizations. HRM practices resulting from such laws and regulations are not reformed in a vacuum but must represent the organizational culture in which they are embedded.

HRM laws, regulations, and policy differ from country to country. More specifically, labor laws, pay structure, various acts, and social security systems are based on government policies that vary from one to another country. For example India/Pakistan/China and the United States have different types of governments and their laws are different, and HRM rules in view of this are different as well. And this poses challenges for international organizations and HRM professionals as they try to navigate the various HRM laws and regulations.

International HRM is not simply HRM on a grander scale. One need only consider the reality that several familiar aspects of HRM, such as recruitment, selection, and employee relations may actually be outside the scope of international HRM because of the different (primarily national) legislative frameworks to which they must adhere. Employees are selected in one country or another, and wherever the selection is undertaken, there are a range of conventions and legal requirements that have to be met. The person appointed will usually have a contract of employment that will fit within the legal framework of one country but probably not another. Of course, supranational bodies such as the European Union are attempting to "harmonize" such differences out of existence. Yet, despite the differences one might find among countries and within a country, HRM laws and regulations require organizational change, and such change might well require taking a serious look at the existing organizational culture. HRM professionals can and should accept the responsibility of being the "agents of change" for their organizations, by helping not only to set the tone related to HRM laws and regulations, but more importantly by making use of the HRM levers that are so ingrained in the fabric of every organization.

In conclusion, there is an old saying: *Ignorance is bliss.* While that statement may be true, HRM professionals must make sure its organizational leaders and others understand that ignorance is *not* a good defense to a noncompliance violation of any of the HRM laws and regulations. All of the HRM regulations and laws presume the organization knows what its compliance requirements are and is in compliance with those requirements. "Oh, we didn't know that we were supposed to be doing this" or "Oh, we didn't know we were not supposed to be doing this" are *not* appropriate responses to noncompliance charges/claims/allegations *or* to charges/claims/allegations of discrimination, harassment, or wrongful employment practices. HRM laws and regulations are here to stay, and there is no doubt that HRM professionals must know what to do and must do what needs to be done to prepare their organizations to effectively translate them into HRM practices, and when necessary set the tone and change the entire organizational culture if necessary. Anything less is not true professionalism.

REFERENCES

Answers.com. (2014). Managing organizational change. Retrieved from http://www.answers.com/topic/managing-organizational-change

Bateman, T. S., & Zeithaml, C. P. (1990). *Management: Function and strategy.* Homewood, IL: Irwin.

BNA Communications. (1992). What is sexual harassment? Retrieved from http://www.un.org/womenwatch/osagi/pdf/whatissh.pdf

Dibbs, P. (2012). The dangers of received wisdom. *Bdaily Business Network.* Retrieved from http://bdaily.co.uk/news/business/07-08-2012/the-dangers-of-received-wisdom/

Goffee, R., & Jones, G. (1998). *The character of a corporation.* New York, NY: Harper Business.

Goffman, D. (1997). *Vital lies, simple truths: The psychology of self-deception.* London, UK: Bloomsbury.

Janis, I. L. (1982). *Groupthink: Psychological studies of policy decisions and fiascoes* (2nd ed.). Boston, MA: Houghton Mifflin.

Kangis, P., & O'Reilly, M. D. (2003). Strategies in a dynamic marketplace: A case study in the airline industry. *Journal of Business Research, 56*(2), 105–111.

Krech, D., Crutchfield, R. S., & Ballachey, E. L. (1962). Culture. In D. Krech, R. S. Crutchfield, & E. L. Ballachey (Eds.), *Individual in society* (pp. 339–380). New York, NY: McGraw-Hill.

Lehrer, J. (2012a, January 30). Groupthink: The brainstorming myth. *The New Yorker.* Retrieved August 15, 2012 from: http://www.newyorker.com/reporting/2012/01/30/120130fa_fact_lehrer

Lehrer, J. (2012b, March 26). Royal flush: How Roger Thomas redesigned Vegas. *The New Yorker.* Retrieved August 15, 2013 from: http://www.newyorker.com/reporting/2012/03/26/120326fa_fact_lehrer

Majumdar. S. K. (2000). Sluggish giants, sticky cultures, and dynamic capability transformation. *Journal of Business Venturing, 15*(1), 59–78.

Martin, M. J. (2006). The way we do things around here. Electronic Journal of Academic and *Special Librarianship, 7*(1). Retrieved from http://southernlibrarianship.icaap.org/content/v07n01/martin_m01.htm

McGuire, W. J. (1969). The nature of attitudes and attitude change. In G. Lindzey & E. Aronson (Eds.), *The handbook of social psychology: Vol. 3. The individual in a social context* (2nd ed., pp. 136–314). Reading, MA: Addison-Wesley.

Murphy, P. E. (1988). Implementing business ethics. *Journal of Business Ethics, 7*(12), 907–915.

Osborn, A. F. (1963). Applied imagination: Principles and procedures of creative problem solving (3rd ed.). New York, NY: Charles Schribner & Sons.

Pil, F. K., & Holweg, M. (2003). Exploring scale—The advantages of thinking small. *MIT Sloan Management Review, 44*(2), 33–39.

Rivkin, J. W., & Siggelkow, N. (2003). Balancing search and stability: Interdependencies among elements of organizational design. *Management Science, 49*(3), 290–311.

Romme, A. G. L. (1999). Domination, self-determination, and circular organizing. *Organization Studies, 20,* 801–832.

Rowe, G., & Wright, G. (2001). Differences in expert and lay judgments of risk: Myth or reality? *Risk Analysis, 27,* 341–356.

Sanchez, P. (2004). Defining corporate culture. *Communication World, 21*(6), 18–21.

Sauser, W. I., Jr. (2008). Crafting a culture of character: The role of the executive suite. In S. Quatro & R. R. Sims (Eds.), *Executive ethics: Ethical dilemmas and challenges for the c-suite* (pp. 1–17). Charlotte, NC: Information Age.

Schein, E. (1992). *Organizational culture and leadership.* San Francisco, CA. Jossey-Bass.

Schein, E. (1999). *The corporate culture survival guide.* San Francisco, CA. Jossey-Bass.

Schermerhorn, J. R., Jr. (2005). *Management (8th ed.).* New York: Wiley.

Silvestro, R. (2002). Dispelling the modem myth: Employee satisfaction and loyalty drive service profitability. *International Journal of Operations & Production Management, 22*(1), 30–49.

Sims, R. R., & Sauser, W. I., Jr. (2010). Enabling business to craft an organizational culture of character. *2011 Global Business & Economics Anthology, 1*(1), 8–18.

Skoogland, C. (2003, October 16). *Establishing an ethical organization.* Plenary address presented at the Conference on Ethics and Social Responsibility in Engineering and Technology, New Orleans, LA.

Smith, R. A., & Davis, S. F. (2003). *The psychologist as detective: An introduction to conducting research in psychology.* Upper Saddle River, NJ: Pearson/Prentice-Hall.

Svyantek, D. J., & Bott, J. (2004). Received wisdom and the relationship between diversity and organizational performance. *Organizational Analysis, 12*(3), 295–317.

Taylor, D. W., Berry, P. C., & Block, C. H. (1958). Does group participation when using brainstorming facilitate or inhibit creative thinking? Administrative Science Quarterly, *3*(1), 23–47.

Things fall apart: What if the dark energy and dark matter essential to modern explanations of the universe don't really exist? (2004). *The Economist, 70*(8361), 75–76.

Weinberger, J. (2000). William James and the unconscious: Redressing a century-old misunderstanding. *Psychological Science, 11*(6), 439–445.

ABOUT THE CONTRIBUTORS

Martinique "Marty" Alber is a test administration and assessment coordinator with the Personnel Board of Jefferson County in Birmingham, Alabama. She received her Master of Science degree and PhD in Industrial and organizational psychology from Auburn University. Marty's experience and expertise lie in personnel selection, assessment, and psychometrics. She has served as a consultant for the State of Alabama, State of Mississippi, and DeKalb County, Georgia. Marty has presented research to multiple professional associations including the Society of Industrial Organizational Psychology and the International Personnel Assessment Council. She serves as a frequent guest lecturer to graduate programs in industrial/organizational psychology in the area of assessment centers and employee selection.

Sue Ann Balch holds a BA degree in history and political science from Auburn University and a JD from Faulkner University's Thomas Goode Jones School of Law. She is authorized to practice law by the Supreme Court of the United States, the Federal Middle District Court of Alabama, and the Alabama Supreme Court. She has been a member of the American Immigration Lawyers Association since 2002 and the Federal Bar Association Immigration and Employment Law Sections since 2010. She is also a member of the National Association of Foreign Student Advisors and is a past president of both the Alabama Association of Foreign Student Advisors and the Lee County Bar Association. She is a current member in good standing of the Alabama Bar Association.

Legal and Regulatory Issues in Human Resources Management, pages 457–464
Copyright © 2015 by Information Age Publishing
457

Brian Lee Bellenger, PhD, has extensive experience in the field of employee selection, specializing in high fidelity assessment tools incorporating video technology. Dr. Bellenger has worked with multiple public and private sector organizations, including The Southern Company, Auburn University, DeKalb County, Georgia, the State of Mississippi, and the State of Alabama. Over the course of his career, Dr. Bellenger has served as an expert in several employment discrimination cases and has successfully led project teams in developing valid, nondiscriminatory selection tools under federal court scrutiny. Dr. Bellenger received his doctoral degree in industrial and organizational psychology from Auburn University. He currently serves as the manager of performance measurement with the Personnel Board of Jefferson County in Birmingham, Alabama, and he is a partner and principal consultant in Centrus Personnel Solutions, LLC, a human resources consulting firm specializing in public safety testing.

Sheri Bias, PhD, SPHR is an assistant professor at Saint Leo University. She has been a senior-level executive in human resources management with over 25 years of experience and an extensive background in business. She previously led human resources initiatives in companies such as Philip Morris USA and Anheuser-Busch. She was a management consultant with Price-Waterhouse Coopers where her primary focus was performance improvement and technology implementations for Fortune 500 companies. Dr. Bias received her PhD from The Fielding Graduate University, where she studied a variety of human resources topics focusing specifically on the impacts of diversity and social justice. She possesses an MBA from the College of William and Mary and a MA in Education and Human Development from the George Washington University. Bias also taught business and human resources courses at the College of William and Mary, the George Washington University, University of Virginia, and Hampton University.

Karin Bogue, Esq., is an assistant professor at South University and provides consulting trade compliance services to multinational organizations. Karin earned a BBA in Accounting and an MBA in Management from the University of Memphis. She also earned a JD from the Cecil C. Humprhey's School of Law at the University of Memphis, is licensed to practice law by the state of Tennessee, and is currently pursuing a DBA in international business. Karin is a licensed customs broker with over 30 years of experience working in international trade and compliance. She created and organized import compliance departments, directed cross-functional international compliance teams, developed training programs for import compliance, and served as a trade compliance consultant to a variety of international corporations. She is also the author of trade articles, training manuals, textbooks, and online courses for international trade compliance. Karin is a resident of Florida, where she enjoys long distance running (17 marathons and 5 ultramarathons), dogs, disaster relief work, home improvement projects, community service, and the beach.

James S. Bowman is professor of public administration at the Askew School of Public Administration and Policy, Florida State University. Noted for his work in ethics and human resource management, Dr. Bowman is author of over 100 journal articles and book chapters, as well as editor of six anthologies. Bowman is coauthor of *Human Resource Management in Public Service: Paradoxes, Processes and Problems* (4rd ed., Sage, 2012) and *The Professional Edge: Competencies in Public Service* (2nd ed., Sharpe, 2010). His most recent book, with Jonathan P. West, is *Public Service Ethics: Individual and Institutional Responsibilities* (Sage, in press). He is editor-in-chief of *Public Integrity*. A past National Association of Schools of Public Affairs and Administration Fellow, as well as a Kellogg Foundation Fellow, he has experience in the military, civil service, and business.

C. Kevin Coonrod married careers in the law and facilitative mediation to make a difference within a community as ombudsperson at Auburn University. After practicing commercial law in Seattle, Washington, he managed court and Foreclosure Fairness Act mediation programs for the Dispute Resolution Center of King County. Coonrod credits his education and experience at the Dispute Resolution Center in substantial part for giving him the skills to actively listen, empathize, and assist parties in serious conflict, all of which are necessary attributes for the art of organizational ombudsing. He received his BA from the University of Washington and his JD from the Idaho College of Law.

Kristin L. Cullen, PhD, received her degree from Auburn University in 2011. She joined the Center for Creative Leadership (CCL) as a postdoctoral research fellow after graduation and is now a faculty member in research, innovation, and product development at CCL. Kristin's work focuses on leadership development, including improving leaders' understanding of organizational networks and the ability of organizations to facilitate collective leadership, complex collaboration, and change across organizational boundaries. She conducts research and consults with organizations in these areas. Her research has been published in journals such as the *Journal of Management, Leadership Quarterly, Journal of Vocational Behavior,* and the *Journal of Business and Psychology*. She is currently on the review board of the *Journal of Business and Psychology* and is an ad-hoc reviewer for *Leadership Quarterly* and the *Journal of Organizational Behavior*.

George Denninghoff, JD, MPA, SPHR founded HR Synergy in 1995 as a human resource and management consulting firm. The primary focus of the firm has been the utilization of systems approaches to create integrated solutions in strategic planning, organizational development with compliance, performance, and change management. HR Synergy has received Dunn and Bradstreet's highest possible past performance rating. Among the firm's clients are healthcare, sales, communications, manufacturing, education, and aerospace companies, including the American Council on Education, Alcoa, the Center for Naval Analysis, Anheuser-Bush, Phillip Morris, and Liebherr Mining Equipment. He has also consulted with NASA and its partners on public and private consortiums and alliances such as the Small Aircraft Transportation System and the AGATE Alliance. He was recently retained to assist NASA's strategic relationships office in designing the workplace of the future and was a thought leader for NASA's first TE-Dex. Mr. Denninghoff has lectured for the George Washington University Graduate School on human resource development and the law, consulting skills, and strategic human resource strategies. He has served on the board of directors of the Human Resource Certification Institute and was selected to participate in the SHRM Foundation's Thought Leader Conferences.

Alexa J. Doerr is a PhD student at Auburn University. Her research interests include selection, leadership, person–environment fit, and organizational culture. Within these broader interests, she is specifically concerned with the creation and maintenance of an organizational culture for safety. Prior to her graduate studies, she worked at American Institutes for Research as a research assistant. Among others, her projects included one with the goal of improving patient safety through team training among healthcare providers, and another with the purpose of enhancing a selection process for an airport security position.

Sally C. Gertz is clinical professor at the Florida State University College of Law where she teaches in the school's judicial, government, public interest, and corporate externship programs. Her research has been published in the *Justice System Journal, International Journal of Public Administration*, and *Review of Public Personnel Administration* (with Bowman, Gertz, & Williams). Most recently, she wrote a book chapter for *Human Resource Management in Public Service: Paradoxes, Processes, and Problems* (4th ed., Sage, 2012). She served as a commissioner on Florida's Public Employees Relations Commission, and as in-house counsel to a statewide school employees' union. As a member of the Florida Supreme Court Standard Jury Instructions Committee, she drafted uniform jury instructions for employment cases.

Barry Hoy, PhD, is a retired naval officer and the present chair of the department of administrative studies for Saint Leo University. He has taught at a total of five different post-secondary institutions and is the author of the dissertation section of Saint Leo's doctorate in business administration program. For seven years, he was the training director and EEO manager for Virginia's largest heavy construction company. Dr. Hoy holds a PhD in management with a concentration in learning management from Walden University. His Master of Science in human resources management was conferred by Troy University. He also holds a BS in adult education from Southern Illinois University and is pursuing an MS in computer information systems. Barry is a published author on the topic of conditioned head turn technique. His dissertation involved the value of apprenticeships. As a veteran of 26 years of naval service, Dr. Hoy is in tune with veterans' issues. While employed in the construction industry, he operated internships and apprenticeships in the private sector. He knows the value these programs can bring to the candidate. With more than 18 years experience in post-secondary education, he is qualified to speak to the challenges presented by academia as well as the vital contribution that education can make.

Sara R. Jordan is currently a visiting assistant professor in the department of political science at the University of Miami. Her research interest is to define standards of ethics for high technology and high risk areas of government activity, such as predictive analytics and clinical trials of drugs and devices. Sara's research can be found in a range of venues from *Accountability in Research* to *Public Management Review* to *Administrative Theory & Praxis.*

Christine L. Rush, PhD, is an assistant professor of public administration in the department of political science and public administration at Mississippi State University. Her research interests include the influence of law on public managers, workforce diversity, and the implementation of equal employment opportunity law in the public sector. Her work appears in the *Review of Public Personnel Administration, Public Administration Review,* the *American Review of Public Administration,* and *The Public Manager.* Prior to joining the faculty at Mississippi State University, Dr. Rush served as the compensation officer for the United States Courts where she worked to develop and implement human resource policy for the employees of the federal courts nationwide. She received her PhD in public administration from the School of Public and International Affairs at the University of Georgia, and her JD from Emory University School of Law.

William I. Sauser, Jr., PhD, is professor of management in the Harbert College of Business at Auburn University. Dr. Sauser earned his BS in management and MS and PhD in industrial/organizational psychology at the

Georgia Institute of Technology and an MA in business ethics from the University of Wales. He is licensed to practice psychology in Alabama and holds specialty diplomas in industrial/organizational psychology and organizational and business consulting psychology from the American Board of Professional Psychology. Dr. Sauser's interests include organizational development, strategic planning, human relations in the workplace, business ethics, and continuing professional education. He is a fellow of the American Council on Education and the Society for Advancement of Management. Dr. Sauser is also a commissioned ruling elder in the Presbyterian Church (USA) and serves as pastor of the Union Springs (Alabama) Presbyterian Church. He was awarded the 2003 Frederick W. Taylor Key by the Society for Advancement of Management and the 2013 External Consulting Award and 2014 Algernon Sydney Sullivan Award by Auburn University.

Ronald R. Sims is the Floyd Dewey Gottwald Senior Professor in the Mason School of Business at the College of William and Mary. He received his PhD in organizational behavior from Case Western Reserve University. His research and consultation focuses on a variety of topics, to include leadership and change management, HRM, business ethics, employee training, management and leadership development (i.e., human resource development), learning styles, and experiential learning. Dr. Sims is the author or coauthor of 32 books and more than 165 articles and book chapters.

Daniel J. Svyantek, PhD, received his degree from the University of Houston in 1987. He was a faculty member in the industrial/organizational psychology PhD program at the University of Akron from 1987 to 2003. He is currently a full professor in the psychology department of Auburn University. He served as the program director of the industrial/organizational psychology PhD program from 2003 to 2008. He is currently serving as chair of the Auburn University psychology department. He has published in journals such as the *Journal of Applied Psychology, Journal of Vocational Behavior, Journal of Applied Behavioral Sciences,* and *Human Relations.* He has served as editor of the journal *Organizational Analysis* and is currently series editor for the annual series, *Research in Organizational Sciences.* He has consulted with several organizations on organizational change projects in the areas of problem-solving, compensation systems, and implementing work teams. He is particularly interested in the development of new evaluation methods for assessing the practical value of applied research within applied contexts. In addition, his research interest areas include person–organization fit issues and the role of organizational culture and climate as the context for the expression of individual behavior in organizations.

Robert A. Tufts is an attorney and associate professor in the School of Forestry and Wildlife Sciences at Auburn University. He earned a BS and an MS in forestry from Louisiana State University and a PhD in forestry from Virginia Tech. He earned a JD from Jones School of Law, Faulkner University and an LLM (tax) from the University of Alabama. Robert teaches classes and presents workshops on estate planning, agricultural law, property law, choice of business entity, taxation of timber, environmental law, senior capstone course, and surveying. He also has a part-time law practice concentrating in estate planning and issues affecting landowners.

John G. Veres III has served as the chancellor of Auburn University Montgomery since July 1, 2006, and is the first Auburn Montgomery alumnus to do so. He received his PhD in industrial/organizational psychology from Auburn University in 1983. Dr. Veres has over 30 years' experience as a consultant to organizations. He has published on human resources management topics, including some 40 articles in scholarly journals, as well as nine book chapters, two edited volumes, and one book. Dr. Veres has consulted in approximately 80 employment discrimination lawsuits, testifying on assessing adverse impact, selection procedure validity, and other issues regarding equal employment opportunity. He currently serves as special master to a federal district court in the Northern Division of Alabama.

Jonathan P. West is professor and chair of political science and director of the MPA program at the University of Miami. His research interests include human resource management, productivity, local government, and ethics. Professor West has published eight books and over 100 articles and book chapters. His most recent books are co-edited with Bowman, *American Public Service: Radical Reform and the Merit System* (Taylor & Francis) in 2007 and with Berman, *The Ethics Edge* (ICMA) in 2006. Other recent books with Berman, Bowman, and Van Wart are *Human Resource Management: Paradoxes, Processes, and Problems* (4th ed., Sage) in 2012 and *Competencies in Public Service: The Professional Edge* (Sharpe) in 2010. He is the managing editor of *Public Integrity*. He taught previously at the University of Houston and University of Arizona and served as a management analyst in the U. S. Surgeon General's office, Department of the Army, Washington, D.C.

William J. Woska, JD, has been a faculty member at several colleges and universities including the University of California, Berkeley, Saint Mary's College, Moraga, Golden Gate University, San Francisco, and San Diego State University. He is presently on the faculty at Cabrillo College in Aptos, California. He has more than 30 years of experience representing employers in employment and labor law matters. His articles have been published in a number of publications including *Public Personnel Management, Police Chief,*

Labor Law Journal, Public Administration Review, Lincoln Law Review, Labor-Relations News, HR News, and the *Public Personnel Review.* He is a member of the Labor and Employment Law Section of The State Bar of California.

Kenneth P. Yusko, PhD, is currently a professor of Human Resources and Management in the School of Business Administration at Marymount University and co-principal of Siena Consulting, a human capital consulting firm. An expert in the design of personnel selection, development, and performance management systems, Ken's recent clients include S.C. Johnson, the National Football League, Diageo, Merck, the U.S. Department of Agriculture, and the NYC Department of Education. Dr. Yusko has authored two books on human resource and human capital management practices and is a frequent contributor to both trade and research journals on the topic of employee selection. Ken and his team were recently awarded the M. Scott Myers Award for Applied Research from the Society of Industrial/Organizational Psychology and the International Personnel Assessment Council's Innovations Award for their work in developing and implementing the Siena Reasoning Test (SRT), a cognitive ability test that substantially enhances diversity in hiring.

INDEX

Legal and Regulatory Issues in Human Resources Management, pages 465–469
Copyright © 2015 by Information Age Publishing
All rights of reproduction in any form reserved.

P

R

S

T

Task performance, 325
Taylor, Frederick W., 5
Technology policy, 261–262
Test administration, 128–129, 236–240
Test development, 126–128
Training and development, 451–452
Turnover, 324, 331

U

U.S. Department of Labor, 5

V

Validity, 120, 122–123, 124, 234, 257,
    428, 430

Values, 77–79, 88, 94
Visas, types of, 158–162

W

Web cams, 259–260
Work/life balance, 308
Workplace conflict, 395–397

Z

Zero tolerance, 225